AF479137

MICHELANGELO PISTOLETTO

Michelangelo Pistoletto

From One to Many, 1956–1974

Edited by Carlos Basualdo

Essays by Carlos Basualdo, Jean-François Chevrier, Claire Gilman, Gabriele Guercio, Suzanne Penn, and Angela Vettese

Chronologies by Marco Farano and Luigia Lonardelli

Philadelphia Museum of Art
in association with
Yale University Press, New Haven and London

Published on the occasion of the exhibition
Michelangelo Pistoletto: From One to Many, 1956–1974

Philadelphia Museum of Art, November 2, 2010–January 16, 2011
MAXXI—Museo Nazionale delle Arti del XXI Secolo, Rome, March 3–June 26, 2011

The exhibition was organized by the Philadelphia Museum of Art and MAXXI—Museo Nazionale delle Arti del XXI Secolo, Rome.

In Philadelphia the exhibition was made possible by The Pew Center for Arts & Heritage through the Philadelphia Exhibitions Initiative, and by The Andy Warhol Foundation for the Visual Arts and The Kathleen C. and John J. F. Sherrerd Fund for Exhibitions. Additional support was provided by Galleria Lia Rumma and GALLERIA CONTINUA, San Gimignano / Beijing / Le Moulin; by Christie's, Luhring Augustine, Galleria Christian Stein, and Simon Lee Gallery; by Lynne and Harold Honickman, Jane and Leonard Korman, Harriet and Larry Weiss, and Sankey and Connie Williams; and by the Philip and Muriel Berman Foundation, Jill and Sheldon Bonovitz, and Jaimie and David Field.

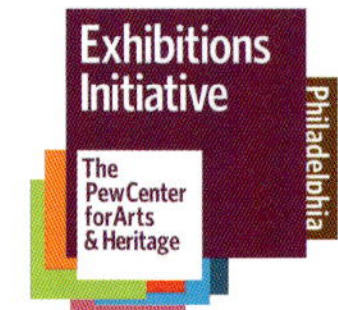

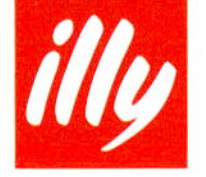

The English-language edition of the catalogue was made possible by illycaffè and by The Andrew W. Mellon Fund for Scholarly Publications.

Credits as of September 2, 2010

Produced by the Publishing Department of the
Philadelphia Museum of Art
2525 Pennsylvania Avenue
Philadelphia, PA 19130 USA
www.philamuseum.org

Published in association with
Yale University Press
P.O. Box 209040
New Haven, CT 06520 USA
www.yalebooks.com

Edited by Kathleen Krattenmaker
Editorial assistance by Roberta Nuzzaci
and Erica F. Battle
Assistance with translations from
the Italian by Roberta Nuzzaci
Production by Richard Bonk
Design by Abbott Miller and Christine Moog,
Pentagram, New York
Color separations, printing, and binding by
Tien Wah Press Pte Ltd, Singapore
Composed in Kievet
Printed on 150 gsm Lumisilk Matt Art

An Italian-language edition was published by Electa
with the Publishing and Research Office
MAXXI—Museo Nazionale delle Arti del XXI Secolo
Carolina Italiano, Luigia Lonardelli, Carlotta Sylos Calò
Via Guido Reni 4A, 00196 Rome ITALY
www.fondazionemaxxi.it

Additional artists' copyrights appear on p. 403.

Cover illustration: Michelangelo Pistoletto,
Biennale 66, 1966 (plate 39). The Sonnabend Collection

Library of Congress Cataloging-in-Publication Data

Pistoletto, Michelangelo, 1933–
Michelangelo Pistoletto : from one to many, 1956–1974 / edited by Carlos Basualdo ; essays by Carlos Basualdo . . . [et al.] ; chronologies by Marco Farano and Luigia Lonardelli.
p. cm.
Published on the occasion of an exhibition held at the Philadelphia Museum of Art, Nov. 2. 2010–Jan. 16, 2011 and at MAXXI—Museo Nazionale delle Arti del XXI Secolo, Rome, Mar. 3–June 26, 2011
Includes index.
ISBN 978-0-87633-223-8 (pma)—ISBN 978-0-300-16616-3 (yale)
1. Pistoletto, Michelangelo, 1933—Exhibitions. 2. Art and society—History—20th century—Exhibitions. I. Basualdo, Carlos, 1964– II. Lonardelli, Luigia. III. Farano, Marco. IV. Philadelphia Museum of Art. V. Museo Nazionale delle Arti del XXI Secolo (Italy) VI. Title. VII. Title: From one to many, 1956–1974.
N6923.P5A4 2010
709.2–dc22

2010021521

CONTENTS

LENDERS TO THE EXHIBITION

Abrams Family Collection, New York

Albright-Knox Art Gallery, Buffalo

Marco and Franca Brignone

Constance R. Caplan

Cittadellarte-Fondazione Pistoletto, Biella

Collezione La Gaia, Busca

Collezione Maramotti, Reggio Emilia

The Detroit Institute of Arts

Fondazione per l'Arte Moderna e Contemporanea—CRT, with Castello di Rivoli Museo d'Arte Contemporanea and GAM—Galleria Civica d'Arte Moderna e Contemporanea, Turin

Fondazione Marconi, Milan

Fundação de Serralves—Museu de Arte Contemporânea, Porto, Portugal

GNAM—Galleria Nazionale d'Arte Moderna e Contemporanea, Rome

Martin Z. Margulies

MART—Museo per l'Arte Contemporanea di Trento e Rovereto, Rovereto, Italy

MAXXI—Museo Nazionale delle Arti del XXI Secolo, Rome

The Robert B. Mayer Family Collection, Chicago

The Menil Collection, Houston

Beatrice Monti della Corte von Rezzori

Museum Boijmans Van Beuningen, Rotterdam

Giorgio and Giorgiana Persano

François Pinault Foundation

Michelangelo Pistoletto

Estate of Robert Rauschenberg

Lia Rumma

Keith L. and Katherine Sachs

San Francisco Museum of Modern Art

The Sonnabend Collection

Pietro Valsecchi

Walker Art Center, Minneapolis

Suzanne Weil

And private individuals and institutions

FOREWORD

If art is life's mirror, then I am the mirror maker.
—Michelangelo Pistoletto, "Division and Multiplication of the Mirror," 1978

Over the past several decades the attention that has been given by American museums to postwar Italian art has been episodic, and thus our understanding of key moments in its development and of the work of key figures such as Michelangelo Pistoletto is, at best, imperfect. Indeed, Pistoletto and the seminal contributions he has made to the art of our time have been the subjects of only two major exhibitions in this country: the first, in 1966, a survey of the artist's mirror paintings organized by Martin Friedman at the Walker Art Center in Minneapolis, and the second, in 1988, a survey curated by Germano Celant at PS1 in New York.

The reason that Pistoletto has not been given the attention he so richly deserves is not due simply to neglect or indifference, although both have certainly played a part in limiting our knowledge of his work and all that he has achieved during a career that now spans nearly six decades. It may have more to do, I suspect, with the seemingly mercurial nature of Pistoletto's activities, especially after the mid-1960s, and with his own rigorous interrogation of the nature and function of art in contemporary society, an enterprise that reveals him to have been one of the most brilliant thinkers of our time on this important matter.

The purpose of this catalogue and the exhibition it accompanies is to provide, first and foremost, a survey of Pistoletto's artistic production from the mid-1950s through the early 1970s. This is long overdue and will no doubt be revelatory both to those who have followed his career and to younger audiences who may be largely unfamiliar with his many accomplishments. Equally significant is the comprehensive account that this publication provides of the impressive range of Pistoletto's activities during this period—the prominent role he played within avant-garde circles in Turin, for example, or his organizing of various collective artistic efforts in the late 1960s—and its thoughtful analysis of the complex social and political contexts in which these took place and to which the artist was clearly responding.

At the heart of the exhibition are Pistoletto's extraordinary mirror paintings. Far from straightforward in either execution or intent, although they might seem so at first glance, these works function in one sense as an extended meditation on the nature of representation and on the duality of human experience that Pistoletto had come to believe was fundamental to our understanding of the world. Addressing this issue in a short essay with the marvelously droll title "Famous Last Words," published in 1967, he observed:

> Man has always attempted to double himself as a means of attaining self-knowledge. . . . When my need to understand things came to include the consideration of life itself, I instinctively

> understood all of the conflicts in the system of doubling all things of the universe. Looking at works of art, I felt the force with which I was compelled to oscillate between one dimension of experience that was abstract and mental and another dimension of experience that was concrete and physical. And it was in the fact of representation that I discovered the poles that were in simultaneous attraction and repulsion—my literal presence as proposed by the mirror, and my intellectual presence as proposed by my painting. These two presences of myself were the two lives that were simultaneously tearing me in two and calling me with urgency to the task of their unification.

To see the mirror paintings together is to understand why they appealed so much to contemporary sensibilities in the 1960s, and why it was so easy at the time to assume their affiliation, both in theme and in spirit, with the emerging Pop art movement in the United States. Yet encountering these works as a series—for this is how Pistoletto came to view them—also enables us to discern the broader purpose that informed their creation and still animates our experience of them today.

With their elegantly reflective surfaces and beautifully rendered figures, the mirror paintings are both seductive and, as if by intent, subtly subversive. By contrast, Pistoletto's *Oggetti in meno* (Minus Objects) of 1965–66 still seem—even at a distance of more than four decades—startlingly radical. The explicit declaration of a new direction in his work that they represented would objectify many of the issues Pistoletto had explored in his mirror paintings and, at the same time, place a far greater emphasis on the active engagement of the viewer. As he noted in 1966 in an essay on these new works titled "The Minus Objects":

> I feel that in my recent works I have entered the mirror and actively penetrated that dimension of time which was merely represented in the mirror-paintings. These recent works bear witness to the need to live and act in accordance with this dimension, i.e. in the light of the unrepeatable quality of each instant of time, each place, and thus of each "present" action.

What came later—the broadening of the boundaries of artistic practice to include various collective actions, including the performances of the group known as Lo Zoo—took the themes explored by Pistoletto in his earlier works as a point of departure and represents the endpoint of the period of time covered by the exhibition and this catalogue. For Pistoletto, however, these actions became the foundation for the work that was to come, including the creation of that remarkable enterprise known as Cittadellarte, and have continued to sustain the creative power of one of the most remarkable artists of our time.

The development and the successful completion of this project have required the contributions of many talented individuals, the support of many generous sponsors, and the participation of many different lenders, both museums and individual collectors. We are deeply grateful to all those who helped in myriad ways. Speaking on behalf of our staff and our Board of Trustees, I would like to thank them for their commitment to sharing Pistoletto's work with audiences in this country and in Italy. A special note of appreciation is owed to our colleagues at MAXXI, the recently opened museum of the art of the twenty-first century in Rome, which collaborated with the Philadelphia Museum of Art on the organization of the exhibition and will present it in early 2011. I would also like to express our deepest appreciation to the several scholars who authored essays for this catalogue and prepared the documentation that is so crucial for the study of the artist's work and career.

Above all, I would like to express our gratitude to two individuals whose vision, commitment, and spirit of cooperation have been essential to the realization of this project. Several years ago Carlos Basualdo, our Keith L. and Katherine Sachs Curator of Contemporary Art, proposed that we mount a major exhibition that would provide audiences with the opportunity to become acquainted with the work Pistoletto produced during an important period in his career, both to broaden understanding of his unique achievement and to highlight the central role he played in the development of Italian art at that time. His recommendation was enthusiastically embraced by my esteemed predecessor, Anne d'Harnoncourt, and it has been my pleasure to see the project through to completion. Mr. Basualdo's detailed understanding of Pistoletto's work and his place in the history of contemporary art is admirable, and so, too, has been his attention to every detail of the preparation of the exhibition and catalogue. We are deeply grateful for all that he has done. Finally, we reserve our greatest thanks for Michelangelo Pistoletto himself, who has fully supported our work and given so generously of his time.

The development of *Michelangelo Pistoletto: From One to Many, 1956–1974*, and its presentation in Philadelphia were made possible by The Pew Center for Arts & Heritage through the Philadelphia Exhibitions Initiative, and by The Andy Warhol Foundation for the Visual Arts and The Kathleen C. and John J. F. Sherrerd Fund for Exhibitions. Additional support was provided by Galleria Lia Rumma, Christie's, Luhring Augustine, Galleria Christian Stein, and Simon Lee Gallery, by Lynne and Harold Honickman, Jane and Leonard Korman, Harriet and Larry Weiss, and Sankey and Connie Williams, and by the Philip and Muriel Berman Foundation, Jill and Sheldon Bonovitz, and Jaimie and David Field. The catalogue was made possible by illycaffè and by The Andrew W. Mellon Fund for Scholarly Publications.

Timothy Rub
The George D. Widener Director and Chief Executive Officer
Philadelphia Museum of Art

FOREWORD

This exhibition of the work of Michelangelo Pistoletto has been an important collaborative project with the Philadelphia Museum of Art. During the time spent defining and organizing the exhibition, our relationship went beyond a mere partnership—in itself so necessary to a wide-ranging undertaking of this kind—to become much more. Indeed, the museums shared their working and administrative procedures, enriching both institutions and providing new professional experiences. In the coming years MAXXI will continue to forge collaborative relationships with other museums, so that this initial experience with the Philadelphia Museum of Art becomes a working model as we move forward. For we are convinced that it is only through sharing and comparison that we can achieve the quality needed for high-level cultural offerings.

The exhibition could not have come about without the willingness of lenders—many of them private individuals—to make their important works of art available to the public. This has been an occasion for bringing together works from the United States and Italy and has fully demonstrated the attention that individual collectors have paid to someone who was, as recently as the 1960s, still an emerging artist.

In addition to sampling Pistoletto's work from a crucial eighteen-year period at the beginning of his career, the exhibition and this catalogue offer an opportunity to take a comprehensive look at his mirror paintings, which constitute some of his best-known work. Indeed, a good portion of the exhibition is devoted to this body of work, which marks the beginning of Pistoletto's meditations on the self and his questioning of the traditional artist-viewer relationship, with the work of art taking its place as an intermediary between these two poles. Over the course of the exhibition Pistoletto's artistic personality as a whole is analyzed, beginning with his early self-portraits—oils on canvas that clarify and elucidate his subsequent reflections on the work of art's role as an intermediary. The mirror paintings attest to the dramatic collision between the intimacy of research, which tends toward the private definition of an artistic self, and the inevitable social component of existence. The figures portrayed in these works seem to emerge from the immediate past, characterized by Italy's postwar "economic miracle"; they are the visual legacy of a postindustrial society we are still coming to terms with and which it is essential to comprehend in order to understand the work of present-day artists.

In fact, although closely tied to Pistoletto's particular biographical path, the mirror paintings can also be interpreted as a sort of commentary on the new visual perception imposed by modern society, which made its appearance in Italy between the 1950s and the 1970s. Pistoletto's first sculptural works, the *Oggetti in meno* (Minus Objects, 1965–66), initially displayed in his studio, speak to us of a desire to move beyond the concept of the exhibition space as a closed place and to eliminate the boundary between public and private. In particular, their challenge to authorship responds to a need to react to and at the same time establish a relationship with the spread of the cultural "industry." In this sense, Pistoletto anticipated a tendency that would fully develop only some years later, in the poetics of Arte Povera.

The exhibition also devotes ample space to creative collaborations and to the investigations carried out by Pistoletto's group Lo Zoo, which convey not only a fundamental artistic experience in the development of Italian art—approaching performative or social practices that deeply involve the viewer—but also a feeling of collectivism, with the group emerging as a unique actor within society.

With the mirror paintings, too, the artist seeks to involve the public in an all-encompassing way, making people feel simultaneously "dentro e fuori lo specchio" (inside and outside the mirror). The message that these works communicate fully corresponds to how we experience the spaces of MAXXI—places where inside and outside, public and private coincide; spaces where the visitor can have a total aesthetic experience, undergoing a transformation from viewer to actor.

If it has been important, on the one hand, to reassert the connection established by Pistoletto between the arts in Italy and the art system in place in the United States in the years 1956–74, what also seemed urgent to us in organizing the exhibition was to focus on an artistic practice that sees the aesthetic endeavor as a collaborative act, as demonstrated by Pistoletto's involvement in the important Deposito d'arte presente (Warehouse of Present Art) project in Turin in the late 1960s. This was an example of how people can create self-managed spaces, areas for promotion and production that unite all the professions around a common purpose. The synergy that led to the definition of the current art system, a network in which the museum is fully involved as a principal player, also stems from the exhibition history of these types of places.

At both MAXXI and the Philadelphia Museum of Art there will be a laboratory space in the exhibition dedicated to Cittadellarte, the project Pistoletto has been involved with since 1998 but which continues to investigate the democratization of art begun in the 1960s. In this section of the exhibition the public will have the opportunity to learn—in a strongly interactive way—about the artist's most recent social commitments, through engaging with the works of art and rediscovering the ontological unity experienced by being reflected in his mirrors.

MAXXI will continue to dedicate itself to the presentation of work by great Italian masters from recent generations. This act of recognition—challenging but more necessary than ever at this historical moment—is undertaken with the conviction that it is important to define and trace a record. If it is true that we understand our past through our current perspective, I believe it is also necessary to consider the work of our youngest artists in relation to the legacies left by the previous generation. The most serious danger for a museum concerned with the contemporary is that it might overlook the causal connection that links events and turns the unfolding of time into a historical path. It is only through elucidating this connection that the museum can fulfill its educational function; the greatest risk would be to surrender to a generic "All" in which the advances and setbacks that characterize individual research are experienced as only chance occurrences.

Anna Mattirolo
Director MAXXI Arte
MAXXI—Museo Nazionale delle Arti del XXI Secolo, Rome

MICHELANGELO PISTOLETTO: FROM ONE TO MANY, 1956–1974

CARLOS BASUALDO

> *If, from a strictly chronological point of view, I am the same individual as the painter of these paintings, the linear passage of time (1912–1952) is not a justification of the identicality of M.D. of 1912 with M.D. 1952. On the contrary, I think there is constant dissociation, if this dissociation is not prevented by superficial thinking and acceptance of the principle of identity.*
>
> —Marcel Duchamp to Helen Freeman, February 12, 1952[1]

Michelangelo Pistoletto: From One to Many, 1956–1974 is an attempt to record and analyze a series of extraordinary passages that, seen through the vantage point of the groundbreaking work of one Italian artist, testify to a deep and lasting social, political, and aesthetic transformation that profoundly affected life in Italy and western Europe in the second half of the twentieth century. It is, first and foremost, the story of the amazing transition in the work of an artist born in 1933 in a small town in the north of Italy, whose early self-portraits, an incisive exploration of the medium of painting and of his own self-representation, gave way in the following years to some of the most influential experiments in art to take place during the extremely prolific decade of the 1960s. From his precise interrogation of the limits of painting to his joyful questioning of the role of art in society, Pistoletto has experimented with photography, theater, artistic collaboration, and multiple authorship, opening along the way many paths that contemporary art has yet to explore fully. In the meantime, everything around him changed. After the war, and most particularly during the period in question, 1956–74, Italy underwent a radical transformation, with accelerated industrialization in the north that produced massive migration from the south and drastically changed the whole of society. The city of Turin, where Pistoletto lived and developed his work during the years under study, with its powerful automotive industry, became the turbulent epicenter of this process. The restlessness of Pistoletto's work during these years finds its perfect match in the environment where it came into being. One mirrors the other, and it is precisely in the territory where reflections and realities coexist that his play unfolds, attempting the impossible task of discerning between illusion and reality, separating voices from their echoes and the reflected face from the hidden self. But "from one to many" also refers to a condition that, clearly insinuated in the artist's early paintings, persists throughout the period analyzed in this exhibition: The tension between singularity and anonymity that, like a fracture, organizes the unstable balance on which the persuasive effect of the successive series of works realized by Pistoletto during this time evidently depend. A tension between individual and collective authorship that his mirror paintings and sculptures, as much as the actions of his group Lo Zoo (The Zoo), insistently reflect, and reflect upon.

Pistoletto does not stop working after 1974—quite the contrary. In November 1972 he moves with his wife, Maria Pioppi, and their one-year-old twins, Armona and Pietra, to the small town of San Sicario, in the mountains of the Susa Valley, where he lives and works for the next six years. With the turmoil of Turin behind him, he sets himself to reestablishing the foundations for his practice, a process that begins in 1973 with a show at Galleria Sperone in Turin titled *Padre e figlio* (*Father and Son*), in which, for the first time, he shows his works together with his father's realistic paintings. By this time the impulse that had taken Pistoletto far from his own early painting and into "actions" and the development of a distinctive form of street theater has temporarily been put to rest; it will be two decades before the writing of his "Progetto Arte" manifesto of 1994[2] and his experiences as a teacher from 1991 to 2001 in the Akademie der bildenden Künste in Vienna prompt him again to develop an institutional experiment in collaboration that continues to this day, under the name Cittadellarte. In the early 1970s, Pistoletto is not the only person to leave Turin. In 1972 the dealer Gian Enzo Sperone, one of the indisputable protagonists of many of the transformations in the Italian art world over the previous decade, moves his gallery to Rome, and is soon followed by the artist Alighiero Boetti. In a short period of time, Turin loses many of the people that had made it an ebullient center of artistic production over the previous ten years.

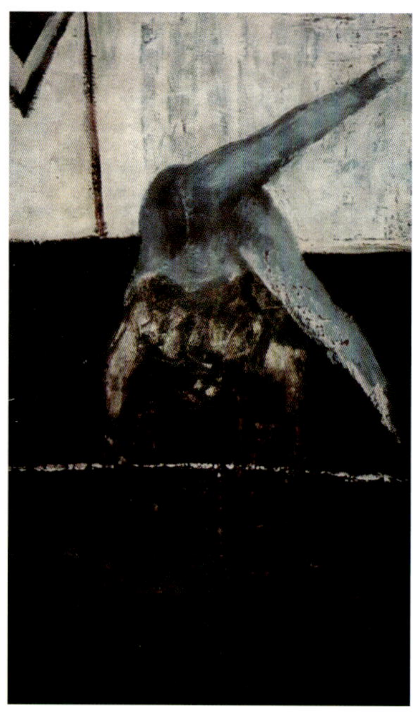

FIG. 1. Michelangelo Pistoletto, *Acrobata azzurro* (*Azur-blue Acrobat*), 1960. Oil on canvas, 43¼ x 27 9/16 inches (110 x 70 cm). Private collection

Turin's most radical transformation in the twentieth century had started two decades earlier. It was in the 1950s that the population of the Piedmontese city grew 42 percent and industrial production increased 36.4 percent. These were the years of the Italian *miracolo economico* (economic miracle), and Turin became, in the popular imagination, "the Italian Detroit."[3] In December 1955, Michelangelo Pistoletto, son of Ettore Olivero Pistoletto, a Turin-based painter and restorer of medieval and Renaissance painting, having recently graduated from a school of advertising directed by the renowned graphic designer Armando Testa—"a passage from antiquity to modernity," in the words of the artist[4]—participates in his first group show with a slim self-portrait, painted on a plank of wood (see fig. 38). These are the years when Art informel, heralded by the French critic Michel Tapié, is making a strong mark on the work of the younger artists in the city. Looking at a slightly later self-portrait of Pistoletto's, from 1956 (plate 1), which shows a barely recognizable face occupying almost the entire surface of the canvas, painfully emerging from a red background thick with heavy brushstrokes and varnish, the lessons of Jean Dubuffet come immediately to mind. Soon after, in 1958, the influential Galleria Galatea at via Viotti 8 in Turin, directed by Mario Tazzoli, exhibits the work of the British painter Francis Bacon, who will have a strong influence on Pistoletto. Pistoletto himself becomes part of the gallery's roster, and he has his first solo show there in 1960, an exhibition that includes a series of almost impersonal self-portraits together with landscapes, a still life, and paintings of acrobats (fig. 1). At this time, Pistoletto still signs his works using his father's full last name, as Michelangelo Olivero Pistoletto.

In 1974—four years after Lo Zoo, the group with which Pistoletto had been realizing actions and spectacles since 1968, finally dissolves—the artist shows a series of recent works at the Sidney Janis Gallery in New York. Coming after a survey of his mirror paintings at the Walker Art Center, Minneapolis, in 1966 (fig. 2), and exhibitions of his work at the Kornblee

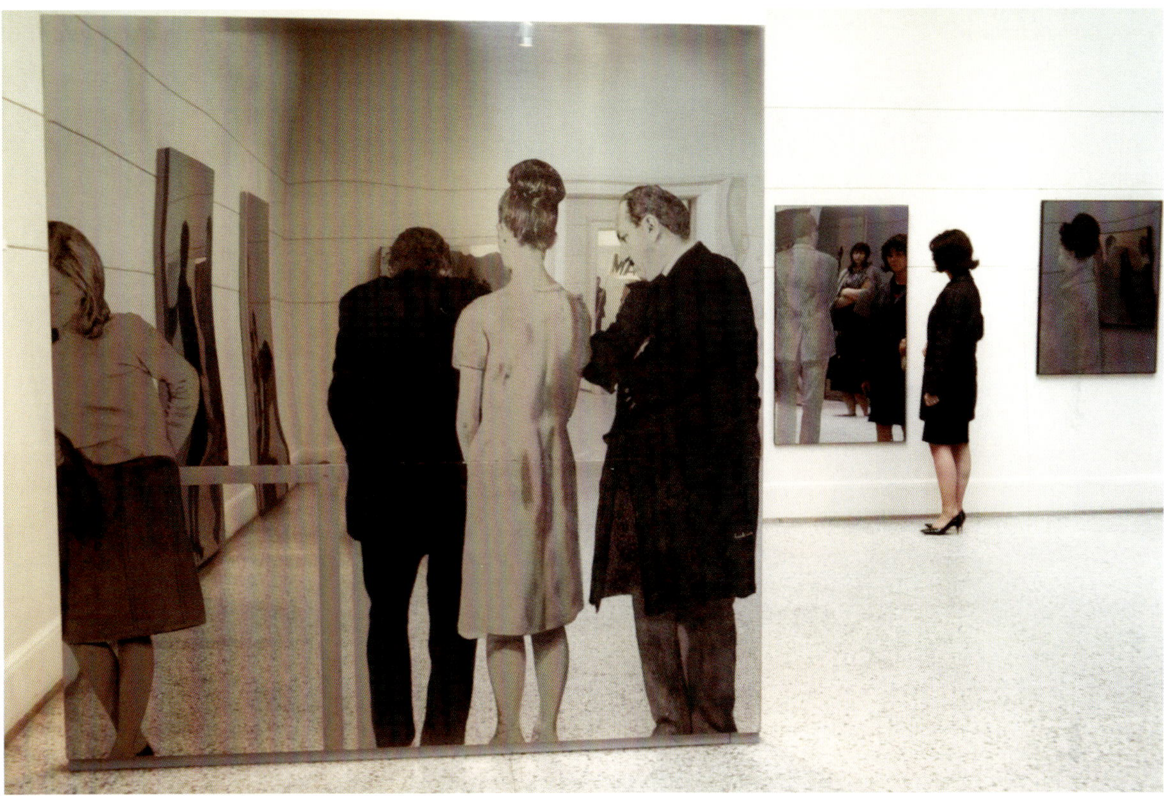

FIG. 2. The exhibition *Michelangelo Pistoletto: A Reflected World* at the Walker Art Center, Minneapolis, spring 1966. Courtesy of the Walker Art Center, Minneapolis

Gallery, New York, in 1967 and 1969, this will be the last show of Pistoletto's in the United States until the end of the decade. The works exhibited in 1974, all of them mirror paintings, include a very large, enveloping *Gabbia* (*Cage*), the menacing *Pericolo di morte* (*Danger of Death*; plate 66), and a solitary *Donna al cimitero* (*Woman in the Cemetery*), among others. The sense of looming danger that seems to pervade these works is made explicit the following year, when Pistoletto opens an exhibition at the Sperone gallery in Turin composed of mirror paintings realized between 1973 and 1974 and entitled *La prigione, il suicidio, il pericolo della morte, l'agguato, il decadimento, gli escrementi, il cimitero, la cattura* (*The Prison, the Suicide, the Danger of Death, the Ambush, the Decay, the Excrement, the Cemetery, the Capture*). The title creates a circular narrative that starts and ends in imprisonment and traverses death, crime, and decay. It is in this same year that the Brigate Rosse (Red Brigades)—a clandestine organization whose goal is to realize communism in Italy by violently abolishing the state and replacing it with a dictatorship of the proletariat—begins their "attack at the heart of the State."[5] The "years of lead,"[6] a long-lasting period of crisis in the political and social life of Italy that had begun in 1969, is then at its height. It will only recede around 1981, leaving behind 450 deaths, 4,500 wounded, and more than 5,000 acts of violence.[7] The temporal arc encompassed by this exhibition takes us, through Pistoletto's evolving work, from one of these extremes to the other, and cannot be traversed without an impending sense of anxiety, and then hope, and fear—with all these feelings constantly present in the most complex and recurrent combinations of art and life.

MIRROR PAINTINGS

There is a definitive quality in Renaissance self-portraiture that is clearly missing in the genre in modern times, and Pistoletto's paintings from the late 1950s are no exception. Titian's late self-portraits, for example—excluding his last, pathetic self-representation as a supplicant in his unfinished Pietà—exude a sense of assurance that is practically the opposite of Rembrandt's doubtful self-depictions in old age. But in both cases the painted semblance stands firmly for the artist; it is one with its subject and is proposed as such to the viewer, without hesitancy. Pistoletto's self-portraits, beginning in 1955, are painfully incomplete, as if his need to find himself in the depicted image could not but be constantly frustrated by delays and the heavy burden of anonymity that modern society mandatorily confers as an ambiguous gift. That sense of incompletion makes the continuation of the series a structural need. It is as if, in contrast to the self-portraiture of the past, destined to deliver a stable image to posterity, these paintings are condemned to imagine an endlessly unraveling future, anxiously enmeshed with the unavoidable past. The self-portrait of 1956 (plate 1) is ageless, and could perhaps equally represent Michelangelo or his father, Ettore Olivero Pistoletto—a confusion enhanced by the fact that Pistoletto signs his early paintings using his full name. By 1960, the son will

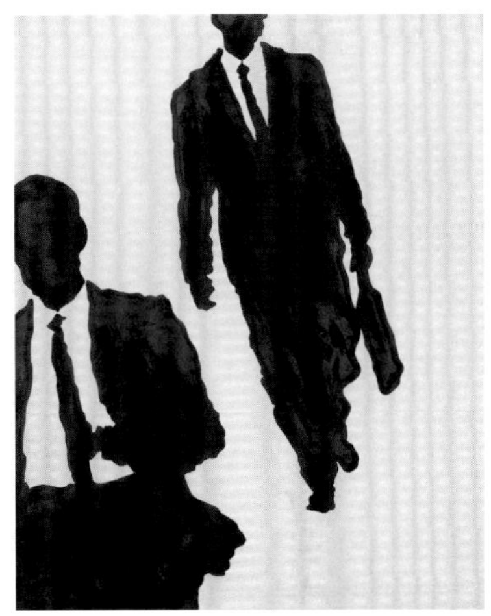

FIG. 3. Sergio Lombardo (Italian, b. 1930). *I Vip* (*The VIPs*), 1962. Enamel on canvas, 63 x 51⅛ inches (160 x 130 cm). Courtesy of Galleria La Nuvola, Rome

have assertively dropped the Olivero, but in *Esperimento* (*Experiment*; plate 3) of 1959, it is still a dark silhouette on a silver background that stands for the artist, confined behind a series of elegant vertical lines—a shadow trapped in shadows. The anonymous figure that appears in his paintings around 1960, and whose impersonality has been compared repeatedly to that of a character in a film by Michelangelo Antonioni, will acquire a clearly distinguishable physiognomy only in the mirror paintings executed toward the end of the decade. Truly, Pistoletto is not the only Italian artist depicting impersonal men in suits at this time; Sergio Lombardo's paintings (fig. 3) and Mario Ceroli's wood constructions also abound in that species, but the fact that in Pistoletto's case they primarily assume the role of standing for the artist himself gives these images a special poignancy. Whether reflections of a culture confronting itself with the enforced anonymity of advanced capitalism or a literal representation of the hesitations of a young artist in the process of emerging from the constrictions imposed by the traditional artistic training he received from his father, Pistoletto's self-portraits frustrate the viewer's expectations of ultimate disclosure associated with the genre, as much as they must have frustrated the artist himself in his search for a self-contained image. We could possibly find in this group of works the first of many series that will define and articulate Pistoletto's work from now on. Most important, there is in these paintings an intimate struggle with endlessness and incompleteness that will forever encircle Pistoletto's practice and manifest itself in his recurrent references to the notion of totality or wholeness, its dialectical opposite.

Considering the tension from which these paintings emerge, it is perhaps predictable that the breakthrough will come not from inside the image but from its context. From 1959 until 1961, Pistoletto seems to have embarked on a laborious exploration of the relation between figure and background that finds its echo in many of the most prolific researches of modernism. First, he makes the anonymous image occupy the entire surface of the painting, as in *La folla* (*The Crowd*; plate 2) of 1959, whose allover composition denotes a disquieting equivalency between the contained but absent self-portrait and the oceanic crowd, unequivocally pointing to a passage from the singular to the plural that seems to have been set as a condition for Pistoletto's practice from the very beginning. The figures in *La folla* do not simply occupy the background of the painting, they become one with it. That solution is temporarily abandoned—it will take almost a decade for Pistoletto to explore the possible ramifications of this strategy, in the works of Lo Zoo—in favor of isolating a lonely standing figure as a character lost in front of a vacated background. In an unmistakable reference to medieval icons, the background is depicted with metallic colors—silver, gold, bronze—in a series of works from the early 1960s (see plates 4–6). Finally, a dark, profound surface, thick with varnish, offers for view an apparently thin veneer of paint depicting the same hieratic figure, in his *Il presente* (*The Present*) paintings (see fig. 46; plates 7–9). It is at this time that Pistoletto is confronted with the reflective possibilities of such a background, and ultimately finds there a way out of the painful disjunction between figure and ground. Seen in this light, the subsequent replacement of the canvas with polished stainless steel that will initiate the unending series of his mirrors constitutes an impossible resolution of the tension between figure and background, which now are forced to coexist in a forever unstable space, hungry to be constantly—and always impermanently—inhabited. A reconciliation of opposites is accomplished, at the price of subjecting the image to a lack of structural stability. The fact that Pistoletto was involved in this meticulous search in isolation, as many of his self-portraits were not exhibited at the time, gives these works a particularly poignant meaning.

The history of modernism teaches that real space starts to haunt the artist as soon as the tension between figure and background is identified as a problem to be resolved within the work. Lygia Clark, a contemporary of Pistoletto, is also exemplary in articulating a meticulous investigation of this tension, which takes her from an exploration of the structural aspects of the picture frame in the 1950s toward interactivity and the space of the spectator in the following decade, and concludes, in the late 1970s, in the development of a therapeutic methodology involving objects.[8] Similarly, Pistoletto's mirror paintings are recast by the artist as a step in a progression from traditional painting to participation and collaborative actions that reaches its apex in the actions of Lo Zoo toward the end of the 1960s. But while in Clark's case her artistic path seems inevitable, the generosity of Pistoletto's development seems, although equally precise, infinitely more open to the circumstances of his life. The effectiveness of the mirror paintings in restaging the tension between figure and ground on a plane that can be described as both literal and metaphysical appears somewhat definitive. In order to realize their promise—that of portraying anything and everything—the mirrors had to become part of an indefinite series, which is exactly the way in which Pistoletto has gone about making them. As much as they may lead to a further exploration of real space, they are in themselves a solution, and as such they constitute their own closed system. A passage that interests us particularly, though, is that from the early mirror paintings, in which the image on the surface of the polished stainless steel is amorously depicted by hand, in a process that is precisely elucidated in one of the essays in this volume (see pp. 143–67 below), to the moment when the artist replaces the last traces of pictorial craft with the impersonal process of mechanical reproduction. It is only then that the anonymity of the early self-portraits ends up completely taking over the logic by which these objects are produced. An endless series is then superimposed on an endlessly reproducible system of image making, in a mirroring logic that brings these works to their tautological completion. One can speculate that the violence of this doubling coincides, in 1973 and 1974, with the violence portrayed by the subjects of the mirrors. A society entrapped by revolutionary violence is faithfully reflected in a series of works—endlessly reproducible in their tragic anonymity—that make imprisonment and decay their leitmotif.

"Angels have no backs" goes a popular saying in Argentina, and so it must be with the insistent depiction of anonymous "angels" that concerns Pistoletto in his early mirror paintings. That makes the self-portrait of 1962

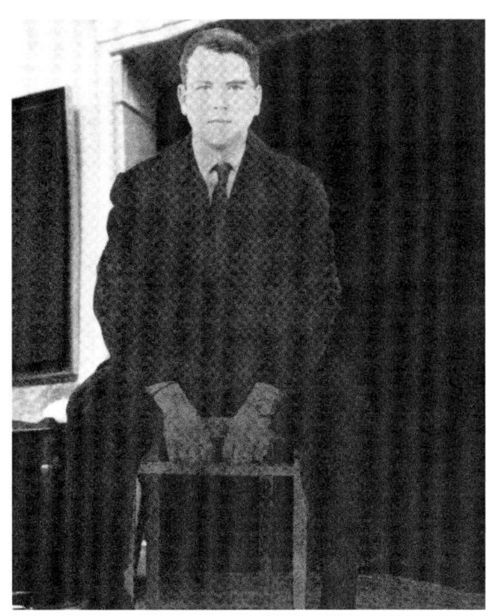

FIG. 4. Michelangelo Pistoletto, *Autoritratto (Self-Portrait)*, 1962. Painted tissue paper on polished stainless steel, 47¼ x 39⅜ inches (120 x 100 cm). Collection unknown

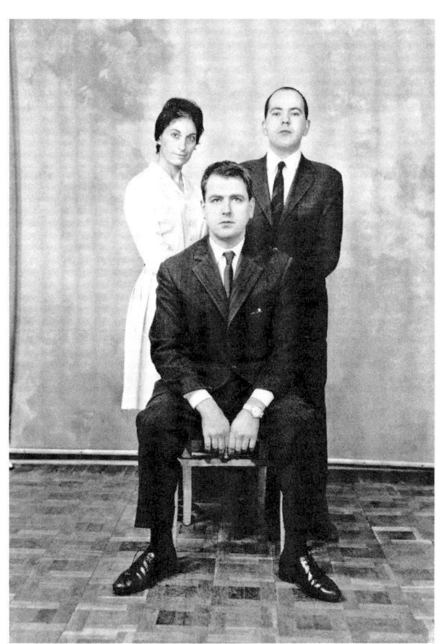

FIG. 5. The source photograph for *Autoritratto (Self-Portrait*, 1962; fig. 4). Courtesy of Cittadellarte-Fondazione Pistoletto, Biella

(fig. 4), in which a seated Pistoletto looks directly at the viewer in a pose that had appeared once before, in *Verso il presente* (*Toward the Present*; plate 7) of 1961, a notable exception. Looking at the original picture by Paolo Bressano (fig. 5), the photographer in whose studio Pistoletto staged the subjects of most of his early mirror paintings, we see two additional figures standing by the artist's side: his first wife, Marzia Calleri, whom Pistoletto, a consummate skier, had met while practicing that sport in the Italian Alps; and Renato Rinaldi, an artist whom Pistoletto had befriended at the Testa school of advertising. The image of Rinaldi standing, looking straight up, his hands clutched behind his back, will in fact appear cropped in a beautiful drawing of the same year (plate 10), one of a small, masterful series that Pistoletto made in conjunction with the production of the first mirror paintings. Marzia, her hair cut fashionably short, is the subject of many of the early works in that series, shown in a variety of poses—dressed and undressed, holding their baby girl, Cristina (plate 24), looking over an illusory balcony (in the sense that the balcony was fabricated by the artist *a posteriori* directly on the surface of the work) as a nurse holding a convalescent girl—in some of Pistoletto's most beautiful works and ambitious early mirror paintings.

The seated figure in that early self-portrait is clearly a transitional one. He looks at us, and when we look back, we see ourselves reflected behind him. When we look at our reflection on the painting's surface, his penetrating absent gaze thus seems directed not at us, but at the space right behind us. Pistoletto's repeated use of figures that give their backs to the spectator might have been at least partly a response to this disjunction between the spaces that his seated character and the viewers occupy. When we look at many of his early mirrors with the figures turning their backs to the viewers (see plates 17, 18, 20, 24–27), their faces averted modestly from our scrutiny, they seem instead to be looking directly at our reflections in the polished stainless steel, and then fully enclosing us in the space of representation. Our space then becomes fully theirs, and the space between us and them collapses. This is exactly what Pistoletto seems to have been looking for, aided in his search by the anxious sense of anonymity that he carried with him from the time of his painted self-portraits.

That enchanted space eluded Tazzoli, who does not seem to have been in the least enthusiastic about Pistoletto's first mirror paintings, shown at Galleria Galatea in April 1963—a lack of support that takes Pistoletto to Paris and propels him to a somewhat accidental encounter with Michael and Ileana Sonnabend that profoundly affects not only the course of his life but also, arguably, the history of postwar Italian art. The Sonnabends subsequently visit Turin and acquire the entire exhibition at Galatea, initiating Pistoletto's itinerary in the United States as well as the misperception of his work as Pop art. In March 1964, Pistoletto opens his first exhibition at the Galerie Sonnabend in Paris, inaugurating a long season of solo and group exhibitions of his work in both Europe and the United States. While in Italy his work is connected to a rich genealogy and analyzed mostly in metaphysical terms, in the United States it is commonly described in a straightforward and literal manner, as a sort of ingenious European variant of Pop, a notable exception being the extraordinary exhibition of his early mirror paintings organized by Martin Friedman at the Walker Art Center in Minneapolis in April 1966 (see fig. 106). In his brilliantly perceptive essay for the show, Friedman in fact makes a special effort to distinguish Pistoletto from American Pop and to relate his practice instead to Surrealism and artists such as René Magritte and Giorgio de Chirico.[9] The discrepancy between these opposing interpretations speaks eloquently of the differences in artistic reception in the United States and Europe at the time, with the Europeans both admiring of but antagonistic to Pop art and what it seemingly represents in terms of cultural colonialism, and the Americans aggressively defensive of their artists and partially deaf to the nuances of the artistic landscape across the ocean. Commercially successful but fundamentally misunderstood, Pistoletto's mirror paintings seem to become in those years a sort of golden cage for the artist, an enchantment that he will be able to lift only by asserting the presence of the spectator in his work ever more disruptively, first with his cerebral Plexiglas works in 1964 (plates 68–74) and, later, with the extraordinarily liberating *Oggetti in meno*—the so-called Minus Objects—of 1965–66 (plates 75–97).

During the period under study, Pistoletto never ceases to experiment with the technique and subject matter of his mirror paintings. It is interesting to note that while he is systematically exploring the relation between simulacra, representation, and real space with his Plexiglas works of 1964, he is also producing one of the most extraordinary series of early mirrors, initially presented in February 1965 at the Sala Espressioni of the Ideal Standard company at via Hoepli 6 in Milan. Similarly, the powerful *Comizi* (Demonstrations) series of 1965–66 (see fig. 144; plates 32–34, 37), representing scenes from what seem to be some of the political protests disrupting public urban spaces across Italy at the time, is contemporaneous with the production of the Oggetti in meno. The solitary figures of the first mirrors, colorless and isolated, are progressively joined by a profusion of colorful and more easily identifiable characters, including Pistoletto's mother in *Due persone in coda* (*Two People in Line*, 1964; plate 28; see fig. 130). By 1967, the mood of the figures represented in the mirrors seems to change, in consonance with the profound transformations affecting Italian society. The use of color that had characterized the mirror paintings from the mid-1960s is perfected toward the end of the decade, a change attested by the glorious greens of *Ragazza che cammina* (*Girl Walking*; plate 40) of 1966, and the perfectly modulated skin tone of the figure in *Maria nuda* (*Maria Nude*; plate 45) of 1967, which is truly monumental in its serene sensuality, evoking the contained lusciousness of Titian's *Flora*, while the pose clearly recalls his *Venere di Urbino* (*Venus of Urbino*). The mirrors are increasingly inhabited by couples—some blatantly young—embracing (see plate 47), kissing, or simply staring attentively at each other. The extreme pictorial sophistication of these works can only retrospectively be recast as announcing the complete demise of painting in Pistoletto's work that takes place beginning in 1969, when the artist produces his first serigraphic edition with Mazzotta in Milan. It is a self-portrait, yet again, that signals the abandonment of any remaining residue of pictorial craft in these works and its replacement with a mechanical technique of reproduction (fig. 6).[10]

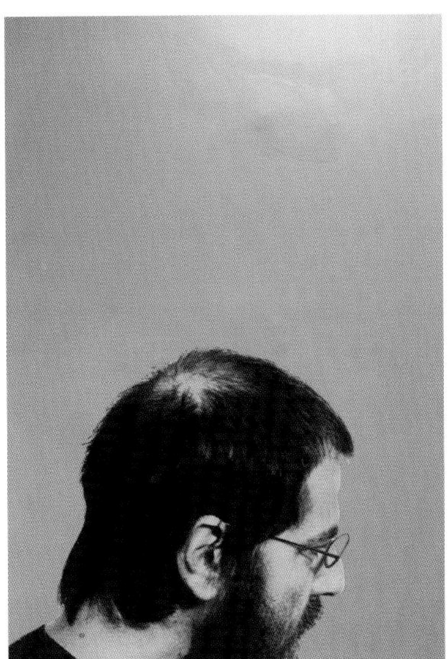

FIG. 6. MIchelangelo Pistoletto, *Autoritratto* (*Self-Portrait*), 1969/1970. Silkscreen on nickel-plated copper, 19¹¹⁄₁₆ x 13¾ inches (50 x 35 cm). Edition of 100. Edition by Gabriele Mazzotta Editore, Milan. Printed by Colophon Arte Moltiplicata, Milan

Coincidentally, it is at this time that Pistoletto concludes his long collaboration with Bressano and starts working with Paolo Mussat Sartor, a photographer associated with the Sperone gallery in Turin. Pistoletto had originally met Bressano through his father, who used the photographer to document his restoration work. For a decade, Bressano continued to work closely with Pistoletto, a sympathetic witness to the artist's development, so it is perhaps telling that Pistoletto's decision to replace the laborious process of staging, photographing, and then painting the figures of his mirrors with the faster and more mechanical rhythms of the silkscreen technique also signals the end of his collaboration with a photographer who, in many ways, may paradoxically have represented his early attachment to the craft of painting—and to his father.

In the early mirror paintings, the tension between figure and ground is provisionally resolved by recourse to a methodology that involves mechanical reproduction as much as painting, in a painfully slow and detailed process that points to a profound interdependency between painting and photography, in which each of the coexisting mediums allows the viewer to appreciate the specific qualities of the other. The endless series of mirrors then finds its correlate in the inescapable singularity of the painted figures. With the use of serigraphy the balance is subtly but enduringly reversed. It is then the possibility of endless reproductions that looms over a series destined to extend itself indefinitely. Possibly reflecting, once more, on the increasing occupation of the Italian landscape by a myriad of commodities and their ghostly representations, the mirrors, like Pistoletto's Plexiglas objects, become less of a presence and more of a simulacrum.

But it is perhaps in the group of mirror paintings that Pistoletto exhibited in the Sala Espressioni in Milan in 1965 (fig. 7), commonly identified as *Balconate* (Balconies; fig. 8), that the joint changing of the guard and the forms of production affecting Italian society are most clearly identifiable. The men and women in *Quattro persone alla balconata* (*Four People on a Balcony*, 1964; plate 26) all seem to come from Pistoletto's past. Their backs to the viewer, they are nonetheless eerily together. The three figures on the right seem to be touching, yet very few mirror paintings succeed in creating such a poignant feeling of isolation. Looking at the source photographs, taken in Bressano's studio, we see that in fact the two men and two women were initially photographed individually (see fig. 135). The man at the right is none other than Bressano himself, looking warily down at a point that is noticeably absent in the finished composition. The woman at the center of the mirror, her dress reaching below the knee and her hair gathered in a topknot, is standing in a pose that notably echoes that of the female character in *Due persone* (*Two People*; plate 20), a mirror painting of 1963–64. As Suzanne Penn describes in her essay (p. 153 below), Pistoletto used two horizontal mirrors for these compositions and with tissue paper fabricated a wooden balcony that does not appear in the source images, whose figures were photographed in poses that seem to indicate that he already had the ultimate arrangement in mind. Originally, the *Balconate* were installed on an elevated platform in front of a window, so that the spectators on the street would look at these figures from below—and by looking become integrated with the lower part of the composition. The overall effect is elegiac. The characters seem to gaze at something that might be vanishing, but it is they themselves who become mysteriously evanescent. They look ahead at their demise. To find a similar atmosphere in a painting one would have to bring to mind the beautifully pathetic self-absorption of the characters in Giandomenico Tiepolo's *Mondo Novo* of 1791 (fig. 9). In both these works, it is a new world that brings about the obsolescence of everything these people seem to stand for: A world that decrees the obliteration of the precious materiality of Bressano's glass plates, in which the rumors of a preindustrial form of labor can still be heard; and of the amorous dedication to the slowness of craft that Pistoletto had inherited, willingly or unwillingly, from the teachings of his father. An anxious world confronted with its inescapable future, which will certainly be louder, brighter, more colorful, and endlessly and more deeply threatening. As the poet and filmmaker Pier Paolo Pasolini declared in his last interview, on November 1, 1975, only a few hours before he was killed: "Forse sono io che sbaglio. Ma io continuo a dire che siamo tutti in pericolo" (Perhaps it is I who am mistaken. But I continue to say that all of us are in danger).[11]

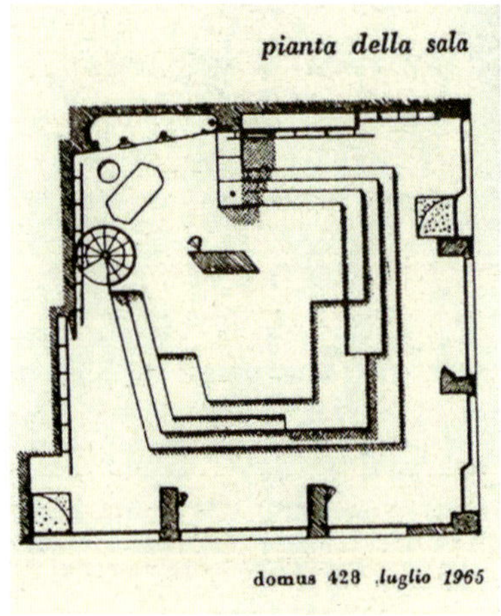

FIG. 7. The floor plan of the Sala Espressioni of the Ideal Standard company, via Hoepli 6, Milan. Courtesy of the Gio Ponti Archives, Milan

OGGETTI IN MENO

Anything and everything can be reflected in a mirror. It is as if the very notion of "possibility" were primordially encapsulated in a reflective surface. Its proverbial faithfulness corresponds to the lightness with which mirrors attach themselves to any given reflection. On their surfaces everything glitters and goes, like a furtive glance stolen in the street, or shimmering leaves on the surface of a river. Pistoletto may have been mesmerized by the endless possibilities of his mirrors, and by the way in which they amplify the unfinished nature of his early self-portraits, expanding it in both temporal and spatial dimensions. In the mirror paintings, it is not only he, looking at the increasingly reflective surface of a varnished canvas, who becomes a fleeting part of the pictorial composition, but a whole multitude of things and people that can instantaneously be trapped by their polished metal surfaces.[12] It is impossible not to notice that Pistoletto's mirrors invite participation (they were frequently described by contemporary critics as enacting a sort of frozen "Happening").[13] The narrative possibilities offered by a combination of several mirrors and their ephemeral reflections when placed in the same room were also evident at the time. These are but two ways in which the ghost of theater seems to be invoked in their presence. The nature of the photography sessions by which the images on the surfaces of the mirrors were obtained only reinforces that impression. The characters in the mirror paintings posed for Bressano's lens, rehearsing carefully designed gestures that deliberately mimic common situations and actions. The photography studio became a precisely controlled stage on which the artist directed a small cast of improvised actors to play, anonymously, everyday life, to be performed in front of a

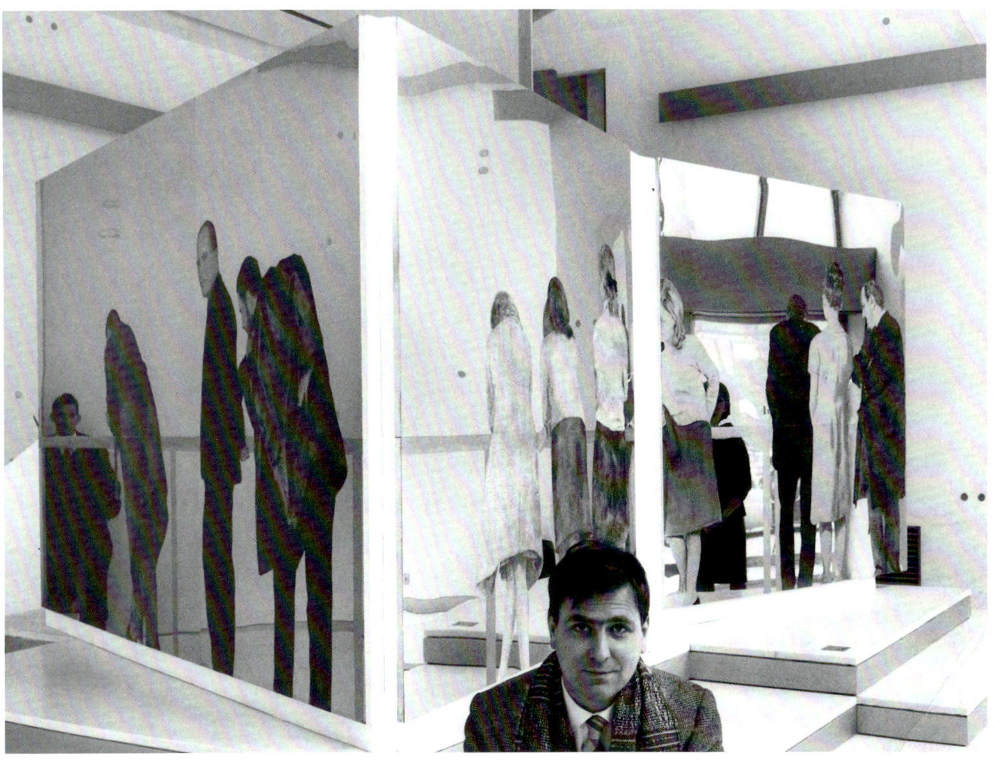

FIG. 8. Pistoletto's exhibition at the Sala Espressioni in the Ideal-Standard showroom, Milan, winter 1965. Courtesy of Cittadellarte-Fondazione Pistoletto, Biella

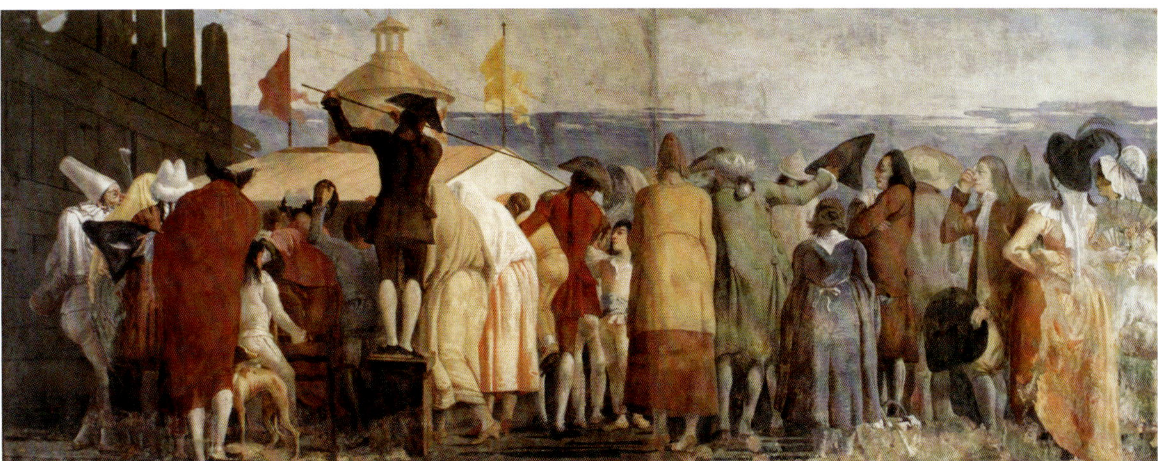

FIG. 9. Giandomenico Tiepolo (Italian, 1727–1804). *Mondo Novo* (*New World*), 1791. Detached fresco, 80¾ x 206¾ inches (205 x 525 cm). Venice, Ca' Rezzonico—Museum of Eighteenth-Century Venice. The Villa in Zianigo-Portico

mutable audience of fleeting spectators. The figures' poses, which may find echoes in classical sculpture and Renaissance portraiture (figs. 10–12), were used and reused by Pistoletto, arranged or simply framed in different formats and compositions, in a process that cannot help but remind us of the graphic possibilities that, decades later, would be available through electronic media.

The operations by which the photographic images were ultimately transferred onto sheets of stainless steel were extremely time-consuming, imposing a temporality in the fabrication of the objects that contrasts with the swiftness with which images pass over their reflective surfaces. That changed after Pistoletto began using serigraphy in the 1970s. At first, the use of this technique was limited to the editions that he started producing in 1969, and it took him three years (an eternity, measured by the speed with which his mirrors evolved during the 1960s) to finally abandon any remaining trace of pictorial craft to rely exclusively on mechanical reproduction in their making. It is hard not to think that the violence implied in the possibility of an endless reproduction is mirrored somehow in the subject matter of the works he made at that time. It is also hard not to link that possibility to Pistoletto's decision to discontinue producing multiples of the mirrors. Each silkscreen was to be unique—a paradoxical decision that contradicts the very nature of mechanical reproduction. In order for the series of mirror paintings to become endless, each individual object must aspire to embody singularity, almost negating itself. The anxiety of self-portraiture seems to have been transferred fully to that renewed tension between one and many.

Oggetti in meno can hardly be translated by the expression "Minus Objects." A "minus object" seems to imply a negative object, like any symbol carrying a minus sign before it. In *oggetti in meno* there is a somewhat self-contradictory assertion of the positivity of the object, as if the minus sign comes after and not before a number. First comes the object, and then we are made to believe that it has been extracted from an absent totality. A better translation might have been "substracted object," though here, too, the action precedes its supposedly passive recipient. In *oggetti in meno*, the simple evidence of the presence of the object comes first, and only then is it folded back within the immaterial field of possibility from which it seems to have become manifest. Once again, Pistoletto's work confronts the fragmented and ultimately frustrating openness of the modern experience of knowledge—and self-knowledge—by returning to the world its mirror image.

With the Oggetti in meno, Pistoletto's work gloriously conquers the space that his Plexiglas works had only hesitantly come to occupy, through the progressive dissolution of their materiality and the transformation of objects into images—simulacra. The Oggetti in meno do not pretend, they are simply there, right in the space of the spectator, brash and surprisingly beautiful, intellectually complex and full of lightness and play. It is not only that they occupy, literally or experientially, the space of the viewer, but also that they resonate explosively in the imagination. Their multidimensionality continues to grow as we contemplate them. The first one,

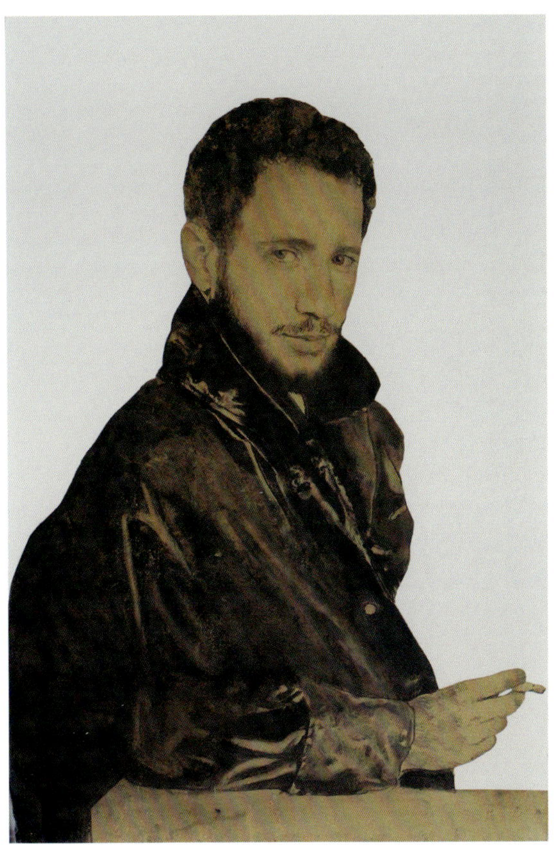

FIG. 10. Michelangelo Pistoletto, *Ritratto di Clino* (*Portrait of Clino*, 1963; plate 15). The subject is Clino Trini Castelli.

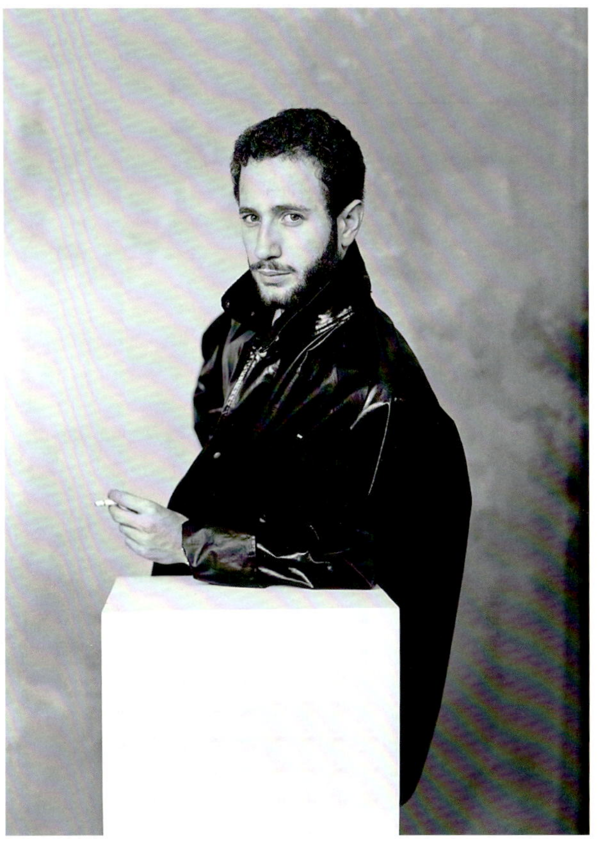

FIG. 11. Source photograph for *Ritratto di Clino* (*Portrait of Clino*, 1963; plate 15). Courtesy of Cittadellarte-Fondazione Pistoletto, Biella

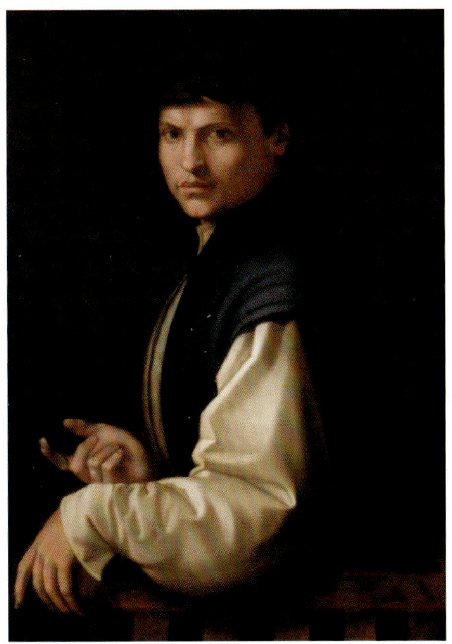

FIG. 12. Jacopino del Conte (Italian, active Florence and Rome, 1510–1598). *Portrait of a Gentleman*, c. 1535. Oil on panel, 26 x 18 3/8 inches (66 x 46.7 cm). Philadelphia Museum of Art. John G. Johnson Collection, 1917

Quadro da pranzo (*Lunch Painting*, 1965; plate 75), is an untranslatable pun. In Italian, *quadro* means both "frame" and "painting." A *quadro da pranzo* is both a frame that creates a space where people can eat—as they probably could if physically entering the work—or a painting in which people can be seen while eating. The work mocks the mannerisms of contemporary object design while joyfully throwing darts at Novecento painting, with its artful scenes of daily life in the Italian countryside. In one gesture, the object encompasses Pistoletto's present and past and asserts itself as a materialization of his wit and imagination.

The Oggetti in meno do not differentiate between the particular and the generic; on the contrary, they seem predicated on the erasure of the boundaries between these apparently opposite terms. *Casa a misura d'uomo* (*House on a Human Scale*, 1965–66; plate 93) is both archetypal and extremely individual in the sense that its dimensions correspond to that of one man—again, the English translation misses the nuances of the Italian, in which the singularity of *uomo* (man) persuasively pervades the characteristics attributed to the noun *casa* (house), so that the object is both an ideal model and a specific reference to an invisible body from which its measures may have emerged. A similar tension between one and many seems to be enacted by *Ti amo* (*I Love You*, 1965–66; plate 90), an apparently straightforward painting on canvas whose effective graphic nature brings to mind Pistoletto's training in advertising. A naked rectangular frame in black and white proudly and anonymously displays, in loud letters, the most intimate message—"I love you." But who loves whom, or what? Where does the I that loves come from? Is it the fragmented I that created the Oggetti in meno—that series, arbitrarily interrupted, of completely dissimilar objects? The enunciating subject is centerless, inhabiting difference and dispersal. The recipient is unknown, but clearly there must be one. The Oggetti in meno as a whole could be considered as a series of open letters with no particular recipient, containing verses, calling for action, unveiling secrets. Their vitality is clearer when contrasted with Minimalism's "specific objects"[14] and the literality with which these address both the spectator and the industrial mode of production. Pistoletto's objects correspond to a society in transition, where the industrial has not entirely replaced the artisanal, and where advanced industrial and popular-culture design coexist with manual labor. A similar complexity can perhaps be exceptionally found in Hélio Oiticica's *Tropicália* (fig. 13), an installation, first presented at the Museu de Arte Moderna, Rio de Janeiro, in 1967, that addressed Brazilian national identity in terms of a dialogue between the modern and the archaic.

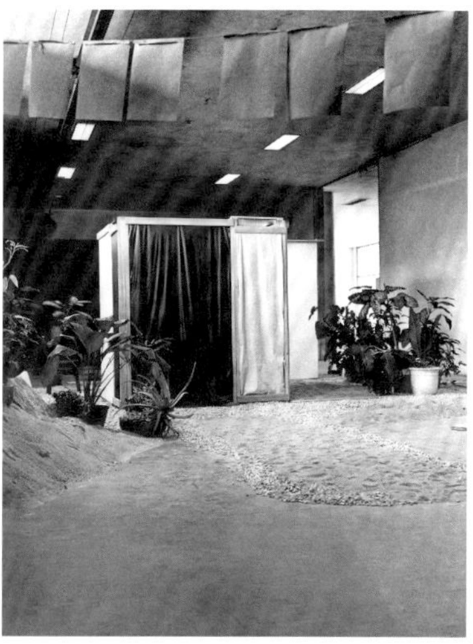

FIG. 13. Hélio Oiticica (Brazilian, 1937–1980). *Tropicália, Pentraveis PN 2 "Pureza é um mito" e PN 3 "Imagético"* (*Tropicália, Penetrables PN 2 Purity is a myth' and PN 3 Imagetical*), 1966–67, during the exhibition *Nova Objetividade* (*New Objectivity*) at the Museu de Arte Moderna, Rio de Janeiro, January 1967. Courtesy of Projeto Hélio Oiticica

Oiticica's installation was intended to become a space for action. He conceived it as a participatory platform in which friends—many of them samba dancers from the shantytown of Mangueira—and other artists would be invited to participate. It is hard not to imagine that Pistoletto had a similar conception for his Oggetti in meno. Produced in December 1965 and January 1966, they were photographed in various permutations in his studio—at that time located at via Reymond 13 in Turin. (It is in this studio that some of the actors of the Living Theatre will temporarily make

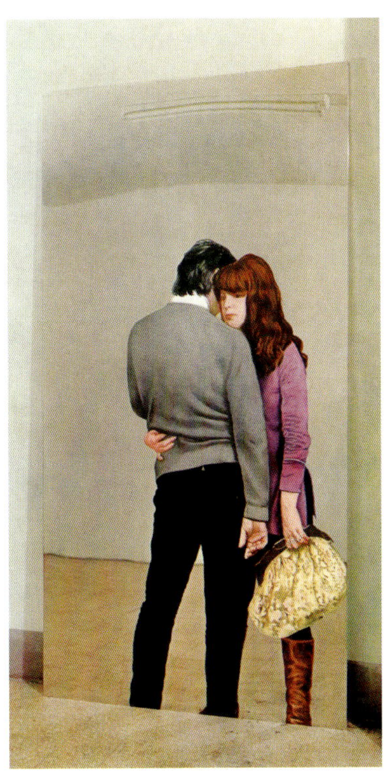

FIG. 14. Michelangelo Pistoletto, *Autoritratto con Souzka* (*Self-Portrait with Souzka*), 1967. Painted tissue paper on polished stainless steel, 90$^{9}/_{16}$ x 47¼ inches (230 x 120 cm). Private collection

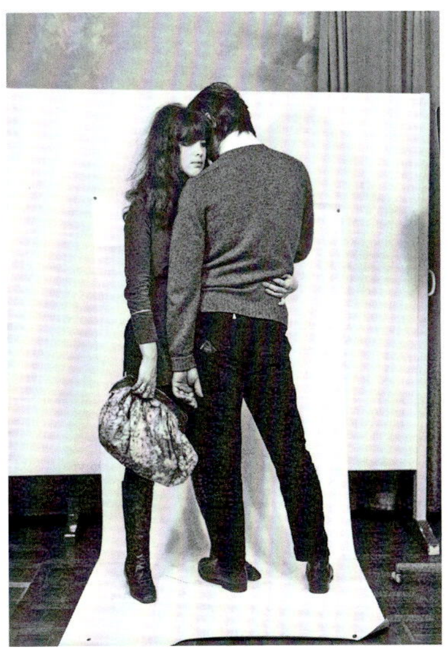

FIG. 15. Source photograph for *Autoritratto con Souzka* (*Self-Portrait with Souzka*; 1967; fig. 14). Courtesy of Cittadellarte-Fondazione Pistoletto, Biella

their quarters—a mirror painting from 1967 shows Pistoletto tenderly embracing Souzka, one of the members of the Living Theatre troupe; figs. 14, 15.) Pistoletto shows only a small selection of them, together with objects of a later series called *Versioni* (Versions; see figs. 59, 60)—in which the chosen object is partially altered with the use of a mirror—a year after, at Galleria La Bertesca in Genoa, together with a group of his mirror paintings, in a practice that will be extended for years to come. A few months later, on March 6, 1967, he realizes the first of his actions at the Piper Pluriclub (figs. 16, 17), a multifunctional space in Turin built by the architect Piero Derossi the year before. This is the same space where the Living Theatre performs *Mysteries . . . and Smaller Pieces* less than ten days after Pistoletto's action, on March 15, 1967 (fig. 18).

Resisted by his dealers and by some of his critics, Pistoletto's Oggetti in meno insistently point to the emergence of a new form of theatricality in his work, one in which the space for art is progressively conceived as a space for action. It is a conception of action that does not intend to locate itself outside art, or to confuse the boundaries between art and life, but one that, assuming the form of play, makes of action a performative reflection on the possibilities open to art in contemporary society. That Pistoletto seems increasingly to have understood art as a staged interrogation of its own nature and transformative potential is made clear by the fact that after 1967 the exhibitions of his work systematically assume the form of plays. This is evidenced first by his participation in *Con-temp-l'azione*, an exhibition that took place in December 1967 at three galleries in Turin, in which the artist made a ball of newspaper (*Sfera di giornali*, see fig. 64) to roll between the exhibition spaces—an action that he repeats a month later, in January, this time in the company of his partner Maria Pioppi. A wonderfully playful film by Ugo Nespolo, *Buongiorno, Michelangelo* (*Good Morning, Michelangelo*, 1968), shows the entire sequence of action, from Pistoletto shaving in front of one of his mirrors to a delirious night scene in which the rolling sculpture becomes a circus prop, a magnified soccer ball, and a shining moon to be carried along the endless Turinese arcades (fig. 19). Subsequently, at the time of his solo show at the Sperone gallery, also in December 1967, Pistoletto publishes a manifesto announcing that he has opened his studio as a place for encounter and collaboration (fig. 20). In February of the following year, his solo exhibition at Galleria L'Attico in Rome is conceived literally as a stage for action, complete with sets and costumes borrowed from Cinecittà (see figs. 92, 112). Finally, on May 8, the first action of the newly formed group Lo Zoo, *Cocapicco e vestitorito*, takes place at the Piper Pluriclub (see fig. 76).

Buongiorno, Michelangelo shows the *Sfera di giornali* used, as if by a modern Theseus, to unravel through day and night the urban labyrinth of Turin's streets. Toward the end of the film, it is Pistoletto's *Rosa bruciata* (*Burnt Rose*, 1965; plate 76) that becomes the main character, denouncing a clear theatrical vocation for this group of objects. Interestingly, several of the Oggetti in meno—*Lampada a mercurio* (*Mercury Lamp*, 1965; plate 79), *Struttura per parlare in piedi* (*Structure for Talking while Standing*, 1965–66; plate 87), *Corpo a pera* (*Pear Body*, 1965–66), *Casa a misura d'uomo* (*House

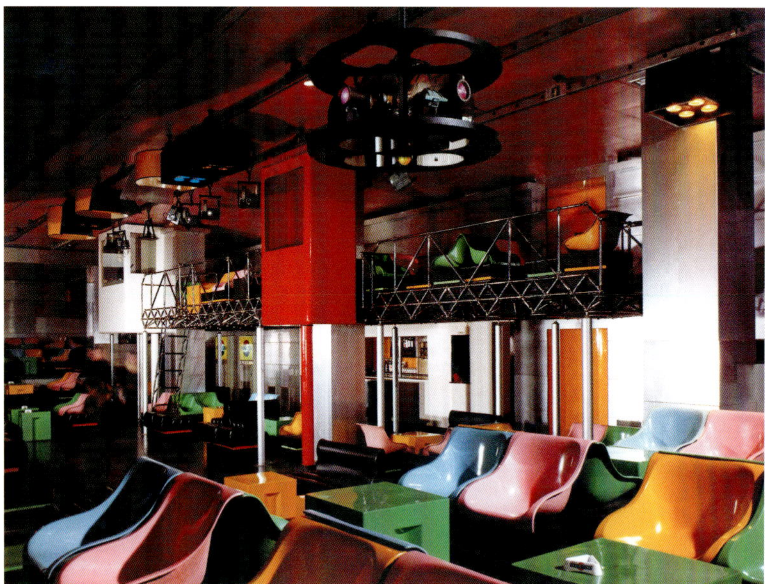

FIG. 16. Interior of the Piper Pluriclub, Turin, 1966. Photograph by Renato Rinaldi. Courtesy of Derossi Associati, Turin

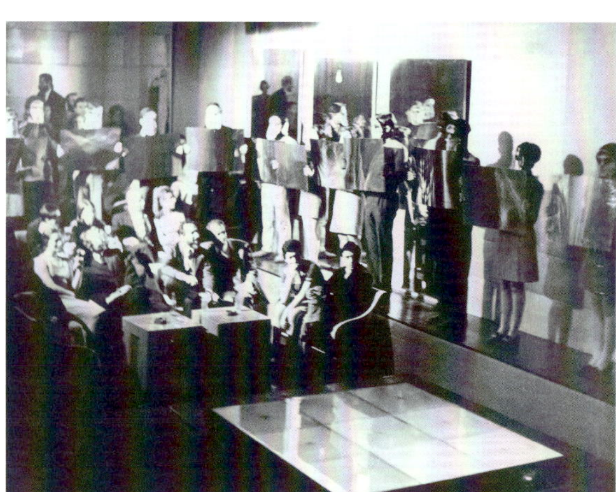

FIG. 17. Pistoletto's action *La fine di Pistoletto* (*The End of Pistoletto*) at the Piper Pluriclub, Turin, March 6, 1967. Photograph by Renato Rinaldi. Courtesy of Cittadellarte-Fondazione Pistoletto, Biella

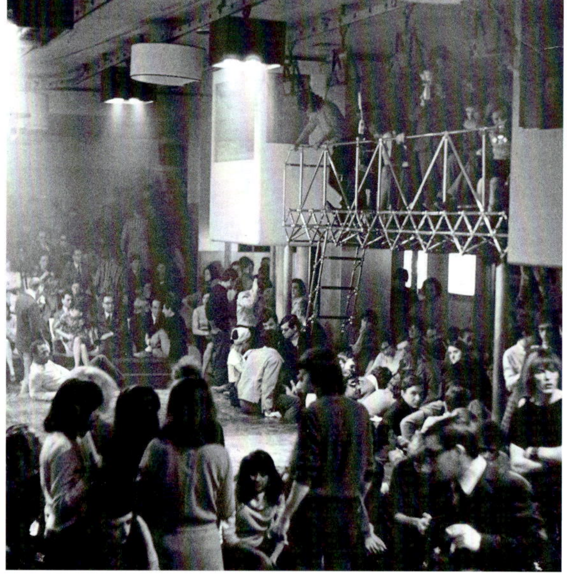

FIG. 18. The Living Theatre's performance of *Mysteries . . . and Smaller Pieces* at the Piper Pluriclub, Turin, March 15, 1967. Photograph by Renato Rinaldi. Courtesy of Derossi Associati, Turin

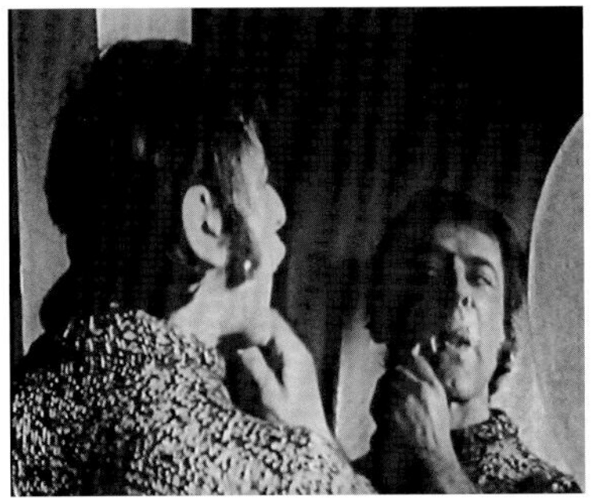

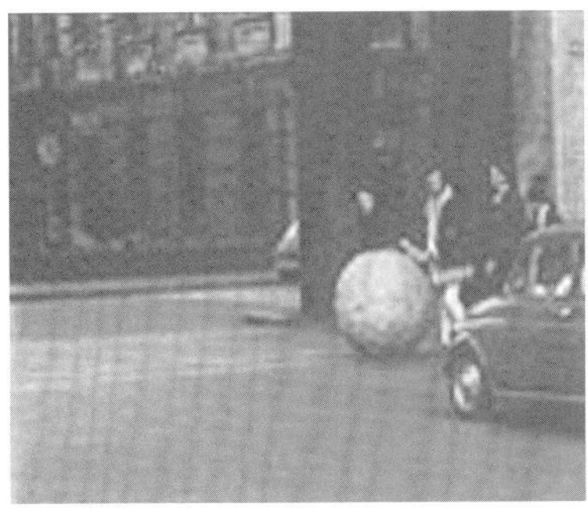

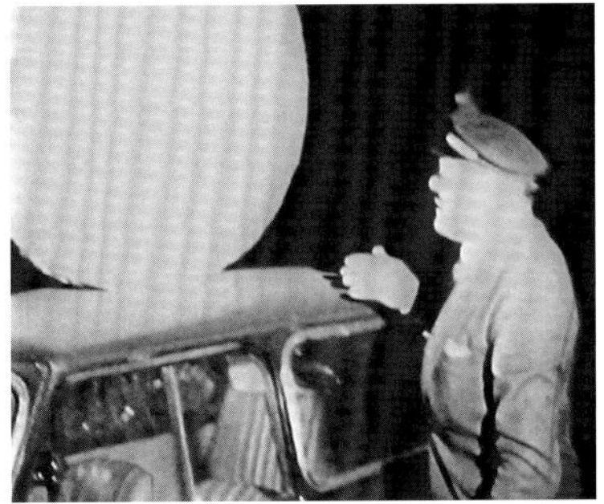

FIG. 19. Stills from the film *Buongiorno, Michelangelo* (1968), by Ugo Nespolo. Courtesy of Cittadellarte-Fondazione Pistoletto, Biella

on a Human Scale, 1965–66; plate 93), and *Metrocubo d'infinito* (*Cubic Meter of Infinity*, 1966; plate 96)—finally find their way on stage when Lo Zoo presents *Play* at the Deposito d'arte presente (Warehouse of Present Art) in Turin in December 1968 (fig. 21). Once again, they are used as an instigation for action, in a manner that recalls the constructions that Robert Rauschenberg created for the Merce Cunningham dance company on the occasion of its 1954 presentation of *Minutiae*—an important landmark in its ongoing collaboration that was certainly relevant to the work of many artists across the Atlantic.

The specific form of theatricality that Pistoletto develops during this period seems to have been contained, in essence, in the first installation of his Oggetti in meno in his studio, and is reflected in the photographs taken on that occasion (see fig. 52). There they are, much as actors waiting for a curtain call, coming and going in a variety of arrangements that inescapably point to their own semantic instability, their existence stolen from a remote field of endless possibility, their itinerant being in the world. It is perhaps possible to imagine that Pistoletto was able to recognize some of those same qualities in the work of the young artist he accidentally meets in Rome in 1965, on the occasion of the opening of a group exhibition in a space near Piazza del Popolo. Only two years Pino Pascali's senior, Pistoletto is at the time a much better-known artist, still mostly identified with his mirrors. Pascali introduces himself and, surprisingly, persuades Pistoletto to leave the party and walk to his nearby studio to see his recent work. Pistoletto is stunned to see a courtyard full of weapons—cannons, bombs, machine guns—all realistically assembled with scraps of metal and painted wood, complete with all the paraphernalia of war, including what look like camouflage nets. Amused, Pascali tells Pistoletto that the weapons are all fakes, made with discarded materials, bits and pieces of anything he can get his hands on. Pistoletto goes back to Turin to tell Gian Enzo Sperone about this extraordinary artist, whose exhibition the dealer arranges for January of the following year.

A year earlier, in January 1965, Pascali had exhibited his sculptures and pictorial reliefs at the legendary gallery La Tartaruga in Rome, his first solo show. The disparate works included in the exhibition—a large model of the Colosseum, a number of objects composing a still life, and large stretched canvases reproducing female body parts—apparently have in common only their precarious materiality. The objects, comprising champagne bottles made of plastic, fruits embalmed with wax, and a *triccheballacche* (a popular Neapolitan musical instrument made of wood), are called *Gruppo di personaggi* (*Group of Characters*, 1964; fig. 23), and some of them have an opportunity to perform the following April, when Pascali shows his *Teatrino* (*Puppet Theater*, 1964; fig. 22) at the Feltrinelli library in Rome, on the occasion of a group exhibition appropriately titled *Realtà dell'immagine* (*Reality of the Image*). In July 1965, Pascali performs a ritualistic action—described by the art historian Livia Velani as the first Happening in Rome[15]—on the path of the Living Theatre's recent presentation of *Mysteries*, in front of one of his sculptures, a presumptive funeral monument in honor of Corrado V, a medieval ruler of Naples. Clearly, theater was very much on Pascali's mind.

It could hardly have been otherwise, considering that Pascali had studied stage design with the artist Toti Scialoja at the Accademia di Belle Arti in Rome—an apprenticeship in which he was joined by Jannis Kounellis and Maria Pioppi—and had been creating sets for Italian television since 1964. As with Pistoletto, advertising provided Pascali with privileged access to the brave new modern world of consumer culture that was rapidly taking over life on the Italian peninsula. His early sculptures have repeatedly been characterized as an Italian response to Pop art, whose impact was strongly felt throughout the country after 1964, when the Grand Prix of painting was awarded to Robert Rauschenberg at the Venice Biennale. It is hard to think solely of Pop when looking at Pascali's *Teatrino* of 1964, with its bright orange curtain, its lemony yellow proscenium, and its carefully crafted, almost archaic character. Composed of two segments, a dark pedestal and the bright, towering arc of the proscenium, the sculpture has an ancient, almost phallic solar quality. Its pathetic cast of characters, including embalmed fruit and plastic bottles, immediately brings to mind street theater and the Commedia dell'Arte. During his short life, Pascali constantly negotiated between consumer and popular culture in his work. The elements reminiscent of Pop were to be consumed by an infinitely profound and archaic fire, filtered and transformed by an anthropological conception of art that is clearly manifest in the series of works realized toward the end of his life: sculptures evoking primitive tools in an exploration of the aesthetic dimension of the act of making, regardless of the object's ultimate functionality, or lack thereof.

Pistoletto must have recognized in Pascali's work some of the qualities that his mirrors undoubtedly harbor, transposed to the actual gallery space, so that the exhibition becomes a stage ready to be occupied by the spectator/participant—as Palma Buccarelli brilliantly describes in his introduction to the first retrospective of Pascali's work,[16] at the Galleria Nazionale d'Arte Moderna in Rome, soon after the artist's tragic death following a motorcycle accident at the Porta Pinciana tunnel on August 30, 1968. The similarities in Pistoletto's and Pascali's artistic research made their encounter the beginning of a close and intense friendship that lasted as long as the latter's life.

With the benefit of hindsight, it is possible to identify a similar notion of the exhibition space in a show that would leave profound traces in the history of the reception of conceptual art and post-Minimalism in Europe: *Live in Your Head: When Attitudes Become Form*, organized by Harald Szeemann, the young director of the Kunsthalle Bern, in March 1969.[17] Artists were invited to fabricate or re-create their works directly in the galleries of the museum, which became a stage for action more than a contemplative space. More than a year and half earlier, toward the end of 1967, the collector Marcello Levi, seemingly motivated by a group of artists that included Pistoletto and Piero Gilardi, and in association with Gian Enzo Sperone, had opened the Deposito d'arte presente at via San Fermo 3, in a former car dealership (fig. 26). It was destined to become simultaneously an open studio and an exhibition space for artists, many of whom had previously taken part in the first presentation of Arte Povera that the critic Germano Celant organized at Galleria La Bertesca in October 1967.

PISTOLETTO

dal 22 dicembre 1967
alla Galleria Sperone
TORINO

Con questa mostra io ho liberato il mio studio, che si apre per accoglierci i giovani che vogliono presentare il loro lavoro, fare delle cose, trovarsi.

PISTOLETTO
Via Carlo Reymond, 13
Torino - Tel. 63.51.05

GALLERIA SPERONE - VIA CESARE BATTISTI, 15 - TEL. 54.76.21

FIG. 20. The announcement of the opening of Pistoletto's studio to the public on December 22, 1967, in the context of his exhibition at Galleria Sperone, Turin. Courtesy of Cittadellarte-Fondazione Pistoletto, Biella

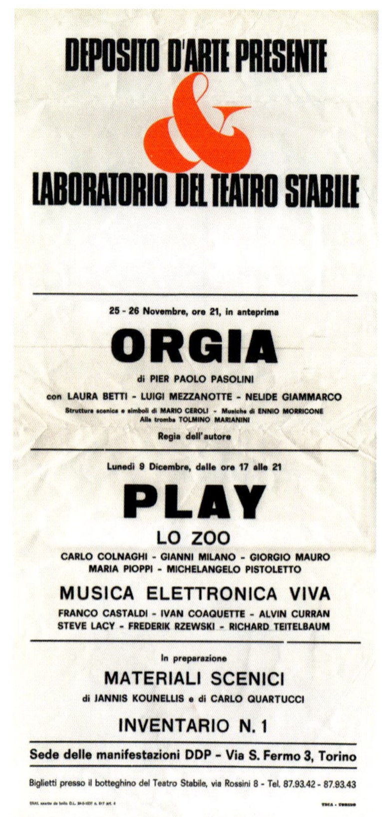

FIG. 21. The poster for Lo Zoo's performance of *Play* at the Deposito d'arte presente (Warehouse of Present Art) in Turin, December 1968. Courtesy of Cittadellarte-Fondazione Pistoletto, Biella

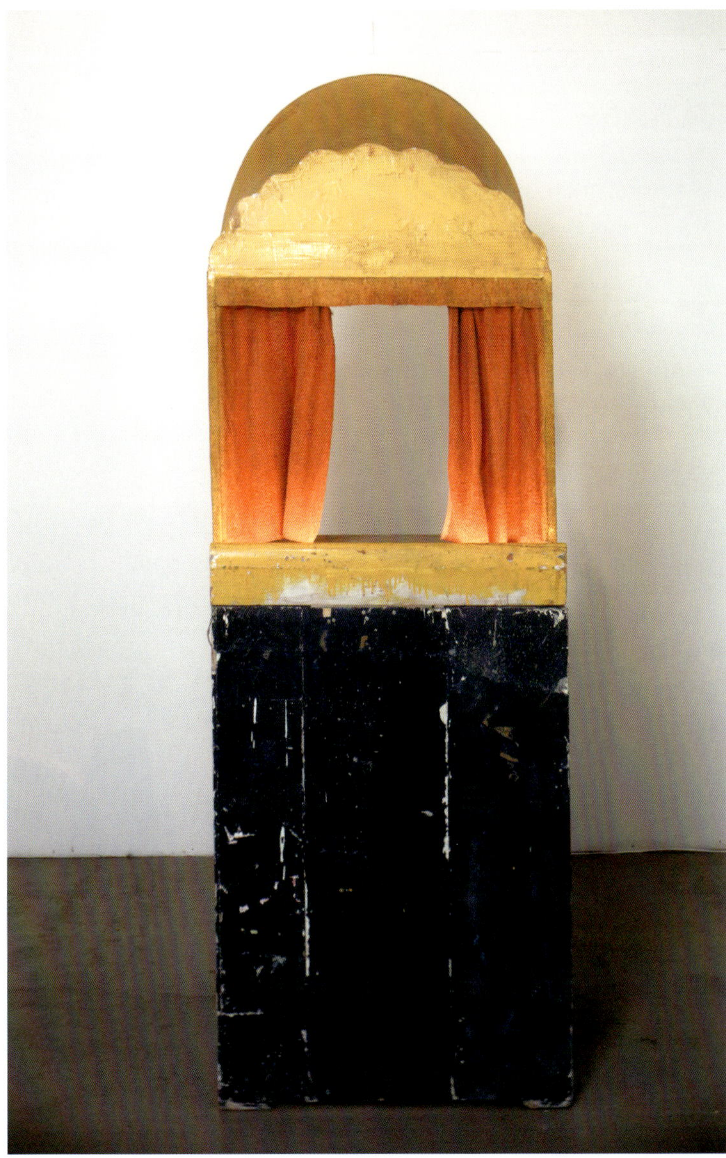

FIG. 22. Pino Pascali, *Teatrino (Theâtre de Guignol)* (*Puppet Theater [Theâtre de Guignol]*), 1964. Wood and painted canvas, 85 7/16 x 29 1/8 x 28 3/8 inches (217 x 74 x 72 cm). Collection of Liliane and Michel Durand-Dessert, Paris

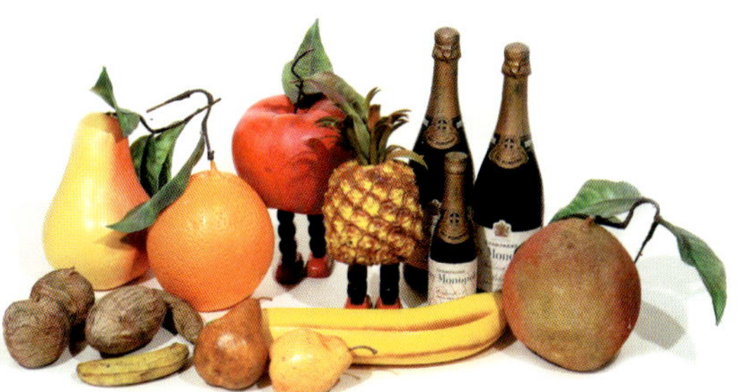

FIG. 23. Pino Pascali (Italian, 1935–1968). *Gruppo di personaggi* (*Group of Characters*), 1964. Various mediums and sizes. GNAM—Galleria Nazionale d'Arte Moderna e Contemporanea, Rome

Gilardi himself, in a recent interview with the critic and curator Francesco Manacorda,[18] locates in Pistoletto's use of his studio around 1966—as a place for meeting and production—the inaugural instances of such modality. Pistoletto did not use his studio simply as a space for action but conceived of those actions as a reflection on the meaning of artistic practice, a reflection he would articulate around the notion of collaboration and which constitutes an investigation into the possibilities of collective authorship.

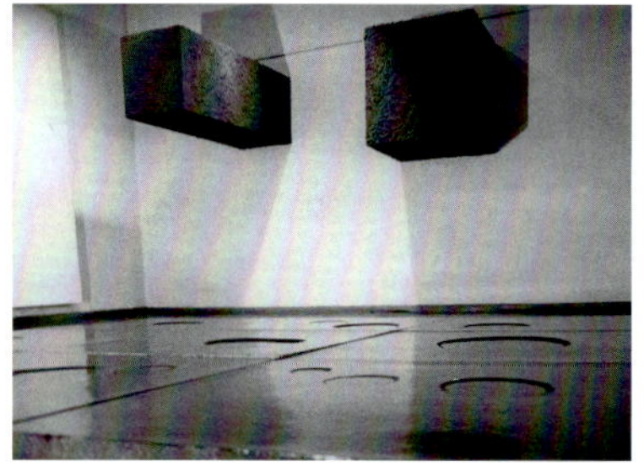

FIG. 24. The exhibition *Fuoco immagine acqua terra* (*Fire Image Water Earth*) at Galleria L'Attico, Rome, June 1967. Courtesy of L'Attico Archive-Fabio Sargentini, Rome

While keenly aware of the radical nature and relevance of his Oggetti in meno, Pistoletto seems to have been equally concerned about their reception beyond the circle of his artist friends. That hesitancy is made clear by the fact that he did not show them outside the studio immediately after they were created, instead producing a number of *Versioni* in which the objects were altered with mirrors for inclusion in an exhibition at La Bertesca at the end of 1966, and which evidently were intended to mediate, materially and metaphorically, between the artist's two bodies of work. He would agree instead to show just one mirror painting at the groundbreaking exhibition *Fuoco immagine acqua terra* (*Fire Image Water Earth*) at L'Attico in June 1967 (fig. 24), and only two Oggetti in meno, *Pozzo* and *Sarcofago* (*Well* and *Sarcophagus*; plates 78, 94), together with a group of mirrors, would be displayed at his second solo exhibition at Galerie Sonnabend, Paris, in December. (Pistoletto later reacquired both objects from the gallery, with the intention of assembling a complete set of them.) A retrospective in 1976 at the Palazzo Grassi in Venice (fig. 27) became the first opportunity to see the Oggetti in meno as a whole, and was followed by an exhibition entirely devoted to them at the Los Angeles Institute of Contemporary Art three years later, in 1979. But if their relevance was not entirely evident to important supporters of Pistoletto work, such as Ileana Sonnabend, it was extremely clear to another artist from Turin, Alighiero Boetti, whose artistic development was profoundly affected by his encounter with the sculptures in Pistoletto's studio and those of Pascali at the Sperone exhibition in 1966. On January 19, 1967, Boetti's first solo exhibition opened at Christian Stein's gallery in Turin. Among the sculptures exhibited were *Catasta* (*Heap*, 1967), *Lampada annuale* (*Annual Lamp*, 1966), *Mazzo di tubi* (*Bouquet of Tubes*, 1966), *Rotolo di cartone ondulato* (*Roll of Corrugated Cardboard*, 1966), *Scala* (*Ladder*, 1966; fig. 25), and *Sedia* (*Chair*, 1966; fig. 25). The correspondence between Boetti's objects and Pistoletto's is clear—although Boetti's beautifully evocative objects lack the anarchic inventiveness and clarity of execution present in the Oggetti in meno. The wild diversity of Pistoletto's Oggetti in meno, each of them a synthetic solution to a complex sculptural problem, seems to have been the spark that ultimately prompted Boetti to develop his own fertile artistic path. A work by Boetti from 1968, *Shaman/Showman*—a photomontage showing the artist as a figure on a tarot card—perhaps constitutes a renewed homage to, and literalization of, the potential implications of Pistoletto's Oggetti in meno.[19] *Shaman/Showman*—the title contains a succinct reference to the duality assumed by the artist when the space of art is ultimately conceived as a reflection on the possibility of action, and vice versa.

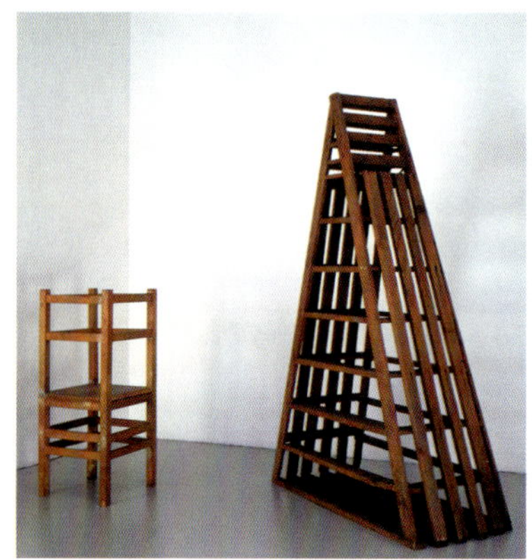

FIG. 25. Alighiero Boetti (Italian, 1940–1994). *Scala* (*Ladder*); *Sedia* (*Chair*), 1966. Wood, 35¼ x 14 9/16 x 15 3/8 inches (89.5 x 37 x 39 cm); 67 15/16 x 43 11/16 x 18 7/8 inches (172.5 x 111 x 48 cm). Collection of Margherita Stein; property of Fondazione CRT, Progetto Arte Moderna e Contemporanea. On permanent loan to Castello di Rivoli Museo d'Arte Contemporanea, Rivoli, and Galleria Civica d'Arte Moderna e Contemporanea, Turin

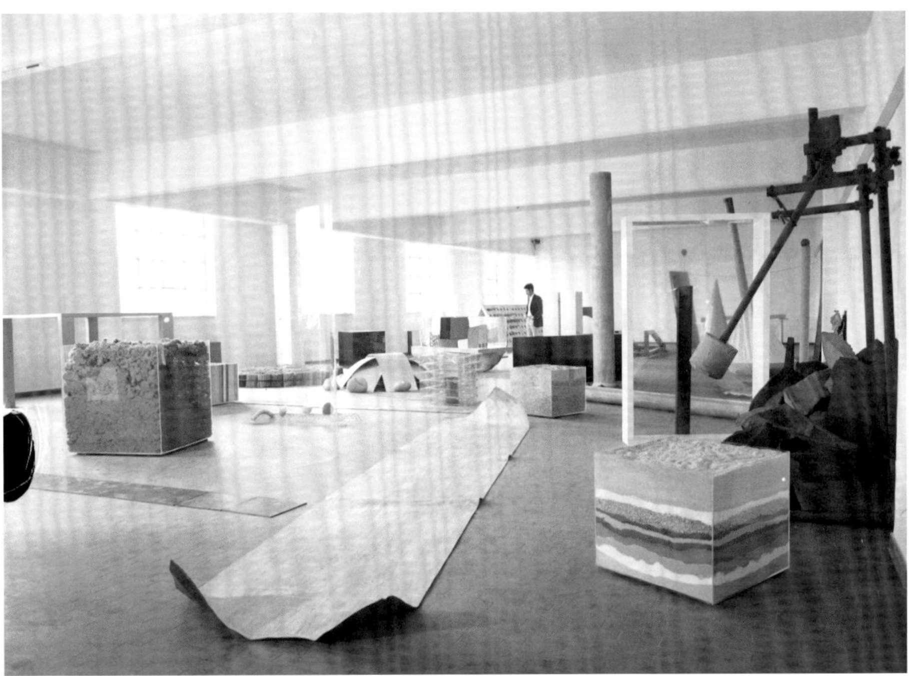

FIG. 26. The Deposito d'arte presente (Warehouse of Present Art), at via San Fermo 3, Turin. Pistoletto's *Bagna-barca* (*Bath-Boat*, 1968) is visible in the background. The figure in the far background is Gian Enzo Sperone. Photograph by Paolo Bressano. Courtesy of Cittadellarte-Fondazione Pistoletto, Biella

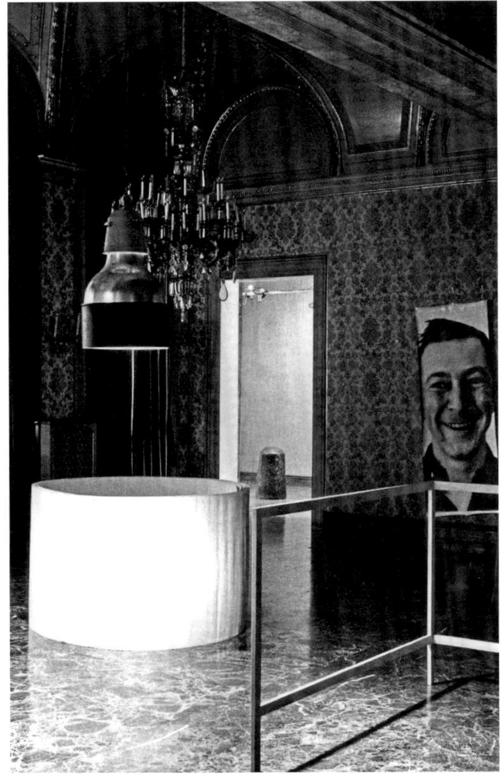

FIG. 27. Pistoletto's retrospective at the Palazzo Grassi, Venice, summer 1976. Photograph by Paolo Pellion. Courtesy of Cittadellarte-Fondazione Pistoletto, Biella

UOMO NERO

> *Ho affrontato la vita come teatro. Ho indossato innumerevoli maschere. A volte la gente non mi riconosce, perché cambio maschera, cambio costume, cambio attegiamento. Ma é istintivo, non conosco che maschere, non vedo che maschere, che atteggiamenti, che costumi, non vedo mai un volto, un uomo.*
> *(I've faced life as though it were theater. I've worn countless masks. Sometimes people don't recognize me, because I changed my mask, my costume, my pose. But it's instinctive, I know only masks, I see only masks, poses, costumes, I never see a face, a person.)*
>
> —Michelangelo Pistoletto, *L'Uomo nero, il lato insopportabile* [20]

The "Uomo nero" seems to have insinuated himself for the first time on May 13, 1969, when Lo Zoo presented their play *I ratti baratti* (*The Bartering Rats*) at De Lantaren in Rotterdam (see fig. 91). As with many of the actions of this group, *I ratti baratti* was based on a loose script that was used as a starting point for improvisation, including the hyperbolic rehearsal of otherwise common gestures, absurd activities, and lyrical fragments clearly reminiscent of the enchanted world of fairytales. On this occasion, the Uomo nero was incarnated by the actor Lionello Gennero, one of the members of Lo Zoo, who at the start of the play emerged ominously onto the stage from the space traditionally used by the prompter, wearing what later becomes his characteristic black apron and bare feet. His subsequent actions seemed to be intended to negotiate the space between the stage and the audience until, giving his back to the spectators, he opened the curtains on the stage with the movement of a baton, revealing only a dark, deep, empty space. Gennero left Lo Zoo after its European tour finished at the end of the month. Back in Italy, the rest of the group remained in the small town of Corniglia, near Genoa, engaged in a collective experiment that they chose to describe as *La ricerca dell'Uomo nero* (*The Research of the Minus Man*; see figs. 89, 90).

The action seems to begin as a game. One of the members of Lo Zoo inscribes a circle with chalk on the floor, and the others promptly enter the marked space to create their own circles, in a clumsy race in which the first one to finish is declared the winner. But the winner's prize is to be beaten by the rest of the players. Then, while they leave to sleep, he stands up and improvises an individual action. Awakened from their lethargy, the rest of the group respond, collectively (fig. 28). The action begins anew, and once it is concluded, a new Uomo nero is designated to start the whole sequence over again. The entire group rehearsed the game daily, from 4:00 to 7:30 p.m., for the duration of four months.

Having made his buffoonish but certainly anxious and somewhat threatening entry into Pistoletto's work, the Uomo nero appears and reappears insistently for years to come, like a disquieting image from a childhood dream (fig. 29). On October 25, Lo Zoo presents the spectacle *Lo Zoo scopre l'Uomo nero* (*Lo Zoo Discovers the Minus Man*) at Galleria

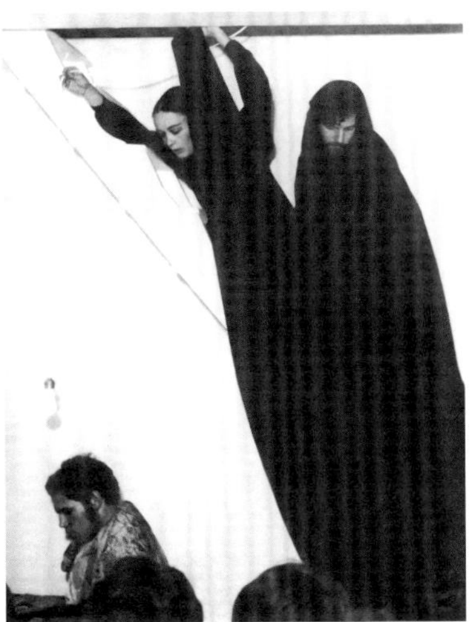

FIG. 28. Lo Zoo's performance of *L'Uomo nero* (*The Minus Man*) at Artestudio, Macerata, November 14 1969, with (from left) Dennis Kaufman, Maria Pioppi, and Lele Vacchetto. Photograph by Raul Morichetti. Courtesy of Cittadellarte-Fondazione Pistoletto, Biella

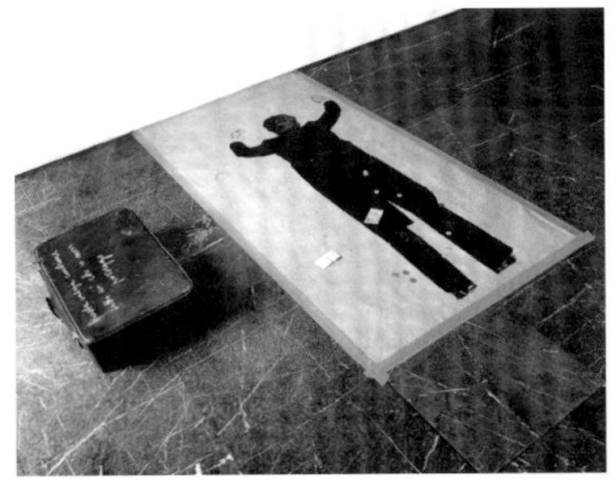

FIG. 29. Michelangelo Pistoletto. Left: *Valigia dell'Uomo nero* (*Suitcase of the Minus Man*), 1969. Suitcase with writing in chalk, 7½ x 26¾ x 16⁹⁄₁₆ inches (19 x 68 x 42 cm). Right: *Il direttore d'orchestra* (*The Conductor*), 1976. Silkscreen on paper, 91⅜ x 47¼ inches (232 x 120 cm). Private collection. Installation, Palazzo Grassi, Venice, 1976. Photograph by Paolo Mussat Sartor

Sperone in Turin. Subsequently, Lo Zoo introduces their Uomo nero in the city of Macerata, near Ancona, on November 14. In 1969, Pistoletto dedicates exactly one month to daily writing a book with as many pages as there are days in a calendar year. The book is titled *L'Uomo nero, il lato insopportabile* (*The Minus Man, the Unbearable Side*; fig. 30). At Bologna, in 1970, he introduces audiences to the working quarters of his Uomo nero by presenting at the Museo Civico his *Ufficio dell'Uomo nero* (*Office of the Minus Man*; see fig. 67), a staged world inhabited by the Oggetti in meno—and possibly the reason why in many texts *Uomo nero* is translated as "Minus Man," an expression that, more than anything, involves a conscious act of interpretation. It will take almost three decades for the Uomo nero to reappear, finally disguised as Pistoletto, in a film on the artist realized by Pierre Colibeuf between 1996 and 1998. By this time, the association between the Uomo nero and Pistoletto would seem to have become natural. In 1997, a 1970 photograph of Pistoletto dressed as a goofy nineteenth-century gentleman or general, with the abundant beard of a patriarch and holding an umbrella with a sculpted rose for a handle, will make a decisive appearance on the cover of the German edition of his book (fig. 31). Becoming the Uomo nero was, for Pistoletto, clearly an irresistible but ultimately unbearable option.

But if the Uomo nero is that character which the artist can never fully enact, even if his work irresistibly moves in his direction, it is because his ambiguous persona has come to represent a central figure in the development of Pistoletto's practice. The atavism of the Uomo nero is a mark of freedom—first and foremost a liberation from the set of cultural conventions that correspond to his obsolete formal dress. He stands for the emancipation process that Pistoletto's artistic development has passionately aimed at since the 1950s—an emancipation from the constraints of art conceived as a purely contemplative activity, produced in isolation by a single individual. Pistoletto has written that Lo Zoo was born of a sardonic remark by another actor, Carlo Colnaghi, who would become one of its most active members: "I am in the same position as a lion in a cage."[21] The Uomo nero is both the guardian and the prisoner. The Uomo nero is, in fact, to borrow a term used by Marcel Duchamp toward the end of his life to account for his own work, an *anartiste*. For the French refers less to a character than to a position that expresses a paradoxical tension between the simultaneous affirmation and negation of what exists. In the case of Pistoletto, the Uomo nero expresses the tension between one and many, self-portraiture and anonymity, between subjective reveries and collective authorship. *La ricerca dell'Uomo nero* is not only a play in the sense of being both an invented game and a spectacle; it is a play whose rules are constantly to be reinvented and located in the endless negotiations between tradition and innovation, individual authorship and collective practice, between repetition and improvisation.

Undoubtedly, the Uomo nero temporarily incarnates the centerless author of the Oggetti in meno, but there is something deeper and darker in the clownish severity with which he imposes his presence, even momentarily, on the other members of the group. After all, he is supposed to be the exact opposite of who we are. He is always already marked—a foreigner, a menace. He asserts his precarious sovereignty outside of any cultural convention, outside of language itself, a boundless power to be responded to with sheer violence. He then ceases to be, only to be reborn. In the northern Italy of the 1960s, a traditional society undergoing an accelerated process of transformation, a reference to a "black man" must inevitably have conjured colonial undertones, an unmistakable reference to Africa as the dark continent of Joseph Conrad, the threatening unknown. The Uomo nero is the "other" mirror that reflects oneself, that gives one back a sense of self in an image in which no fulfilling self-recognition is ever possible. It is understandable, then, that his irruption prefigures the ultimate dissolution of Lo Zoo, and makes a lasting mark in Pistoletto's artistic evolution. His *L'Uomo nero, il lato insopportabile*, a remarkable incursion in experimental writing, has the mission of placating that inscrutable presence, and was written in the context of a society that was increasingly resorting to all forms of violence to resolve its own tension between traditional and revolutionary ideals. In the fall of 1969, exactly at the time that Lo Zoo is insistently looking for the Uomo nero in the idyllic small town of Corniglia overlooking the Mediterranean sea, an extensive workers' strike in Turin marks the beginning of the Italian "Autunno Caldo" (Hot Autumn), a season of social and political unrest. At the end of that year, in December, a bomb exploding in the atrium of the Banca Nazionale dell'Agricoltura e Pesca in Milan kills seventeen people. Two years later, the Red Brigades organize their first kidnapping. The force of an irrational violence progressively obliterates the dreams of social equality and collective emancipation that had characterized the earlier part of the decade.

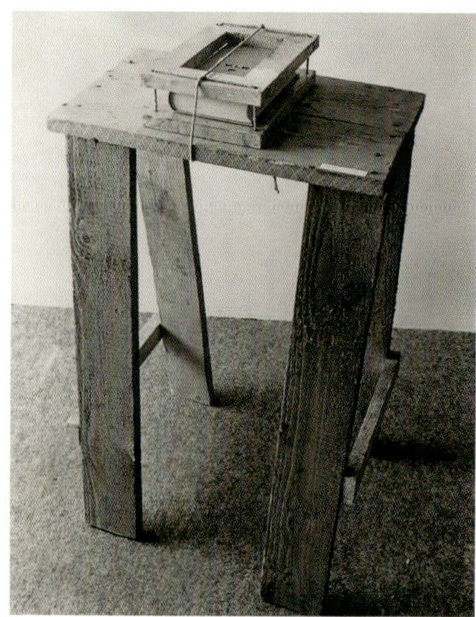

FIG. 30. Michelangelo Pistoletto, *Manuscript of "L'Uomo nero, il lato insopportabile,"* 1970. Wood, string, and book. Collection of the artist

In his book, Pistoletto imagines that the game in Corniglia slowly becomes the main activity around which the town lives. First its youth, and eventually the entire population of the town, come to participate in the interminable game. Pistoletto's endless book, whose final pages were written halfway through the process, so that the reader, finally arriving at the end, finds it connected to the beginning in a seamless loop, is an exercise in a purely performative form of writing. Pistoletto writes to bring to action those aspects of his past experiences that cannot possibly be reenacted. He uses the means of a confessional form of literature, a form of diary, to imagine an ideal community, closely united around the unstable blessing of the Uomo nero—"Ma le storie belle finiscono presto" (But beautiful stories are soon over).[22]

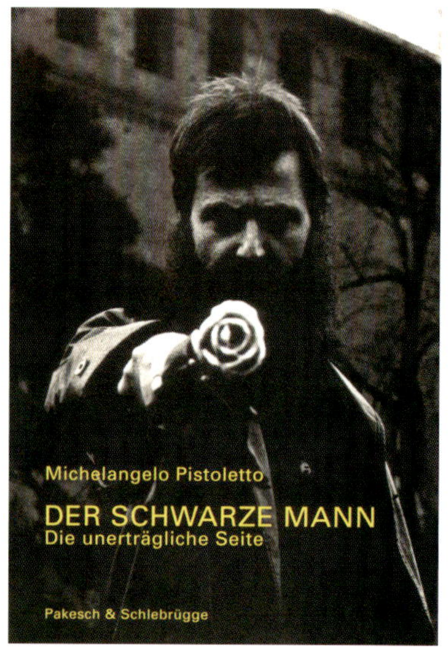

FIG. 31. The cover of the 1997 German translation of Pistoletto's book *L'Uomo nero, il lato insopportabile* (1970). The photograph of Pistoletto is by Paolo Mussat Sartor. Courtesy of Cittadellarte-Fondazione Pistoletto, Biella

CODA

This exhibition and its accompanying publication were set the task of tracing the passage from painting to collaboration in Pistoletto's work, a passage that took place from the latter part of the 1950s through the early 1970s and is better understood not teleologically, but as the repeated actualization—in the context of an increasingly unstable political and social environment—of the tension between self-recognition and anonymity that seems to have permeated his artistic practice during those years. Felt throughout the works that Pistoletto produced in this period are both the playful positivity of invention and the productive anxiety of a lack, signified by the impossibility of assuming a stable identity in his practice. His works—paintings, sculptures, and actions—could be considered an accurate expression of the tension between self-portraiture and collective authorship in a society in tension. It is precisely the impossibility of self-recognition, structurally inscribed in modern portraiture, that ultimately becomes, in the context of Pistoletto's work, a liberating impulse, the instrument of a constant search for emancipation. As such, it manifests itself first as a negation of the nihilistic existentialism of Art informel and then of the reductivism of Pop and Minimalism, ultimately to coalesce around an open interrogation, still pertinent today, concerning the relationship between art and collective action. In their profound joy and insistent anxiety, these works are deeply inscribed in the historical and geographical context in which they were produced, while at the same time opening up many fruitful possibilities that are yet to be explored. In the story of the series of contingent and diverse incarnations that Pistoletto's work traverses from 1956 to 1974, we are perhaps able to find not only a reflection of the trials and tribulations undergone by a rapidly transforming society, but also a key to our contemporary situation.

The goal of this publication has been precisely to open up new avenues for the interpretation of Pistoletto's work. The scholarly essays in this book certainly aspire to accomplish that objective. Angela Vettese wonderfully illuminates the interlude that predates the production of the first mirror paintings in the early 1960s, allowing the reader to grasp the significance of the events in that period of Pistoletto's life as well as the artistic context of postwar Turin. Jean-François Chevrier forcefully returns to Pistoletto, an artist to whom he has already devoted a number of insightful essays, in the most comprehensive exploration of the Oggetti in meno to date, positioning these works in relation to other series, like the mirror paintings and Plexiglas works, while addressing their place in the context of American Minimalism, conceptual art, and Pop. Claire Gilman analyzes the actions and spectacles of Lo Zoo, specifically in connection with the "Poor Theatre" of Jerzy Grotowski and the activities of the Living Theatre, locating in Pistoletto's performances of the mid- to late 1960s the genesis of his beautiful *stracci* (rag) works. Gabriele Guercio's essay allows for the possibility of a contemporary understanding of Pistoletto's work as the embodiment of a model of original forms of community and collective action. Suzanne Penn's richly detailed account of the process involved in the creation of Pistoletto's mirror paintings constitutes an inaugural contribution to a central subject in our understanding of the artist, one that has never before been properly addressed. The essays are complemented by Marco Farano's and Luigia Lonardelli's thoughtful chronologies of the period under study. While Farano concentrates on the events of Pistoletto's life and career, Lonardelli gives the reader information about the wider political and cultural situation of Italy. Finally, a selection of Pistoletto's extraordinarily perceptive writings from the years 1956–74 are included, so that the eloquent voice of the artist can be heard in its exemplary clarity. Always insightful and almost painfully lucid, at times vehement but tirelessly playful and endlessly inventive, Pistoletto's texts are among the most important reflections on art rehearsed at a time already indelibly marked by an extraordinary number of critical texts by both artists and writers.

The texts in this catalogue do not aspire to provide a unique perspective from which to access the works that Pistoletto created from 1956 through 1974. The richness and complexity of his practice do not allow such forms of reductivism. In the ongoing conversation that they hopefully establish, with its partial agreements and deliberate contradictions, they perhaps perform the desired task of opening another chapter in the critical interpretations of the work of one of the key figures in art history of the postwar period. That they manage to do so without historicizing Pistoletto, but rather by rendering a careful consideration of his practice from today's perspective ever more urgent, is the best possible testimony to the continuing relevance of his work.

I am profoundly indebted to many people with whom I had the invaluable opportunity to engage in wonderfully illuminating conversations about Pistoletto and the period under consideration in this exhibition. First and foremost, my thanks go to Michelangelo and his wife, Maria Pioppi, to whom I owe much more than I can possibly account for with just a few words. Since 2006, they have patiently answered all my questions, hosted me at their house in Biella, and aided me in every imaginable aspect of the exhibition and this publication. Clino Trini Castelli, Germano Celant, Martin Friedman, Antonio Homem, Marcello Levi, Pier Luigi Pero, Valentina Pero, Giorgio Persano, Fabio Sargentini, Paolo Mussat Sartor, and Gian Enzo Sperone all generously agreed to be interviewed at different times during the preparations for this project. To Kathleen Krattenmaker and Roberta Nuzzaci, I owe thanks for many invaluable suggestions on this text. Lastly, I am grateful to Anna Mattirolo for her constant support and the expert advice that allowed me to bring this exhibition to fruition.

1 Marcel Duchamp to Helen Freeman, February 12, 1952, in *Affectionately Marcel: The Selected Correspondence of Marcel Duchamp*, ed. Francis M. Naumann and Hector Obalk, trans. Jill Taylor (Ghent, Amsterdam: Ludion Press, 2000), pp. 308–9.

2 See Michelangelo Pistoletto, "Progetto Arte," at www.pistoletto.it/it/testi/progetto_arte.pdf; and for the translation, www.pistoletto.it/eng/testi/the_progetto_arte_manifesto.pdf.

3 Alberto Papuzzi, "Lo scrutatore nella nuvola d'ira (Torino, 1950–1970)," in *Un'avventura internazionale: Torino e le arti, 1950–1970* (Milan: Charta, 1993), pp. 35–42.

4 Michelangelo Pistoletto, "Per Armando Testa," in *Armando Testa*, exh. cat. (Milan: Charta, 2001), p. 66.

5 Marco Belpoliti, Gianni Canova, and Stefano Chiodi, *Annisettanta: il decennio lungo del secolo breve*, exh. cat. (Milan: Skira, 2007), p. 77.

6 Initially called *Opposti Estremismi* (Opposing Extremisms), the period was later renamed the *anni piombo* (years of lead) after the film *Marianne and Juliane* (1981) by Margarethe von Trotta (called *Die bleierne Zeit* in the original German).

7 See Belpoliti, Canova, and Chiodi, *Annisettanta.*

8 See Fundació Antoni Tàpies, *Lygia Clark*, exh. cat. (Barcelona: Fundació Antoni Tàpies, 1997).

9 Martin Friedman, "Michelangelo Pistoletto," in *Michelangelo Pistoletto: A Reflected World*, exh. cat. (Minneapolis: Walker Art Center, 1966).

10 This self-portrait has been variously dated to 1969 or 1970. It was first exhibited in *New Multiple Art* at the Whitechapel Art Gallery, London, in November 1970, when it was dated to 1970.

11 Pier Paolo Pasolini, interview by Furio Colombo, November 1, 1975, in *Tuttolibri*, a supplement to the newspaper *La Stampa*, November 8, 1975.

12 Pistoletto has described many times the precise moment in which he realized that the varnished surface of his paintings had become reflective enough that he no longer needed to resort to a mirror to make a self-portrait. That realization initiated a radical passage that would be completed with his mirror paintings, which were destined to introduce a fundamental and lasting break in his artistic practice as a whole.

13 Grace Glueck, "Highways, Mirrors and. . . Gee," *New York Times*, February 2, 1969.

14 The phrase comes from Donald Judd's seminal essay "Specific Objects," published in *Arts Yearbook* 8 (1965), pp. 74–82.

15 See Livia Velandi, "'Ho letto così tutto di Botto. . .,'" in *Pino Pascali: Napoli, Castel Sant'Elmo*, ed. Achille Bonito Oliva, Angela Tecce, and Livia Velani, exh. cat. (Milan: Electa, 2004), p. 103.

16 Palma Buccarelli, *Mostra di Pino Pascali*, exh. cat. (Rome: De Luca, 1969), pp. 5–12, esp. p. 6.

17 Harald Szeemann, *Live in Your Head: When Attitudes Become Form; Works, Concepts, Processes, Situations, Information*, exh. cat. (Bern: Kunsthalle, 1969).

18 "Temporary Artistic Communities: Francesco Manacorda Interviews Piero Gilardi," Turin, November 8, 2008, unpublished transcript.

19 See Jean Christophe Amman, *Alighiero Boetti: catalogo generale*, vol. 1 (Milan: Electa, 2009), pl. 194.

20 Michelangelo Pistoletto, *L'Uomo nero, il lato insopportabile* (Salerno: Rumma, 1970), p. 129; translation from "The Minus Man, the Unbearable Side," in *Michelangelo Pistoletto: A Minus Artist* (Florence: hopefulmonster, 1988), pp. 128–29.

21 See Maria Teresa Roberto, "Davanti allo specchio, al di qua delle sbarre: Lo Zoo dagli antefatti a *L'Uomo nero*, 1966/1970," in *Michelangelo Pistoletto: il varco dello specchio*, p. 21 (my translation).

22 Pistoletto, *L'Uomo nero, il lato insopportabile*, p. 51; translation from "The Minus Man," p. 51 (modified slightly).

FROM THE EARLY PAINTINGS TO THE FIRST REFLECTIVE SURFACES

ANGELA VETTESE

This essay traces the development of Michelangelo Pistoletto's poetics through an interpretation of specific works, each taken as an exemplum of the artist's efforts when he was on the threshold of creating his mirror paintings.[1] Reading each of these paintings individually, considering Pistoletto's work during a five-year gestational period from 1956 to 1961, one can discern nearly all the themes, stylistic and formal developments, and technical devices that led to his mature work.

In 1947, Pistoletto began working with his father, Ettore Olivero Pistoletto, a Turinese painter who had created, among other works, a gallery of paintings on the history of the art of wool-making for the Ermenegildo Zegna company in Biella. Hostile to modern painting trends, the elder Pistoletto would never have allowed his son to attend the Accademia di Belle Arti (Academy of the Fine Arts) in their city of Turin, or other centers for art education. He taught his son the classical fundamentals of painting himself, from anatomy to the rendering of chiaroscuro, and introduced him to various styles from the past through his work as an art restorer. By the time Michelangelo was fourteen, his father had encouraged him to draw a self-portrait (now lost) in sanguine pencil.[2] Indeed, it was through his exploration of the subject of the self-portrait that the younger Pistoletto subsequently discovered his own fully autonomous path.

Pistoletto was able to take advantage of his father's training on numerous occasions, above all in an attempt to strike out on his own. In 1953, his mother enrolled him at an advertising school opened by the designer Armando Testa, the most important advertising figure in Italy. Testa was responsible for some of the country's most characteristic slogans and cartoon personalities and had enormous powers of synthesis and persuasion, particularly in the use of images that got to the heart of the significance of mid-century Italian design. He had started what can be considered the first true school of advertising in Italy, mainly to identify talented young people to bring into his professional practice. A painter himself, he was knowledgeable about art history and encouraged his young students to familiarize themselves with the subject. Pistoletto's previous experiences with images and their construction were such that, after just one year (the school called for a two-year program), he was invited to become a member of Testa's staff. He turned down the opportunity, however, after another advertising figure offered him complete control over his agency and clientele.

Pistoletto's advertising-school experience was significant for his artistic production above all because it put him in contact with a lively group of contemporaries eager for new knowledge and experiences. Attempting to rejuvenate the advertising image through visual art, they exchanged information and opinions, discussing artists such as Fernand Léger, Henri Matisse, Georges Rouault, and others who were exhibiting in the local galleries.[3] Some of them also spent time at the library of the United States Information Service (USIS) in Turin, where they had access to specialized magazines; others consulted international art catalogues.

The school also proved essential to Pistoletto's development because the language of advertising imposed on the mostly figurative image the need to communicate clearly and effectively in order to establish a strong relationship with the viewer. In advertising, unlike art, which may come into being without a client, proposing images disagreeable to the public is not a feasible option. For this reason, too, Pistoletto's first autonomous explorations were inclined to focus on a single subject and to devise a system in which the representation of reality combined with viewer interaction to engage the onlooker, an approach he would develop fully in his mature production.

The cultural environment of postwar Italy was another crucial factor in Pistoletto's development as an artist. The visual art of Italy in the years following World War II had revealed profound disappointment, rage, and a rejection of life as it was currently lived. While Pistoletto had experienced the war years as an evacuee in the Piedmontese town of Susa, along a frontier ravaged by German reprisals, he managed to escape the influence of this particular cultural climate, in part thanks to the pragmatic lessons offered by the advertising world through its contact with the world of industry. Through his advertising work, Pistoletto experienced the first stages of the postwar economic boom generated by the Marshall Plan and the dynamic reconstruction of European manufacturing.

For the autonomous, almost autodidactic aspects of his education, Pistoletto was able to learn through witnessing the results of Art informel and Abstract Expressionist currents in Turin. Profoundly marked by its role as an automobile capital and by the development of a working class plagued by unrest due to a large influx of immigrants from southern Italy, the town seems to have employed art and culture for the purposes of unifying three rather divergent classes: the urban proletariat, the upper middle class, and a very ancient aristocracy that had been charged with carrying out the unification of Italy in the mid-nineteenth century. Over time, this generated a great deal of attention to humanistic culture, particularly apparent in the activities of the Einaudi publishing house, which for years was one of the beacons of cultural renewal in Italy. In Turin, Pistoletto experienced, at least indirectly, the effects of an atmosphere in which, beginning in the second half of the 1940s, writers and philosophers such as Norberto Bobbio, Italo Calvino, Natalia Ginzburg, Cesare Pavese, and Elio Vittorini worked together at Einaudi as authors, editors, and consultants for book projects. These men and women frequently came from the ranks of the Resistance, even if, as in the case of Calvino in 1957, they just as often vehemently distanced themselves from the Communist party, which fostered a culture that could sometimes become quite authoritarian. Pistoletto never embraced an ideology of this kind, always preferring a social engagement free of dogmatic formulations.

This patchwork of complex and often contradictory but undoubtedly stimulating conditions resulted in various manifestations of contemporary art in Turin, supported by the public sector and available to all. Already in

1953, this environment saw some of the *Arte in vetrina* (*Art in the Window*) exhibitions in major downtown shops in Turin.[4] Pistoletto recalls seeing one of Lucio Fontana's large monochrome "hole" paintings on via Roma, in the Galtrucco fabric outlet.

Private initiatives cropped up around public ventures, sometimes backed by funding from the automaker Fiat and its satellite industries. Galleria Notizie, run by Luciano Pistoi, a critic for the Communist newspaper *L'Unità*, brought Adolf Gottlieb and Franz Kline to Turin, while Galleria La Bussola exhibited Giuseppe Capogrossi's extremely personal and anti-tragic paintings, with their characteristic forklike signs (see fig. 57), the magical-realist canvases of Mario Mafai, and works by Alberto Burri, whose lacerated paintings encouraged a way out of the strict two-dimensionality of the canvas. In 1960, the French critic Michel Tapié opened a space in Turin, the International Center of Aesthetic Research, where he showed works by the Japanese Gutai group, French and European Art informel, some Americans, and even Ikebana artists. At the Museo Civico in Turin, the critic Luigi Carluccio presented a series of exhibitions focusing on a comparison between the art of Italy and France in which it was possible to see works by Georges Mathieu and Hans Hartung, among many others. Further stimulation came from the young Italians in the Arte Nucleare group, led by Enrico Baj, which provided continuity with Fontana's spatialism but demonstrated greater faith in science and an appreciation of irony, opposed to any late Romantic or existentialist rhetoric.

This panorama nurtured the basic steps of Pistoletto's beginnings, whose foundations may be detected in certain traits: the choice, above all, to not abandon figuration; the desire to renew figuration through the aesthetic and the physical before the conceptual; and the need to reflect on the icon, which the artist experienced as a form still rich in expressive possibilities, capable of communicating a laic spirituality even with the loss of religious faith. Indeed, Pistoletto's beliefs have always been oriented to man as the proponent of his own destiny.

AUTORITRATTO (SELF-PORTRAIT), 1956

In 1956, Pistoletto painted a large—more than four-and-a-half-feet tall—self-portrait (plate 1), vertical in format, in which the face is rendered with gestural brushstrokes in yellow, brown, and black tones against a red background. We are presented with a work at a crossroads. On one hand, the materiality that Pistoletto had explored in the preceding works is still abundantly present, especially relative to what he was seeing around him in the Turin galleries. Pistoletto says he was very struck by the treatment of pictorial material in the work of the Tachist painter Jean Fautrier, who turned his medium into a projecting and fleshy element of the canvas. At the same time, the young Pistoletto demonstrates, specifically in this self-portrait, a desire to push in the opposite direction. Indeed, the background appears here as a flat field, with a relationship of absolute differentiation from the more material rendering of the figure. In both the frontality and immobility of the figure and the deliberate flatness of the background, the painting brings to mind medieval devotional images.

The immediate precedent for this work is another 1956 self-portrait by Pistoletto, an oil on canvas (later destroyed) that is now visible only in a photograph titled *Autoritratto senza tempo* (*Self-Portrait without Time*; fig. 32). For a certain period the painting was a constant point of reference for the artist. Here we can recognize an oval, flattened toward the top, its edges close to the confines of the canvas—a clear sign emerging from a tangle of *informel*-style brushstrokes. The same face, with a flatter head and a more pointed chin—in other words, made more geometric—appears in a strongly vertical self-portrait from 1957 (fig. 33) in which red, blue, black, and brown muddle together in the face, the resulting magma standing out from a white field. The color is scraped in places, and the lumpy paint contrasts with the confined figure. A visual dialectic arises between what is "completely full" and what is "completely empty."

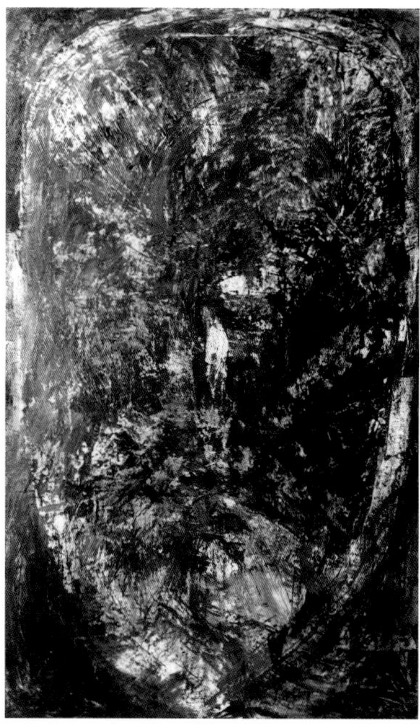

FIG. 32. *Autoritratto senza tempo* (*Self-Portrait without Time*), a photograph of Pistoletto's destroyed self-portrait from 1956. Photograph by Paolo Bressano. Collection of the artist

Pistoletto went on to create a number of works that Luigi Carluccio considered convincing. After seeing one of them, *Uomo seduto* (*Seated Man*, 1958), exhibited at the Premio San Fedele in Milan in 1958, he put Pistoletto in touch with Mario Tazzoli of the Galleria Galatea in Turin. This was the same gallery that showed the paintings of Francis Bacon and the sculptures of Alberto Giacometti, and among whose patrons was Gianni Agnelli, the president of Fiat and the most powerful industrialist in Italy at the time. And so in 1958 Pistoletto was encouraged to leave his work in advertising and to make a living as an artist, thanks to an exclusive contract for the sale of his work and the payment of a monthly stipend from the gallery. His first exhibition at Galatea opened two years later, in March 1960. His second and last show with the gallery was held in April 1963, when he had already begun to create his mirror paintings. Because Tazzoli did not understand the mirror paintings' impersonality and deliberate remove from the pictorial mastery that had initially impressed him (in fact, he seemed embarrassed to present these works to his clientele), he offered no objection when Pistoletto requested that his contract with the gallery be canceled.

It should be noted that although the Pop aesthetic had by this time made significant inroads into Italy—particularly with the work of Mimmo Rotella in the late 1950s—it did not enter the common sensibility until after the 1964 Venice Biennale, when it was reimported to Italy from the United States. Although it is debatable whether Pistoletto ever participated in this movement, his abandonment of individual sensibility in order to connect to a collective mythology, and his use of photographic and "objective" images rather than those created with a strong subjective emphasis, as well as other elements in his work, bring him close to Pop art. This approach was incomprehensible to Italian art dealers—and to Tazzoli in particular—who were still attached to the aesthetic of Art informel and

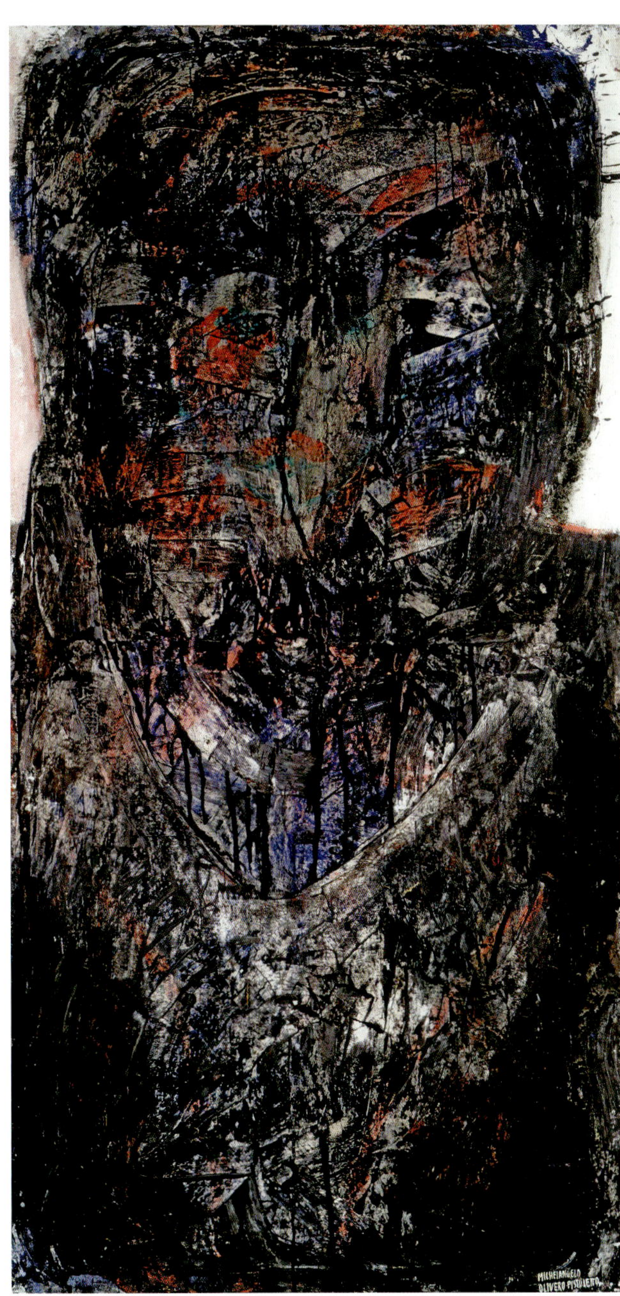

FIG. 33. Michelangelo Pistoletto. *Autoritratto* (*Self-Portrait*), 1957. Oil and acrylic on canvas, 78¾ x 39⅜ inches (200 x 100 cm). Collection of the artist

not yet immersed in the mass-market imagery of twentieth-century consumerism common in the United States and the more affluent countries of Europe, while it was relatively easy for American and international viewers to appreciate.[5] During a trip to Paris in 1963, and almost by chance, Pistoletto met Ileana Sonnabend and left her a small painting that he had with him. This encounter piqued her interest in his work, and, encouraged by a mutual affinity, the two soon signed an exclusive contract. It was Sonnabend's idea that she would include Pistoletto among her leading artists in the coming years, which subsequently happened, though Pistoletto would reject the suggestion of her U.S. representative, Leo Castelli, that he move to New York. He first participated in an exhibition at Sonnabend's Paris gallery in 1963, shortly after his second and final show at Galatea. His inclusion in the Paris exhibition, titled *Dessins pop*, was an attempt to link him stylistically to that movement and marked the beginning of his international career. In 1964, his work was again shown at Sonnabend in Paris, this time introduced by a text by Alain Jouffroy,[6] a much-esteemed critic who was close to the remaining members of the Surrealist circle. Later that same year, Pistoletto exhibited at important public venues in Ghent, The Hague, Paris, Pittsburgh, and Vienna.

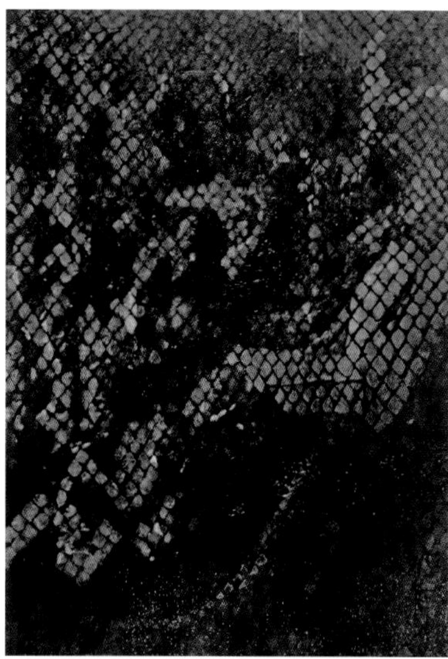

FIG. 34. Michelangelo Pistoletto. *La folla ingrata* (*The Thankless Crowd*), 1958–59. Oil and acrylic on canvas, 55⅛ x 39⅜ inches (140 x 100 cm). Collection of the artist

LA FOLLA (THE CROWD), 1959

Having jumped forward, we must now go back to pick up the trail of the early works that first helped Pistoletto to penetrate art circles in Turin and elsewhere in Italy. *La folla* (*The Crowd*, 1959; plate 2) is an oblong canvas painted in oil and acrylic in brown, black, and ocher tones. It is a vast gathering of heads that has a rhythm not unlike that found in certain American examples of Abstract Expressionism. There is a lack of hierarchy between center and edges that brings to mind the allover work not only of Jackson Pollock but also of Willem de Kooning and Mark Tobey. Compared to the earlier self-portraits, a sense of the multitude—of its chaos and mobility—now prevails.

La folla shows the same tolerance for disorder that is found in the slightly earlier canvas *La folla ingrata* (*The Thankless Crowd*, 1958–59; fig. 34), in which the artist constructs a pattern of prisms, an almost regular web of dark rhombic shapes behind which one can intuit a fluid mass of bodies. Here, the shapes somewhat recall the stained-glass windows of a cathedral, a theme found in other works by the young Pistoletto, such as *Uomo coricato sotto la finestra* (*Man Lying beneath the Window*, 1957–58; fig. 35), a painting on Masonite with a vast area of pentimento, left unfinished, in which almost half the surface is taken up by the grid of a leaded window. Simultaneously prison and light, it depicts the place in his father's studio where the artist used to rest and therefore can ultimately be considered another self-portrait.

In *Uomo sul sofà* (*Man on the Sofa*, 1958; see fig. 117), the upper portion of the canvas is again occupied by a window, from which a pink, oval light

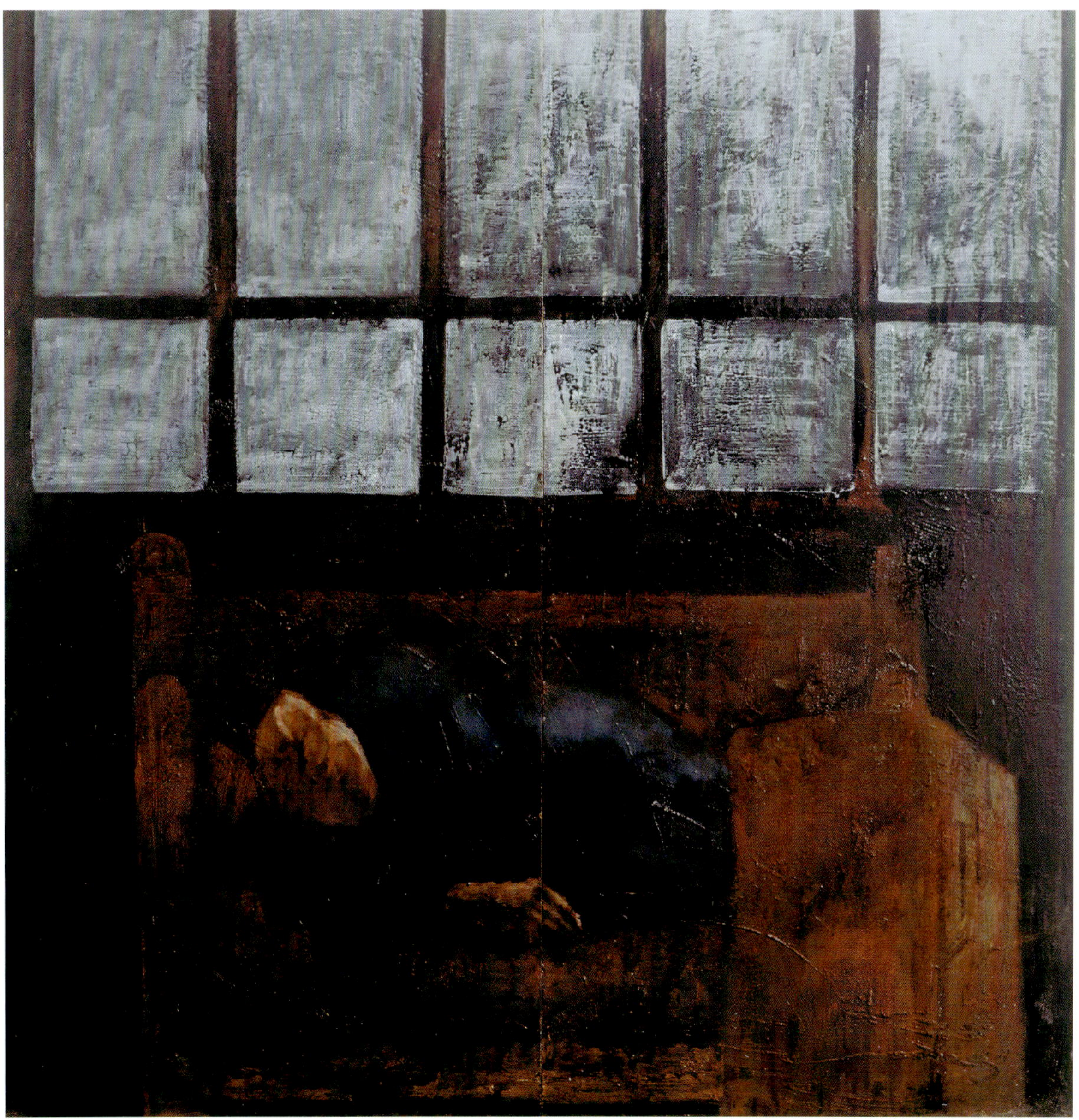

FIG. 35. Michelangelo Pistoletto. *Uomo coricato sotto la finestra* (*Man Lying beneath the Window*), 1957–58. Oil and acrylic on Masonite, 78¾ x 78¾ inches (200 x 200 cm). Collection of the artist

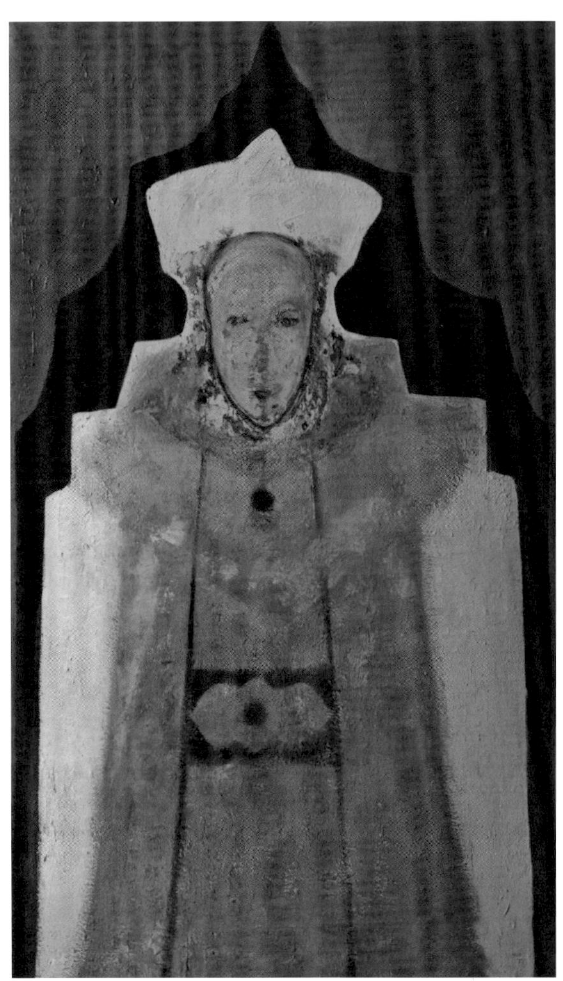

FIG. 36. Michelangelo Pistoletto. *Sacerdote* (*Priest*), 1957. Oil and acrylic on canvas, 78¾ x 47¼ inches (200 x 120 cm). Collection of the artist

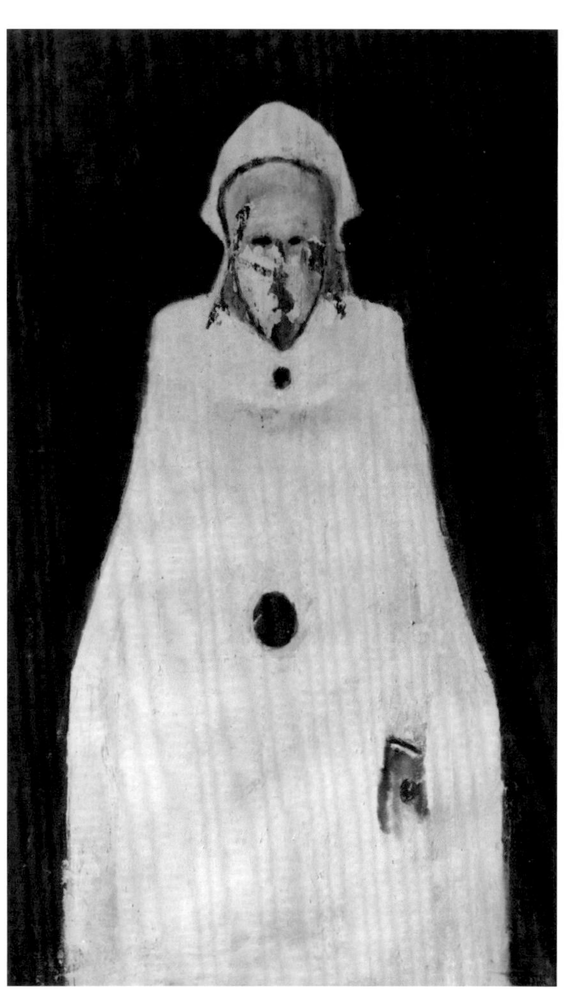

FIG. 37. Michelangelo Pistoletto. *Il santo* (*The Saint*), 1957. Oil and acrylic on canvas, 78¾ x 47¼ inches (200 x 120 cm). Collection of Renato Rinaldi, Milan

emerges, surrounded by a celestial crown of lozenge shapes. Both the light and the crown are concentric forms, interrupted by dark markings of what are probably intimations of the leaded divisions of glass panes and framed by two brown bands. The man, again probably the artist, is portrayed attempting to relax but also at the moment of his greatest emotional compression, closed off within himself, as if drowning in problems, although the painting is deliberately non-tragic. Pistoletto has never been drawn to an expressionist rendering of the body; he has never been interested in the decay of flesh, frenzy, or other Dionysian aspects of the human spirit. Rather, his research has been a constant investigation of Apollonian forms and spirituality. The atmosphere that Pistoletto feels he is conveying is similar to that which animates Michelangelo Antonioni's film *L'avventura* (*The Adventure*, 1960), where in one scene, lost amid the cliffs of Basiluzzo in the Aeolian Islands, the actress Monica Vitti's white face forms a smooth oval against the rough rock, a living element in contrast to the island's sedimentary fault lines, a glance without serenity but also without dramatic urgency. Pistoletto's lying or seated figures have little in common with the agitated figures of Bacon, except for the cage of lines that surround them. His crowds likewise have little in common with those of James Ensor (as in *Self-Portrait with Masks*, 1899), other than the idea of a compressed mob.

ESPERIMENTO (EXPERIMENT), 1959

Free to focus solely on art, Pistoletto intensified his experimental activity beginning in 1958. His investigations focused on the figure-ground relationship and involved his first attempts to move away from traditional materials and techniques. He increasingly sought to escape the dichotomy between abstraction and figuration, which in the Italian context was still very much alive. *Esperimento* (*Experiment*; plate 3) is not strictly a painting but rather an assemblage of materials. At the center of a small canvas with classical proportions is a head, a form obtained by surrounding with silver paint the shadow projected on the canvas by the artist while he was painting. The emptiness of the background allows the emergence of a layer of gray that had been applied prior to the silver. The central placement of the image is compatible with the portrait bust from Leonardo da Vinci to Jean-Auguste-Dominique Ingres. Pistoletto had already used the bust form in two anomalous works, both from 1957: *Sacerdote* (*Priest*; fig. 36) and *Il santo* (*The Saint*; fig. 37). At the center of each is a hieratic, frontal, still figure, strongly referencing the symmetrical architecture of churches, almost as if the stylized body were coinciding with the profile of a spired structure, reaching upward and toward the Absolute.

In *Esperimento*, however, the bust does not extend as far as the abdomen but is cut off at the shoulders. Moreover, the facial features vanish in the uniform application of paint, although this too might be seen as part of a system for sanctifying the figure. In front of this form, strings have been attached at either end to wood boards affixed to the top and bottom edges of the work. These strings, along with a sort of stick or wood dowel on one side, project above the painting's surface, imbuing the work with three-dimensionality and giving expression to an investigation of space (see fig. 120). They cut the figure vertically, creating an almost syncopated visual rhythm and breaking up its unity.

One of the most significant elements of the composition, however, is its silver-painted background (once again we find ourselves confronting a memory of the gold ground of medieval icons). The use of silver might lead one to suspect that the work was already approaching the mirror paintings, but the artist was still three years away from his first *quadro specchiante*.

Esperimento contains an opposition between the static and the dynamic, the absolute and the relative, which is precisely what will be developed later in the mirror paintings (and is the same mechanism that will also be fundamental to the artist's *Venere degli stracci* [*Venus of the Rags*], 1967; plate 99). But in *Esperimento*, unlike in the mirror paintings, it is the background that is still, whereas the figure gains motion through the dynamic brushstrokes and above all through the way the strings interfere with the viewer's perception. This was a period when research on the phenomenon of vision was emerging from various avenues, which clearly had an effect on optical-kinetic art and, in the theoretical field, on Gestalt theory and its investigations into the relationship of figure and ground, fixity and movement. Without being directly aware of these developments, Pistoletto was working along some of the same lines.[7]

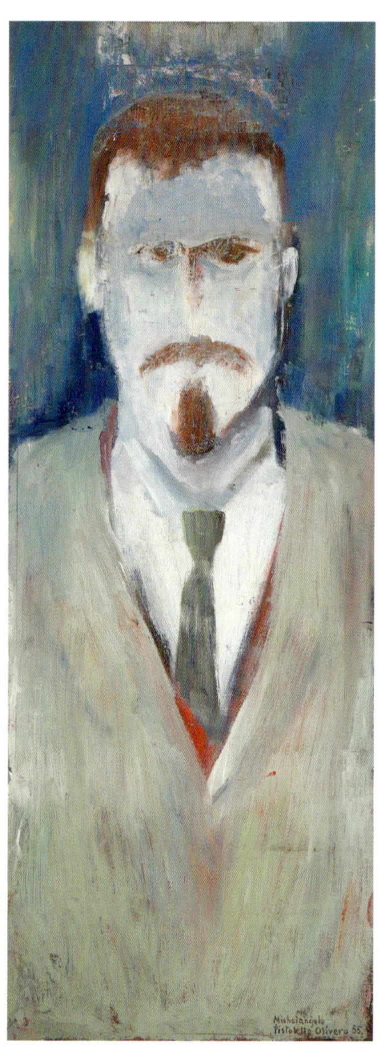

FIG. 38. Michelangelo Pistoletto. *Autoritratto* (*Self-Portrait*), 1955. Oil on wood, 25⅝ x 9⅝ inches (65 x 24.5 cm). Collection of the artist

AUTORITRATTO ARGENTO (SILVER SELF-PORTRAIT), 1960

Pistoletto has continued to use silver for the background over the years, specifically to give greater emphasis to a figure who abandons the crowd, the grid, and the multitude of signs as background components. In turn, the figure is presented from the front and rendered neutral by conventional clothing. In *Autoritratto argento* (*Silver Self-Portrait*, 1960; plate 4), the brush still moves freely over the folds of the garment and the lighter area of the face, which is deliberately inexpressive, distant from any desire for emotional autobiography; the figure, however, is rendered realistically, with no trace of *informel* gesture. The image does not need to occupy the center of the canvas but is positioned to one side. Paradoxically, in order for the figure to appear objective, it must be anchored to certain precise physiognomic signs. This is one more reason the artist uses himself as a model. His person, in the painting, stands for the human being in general, for an individual who potentially represents all individuals. To locate the genesis of this work, we need to go back to the aforementioned self-portraits, but first we must go back even further, to a self-portrait from 1955 (fig. 38), an oblong oil painting on board in which the facial features

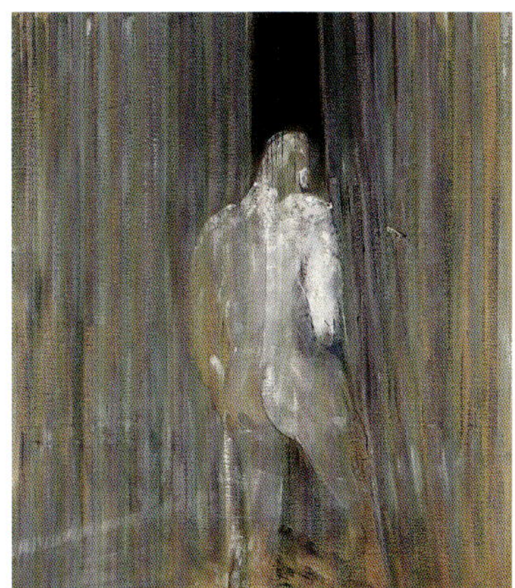

FIG. 39. Francis Bacon (English, born Ireland, 1909–1992). *Study from the Human Body*, 1949. Oil on canvas, 57⅞ x 52⅞ inches (147 x 134.2 cm). National Gallery of Victoria, Melbourne. Purchased 1953

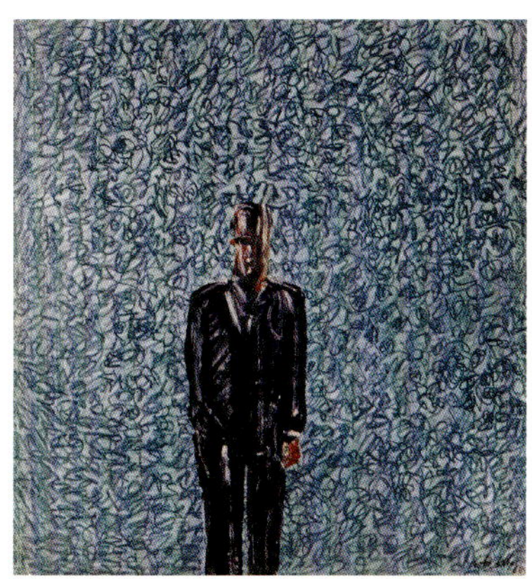

FIG. 40. Michelangelo Pistoletto. *Autoritratto su fondo verde* (*Self-Portrait against Green Background*), 1960. Mixed media on paper, 19 11/16 x 18½ inches (50 x 47 cm). Private collection

are rather realistic if extremely summary, connoted by the dry geometry of the eyes, the mustache and beard, and here, too, by neutral clothing consisting of a jacket and tie.

The phenomenology is that of the everyman, René Magritte's bourgeois, treated without irony—indeed, with absolute seriousness—the "One, No One, and One Hundred Thousand" described by Luigi Pirandello in his novel of 1926.[8] Nor is there any narcissistic smugness, in a self-destructive or mocking sense, as with the main character in Italo Svevo's greatest novel, *Zeno's Conscience* (1923).[9] In Pistoletto's figure there is no intimate diary of the dramas of the body, and even less a confession of mental malaise, as in the solitary figures of Francis Bacon (fig. 39). There is neither obsession nor desperation, and none of the degradation characteristic of the writings of Georges Bataille, but rather its opposite. Here one moves toward life with a glance that looks forward, not backward. In earlier or contemporary works by Pistoletto, we find very similar figures, cut off below the knees—as in the drawing *Autoritratto su fondo verde* (*Self-Portrait against Green Background*, 1960; fig. 40) and the painting *Autoritratto linoleum* (*Linoleum Self-Portrait*, 1960; fig. 41)—or with the arms crossed and the figure cut off at the bottom edge of the jacket and placed very low, beneath the midpoint of the figurative space, as in a self-portrait of 1960 (fig. 42).

These works demonstrate a concern with finding an optimal placement for the figure within the pictorial space. Beyond the high-low or right-left shifts, what one notes is that the work must be hung so that the viewer observes the figure at eye level—eye to eye. In practice, if the figure were full-length, the painting would have to rest on the floor. Precisely in order to avoid the problem of the horizontal angle of the feet where they are seen to rest on the floor, Pistoletto excludes them, cutting off the body above the ankles. Clearly, the self that is portrayed wants to come down from any pedestal or elevated plane; it has no intention of passing above the life of others, but rather seeks to join in—to place itself at the viewer's level.

Pistoletto's icon, in traditional fashion and in keeping with the icon's role in devotional practices, remains an invitation to thought, an intermediary toward meditation. But it is no longer in an aulic place or physically elevated, or even, as with some icons, placed at the intersection of two walls with the ceiling. Rather, it is available to mix with the world, having literally descended to human level. This is a course the artist continued to pursue and that is fundamental to the functioning of his subsequent mirror paintings.

Another focus of Pistoletto's early works is the search for a solution to the still-unresolved problem of the background. In the case of the 1960 *Autoritratto* (see fig. 42), there is once again a silver background, but it is treated in an almost material fashion, with the paint applied over a canvas on which Pistoletto had arranged lumps of plaster. A similar effect of opacity mixed with the accentuated luminescence of metallic paint is seen in *Autoritratto oro* (*Gold Self-Portrait*, 1960; plate 5) and *Autoritratto bronzo* (*Bronze Self-Portrait*, 1961; plate 6). In both cases, the realism of the figure is reduced to its outline, while the facial features are lost and the silhouette

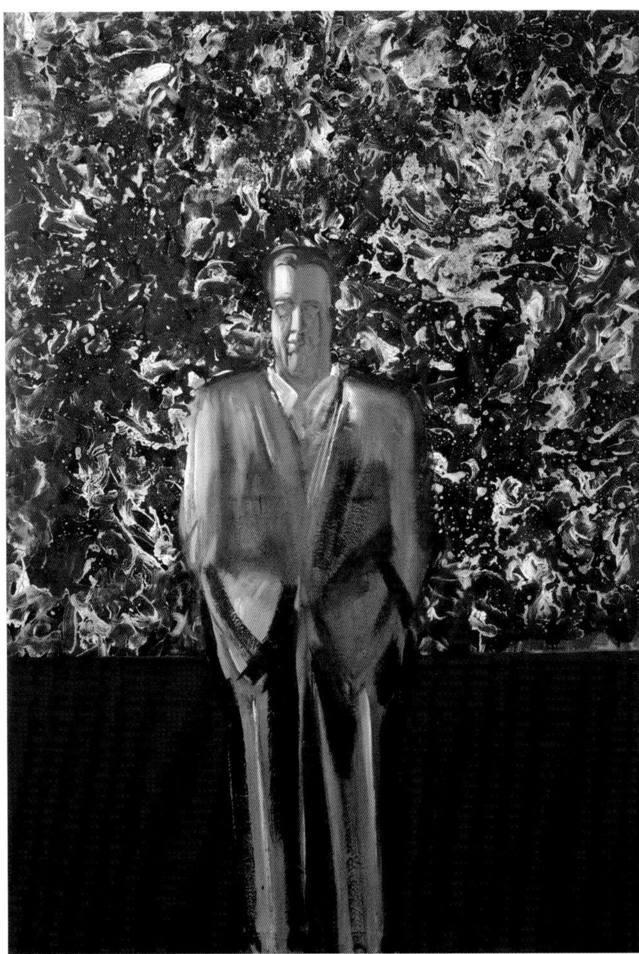

FIG. 41. Michelangelo Pistoletto. *Autoritratto linoleum* (*Linoleum Self-Portrait*), 1960. Oil and acrylic on canvas, 78¾ x 59 inches (200 x 150 cm). Goetz Collection, Munich

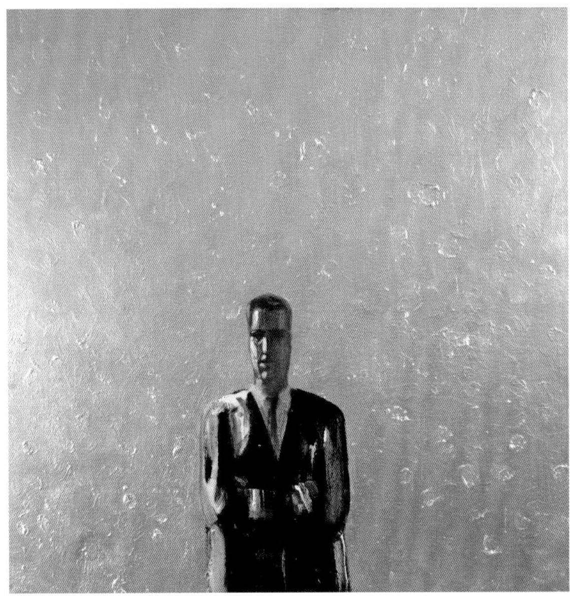

FIG. 42. Michelangelo Pistoletto. *Autoritratto* (*Self-Portrait*), 1960. Acrylic and silver on canvas, 59 x 59 inches (150 x 150 cm). Collection of the artist

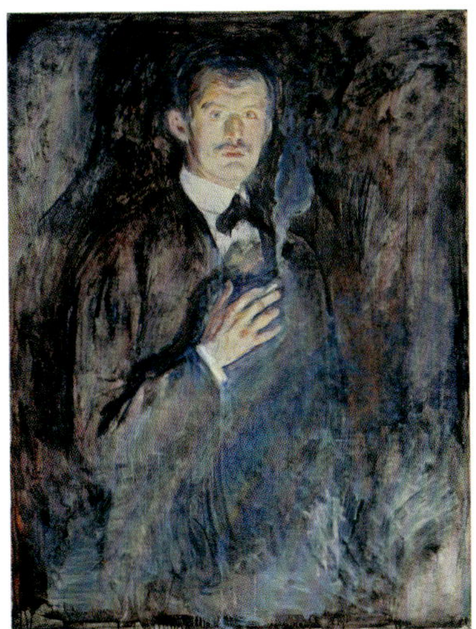

FIG. 43. Edvard Munch (Norwegian, 1963–1944). *Self-Portrait with Cigarette*, 1895. Oil on canvas, $43\frac{1}{2}$ x $33\frac{5}{8}$ inches (110.5 x 85.5 cm). The National Museum of Art, Architecture and Design, Oslo

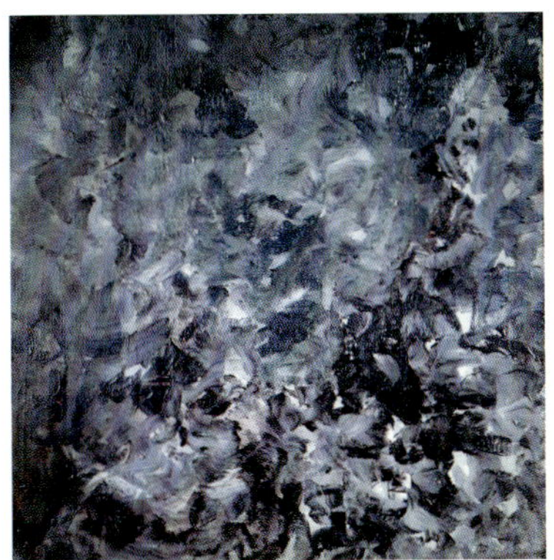

FIG. 44. Michelangelo Pistoletto. *Linoleum*, 1960. Acrylic on canvas, $39\frac{3}{8}$ x $39\frac{3}{8}$ inches (100 x 100 cm). Collection of the artist

emerges as if through a play of light, creating a ghostly appearance that, except for the objective and non-romantic nature of the painting, brings to mind Edvard Munch's youthful self-portrait (fig. 43).

During this same period, Pistoletto—working in a direction opposite from that informing these paintings on monochrome and luminous grounds—was also investigating very worked backgrounds, conceived as allover fields inspired by the tone-on-tone marbling typical of certain linoleums. In a one-meter-square painting of 1960 explicitly titled *Linoleum* (fig. 44), the artist mixed a pearly color with silver paint. The rhythm of this deliberately chaotic abstraction somewhat recalls the dancing heads in *La folla* of 1959 (plate 2). *Autoritratto linoleum* associates this pattern with the figure, although there is a burgundy baseboard at leg level in this painting that might also imply a sort of boiserie, or sculptured wood paneling, characteristic of a bourgeois apartment, which thus assigns the linoleum a role similar to that of wallpaper. The gestural and obsessive scribbling that appears unadorned and without baseboard in the earlier colored pencil drawing *Autoritratto su fondo verde* (see fig. 40) is more courageous and drastic. Here we have arrived at another element that will characterize all of the mirror paintings and much of the artist's later output, from the *Venere degli stracci* to other works conceived as capable of welcoming the public and movement, from *Quadro da pranzo* (*Lunch Painting*, 1965; plate 75) to *Anno bianco* (*White Year*, 1989; see fig. 45)—that is, the decisive contrast between the order of the figure and the disorder of the background.[10] It comes as no surprise that the terms *order* and *disorder* were also present in Alighiero Boetti's work, as this was a frequent topic in the discussions of the group of artists that began meeting in the mid-1960s in Turin. *Quadro da pranzo* is a shallow wooden structure comprising a table and two chairs within a frame; its ordered construction welcomes the disorder of a discussion, of a meal, of a relationship between two people, while framing any activity within as a painting (*quadro* in Italian means both "square" and "painting").

The concept of the frame also informed *Anno bianco*, which was basically a readymade that included the element of time: the year 1989 was conceived from its beginning as a work of art, with Pistoletto presenting it as a whole in his installation. The word *white* in the title functions as it does in the white paintings of Robert Rauschenberg, which were conceived to be mirrors of whatever might happen in front of and within their reflective surfaces. *Anno bianco* is a frame in which everything is transformed into a work of art, in exactly the way that a mirror transforms—as a sort of painting—whatever passes by and thus enters its reflecting surface, including passing time.

VERSO IL PRESENTE (TOWARD THE PRESENT), 1961

The painting *Verso il presente* (*Toward the Present*, 1961; plate 7) brings us to our first encounter with the *Uomo nero* (literally, "Black Man," but translated as "Minus Man"), Pistoletto's alter ego but also his negation as a single, defined individual. The *Uomo nero* is an absence (of individuation) that contains all presence, or every possible way of being in the world. The work places us before an intuition—casually discovered but long sought, at least unconsciously—of a background capable of reflecting and thus of surrounding a static self-portrait with the extremely mobile comings and goings of the world. Pistoletto's painting surface is now regularly large enough to accommodate a life-size figure with whom viewers can relate on an equal footing. The search for realism—which can be understood as the painting's contact and interrelationship with reality more than as a copying of reality—advanced, thanks to technical choices such as those made in this work. The fundamental step was the choice of the color black, as announced in this oil on canvas in which the by now stereotypical image of the artist appears seated, his hands on his knees, which protrude outward in a way that brings the image closer to the viewer. As revealed by the lowering of the figure within the parameters of the painting, and by the canvas's position on the wall, the painting's descent from window to door height—or from the level of the altar (where ancient altarpieces but also the blue monochromes of Yves Klein were placed) to the level of base materiality—is now complete.

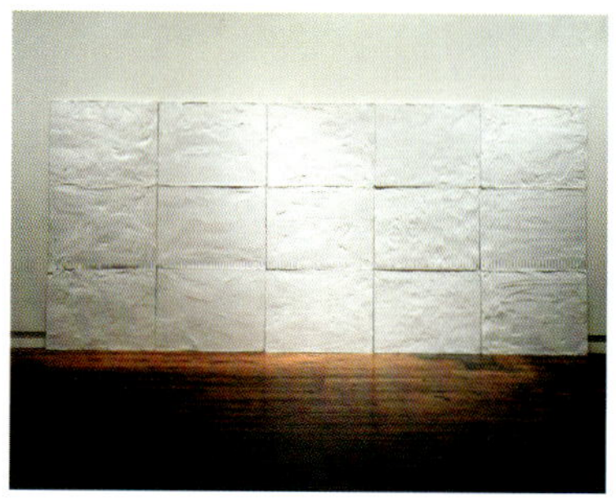

FIG. 45. Michelangelo Pistoletto, *Rilievo orizzontale* (*Horizontal Relief*), 1989. Gesso, 70⅞ x 157½ x 1⅝ inches (180 x 400 x 4 cm). Private collection. From the installation *Anno bianco* (*White Year*) at the Jay Gorney Modern Art, New York, February 1989. Photograph by A. Marcopoulos

The uniformly applied black paint of the background was the final step along a path begun many years earlier, when Pistoletto was brought by this father to the local art museum. The first rooms of the gallery were filled with medieval paintings on gold grounds. What the young Pistoletto loved best were the Flemish still lifes in the rooms that followed, but he fully absorbed the allure of those isolated medieval figures, immersed in the light of the divine and, like Dante's Charon, capable of ferrying one across to the banks of the transcendent. But the bank toward which Pistoletto intends to ferry the observer does not pertain to a state that is to be embraced ever after, in eternity. On the contrary, he takes us toward the pure present, the here and now, the only thing one can believe in but which is also able to contain, as we will see, the future and the past.

IL PRESENTE—UOMO DI FRONTE (THE PRESENT—MAN FROM THE FRONT), 1961

Pistoletto's abandonment of craft was very gradual and can be traced in the slow loss of the authority of the canvas and the lessening importance of drawing during the period of the mirror paintings. For as long as possible, and with rare exceptions, he utilized a traditional support such as canvas stretched on a frame. But while following tradition, he introduced

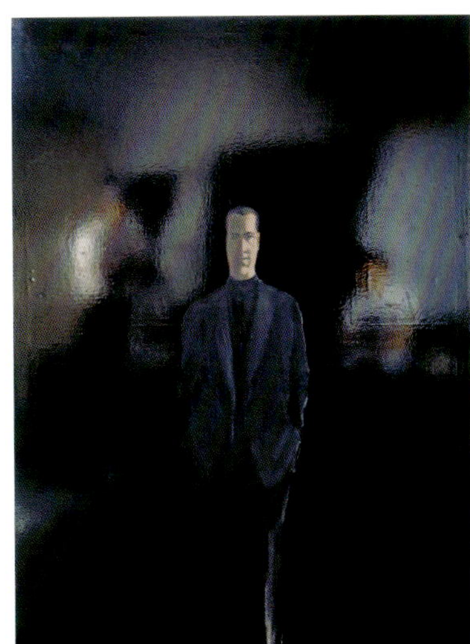

FIG. 46. Michelangelo Pistoletto. *Il presente—Uomo di fronte* (*The Present—Man from the Front*), 1961. Acrylic and plastic varnish on canvas, 78¾ x 59 inches (200 x 150 cm). Private collection

materials extraneous to the history of fine-art painting, such as a particular "plastic boat varnish" that is shiny to the point of being reflective.[11] Pistoletto relates that while he was painting the self-portrait *Il presente—Uomo di fronte* (*The Present—Man from the Front*, 1961; fig. 46), with the figure centered and cut off at ankle level, he immediately understood the invention he was moving toward and, astonished, had to abandon the work. The protagonist was no longer the depicted figure—now almost a mere accessory in a painting whose title drops any reference to the self-portrait—but rather the figure's reflective surroundings. Space, or all of the environments in which the surface will find itself existing and thus also reflecting, enters the painting. And with space comes time, as well as movement and the passage of things.

The pictorial composition of *Uomo di fronte* is divided into two parts, both desired by the artist: the figure, which is completely under his control; and the reflecting space of the background, made up of chaotic transitions of light, people, facts, days, and years, over which he exercises no control at all. It is at this point that all reference to the self-portrait disappears from Pistoletto's titles and is found only in the subtitles. The work, in fact, also becomes a portrait of the viewer, and thus a place of encounter and relationship; there is a transition from individual and authorial self-portrait to collective portrait. The figure is no longer isolated but is found within a potential relationship of dialogue. One thinks again of the two "crowds" of the still-material paintings (see fig. 34; plate 2). That multiplicity returns to face itself in the painting, in contrast with, or more precisely accompanying, the single unit. The I no longer exists without a you. Simultaneously, the material of the painting desperately seeks flatness and simplification, following a direction that will find completion only with the use of photographic tracing as an "objective" aid to the subjectivity of the drawing. The same effect will come to be used in other works, such as *Il presente—Autoritratto in camicia* (*The Present—Self-Portrait in Shirt*, 1961; plate 8), one of the first to employ this technique.

With reflections of the world introduced into the painting, we also have the involvement of a spectator who, in his living, mobile form, becomes a participant and even a protagonist in the work. In this sense, Pistoletto shows his involvement in the way of thinking that led Umberto Eco to consider the idea of the "open work" (*opera aperta*), open above all in the sense that it is amenable to interpretation and even reconstruction by the reader, or viewer, as well as capable of being redefined over time.[12] We have, too, the involvement of the passage of time: a painting that is shiny to the point of being reflective receives whatever is in front of it, encompassing the present moment, bearing a memory of the past that has flowed within it, and promising to receive future moments as they materialize. Finally, since part of the pictorial composition is destined always to be indeterminate, this work embraces the involvement of chance; in this sense we cannot help but recall Robert Rauschenberg's white monochromes (fig. 47), which were intended ideally to reflect everything that happens to them and all of life that passes before them, but which in fact remain opaque screens. A certain line of musical theory is very close to the conceptual structure of Pistoletto's reflective paintings, beginning with the Futurist composer Luigi Russolo and extending to John Cage's chance operations and his composition *4'33"*, with its three movements of silence.

FIG. 47. Robert Rauschenberg (American 1925–2008). *White Painting (Three Panel)*, 1951. Oil on canvas, 72 x 108 inches (182.9 x 274.3 cm). San Francisco Museum of Modern Art. Purchased through a gift of Phyllis Wattis © Estate of Robert Rauschenberg / Licensed by VAGA, New York

IL PRESENTE—UOMO DI SCHIENA (THE PRESENT—MAN FROM THE BACK), 1961

In *Il presente—Uomo di schiena* (*The Present—Man from the Back*, 1961; plate 9), the individual becomes a general being. The artist depicts himself with his back to the viewer, refusing to show the physiognomy of his face, which is no longer necessary and would indeed be counterproductive. It is the viewer—more or less equal in dimension to the painted figure—who makes his own face present through the reflection in the glossy varnish used by Pistoletto. Thus both the painted image and the spectator face in the same direction rather than facing one another. Any heroism of the ego has ceased completely, if indeed it was ever present after those early, large, hieratic faces. It is not without reason that Pistoletto's next work is no longer a self-portrait but a simple *Uomo grigio di schiena* (*Gray Man from the Back*, 1961; fig. 48). While both the viewer and the figure of *Il presente—Uomo di schiena* look toward the future, the varnished surface reflects, albeit not yet perfectly, a present that becomes past; the three temporal dimensions now coexist very explicitly in the painting. A new perspective also emerges, diverging from classical perspective with its central vanishing point. This is not a question of allowing the viewer to see beyond the painting, as in, for example, Marcel Duchamp's *The Bride Stripped Bare by Her Bachelors, Even (The Large Glass)* (1915–23). In Pistoletto's painting, the glance ahead does not lead toward a door or an empty space but is blocked by a sheet of varnish that refers us backward, toward a context and a past that are part of us, that we comprise, and that are both otherness and our essence. The man who looks forward carries with him the responsibility of history, summarized in the vista that lies behind him and that he bears, literally, on his shoulders.

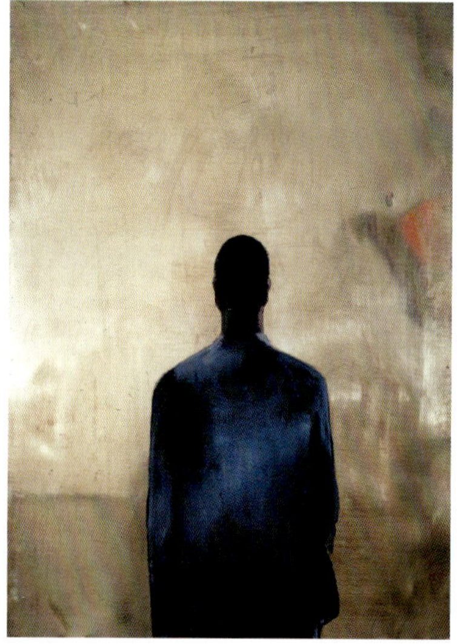

FIG. 48. Michelangelo Pistoletto. *Uomo grigio di schiena* (*Gray Man from the Back*), 1961. Oil and aluminum on canvas, 55⅛ x 39⅜ inches (140 x 100 cm). Collection of the artist

In a process that has taken place entirely within tradition, within the relationship of material and form, the religious icon has evolved in Pistoletto's work to the point of becoming a sign that conveys a laic state. The relationship that, finally, is emphasized is not that of transcendence and magical thinking but that of immanence and logical thinking. Through a process of reversal, the opaque gold that stands for divine light has become a black varnish that stands for terrestrial light. In the same way, the person who, standing before a traditional icon, implores God and is annulled in Him, here becomes an individual responsible for him- or herself and for the world.[13] The absolute is converted to the relative. After the Gothic, which looked upward, toward a providential divinity, Pistoletto seeks a new idea of the classical, based on a glance at the human level and on a sense of our self-sufficiency.

TOWARD A PERFORMATIVE ART

In Byzantine mosaics, Gothic polyptychs, religious icons, and even the small images that Orthodox Christians keep in their houses as votive objects, the gold ground symbolizes a specific metaphysical concept, whereby a superior, nonhuman, and therefore non-anthropomorphic being exists, whose best expression in painting occurs through an emanating plane of light. God is represented as light, as pervasive energy, as a ubiquitous and omnipotent presence.

Pistoletto took from this historical form the intuition that the artist's conception of life, history, and the world as a whole is manifested in the background of the work of art. Since Pistoletto's sense of spirituality does not involve a superior being, it does not imply a metaphysics but is completely internal to physics; thus it is understandable that he sought a solution through which his backgrounds do not seek to portray any Being, but rather the "being" of whoever is required to "be in the world."[14] Positive critical responses to his first show at Galatea tended to recognize his solitary figures as attempts to represent the human condition without illusions or pretense.[15] What is merely hinted at in Pistoletto's black, shiny paintings—an attempt to expose the world in the way it appears as an optical phenomenon, always in motion, compared with a stable element such as the figure—is made obvious in the mirror paintings, where the place of the sacred and of spirituality, a background made of light, has lost all immobility. The background of the mirror paintings is the place not of the absolute but of that which is transitory. What remains is the surface, which speaks of the nature of being but deprives being of any constant aspect. The only thing that remains constant, or rather, reliably recurrent, is chance. The basic oxymoron of this new "theology" is that the most stable aspect of being is movement. There is no certainty, but only the probable; nothing sure, but only the aleatory. The light of the gold background becomes an alternation of light and darkness that responds to the conditions of the space in which the painting finds itself. The phenomenological aspect of the painting depends in good part on the space itself.

The course from Pistoletto's first self-portrait to the discovery of the mirroring surface is, in the artist's mind, the progress toward a mature way of understanding life, wherein certain constant aspects are central: chance occurrence; faith in a view of reality that is objective and rational, cleansed of any emotional complacency and almost pushed to a negation of personal emotionality; the possibility, or rather the moral duty, to make visually harmonious aspects of reality that might seem incompatible; and the acceptance of our loss of control over parts of existence, an attitude in which non-censoriousness of the different or the unexpected is implied.

Through all these elements—already present in the black-ground paintings and flowing so naturally into the mirror paintings—the performative aspect of Pistoletto's work emerges, an aspect that entails a presupposition of the abandonment of the work as hypostasis, as a still and assertive moment of reality, and indeed transforms the work into an homage to change as an ineluctable law of life.

The performative aspect of Pistoletto's work has gradually divested itself of the painted figure. While it is true that the mirror paintings and the artist's work with mirrors in general have never been abandoned, it is also true that along with his focus and clarifying of its values, he began in 1965 a mode of operation that we can define in many ways—as "context-specific, site-oriented, site-responsive and socially engaged," to use some definitions favored by recent critics.[16]

The reflected bodies that move within the painting and that transfom it into a transitory image began to transform Pistoletto's work into a kind of extremely concise theater piece, tied to the coexistence in the painting of three temporal phases: present, past (what lies behind the viewer and what the viewer sees reflected), and future (represented by the viewer's own forward glance). The time factor thus entered into the black paintings, as it would in the mirror works, presenting precise foundations for what will come later. (It has already been noted that some of the Minus Objects, created in 1965 and 1966, portend movement and participation.) A space such as the Deposito d'arte presente (Warehouse of Present Art), whose opening in Turin Pistoletto had strongly supported, invited people to move around the works on display, to experience their physicality, in direct contrast to the untouchable, static nature of traditional paintings and exhibitions and the viewer's usual contemplative stance. In this regard, the activities of Lo Zoo, a theater group that Pistoletto conceived, separate from his own persona but congruent with it,[17] was prescient (see pp. 81–107). It is obvious, however, that Pistoletto's work emerged and matured on two tracks, one tied to the image and the other to action. Sometimes these two directions interweave or run together, as is evident in a comparison of the black paintings and the mirror paintings. But sometimes they separate, as in collective performances such as those he presented at Amalfi's *Arte Povera + Azioni Povere*[18] and at Rotterdam's *Labirinto Azione* in 1968 and 1969,[19] up to exhibitions that have a strong emphasis on the temporal aspect, such as *Le stanze* (*The Rooms*) at Galleria Christian Stein in Turin in 1975–76 (fig. 49) and true theater pieces such as *Anno uno* (*Year One*), interpreted by the inhabitants of Corniglia in 1981 and reinterpreted in subsequent years.[20]

It is this performative aspect in Pistoletto's work that took off in the 1990s and the following decade. The birth and development of Cittadellarte as a center for production, training, and the integration of various social sectors would not be comprehensible within a consistent framework were we not to begin with those first movements of light on the painted canvas. There is not a Pistoletto of the early work, a Pistoletto of the mirror pieces,

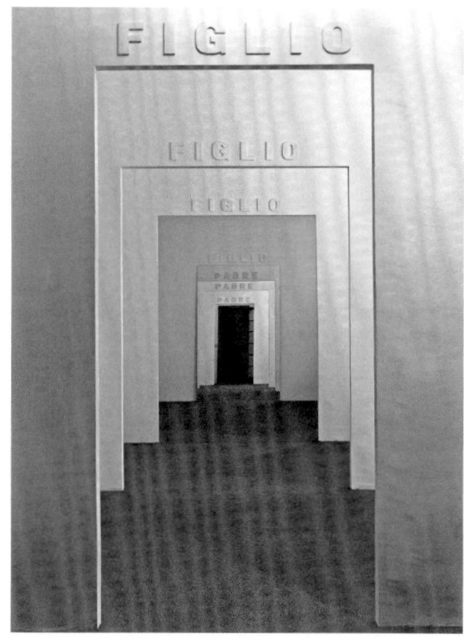

FIG. 49. Pistoletto's *Le stanze: dodici mostre consecutive* (*The Rooms: Twelve Consecutive Exhibitions*), installation view of the third exhibition, Galleria Christian Stein, Turin, December 1975. Photograph by Paolo Mussat Sartor. Courtesy of Cittadellarte-Fondazione Pistoletto, Biella.

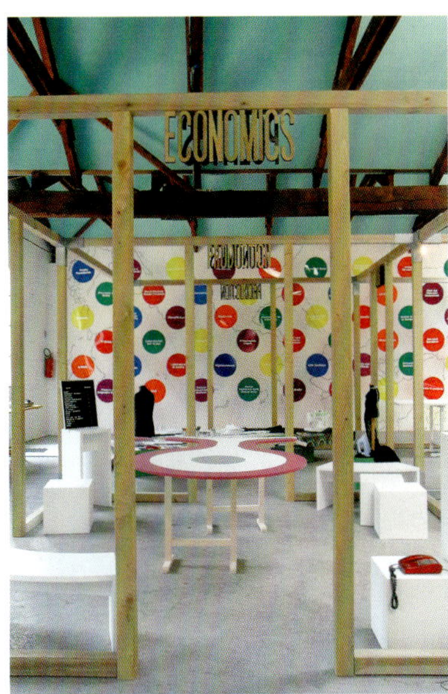

FIG. 50. Interior of Cittadellarte, Biella, 2005. Courtesy of Cittadellarte-Fondazione Pistoletto, Biella

a Pistoletto of the actions or performances, and another who established the multi-entrepreneurial factory known as Cittadellarte (fig. 50). There is only one artist who has steadily invented, welcomed, and developed what has been defined—without, however, giving him sufficient credit—as "collaborative creativity."[21]

Seen from this perspective, Pistoletto's work emerges in full harmony with the scientific revolution of the last century, in which we are still immersed. In the reflections in his varnished paintings, he envisions a conception of the world that is compatible with many of the themes of the new science, including the principle of indeterminacy, quantum mechanics, the dual nature of light, the concept of time as relative, and in general an idea of energy as a symmetric pole not contradictory to static matter. The medieval wood statues that Pistoletto began to collect as a boy and that he still keeps in his house, which are three-dimensional versions of the painted gold-ground icon, were a great source of inspiration but also a manifestation of the fixidness of the work he was to abandon and overcome.

The reflection of the All in the black-varnish of Pistoletto's early paintings signifies that the person of the self-portrait is not an isolated I but part of a whole that is in a state of continuous flux. It is this perpetual change that animates the paintings, revealing a conception of life as a mutable condition, without an intelligent and providential guarantor in the heavens, whose horizon lies in our own hands and in the possibility of seeing things as they are—to follow, without fear, the path that knowledge offers us.

Translated from the Italian by Marguerite Shore.

1 Most of the information in this essay came from numerous conversations that I had with the artist, especially in Biella (September 2000), Modena (September 2005), Venice (March 2006), Faenza (May 2008), Corniglia (August 2009), and again in Biella (October 2009). Regarding general developments in Michelangelo Pistoletto's work, see Angela Vettese, "Into the Looking Glass," in *Io sono l'altro*, exh. cat. (Turin: Galleria Civica d'arte Moderna e Contemporanea, 2000), pp. 10–34.

2 Michelangelo Pistoletto, conversations with the author, Corniglia, August 2009, and Biella, October 2009. Sanguine pencil is a type of fabricated red-chalk pencil that produces an antique look.

3 Many of these artists had had contact with Michel Tapié, the French critic who invented the term *Art informel* and whose theory was based on the legacy of such artists. Tapié had always been a presence in Turin through galerists and critics.

4 The *Arte in vetrina* exhibitions began in 1951 through an association of the main shops in Turin with the help of the municipality, in order to mix culture and shopping on via Roma, a very elegant street. We can still find a trace of this kind of initiative in the *Luci d'artista* show that has taken place since the 1990s in the main streets of Turin every year at Christmastime.

5 It was difficult for the Italian public to detach itself from the aesthetic of Art informel and embrace a new use of the figure. In particular, the packaging, publicity, and selling of goods were still linked to artisanal production. Consumerism was not yet an option or a habit in a country that was still poor and only just beginning to emerge from a period of postwar reconstruction. Italy was thus not as familiar with the kind of realism that was implicit in the images linked to the new circulation of goods and that also was typical of certain media (television, posters, magazines). Much of Pistoletto's own familiarity with the new form of realism came from his strong and early association with the language of an avant-garde kind of advertisement.

6 Alain Jouffroy, Tommaso Trini Castelli, and Michael Sonnabend, *Michelangelo Pistoletto* (Paris: Galerie Sonnabend, 1964).

7 It should be noted that some important exhibitions of optical-kinetic art had already taken place, such as *Le mouvement*, curated by Pontus Hulten in 1955 at the Galerie Denise René, Paris (this show included works by Alexander Calder, Robert Jacobsen, Victor Vasarely, Jesus Raphael Soto, Yacov Agam, and Pol Bury). Moreover, the first edition of Rudolf Arnheim's *Art and Visual Perception*, which would become a point of reference for this area of artistic research, tangentially touched upon by Pistoletto, was published in 1954 (it did not appear in Italian translation until 1962).

8 See Luigi Pirandello, *One, No One, and One Hundred Thousand*, trans. William Weaver (Boston: Eridanos Press, 1990); originally published as *Uno, nessuno e centomila* (Firenze: R. Bemporad e Figlio, 1926).

9 See Italo Svevo, *Zeno's Conscience*, trans. William Weaver (New York: Alfred A. Knopf, 2001); originally published as *La coscienza di Zeno* (Bologna: Licinio Cappelli, 1923). Earlier translations give the title as *Confessions of Zeno*.

10 See the text that accompanied the exhibition at Galleria Galatea (Turin, 1960), signed by Luigi Carluccio. The same critic later wrote texts for other exhibitions that included works by Pistoletto, such as *Aspetti dell'arte torinese* at the Galleria Narciso in Turin (1960) and *Giovani pittori in Piemonte* in Ivrea (1962). The texts contain traces of a lucid but somewhat traditional reading of the works, closely tied to a late *informel* climate. Carluccio in effect ceased following developments in Pistoletto's work after the mirror paintings.

11 See Suzanne Penn, "'The Complicity of the Materials' in Pistoletto's Paintings and Mirror Paintings," pp. 146–47 below.

12 See Umberto Eco, *The Open Work* (Cambridge, Mass.: Harvard University Press, 1989); originally published as *Opera aperta: forma e indeterminazione nelle poetiche contemporanee* (Milan: Bompiani, 1962).

13 In this regard, see the first text written by Michelangelo Pistoletto, "S.T.," in *Presenze* (Turin), July 1957. The journal *Presenze* was published by Pistoletto and other Turinese artists and intellectuals for a brief period.

14 The phrases in quotations clearly relate to the ideas of Martin Heidegger and Maurice Merleau-Ponty. I have taken the liberty of making this connection, which seems pertinent to me because of the absolute laic nature—but also the spirituality without God—that the Turin artist shares with the Heidegger of *Sein und Zeit* (*Being and Time*, 1927) even more than with the latter's writings on art from the 1930s. As for Merleau-Ponty, his "being in the world," as described in his *Phenomenology of Perception* (1945), is tied to the manner in which phenomena appear to man in relation to his physical form and thus in relation to the limits and characteristics of his perceptual actions. That the paintings have a vertical axis, symmetry, and a front and a back, that certain parts of ourselves remain invisible (namely the back), and that there is a direction to the glance that, given the specific position of the visual apparatus in relation to the body, pushes forward like a vector all make the French philosopher relevant. Pistoletto, however, maintains that he has "never read anything"—that is, that his artistic work has not been supported by literary or philosophical positions suggested by the texts of others. Thus every reference, including to authors and discoveries in the realm of science, should be interpreted as possible suggestions and not as certain sources for the works.

15 The exhibition was enthusiastically received by the local press. It should be noted that the artist had not yet established his signature, which appeared on the works in three different ways: Michelangelo Pistoletto Olivero, Michelangelo Olivero, and Michelangelo Olivero Pistoletto. The subsequent decision to go with only the second surname, calling himself Michelangelo Pistoletto, should probably be attributed to his desire to differentiate himself from his father, who signed his

works Ettore Olivero or Ettore Olivero Pistoletto. The main articles that came out following the show at Galatea were "Atleti e Acrobati," in *Stampa Sera*, March 31, 1960, a positive review signed "An. Dra."; "Ritorna l'immagine umana," in *La Stampa*, March 31, 1960, p. 4, signed "Mar. Ber.," a very positive piece that emphasizes Pistoletto's abandonment of subjective painting in favor of the realistic figure and that encourages the artist to discard "superfluous stylistic features" and continue in the direction he has undertaken; and "M. Olivero espone a Torino," by Vittorio Renier, in *Il Biellese*, April 12, 1960, p. 5. These positively underscore Pistoletto's solitary path, not acquiescing to fashions, with his use of the solitary figure, which he will develop along with his capacity to use materials, only to abandon the latter. Another response was "Mostre d'arte Pistoletto alla Galleria Galatea," in *Gazzetta del Popolo*, April 3, 1960, signed "L.C." (the same critic who wrote the introduction to the exhibition, probably Luigi Carluccio), in which the author emphasizes "the state of solitude, of difficult and yet necessary rebirth," pointing out the solitary figure as something already present in works by Francis Bacon, Balthus, Jean Dubuffet, and Alberto Giacometti. However, a few years later, reviewing the early mirror paintings in a catalogue for Galleria Galatea, Turin, April 1963, the same critic distanced himself somewht, repeatedly describing the works as "disconcerting" because "the revival of the human figure seems to be carried out beyond every limit of prudence and caution." Only three years earlier, introducing Pistoletto's first show at the same gallery, he had written some phrases that, while in a context of general appreciation, played it safe: "I said that this is an experience that can arouse wariness, but I admire it . . . because it is the experience of a young artist who accepts maintaining an aloof stance and appearing unacceptable." Both texts appear in Anna Imponente, with Francesca Floreani, eds., *Michelangelo Pistoletto*, exh. cat. (Rome: Electa, 1990), p. 31.

16 See Claire Doherty, "The New Situationists," in *Contemporary Art: From Studio to Situation*, ed. Claire Doherty (London: Black Dog, 2004), p. 10.

17 Pistoletto thought of his role in Lo Zoo as that of director and animator, in such a specific way that in Germano Celant's book *Arte povera* (Milan: Mazzotta, 1969), he requested specific pages to witness the activities of Lo Zoo, conceived as an independent artistic subject even if he was its founder and main director. In the published book there are six pages at the front under the heading "Michelangelo Pistoletto," assigned to him as an individual artist, while at the back of the book are ten pages on "Lo Zoo"—a one-page statement and nine pictures—with an emphasis on the idea of group, and therefore with an implicit critique of the idea of the individual author. The latter has never been abandoned by Pistoletto but has always found a balance in his non-signed group activities, which have their last and most complete legacy in the concept behind the "factory" Cittadellarte.

18 The exhibition *Arte Povera + Azioni Povere*, which took place at Amalfi in September 1968, was based on a concept by the art publisher and curator Marcello Rumma.

19 The exhibition *Labirinto Azione* took place at the Museum Boijmans Van Beuningen, Rotterdam, in March 1969.

20 Pistoletto's *Anno uno* was subsequently presented in 1989, 1991, 1994, and, most recently, in November 2009, on the occasion of *Artissima* 16 at the Teatro Regio Torino.

21 See Claire Bishop, "Introduction: Viewers as Producers," in *Participation*, ed. Claire Bishop (London: Whitechapel; Cambridge, Mass.: MIT Press, 2006), p. 12.

THE MINUS OBJECTS: THE DIMENSION OF TIME

JEAN-FRANÇOIS CHEVRIER

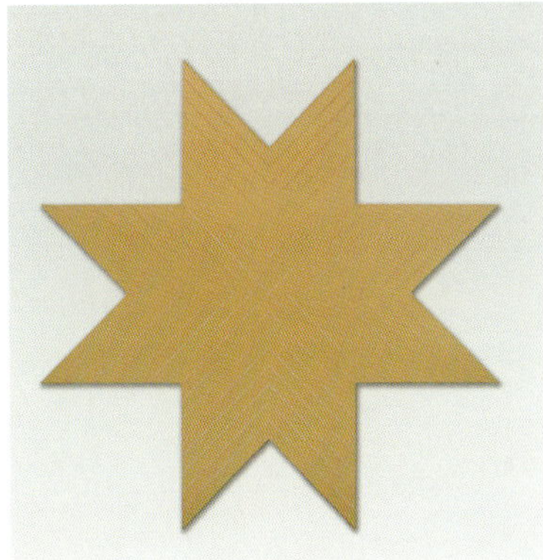

FIG. 51. Frank Stella (American, born 1936). *Plant City*, 1963. Zinc chromate on canvas, 102½ x 102½ inches (260.4 x 260.4 cm). Philadelphia Museum of Art. Gift of Agnes Gund in memory of Anne d'Harnoncourt, 2008

Michelangelo Pistoletto invented the mirror painting (*quadro specchiante*) in the early 1960s. The transformation from painting to mirror is a radicalization of the reflective effect producible by any surface covered in paint. Robert Rauschenberg had revealed this potential in his 1951 monochromes, the *White Paintings* (see fig. 47). Pistoletto, meanwhile, first experimented with it in 1961 with the two self-portraits—front and back (see fig. 46; plate 9)—on a varnished black ground, titled *Il presente* (*The Present*). The frontal self-portrait, *Il presente—Uomo di fronte* (*The Present—Man from the Front*; fig. 46), was exhibited in Turin in 1962. Four years later, on the occasion of his exhibition at Galleria La Bertesca in Genoa, Pistoletto christened it "il primo quadro specchiante" (the first mirror painting).[1]

The mirror painting thus grew out of the ground of a self-portrait; it was also born of an alternative use of the black surface normally associated with the idea of opacity of the paint medium. In the early 1960s, Frank Stella's *Black Paintings* and shaped canvases had seemingly achieved an anti-illusionist ideal (fig. 51). In Pistoletto's case, the idea was not to establish the painting in its literal actuality, rid of representation, but to expose it to the variable actuality of its presentation by stimulating the sensitivity of the pictorial field.

The christening of the "first mirror painting" dates from the artist's definition of the *Oggetti in meno* (Minus Objects) in a statement that accompanied their initial presentation in his studio in 1965–66 (fig. 52).[2] Everything is about the present, and presentation. Pistolettlo affirms the "dimension of time," fulfilled within the objects:

> I feel that in my recent works I have entered the mirror and actively penetrated that dimension of time which was merely represented in the mirror-paintings. These recent works bear witness to the need to live and act in accordance with this dimension, i.e. in the light of the unrepeatable quality of each instant of time, each place, and thus of each "present" action.[3]

In 1966, the mirror paintings had a form that was settled, constituted—defined by its material components: a *fotogramma* (photographic image) painted onto a piece of tissue paper (replaced in the early 1970s by a silkscreen of a photograph) that was then applied to a panel of polished stainless steel. Two years earlier, Pistoletto had shown photographic reproductions of objects cut out and affixed to Plexiglas plates at Galleria Sperone in Turin (plates 68–74). That exhibition marked a decisive step between the mirror paintings and the Minus Objects.

The mirror paintings combined, in a "relationship of instantaneousness,"[4] the photographic image—fixed, immobile, the product of the recording of a past moment—and the reproduction in the present of bodies in motion. They introduced the present-past of recording into the present-in-the-process-of-passing of reproduction. Therein is constituted

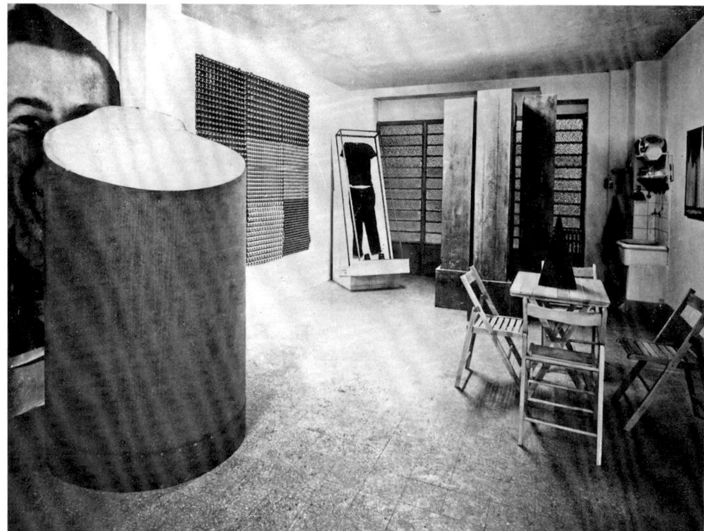

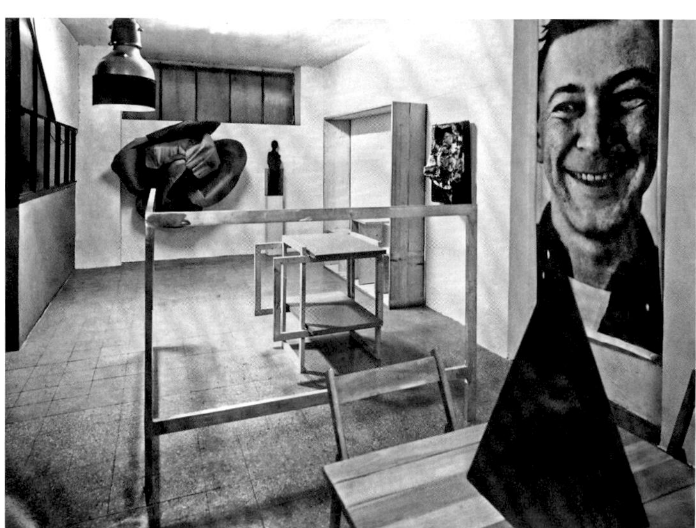

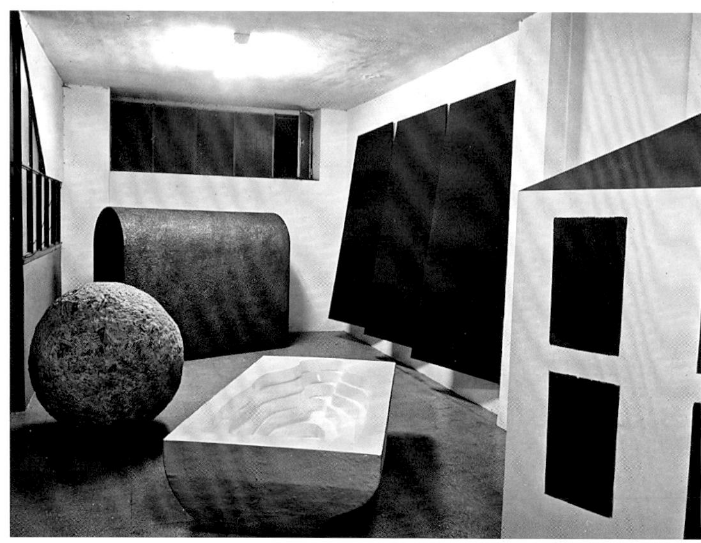

FIG. 52. The Minus Objects (1965–66) in Pistoletto's studio in Turin, January 1966. Photographs by Paolo Bressano. Courtesy of Cittadellarte-Fondazione Pistoletto, Biella

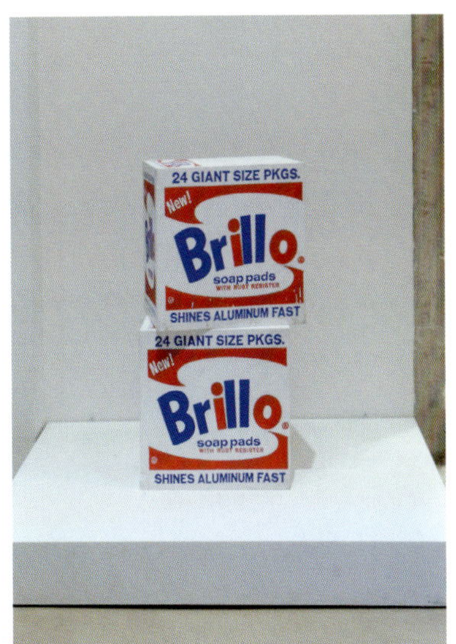

FIG. 53. Andy Warhol (American, 1928–1987). *Brillo Boxes*, 1964. Silkscreen and ink on wood, each 17 x 17 x 14 inches (43.2 x 43.2 x 35.6 cm). Philadelphia Museum of Art. Acquired with funds contributed by the Committee on Twentieth-Century Art and as a partial gift of the Andy Warhol Foundation for the Visual Arts, Inc., 1994

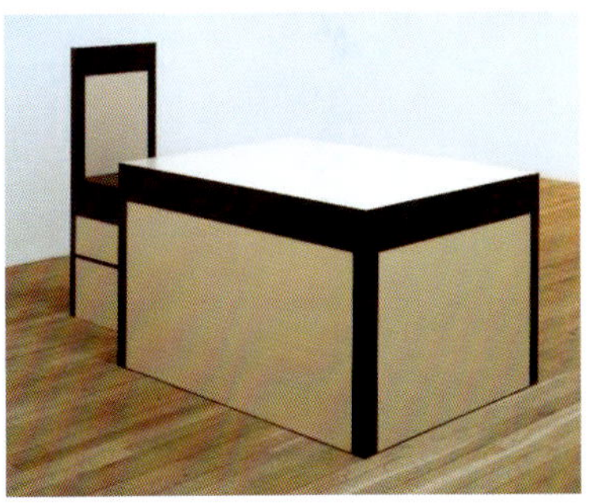

FIG. 54. Richard Artschwager (American, born 1924). *Table and Chair*, 1963–64. Melamine laminate over wood; table 29¾ x 52 x 37½ inches (75.5 x 132 x 95.2 cm); chair 45 x 17¼ x 21 inches (114.3 x 43.8 x 53.3 cm). Tate, London. Purchased 1983

"the dimension of time." For Pistoletto, the Minus Objects were a way of rendering that dimension more tangible—of giving it *place*. He had, to take up an expression that he would use again and again, "entered the mirror."

That particular evolution, specific to the artist, would result in encounters with and a condensing of other experiments conducted in the late 1960s—which were to varying degrees speculative—on the object and its theatricality, whether real or of the imagination.

The 1966 essay introducing the Minus Objects asserted the production of a *place* in conformity with the idea of time as a whole:

> One must bear in mind that every place is created by virtue of a movement: to put it another way, every distance is measurable in relation to the speed at which it is covered. In my mirror-paintings the dynamic reflection does not create a place, because it only reflects a place which already exists—the static silhouette does no more than re-propose an already existing place. But I can create a place by bringing about a passage between the photograph and the mirror: this place is whole time [*tempo intero*].[5]

By the very order of their production and appearance, from the electric wire, to the stack of records, to the coffee table and wall sign marked with a red dot, the objects in the Plexiglas series were a progressive bringing-to-light of that place where the transformation of objects into images reveals the action of time (see plates 68–74). But there remained to be produced a place common to the image-objects (the mirror paintings) and the object-images (the Plexiglas works). That reversibility is characteristic of the mirroring operation of the Minus Objects.

The Plexiglas works are simulacra. This idea was part of the 1960s zeitgeist. Early in the decade, several artists had similarly experimented with life-size reproductions of everyday objects. Warhol's *Brillo Boxes* (1964; fig. 53) were empty cubes covered with the silkscreened brand name. Around the same time, Richard Artschwager showed *Table and Chair* (1963–64; fig. 54), composed of melamine laminate over wood, combining in a single compact block the shape of the furniture and the empty (negative) space between the legs. Pistoletto's Plexiglas coffee table (1964; plate 73) produced a similar filling-in of a hollow structure, with an additional effect of illusion due to the transparency of the material. But the Plexiglas works stood apart from Pop objects by way of their speculative function in a process devoted to the revelation of time. Like the Pop artists, Pistoletto asserted the present and the strange presence of the object-simulacrum. He was also part of the long history of speculations on the mirror—the effervescent history of catoptrics reconstituted by Jurgis Baltrušaitis (fig. 55).[6] For Pistoletto, artistic activity is part of an experience at once specular and speculative. The image-object's actuality is inseparable from the virtual image in the mirror.

The subtraction indicated by the title Minus Objects stems from the simple observation that the experience of the present is not self-presence: the lived present always contains a share of anachronism; it proceeds from an abstraction (it is abstracted, cut off from duration) and, Pistoletto adds, a division. In the mirror paintings, the present of the reflection in the mirror is counteracted, interrupted by the image fixed to the reflecting surface: the photograph is at once the fixed point of a moving representation and, as the already occupied portion of the mirror, the blind spot of the representation. Confronted with this composite picture, made up of a partially blind mirror, the viewer himself becomes divided. Where Stella sought to ban any projection in the image by rescinding illusionism, Pistoletto set up an ambiguous space of reflection that exposes the viewer to his own (virtual) image, while forcing him to consider another (actual) image that is coexistent and anachronous.

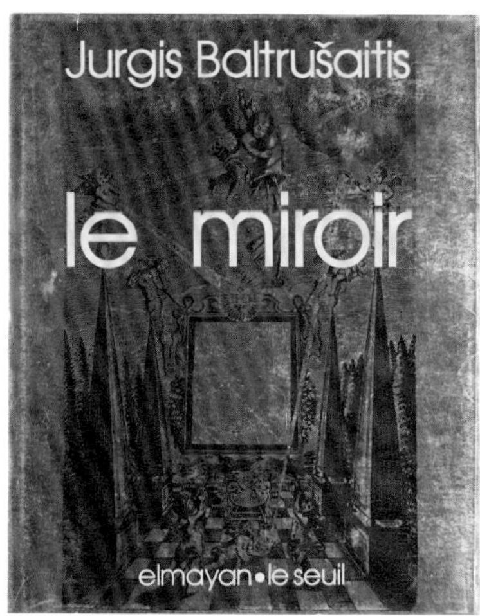

FIG. 55. Jurgis Baltrušaitis (Lithuanian, 1903–1988). *Le miroir: essai sur une légende scientifique* (Paris: Elmayan, 1978). Courtesy of Élia Pijollet and Jean-François Chevrier

The mirror painting's divided present—actual and virtual—is thus the *speculative* (and specular) *frame* of the Minus Objects. This is explicit in Pistoletto's 1966 text, in which he asserts the critical alternative of an "individual dynamic system"[7] in the context of a blind rush to actuality:

> I do not feel able to subscribe to any pre-determined concept of actuality: in the best of cases, any such pre-determination dramatizes the present in the tension of breaking with the past and the hope of a fuller realization in the future. What I am interested in is situating my own action outside of time as conventionally defined. It is of no importance to me whether or not a work of mine answers the current general need: what I strive for in each work is the expression of a real contingent perception: if my action is perpetually authentic, it will not need to be repeated, for its very accomplishment will have effectively exhausted the possibilities it contains.[8]

Pistoletto speaks of "frame" and "action"; he defines the conditions for an *artistic activity* no longer subjected to standards of production. His "individual dynamic system" is a miniature war machine, armed against the cult of the present reduced to actualism, itself subjected to the commercial exigencies of constant renewal of supply. As much as any artistic method, this alternative "system" points the way to an art of living opposed to the programs that seek to impose evolutionary laws while denying the contingencies of subjective duration. The call to contingency is a way of unhooking the activity, to the extent that this is possible, from any and all programs of production. Every object is contingent insofar as it is specific, singular—to the extent that it proceeds out of the artist's necessity in a given time and place. Pistoletto alternates between the terms *necessity* and *possibility*; the two are not equivalent, but one can switch from one to the other: necessity appears in retrospect as a possibility once the object has been created.[9] Each "minus" object accomplishes an action;

it is called "minus" precisely because it has exhausted the possibilities of that action. It is one less thing to be done.

The "minus" object is thus subtracted from the system of programmed accumulation of differences that governs the production of "newness" in the art world, at the same time as it reduces—minutely—the vast domain of all possible objects. Pistoletto's humor has never been so logical.

An example of humorous respect of contingency in the Minus Objects is the photographic portrait of Jasper Johns, of which two versions exist. The first shows the central part of the face (see fig. 52, center; plate 95); the second, only the ears (and part of the shoulders) on either side of a void corresponding to the first picture. This divided reproduction stemmed from a technical constraint: the lab technician who made the enlargement of the portrait did not have a sheet of photographic paper large enough, and so he had to produce the proof in three parts.

The Minus Objects today make up an ensemble.[10] But they were not designed for that purpose; they were produced individually, one after the other, with no plan to create a larger project. Pistoletto's theoretical text that accompanied their presentation in 1966 should not be construed to mean that the objects resulted from any strategic intention. As assembled, they are part of an assertion of a particular stance in the world of art, but that stance was stated after the fact, when the objects already existed and could indeed constitute an ensemble—subject, incidentally, to remakes and "variations."

In his 1966 text, Pistoletto distances himself from an art history that was not his own. A few months earlier, the Walker Art Center in Minneapolis had presented the exhibition *Michelangelo Pistoletto: A Reflected World,* which endorsed the view that the Turinese artist moved in Pop art circles.[11] That critical assimilation had begun in 1963, when he was the only European included in the exhibition *Dessins pop* at Galerie Sonnabend in Paris.[12] In the early 1960s, Pistoletto had seen fit to cleave to the new demand for "realism" or "actualism" that had appeared in art, in Paris with the Nouveaux Réalistes, and in New York within the Pop movement.[13] He saw in this trend a willingness to reengage with objectivity, against the gestural pathos and subjective dramatization of abstraction. But this idea of objectivity, to which he attaches great importance, was for him part of a long history of art, stretching back at least to the Quattrocento artists' development of geometrical perspective. Pistoletto has always seen himself as part of the lineage begun by Piero della Francesca, having referred often to Piero's painting *The Flagellation of Christ* (fig. 56), displayed in the Palazzo Ducale in Urbino. As he told me during a 1993 interview: "The gesture of the man with the whip is suspended, without giving rise to any tension. I understood much later, when I began to make the mirror paintings, that the frozen gesture of the whip could move and develop itself in the perspective opened up by Piero."[14] The mirror-painting form was for Pistoletto a means of intervening in that history, allowing him to draw the main subject (the photographic figure) toward the foreground of the

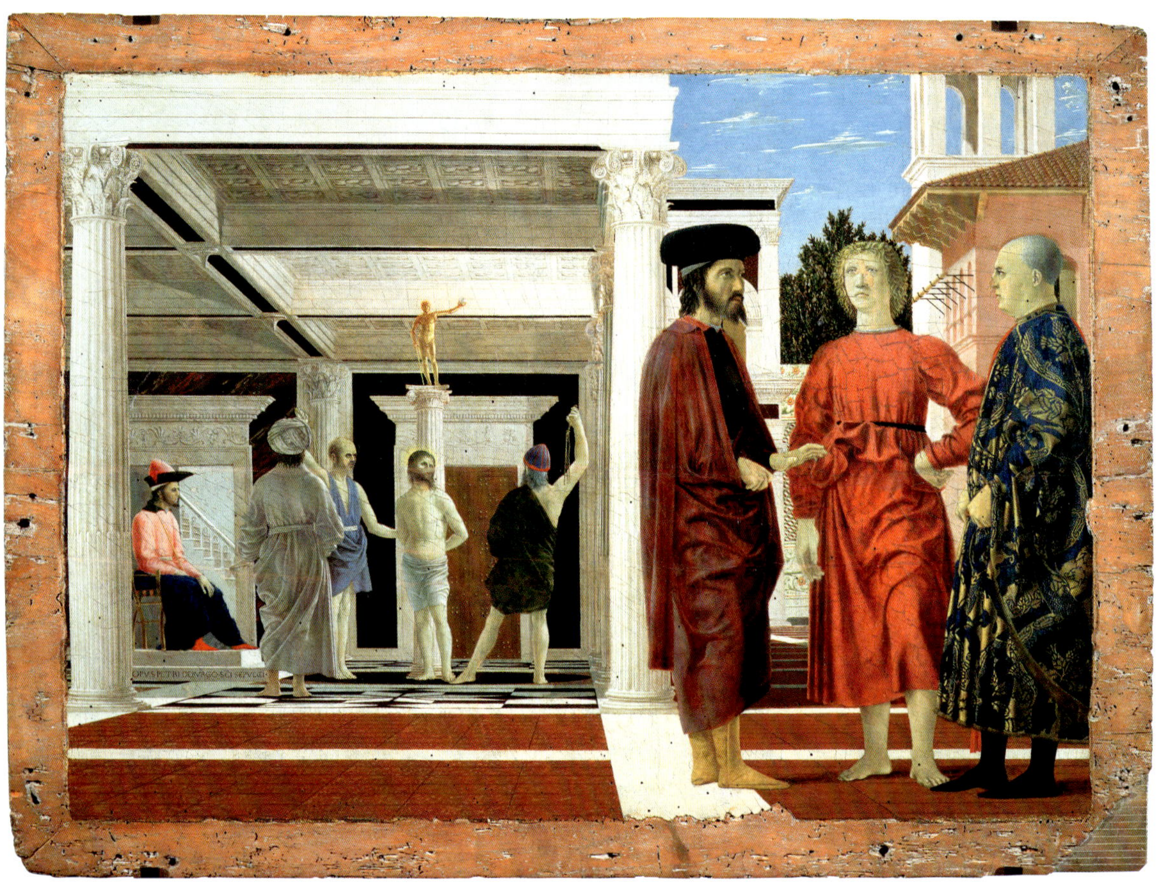

FIG. 56. Piero della Francesca (Italian, c. 1415–1492). *The Flagellation of Christ*, 1455–60. Oil and tempera on panel, 23 x 32⅛ inches (58.4 x 81.5 cm). Galleria Nazionale delle Marche (Palazzo Ducale), Urbino

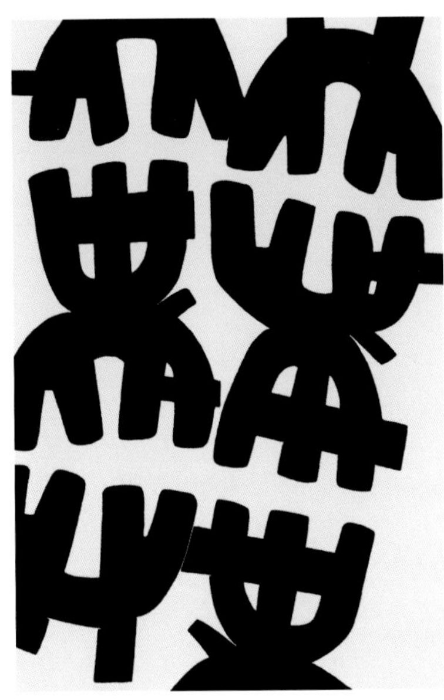

FIG. 57. Giuseppe Capogrossi (Italian, 1900–1972). *Superficie 290* (*Surfaces 290*), 1952–62. Oil on canvas, 106¼ x 70⅞ inches (270 x 180 cm). GNAM—Galleria Nazionale d'Arte Moderna e Contemporanea, Rome

painting, not push it to the rear of the perspective: "With the mirror, the logic of perspective is both fulfilled and reversed: one penetrates the ground of the picture by drawing away, or in other words, one enters the picture—and sees oneself entering it—to the extent that one draws away"[15]

At the beginning of the 1960s, Pistoletto had been seeking an exit from the drama of abstraction, which he connected with the imagery of Francis Bacon.[16] But that dramatic dimension could not be resolved by an amnesiac celebration of media imagery (Pop art) or by variations on *folklore industriel* (industrial folklore), to take up an expression used by the Nouveau Réalisme theoretician Pierre Restany. Pistoletto's 1966 text thus registered a discontinuity. It signaled and interpreted a historical rupture: the Minus Objects, as described by the artist, contradict the cumulative idea of Pop art, just as they oppose the serial model that had enabled the convergence of Pop and Minimalism. The elements that were to make Arte Povera a political response to the triumph of Pop art, and an alternative to Minimalism, were already there in the 1966 text. In privileging materials and energy, however, the "Arte Poveristi" often lost sight of the object; hewing to a Marxist vulgate, they assimilated the object to commodity fetishism. The famous slogan of the May 1968 Paris protests, *Objet cache-toi* (Object hide yourself), emblazoned by Mario Merz on one of his first igloos, sums up that rejection.[17] Pistoletto's attitude before 1968 was different.

The Minus Objects reject the model of *coherence* according to which an artist should develop a recognizable style, a brand (by the 1960s, the art market already equated style with brand image). In 1965, Pistoletto ran the risk of becoming "the mirror artist." The history of art is replete with artists who have been content to produce variations on a prototype throughout their careers. This mode of production was especially prevalent in the "bourgeois" Dutch art of the seventeenth century. Two centuries later, the system was linked to the concept of "pure painting," for it had the advantage of allowing one to forget the subject and appreciate the painter's art for its own sake.[18] In the twentieth century, after the nomenclature of genres had become obsolete, the recurrence of theme and style was supplanted by a principle of variations on the "sign," the prime exponent of this attitude in 1950s Italian art being Giuseppe Capogrossi (fig. 57). In the 1990s, Pistoletto himself reclaimed this idea of the sign, in his own way, by inventing a *segno arte* (art sign). In 1965, however, he was chiefly concerned with disengaging from an image of himself as a "specialist." Other artists had similar worries, as seen in a statement by Pino Pascali in 1968: "Talking with Pistoletto, we agreed that our work has one thing in common: the impossibility of relating to identical objects. It is dangerous to identify with a manual technique."[19]

In the years leading up to 1968 and through 1975, many artists mounted more or less elaborate critiques of the institutional standards of artistic production and communication. From a perspective of systematic opposition to the "system of art," the French group BMPT—(Daniel) Buren, (Olivier) Mosset, (Michel) Parmentier, and (Niele) Toroni—took a critical-materialist stance at the 1967 Paris Biennale: the four artists radicalized the motif-to-sign reduction so as to adopt a tool and procedures.[20] That vocabulary is not entirely absent in Pistoletto's work. He too sought to implement a system, but at the empirical level of individual experience. This is why he recognized a kinship with Pascali, an artist of doing and making rather than of analysis and deconstruction. In Pascali's series *Armi* (Weapons, 1965; fig. 58), Pistoletto identified the amplified strength of the simulacrum, on which his own Plexiglas works rely.[21] In fact, Pascali's works prior to the *Armi* had already revealed affinities with the Minus Objects—notably in their theatricality. In both artists' work, one can detect the idea of repositioning the painting within a genealogy of objects lying between plastic forms and simulacra; hence the importance of the relief painting to both artists.[22] The difference lies in the decorative effect, which is emphasized to a greater degree in Pascali; indeed, he was at that time working as a set decorator for the Italian television network RAI.

In 1964, Rauschenberg had triumphed at the Venice Biennale, becoming the first American to win the Grand Prix, and the gallery owner Leo Castelli was conducting his "grand maneuvers." Pistoletto was the Italian artist who appeared to be most easily assimilable to the gallery's stance. Castelli tried to persuade him that, in order to advance his career, he should take up with the "family" of American Pop artists and settle in New York. Today, Pistoletto recounts this episode with no less bitterness than he felt at the time, but he also notes that the Minus Objects were not a riposte to Castelli's unacceptable summons: their necessity extended beyond the strategic games of the art world, and they cannot be made prisoners of a historic moment, no matter how significant. They also should not be viewed exclusively as the offspring of Arte Povera.

The first of what were later to be known as the "minus" objects, *Quadro da pranzo* (*Lunch Painting*; plate 75), appeared in 1965. Before the end of the year, Pistoletto would produce *Rosa bruciata* (*Burnt Rose*; plate 76), *Colonne di cemento* (*Concrete Columns*; plate 81), *Paesaggio* (*Landscape*; plate 77), *Lampada a mercurio* (*Mercury Lamp*; plate 79), *Piramide verde* (*Green Pyramid*; plate 80), *Specchio* (*Mirror*), and *Pozzo* (*Well*; plate 78). At the time, he had a studio in Turin on via Cibrario. He recalls:

> It was a former typesetting workshop, with small windows at the tops of the walls, which on the street side were at ground level, but in the back were higher up. There was a main entrance that led downward, and I entered from the back, through a large door that, at the time, allowed me to unload materials. There were two sizable rooms, one medium size and the other larger; between them was a glassed-in office cubicle, and that is where I lived. I had a bed, a table, a small camping chest, a camp table, and a camp stove—I was camping. The little sphere of newspapers,

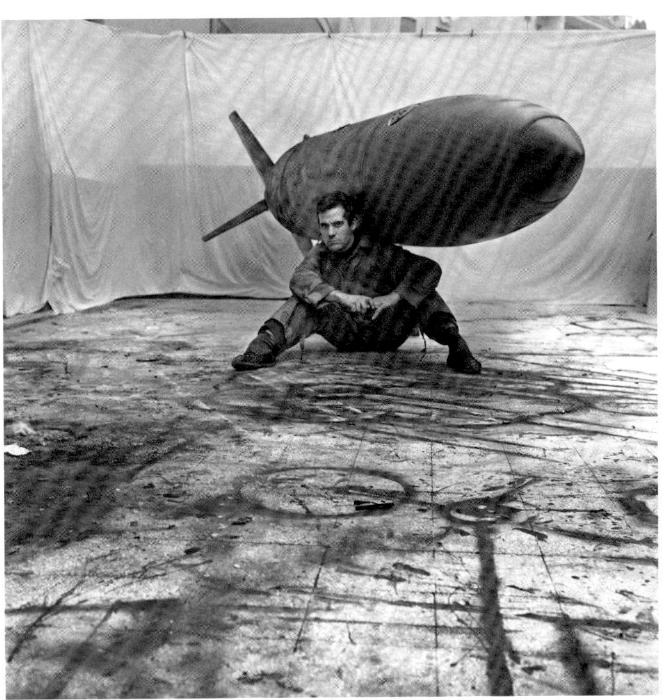

FIG. 58. Pino Pascali in his studio with one of his *Armi* (Weapons), *Missile Colomba della Pace* (*Missile Dove of Peace*, 1965), made of painted found objects, Rome, 1965. Photograph by Claudio Abate

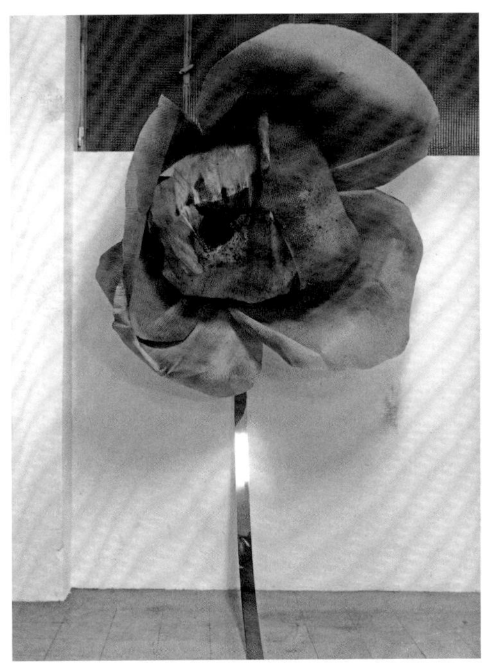

FIG. 59. Michelangelo Pistoletto, version of *Rosa bruciata* (*Burnt Rose*), c. 1968. Spray-painted, corrugated cardboard, polished stainless steel, and mirror; 98 7/16 x 55 1/8 x 39 3/8 inches (250 x 140 x 100 cm). Photograph by Paolo Bressano. Courtesy of Cittadellarte-Fondazione Pistoletto, Biella

> *Sfera sotto il letto* [*Sphere under the Bed*], really was under my bed; I shone a lamp on it to light it. It was like a small gallery, a fourth space with a work [under the bed].[23]

The objects Pistoletto created in his Turin studio shared their early lives with the artist, but only one, the compact sphere under the bed, was shown in the living quarters, or private area, of the studio. Later, when the objects left the studio, Pistoletto built a bed to go with the sphere, which remained lit by a lamp. This evolutive dimension of the object caused a distancing of the impulses and interests that allowed it to be born (I employ this word intentionally). One might say that the object *had its life to live*. This way of putting it indicates that the object is disengaged from the person who made it, that it is endowed with an individual form and existence, both anthropomorphic.[24] At the same time, the very idea of "a life to live" points to a doubling that is analogous to the alienating experience of the mirror.[25] An ongoing exchange was established between the undefined class of the Minus Objects and the family of photo-objects affixed to the virtual space of the mirror in Pistoletto's mirror paintings. Everyday objects circulated in a space that was no longer that of usage but rather that of the image, and of the animated image-simulacrum.

In Pistoletto's wake, other Italian artists, most notably Alighiero Boetti, speculated about a specific biography of the object as distinct simultaneously from the work of art, from artisanal manufacturing, and from serial anonymity. Boetti's work, however, was more conceptual and more lyrical than Pistoletto's. Boetti is surely the artist whose objects, at that point in the late 1960s, owed the most to Pistoletto's example, but his conceptual inspiration took a more epigrammatic, paradoxical (or enigmatic) turn, whereas Pistoletto favored a more prosaic attitude, grounded in the relationships between the figurative performances of the mirror and the narrative expansions of fable.[26] Among the "Poveristi" with whom Pistoletto was friendly—and, as it happens, the one with whom he would also collaborate, in the 1990s—was Pier Paolo Calzolari, who had developed the idea of the biographical object most fully, showing parallels with the work of Joseph Beuys. As with Beuys, Calzolari's objects are bound together by the mythopoetic tenor of the materials. Pistoletto's objects are more sober: the materials retain a disparate character, never coalescing into a harmonious grouping, a syntax; the objects remain at a distance—the distance of the image.

When he decided to show the Minus Objects in a gallery, at La Bertesca in Genoa in 1966, Pistoletto made what he called *versioni* (versions) of them (figs. 59, 60).[27] The difference lay in the addition of mirrors: between the *Colonne di cemento* (*Concrete Columns*; plate 81), renamed *Portico*; on the front side of the *Vetrina* (*Display Case*; plate 88); between the *Semisfere decorative* (*Decorative Semispheres*; plate 82) and the wall; and so on. In the case of *Pozzo specchio* (*Mirror Well*), the mirror stands in for the initial object: the cardboard wall of the original well was replaced with a circular

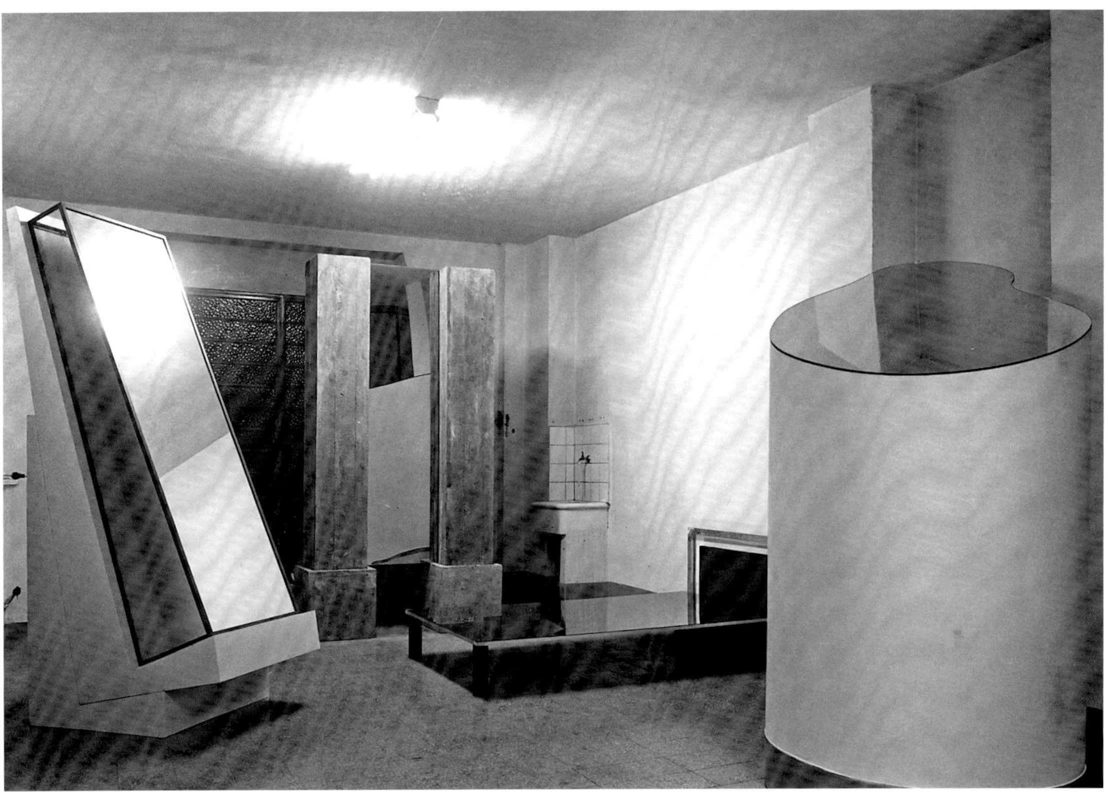

FIG. 60. *Versioni* (Versions) of the Minus Objects in Pistoletto's studio, with *Corpo a pera* (*Pear Body*) on the right, Turin, late 1968. Photograph by Paolo Bressano. Courtesy of Cittadellarte-Fondazione Pistoletto, Biella

mirror placed on the floor—the reflecting bottom of an absent well. Today, Pistoletto offers no justification for these transformations. Their effect, at any rate, was to link the Minus Objects, which had become public objects, to the family of the mirror paintings. Contradictorily, this foregrounded their initial private character. *Rosa bruciata* was the materialization of an object seen in a dream the night before its creation; *Paesaggio* is a Nativity scene with the religious figurines absent, Pistoletto's idea being to rid himself of a childhood image.

In 1965, the year the first Minus Objects were created, Donald Judd published his well-known essay "Specific Objects."[28] Without having directly responded to that text—which he told me he has not read—Pistoletto showed that *specificity* lies not in that which distinguishes an art object from the generic categories of painting and sculpture, nor in some plastic singularity disengaged from illusionism and composition, but in the contingency of an action. The so-called *minus* object is not an added object, nor an object that has been given supplementary presence—insofar as it is freed from illusionism and is outside the bounds of categories—but rather is an object from which the artist, in the act of creating it, has liberated, detached, and undone *himself*. Pistoletto has observed that literalism, in its amnesiac actuality, equates with a desire for affirmation that is too insistent, urgent, and authoritarian:

> My works are not constructions or fabrications of new ideas, any more than they are objects which represent me, intended to be imposed and to impose me on others. Rather, they are objects through whose agency I free myself from something—not constructions, then, but liberations. I do not consider them more but less, not pluses but minuses, in that they bring with them a sense of a perceptual experience which has been definitively manifested once and for all.
>
> According to my idea of time, one must learn how to free oneself from a position even while one is engaged in conquering it.[29]

The aim of the Minus Objects was not to "get clear" of painting, as Judd suggested;[30] that "position" had already been "conquered" with the Plexiglas series. The *Quadro da pranzo* (*Lunch Painting;* plate 75), incidentally, is a framed painting that one can enter and sit down in. The intent was not to reduce illusionism, or even to exaggerate it or drive it to its limits, as the Photorealist painters did, but rather to occupy its space—to live in it, almost—as one occupies a position, temporarily, among other possible positions. It is pointless to confront those who wish to ascertain the existence of a new, hyperreal reality with a negation of or a systematic contempt for the object. The logic of subtraction is subtler. It asserts that negation is an "addition of thinking" because a "minus object" is a real, actual object, augmented by the mental operation that subtracted it, to ensure its existence, from the vast domain of possible objects.

The Minus Objects are not antiobjects. They have no place in the history of conceptual art.[31] Pistoletto made them, sometimes calling on outside assistance (for the reproduction of Jasper Johns's portrait, for example); occasionally they are entirely "manufactured," and some of them also resulted from appropriation and alteration, after the fashion of Marcel Duchamp's "assisted" ready-mades. They are the clear antithesis of a productivist model, but they are still objects, not antiobjects. In every case, they exist; they have even been "produced," in the sense in which one speaks of "production" in the performing arts. Pistoletto had not gone to war against the fetishized object of consumer society, or against the "Society of the Spectacle" vilified during the same period by Guy Debord. He avoided that polemical front, sidestepping the confrontational posture of militant criticism. By their title, the Minus Objects reveal a paradoxical aspect, but the paradox is specifically logical; it does not aim for derisive effect.

Likewise, Pistoletto skirted the empty/full alternative so spectacularly exploited by the Nouveaux Réalistes. Clearly, his aim was not to take up some tabula rasa project, nor even to perpetuate the ascetic attitude adopted—quite legitimately—by artists who sought to withdraw, to *disencumber*, the environment of modern life by opposing decorative and eclectic overload.[32] The Minus Objects, on the contrary, seemed quietly to contribute to the diversity, if not the eclecticism, of the so-called postmodern environment. In reality, Pistoletto was above all seeking a mental mobility, corresponding to the freedom of a stroll *between the objects*. To this day, the quality of the Minus Objects resides largely in the multiplicity of their interrelationships in space—that is, in a given place as well.

One object, however, emerged from the rest of the ensemble as the most symbolic and most ambitious: *Metrocubo d'infinito* (*Cubic Meter of Infinity*; plate 96). In 1966, it marked a conclusion, a synthesis—because it represents *infinity minus one*. Pistoletto believes today that it was this object, with its inward-facing mirrors, that enabled him to work with the mirror once again. It is the star among the Minus Objects, the one most often exhibited. It corresponds to Pistoletto's expression "Art Takes on Religion," which in 1978 marked the culmination of the process of artistic expansion begun with the speculations on the mirror.[33] In 2000, a replica of this work was placed at the center of a multi-confessional meditation space designed for the Institut Paoli-Calmettes, a medical center in Marseille, in the south of France (fig. 61).[34]

The Minus Objects belong to a kind of art that promotes the act of making over the work of art, without negating the object. They give precedence to mental and artisanal processes over the iconic value exemplified by the painting, without negating the painting. Underpinning that stance is a theatrical performance model. Pistoletto laid no claim to the ambiguous heritage of Futurism; his system is a "dynamic" one, but he made no attempt to update the concept of modern life adduced by the artists who were

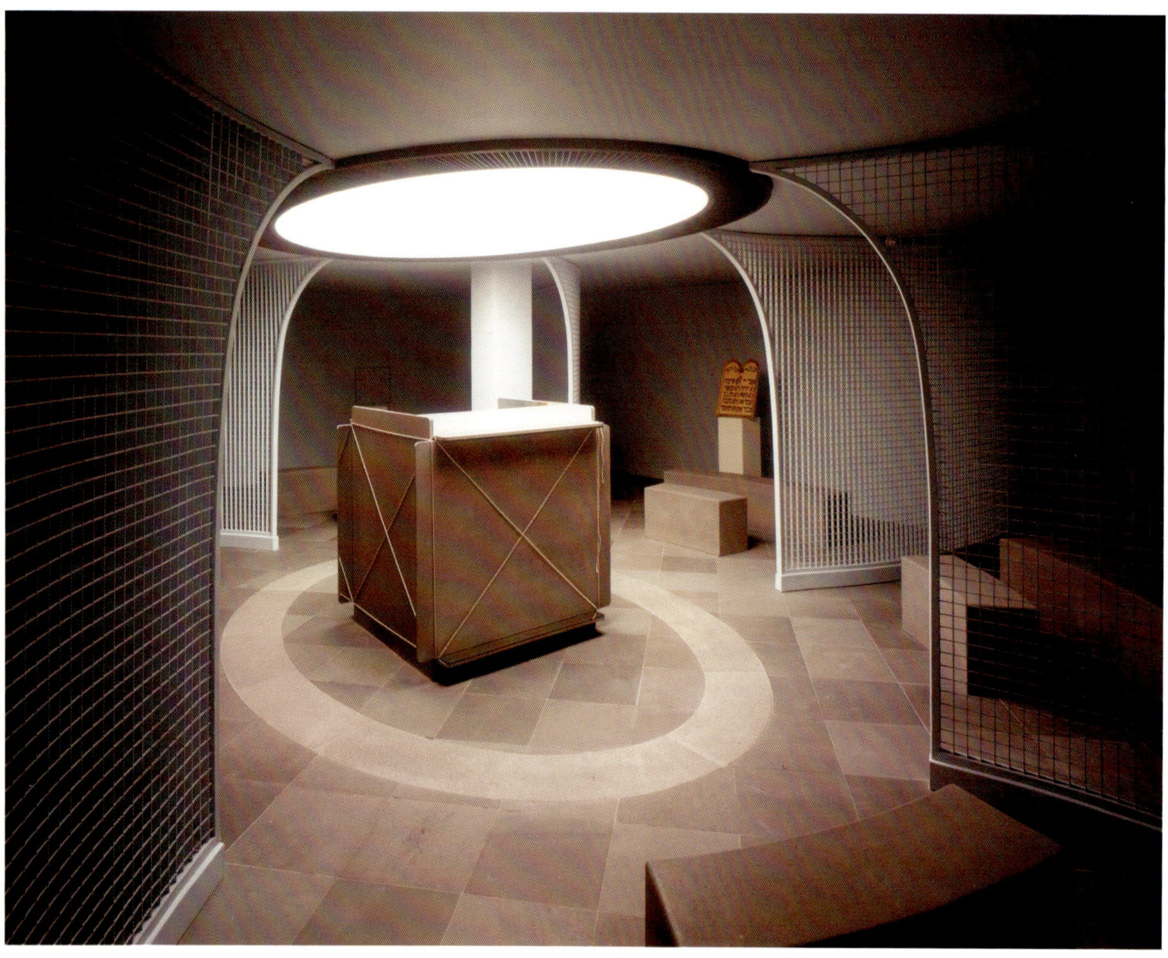

FIG. 61. Michelangelo Pistoletto, *Luogo di raccoglimento e di preghiera* (*Place of Meditation and Prayer*), 2000. Permanent installation, Institut Paoli-Calmettes (oncology center), Marseille, France. Photograph by Margherita Spiluttini. Courtesy of Cittadellarte-Fondazione Pistoletto, Biella

interested in the movement as such. On the other hand, his conception of the object is related to a definition of stage space that owes much to the great reform in theater since the early twentieth century. In 1919, Adolphe Appia wrote: "To receive its portion of life from the living body, space must oppose this body. . . . But opposition to the body gives life to the inanimate forms of space. *Living* space is the victory of bodily forms over inanimate forms. The mutuality is complete."[35]

The theater reform advanced by Appia essentially aimed to disencumber the stage space to allow more room for actors' movements. But the end result of such disencumbrance is not emptiness.[36] The stage space is not an inert container brought to life by bodies in motion; the two components of theatrical action interact in reciprocal opposition: one *objects* to the other. So it is, also, that objects plot a path through the very space in which they are presented and arranged: the objects lend the exhibition site its spatial quality by simultaneously being obstacles and markers.

In transposing these acquisitions from modern theater to the visual arts, Pistoletto put into practice the dialectics of space and place posited subsequently—in the late 1970s—by theoreticians such as Yi-Fu Tuan, author of *Space and Place* (1977), and Michel de Certeau. The latter writes, in *The Practice of Everyday Life* (1980):

> A place (*lieu*) is the order (of whatever kind) in accord with which elements are distributed in relationships of coexistence. It thus excludes the possibility of two things being in the same location (*place*). The law of the "proper" rules in the place: the elements taken into consideration are *beside* one another, each situated in its own "proper" and distinct location, a location it defines. . . .
> A *space* exists when one takes into consideration vectors of direction, velocities, and time variables. Thus space is composed of intersections of mobile elements. It is in a sense actuated by the ensemble of movements deployed within it.[37]

Certeau concludes by positing that "space is a practiced place." Space therefore designates the dimension of time as it is lived as part of the experience of place.

Consistent with this spatialization of place, one of the salient features of the Minus Objects is their diversity: diversity of forms, functions, and materials. The ensemble is inclusive and open. It is in that diversity that Pistoletto's way of thinking found its greatest mobility. It also found a *speed*, which is located between the virtual swiftness of the reflected images and the slow pace of the image returned from the past, constituted by the arresting action of the photographic image. The mirror painting combines the mobility of virtual images with the immutability of the actual image. The subtractive logic of the Minus Objects relates to a constrained duration and a reduced speed. At the same time, the heterogeneity of the materials used, from cement to glass, underscores the existence of a further parameter: the slowness-swiftness relationship is overlaid by one of opacity-transparency, already evident in the interplay of the double ground (wall and panel) in the Plexiglas works—a relationship that is also at work in the mirror paintings, where the transparency of the reflection is interrupted by the opaque, blind area of the photographic image.[38]

Speed is held to be a distinctive trait of modernity—present in art since Futurism—and a manifestation of the fleetness of thought. But speed is relative: like light, it becomes perceptible only by contrast. We are back to the logic of reciprocal opposition and stimulation of bodies and space asserted by Appia.

With the Minus Objects, Pistoletto gave himself the freedom of movement of one who has made himself available to circumstances, who takes advantage of occasions and can transform a constraint into an opportunity. He put into practice a plastic thought that pertains to "everyday tactics," to use de Certeau's expression. De Certeau quite rightly connects this concept to the example of "the cunning of the ancients" (Greek *mêtis*), citing the Hellenists Marcel Detienne and Jean-Pierre Vernant:

> There is no doubt that *mêtis* is a type of intelligence and of thought, a way of knowing; it implies a complex but very coherent body of mental attitudes and intellectual behaviour which combine flair, wisdom, forethought, subtlety of mind, deception, resourcefulness, vigilance, opportunism, various skills, and experience acquired over the years. It is applied to situations which are transient, shifting, disconcerting and ambiguous, situations which do not lend themselves to precise measurement, exact calculation or rigorous logic.[39]

The Minus Objects are a defense and an illustration of artistic activity that is unbound from the lofty values of Art, as much as from the negative compulsions of antiart or the paradoxical cult of the insignificant. *Mêtis,* as an everyday practice, ignores dogmatic seriousness but does not claim to subvert it, because it does not proceed from an intent to "radically" transform thinking habits. Humor, here, is not the carnivalesque, grotesque laughter of popular culture, which the philosopher Mikhail Bakhtin placed in opposition to learned culture.[40]

For Pistoletto, every opportunity is worth seizing if it permits thought to be *applied,* the better to become *detached.* He favors neither high nor low. Bakhtin's theory of the grotesque has found echoes in an artistic trend that has endured since the end of the nineteenth century, from Alfred Jarry's *Ubu Roi* (1896) to Paul McCarthy's scatological orgies. Carnivalesque theatricality is not alien to Pistoletto, who has cultivated a protean exuberance in the various, often buffoonish characters found in his performances and other role-plays (see pp. 81–107 below). He has consistently blended parody and burlesque comedy with the pathos of the hieratic figure. But the humor of the Minus Objects is more akin to what Bakhtin terms

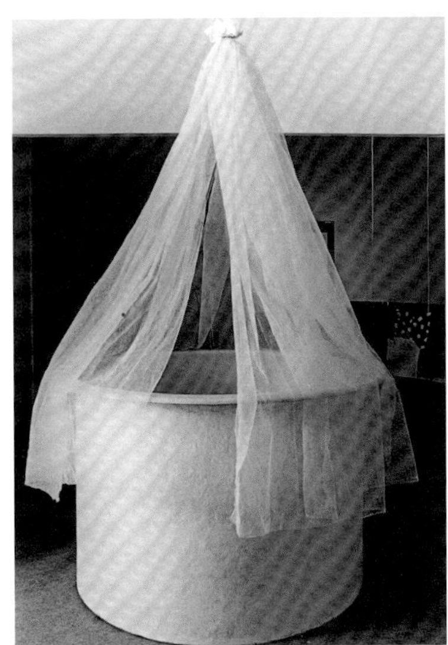

FIG. 62. Michelangelo Pistoletto, *Pozzo culla* (*Well Cradle*), 1966–68. Fiberglass, mirror, and gauze, 118⅛ x 65¾ inches (300 x 167 cm). Collection of the artist. Photograph by Mimmo Jodice

"reduced laughter"—that is, an attenuated, muffled form of grotesque humor. Bakhtin remarks: "The most extensive form of reduced laughter in modern times (especially starting with Romanticism) is *irony*."[41] Irony is rare in Pistoletto's oeuvre. Rather, he oscillates between seriousness and humor. On the other hand, he validates Bakhtin's definition of "open seriousness," as opposed to "dogmatic seriousness": "True open seriousness fears neither parody, nor irony, nor any other form of reduced laughter, for it is aware of being part of an uncompleted whole."[42]

Pistoletto's *Sarcofago* (*Sarcophagus*; plate 94) gives material expression to the muffled character of "reduced laughter" when confronted with the ambivalent motif of death and the desire for eternity; the mummy in the sarcophagus is not visible, any more than are the reflecting surfaces of the inward-facing mirrors of *Metrocubo d'infinito*. The wooden sarcophagus is shining, covered in mica; it is, as Pistoletto said, "a Sunday sarcophagus, dressed up for a party."[43] It replies to the well (*pozzo*), shrouded in a veil, transformed into a cradle (*culla*)—*Pozzo culla* (fig. 62). The ambivalent relationship of death to birth (or rebirth) lies at the heart of Bakhtin's concept of the grotesque.[44]

After the Minus Objects, and thanks to them, Pistoletto launched himself into a space-time with no fixed objects, in which objects could be used, like props; he could take the stage, just as he had entered the mirror. This confidence sustained the collaborations he directed in 1967 and during the period when his theater troupe Lo Zoo was active (1968–70; fig. 63).[45] In December 1967, for the exhibition *Con-temp-l'azione*, on view in three separate Turin galleries, the *Sfera di giornali* left the private space of the bedroom (under the bed) and ventured out into the street. The new "ball" (*palla*) created for the occasion was bigger, one meter in diameter (fig. 64). On opening night, Pistoletto took it for a (st)roll through the streets of Turin from one gallery to the next, joined along the way by some of the exhibition artists and organizers: the *palla* had become a sort of poor *pala* (retable). The object had left the studio for the theater of the street (fig. 65).[46]

Street theater is not—contrary to an old activist fantasy—the ideal venue for reconciling art with the people, with the intention of effecting social change. Pistoletto has always aspired to a dedramatization of art, through objectification and subjective detachment. But *drama*, in both senses of the term, is constituent of a type of theater that cannot be confined to entertainment—that remains engaged with the world and actuality. The drama is in the very heart of "things," private or public; it is distilled in the work (or the art object). Bakhtin's observation that "reduced laughter in carnivalized literature by no means excludes the possibility of somber colors within a work"[47] finds echoes in the staging of the Minus Objects at the February 1970 Biennale in Bologna, where Pistoletto showed *Ufficio dell'Uomo nero* (*Office of the Minus Man*; fig. 67).

The theater experiment of Lo Zoo was bound to lead to a literary revival (*ripresa*, in Italian, meaning "revival" but also "shot" in the

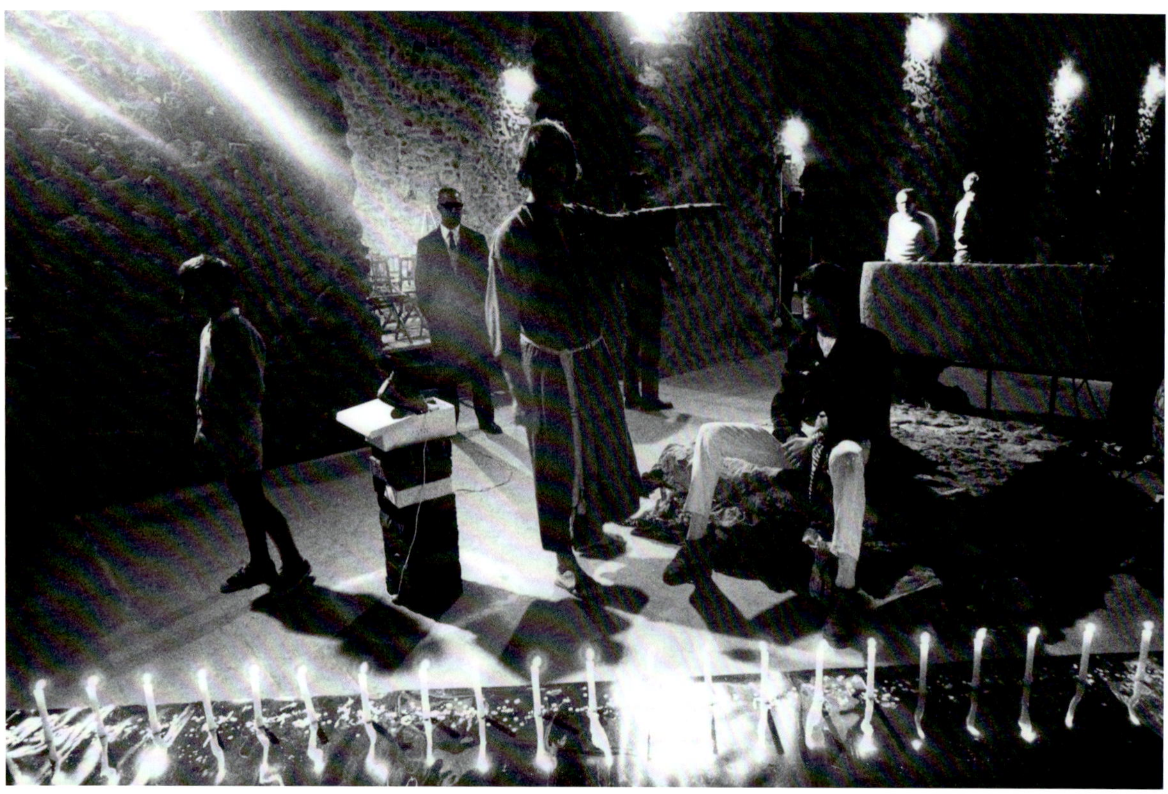

FIG. 63. Pistoletto's installation at *Arte Povera + Azioni Povere*, Arsenali dell'Antica Repubblica, Amalfi, October 4, 1968. Among the works exhibited are *Monumentino* (*Small Monument*); *Capitello e stracci* (*Capital and Rags*); *Sarcofago e stracci* (*Sarcophagus and Rags*); *Mappamondo* (*Globe*); and *Candele* (*Candles*). Photograph by Claudio Abate. Courtesy of Cittadellarte-Fondazione Pistoletto, Biella

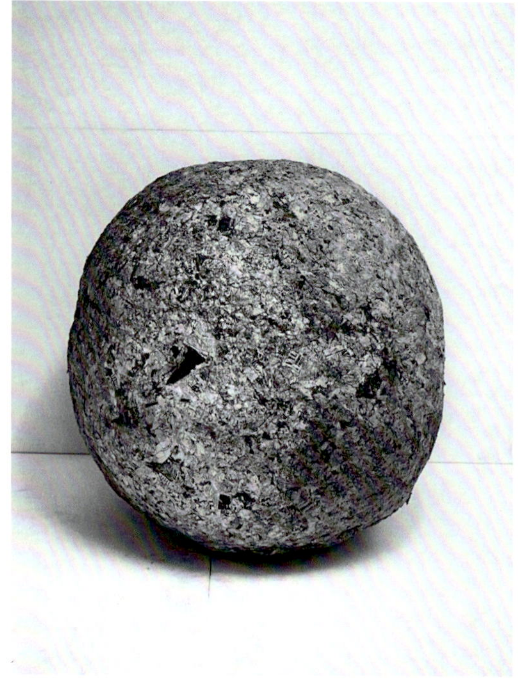

FIG. 64. Michelangelo Pistoletto, *Sfera di giornali* (*Newspaper Ball*), 1966. Pressed newspapers, diam. 39 3/8 inches (100 cm). Photograph by Paolo Bressano. Courtesy of Cittadellarte-Fondazione Pistoletto, Biella

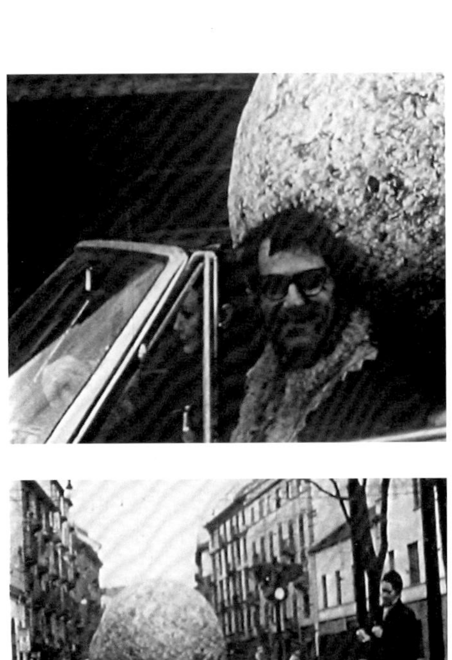

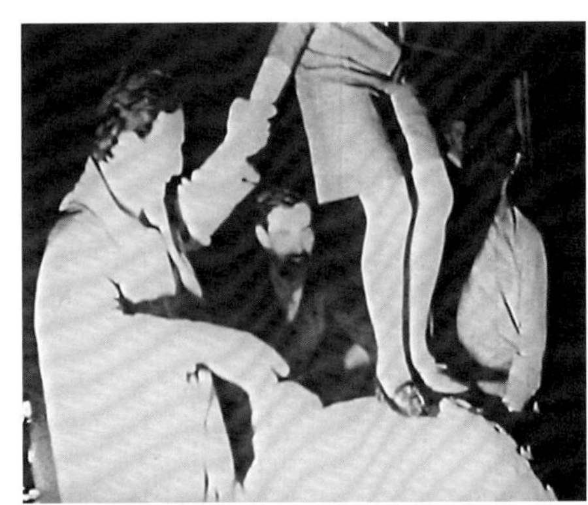

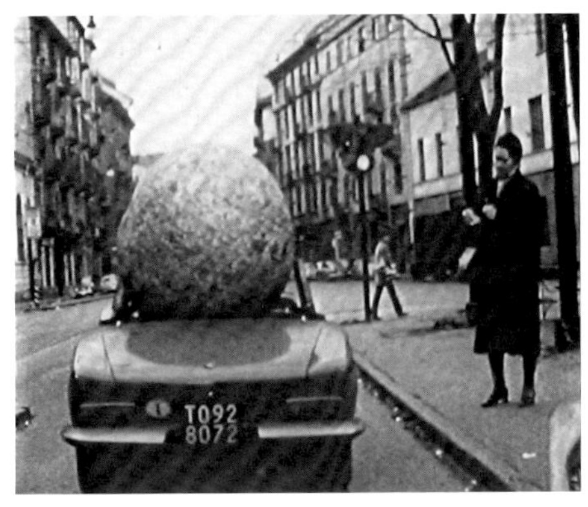

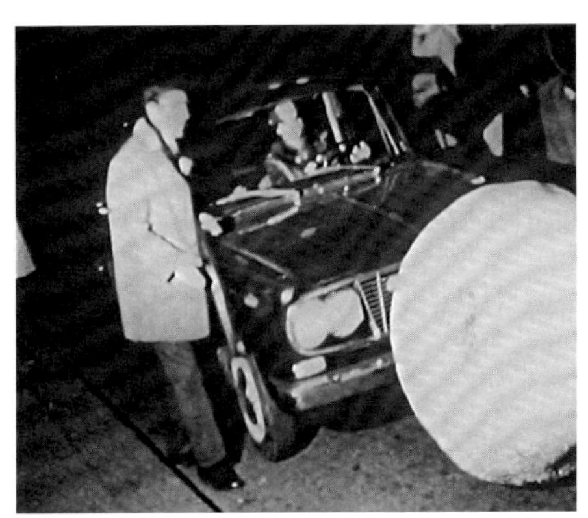

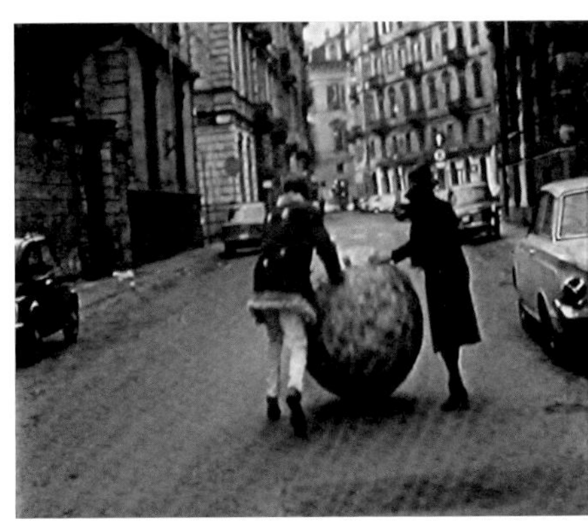

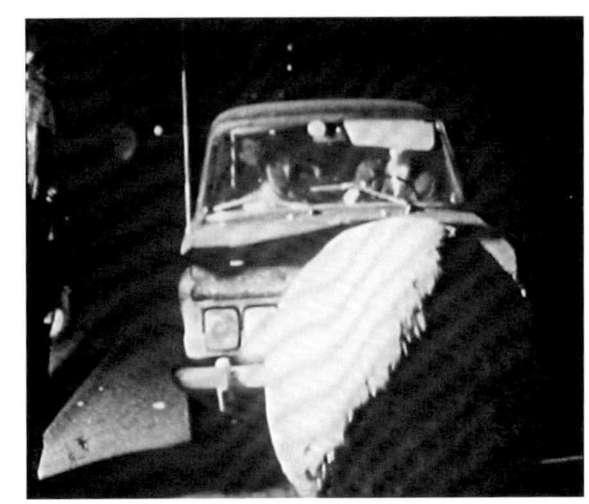

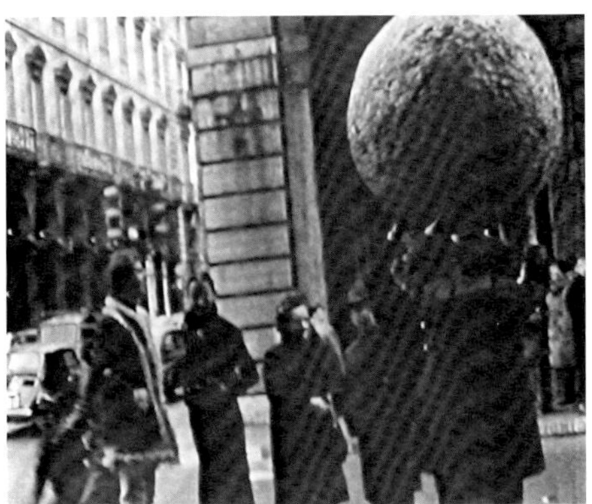

FIG. 65. Lo Zoo, *Scultura da passeggio* (*Walking Sculpture*), two actions in the streets of Turin, December 1967 and January 1968. Stills from the film *Buongiorno, Michelangelo* (*Good Morning, Michelangelo*, 1968), by Ugo Nespolo. Courtesy of Cittadellarte-Fondazione Pistoletto, Biella

cinematic sense). Enter the "Minus Man," a theatrical character who is "unbearable" (*insopportabile*), given voice in a book Pistoletto wrote in December 1969 and January 1970, *L'Uomo nero, il lato insopportabile*.[48] This is the big bad wolf—*l'uomo nero*, or "the man in black" (later translated as "the Minus Man")—the emissary of dark forces without whom the experience of the present is confined to the progressive pretenses of a clear, objectivized conscience. It is also the "other stage," the stage of the unconscious, and the "other side of the painting," the literary side.[49]

At the time of the Bologna Biennale, the Minus Man disengaged himself from his actions and his works, took stock, and administered his past. Two walls of the exhibition space were occupied by large, full-scale prints of two photographs of the Minus Objects exhibited in Pistoletto's studio in 1965–66 (see fig. 67). Like arrested mirrors, they opened up the actual space of the "office" to the moment when the Minus Objects came into existence. The delay inherent in the prerecorded image, always poised to return, is the shadow of the past in the present. It also plots a vanishing line—an ideal horizon or a gauge for the present. *La terra e la luna* (*The Earth and the Moon*; fig. 66), a version of *Mappamondo* (*Globe;* plate 97) with the ball caged after having rolled along for so long, amplifies, in a minor key, the play of scales. One cannot move away from the reproduction, with its immediate doubling of actuality, without entering even deeper into the mirror.[50]

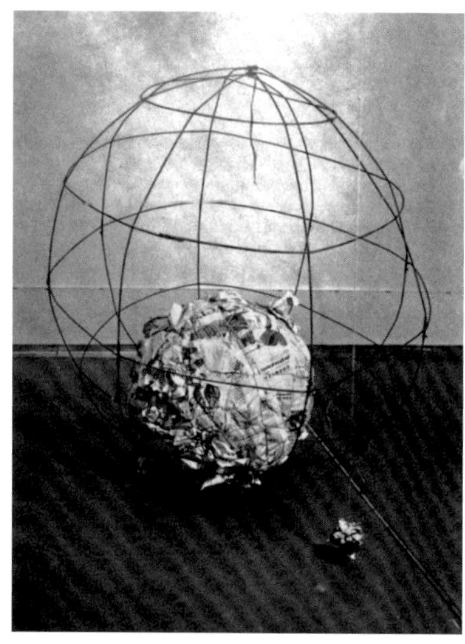

FIG. 66. Michelangelo Pistoletto, *La terra e la luna* (*The Earth and the Moon*), 1966–68. Iron, newspaper, and cord, 70 ⅞ x 70 ⅞ x 94½ inches (180 x 180 x 240 cm). Collection of the artist. Photograph by Paolo Mussat Sartor. Courtesy of Cittadellarte-Fondazione Pistoletto, Biella

Pistoletto explains that the idea for *Struttura per parlare in piedi* (*Structure for Talking while Standing*; plate 87) came to him when he noticed the handprints visitors left after they had leaned against gallery walls. The object seems to have come from some bricolage competition to find the most ingeniously superfluous, even useless, object. In 1960s Italy, the activity of bricolage, or constructing something from whatever is at hand—popularized in Claude Lévi-Strauss's *La pensée sauvage* (*The Savage Mind*), published in 1962—was an alternative to the design and antidesign trends in so-called Programmed Art.[51] Pistoletto did not situate his practice between programming and chance. Similarly, he did not think in terms of *montage*. After the mirror paintings, which proceeded from collage, the ensemble of the Minus Objects took shape according to a paradoxical mode of concentrated dispersion, not through a montage procedure whereby space and duration are governed by the notion of intervals.[52] Bricolage in the Minus Objects testifies above all to the persistence of an artisanal dimension in the mental processes of art-making. The *bricoleur*'s ingenious "idea" is not the cumbersome machinery of the operative concept. Rather, it adopts the pretext of a utilitarian motif to give free rein to the whimsy of art.

When Walter Pach expressed surprise and regret that Duchamp had given up painting, the latter replied: "I have not stopped painting. Every picture has to exist in the mind before it is put on canvas, and it always loses something when it is turned into paint. I prefer to see my pictures

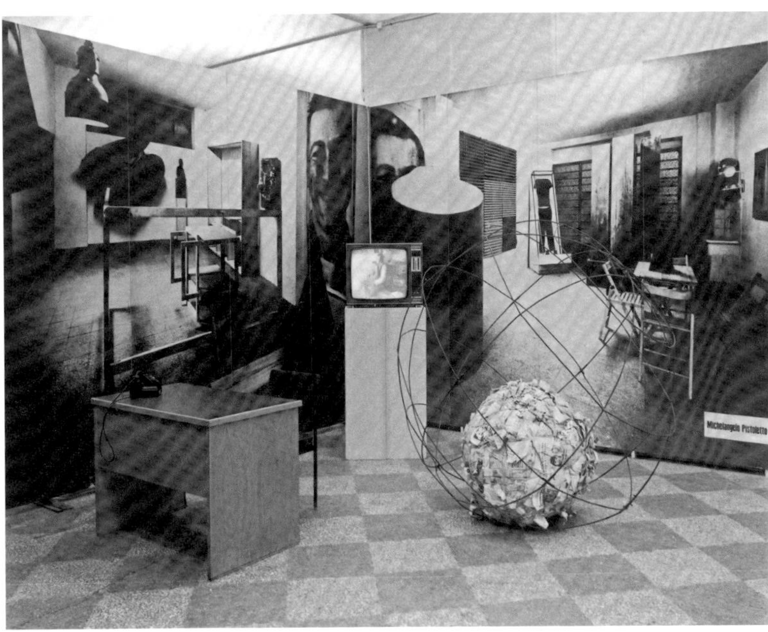

FIG. 67. Michelangelo Pistoletto, *Ufficio dell'Uomo nero* (*Office of the Minus Man*), 1970. Installation, III Biennale, Museo Civico di Bologna, 1970. Photograph by Paolo Mussat Sartor. Courtesy of Cittadellarte-Fondazione Pistoletto, Biella

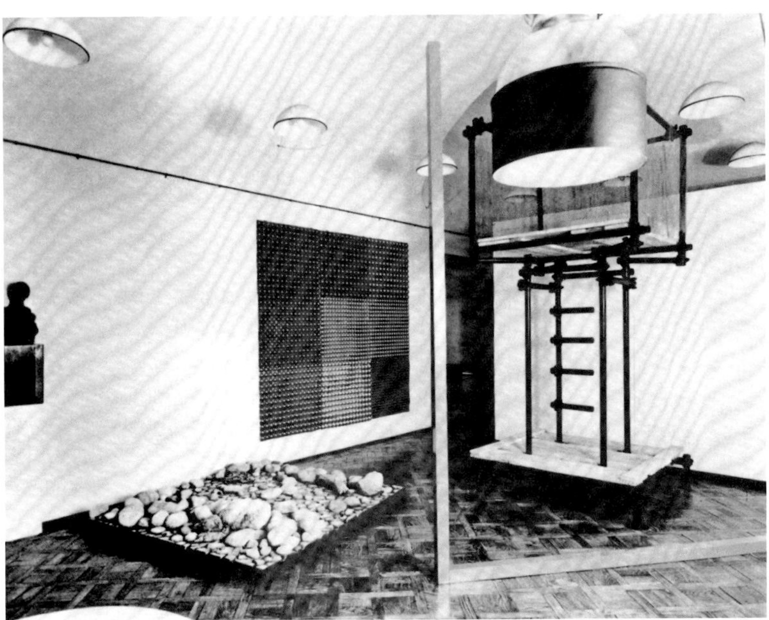

FIG. 68. Installation of the exhibition *Arte abitabile* (*Inhabitable Art*), Galleria Sperone, Turin, June–July 1966, with (from left to right) Pistoletto's *Scultura lignea* (*Wood Sculpture*, 1965–66; plate 91); a work by Gianni Piacentino; Pistoletto's *Semisfere decorative* (*Decorative Semispheres*, 1965–66; plate 82); and a work by Piero Gilardi. Courtesy of Courtesy of Cittadellarte-Fondazione Pistoletto, Biella

without that muddying."[53] In the Minus Objects, this idealized mental painting took material form, at the same time being extended to the infinite ensemble of virtual objects (produced by the mirror).

Pistoletto distilled from the Minus Objects the idea of "inhabitable art" (*arte abitabile*), exemplified in the June–July 1966 show at Galleria Sperone in Turin, mounted in collaboration with Piero Gilardi and Gianni Piacentino, the two artists with whom he was closest at the time (fig. 68).[54] The adjective *inhabitable* qualifies art "subtracted" from the sphere of mercantile accumulation. The danger lay in naively placing an art that was useful and functional in opposition to an object of pure contemplation. In fact, the idea was especially to mark the crossing of a threshold within a space-time continuum linking art to life. That crossing is exactly what the Minus Objects produced.

Pistoletto had created objects where he lived; he had lived with them, if not among them (since his central living quarters corresponded to the former offices of the typesetter, distinct from the adjacent workshops). If art is no longer an "elsewhere," then the domestic place has simultaneously lost its private nature; it is no longer distinct from public space. The private-public partition tends toward effacement in a space that melds painterly imagination with objectified signs of the everyday.

One of the objects, *Lampada a mercurio* (*Mercury Lamp*; plate 79), is functional. Most of the others are linked to the tradition of the autonomous art object, all while referencing an everyday utility. Between those two poles unfurls a wide array of possibilities. The serving table with its twin trays of painted fabric (*Mobile, or Furniture*; plate 84) is hardly useful, while *Quadro da pranzo* (*Lunch Painting*; plate 75) suggests that one can physically enter the imaginary space of the picture. The picture form shows up in the three *Teletorte* (*Twisted Canvases*; plate 83) and in *Mica* (plate 86), with its play of flakes, as well as in *Ti amo* (*I Love You*; plate 90), *Semisfere decorative* (*Decorative Semispheres*; plate 82), and *Fontana luminosa* (*Luminous Fountain*; plate 89). Pistoletto was playing with painterly styles: Pop art word painting, kinetic effects, psychedelic colors. The mirror (*Specchio*) is a real mirror. *Paesaggio*, the little nativity landscape (plate 77), is perhaps in dialogue with *Scultura lignea* (*Wood Sculpture*; plate 91); both are ancient images testifying to a religious folklore. The enlarged photographic portrait of Jasper Johns (plate 95) is in another, profane register. *Rosa bruciata* (*Burnt Rose;* plate 76) introduces a fantastical, oneiric characteristic echoing around the work. The frontier meant to separate (or protect) familiar reality from the imaginary has been abolished. The ensemble is not an inventory but the concentrated experience of diversity, and the reassembling of dispersion. The scale of the human body is insistent, but it is altered, perturbed by sudden variations.

Unlike Claes Oldenburg, Pistoletto does not make systematic use of distortions of scale—he does not produce monsters. In the tradition of collage and assemblage to which Oldenburg belongs, everyday objects are submitted to a process of metamorphosis (fig. 69). The Minus Objects are

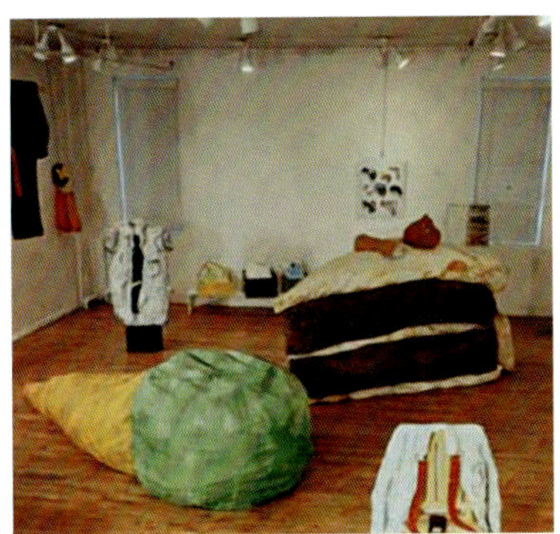

FIG. 69. Installation of Claes Oldenburg's exhibition at the Green Gallery, New York, fall 1962, with *Floor Cone* and *Floor Cake* at center

evolutive, but they do not aim at a poetics of the bizarre that upsets and transfigures the stable appearances of the everyday; they do not testify to the power of some constrained or repressed whim. Each marks a gap, and the whole constitutes an "other" space, in the meaning intended by Michel Foucault when he posited his heterotopias in 1967.[55] An "other space," though, is not another world, a utopian one, radically concealed from utilitarian norms and naturalist verisimilitude. Up to and including Pop simulacra, the art of the object has consistently swung back and forth between the fantastical rupturing of the everyday and the alternative of the marvelous. In 1936, André Breton pointed to a "crisis of the object" conducive to the Surrealist concept of the marvelous; the intent of art could be replaced, he said, by a "*desire to objectify*," the prime expression of which is the fabrication and circulation of objects appearing in dreams. *Rosa bruciata* pertains to that "objectification of the very act of dreaming."[56] But it is one object among many. In the ensemble, the marvelous and the fantastical appear on the periphery of an *experiential mean*.

"The objects brought together in this way," Breton writes, "have one thing in common: they derive from the objects which surround us but succeed in achieving a separate identity simply through a *change of role*."[57] Among the many expressions of Surrealistic poetics, this is doubtless the only one applicable to the Minus Objects—on the condition, naturally, that one does not equate the "change of role" with a process of appropriation (for Breton himself did not restrict the gamut of Surrealist objects to found objects). This phrase designates the heterotopian mechanism of the mirror; it is why Pistoletto states that the Minus Objects allowed him to "enter the mirror." The wellspring of the ensemble is a change of role that works in both directions, between the everyday object and its altered double—which is to say, between two experiential modes as well: dispersion and concentration. Each of the Minus Objects is at once a concentration and the moment of a dispersion produced by the coexistence of heterogeneous, disparate objects.[58]

The artists grouped under the Arte Povera label often professed to an interpretation of dispersion in conformity with their preference for flexible, shapeless materials; dispersion in those cases emerged from the effects of chance and entropy. In the Minus Objects, dispersion pertains particularly to a rupturing of syntactical continuity, which gives rise to a principle of *constellation*: chance is outwitted. An ensemble was finally constituted, and distilled into an ultimate object, the *Metrocubo d'infinito*. The experiential mean is thus located between dispersion and concentration. This approach to activity is similar to playing; it corresponds to the enterprise of dedramatization begun with the mirror paintings. Here again, we see the kinship with Pascali. His *Armi* are outsized toys: the artist was playing at war and against it. One perceives simultaneously a dramatization (in the sense of theatricalization) of critical thinking and a playful dedramatization of polemical (in the etymological sense of the term) thinking.

In the mirror paintings, Pistoletto had investigated the spatial relationship of near to far, of here to there, inscribed in time. This relationship is the crux of the phenomenological description of the perceptual and spatial experience *of the body-subject*, perceiving and perceived at once, *in time*. As Maurice Merleau-Ponty wrote in *Phenomenology of Perception* (1945): "The 'order of co-existents' is inseparable from the 'order of sequences', or rather time is not only the consciousness of a sequence. Perception provides me with a 'field of presence' in the broad sense, extending in two dimensions: the here-there dimension and the past-present-future dimension."[59]

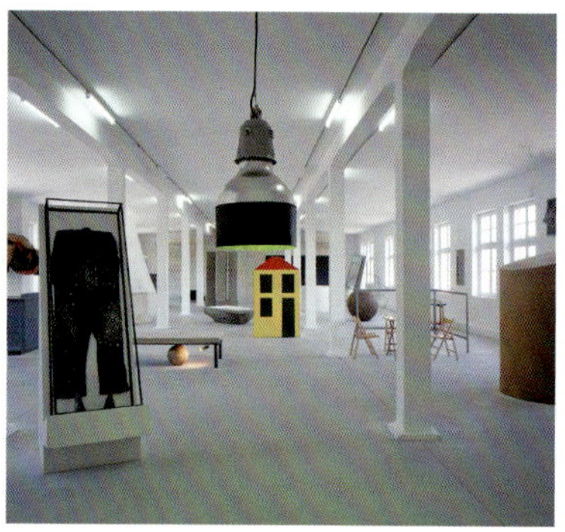

FIG. 70. Pistoletto's Minus Objects exhibited at *Documenta 10*, Kassel, Germany, 1997. Photograph by Monica Nikolic. Courtesy of Cittadellarte-Fondazione Pistoletto, Biella

At the same time, the body-subject is always already other, alienated, ensnared by image and the imaginary dimension. The Minus Objects explore a division of the body between the "proper" (*le propre*)—which characterizes place, as de Certeau noted—and the otherness of imaginary space, made up of objects (object-images and image-objects). Merleau-Ponty drew a distinction between the body-subject (*le corps propre*) and the world of objects:

> In so far as it stands before me and presents its systematic variations to the observer, the external object lends itself to a cursory mental examination of its elements and it may, at least by way of preliminary approximation, be defined in terms of the law of their variation. But I am not in front of my body, I am in it, or rather I am it. Neither its variations nor their constant can, therefore, be expressly posited.[60]

The Minus Objects repudiate that distinction insofar as they make up another space, an imaginary space (fig. 70). They are not on the side of "the object" against "man," nor are they in the contrary position. They unmake these ideological categories; they are elsewhere, in an ambiguous space that merges the *body-image* with object-images.[61] Pistoletto had gone to dwell on "the other side of the mirror"—"through the looking-glass," as Lewis Carroll imagined it.[62] The here-there depth dimension was augmented by an inside-outside relationship referring to another, more primitive body-image; the plane of the projected mental image (of the hallucinatory kind) replaced the depth of the perceptual space.[63]

The scale of the body standing in space is one among many; it is the scale that allows a pear shape, the *Corpo a pera* (*Pear Body*; see fig. 60), to also stand in a dimension that is analogous if not identical to the *Casa a misura d'uomo* (*House on a Human Scale*; plate 93). Like the *Rosa bruciata*, object-images are the materialization (the objectification) of mental images; this is why they are more in the realm of hallucination than in that of perception. In his 1967 text "Le ultime parole famose" ("Famous Last Words"), Pistoletto links this hallucinatory dimension to that of time.[64]

The Minus Objects were a moment of euphoric retreat in Pistoletto's oeuvre: a retreat away from his public (or brand) image, the euphoria of a stroll through the expansive realm of the possible. That world of object-images was proof of an opening up of private (but not privative) space to a public dimension. Pistoletto subsequently sought to share his "individual dynamic system." The experience of Lo Zoo, however, revealed that the "other side," the other side of the mirror, is also the "unbearable" facet haunted—one might also say inhabited—by the Minus Man. Dedramatization here reached its limits. It was inevitable. The means of the theater, even when used outside the theater, lead back to drama.

Translated from the French by Michael Gilson.

1 See Michelangelo Pistoletto, "Gli oggetti in meno," first published in *Michelangelo Pistoletto*, exh. cat. (Genoa: Galleria La Bertesca, 1966); republished, as were all of Pistoletto's texts through 1988, under the title "Oggetti in meno," in *Pistoletto: un artista in meno* (Florence: hopefulmonster, 1989), p. 12; hereafter cited from the translation "The Minus Objects," in *Michelangelo Pistoletto: A Minus Artist*, trans. P. Blanchard (Florence: hopefulmonster, 1988), p. 12.

2 See Pistoletto, "The Minus Objects," pp. 12–14.

3 Ibid., p. 12.

4 Ibid.

5 Ibid., pp. 12–13. The idea of "whole time" or "time as a whole" (*tempo intero*) can be read as an echo of Bergsonian thought and of the revelation of "Time" in Marcel Proust's *À la recherche du temps perdu* (*In Search of Lost Time*), itself inspired in part by Henri Bergson's writings and theories. The mechanism of the mirror painting, however, employs the spatial interpretation of duration rejected by Bergson. To him, "pure time" is in opposition to division into small spaces of time; it corresponds to the integral preservation of the past, in a duration that runs counter to the abstraction of spatialized time. See, for example, the pages on "the survival of the past" in Bergson's 1911 lecture "The Perception of Change," published in *The Creative Mind: An Introduction to Metaphysics*, trans. Mabelle L. Andison (New York: Kensington, 1946), and in *Henri Bergson: Key Writings*, ed. Keith Ansell-Pearson and John Mullarkey (London: Continuum, 2002); originally published as *La pensée et le mouvant: essais et conférences* (Paris: F. Alcan, 1934). The mirror painting is a divided form that divides time, whereas Bergson insisted on the indivisibility of change. To reconsider "change" in his own way, Pistoletto had to equip himself with a time-division operator: the mirror. He was keen on the fact that time should be represented in space, because that is what enabled him to speculate on a reversal, in the mirror, of the past-future relationship.

6 Jurgis Baltrušaitis, *Le miroir: essai sur une légende scientifique; révélations, science-fiction et fallacies* (Paris: Elmayan, 1978). This history of the mirror reveals the inevitable "abuses" of systematic experimentation. Writing about the "catoptric" museums and theaters of the sixteenth century—the era of cabinets of curiosity—the author remarks: "Multiplications, substitutions, reversals, enlargements, reductions, dilatations, strangled shapes—all the operations are presented as a technical demonstration of the laws of reflection in a savant's cabinet" (p. 38; loosely translated). Though more austere, the mirror "operations" conducted by Pistoletto in the 1970s produced a similar questioning of specular knowledge: as it is divided, the mirror multiplies doubles, to the point of undoing the very idea of the double (and of doubling).

7 Pistoletto, "The Minus Objects," p. 13.

8 Ibid., pp. 13–14. A slight amendment has been made to the published translation: where *attualità* was translated as "topicality," here "actuality" has been used.

9 Such a retrospective constitution of the possible had been noted and impugned by Bergson in *The Creative Mind*, chap. 3 ("The Possible and the Real"). Bergson compares the possible, "the mirage of the present in the past," with the virtual image of the mirror. This validates the notion that Pistoletto's brand of Bergsonism is heterodox, to say the least. He has nonetheless defined himself as being part of a strongly Bergsonian culture, since Futurism. As I was able to confirm at our most recent meeting (in Biella, July 2009), Pistoletto conceives of his "individual dynamic system" in reference to Futurism; he does not mention metaphysics, which was the other (contrary) road taken by the original Italian avant-gardists. He implemented a dynamic founded on retrospection—not, as in Bergson (as interpreted by the Futurists), on an adherence to "becoming." He repudiates the idea of "progress" underpinning the Futurist cult of mechanized (and military) modernity. These differences, however, are themselves constituent elements of his "system."

10 In the early 1980s, Pistoletto repurchased from Ileana Sonnabend, through Giorgio Persano, three of the objects that he had given her in the 1960s to honor the contract binding him to the gallery: *Sarcofago* (*Sarcophagus*; plate 94), one of the *Pozzos* (*Wells*), and *Colonne di cemento* (*Concrete Columns*; plate 81).

11 In the catalogue of the exhibition, Martin Friedman, director of the Walker Art Center, noted the difference between the mirror paintings and Pop painting: *Michelangelo Pistoletto: A Reflected World*, exh. cat. (Minneapolis: Walker Art Center, 1966), n.p. But the reception of Pistoletto's work tended toward an assimilation into the Pop genre.
12 The other artists were Lee Bontecou, Jim Dine, Jasper Johns, Roy Lichtenstein, Claes Oldenburg, Robert Rauschenberg, George Segal, and Andy Warhol.
13 Pistoletto as yet had no direct knowledge of the New York scene, but he was well acquainted with Parisian art circles, which were more accessible to him owing to the fact that he was conversant in French. He kept up, for example, with exhibitions at Galerie J on rue Montfaucon (on the Left Bank), founded in 1961 by Pierre Restany and Jeannine de Goldschmidt.
14 Jean-François Chevrier, "Michelangelo Pistoletto: trente ans dans le miroir / Thirty Years in the Mirror," *Galeries Magazine* 54 (April–May 1993), p. 72.
15 Ibid., p. 76.
16 Pistoletto had discovered Bacon's paintings in 1958, at the British artist's first Italian exhibition, at Galleria Galatea in Turin, the same space in which Pistoletto had his first one-man show in 1960. In our 1993 conversation, he told me: "I situated myself with respect to Bacon. In his work I found an image of man in natural dimensions, as in my paintings. But this image was highly dramatized. I then began to understand what I wanted to do. I wanted to avoid all dramatization. I definitively opted for an unexpressive, hieratic figuration, attempting to produce an emptiness around the figure that would no longer be the emptiness of the perspectival space of the Renaissance, but a space around man which would allow him to get out of the cage in which Bacon had enclosed him. For me, the non-figurative artists aligned themselves along the drama figured by Bacon, they shared in the same existential situation" (ibid., pp. 72, 76).
17 The igloo, dated 1968, bears the neon inscription "Objet cache-toi" (Object hide yourself); a reproduction can be seen in the book by Germano Celant, *Arte Povera* (New York: Praeger, 1969), p. 38.
18 This opinion was forcefully expressed by Eugène Fromentin in *Les maîtres d'autrefois* (Paris: E. Plon, 1876); translated as *The Masters of Past Time: Dutch and Flemish Painting from Van Eyck to Rembrandt*, trans. Andrew Boyle (London: Phaidon, 1948).
19 Pino Pascali, interview with Marisa Volpi in *Marcatrè* (Milan) 37–40 (May 1968), p. 73 (loosely translated).
20 For illustrations and a brief discussion of the four identically sized canvases displayed by these artists at the Musée d'art moderne de la Ville de Paris in September 1967, each with its individual logo, see Benjamin H. D. Buchloh, "The Group That Was (Not) One: Daniel Buren and BMPT," *Artforum* 46 (May 2008), p. 313.
21 Pistoletto first saw the *Armi* in Pascali's Rome studio in late 1965 and told Gian Enzo Sperone about them (Sperone notes that Pistoletto was his key counsel in his first years as a dealer); Sperone showed them in his Turin gallery in January 1966. See Sperone's conversation with Ida Gianelli in *Un'avventura internazionale: Torino e le arti, 1950–1970*, ed. Ida Gianelli, exh. cat. (Milan and Florence: Charta, 1993), p. 169. For more on the *Armi*, see www.museopinopascali.it/fe/pascali/opere/04_armi/default.php.
22 The principle of the relief painting, often monochromatic and featuring a canvas distended by salient points or volumes, was first explored by Enrico Castellani in 1960. Among the Minus Objects, the *Teletorte* (plate 83) are a rather humorous interpretation of this model.
23 Michelangelo Pistoletto, in conversation with the author, Biella, July 2009.
24 Italian folklore had of course already given us the character of a toy that comes to life—Carlo Collodi's celebrated 1881 creation, Pinocchio, who can be compared to Lewis Carroll's Alice.
25 Jean-Luc Godard film's *Vivre sa vie* (*My Life to Live*) was released in France in 1962 and in Italy later that year.
26 This divergence between the two artists was accentuated during the 1970s, when Pistoletto began developing artistic action scenarios in the form of cycles, whereas Boetti preferred a geopoetic expansion, emphasizing graphic and ornamental forms. Drawing, omnipresent in Boetti, is practically absent from Pistoletto's work.
27 The exhibition at Galleria La Bertesca opened in December 1966. By then, the full ensemble of twenty-seven Minus Objects was definitively constituted. Gian Enzo Sperone had already shown a few of them in his galleries in Turin and Milan in isolated fashion, without presenting them as a group: *Lampada a mercurio, Semisfere decorative*, and *Scultura lignea* in June–July 1966 in Turin, as part of the exhibition *Arte abitabile*, which also featured Piero Gilardi and Gianni Piacentino; and *Bagno, Struttura per parlare in piedi*, and *Corpo a pera* in November of that year in Milan, in a one-person show of Pistoletto's work. It was for the latter exhibition that Pistoletto created the first of the *versioni*, *Pozzo cartone e specchio* (*Cardboard and Mirror Well*). Each of the twelve Minus Objects of the limited but representative ensemble shown the following month at La Bertesca included a mirror. Of the objects in the original group, two (*Specchio* and *Letto*) already contained a mirror and were not modified; others (*Rosa bruciata, Paesaggio, Bagno, Struttura per parlare in piedi*, and *Ti amo*) were "arranged" for the occasion; and still others gave rise to *versioni* incorporating a mirror (*Portico, Vetrina specchio, Corpo a pera specchio, Pozzo specchio*, and *Semisfere decorative sospese*). The full ensemble of fourteen *versioni* was completed in 1968 with *La terra e la luna* (see fig. 66), the final variation on the *Sfera di giornali*. It should be noted that these series of alterations did not preclude other uses and "reprises" (theatrical in nature) in the contexts of performances and installations.

28 Donald Judd, "Specific Objects," in *Contemporary Sculpture*, Arts Yearbook 8 (New York: Art Digest, 1965), pp. 74–90; republished in *Donald Judd: The Early Work, 1955–1968*, ed. Thomas Kellein (New York: D.A.P., 2002), pp. 87–97.

29 Pistoletto, "The Minus Objects," p. 14.

30 Judd, "Specific Objects," p. 74.

31 Pistoletto's name very rarely crops up in books about conceptual art. He is absent, for instance, from the survey published by Peter Osborne in the Phaidon "Themes and Movements" collection (2002), despite its all-inclusiveness. Nor is he to be found in the (admittedly less catholic) volume by Anne Rorimer, *New Art in the 60s and 70s: Redefining Reality* (New York: Thames and Hudson, 2001). Pistoletto did, however, rate a mention in Lucy Lippard's *Six Years: The Dematerialization of the Art Object from 1966 to 1972* (New York: Praeger, 1973), on the strength of his 1967 essay "Le ultime parole famose" ("Famous Last Words"; see *Michelangelo Pistoletto: A Minus Artist*, pp. 17–20). Pistoletto had previously been represented in *Information*, an exhibition of conceptual art at the Museum of Modern Art, New York, in 1970.

32 The seminal text in this movement is an essay of 1895 by Henry van de Velde, "Déblaiement d'art" ("Clearing Away with Art"), republished in *Déblaiement d'art: suivi de, La Triple Offense à la beauté, Le Nouveau, Max Elskamp, La Voie sacrée, La Colonne*, 2nd ed. (Brussels: Éditions des Archives d'architecture moderne, 1979).

33 See the English translation of "L'arte assume la religione" (1978) in *Michelangelo Pistoletto: A Minus Artist*, pp. 216–18.

34 The Institut Paoli-Calmettes is a regional cancer-care center. The Pistoletto-designed "place of meditation and prayer" consists of five rooms and an access corridor radiating outward from an elliptical light well. The *versione* of the *Metrocubo d'infinito* sits at the center of the ellipse. Three of the rooms are destined for practitioners of the main monotheistic religions—Christianity, Judaism, and Islam—each identified by a symbolic object and sign. The fourth is open to other faiths, including Buddhism. The fifth is a meditation and reading space dedicated to secular thought. See the brochure published by the institute, accessible online at www.bureaudescompetences.org/laventureici/projetrealises/lieuderecueillement/Publication_Pistoletto.pdf.

35 Adolphe Appia, *"The Work of Living Art": A Theory of the Theatre*, trans. H. D. Albright, ed. Barnard Hewitt (Coral Gables, Fla.: University of Miami Press, 1960), p. 27. For the original French, see *L'Oeuvre d'art vivant* (1921), published in *Oeuvres complètes*, vol. 3, 1906–1921, ed. Marie L. Bablet-Hahn (Lausanne: L'Âge d'Homme, 1988), p. 372.

36 In 1968, in London, Peter Brook published a collection of essays on the theater that he titled *The Empty Space*. Of course, these texts did not call for the negation of the theater, but for its disencumbrance and an adoption of new ways of doing things that broke from sterile conventions, following the trails blazed in divergent directions by Bertolt Brecht and Antonin Artaud. Remarkably, when Germano Celant propounded the idea of "poor art" (*arte povera*) in 1967, it was in reference to the "poor theatre" of another greater theater director, Polish-born Jerzy Grotowski, who, as it happens, worked with Brook. But Pistoletto was more influenced by the Living Theatre of Julian Beck and Judith Malina than by the acting exercises conducted in Grotowski's theater-laboratory, which he decried as elitist (see Pistoletto's response to the investigation, "Il momento della negazione? Inchiesta sulla situazione del teatro di prosa in Italia oggi," *Sipario* 268–69 [August–September 1968], pp. 16–17). More broadly, he steered clear of professional theater, never working *for* the theater. In the late 1960s, he founded his own troupe, Lo Zoo, because he did not care to be beholden to theater institutions, as he explained in a note published in 1976: "I had been called in as a painter at the Teatro Stabile in Turin to work on a set design; this was one of the reasons that Lo Zoo came into being. My sense of my own work as a painter prevented me from accepting the assignment, but it wasn't enough to turn it down; I had to announce an alternative"; see *Pistoletto*, exh. cat. (Milan: Electa, 1976), p. 45; I thank Roberta Nuzzaci for her help with this translation from the Italian. Pistoletto incorporated theater (theatrical action) into a system of expanded artistic activity, so as to rupture the division between art and spectacle, object and performance. A similar attitude toward literature and the institution of literature would later lead him to write *L'uomo nero, il lato insopportabile* (*The Minus Man, the Unbearable Side*) in 1970; see "The Minus Man: The Unbearable Side," in *Michelangelo Pistoletto: A Minus Artist*, pp. 27–158. For more on Pistoletto's performances and actions, see Claire Gilman's essay in this volume (pp. 81–107 below).

37 Michel de Certeau, *The Practice of Everyday Life*, trans. Steven Rendall (Berkeley: University of California Press, 1984), p. 117; originally published as *L'Invention du quotidien* (Paris: Union générale d'éditions, 1980), pp. 172–73.

38 Pistoletto always kept in mind the initial observations he had made in the early 1960s, when, in his paintings, the luminosity of light backgrounds with shaded figures was supplanted by the reflecting action of a black ground (in *Il presente*). The same necessity is valid for light and movement: both, in order to be thought of (to be reflected), need to come up against an obstacle, either fixed or opaque. A movement can be slower or faster in the same way a material is more or less opaque.

39 Marcel Detienne and Jean-Pierre Vernant, *Cunning Intelligence in Greek Culture and Society*, trans. Janet Lloyd (Chicago: University of Chicago Press, 1991), pp. 3–4; originally published as *Les ruses de l'intelligence: la mètis des Grecs* (Paris: Flammarion, 1974), p. 10. The authors begin by discouraging any expectations of textual evidence for the concept: "There are no treatises on *mêtis* as there are treatises on logic, nor are there any philosophical systems based on the principles of

wiley intelligence. It is not difficult to detect the presence of *mêtis* at the heart of the Greek mental world in the interplay of social and intellectual customs where its influence is sometimes all-pervasive. But there is no text which reveals straightforwardly its fundamental characteristics and its origins" (ibid., p. 3).

40 Bakhtin's works—in particular his two masterworks on Fyodor Dostoevsky and François Rabelais—were late in coming to prominence in Western European countries, but, in the context of the 1960s and 1970s counterculture, their impact was immediate.

41 Mikhail Bakhtin, *Rabelais and His World,* trans. Hélène Iswolsky (Bloomington: Indiana University Press, 1984), p. 120 n. 63 (my italics); originally published as *Tvorchestvo Fransua Rable i narodnaia kul'tura srednevekov'ia i Renessansa* (Moscow: Khudozh, 1990).

42 Ibid., p. 122.

43 Pistoletto, in conversation with the author, Biella, July 2009. *Sarcofago* was the only object that Pistoletto sent to Ileanna Sonnabend, to whom he was contractually bound, when she wanted to show the Minus Objects in her Paris gallery in 1967. The sign of defiance could not have been clearer. An exhibition was nonetheless arranged: *Sarcofago* was shown along with the mirror paintings.

44 About the veil covering the well as it would a crib, Pistoletto explained to me: "It is to protect birth, because we come from water" (ibid.). The (Christless) nativity of *Paesaggio* is also connected to the birth theme.

45 On this aspect of Pistoletto's oeuvre, see *Michelangelo Pistoletto: il varco dello specchio; azioni e collaborazioni, 1967–2004,* ed. Marco Farano, Maria Cristina Mundici, and Maria Teresa Roberto (Turin: Fondazione Torino Musei, 2005); and Claire Gilman's essay in this volume (pp. 81–107 below).

46 This initial outing of the *Palla di giornali* (it bears this title in the catalogue of the 1976 Pistoletto exhibition at the Palazzo Grassi, Venice, p. 46) was followed by a second, a month later, with Maria Pioppi, again in the streets of Turin but along another route, open to the vagaries of strolling lovers and chance meetings. A film, *Buongiorno Michelangelo,* directed by Ugo Nespolo and produced by the three galleries in which the exhibition *Con-temp-l'azione* was held (Sperone, Stein, and Il punto), documents the tribulations of the *palla.* It begins in Pistoletto's studio, with shots showing a mirror painting and the *Scultura lignea.* It ends with the *Rosa bruciata,* taken out through the window of Galleria Stein and passed to Pioppi, who improvises a few movements with it on the Piazza San Carlo. The *Sfera* or *Palla di giornali* ended its journey in Amalfi (Campania), during the three-day event *Arte Povera + Azioni povere* (October 4–6, 1968). Purchased by the festival's organizer, it was rechristened *Mappamondo* (*Globe*) and enclosed in a large wireframe sphere in which the wires are analogous to meridians and circles of latitude; *Mappamondo* is today one of the *versioni.* Pistoletto gave the following caption to the photograph reproduced by Germano Celant in *Arte Povera* (Milan: Mazzotta, 1969), pp. 7, 20: "Il mondo d'oro, la palla che prima andava in giro per la strada è entrata nella gabbia" (The golden world, the ball that once rolled through the street, has entered the cage).

47 Mikhail Bakhtin, *Problems of Dostoevsky's Poetics,* trans. Caryl Emerson (Minneapolis: University of Minnesota Press, 1984), p. 166.

48 Pistoletto, "The Minus Man: The Unbearable Side," in *Michelangelo Pistoletto: A Minus Artist,* pp. 27–158.

49 The "literary side" is *the other side,* corresponding to the Minus Man's place. In 1970, Pistoletto produced a work titled *Un libro, il lato letterario del quadro* (*The Book, the Literary Side of the Painting*): thirty-one blank canvases (200 x 20 cm) lined up against the wall, upside down, with the frames bearing handwritten notes apparently excerpted from the artist's diary (reproduced in *Michelangelo Pistoletto: A Minus Artist,* p. 163).

50 A monitor positioned along the axis of the two photographs shows a video panorama in which Pistoletto shot his reflection in a mirror and then turned in place until the camera focused on a monitor showing the live image, thus generating infinitely regressing reproductions of the image of the artist filming his image. Any distance taken with respect to oneself must be played over again, like the revival of a theater play.

51 *La pensée sauvage* (1962) was issued in Italian in 1964 by the Milanese publisher Il Saggiatore as *Il pensiero selvaggio.* In the vocabulary of Italian art styles, *Arte Programmata* encompasses experimentations with kinetic art.

52 During our July 2009 conversations in Biella, Pistoletto repudiated the idea of interval in qualifying the spatial (or spatiotemporal) relationship of the Minus Objects.

53 Walter Pach, *Queer Thing, Painting* (New York: Harper, 1938), p. 155. The statement is often quoted without including the first sentence. Duchamp was taking up the idea of painting as a "mental thing" (*cosa mentale*), upheld by Leonardo da Vinci when the artist needed to disengage from artisanal corporatism and move into the realm of the liberal arts. Pistoletto links himself, explicitly, to that anticorporatist tradition. At the same time, however, he assimilates the legacy of the artisanal know-how transmitted by his father, Ettore Oliviero Pistoletto, who was a painter and art restorer. Indeed, in 1973 he had a joint exhibition with his father, *Padre e figlio* (*Father and Son*), at Galleria Sperone in Turin. At the Ermenegildo Zegna foundation in Trivero, near Biella (Michelangelo Pistoletto's native city), one can still view a collection of murals depicting wool-working, painted in 1931–33 by the elder Pistoletto.

54 On *Arte abitabile,* see note 27 above.

55 "Of Other Spaces," the basis of a March 1967 lecture by Foucault, was published in English (translated by Jay Miskowiec) in *Diacritics* 16, no. 1 (1986), and was reprinted in *Politics-Poetics:*

Documenta X—The Book, ed. Jean-François Chevrier (Ostfildern-Ruit: Cantz, 1997), pp. 262–72. The contemporaneity of that lecture and the public presentation of the Minus Objects is remarkable. Foucault sees in the mirror the prototype of his "other spaces": "In the mirror, I see myself there where I am not, in an unreal, virtual space that opens up behind the surface: I am over there, there where I am not, a sort of shadow that gives my own visibility to myself, that enables me to see myself there where I am absent: such is the utopia of the mirror. But it is also a heterotopia in so far as the mirror does exist in reality, where it exerts a sort of counteraction on the position that I occupy. From the standpoint of the mirror I discover my absence from the place where I am since I see myself over there" (ibid., in *Politics-Poetics*, p. 266).

56 André Breton, "Crisis of the Object," first published as "Crise de l'objet" in *Cahiers d'art* 1–2 (1936), on the occasion of the *Exposition surréaliste d'objets* at Galerie Charles Ratton (May 22–29, 1936); published in English in *Surrealism and Painting,* trans. Simon Watson-Taylor (New York: Harper & Row, 1972), p. 277 (emphasis in original).

57 Ibid., in *Surrealism and Painting*, p. 280 (emphasis in original).

58 The idea of the *disparate* once again has echoes in Foucauldian writings from the same period as these works by Pistoletto (although neither of the two, as far as I know, was acquainted with the other's work). Foucault first posited the idea of heterotopia in the preface to *Les mots et les choses* (translated as *The Order of Things*), published in 1966, deducing it from a disorder introduced into the rational arrangement of things uttered, named, and identified. Foucault described a phenomenon of *dispersion* of knowledge.

59 Maurice Merleau-Ponty, *Phenomenology of Perception*, trans. Colin Smith (London and New York: Routledge Classics, 2002; repr. 2006), p. 309 ("Space"); originally published as *Phénoménologie de la perception* (Paris: Gallimard, 1945).

60 Ibid., p. 173 ("The Synthesis of One's Own Body").

61 I use "body-image" in the same sense that psychoanalysts have employed since the publication of Paul Schilder's *The Image and Appearance of the Human Body: Studies in the Constructive Energies of the Psyche* (New York: International Universities Press, 1950).

62 In 1969, Lo Zoo dedicated a performance, *Il tè di Alice* (*Alice's Tea*; figs. 74, 75 below), to the Mad Tea Party episode in *Alice's Adventures in Wonderland* (1865).

63 This distinction between "imaginary" space and phenomenological space has been mapped out by the psychoanalyst Sami Ali in *L'Espace imaginaire* (Paris: Gallimard, 1974). Besides presenting the purely analytical material provided by patients of his, the author delves into the work of Lewis Carroll, noting: "In *Through the Looking-Glass,* the accent shifts from the body-subject to a representation of space subjected to the distorting effects of specular doubling" (p. 211; loosely translated).

64 Pistoletto, "Famous Last Words," in *Michelangelo Pistoletto: A Minus Artist*, pp. 17–20.

PISTOLETTO'S OBJECT THEATER

CLAIRE GILMAN

Scholars of postwar Italian art typically observe a fundamental shift in Michelangelo Pistoletto's work following his move beyond painting in 1965. First came the *Oggetti in meno* (Minus Objects), whose makeshift appearance and random accumulation contradicted the studied investigation into the nature of pictorial representation that had characterized the artist's mirrors, with their painted figures collaged on stainless steel grounds (plates 13–67). Then in 1967 the artist created the first of his rag sculptures (plates 99–102), which seemed to mark a full-scale transition away from his preoccupation with illusionistic representation and toward an Arte Povera aesthetic rooted in the pursuit of unmanipulated form and antirhetorical immediacy.[1] As defined by Germano Celant, the Genoese critic and curator who coined the term in 1967 and organized the group's first exhibitions, Arte Povera was resolutely antirepresentational and responded to the new consumer landscape by eliminating artifice and embracing natural elements and unprogrammed behavior. The rag sculptures were the quintessential "poor art," incarnating Arte Povera's agenda in their very choice of material.

It is less often mentioned that the rags made their first public appearance in theatrical experiments that Pistoletto undertook as part of Lo Zoo, a group he founded and collaborated with from 1968 to 1970 (Lo Zoo's first performance took place in May 1968, their last in October 1970). Always present in Pistoletto's studio, where they were used to polish the mirror paintings, the rags served in Lo Zoo's earliest productions as costumes, set decorations, and props intended to illustrate the narratives being enacted and to provide visual focus. Although Arte Povera repudiated artifice, it did not reject theater per se. On the contrary, on the occasion of the three-day event *Arte Povera + Azioni Povere* in October 1968 at the Arsenali in Amalfi, where Lo Zoo performed, Celant lauded the anarchic spirit of the new theater and called for the abolition of objects in favor of unrestricted action and behavior.[2] But this appeal to spontaneous behavior is entirely distinct from Lo Zoo's incorporation of fantasy, narrative, and role-playing. Moreover, Pistoletto has asserted that in trying his hand at sculpture, and later theater, he did not aim to eliminate pictorial illusionism but rather to extend its requirements into wider space. Indeed, although painting took a back seat during his three years with Lo Zoo, Pistoletto made mirror paintings throughout this period and continues into the present day.

Taking into account the artist's own statements, I contend that the conventional view of Pistoletto's work from this period is fundamentally misleading. Not only is the sculpture he produced in and around 1968 deeply intertwined with his theatrical activities and vice versa, but also, rather than representing a sharp break with his painting, this work is consistent with the concerns that have motivated the artist's production from the beginning. Indeed, the imbrication of material form, pictorial space, and theatrical gesture in Pistoletto's work can be understood as providing a conscious alternative to Arte Povera's more typically neo–avant-garde conflation of art and life—a position, we will see, that had its skeptics within Italy's leftist intellectual community. Ultimately, I believe that Pistoletto's work assumes an unorthodox political imperative, one in which spontaneous action is always tempered by moments of arrest, and in which the acknowledgment of physical limitations and representational distance is a precondition for commitment—artistic, political, or otherwise.

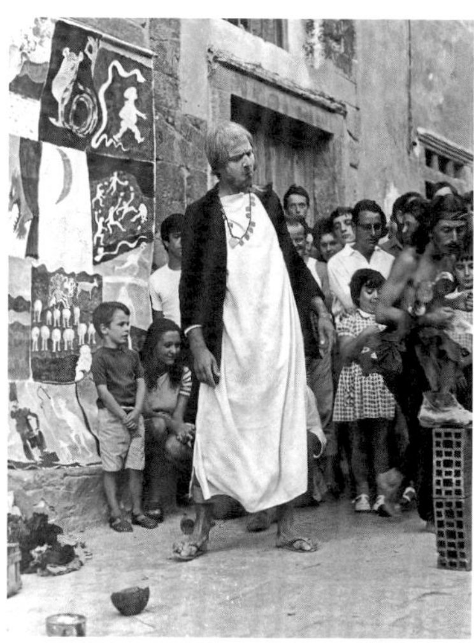

FIG. 71. Lo Zoo, *L'Uomo ammaestrato* (*The Trained Man*), with Pistoletto (center) and Gianni Milano (right), in the square of Vernazza, August 8, 1968. Photograph by B. Scagliola. Courtesy of Cittadellarte-Fondazione Pistoletto, Biella

Pistoletto has recounted that Lo Zoo emerged in 1968 as an alternative to the Teatro Stabile, Turin's municipal theater, renowned for its innovative productions of both contemporary and classical European theater, whose offers to collaborate he had rejected in 1967 because of creative differences.[3] More specifically, Lo Zoo came together after a month-long series of events in December 1967 in which Pistoletto opened his Turin studio to artists of all disciplines—poets, filmmakers, musicians, actors, directors, and visual artists. Frequent visitors included the poet Gianni Milano and the actor Carlo Colnaghi, both of whom would feature prominently in Lo Zoo's early productions. In fact, Lo Zoo never evolved into a conventional theater company. Instead, it styled itself as a band of players with fluctuating membership, a traveling troupe modeled on traditional Italian street theater that performed its scenarios in village streets, city squares, and, less commonly, mainstream theaters both within and outside Italy.[4] Although Lo Zoo's performances in art spaces and theaters drew an art-savvy audience, many of the group's street productions occurred spontaneously before an audience of local passersby. The constant throughout Lo Zoo's roughly two-and-one-half-year lifespan was Pistoletto himself, who along with his wife, Maria Pioppi, participated in all of Lo Zoo's performances and served as artistic director, guiding the group's overall vision if not always its specific narratives.

Typical of Lo Zoo's approach was *L'Uomo ammaestrato* (*The Trained Man*; figs. 71–73), a performance initially staged in the northwestern Italian fishing village of Vernazza, where Pistoletto was staying with friends during the summer of 1968. The group arrived at the story somewhat spontaneously, developing a loose narrative about a man, abandoned in the forest as a baby and found years later by traveling minstrels, who was only now encountering the wider world and discovering how to operate within it: beginning to speak, recognizing colors, learning to play the trumpet.[5] The performance began with the actors singing, dancing, and calling out for an audience as they walked down to the village from the cottage where they were staying. On reaching the piazza, they indicated the performance space with white chalk and set up a colorful gridded storyboard. Pistoletto followed the action on the storyboard as it unfolded, serving as the audience's visual guide, while Colnaghi narrated, presenting to the public Gianni Milano—the newly civilized protagonist—in a comedic pas de deux. Meanwhile, Pioppi sat at center stage, swathed in a Persian robe held together by rags and holding a kitten (fig. 73). Throughout the performance,

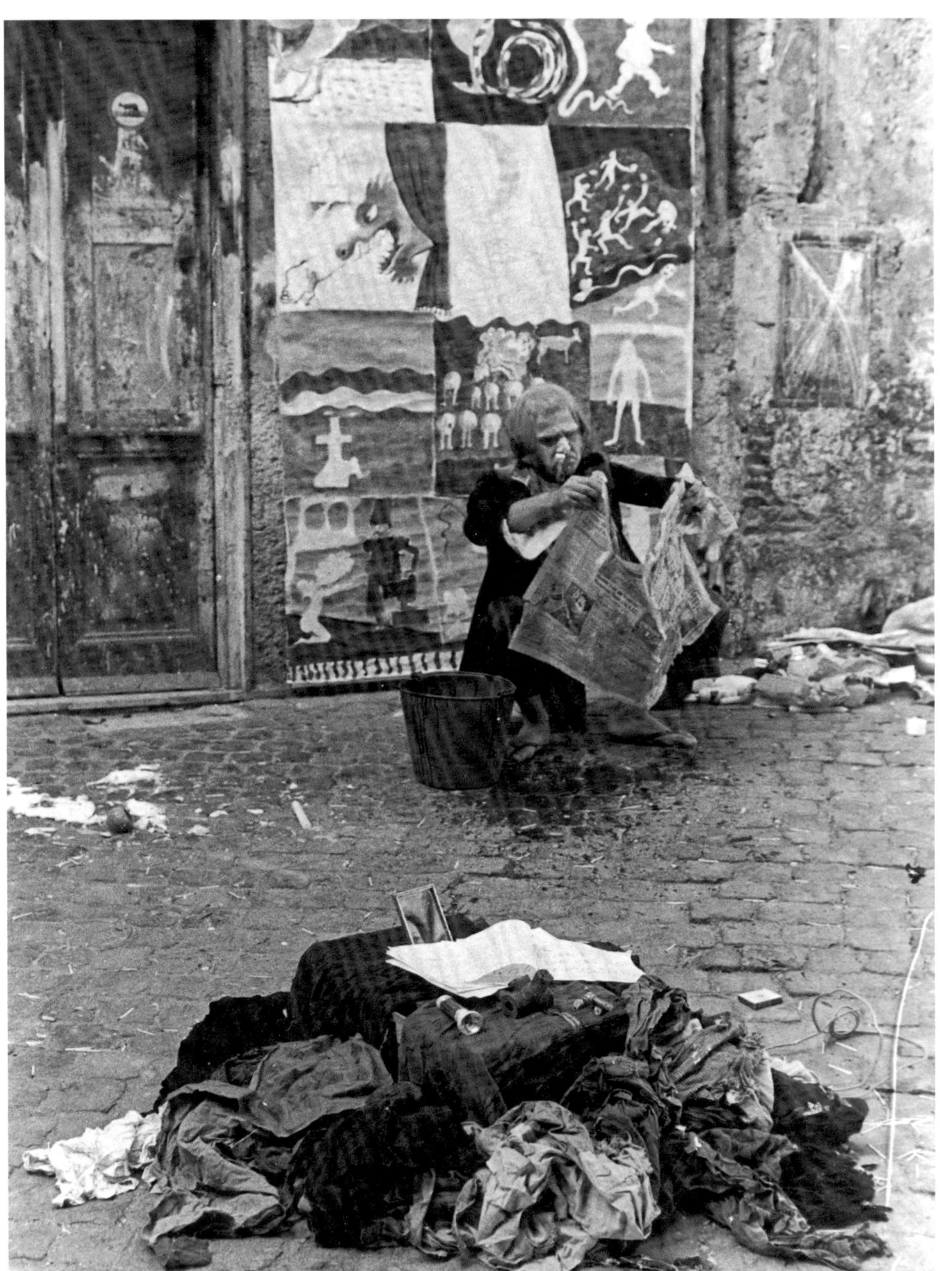

FIG. 72. Lo Zoo, *L'Uomo ammaestrato* (*The Trained Man*), with Pistoletto reading a newspaper in Dell'Atleta alley; Rome, October 1969. Photograph by M. Cresci. Courtesy of Cittadellarte-Fondazione Pistoletto, Biella

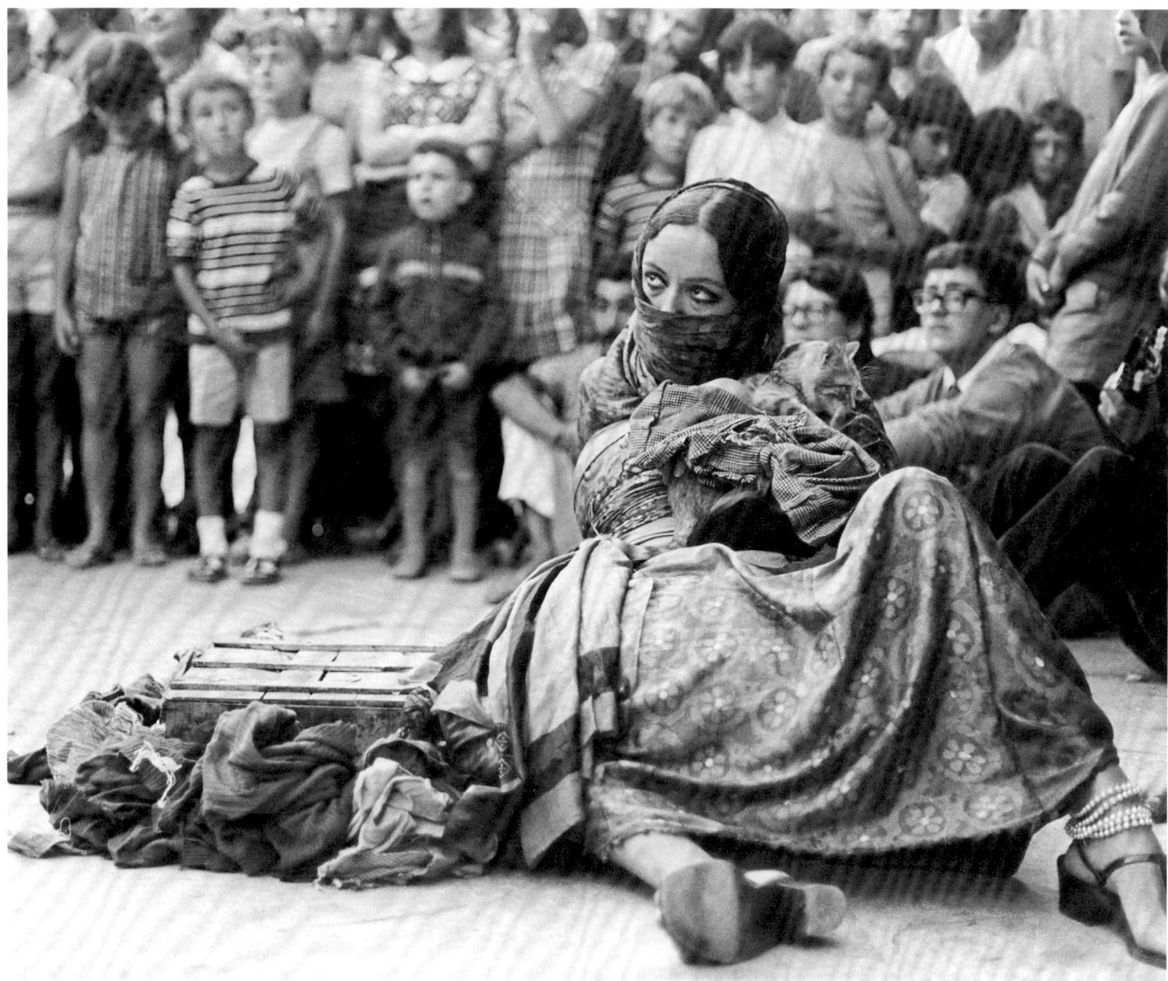

FIG. 73. Lo Zoo, *L'Uomo ammaestrato* (*The Trained Man*), with Maria Pioppi at center stage, in the square of Vernazza, August 8, 1968. Photograph by B. Scagliola. Courtesy of Cittadellarte-Fondazione Pistoletto, Biella

Pistoletto engaged in a series of mini actions, such as dipping a newspaper into water and reading it wet (fig. 72); making noises on a bird caller; tying rags to tiny flashlights and throwing them around the "stage"; lighting fires with matches; and constructing makeshift "sculptures," including a wooden pallet surrounded by rags against which Pioppi reclined, and a little tower of bricks topped by an old shoe (see fig. 71). At the end of the performance, the troupe collected money in a hat.

From the beginning, Lo Zoo's loose, spontaneous approach prompted association with the anti-illusionistic direction in 1960s theater. Exemplifying the trend were Antonin Artaud's Theater of Cruelty; Polish director Jerzy Grotowski's "poor theatre," which directly inspired Arte Povera's own name; and the Living Theatre, an American company whose co-founders, the actor Judith Malina and the painter and poet Julian Beck, were frequent presences in Rome and Turin at the time.[6] In their own way, each of the aforementioned strove to overcome artifice in favor of a communal, ritualistic aesthetic aimed to shatter hierarchical systems and conventional forms of representation. Energetic movement, raw physical gesture, and intense vocalization were employed as means of attaining an anti-ideological fusion of self and world.

This kind of work had already been embraced by key members of the international avant-garde, and contemporary commentators saw in Pistoletto's troupe yet another variant on an increasingly familiar theme. In 1966, Martin Friedman, then director of the Walker Art Center in Minneapolis, likened the experience of being in front of Pistoletto's mirror paintings to participating in Allan Kaprow's and Jim Dine's Happenings, in which disconnected actions and chance disruptions incorporated audience members as integral players.[7] Three years later, the Italian artist and theoretician Gillo Dorfles declared that the penchant for "the absurd, the incomprehensible, the playful and the occult" that defined the Japanese Gutai movement, as well as Jack Kerouac's writings and the Living Theatre, had found its Italian expression in Pistoletto's "'poor' theatrical creations."[8]

Celant was equally intent on characterizing Lo Zoo as radically anti-theatrical, maintaining of the artist's work: "Pistoletto does not play at being someone. . . . He is not concerned with representing, either. He does not want to go on acting."[9] By contrast with traditional theater, Celant asserted, performance in the manner of Lo Zoo refused representational distance. Instead of engaging in role-playing, Lo Zoo's actions sought to access the actor's "perceptual self-realization," so that every task "would be the contingent and liberatory satisfaction of the group's psycho-physical needs." As Celant described it, Lo Zoo incorporated "music, dialogue, action, singing, and dancing," but not as illusionistic devices. Rather, the performances overcame narrative, so that the actors became "a happy and unalienated mirror of the public that perceives and experiences it . . . in a continuous co-fusion of the group with the environment and the environment with the group."[10] Like his peers, in other words, Celant celebrated Lo Zoo for liberating theatrical performance from obstacles and directives. This new theater, Celant proclaimed, "has the goal of creating a new class in which linguistic and gnoseological nomadism will accompany the nomadism of action." "At last," he concluded, "there will be no more objects."[11]

For the members of Lo Zoo, however, such pronouncements missed the mark. In an early interview, Pistoletto disputed the notion that such a thing as unalienated production exists, asserting: "Even American Happenings, while giving the illusion of seeing everything and participating in everything, are in reality nothing other than a work of distraction with respect to . . . the technical and political means that they incorporate."[12] The artist was equally critical of Grotowski's ritualistic, mass-oriented aesthetic, which he faulted for obscuring its elitist foundations.[13] Lo Zoo, by contrast, chose to emphasize rather than deny the constructed nature of theatrical experience. As one of the original participants, Henry Martin, explained: "It is important to think of the spectacles realized by the Zoo not as a natural terrain for the transubstantiation of conflict in creativity, but rather as a stage created artificially in which is constructed an area of halting/stopping/respite that did not exist before. It must be thought of as a 'work' or a 'representation.'"[14] Similarly, Lo Zoo's "manifesto" directly contradicts Celant's model of happy, liberated coexistence: "When you see, hear, and smell a piece performed by the Zoo, what you think you understand is only the exterior covering, the wrapping. You will never really know that happened until you, too, become actors and audience on this side of the bars."[15]

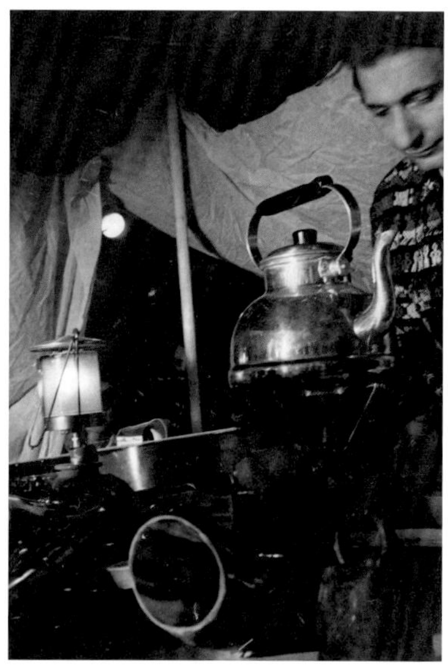

FIG. 74. Lo Zoo, *Il tè di Alice* (*Alice's Tea*), with a large table positioned under a translucent canopy, a small child's table and chairs placed beneath it, Galleria Il Centro, Naples, March 1, 1969. Courtesy of Cittadellarte-Fondazione Pistoletto, Biella

In other words, unlike the Happenings, which aimed to eradicate distance—"the line between art and life should be kept as fluid, and perhaps indistinct, as possible," Kaprow observed[16]—Lo Zoo retained a separation between audience and actor while encouraging conversation. Indeed, the idea of division is implicit in the group's title. "The goal was not to break down the barrier," Pistoletto has explained, "but to recognize it."[17] Again and again, Lo Zoo's performances relied on scenic devices such as chalk circles, bed sheets, curtains, ladders, and baskets to reinforce the separation between actors and spectators. In Lo Zoo's first production, *Cocapicco e vestitorito*,[18] presented in May 1968 at the Piper Pluriclub, a Turin nightclub that hosted art performances, Pioppi was situated above the audience and the other actors on a tall ladder, wrapped in a voluminous cellophane cloak (fig. 76). Similarly, in *Il tè di Alice* (*Alice's Tea*; first staged in March 1969 at Naples's Galleria Il Centro), a creative interpretation of *Alice in Wonderland*, a huge table positioned under a translucent canopy—with a small child's table and chairs beneath—separated the actors from the audience. The actors performed on top of and under the table and on a large ladder alongside it, while the audience looked on through the canopy curtains, which the actors opened and closed at various moments throughout the performance (figs. 74, 75). Even in an unscripted action such as *Teatro baldacchino* (*Canopy Theater*, 1968), in which Pistoletto and some friends wandered through the streets of Turin playing music and making up stories, the group was distinguished from passersby via fanciful costumes, props, and a handheld canopy (figs. 77, 78).

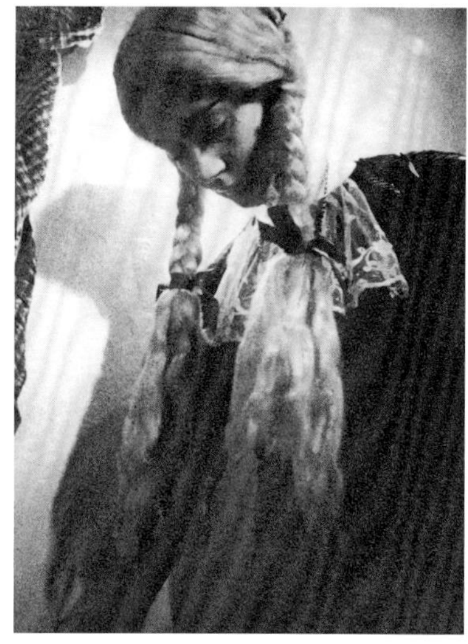

FIG. 75. Lo Zoo, *Il tè di Alice* (*Alice's Tea*), Galleria Il Centro, Naples, March 1, 1969. Courtesy of Cittadellarte-Fondazione Pistoletto, Biella

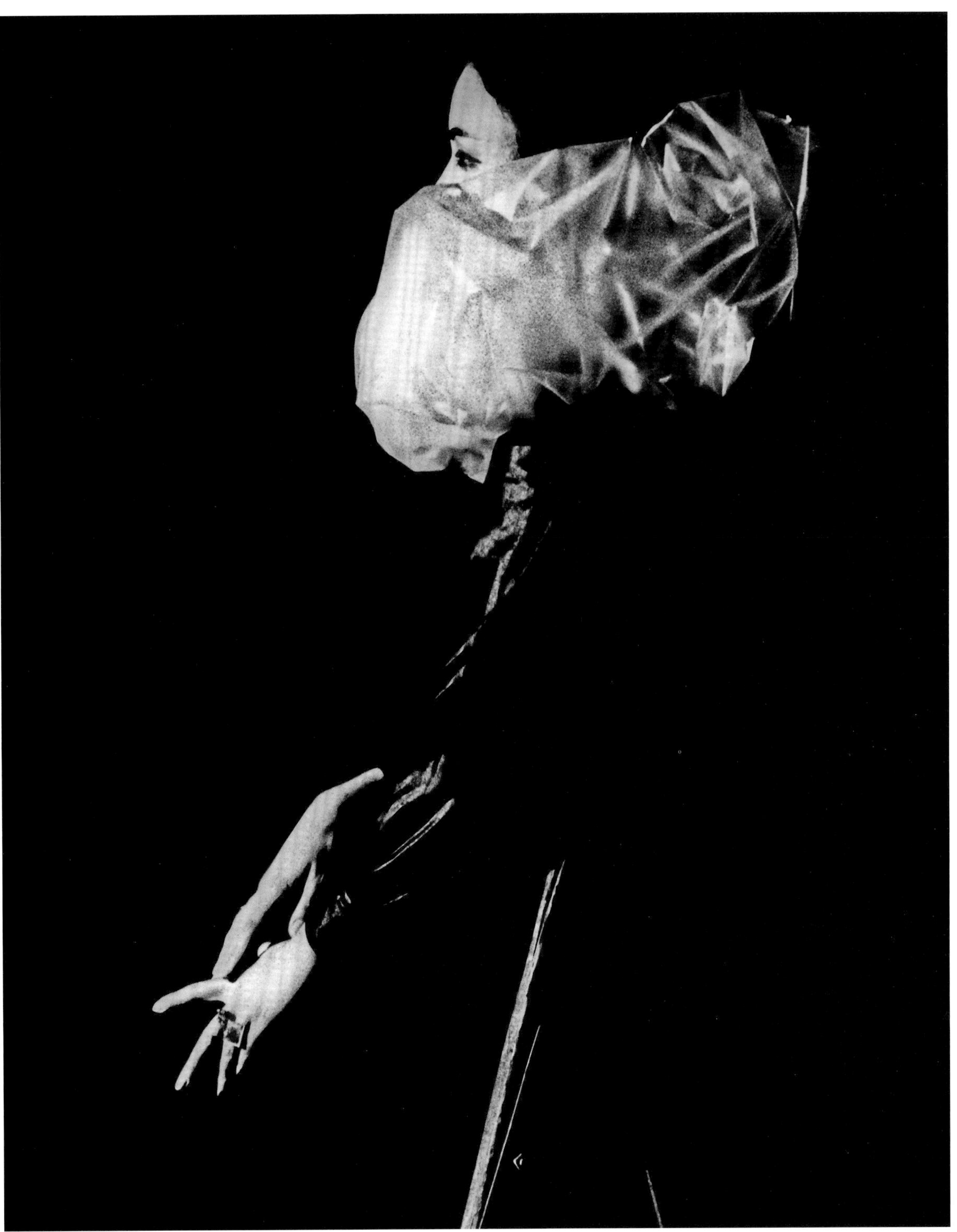

FIG. 76. Maria Pioppi in Lo Zoo's performance of *Cocapicco e vestitorito* at the Piper Pluriclub, Turin, May 8, 1968. Courtesy of Cittadellarte-Fondazione Pistoletto, Biella

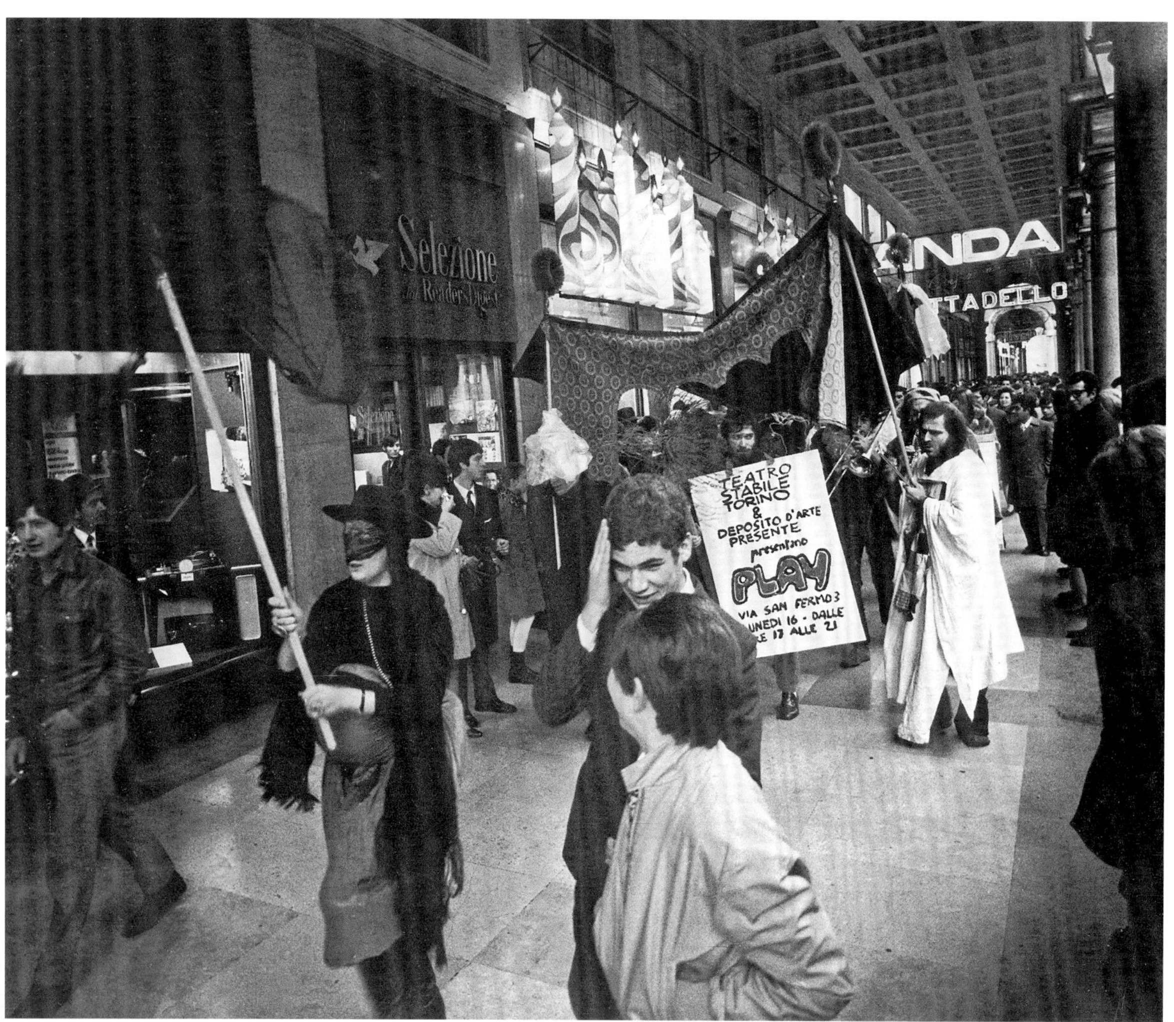

FIG. 77. Lo Zoo and MEV (Musica Elettronica Viva), *Teatro baldacchino* (*Canopy Theater*), Turin, December 15, 1968. Photograph by Claudio Abate. Courtesy of Cittadellarte-Fondazione Pistoletto, Biella

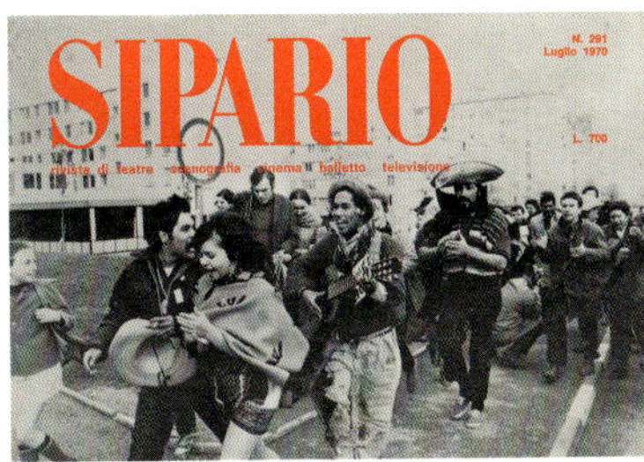

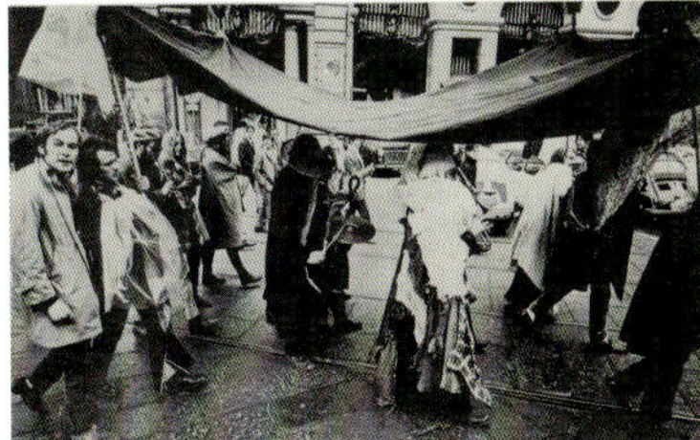

FIG. 78. Lo Zoo and MEV (Musica Elettronica Viva), *Teatro baldacchino* (*Canopy Theater*), Turin, December 15, 1968. Cover of the magazine *Sipario* 291 (July 1970). Courtesy of Cittadellarte-Fondazione Pistoletto, Biella

These devices are neither trivial efforts meant to entertain nor signifiers of carnivalesque celebration. Rather, they reflect a carefully constructed approach to the world, one in which narrative, or representation more generally, mediates social encounters. This is not to say that Lo Zoo's plots were linear or traditionally cohesive. On the contrary, side actions frequently interrupted the central narrative, while the dialogue cited sources as diverse as Sophocles, William Shakespeare, Carlo Goldoni, Lewis Carroll, Luigi Pirandello, Bertolt Brecht, and Albert Camus, often within the same performance. Like the scenarios of the sixteenth-century commedia dell'arte, which employed set types in diverse roles and circumstances, Lo Zoo actors assumed identifiable roles—Pioppi as the Persian gypsy, Pistoletto as the eccentric leader—which they modified according to the specific production. As Martin remembers it, Pistoletto, serving as master of ceremonies, directed the action from the orchestra pit, encouraging the actors to repeat phrases in a variety of styles. A lamentation, an operatic aria, or a Shakespearean aside together presented "x points of view with x different ways of seeing things."[19] A similar motivation guided the staging and costuming. Describing the cellophane cloak Pioppi wore in *Cocapicco e vestitorito* as a "transparent mantle" that framed two "scenes"—the pristine Pioppi above versus the writhing mass below—Pistoletto explained that what was most important was to create an image.[20] The goal, he said, was to concentrate the action in order to enable the audience to "see" and, by extension, to "react."[21]

This emphasis on the production of *things* and an awareness that such production takes place within a social context were fundamental to the group's aesthetic. Consider *L'Uomo ammaestrato*. The play's overt theme is undoubtedly the brutality of the "civilizing" process. And yet the ultimate message is not that we should protect the trained man's innocence by isolating him in his native forest, out of public view. On the contrary, the lessons that the man masters throughout the course of the play, such as playing an instrument and identifying sign systems, are valuable. These learned skills are rooted in convention, and as such they allow one to function in the world. Moreover, the self-motivated creativity that the protagonist employs in mastering them contrasts positively with Colnaghi's vulgar disciplinary method, in which he alternately orders, berates, and praises his charge.

It is here that the side actions that occupy Pistoletto throughout *L'Uomo ammaestrato*—what he has described as "little exhibitions" or loci of narrative "punctuation" outside the main storyline—assume relevance.[22] If, for someone like Celant, the goal was to overcome fixed parameters by leaving things to develop as they may, Pistoletto, in piling up rags or creating small sculptures out of rusty bricks and old shoes, demonstrates a rather different lesson: the necessity of communicating with available means. Pistoletto's materials may be rough, but they are not unmanipulated. Rather, they are all the more worked over for having started out so unrefined. It is instructive that Pistoletto refers to his objects in narrative terms, by which he does not mean to say that they convey a certain message. On the contrary, the objects he manipulated in the performance at Vernazza were intentionally obscure, and he no longer recalls their specific inspiration. The point is that they were subject to a guiding consciousness and, once completed and set aside, they created a visual stopping point. Like the storyboard that divided the overall narrative into separate scenes, the mini actions and their resultant objects disrupted the narrative flow and served as visual reminders of what had taken place, even as the story moved forward. Pistoletto's assemblages were crucial to the theatrical experience precisely because their creation halted the action, requiring the audience to reflect for a moment on the constructed nature of the whole.

Equally important is that Pistoletto's actions, in their very opacity, shifted the focus from a specific story about a man encountering the world to the process by which meaning is acquired, with his whimsical gestures and assemblages taking their place alongside the main action as an equivalent form of communication. It was not necessary that the audience understand what Pistoletto was doing, only *that* he was doing; indeed, his relationship with his objects remained opaque, but his investment in them was necessarily familiar. The spectator was initiated into Lo Zoo's performances not by being invited up on stage as part of some "happy and unalienated" company, as Celant described, but rather because Pistoletto was revealed to be a bit like them, alternately engaging with and stepping back to observe the main action. This kind of autonomous coexistence was built into all of Lo Zoo's productions, as the various members broke off from the central storyline to sing songs, play instruments, make objects, recite lines, and stop and look at what was going on around them, all of them united in their concentration rather than in their specific behavior.[23]

Lo Zoo restaged *L'Uomo ammaestrato* five times over a two-year period, with different actors performing the role of the trained man. The most ambitious staging took place on the second day of the aforementioned *Arte Povera + Azioni Povere* event in Amalfi, for which Pistoletto also produced a group of site-specific sculptures (fig. 79). This was his public introduction of the "rag sculptures," and his description of the experience is worth recounting at length:

> We arrived in Amalfi late, when everybody had already chosen their space in the designated exhibition area. . . . I hadn't brought objects, only some bricks, some candles, and a ball made of papier-mâché—about one meter in diameter—that we had used before in a performance in the streets of Turin and that had passed through the hands of children who had played with it. Since it had already made its journey, the mobile sculpture couldn't be used as before. So I built a circular cage around it that allowed it to roll, but only minimally. . . . But coming back to the beginning of the story, when I arrived in Amalfi I had this bundle of rags, and I thought I could make something with them

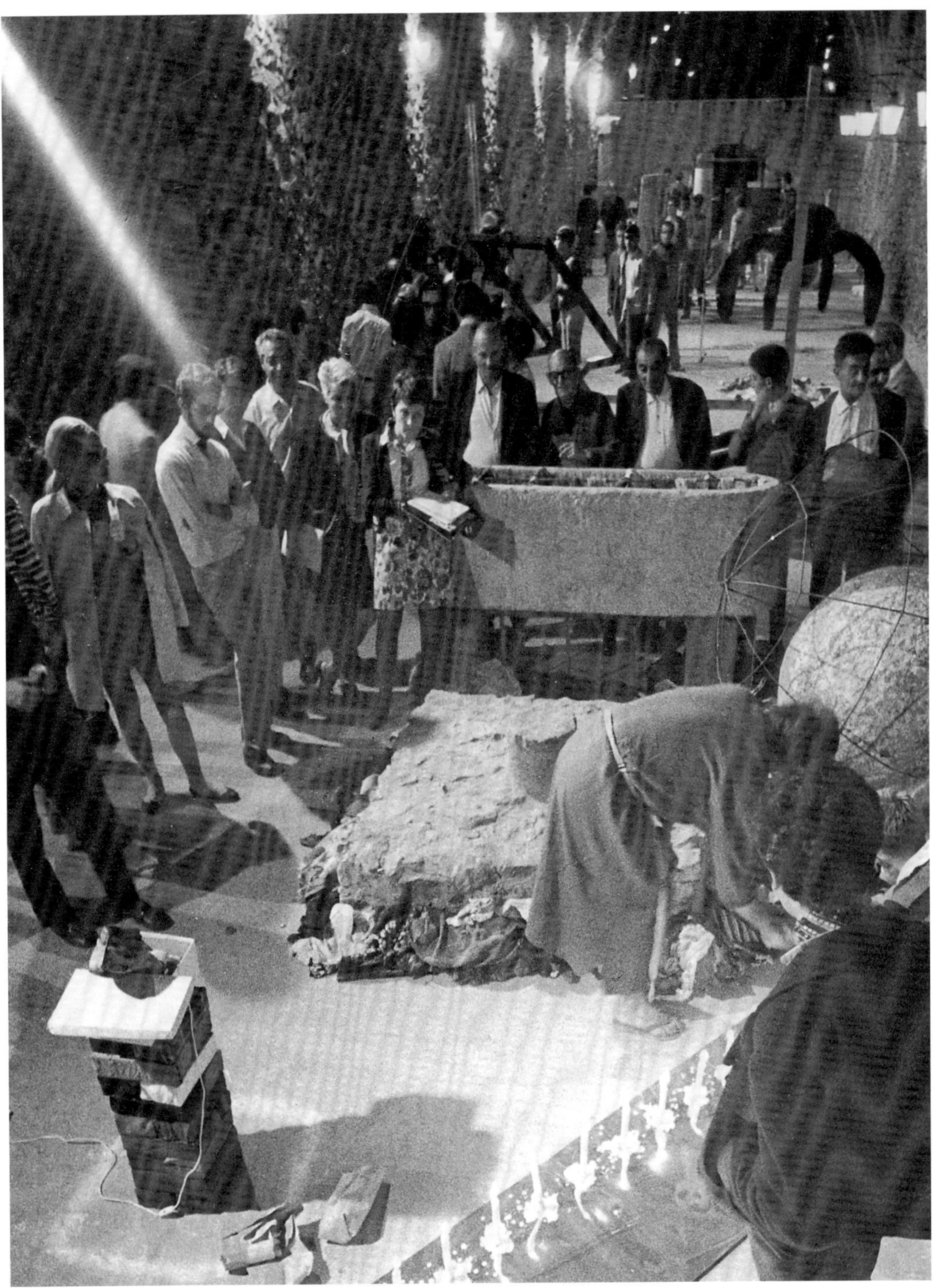

FIG. 79. A group of site-specific sculptures produced by Pistoletto for *Arte Povera + Azioni Povere*, Arsenali dell'Antica Repubblica, Amalfi, October 4, 1968. Photograph by Claudio Abate. Courtesy of Cittadellarte-Fondazione Pistoletto, Biella

> but I didn't know exactly what. . . . All the space was occupied already, except for one small area, which, to the misfortune of all the other artists, contained the remains of Roman ruins. . . . The ruins were in a square and were about a half-meter high, and to the side was a Roman sarcophagus. If I had arrived with my proper objects, I wouldn't have known where to put them, but with my rags I could decorate the Roman objects, hang them on the inside, and in this way create my own little set design. I had arranged my own little theater; the Roman ruins became just like the rags I had arranged all around them, and in this way what should have been an obstacle became an aid.[24]

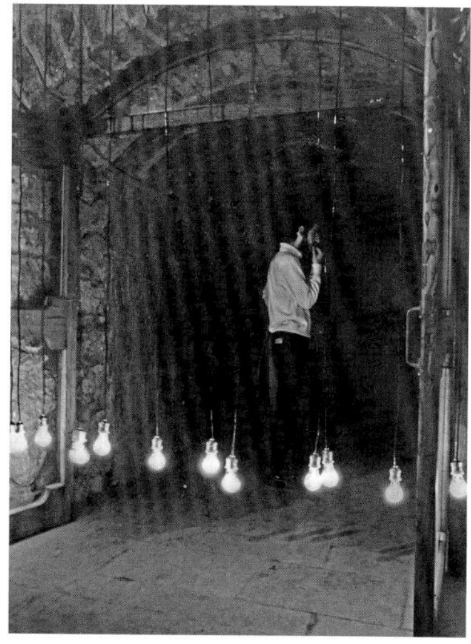

FIG. 80. Pistoletto's *Tenda di lampadine* (*Lightbulb Curtain*) suspended outside the entrance to the Arsenali dell'Antica Repubblica during *Arte Povera + Azioni Povere*, Amalfi, October 4, 1968. Photograph by Claudio Abate. Courtesy of Cittadellarte-Fondazione Pistoletto, Biella

In the end, Pistoletto created six objects for the space, only one of which, *Sfera di giornali* (*Newspaper Ball*, 1966; see fig. 64), had been selected ahead of time.[25] The other sculptures included *Tenda di lampadine* (*Lightbulb Curtain*), which the artist suspended outside the entrance to the Arsenali (fig. 80); *Candele* (*Candles*), a piece of mylar lined with candles that were lit on opening night; *Sarcofago e stracci* (*Sarcophagus and Rags*) and *Capitello e stracci* (*Capital and Rags*), a found sarcophagus and a broken column capital, each of which Pistoletto adorned with rags (see fig. 79); and, finally, *Monumentino* (*Little Monument*), a version of the shoe column from *L'Uomo ammaestrato* to which Pistoletto added a humidifier and, around the column's base, a line of insect powder (DDT) to "protect" it from the other exhibiting artists (fig. 81). The day after the opening, Pistoletto and his troupe marched from the Arsenali to the village piazza, where they performed their play (fig. 82). En route, Pioppi sang the "Papaciani," a Persian revolutionary song (so called by Pistoletto) that she had learned while living in Iran from 1962 to 1964, and that she reprised in numerous Zoo productions. As usual, Pistoletto marked off the stage from the audience, this time with protective DDT powder, before the performance commenced.

Pistoletto's performance and sculptures represented distinct contributions to the Amalfi exhibition, but his anecdote indicates that he saw them as aligned. His perception of an interrelationship is as instructive for his sculptural aesthetic as it is for his theatrical endeavors. Whereas in the plays the objects interrupt the action, providing a necessary locus for reflection, it would seem that in the sculptures the dynamic is reversed, with Pistoletto activating his sculptural displays via theatrical terminology. Ultimately, however, the effect is the same: in each case, there is a deliberate balance between freedom and control, action and stasis, formlessness checked by the organizing power of form. In his comments regarding his sculptural display in Amalfi, Pistoletto emphasizes his creative spontaneity when he describes arriving at the Arsenali with his bag of odds and ends and proceeding to enliven the found Roman objects. At the same time, however, this very gesture served to reaestheticize the space, making of it, in Pistoletto's words, "my own little set design . . . my own little theater." Formless in themselves, the rags functioned like Lo Zoo's objects: they

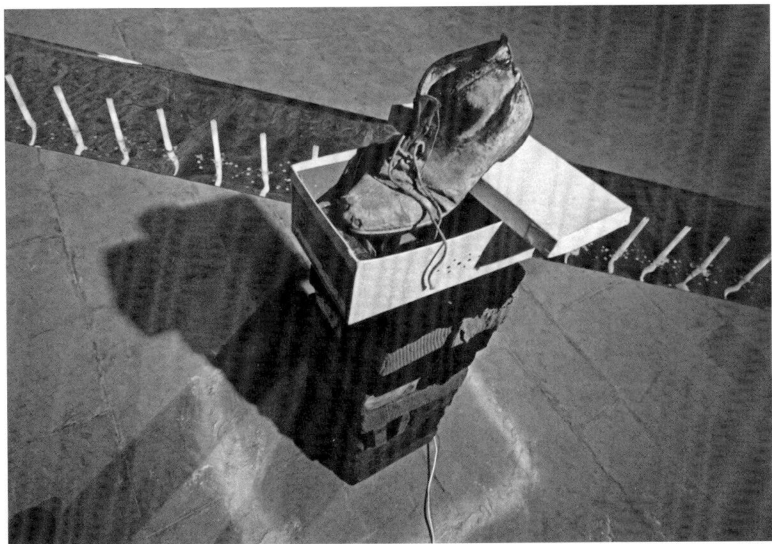

FIG. 81. Pistoletto's *Monumentino* (*Little Monument*) at *Arte Povera + Azioni Povere*, Arsenali dell'Antica Repubblica, Amalfi, October 4, 1968. Photograph by Claudio Abate. Courtesy of Cittadellarte-Fondazione Pistoletto, Biella

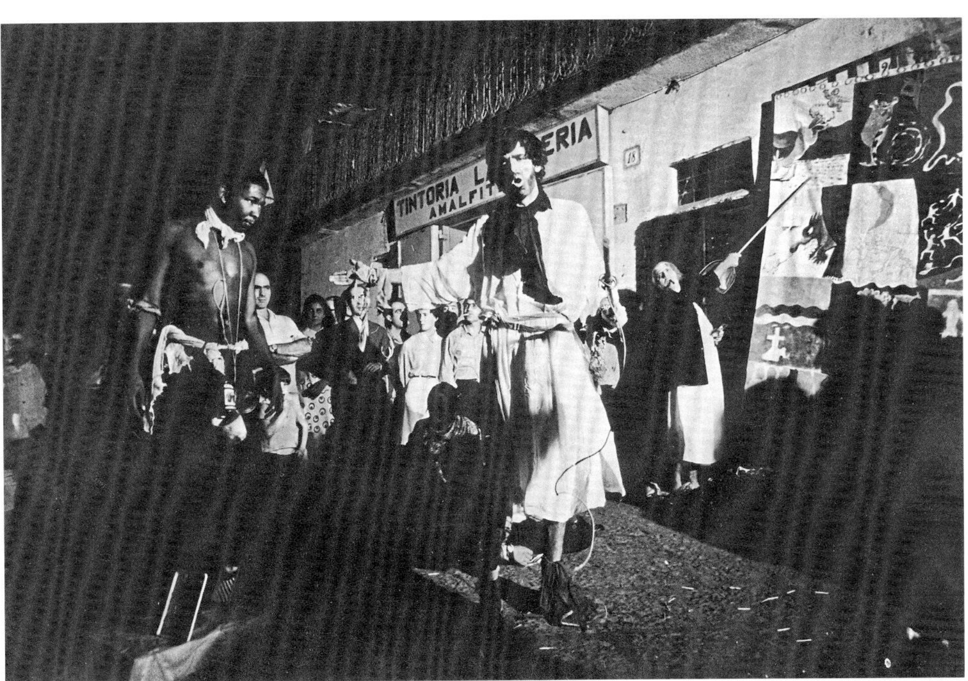

FIG. 82. Lo Zoo, *L'Uomo ammaestrato* (*The Trained Man*), performed at *Arte Povera + Azioni Povere*, Amalfi, October 5, 1968. At center is Carlo Colnaghi, as narrator; to the left is Henry Martin, as the protagonist; and to the right is Pistoletto at the storyboard. Photograph by Claudio Abate. Courtesy of Cittadellarte-Fondazione Pistoletto, Biella

activated their surroundings while simultaneously illuminating the forming process; they served as adornments, focusing vision and drawing attention to the Arsenali as a space. When Pistoletto refers to the decorative quality of the rags, he does not mean it pejoratively. Rather, he is celebrating the presentational aspect of life wherein things are not simply found but are given intention—reconstructed in and through the act of perception.[26]

Pistoletto's role vis-à-vis the other exhibiting artists was equally complex. In his account, he presents himself as a free spirit who takes up residence in an area rejected by the other participants, who have brought conventionally finished works. At the same time, however, he is intent on safeguarding his haphazard display. The DDT powder is a humorous touch, of course, but it is also a serious gesture. Pistoletto has described how the other artists began to play ball in and around the sculptures in the Arsenali and how, when they got to his *Monumentino*, they moved it aside. The members of Lo Zoo were furious at their thoughtlessness, but Pistoletto remained calm, simply moving the sculpture back into place.[27] In other words, he neither overreacted nor chose to join in the free-spirited antics but instead studiously protected and maintained the boundaries he had established and his rights as an artist. "There was a lot of freedom inside both exhibition spaces," he observed, "but it was a guarded freedom."[28]

This dialogue between freedom and control also guides Pistoletto's mature rag sculptures, such as *Orchestra di stracci* (*Orchestra of Rags*, 1968; plate 100), which made its first public appearance in Lo Zoo's four-hour improvisational collaboration with the Rome-based collective Musica Elettronica Viva (MEV), held at Turin's Deposito d'arte presente (Warehouse of Present Art) in December 1968. The artist claims that the sculpture, made of steaming teakettles placed amid rags and topped by a piece of glass, was directly inspired by his experiences in Amalfi. In his words, the work provided "a good example of what the performances in Amalfi were like on a small scale."[29] In part, this statement indicates the interactive nature of the sculpture, with its whistling teakettles and musty olfactory sensations. But the crucial point is that the performance is contained, much as it is in Pistoletto's theatrical arenas. *Orchestra di stracci*'s action is nearly explosive, as the steam pushes up against the teakettles and is in turn absorbed by the rags beneath, but total release never happens. Rather, the action takes place in the here and now, in the space demarcated by the glass square and within the sculpture's form.

This condition recalls the fate assigned to the artist's ball of newspapers, which, set free during its 1967 tour through the streets of Turin (fig. 83), reappeared in Amalfi restrained in a steel cage. Significantly, the sculpture's various titles reflect its altered states. Called *Sfera di giornali* when it was first shown, the work was renamed *Scultura da passeggio* (*Walking Sculpture*) during its tour through the Turin streets, and finally, in Amalfi, "Il mondo d'oro, la palla che prima andava in giro per strada è entrata nella gabbia" (Golden world, the ball that first toured the streets has entered a cage; fig. 84).[30] The final whimsical but cumbersome moniker

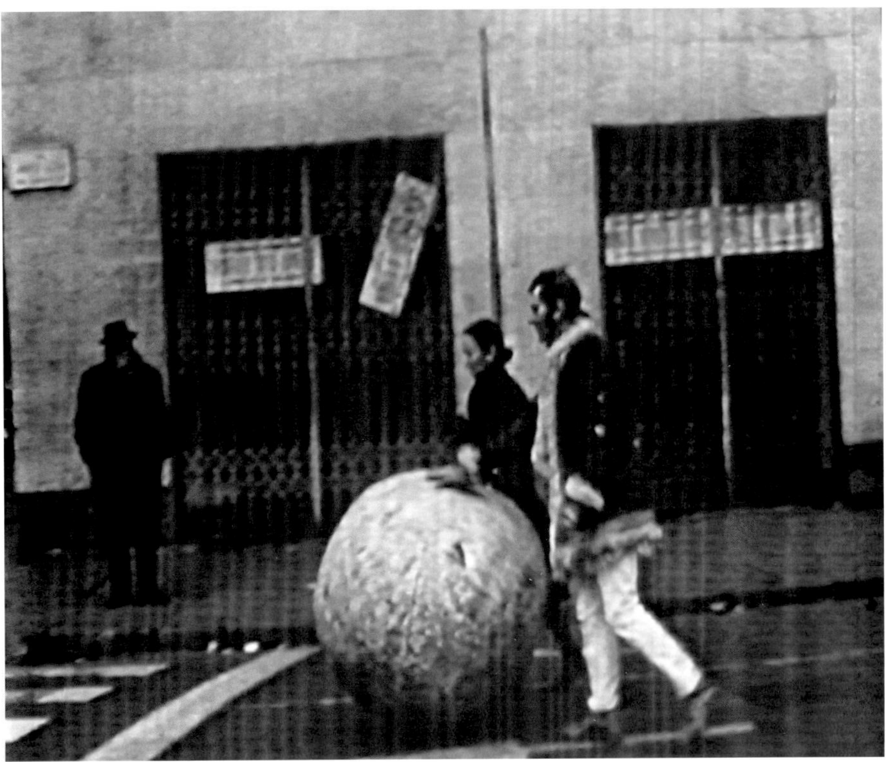

FIG. 83. Lo Zoo, *Scultura da passeggio* (*Walking Sculpture*), two actions in the streets of Turin, December 1967 and January 1968. Still from the film *Buongiorno, Michelangelo* (*Good Morning, Michelangelo*, 1968), by Ugo Nespolo. Courtesy of Cittadellarte-Fondazione Pistoletto, Biella

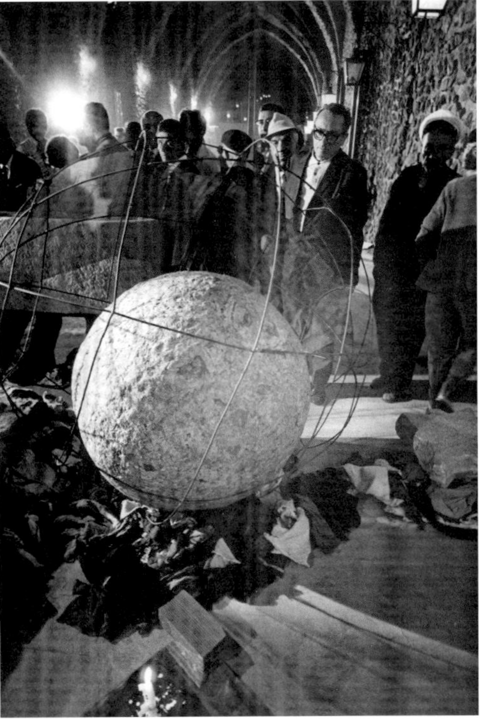

FIG. 84. Lo Zoo with Pistoletto's *Mappamondo* (*Globe*), Arsenali dell'Antica Repubblica, Amalfi, October 4, 1968. Photograph by Claudio Abate. Courtesy of Cittadellarte-Fondazione Pistoletto, Biella

deliberately challenges the notion of a perpetual present and instead gives the object a narrative and subjects it to specific temporal conditions.

Other rag sculptures include *Monumentino* (*Little Monument*, 1968; plate 101), yet another version of the shoe column from *L'Uomo ammaestrato*, made in this case of rag-covered bricks topped with an old boot; and *Muretto di stracci* (*Small Wall of Rags*, 1968; plate 102), a wall of cloth-covered bricks reminiscent of Pioppi's wooden pallet or of *Sarcofago e stracci* and *Capitello e stracci* from Amalfi. In these works, the material is physically controlled, molded into rigid columns or placed up against rag-covered walls, conveying the sense that both forms are valid—the amorphous rags and the structures that have been built out of them—and signaling a process of making and unmaking that is ongoing. And then there is *Venere degli stracci* (*Venus of the Rags*, 1967; plate 99), Pistoletto's famous sculpture of a found replica of a classical Greek nude turned toward the wall, her face buried in a heap of rags that she seems to struggle to keep in position. Like *Muretto di stracci*, *Venere degli stracci* foregrounds the mutual dependence of materials—as statue and rags appear to support each other—rather than their polar opposition. At the same time, the tattered rags, pressing up against the canonical Greek sculpture, are brought within the orbit of a history of representation. In this way, and for all their practical use, the rags enter Pistoletto's sculpture as an aesthetic form removed from the flux of life.

None of this is to say that Pistoletto's work is unresponsive to its immediate social and political context. On the contrary, his work from this period consistently references the charged environment in which he was living and working. His rags, bricks, and walls inevitably recall the student radicals of the late 1960s, for whom bricks and barricades served as makeshift tools of political dissent. Indeed, Pistoletto has spoken of the multiple political associations of the wall motif and has confirmed that a barricade comprised of cement-filled sacks that he constructed for a group exhibition at Rome's Galleria Arco D'Alibert in 1968 was a response to the current protests.[31]

In the same vein, Lo Zoo's theatrical scenarios repeatedly evoked revolutionary struggles of both past and present. Take for example, *Il principe pazzo* (*The Crazy Prince*), first staged at Naples's Galleria Il Centro in February 1969, which told the story of a prince who turns his throne over to the general populace (figs. 85–88). Or consider Lo Zoo's experiment *La ricerca dell'Uomo nero* (*The Research of the Minus Man*),[32] which took place in a piazza in Corniglia from May through October 1969 (figs. 89, 90). In this daily "performance," which was more of a collective experiment than a presentation intended for an audience, each participant assumed the role of the *Uomo nero*, a temporary leader who guided the others in a self-invented game before being overcome and replaced at the end of each day. Pistoletto has described this series of actions as simulating the cyclical conditions of government, in which rules and regimes are established, observed, and eventually undone. There were also smaller instances of

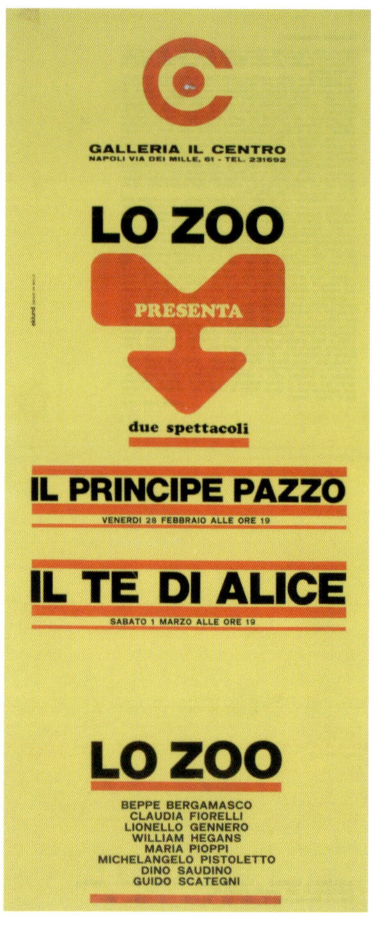

FIG. 85. The poster for Lo Zoo's performances *Il principe pazzo* (*The Crazy Prince*) and *Il tè di Alice* (*Alice's Tea*), 1969. Private collection

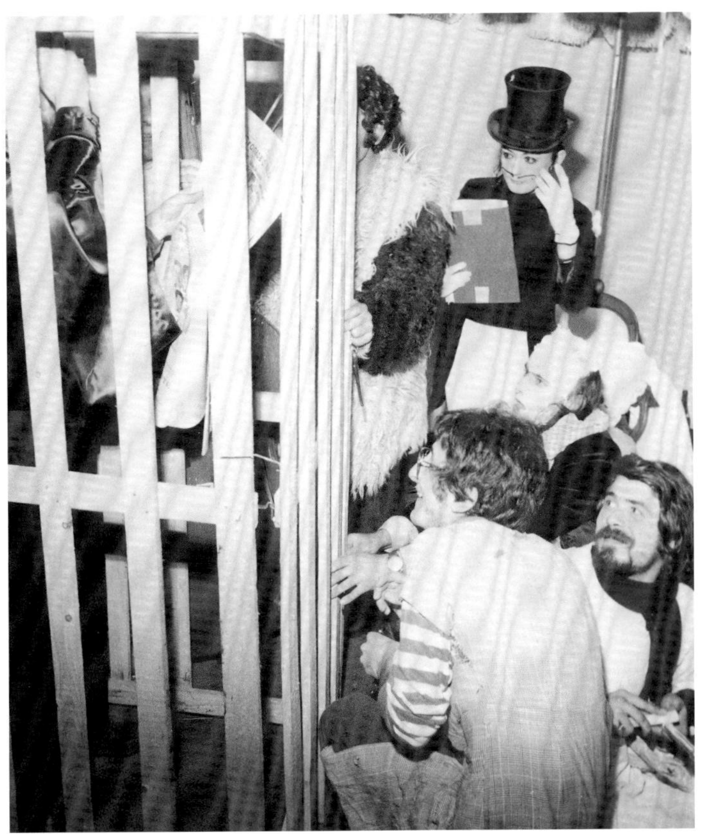

FIG. 86. Lo Zoo, *Il principe pazzo* (*The Crazy Prince*), Galleria Il Centro, Naples, February 28, 1969. Photograph by Fabio Donato. Courtesy of Cittadellarte-Fondazione Pistoletto, Biella

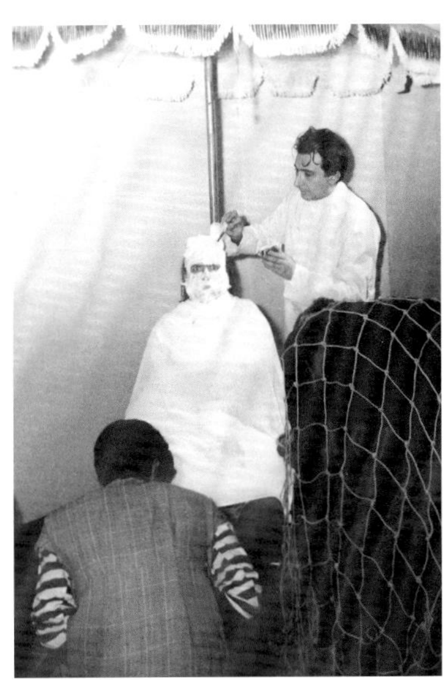

FIG. 87. Lo Zoo, *Il principe pazzo* (*The Crazy Prince*), Galleria Il Centro, Naples, February 28, 1969. Photograph by Fabio Donato. Courtesy of Cittadellarte-Fondazione Pistoletto, Biella

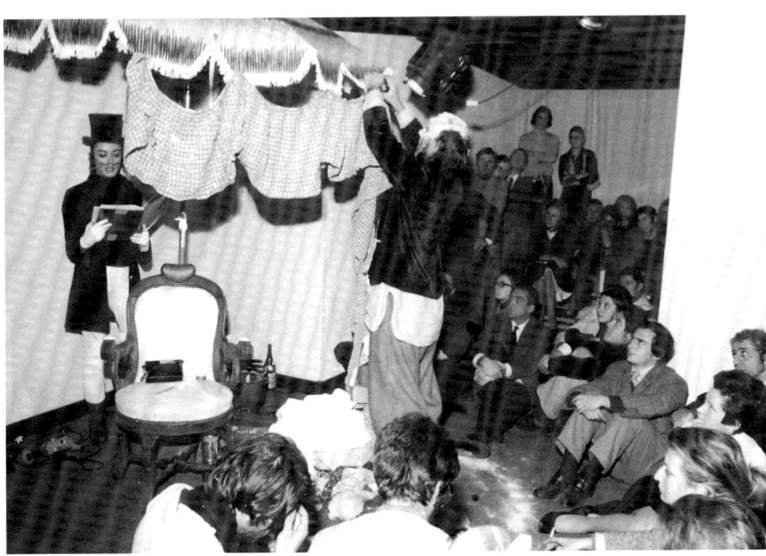

FIG. 88. Lo Zoo, *Il principe pazzo* (*The Crazy Prince*), Galleria Il Centro, Naples, February 28, 1969. Photograph by Fabio Donato. Courtesy of Cittadellarte-Fondazione Pistoletto, Biella

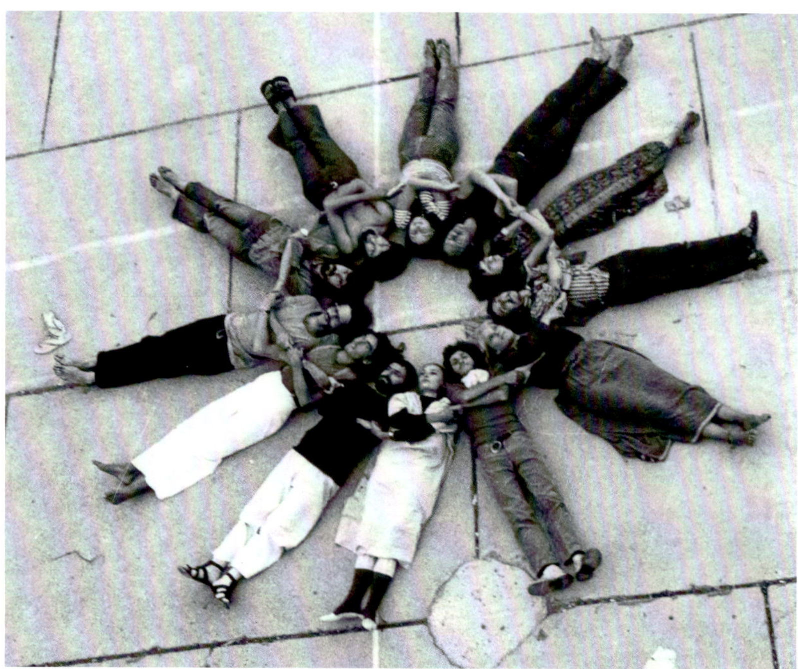

FIG. 89. Lo Zoo, *La ricerca dell'Uomo nero* (*The Research of the Minus Man*), Corniglia, May–October 1969. Photograph by Paolo Mussat Sartor. Courtesy of Cittadellarte-Fondazione Pistoletto, Biella

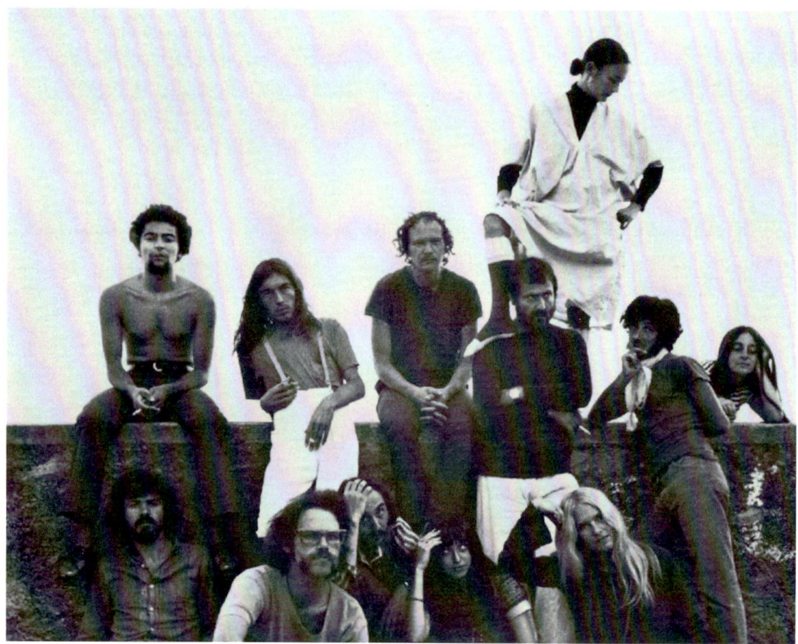

FIG. 90. Lo Zoo, *La ricerca dell'Uomo nero* (*The Research of the Minus Man*), Corniglia, May–October 1969. Photograph by Paolo Mussat Sartor. Courtesy of Cittadellarte-Fondazione Pistoletto, Biella

protest in Lo Zoo's productions, as when Pioppi sang her Persian revolutionary song—"A flower at the side of the field is about to blossom; I will sacrifice everything for my love, except my rifle, because it serves me to kill the soldier of the government"[33]—or when the characters engaged in fake battles and subsequent peacemaking, something that happened in Lo Zoo's last three productions, which followed a looser narrative than the earlier scenarios.[34]

Accepting these references at face value, one can see why contemporary critics described Lo Zoo as incarnating the kind of nonhierarchical "being-togetherness" typical of the student movements and other radical groups active at the time. Lo Zoo's own manifesto embraced the antiestablishment zeitgeist when it proclaimed that artists are equally capable of doing the job of "architects, designers, technicians, and politicians," who typically "have been the ones who know how to do things."[35] And yet even here there is an acceptance of working within the system that belies an emphatically outsider stance. The manifesto does not advocate overthrowing traditional disciplines so much as promoting art's equivalent capacity. Similarly, it describes Lo Zoo's participants as both "actors and audience" and "producers and consumers"—that is, as intrinsically part of, rather than outside, social life.[36]

Indeed, Lo Zoo's actual encounter with Europe's rebellious youth indicates a less typical avant-garde position. Lo Zoo's principal audience consisted of local communities familiar with street theater or, at the opposite extreme, art-world cognoscenti. But in May 1969 the group's members found themselves in unfamiliar territory while performing *I ratti baratti* (*The Bartering Rats*) in Heidelberg, Germany (see fig. 91). As Pistoletto tells it, they arrived in the gymnasium where they were to perform, only to discover a large group of students gathered there—talking and engaging in political agitation. It was, Pistoletto recalls, complete chaos. Not sure what to do but certain that they needed to "find some sort of organization,"[37] the actors began to unfold a large white sheet square by square. Slowly, the mass of students moved back to make way for the cloth until it was completely spread out. No one stepped on the sheet, the room fell silent, and Lo Zoo proceeded to perform in the designated arena. One by one the performers made their way onto the "stage." Though tentative at first, the action grew more and more intense as the actors constructed little objects out of tinfoil, rags, and lighted matches and then threw the objects up in the air, allowing them to fall about the sheet, adorning the performance space. At one point the group gathered under the sheet, playing musical instruments and posing to create a kind of mobile sculpture beneath it. All the while, the audience remained respectful and attentive.

Discussing his reaction to the Heidelberg students, Pistoletto clarified that he sympathized with their desire for change but was dismayed by the form—or lack of form—their actions assumed. "In '68 there was no meaning, no organizing, no culture in the freedom. What was needed was something productive and organized. The goal was to become free but also

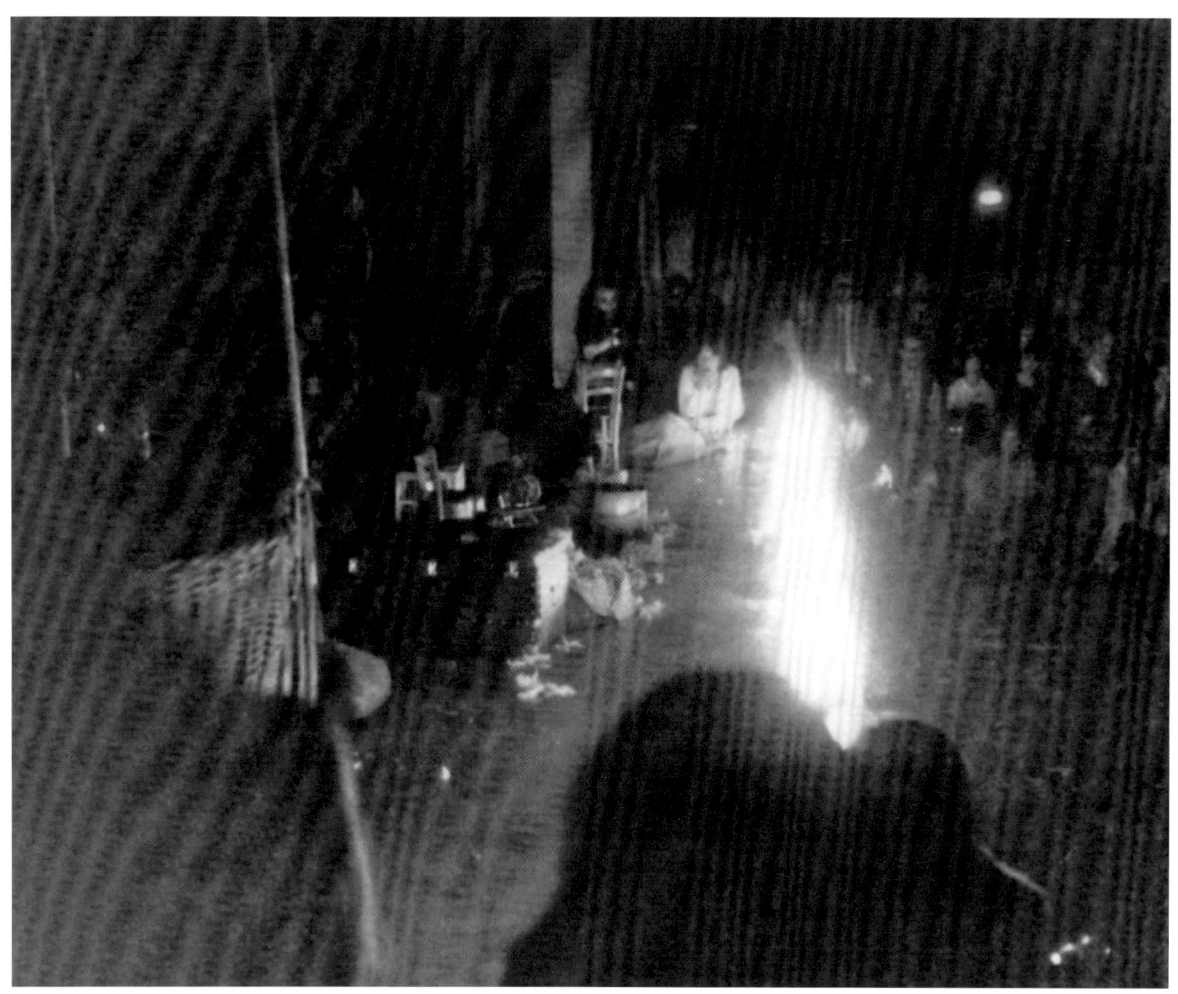

FIG. 91. Lo Zoo, *I ratti baratti* (*The Bartering Rats*), in the performance at De Lantaren, Rotterdam, May 13, 1969, which preceded the Heidelberg performance on May 20. Courtesy of Cittadellarte-Fondazione Pistoletto, Biella

to become conscious; to protect one's space or place; to make a society, something real."[38] In his ambivalence toward the 1960s radicalism, Pistoletto was not alone. Many left-leaning Italian intellectuals expressed skepticism about the irrational, cultlike nature of the 1960s counterculture, which they saw as disturbingly akin to Fascism's imposed consensus and quest for absolutes.[39] For the heretical Marxist filmmaker and writer Pier Paolo Pasolini, fascist authoritarianism, avant-garde progressivism, and consumer mystification were aligned in their parallel refusal to accept Marxism's core faith in otherness. In formulating a response, Pasolini adopted a highly artificial aesthetic that aimed to expose the ideological basis of all modes of cultural production, past and present. Similarly, writers such as Italo Calvino and Umberto Eco promoted a "rational and discriminating consciousness" that would accept the inevitability of social roles and norms while also working to change them.[40]

Like many of Lo Zoo's performances, *I ratti baratti* staged just such an acceptance of social parameters, the spread-out cloth designating an organized space whose limits and conditions the audience had to respect, however temporarily. On the other hand, the actors' formation under the sheet has been described as a kind of "antidiluvian monster . . . that is above all anonymous, undifferentiated," and lacking a "social role."[41] The actors attempted to forge this role as they struck their poses beneath the cloth and, like the "trained man," began to create and communicate via simple materials and gestures. The fact that Lo Zoo observed preset scenarios, however loosely configured, and that the experiments in Corniglia took the form of a game, is not incidental. Like games or politics, Lo Zoo's theatrical experiments were intentionally and emphatically non-natural. There was spontaneity and chaos in the productions, but it was a directed chaos, as in Pistoletto's sculptures. The action was clearly formulated as happening in the here and now, in the context of an event enacted in a particular space at a particular time by particular people—conditions that were reinforced by Lo Zoo's practice of modifying its scenarios according to where the group was performing and who was participating.[42]

These observations bring us full circle, to an aspect of Pistoletto's production referred to at the beginning of this essay: his sustained dialogue with painting. For here Lo Zoo's theater manifests what is fundamental to painting as well—that it is a delimited field in which something takes place. Pistoletto has explained that in moving beyond painting, he was not rejecting the canvas but rather was seeking "a space in which this persona of mine would be able to move," and that he tried his hand at sculpture because he wanted to find a way of doing things "in a public space."[43] The entire trajectory of Pistoletto's early career reveals itself as a progressive testing of presentational space, from his early painted canvases in which solitary figures register against polished grounds (see plates 4–9), to the mirror paintings that situate viewers as witnesses to themselves looking, to the transparent Plexiglas panels that expose the wall itself as subject, or as a medium upon which images are suspended (plates 68–74).

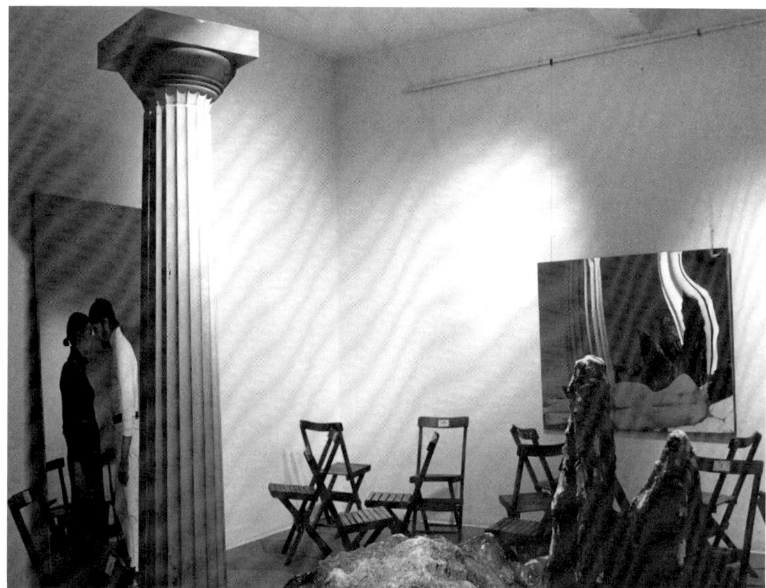

FIG. 92. The installation of Pistoletto's exhibition at Galleria L'Attico, Rome, including props from Cinecittà, February 1968. Photograph by Claudio Abate. Courtesy of Cittadellarte-Fondazione Pistoletto, Biella

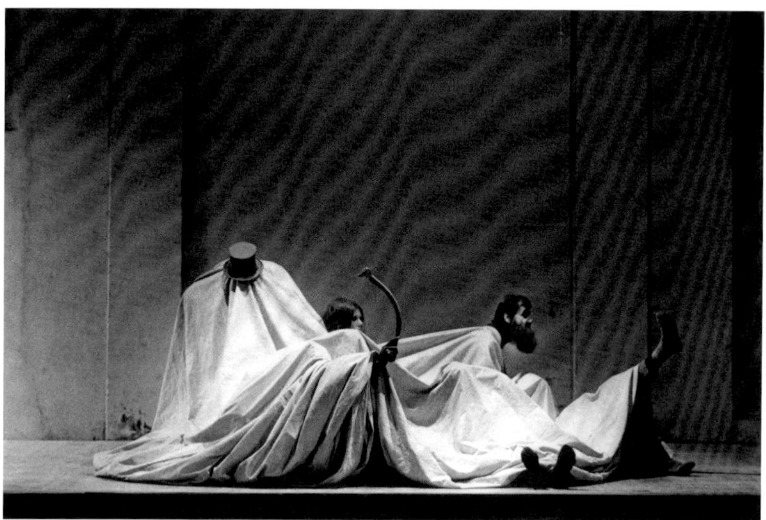

FIG. 93. Lo Zoo, *Bello e basta* (*Beautiful and Enough*), Teatro Uomo, Milan, 1970. Photograph by Ugo Mulas. © Ugo Mulas Heirs. All rights reserved

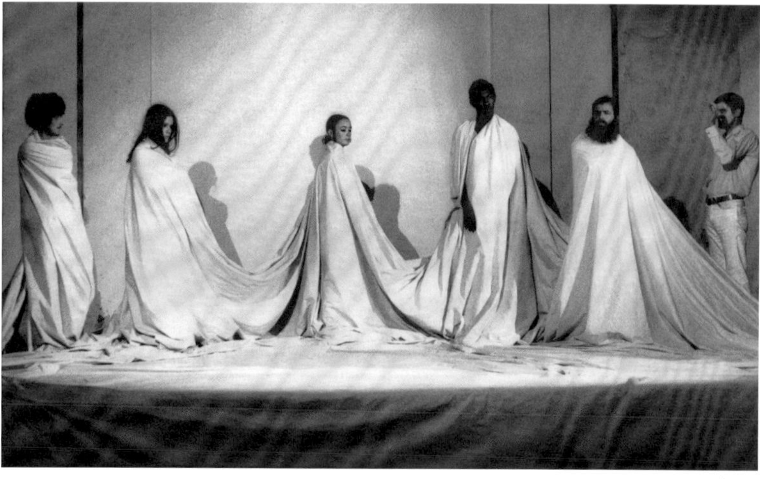

FIG. 94. Lo Zoo, *Bello e basta* (*Beautiful and Enough*), Teatro Uomo, Milan, 1970. Photograph by Paolo Mussat Sartor. Courtesy of Cittadellarte-Fondazione Pistoletto, Biella

In writing about the mirror paintings, critics have tended to emphasize the element of live reflection, downplaying the dialogue between painting, photography, and the reflecting surface. In so doing, they have overlooked the peculiar tension between the viewer's mobile image and the static photo-based silhouettes suspended on the mirroring surface. Whether an effect of the semi-turned-away poses of the individuals depicted, or of the stillness produced by their abrupt isolation against active grounds, the cut-out figures manifest a kind of self-conscious posturing that in turn compels the viewer to reflect on his or her own behavior. Despite the common view that the mirror paintings activate free, mobile perception, they are in fact very much about convention, about the way in which people move, gesture, and take up positions within public space. They highlight, once again, life's presentational aspect.[44]

Pistoletto explicitly aligned painting and theater in an exhibition that took place at Rome's Galleria L'Attico in February 1968, just before he began working with Lo Zoo. The show featured four mirror paintings hung within a fantastical landscape complete with costumes, cardboard rocks, and Roman columns culled from Cinecittà, Rome's legendary film studio (fig. 92). Three cine-cameramen circulated among the crowd (which included Julian Beck and Judith Malina of the Living Theatre), assisting Pistoletto throughout the exhibition's one-month run in making films that were screened on closing night. Suspended amid the action, the mirrors represented focal points of sorts, the isolated figures providing individual, stilled moments in which theatrical flux was revealed as purposeful gesture. Pistoletto has observed: "To be at the same time spectators and actors, producers and consumers, is the spectacle I propose on the stage of my mirror paintings."[45] Understood in this context, the mirror paintings might better be said to envision a world governed not by "free" behavior, but by dialogue and encounter with one's own and other people's images.

Pistoletto's rag columns and walls provide a similar kind of structure in that they offset and contain the rag bundles piled up against them, while works such as *Tenda di lampadine* (*Lightbulb Curtain*; see fig. 80) and *Candele* (*Candles*; plate 103) literally illuminate the limits and conditions of architectural space, exposing another kind of frame. To quote the last line from Lo Zoo's final performance, *Bello e basta* (*Beautiful and Enough*): "There is no light without something for it to fall on" (figs. 93–95).[46] For Pistoletto, Lo Zoo was a way to enact this vision of commitment on a larger scale. It provided an opportunity to widen the arena.

Lo Zoo disbanded in 1970, and its members went their separate ways. But it is suggestive that in recent years, with his creation of Cittadellarte—a foundation featuring offices in such eclectic disciplines as art, ecology, economics, education, fashion, nutrition, and politics—Pistoletto has returned to a collective model of working. Cittadellarte occupies a picturesque building complex in Biella, near Pistoletto's native Turin, which also houses his living quarters and a residency program (fig. 96). It is an idyllic place, but one that the artist has declared is profoundly nonutopian.

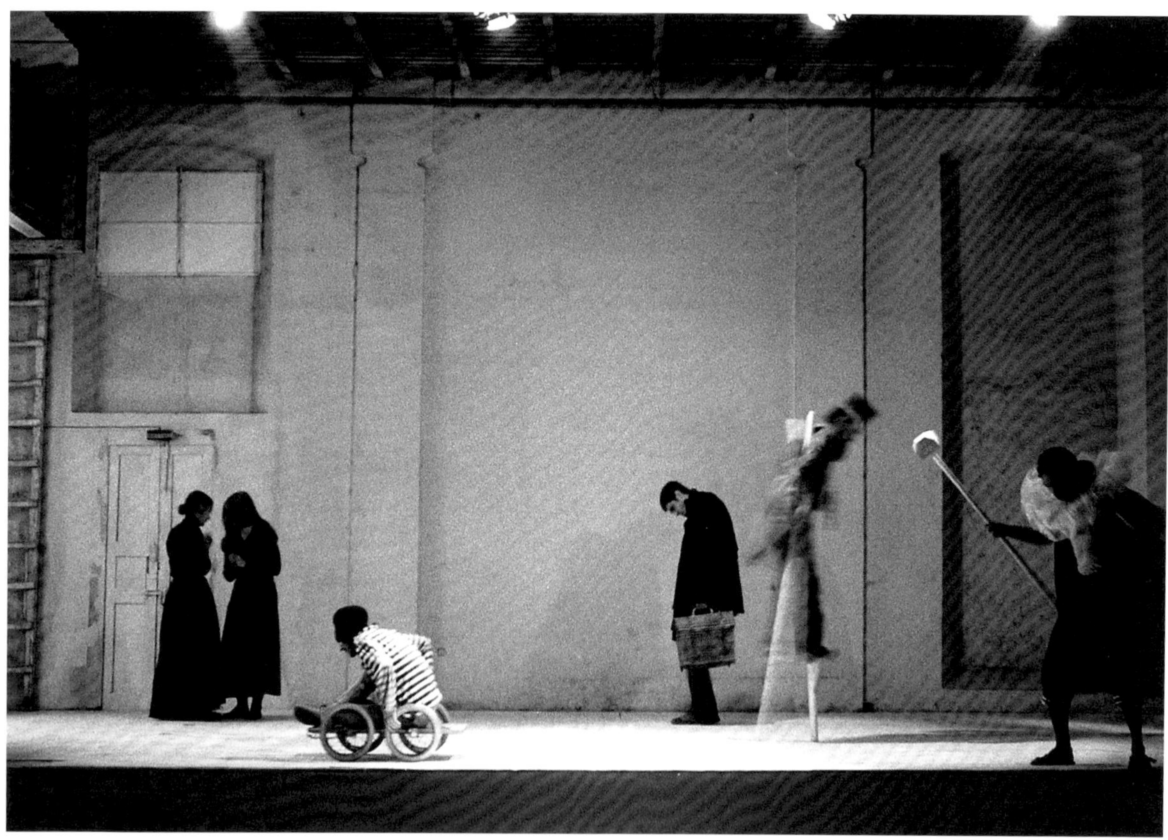

FIG. 95. Lo Zoo, *Bello e basta* (*Beautiful and Enough*), Teatro Uomo, Milan, 1970. Photograph by Ugo Mulas. © Ugo Mulas Heirs.

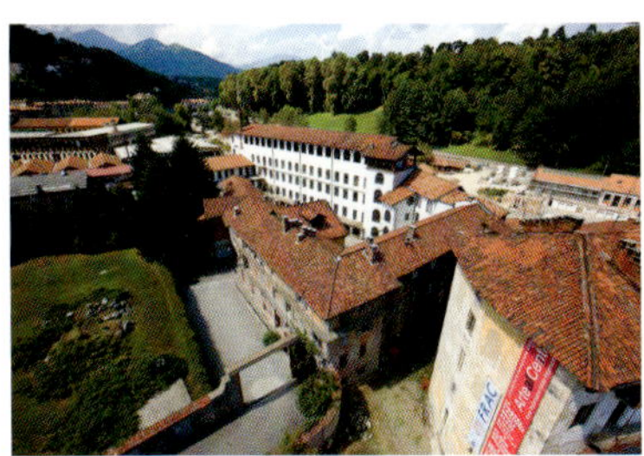

FIG. 96. Cittadellarte, Biella, 2009. Courtesy of Cittadellarte-Fondazione Pistoletto, Biella

Indeed, he has asserted that whereas *utopia* (from the Greek *ou* and *topos*) literally means "no place," the foundation is emphatically geared toward practical goals.[47] The name Cittadellarte was carefully selected for its double meaning. Signifying "city of art," or a place of creativity and limitless possibility, it also references a fortress or citadel. The foundation holds discussions (it recently hosted ten leaders of European banking for a forum on the current economic crisis) and fosters community art activities, but it is careful to respect areas of expertise, encouraging leaders of different fields to come to their own workable solutions.

The foundation also pays close attention to display through typeface, logos, design, and the production of art, fashion, and decorative objects, seeing in these visual forms parallel models of commitment. According to Pistoletto, creating a uniform look is important (the foundation emphasizes sustainable production and natural, recyclable materials) because, apart from function, physical appearance projects anticipated goals. Cittadellarte defines itself on its Web site as "a great *laboratory*, a generator of creative energy," and "a place for the convergence of creative ideas and projects. . . . An organism aimed at *producing* culture activating a responsible social transformation that is necessary and urgent at a local and global level."[48] It is useful here to recall Lo Zoo's definition of art as "knowing how to do things."[49] Beyond its actual achievements, in other words, Cittadellarte is relevant for the way in which it aligns art and politics as systems of production. The same may be said of all Pistoletto's work, from the mirror paintings to his sculptural and theatrical work. Whatever the medium, the primary goal is equivalent: to create and re-create under proscribed conditions, to take a stand, and to make do with the materials at hand.

1 See, for example, Jean-François Chevrier's comments in Benjamin Buchloh, Catherine David, and Jean-François Chevrier, "The Political Potential of Art, Part 2: Interview," in *Politics-Poetics: Documenta X—The Book* (Ostfildern-Ruit: Cantz, 1997), p. 628. See also the section entitled "Gli stracci e l'arte povera," in Bruno Corà, *Michelangelo Pistoletto: lo spazio della riflessione nell'arte* (Ravenna: Agenzia Editoriale Essegi, 1986), pp. 114–19. Here, Corà argues that, like the mirror paintings before them, the rags became the medium of a "new language, and it is more than understandable that an entire climate, that of Arte Povera, was associated with them" (p. 117). He then goes on to explain their wide-ranging influence, citing a sculpture by Robert Wilson made entirely of rags and included in the 1973 group exhibition *Contemporanea* in Rome "as a counterbalance to the rigidity of minimalism" (my translations).

2 See Germano Celant, "Azione Povera," in Celant, *Arte Povera / Art Povera* (Milan: Electa, 1985), p. 89; originally published in *Arte Povera* (Bologna: Galleria de' Foscherari, 1968).

3 See Corà, *Michelangelo Pistoletto: lo spazio della riflessione*, p. 106. More specifically, Pistoletto maintains that since he was a painter first and foremost, he could not join an "official" theater company. This is yet another indication that he did not see painting as irreconcilable with Lo Zoo's brand of theater.

4 For detailed documentation of all of Lo Zoo's productions and of Pistoletto's theater work in general, see Marco Farano, Cristina Mundici, and Maria Teresa Roberts, eds., *Michelangelo Pistoletto: il varco dello specchio; azioni e collaborazioni, 1967–2004* (Turin: Fondazione Torino Musei, 2005).

5 For my discussion of what took place during this and other performances, I am indebted to Marco Farano and Michelangelo Pistoletto, the latter of whom went through the details of his performance work with me in a conversation in June 2009.

6 After the Living Theatre's performance of *Mysteries . . . and Smaller Pieces* at the Piper Pluriclub in March 1967, Pistoletto got to know the members of the troupe, and they stayed with him in his studio on a number of occasions in the following months, while in Turin for various performances.
7 Martin Friedman, *Michelangelo Pistoletto: A Reflected World* (Minneapolis: Walker Art Center, 1966), n.p.
8 Gillo Dorfles, "The Meetings in Amalfi," in *Michelangelo Pistoletto: azioni materiali* (Cologne: Verlag der Buchhandlung Walther König, 1999), p. 73.
9 Celant, "Arte Povera," in Celant, *Arte Povera / Art Povera*, p. 53.
10 Celant, "Zoo," *Sipario* (Milan) 291 (July 1970), p. 19 (my translation).
11 Celant, "Azione Povera," in Celant, *Arte Povera / Art Povera*, p. 89. Note also the similar sentiment expressed by Giuseppe Bertolucci in his article in the same catalogue, in which he associates the need for "poorness" with a "moving further and further away from the object, returning toward behavior, and coming forth again in action." He continues: "Thus it is necessary to shatter the product and bring it toward life, just as it is necessary to undermine life itself and direct it toward action." See Bartolucci, "Poor Action in a Poor Theater," in Celant, *Arte Povera / Art Povera*, pp. 83, 81; originally published as "Azioni povere su un teatro povero," in *Arte povera più azioni povere*, pp. 57–62. One might say that Celant and Bartolucci subscribe to the model of theater as a "choreographic community," wherein, as defined by the philosopher Jacques Rancière, theater is understood to be an exemplary community form, and community is held to be dependent on the elimination of distance between subjects. And yet, as Rancière has clarified: "Distance is not an evil to be abolished, but the normal condition of any communication. Human animals are distant animals who communicate through the forest of signs." For Rancière, true emancipation "begins when we challenge the opposition between viewing and acting," when we understand our commonality to reside not in the group in fusion, but in our unique and equivalent intellectual capacity, a capacity that is stimulated through "a performer deploying her skills and a spectator observing what these skills might produce in a new context among other spectators." See Jacques Rancière, "The Emancipated Spectator," in *The Emancipated Spectator*, trans. Gregory Elliott (London: Verso, 2009), pp. 10, 13, 22; originally published as *Le spectateur émancipé* (Paris: La Fabrique éditions, 2008). I believe that Pistoletto's theater encourages just such an awareness of the relationship between subjects and objects.
12 Pistoletto, "Note di lavoro," in *Pistoletto* (Venezia: Palazzo Grassi, 1976), p. 45 (my translation).
13 After explaining that there is no such thing as complete parity and that the division between audience and actor is an acknowledgment of this disharmony, Pistoletto concludes: "Grotowski, who seems to want a direct relationship between man and man, in reality limits this direct relationship in his theater to a very restricted group of people . . . while the true spectators of Grotowski are those of us who could never have assisted in his productions because we are in the audience. He communicates his myth to us masses by means of the press and other methods of communication and consumption. Moreover, his message is irrelevant when compared with the means used to disseminate it." See Pistoletto, "Il momento della negazione?" *Sipario* (Milan) 268–69 (August–September 1968), pp. 16–17 (my translation).
14 Henry Martin, "Uno Zoo non é una badia," *Data* (Milan) 1, no. 1 (September 1971), p. 61 (my translation).
15 Lo Zoo, "Turin, Late Twentieth Century (Preparing for the Age of Aquarius)," in Celant, *Arte Povera / Art Povera*, p. 127.
16 Allan Kaprow, "Environments, Assemblages, Happenings" (1965), in *Art in Theory, 1900–1990: An Anthology of Changing Ideas*, ed. Charles Harrison and Paul Wood (Cambridge, Mass.: Blackwell, 1992), p. 706.
17 Pistoletto, interview with the author, February 1999.
18 The title *Cocapicco e vestitorito* is a made-up one. The first word combines *coca*, from *Coca-Cola*, and *picco*, from *colare a picco*, meaning "to sink" (in the nautical sense). The second word comes from *vestito*, meaning "dress," and *rito*, meaning "rite"—rite of the dress. In the action, Maria sat at the top of a staircase wearing an extremely long plastic dress, which Pistoletto and his daughter Cristina sewed throughout the action. At the bottom of the stairs a group of participants in a plastic swimming pool poured out Coca-Cola and talcum powder while falling on the floor.
19 Martin, "Uno Zoo non é una badia," p. 60.
20 The full statement, accompanying the first performance of *Cocapicco e vestitorito* in May 1968, reads as follows: "A play in two contemporaneous parts, with slow, magic and contemplative action on a double staircase on one hand; and violent, paranoiac and provocative action on the other. The two scenes come together beneath a transparent mantle, creating a city." Reprinted and translated in Celant, *Arte Povera / Art Povera*, p. 47.
21 Pistoletto, interview with the author, February 1999.
22 Ibid.
23 Again, we are reminded of Rancière, who writes: "The collective power shared by spectators does not stem from the fact that they are members of a collective body or from some specific form of interactivity. It is the power each of them has to translate what she perceives in her own way, to link it to the unique intellectual adventure that makes her similar to all the rest in as much as this adventure is not like any other. This shared power of the equality of intelligence links individuals, makes them exchange their intellectual adventures, in so far as it keeps them separate from one another, equally capable of using the power everyone has to plot her own path. What our performances—be they teaching or playing, speaking, writing, making art or looking at it—verify is not our participation in a power embodied in the community. It is the capacity of anonymous people, the capacity that

makes everyone equal to everyone else. This capacity is exercised through irreducible distances; it is exercised by an unpredictable interplay of associations and dissociations." See Rancière, "The Emancipated Spectator," pp. 16–17.

24 Pistoletto, in conversation with Germano Celant (Genoa, 1971), in *Michelangelo Pistoletto: azioni materiali*, p. 28 (my translation).

25 According to Pistoletto (in conversation with the author, June 2009), Marcello Rumma, one of the show's curators, had asked him to show *Sfera di giornali*, but he ended up altering it by placing it in a steel cage.

26 Interestingly, Pistoletto has also referred to the use of the rags (and other scenic objects) in Lo Zoo's productions as a way of clothing the actors. Once again, the idea would seem to be that the rags served as an embellishment, or a means of enabling something (or someone) to become visible in a public space.

27 For a more complete description of this incident, see Pistoletto's "The Gold Monument," in *Michelangelo Pistoletto: A Minus Artist* (Turin: hopefulmonster, 1988), p. 25; written on the occasion of *Arte Povera + Azioni Povere* in Amalfi under the title "Il monumentino d'oro."

28 Pistoletto, in conversation with the author, June 2009.

29 Ibid.

30 For the latter title, see Maria Teresa Roberto, "Davanti allo specchio, al di qua delle sbarre: Lo Zoo dagli antefatti a *L'uomo nero*, 1966/1970," in *Michelangelo Pistoletto: il varco dello specchio*, p. 22.

31 Ibid.

32 "Minus Man" is Pistoletto's preferred translation of *uomo nero* as it relates to his work.

33 As quoted in *Michelangelo Pistoletto: il varco dello specchio*, p. 86 (my translation).

34 Lo Zoo's last three productions were *I ratti baratti* (*The Bartering Rats*), first performed in Rotterdam in May 1969; *Chi sei tu?* (*Who Are You?*), first performed in Belgrade in September 1970; and *Bello e basta* (*Beautiful and Enough*), first performed in Milan in October 1970.

35 Lo Zoo, "Turin, Late Twentieth Century," p. 127. The full quote reads: "Art means knowing how to do things. For a while now architects, designers, technicians, and politicians have been the ones who know how to do things." The manifesto then goes on to advocate replacing the word *art* with "quack-quack," precisely in order to avoid stereotypical ideas about art—principal among them, that art is dead or no longer necessary. For Lo Zoo, art is a system of making like any other system of production.

36 Ibid.

37 Pistoletto, in conversation with the author, June 2009.

38 Ibid.

39 For an elaboration of this, see my thesis "Arte Povera's Theater: Artifice and Anti-Modernism in Italian Art of the 1960s" (Ph.D. diss., Columbia University, 2006), especially chapter 3, and *Arte Povera: Selections from the Sonnabend Collection* (New York: Miriam and Ira D. Wallach Art Gallery, Columbia University, 2001).

40 This quotation comes from a longer analysis of the work of the fiction writer Carlo Gadda, in which Calvino continues: "From this foundering of the author of letters in the fermentation of the narrated material, a sense of dismay is born. And this sense of dismay is the point of departure of a judgment, so that the reader can . . . make a step forward, reacquire historical distance, declare himself to be different, distinct from the boiling material." See Italo Calvino, "Il mare dell'oggetività," in *Una pietra sopra: discorsi di letteratura e società* (Milan: Arnoldo Mondadori, 1995), p. 50 (my translation); originally published in *Il menabo di letteratura* (Turin) 2 (1960).

41 This description actually references a similar sheet used in Lo Zoo's final production, *Bello e basta* (*Beautiful and Enough*). See Francesco Leonetti, "Teatro d'arte: foglio-recensione di uno spettacolo dello Zoo con Pistoletto capocomico," in *Michelangelo Pistoletto: il varco dello specchio*, p. 128 (my translation); originally published in *Che fare: bollettino di critica e azione d'avanguardia* (Milan) 8–9 (Spring 1971).

42 The contemporary French philosopher Alain Badiou has observed that "the truths lavished by the labor of theatre are essentially political in that they crystallize the dialectics of existence and aim to elucidate our temporal site." In other words, for Badiou, true theater—that is, theater like Lo Zoo's, which reinforces the play element through staging, costumes, and direction—is inherently political because, far from eradicating boundaries, it precisely *localizes* us. Put another way, both politics and theater, in Badiou's sense, defy permanence, requiring participation instead in specific, temporary situations and structures. See Badiou, "Rhapsody for the Theatre: A Short Philosophical Treatise," *Theatre Survey* (Pittsburgh, Pa.) 49, no. 2 (November 2008), p. 200.

43 Barry Schwabsky, "Pistoletto through the Looking Glass: A Conversation on the Art of Subtraction," *Arts Magazine* 63, no. 4 (December 1988), pp. 37, 39.

44 For more on Pistoletto's mirror paintings and their dialogue with theater, see Gilman, "Pistoletto's Staged Subjects," *October* 124 (Spring 2008), pp. 53–74.

45 Pistoletto, interview with F. Prestipino, in *Pistoletto*, ed. Germano Celant, exh. cat. (Florence: Forte Belvedere, 1984), p. 97 (my translation; I thank Roberta Nuzzaci for her help with this); originally published in *Le arte* (Milan) 4 (April 1976).

46 This line in turn constitutes part of the first line of Pistoletto's book *L'uomo nero: il lato insopportabile* (Salerno: Rumma, 1970); see the translation in Pistoletto, *The Minus Man*, pp. 5, 31.

47 Pistoletto, in conversation with the author, June 2009.

48 See www.cittadellarte.it/info.php, and www.cittadellarte.it/info.php?inf=2 (my italics).

49 See note 35 above.

A COMMUNITY OF THE NON-ALL

GABRIELE GUERCIO

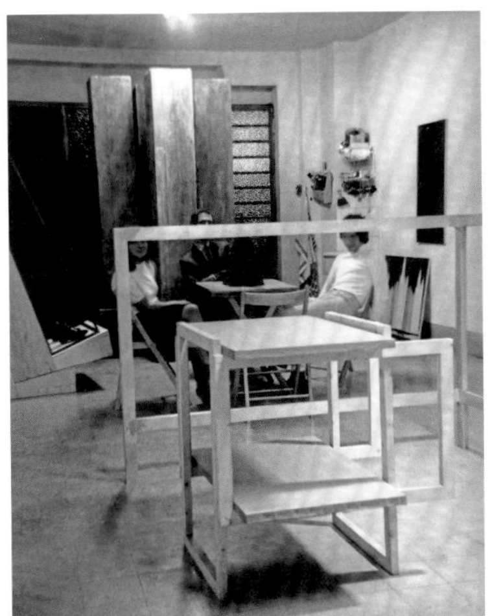

FIG. 97. The Minus Objects (1965–66) installed in Pistoletto's studio in Turin, January 1966. Photograph by Piero Gilardi. Courtesy of Cittadellarte-Fondazione Pistoletto, Biella

THE PUBLIC MIND OF THE ARTIST

Between December 1965 and January 1966, Michelangelo Pistoletto produced a new group of works—the *Oggetti in meno* (Minus Objects)—that he exhibited in an unusual way. Rather than present them in an art gallery, he installed and showed them in his studio in Turin. Paolo Bressano, Pistoletto's friend and photographer, took pictures of the installation (see fig. 52). Bressano's photographs show a studio devoid of people but filled with multifarious artifacts placed seemingly at random on the walls and floor. The images of this heterogeneous aggregate suggest that chaos can be the harbinger of its own eccentric harmony.[1]

By the time Pistoletto installed the Minus Objects in his studio, images of artists' workplaces had become a familiar entity in the modern West, in both artistic and popular culture.[2] While sounding a theme of representation and self-representation to the artists themselves, these images also offered a means of access, via photography, to the other side of creative work—to the actual physical spaces where the most immaterial kind of human activity materializes.[3] Such images might depict the artist mingling with fellow artists or patrons, as was often the case in the nineteenth century, or the studio as a place of retreat and concentration, as was more common in the twentieth century. Showing the artist along with his or her work, or the works alone, these studio images epitomize a cluster of beliefs about inspiration, originality, and inventiveness. But they also function as signifiers of a beginning, of a source or site where the creative emerges and the interplay between artist, work, and world finds its origin.

But the images of the Minus Objects in Pistoletto's studio complicate the detection of a beginning. The artist himself is absent, a fact that enhances the impression of a centerless assemblage that must be taken at face value. In addition, the lack of any shared formal or stylistic characteristics among the exhibited works upsets the concept of the artist's studio as a point of origin. Thirty works of art, collected and shown together despite their conspicuous dissimilarities, are presented as a whole with no explanation.

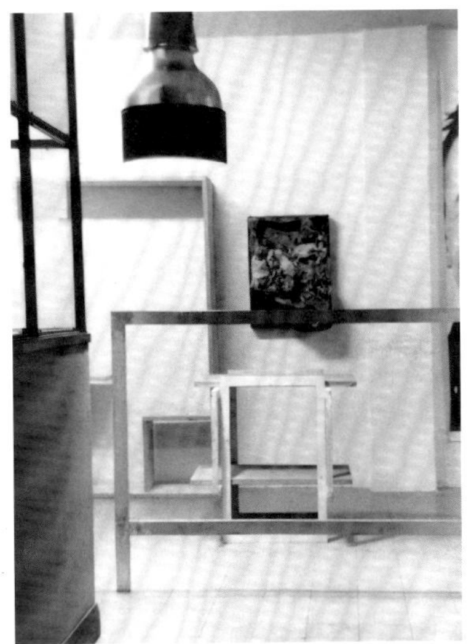

FIG. 98. The Minus Objects (1965–66) installed in Pistoletto's studio in Turin, January 1966. Photograph by Piero Gilardi. Courtesy of Cittadellarte-Fondazione Pistoletto, Biella

The images of the Minus Objects suggest that the emergence of the creative entails a short circuit that (momentarily?) exposes the distance separating the work of art from its maker, this work from that work. Looking at Bressano's and others' photographs (figs. 97, 98), we realize that the works on view dwell in many dimensions as they interweave elements pertaining to both artistic and everyday culture. We are encouraged to regard Pistoletto's studio as an open-ended site, transparent to itself and to the world. It is as if Pistoletto were saying that the origin and destination of the works keep vanishing into a void. The void not only confounds the identities of whoever or whatever partakes of the creative act but also intimates that what appears as a whole in Bressano's photographs is without a center. It cannot appear as one (as an undivided entity) or as a bundle of ones (counting as the many) without compromising its unity and ultimately revealing that the very idea of "being" does not tolerate rigid demarcation between the one and the many: it should be conceived in its "inconsistent multiplicity."[4]

However, the discovery of this inconsistent multiplicity does not necessarily lead us to consider artistic production as relative or completely fortuitous. Nor does it rule out the possibility that the installation of the Minus Objects was aimed at creating a communal domain.[5] On the contrary, the installation may be seen as exploring what is in common or becomes shared through the interplay of artist, work, and world. This exploration seems to go hand in hand with the metamorphosis of the artist's mind into a public mind.[6] The shift from the private to the public is pursued not only by opening the studio to the public—thus eliminating the art gallery as an intermediary in the exhibition of works of art—but also by showing a series of works in which heterogeneous materials have been freely adopted, blended, and reinvented such that the outcome is a collective that cannot be ascribed to a unique source, agency, or property. Just as the artist's mind is projected within the immanence of a transindividual realm—that is, it occupies a realm in which it is not the object of an individual subjectivity—so the work of art is relieved of the burden of firm definitions of ownership or private possession. It may incorporate and trigger a distribution of agencies that connect persons with things or persons with persons via things.[7] The work of art becomes porous to the public, and vice versa, in that they both partake of the same centerlessness.

The two concurrent dynamics of Pistoletto's installation—the opening of the artist's mind to the public and the demeaning of private property—do not, however, result in an equivalence of artist, work, and world such that there is no remainder. Rather, inconsistency and impermanence characterize the gathering of the Minus Objects. And so the questions arise, first, whether community may be imagined without having to surmise it as a representable totality,[8] and second, whether a sense of community may inhere in the very disclosure of its incompleteness and the incompleteness of its components vis-à-vis the nothing or zero of the void in which the one and the many works of art come into existence. In other words, community is not based on determinate principles, on a stable essence of being through which its components can be identified, but rather may consist in the discovery of a shared gap, a quantum of nonbeing to which its components are exposed individually and in their mutual interrelatedness.

In confronting these questions, the present essay addresses the special sense of community that informs Pistoletto's works from 1962 until about 1970: not only the Minus Objects (plates 75–97) but also the mirror paintings (plates 13–67)—a series begun in 1962 and carried on until the present—and the theatrical experience of Lo Zoo from 1968 to 1970 (see figs. 71–95). Pistoletto's works explore whether and how artist and work, work and audience, artistic practice and the world, are bound together, and what this binding may mean.

In Italy and abroad, the 1960s were characterized by outbreaks of political and social unrest pointing to still undeveloped visions of community. In 1962 and 1969 in Turin, the numerous workers' strikes signaled the rise of a different form of struggle, no longer aimed at improving the vexing conditions of factory labor but at rejecting all kinds of alienating activity, if not the notion of work itself.[9] Other manifestations of this unease were the student protests of May 1968 in Paris and other French cities; the civil rights struggle that affected the fabric of American society; the antiwar movement; the Hippie communes; the anti-psychiatric trend; and the spread of manifold countercultures. These and other experiments in alternative modes of being reflected a will to challenge or overcome the forms of life prescribed by the dominant capitalistic culture.

Pistoletto's works, too, defy the assuredness of a status quo, whether artistic, social, or existential. With Pistoletto, however, community acquires yet another sense, one tending to highlight difference, incompleteness, and subtraction as opposed to identity, plenitude, and addition. In retrospect, Pistoletto's works reveal some kinship with a way of thinking about community that, often inspired by the seminal views of Georges Bataille, has in recent years been articulated by such European thinkers as Maurice Blanchot, Jean-Luc Nancy, Giorgio Agamben, and Roberto Esposito.[10] These theorists question customary notions about human co-belonging. Community is seen not as the result of work or production, but rather as taking place in an unworking, in the interruption that dismantles the presumed identity of work (Blanchot). Far from denoting a substance that uniformly underlies the lives of individuals, community entails an exposure to the "in-common"—to a being together that throws one's existence outside of oneself (Nancy). The singular entities forming a community may do so without affirming an identity, indicating that human beings may come together without having to depend on a representable condition of belonging (Agamben). Because it refers not so much to a determinable "public thing" as to the gap that makes the divide between oneself and others perceptible, community generates unity not according to an accumulation or a plus but via the recognition of a minus or a lack (Esposito). Pistoletto's early works address analogous issues of belonging and separation, interposition and withdrawal of the one and the many, through the invention of images and situations that interrogate and transfigure the idea of community's ability to qualify persons as well as things.

A pivotal aspect of Pistoletto's practice in the 1960s is its fresh insights into the eccentric oneness of the work of art, in itself and with regard to what is other-than-itself. The work of art may be said to appear in the singularity of its being one, in that it exemplifies a single possibility out of countless other possibilities that are left uncreated and thus hidden from view. But we would miss the complexity of this appearance if we were to overlook the fact that these countless other possibilities are never completely estranged from the reality of the artwork in the space-time of both its production and its reception. For Pistoletto, the work of art inspires a special kind of computation. It should be counted as one minus infinity or as infinity minus one.[11]

What is remarkable about this computation is that, by including the infinite within the perception of the one and exposing the impermanence of the one within the infinite, it corroborates the view that the ones are transient and that there might be only multiplicities within the zero of a void. In fact, the introduction of a "minus" is crucial. It means that artistic creation is tantamount to a mode of subtraction whose outcome, the work of art, elicits cognizance of an unrestricted multiplicity at the very moment in which it briefly elides that multiplicity. Generating its own self-othering, the work of art formalizes the occurrence of a tension within itself and between it and all the rest. It makes the one appear not as an inflexible unity but as one subtracted from the many, or as the many subtracted from the one. Whichever side of the equation we contemplate, the work of art evinces its ontological incompleteness. It operates as the threshold between what the work has marked and what it has left unmarked, between the domain ahead of its origin and the domain behind its destination.

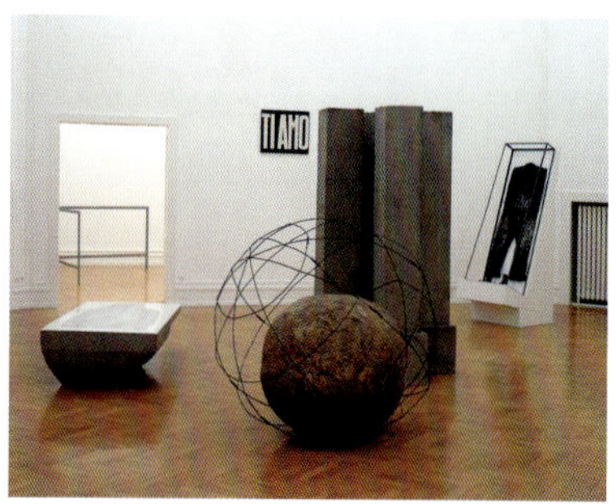

FIG. 99. The Minus Objects in the exhibition *Michelangelo Pistoletto: Oggetti in meno, 1965–1966*, at the Kunsthalle Bern, October–December 1989. Photograph by Roland Aellig. Courtesy of Cittadellarte-Fondazione Pistoletto, Biella

Much of Pistoletto's effort during the 1960s was directed toward the realization of works in which that lying outside the singularity of their being ones remains elusive. Augmenting the sense of the vanishing origin and destination of the work, this elusiveness does more than maintain the work's polysemy. It also intensifies its public, transindividual character—the work's inclination to fluctuate between inside and outside itself and within the void made perceptible by its appearance. With Pistoletto, the becoming-public of the artist's mind is a process that does not comply with the omnipotent impulse to surmise the reality of the given—or that which is regarded as existing in the natural and cultural realms, or both—as a whole that can be represented or mastered in its undivided totality. On the contrary, the process promotes the recognition that any attempt at totalization, or mastery of the All, is a sinister maneuver doomed to failure, or else liable arbitrarily to impose on the given a univocal perspective of sense. Accordingly, the artist's mind becomes public and the work publicizes this becoming because both entities acknowledge that they are simultaneously structured and fractured by a blend of personal and impersonal agencies. Within this commixture, belonging is inextricable from incompleteness. What is shared or in common does not add up, nor can it be established once and forever. It is signaled by a default that the mind or the work envisions as a tension between itself and all the rest.

In light of these considerations, I would argue that the militancy of Pistoletto's practice in the 1960s instances the possibility of a community of the "non-All." I adopt this term from Jacques Lacan, who spoke of the logic of the "non-All" associated with the feminine and opposed to the masculine logic of the master, a logic allured by the prospect of encyclopedic knowledge and eager to subdue all that is in existence to a principle of totalization.[12] A community informed by the logic of the non-All defies the status quo and brings about an ongoing detotalization of the given. It cannot be subjugated by the omnipotent grip of encyclopedic knowledge. Gaining existence through subtraction, through appearing unaccountable

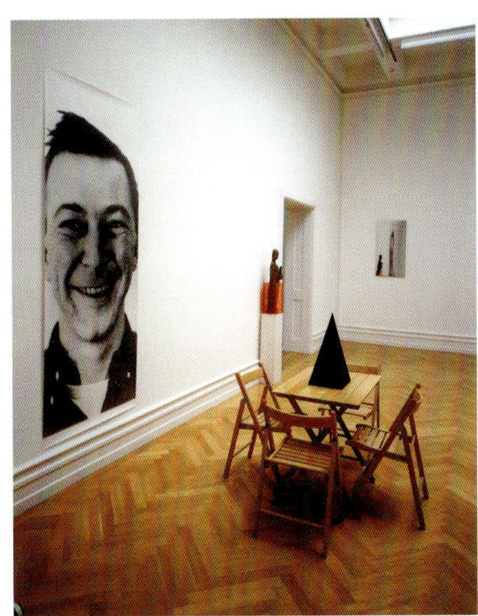

FIG. 100. Installation of the Minus Objects in the exhibition *Michelangelo Pistoletto: Oggetti in meno, 1965–1966*, at the Kunsthalle Bern, October–December 1989. Photograph by Roland Aellig. Courtesy of Cittadellarte-Fondazione Pistoletto, Biella

within a preordered state of affairs, the components of such a community enact a displacement between themselves and all the rest. Who or what partakes of a community of the non-All is or becomes one insofar as it dwells in the void made apparent by the disruptive emergence of its coming into being as one minus infinity or as infinity minus one.

SUBTRACTION AND DEFIANCE

The Minus Objects that Pistoletto showed in his studio in 1965–66 were works that exceeded the disciplinary boundaries of architecture, painting, and sculpture.[13] Nor did they evince a homogeneous mode of expression (figs. 99, 100). To compare, for instance, *Rosa bruciata* (*Burnt Rose*, 1965; plate 76) with *Struttura per parlare in piedi* (*Structure for Talking while Standing*, 1965–66; plate 87) or *Foto di Jasper Johns* (*Photograph of Jasper Johns*, 1966; plate 95) does not help if the purpose is to ascertain a semantic or morphological coherency. Instead of revealing recurrent stylistic traits referencing the identity of a single author, the Minus Objects are so heterogeneous as to look like the production of several authors.[14] Their genericness—that is, their disinclination to adopt a specific semiotic medium or predetermined style—is confirmed by the fact that, in some cases, they appropriated and reworked various artistic idioms current at the time, such as Pop, in *Ti amo* (*I Love You*, 1965–66; plate 90), Abstract Expressionism, in *Fontana luminosa* (*Luminous Fountain*, 1965–66; plate 89), and Minimalism, in *Colonne di cemento* (*Concrete Columns*, 1965; plate 81). Each work exhibits its own contingency: it is the result of a different action and volition. And yet, despite their heterogeneity in form, theme, and materials, and their various titles, these works were linked together by Pistoletto calling them Minus Objects.

If the Minus Objects make up a whole, then it is a whole that cannot be understood through the summation of its parts or by conjecturing a unique source of origin. Indeed, the origin and destination of the Minus Objects are undeterminable. But this blank is productive of sense. It favors the recognition that a work of art may overstep authorial referentiality as well as the valorization of a specific artistic medium (painting, sculpture, drawing). Moreover, the blank of origin and destination allows each of the Minus Objects to manifest its own genericness without conforming to the other objects but rather intensifying the singularity of its being. Each object fits the definition of a being "whatever" that, as Agamben has argued in his meditation on community, not only qualifies the singularity "such as it is" but also carries the implication of a "being such that it always matters."[15]

As an aggregate of generic singularities, the Minus Objects posit the likelihood of a community in which affinities and differences among its components cannot be conceptualized according to an aprioristic essence that transcends or unifies them. On the contrary, affinities and differences occur by means of an unceasing detotalization of the given because such

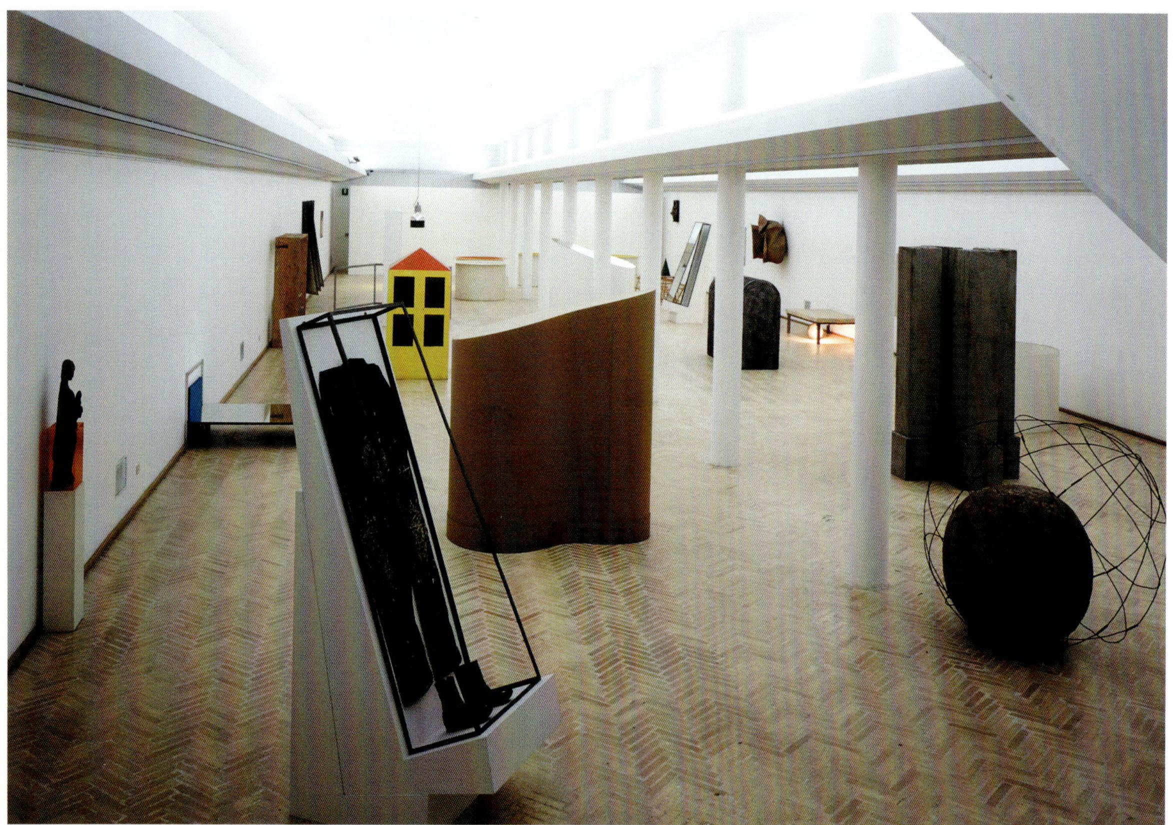

FIG. 101. The Minus Objects in the exhibition *Michelangelo Pistoletto: Oggetti in meno*, 1965–66, at the Galleria Nazionale d'Arte Moderna, Rome, 1990. Photograph by Attilio Maranzano. Courtesy of GNAM—Galleria Nazionale d'Arte Moderna e Contemporanea, Rome

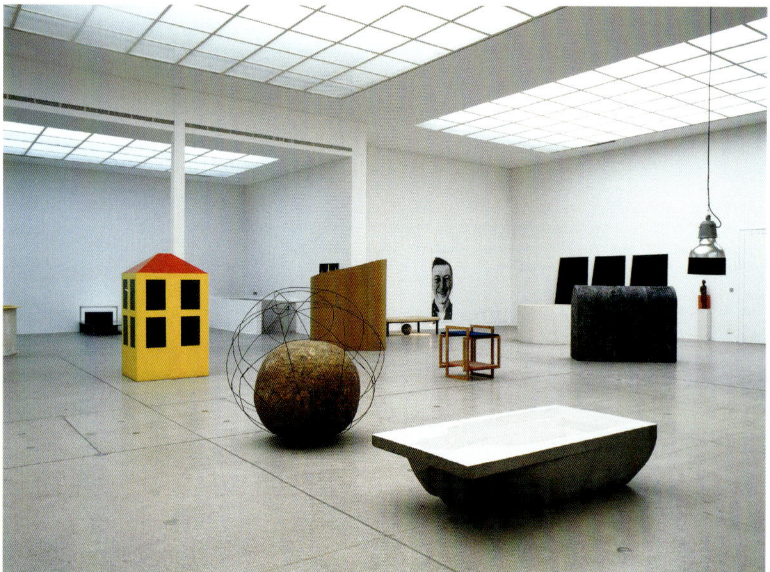

FIG. 102. The Minus Objects in the exhibition *Michelangelo Pistoletto: Oggetti in meno, 1965–1966*, at the Wiener Secession, Vienna, 1990. Photograph by Margherita Spiluttini. Courtesy of Cittadellarte-Fondazione Pistoletto, Biella

a community is without a center. It does not know additions: it exists via subtraction.[16] The repeated element, if any, in the "series" of the Minus Objects is extraneous to the visible traits of its constituent objects and must be sought in the subtraction of an experiential and cognitive space-time that each object epitomizes by becoming countable as one minus the other objects or as the other objects minus one.

Just as the generic singularities of the Minus Objects appear to be subtracted each from the others, so the anarchic collective they form appears to be subtracted with regard to an artist's identity (presumed constant), as well as to an apparatus of codes and expectations that presumably oversees the production and reception of art. The grouping that is the Minus Objects does not hide its incompleteness. It generates gaps between its components, gaps between these and the whole, and gaps between the whole and all the rest. The result is a "being together" in which the one and the many find their definitions within the common gapping that interlocks them. By virtue of that gapping, the multiplicity of the Minus Objects is not a reiteration or multiplication of ones. Singularly and as a whole, the Minus Objects are tied to the zero of a void epitomized by the distance that simultaneously separates and qualifies them.

The very title of the Minus Objects implies a work of subtraction. In 1966, Pistoletto clarified that the Minus Objects "are not constructions or fabrications of new ideas, any more than they are objects which represent me, intended to be imposed and to impose me on others. Rather, they are objects through whose agency I free myself from something—not constructions, then, but liberations. I do not consider them more but less, not pluses but minuses, in that they bring with them the sense of a perceptual experience which has been definitively externalized."[17]

In 1984, in conversation with Germano Celant, Pistoletto recalled how in 1964 the success of his mirror paintings seemed to jeopardize the growth of his work. That year, the New York gallery owner Leo Castelli invited Pistoletto to produce more mirror paintings for an exhibition and later suggested that he immigrate to the United States, arguing that the future of his career depended on his joining the group of artists represented by his gallery. "From that time, for fifteen years," comments Pistoletto, "I have not been back to the United States. This to explain how I went back to Italy, to make the Minus Objects, and how I reacted to a view of the market that empowered a cultural and practical domain that forced you to feel either part of a clan or alone."[18]

Especially if read as a pair, Pistoletto's statements from 1966 and 1984 illustrate how the subtraction that characterizes the Minus Objects entails the defiance of a status quo—of a given state of affairs presumed to be "stable" and identifiable with the conditions of artistic production as well as with its outside reception. The Minus Objects defy a context of reception that requires an artist not only to persist in making the same kind of work over and over again, in order to forge a recognizable stylistic signature that will ensure financial success, but also to share the interests of a "clan" influential in that context. Pistoletto objects to the constraining demands of this clan by affirming the need to operate independently and to imagine, with the Minus Objects, a community that dispenses with hierarchies and centralized agencies. The Minus Objects do not add anything new or original to the world, nor does the artist feel represented by them. Turning a work of art into a generic singularity, Pistoletto sought to disengage himself from having to reiterate a particular artistic form in observance of a market-driven mentality.

The exhibition of the Minus Objects in Pistoletto's studio in 1965–66 represented a break—cultural, ideological, and communicative—between Turin and New York, between a ramified system administering the circulation and appreciation of creative products on an international scale and the private site where the creative emerges. The Minus Objects argue that an artist is not obliged to habituate himself to a "successful" way of working or to ally himself with a powerful group to secure his career. This discovery parallels the realization that a work of art is the proof, contingent and discrete, that the boundary between art and non-art is mobile. In fact, considered individually or together, the Minus Objects operate via both subtraction and defiance toward a given state of affairs. They suggest that, as a generic manifestation of a singular being, as an entity whose origin and destination remain elusive, a work of art may belong to whoever comes into contact with it: it is nobody's and everybody's.

Subtraction and defiance are likewise consonant in surmising another sense of community through the ways the Minus Objects present themselves. For instance, *Scultura lignea* (*Wood Sculpture*, 1965–66; plate 91; see also fig. 101, left) is a fourteenth-century wooden Madonna encased in an orange Plexiglas cube that covers the sculpture for half its height. Whereas the upper part of the Madonna's body is left visible in its untouched albeit deteriorated state, the lower part must be viewed through the orange Plexiglas. If compared or put in relation with the other Minus Objects, *Scultura lignea* marks a distance between the "being one" it epitomizes and the "being many" epitomized by the other objects. The work's belonging to the collective of the Minus Objects cannot be established by means of the criteria of similarity, agreement, and coalition that supposedly sustain a communal entity. By opposing normative criteria of belonging (stylistic, formal, and so on) with the other Minus Objects, *Scultura lignea* is subtracted and thus intensifies the sense that we know nothing about its origin and destination or those of the other works.

But there is more. *Scultura lignea* itself bears evidence of an act of subtraction. The artist has appropriated an artifact from the past, an object related to a certain visual culture and religious context, and placed it within a modern material, Plexiglas. The result is to upset the assuredness of a status quo in which the divide between past and present, sacred and profane, is inviolate. The past loses its stability as unalterable because half of the wooden Madonna appears only through the frame of the orange Plexiglas. The present loses its constancy as a unique moment because

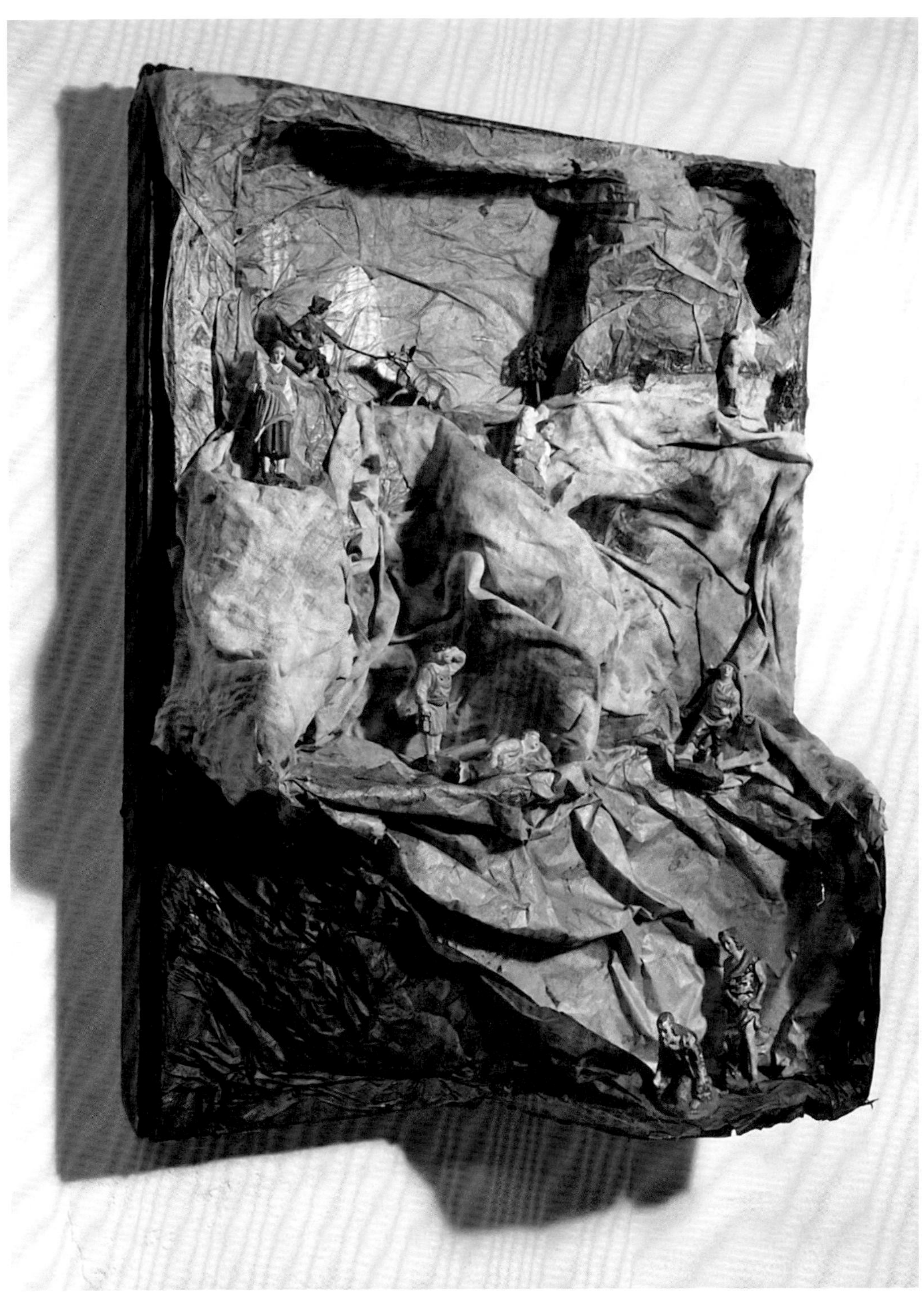

FIG. 103. Michelangelo Pistoletto, *Paesaggio* (*Landscape*), 1965. Cardboard, tissue paper, rags, and clay figures, 27 9/16 x 15¾ x 7⅞ inches (70 x 40 x 20 cm). Cittadellarte-Fondazione Pistoletto, Biella (alternate view of plate 77)

the other half of the Madonna evinces the signs of deterioration of its past-containing nowness. Similarly, just as the profane framework of the Plexiglas cube supersedes the spiritual connotations of the artifact by bracketing its lower half, so the upper half of the Madonna, standing free of the cube, undoes or suspends the secular character of the Plexiglas. *Scultura lignea* does not demand a final accommodation between the identity and difference of its two halves. By canceling out the other half, each half forces the other to disclose its inability to take hold of the whole. Tied up with the perception of a lack, the "being one" of *Scultura lignea* is of a subtractive nature. It can be described as the space or fissure between the work's two halves. *Scultura lignea* is a one that exists in view of the hole or zero denoting the infinity of the non-All within which *Scultura lignea* arises.

The logic of the non-All informing the Minus Objects can be further clarified by examining *Paesaggio* (*Landscape*, 1965; fig. 103; plate 77), a small work consisting of cardboard, colored paper, and clay figures. Cardboard and paper are combined to represent a mountain landscape with tortuous paths and grottoes, while the clay figures depict shepherds and sheep. Pistoletto has related the gestation of *Paesaggio* to the urge to do something with paper. This urge reminded him of how he had used paper as a child, when helping his father to build a *presepio*, or crèche—a naive art form intended to render a three-dimensional model of the Nativity (fig. 104). Some of the clay figures from Pistoletto's childhood had been stored away, and though he was now unmoved by religious feelings, he retrieved them. He knew at this point that, once he had definitively glued them onto cardboard, the figures would build not just another crèche but the "last crèche."[19] Pistoletto's account of *Paesaggio*'s gestation is noteworthy for two reasons. First, it confirms that the Minus Objects entailed the externalization of an experience such that the work of art and its maker are finally detached or subtracted one from the other. Second, it hints at another mechanism of subtraction through which typical elements of a crèche are recast into a landscape that epitomizes the last crèche precisely by withholding the essence of its crèchelike character, the Christ child.

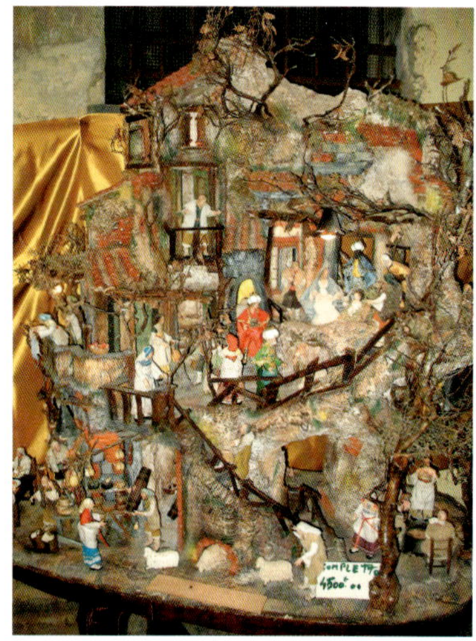

FIG. 104. A Neapolitan crèche photographed on via San Biagio dei Librai in the San Gregorio Armeno district of Naples, a major center for artists and craftsmen, December 30, 2008. Photograph by Riccardo Capitelli. Courtesy of Riccardo Capitelli

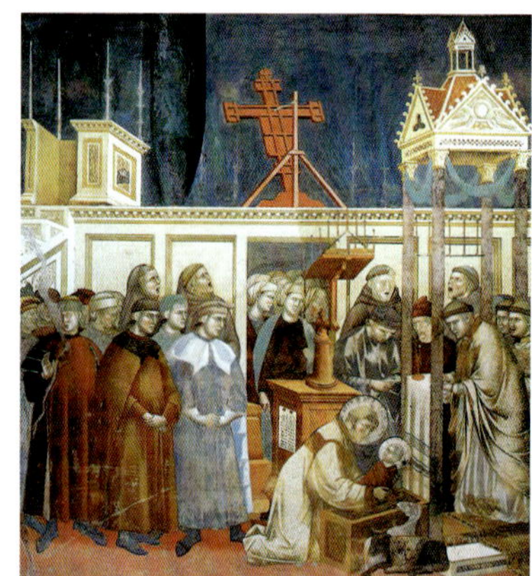

FIG. 105. Giotto di Bondone (Italian, c. 1267–1337). *Il presepe di Greccio* (*Institution of the Crib at Greccio*), from The Legend of Saint Francis (scene 13), c. 1290–95. Fresco, 106¼ x 90½ inches (270 x 230 cm). Basilica Superiore di San Francesco, Assisi

From a Christian viewpoint, the traditional crèche celebrates Christ's birth as the manifestation of God in human form and human history. Saint Francis of Assisi is credited with creating the first Nativity scene—a "living" one—at Greccio in 1223, thus starting the Western tradition of modeling crèches at Christmastime. The legend, depicted by Giotto (fig. 105), carries the implication that probably only Francis, who sided with the oppressed and the outcasts of society, was capable of grasping the message of God being born human into absolute poverty. Francis emulated Christ by practicing and advocating poverty in defiance of wealth, prestige, and the selfish acquisition of property, and he encouraged radical communion between the human, natural, and divine realms. Arguably, the gist of the crèche is Franciscan in that it links the Nativity of Christ with the revolutionary creed of a life lived sharing and upholding the example of the "poor in spirit" of whom Christ spoke. The poor are "blessed" because, in their subtracted station, they can withstand and combat the evil of power. Counting for nothing and having nothing, they cannot be "translated," or represented within a totalizing order of signs. Being poor nullifies the arbitrariness of a status quo. It bears witness to a being non-All, of an incompleteness that inheres to and interconnects human creatures before the point of infinity that Christians identify with God.

Paesaggio, however, does not exhibit the Nativity. There is no Christ child in a crib. It would seem that if *Paesaggio* stands also for a crèche—indeed the "last crèche"—it is because it denies a suprasensory plane of reality and favors either a dissemination of equally valid perspectives of sense or outright nihilism (that is, the two modern options ensuing from Friedrich Nietzsche's decree of the death of God). But the counterargument is that the absence of the Nativity scene does not necessarily erase the Franciscan sense of the crèche from *Paesaggio*. The absence of the infant Jesus encourages another course of speculation: *Paesaggio* is the ultimate crèche because it internalizes and elaborates as a Franciscan invention the revolutionary creed of poverty that the crèche embodies. By blurring origin and destination—of Christ's birth, the tradition of the crèche, its own condition as a work of art—*Paesaggio* does not limit itself to making something felt or present through its absence. Becoming a subtracted or minus crèche, *Paesaggio* stands for a work born in absolute poverty and continuing to testify to poverty. In short, *Paesaggio* is utterly Franciscan. At ease with its own dearth, its incompleteness, the work manifests its being non-All as its irreducible core and as an implement of rebellion against any pretense of mastering the All.

Featuring elements of a crèche without the son of God, *Paesaggio* stages God's absence without vouching for a nihilistic relativization of the given. It asserts its unrestricted detotalization. The loss of the infinite that God's absence would supposedly provoke suggests that, divested of its putative transcendence, the infinite may denote an immanent impossibility that human creatures cannot help confronting in their attempt to make sense of their being in the world. Each new perspective of sense is countable as one minus the infinite—not because the infinite escapes that perspective but because the positing of the one marks a limit that points to its very appearance within the infinite. No longer the symbol of a transcending unity, the one is the figure of a finitude subtracted from all the rest and eccentric to itself. *Paesaggio* is this subtracted, eccentric one.

Thus described, *Paesaggio* indicates that if God's absence leaves humankind with nothing, then the poverty of this nothing may uncover another venue of illumination. This illumination is clearly Franciscan and, I would argue, still Christian, even if not explicitly so. In fact, Christianity is the religion in which God not only becomes human but also dies for humankind. When Christ on the Cross speaks the dramatic words "My God, my God, why hast thou forsaken me?" he is attesting to the absence of God within God.[20] Christ's poverty encompasses both his life and his death and conveys the message of a helpless God. *Paesaggio* brings this message

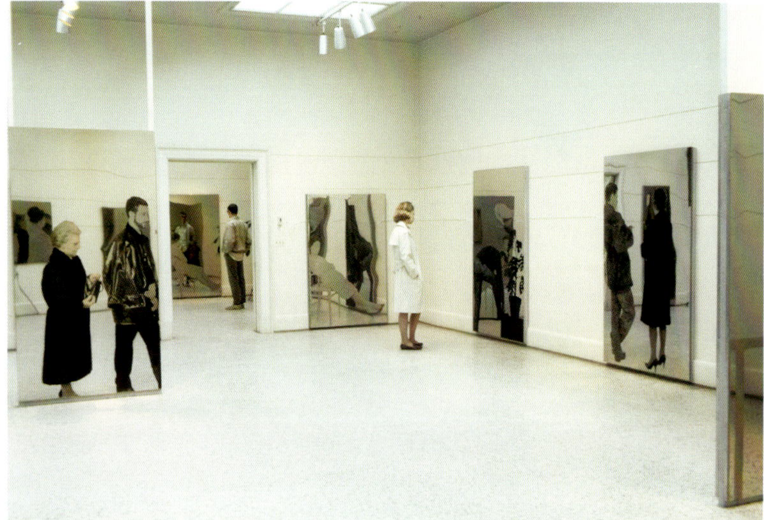

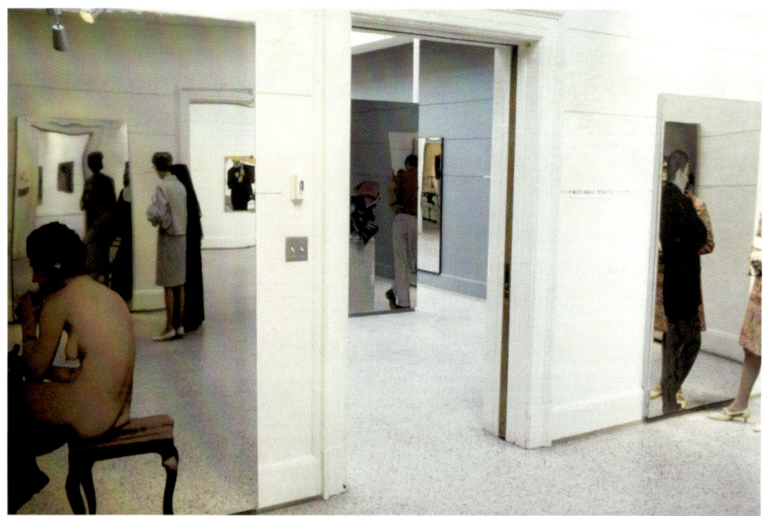

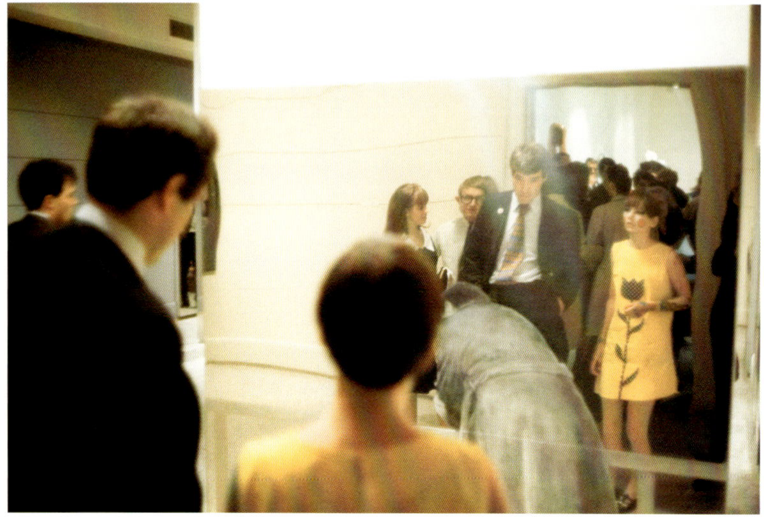

FIG. 106. The exhibition *Michelangelo Pistoletto: A Reflected World*, at the Walker Art Center, Minneapolis, spring 1966. Courtesy of the Walker Art Center, Minneapolis

into the field of human signification, turning it into a principle of art-making by showing that art-making is precisely the occurrence of a breach between the maker and his creations, the exposed and the unexposed elements of a work's composition. In so doing, *Paesaggio* predicates both the recognition and the communication of a poverty in common, of a common gap within the one and between the one and all the rest. The partaking of this shared void defies omnipotence, granting the incompleteness of reality itself while construing the infinite as the ineffable line of default that inspires and defines human endeavors.

As the awareness that being is inextricable from nothing—from a zero within which the ones appear—poverty stands opposite riches, which can be taken here to denote the confidence in being as an undivided transcending one. Poverty is a qualifier not only of *Paesaggio* but also of the relationships entertained among the components that form the Minus Objects.[21] Insofar as it upsets received notions of what is public, of ownership, and of belonging, poverty upholds the community of the non-All that the Minus Objects explore while fostering dynamics of subtraction and defiance of a status quo.

Both the recognition and the communication of a gap in common are key to the becoming-public of the artist's mind and the work of art's capacity to publicize it. Such a becoming, while integrating the singularity of what is unique with the plurality of what is general, entails a transformation of the meaning of *public*. Instead of denoting a plenitude, *public* now means a lack. This shift from plus to minus, as Esposito has demonstrated, illuminates community no longer as a "thing," a realm of counterposing and reciprocal identification among different subjects, but rather as a "non-thing," a realm within the interstices between the thing and nothing, where subjects exit themselves and acknowledge the void, the spacing that connects them in a shared nonbelonging, as the condition and the outcome of community.[22]

Casting community as a "non-thing," the Minus Objects undermine not only the category of private property—of the artist, a group, a collector, an interpreter—but also the notion of a public property expressive of a solidarity of intents or views. The new "public" character of the work, and of the artist's mind, pertains to the faculty of creating a communal being by moving to and fro within the emptiness of a void instead of the fullness of a totality. Each of the Minus Objects can be counted as one insofar as we take it as one minus the other objects and the infinity of all the rest. Each of the Minus Objects can be ascribed to an artist insofar as we take the artist as one minus the artist-authors of the other objects and the infinity of all the rest. If, as Pistoletto indicated, the Minus Objects are "liberations," then it is because they occupy and render visible a *zona franca* where the demarcations between inside and outside, proprietary and nonproprietary, origin and destination, lose their firmness. Belonging and co-belonging are revealed as inextricable from the awareness of a "nothing in common."[23] The cherishing of the poverty of a nothing in common binds the Minus Objects together. It turns their extraneousness into the signifier of a zero that favors their mutual integration by nullifying every totalization and construing them as an inconsistent multiplicity—as the specimens of a community of the non-All.

NOTHING IN COMMON

Even though the Minus Objects were meant by Pistoletto as a break with his previous work, both interrogation and transfiguration of the idea of community also characterize his mirror paintings, begun in 1962.[24] Pistoletto realized the mirror paintings by transposing enlarged photographic silhouettes of people and objects onto thin, translucent paper by means of oil paint and crayon.[25] He then positioned the life-size cutouts on the surfaces of empty, albeit reflective, stainless-steel panels to produce the effect of transparency.[26] The resulting images systematically combine still elements—the cutout figures and objects—with mobile elements represented by whoever or whatever happens to be reflected in the stainless-steel surface, depending on the work's location or place of exhibition (fig. 106). In combining stillness and movement, the mirror paintings endeavor to explore what is shared or in common between artist, work, and world even more explicitly than did the Minus Objects. Through this exploration, the mirror paintings uncover the void of a nothing in common as well as the likelihood of a community of the non-All. Indeed, the leap into a nothing and the logic of the non-All can be seen inhering to the mirror paintings by virtue of both the themes and the compositional structure of these works.

Beginning in the 1960s and until at least about 1974, Pistoletto selected and refashioned for his mirror paintings a number of subjects—mainly friends and associates, household items and pieces of furniture—that are strikingly ordinary.[27] The people, as in *Particolari di persone* (*Details of People*, 1962; plate 14) or *Donna in verde e due persone* (*Woman in Green and Two People*, 1963; fig. 107), seem especially to represent familiar types. It is as if the work of art were showing syntheses of a human being, thus emulating the mind in its dual capacity to filter outside information and develop patterns of identification useful for relating the unknown to the known. Evidently the becoming-public of the artist's mind demands that it mesh with the sphere of the generic and the customary. This enmeshing, while influential also in the contemporaneous imagery of American Pop art, in Pistoletto's work takes up traits of its own because it draws its chief inspiration from the artist's social and cultural milieu.[28]

It would be misleading, however, to assume that the apparent ordinariness of Pistoletto's subjects implies a straightforward equation between the work and a stable world of reference. In their postures and clothing, Pistoletto's cutout figures resist complete detection precisely because they tend to look undistinguished and to convey the impression

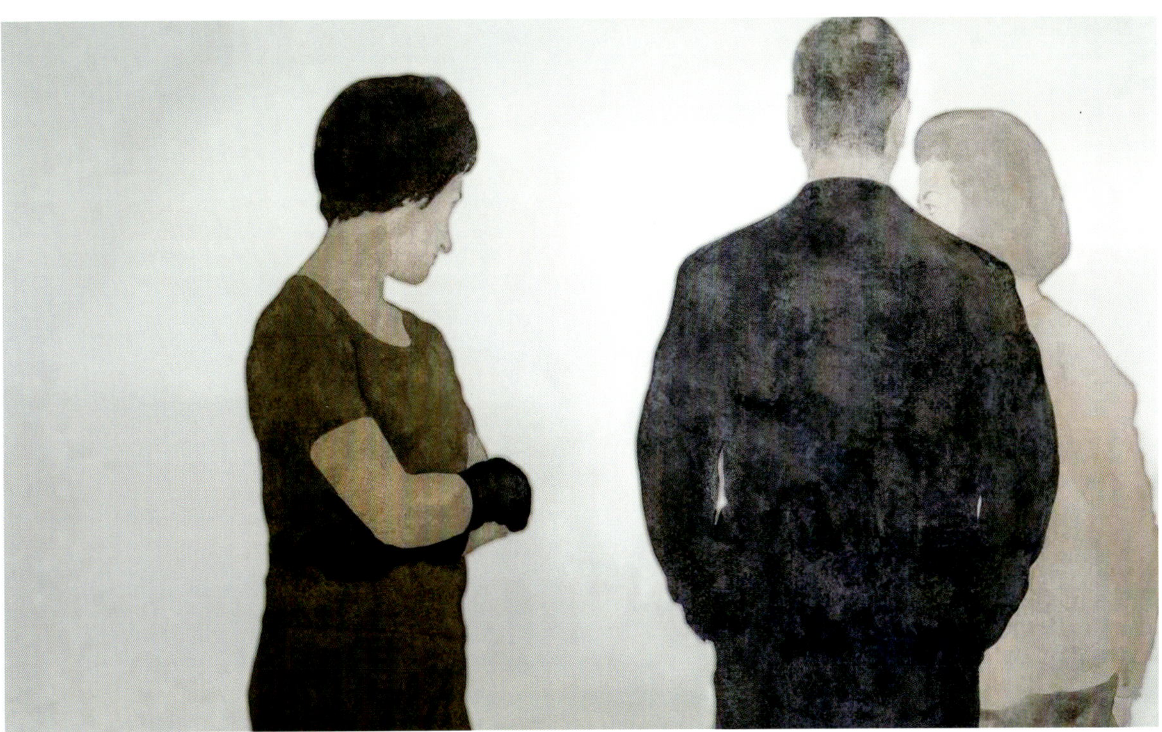

FIG. 107. Michelangelo Pistoletto, *Donna in verde e due persone* (*Woman in Green and Two People*), 1963. Painted tissue paper on polished stainless steel, 39 3/8 x 67 inches (100 x 170 cm). Private collection

of compounding a plurality of types. Nor can we speculate much about their inner states. The more the image seeks to encapsulate the essence of a plurality, the more it inclines toward a nothing and reveals the inconsistent multiplicity of its being.

The nebulousness in which Pistoletto's subjects are partially enveloped brings home the notion that there is a remainder, a margin of unknowability that the image both exposes and cherishes. As Claire Gilman has suggested, the mirror paintings demonstrate that comprehension requires a distance, a detachment on the part of the viewer.[29] By exerting and inspiring critical vigilance, the images resist the overwhelming process of spectacularization (using the term in Guy Debord's sense) that affects Western societies. The illusion induced by the speciousness of spectacle must give way to the realization that the figures comprising the mirror paintings cannot be assumed to be situated entirely within a perspective or worldview that can safely be said to be our own.[30]

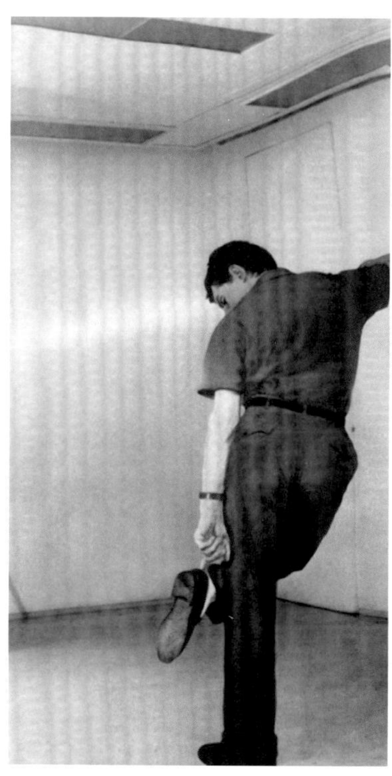

FIG. 108. Michelangelo Pistoletto, *Uomo che si tocca il piede* (*Man Touching His Foot*, 1966; plate 41)

But the dissolving sense of ownership does not result in the instauration of a firm sense of communal distribution. What presents itself as being in common is likewise unstable and unshaped. The undistinguished qualities of Pistoletto's figures point to the presence of something that cannot be fully seized through normative distinctions between what is proprietary and what is nonproprietary, what is private and what is public. Both the seated man who stares at the floor while another male figure stands to the right, his back cut off by the picture's edge (see plate 14), and the woman in green turning her head toward an unfathomable point within the picture while two other figures, a man visible from the back and a woman in profile, direct their heads toward two equally unknowable points (see fig. 107), look as if they were, each in his or her particular way, unconstrained by a representable condition of belonging. This unrepresentability is furthered by the fact that Pistoletto's figures have been extracted as fragments from photographs that sometimes showed more than what the work now incorporates (figs. 108, 109; see also fig. 240; plate 49). The seated man and the woman in green are agents of displacements between themselves and the other figures. They are generic singularities, the personifications of that being "whatever" that I have proposed above as key to the communal nature of the Minus Objects.

The figures of the mirror paintings thus intimate that the signposts of what is shared or in common should be sought in the very gap engendered by their being there. Insofar as they are fragments or entities subtracted from a former whole, the figures become an index not of subjectivity but of the void in which they now operate. Coming into sight within the picture and yet remaining partially unknown, the figures carry an unspecified quantum of nonbeing: the sense of a nothing that marks each figure as one vis-à-vis the zero of a void. But this detotalization of the given is not set forth by the figures alone. Detotalization is concordant with the effects produced by the fact that the surface of the work reflects its outside—that Pistoletto's subjects are cast and offered to view within a mirror. Entering

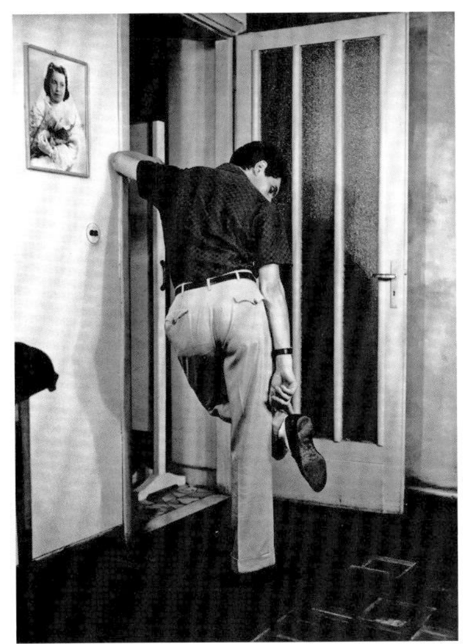

FIG. 109. The source photograph for *Uomo che si tocca il piede* (*Man Touching His Foot*, 1966; plate 41). Courtesy of Cittadellarte-Fondazione Pistoletto, Biella

the mirror, seeing oneself in the picture, does not amount to a mere amalgamation of the inside with the outside. It upsets worn conceptualizations of identity and difference while opening the one and the many to a trial of subtraction.

In fact, just as the cutout figures in the mirror paintings are related to a void, so the work's structure houses a "voided" part corresponding to the mirroring surface without figures. The beholder, whether the work's maker or its user, is reflected within that stainless-steel surface along with whatever is present in the room where the work hangs. Accordingly, the mirroring surface may be regarded as the zone of a communal encounter: the figures or still elements within the picture are joined by the mobile elements epitomized by the beholder and the realm outside the picture. But there is a question concerning the nature of this encounter and what the voided surface actually does in its actualization.

To some extent, the encounter between mobile and still elements promotes a phenomenological experience in which the subject and the object of vision are revealed in their correlation. The work of art is "open" in that, as Umberto Eco demonstrated apropos of literary texts in his paradigmatic 1962 book *L'opera aperta* (*The Open Work*), it maintains a certain degree of semantic indeterminacy so as to leave its interpretation open to public responses or to chance.[31] In 1964 the critic Tommaso Trini could therefore commend Pistoletto's mirror paintings for being a welcome reminder of our own presence within the work of art.[32] A few years later, in 1970, Alberto Boatto pointedly remarked that our entry, and the entry of our environment, into the work of art takes up the connotation and the rhythm of an "event."[33] This line of argument, while rightly underscoring the sense of a lived presence within the work, risks overlooking that the mirror paintings are also tokens of an absence—an absence already implied thematically by the nondescript quality of Pistoletto's figures, their resistance to definition as to their characters, inner states, and motivations.[34] And so it is legitimate to ask whether an unspecified quantum of nonbeing emerges in the encounter between beholder and work of art as well. My answer is that it does, and that this emergence is pivotal in construing the work, the depicted figures, and the beholder as both agents and recipients of a community.

The seated man and his slightly visible companion, and the woman in green and two other people, are positioned so that viewers simultaneously behold the cutout figures, the reflected space outside the work, and their own reflections. But the qualities of this vista are unstable. Arguably, the focal point is not only mobile and shifting within and outside the image but also virtually corresponds to a blank or zero.

Since the viewer is evidently alive—a sensing body-mind moving in space-time—his or her being here and now within the picture becomes countable as one in a subtractive fashion. That is, the moment when one sees oneself reflected in the stainless-steel surface of a mirror painting is also the moment when one realizes that one is never that "same one" in space-time. The realization is twofold. First, it becomes clear that there might be, or might have been, many other "ones" occupying the place within the reflecting surface now occupied by the beholder. Second, the cutout figures look distant from the beholder not only because they remain partially unknown but also because the discontinuity between their stillness and the beholder's mobility makes itself felt. For the beholder, being inside the picture turns into being outside oneself. In the self-reflection within the mirror, the beholder assumes undistinguished features analogous to those perceivable in the cutout figures. Yet, as a generic singularity, the beholder is enabled to experience time affectively, without an external or internally ticking clock.[35] This affective nowness, resistant to a reckoning in terms of progression or addition, arises by virtue of the fact that the beholder perceives him- or herself within and outside the picture as one minus the countless other ones crossed out by the very perception of his or her own transient appearance. The beholder's perception is inextricable from the realization that its focal point, the place in the mirror where he or she is reflected, is virtually empty or voided—the dwelling of an open-ended multiplicity without ones.

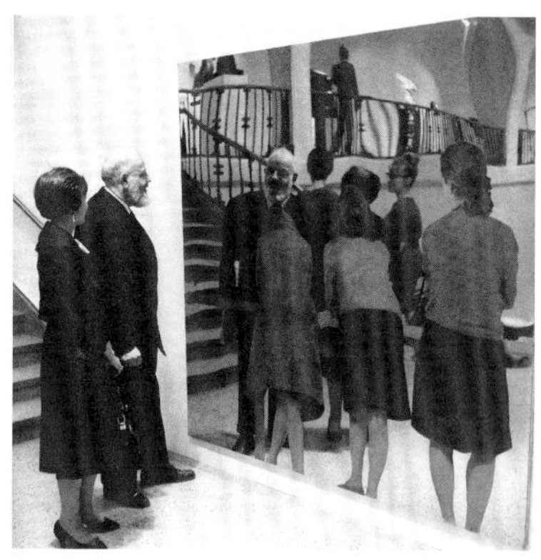

FIG. 110. Installation view of *Tre ragazze alla balconata* (*Three Girls on a Balcony*, 1964; plate 27), in the exhibition *Michelangelo Pistoletto: A Reflected World* at the Walker Art Center, Minneapolis, spring 1966. Courtesy of the Walker Art Center, Minneapolis

That the encounter between beholder and work of art is bracketed by an unspecified quantum of nonbeing is at times evidenced by the very composition of the mirror paintings. In *Tre ragazze alla balconata* (*Three Girls on a Balcony*, 1964; plate 27), for example, and *Lui e lei alla balconata* (*He and She on a Balcony*, 1966), the cutout figures are depicted from the back while either leaning over or standing before the divisory line of a balcony. The line of the balcony rail cuts an edge that separates the figures from another space, which they cannot enter but can only behold. This undetermined space must be figured as a blank or zero from the viewpoint of both the beholder and the cutout figures. By momentarily filling that blank, the beholder discovers his fluctuating status (figs. 110, 111). He perceives himself as the subject of his self-reflection as well as the object included within the gaze of the observed work, in which some of the silhouetted people are presumably looking at the very area that reflects his likeness. By unmitigatingly staring at that blank, the silhouettes do not simply function as doubles of the beholder. They also signal that there is a limit signified, for the silhouettes by the line of the balcony, and for the beholder by the actual frame of the work. Both the cutout figures and the beholder can be described as agent-recipients of a vision of the changeability of the same thing. That is, the beholder looks at the back of the figures and at himself while becoming cognizant that the work is returning his gaze and that his presence within the mirror is passing. The cutout figures, remaining partially nondescript by turning their backs to the beholder, exemplify the possibility of their looking at anyone or anything that may be passing within the blank of the work's mirroring surface.

This same, changeable thing of which the cutout figures and the beholder are agent-recipients is neither inside nor outside the work of art. It is the communal domain of a focal point generated anew each time.

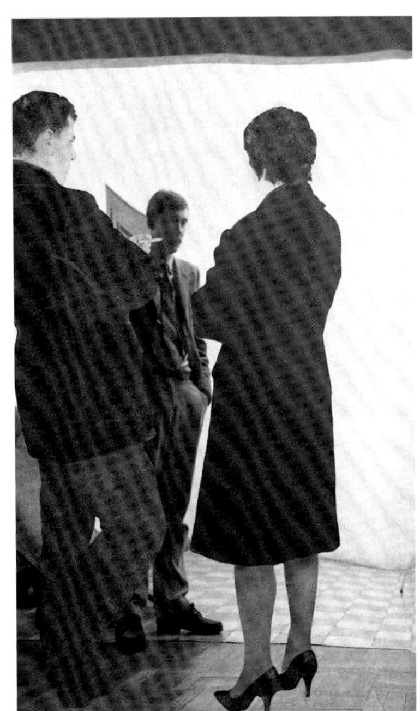

FIG. 111. *Due persone* (*Two People*, 1963–64; plate 20) as photographed in Pistoletto's house on via Cibrario in Turin. The artist Erik Dietmann is reflected between the two painted figures. Photograph by Paolo Bressano. Courtesy of Cittadellarte-Fondazione Pistoletto, Biella

In *Tre ragazze alla balconata* and *Lui e lei alla balconata*, the composition of the work stages its still and mobile components at a crossroads of being and nonbeing. Staring out over the balcony, the cutout figures are the keepers of the unpredictability of what has appeared and what will appear. The work of art is poised to explore the communality of this fleeting appearance, which interlaces distance and closeness, absence and presence, while challenging the establishment of a status quo within and outside the mirroring surface.

The surface of the mirror paintings thus indexes a nothing in common by indicating that any presence visible on its reflecting plane is inscribed within the void of an absence. The beholder shares with whoever or whatever is represented in the mirror paintings the appearance of a space-time that folds itself within the vortex of its being and nonbeing vis-à-vis all the rest. It is in this vortex that the still and the moving components—cutout figures, beholder, and whatever is reflected of the room where the work hangs—come to exist and coexist within the picture. The paradigmatic achievement of the mirror paintings consists in demonstrating that existence and coexistence are not the outcomes of a leveling. Rather, they may occur via dynamics of proximity and remoteness that, answering to a logic of the non-All, evince the work of art's ontological incompleteness.

When he talks about his mirror paintings, Pistoletto suggestively argues that before the mirror we are individuals and also community: we are both viewers and viewed, and we can look ahead and backward, reconsidering the past and sensing the future.[36] Pistoletto's argument grants the mirror paintings the faculty of encompassing heterogeneous dimensions in ways that do not accommodate the omnipotent impulse to totalization but demystify it. The encompassing performed by the mirror paintings shows that a work of art may push the dynamics of appearance so far that it yields the recognition that reality cannot be totalized as a permanent state of things. Who or what appears within the mirror paintings is divided and is impervious to univocal definitions not because there is another reality out there, or hidden behind appearance, but because appearance is the wavering domain in which the mind and the senses may experience reality at its most uncanny. Reality is revealed as unaccountable by perception or conception alone, or through the individuation of a content isolated from form; it is tantamount to a gap within appearance itself, signaling the impossibility of figuring the All that the mirror paintings expose. Such an impossibility is no restraint in the mirror paintings. Rather, it is the hallmark of a poverty. It militates for a community whose components—still and mobile, alone and together—can finally appear as one minus infinity and as infinity minus one.

THE THRESHOLD

In a text of 1968 titled "Between," Pistoletto hinted at the prospect of sharing the experience of the void by calling attention to the oft-neglected gulf of space that lies between two bodies or objects. While he stated his interest in "the passage between objects more than in the objects themselves," he complained that the "vice of considering things only in their fullness does not leave us enough time to consider that in actual fact we can only circulate in the physical channels which are left open to us by objects. . . . We consider only the presence of the objects and not the empty space in which we actually live."[37]

Arguably, the mirror paintings and the Minus Objects had already dealt with the communal implications of that empty space Pistoletto wrote of in 1968. The mirror paintings associate the disclosure of a void with the realization of the impermanence that characterizes the contact between work, beholder, and outside context. The Minus Objects suggest that what is in common lies in the void made apparent by the very gap engendered by each object within itself as well as with regard to its author and the other objects. Whether transfigured within the realm of things, as with the Minus Objects, or surmised in the lived moment of the work's contact with a human being, as with the mirror paintings, the idea of community in Pistoletto's early practice clearly points to something that people may experience. These experiential overtones of Pistoletto's works were given another twist in his solo exhibition at the Galleria L'Attico, Rome, in February 1968.

The L'Attico show invited the active participation of the public in a fantastical mise-en-scène staged by the artist. Pistoletto furnished costumes and hats of various epochs, borrowed from the Cinecittà film studios, and visitors were invited to select their attire (fig. 112). At the gallery's entrance, while dazzled by a 1,000-watt beam of light, visitors would see their own reflections in a mirror painting placed just in front of them. Moving inside the gallery, they would find three other mirror paintings, while the entire space had been transformed into a landscape constructed of cardboard rocks and Roman columns, also from Cinecittà (see fig. 92).[38] Since the visitors could fashion and refashion their guises at will, they were cast in a situation reminiscent of Luigi Pirandello's stories—for instance, his 1924 novel *Uno, nessuno e centomila* (*One, No One, and One Hundred Thousand*)—in which the protagonists reckon with the illusoriness of their belief in a stable personal identity. Pistoletto's show operated as a sort of choreography of the self, as the four mirror paintings provided the means for people to see themselves reflected while shifting between their one and many masked selves.[39]

Reviewing the show, Alberto Boatto argued that Pistoletto's mingling of fiction and reality had an emancipatory effect. For, assuming the camouflaged traits of an artificial self, life "appeared less embarrassed" with itself before the reflecting surface of the four mirror paintings. Inviting

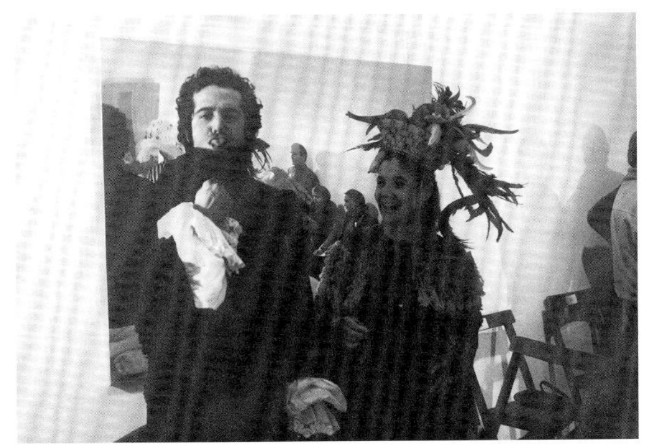
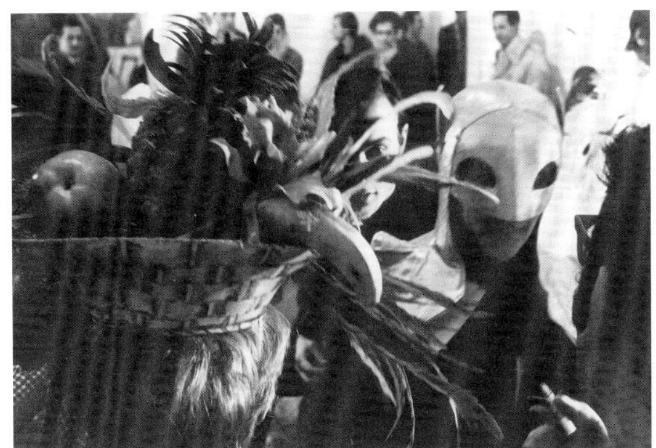
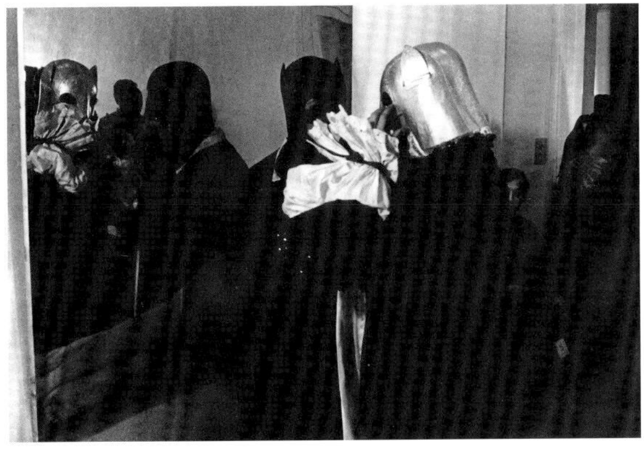
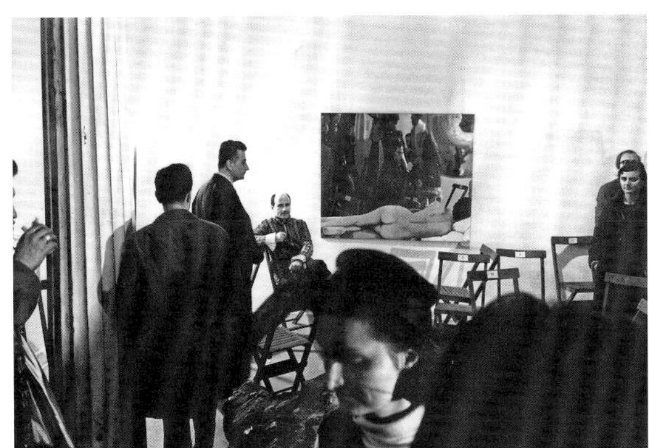

FIG. 112. Visitors in costumes from Cinecittà at the opening of Pistoletto's exhibition at Galleria L'Attico, Rome, February 1968. The figures in the top left photograph are Pino Pascali and Efi Kounellis. Photographs by Claudio Abate. Courtesy of Cittadellarte-Fondazione Pistoletto, Biella

visitors to improvise other possible identities, Pistoletto's mise-en-scène suggested that only by extending fiction and theatricality into the realm of life would it be possible to recover some sense of unity.[40] In the catalogue for the show, Giulio Carlo Argan argued that Pistoletto's modus operandi epitomized a "poetics of the Threshold": it had overcome the need of anchoring artistic activity to this or that kind of work.[41] The artist's installation rendered manifest that one's life occurs within at least two spaces, if not more, and that one always stands at the threshold, neither here nor beyond. As they partook of the fantastical choreography of the self, visitors to the show experienced the gap or void of standing at the threshold, an experience that reminded Argan of death itself. For Argan, Pistoletto was not offering a representation of death but, well aware that "nothing" is not the opposite of "being," made death felt as an imperceptible presence occupying the same space-time as life.[42]

Argan's reference to death is noteworthy. It brings us back to Bataille, the thinker who went furthest into the experience of modern community and whose views are influential in today's thinking about community. For Bataille, the sense of a being-in-common arises when, confronted with the death of a fellow being, a living person can subsist only outside her- or himself.[43] This movement outside of oneself is key to establishing the impossible communion among mortal beings, or death as community. As Jean-Luc Nancy has indicated, commenting on Bataille, community is revealed in the death of others "because death itself is the true community of *I*'s that are not *egos*. It is not a communion that fuses the *egos* into an *Ego* or a higher *We*. It is the community of *others*."[44] Community is not a project of synthesis or a productive and operative subject, but rather "the spacing of the experience of the outside, of the outside-of-self."[45]

Reconsidered via Bataille and Nancy, Argan's insight into the faculty of Pistoletto's works to evoke death provides a further avenue into those works' positing of a sense of community. Argan understands the threshold as the horizon of dislocation for a fluid artistic practice that is neither here nor beyond. Pistoletto's emphasis on the gulf that lies between two bodies or objects conveys the same inclination toward associating what is shared or in common with the spacing of the outside-of-self. If visitors to the L'Attico show could grant Pistoletto's interest in the gulf between different bodies or objects, if they could feel the imperceptible presence of death as suggested by Argan, it was because they went outside themselves. They experienced the spacing of the outside-of-self while observing the impermanence of their costumed selves in the reflecting surfaces of the mirror paintings and vis-à-vis the compound of fiction and reality produced throughout the gallery installation.

The L'Attico show gave a new twist to the performative bent inherent in the mirror paintings as well as the Minus Objects. The poverty of a nothing in common was enacted by the visitors and by the artist himself. As they mingled and separated within the gallery space, they could discover that what they shared was precisely the gap at the threshold

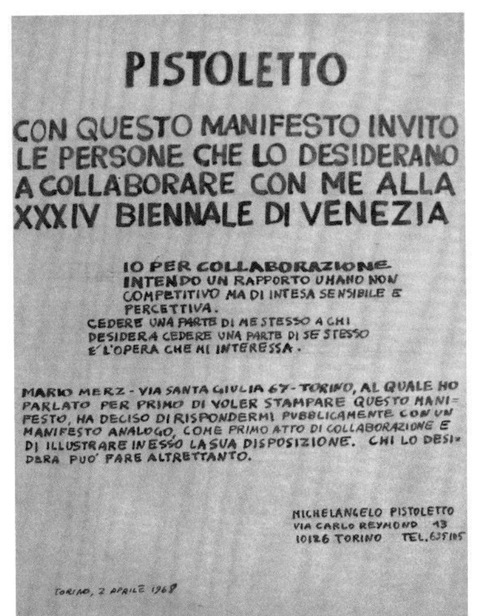

PISTOLETTO

CON QUESTO MANIFESTO INVITO LE PERSONE CHE LO DESIDERANO A COLLABORARE CON ME ALLA XXXIV BIENNALE DI VENEZIA

IO PER COLLABORAZIONE INTENDO UN RAPPORTO UMANO NON COMPETITIVO MA DI INTESA SENSIBILE E PERCETTIVA.
CEDERE UNA PARTE DI ME STESSO A CHI DESIDERA CEDERE UNA PARTE DI SE STESSO E' L'OPERA CHE MI INTERESSA.

MARIO MERZ - VIA SANTA GIULIA 67 - TORINO, AL QUALE HO PARLATO PER PRIMO DI VOLER STAMPARE QUESTO MANIFESTO, HA DECISO DI RISPONDERMI PUBBLICAMENTE CON UN MANIFESTO ANALOGO, COME PRIMO ATTO DI COLLABORAZIONE E DI ILLUSTRARE IN ESSO LA SUA DISPOSIZIONE. CHI LO DESIDERA PUO' FARE ALTRETTANTO.

MICHELANGELO PISTOLETTO
VIA CARLO REYMOND 13
10126 TORINO TEL. 635105

TORINO, 2 APRILE 1968

FIG. 113. "Manifesto della collaborazione" (Manifesto of Collaboration), a flyer printed by Pistoletto prior to the 34th Venice Biennale, summer 1968. Courtesy of Cittadellarte-Fondazione Pistoletto, Biella

between the one and the many appearances of who they were and became in themselves as well as in intercourse with others. In this exhibition, it was no longer objects alone but persons and objects together that publicized the pivotal assumption that community is the disclosure to its members of their finitude, of the impossibility of their gaining mastery of the All. In publicizing a community of the non-All, theater and theatricalization were paramount.

In fact, during the three years following his show at L'Attico, Pistoletto devoted himself almost exclusively to theatrical activities. Already in 1967, together with the actor Carlo Colnaghi, the artist Maria Pioppi, and other friends from diverse backgrounds, Pistoletto had founded a theater troupe called Lo Zoo (The Zoo).[46] From May 1968 to October 1970, Lo Zoo performed seventeen pieces in village squares, cities, discotheques, and mainstream theaters (see pp. 81–107 above).[47] Lo Zoo actors operated in keeping with the medieval tradition of the commedia dell'arte, dressing in extravagant costumes and focusing on storytelling and a few ritualized actions, such as marking the theatrical space with a white canvas spread on the ground and having a master of ceremonies narrate the plot development with the aid of a storyboard.

What is noteworthy for the purposes of this discussion is that, despite its unorthodox modus operandi, Lo Zoo did not try to overcome the gap between fiction and reality. The title "Zoo," as well as its subtitle, "those who stand beyond the cage," derived from a remark by Colnaghi, who had apparently said that he found himself "in the same position as the lion in a cage."[48] While the image of a cage certainly denotes a state of entrapment, Lo Zoo sought not so much simply to break free of the "prison" as to develop an awareness of the cage, which, in its wider ramifications, hampers human psychophysical needs and creative potentials. Accordingly, instead of extending their plays into the environment and joining their audience, Lo Zoo actors encouraged conversations with the public while at the same time highlighting the threshold that separated their performances from the situation of the spectators. At that time, the point of highlighting the threshold was partially missed, as some Italian critics, eager to frame Lo Zoo within an international perspective, linked Pistoletto's theater to the Living Theatre of Julian Beck in the United States and the "poor theatre" of Jerzy Grotowski in Poland.[49] However, Pistoletto distanced himself from these theatrical trends, which aimed at dissolving the barrier between actors and audience.[50] Henry Martin, an art writer and active participant in some of Lo Zoo's performances, insisted that Lo Zoo created an artificial "stage" of uncertainty and pause, an area to be conceived in terms of "work" and "representation."[51]

Lo Zoo did not endorse the attempt to bring art into life that has characterized some of the fringes of avant-garde and neo–avant-garde movements from Dadaism to Situationism and Fluxus. On the contrary, Lo Zoo's radicality lay elsewhere, in recognizing the barrier between the artistic and the living dimensions. Lo Zoo's performances kept the theatrical illusion in order to show its impermanence and fragmentation and to use that illusion as a deterrent against the far more delusional presumption that one might achieve a mastery of the whole. The threshold between the actors and the audience brought home to both the possibility of experiencing the proximity of the outside-of-self. Lo Zoo found in the gap, in the void of a nothing in common, the mobile horizon of a communal distribution that would neither conform to the given nor take for granted the richness of a homogeneous substance that systematically grounds the lives of individuals.

LACK AND EMBARRASSMENT OF RICHES

Defying the assurance of a status quo, Pistoletto's artistic practice in the 1960s uncovered the prospect of construing a communal domain that, rather than striving to achieve a plenitude, would be reflective of the inconsistent multiplicity of being (fig. 113). Community coincides with a lack, and so it draws inspiration from the recognition of the poverty of a nothing in common. Whether it is an object or a theatrical performance, the work of art attests to this nothing in common by emerging as one minus infinity or as infinity minus one. Its oneness is inextricable from the vortex of its being and nonbeing vis-à-vis all the rest. As it exists by means of subtraction, the work of art contains the traces of its inscription within the zero of a void. The artist's mind becomes public and the work of art publicizes this becoming insofar as both share the experience of inhabiting that void. The inclination toward the public and what is in common conveys a fondness for multiplicity and difference.

During the 1960s and 1970s, notwithstanding the strong political climate that characterized those decades (fig. 114), Pistoletto never explicitly linked his work to a precise political ideology, let alone a party. Yet, by addressing the idea of community, his work was intrinsically militant and political. It is noteworthy that the year in which Pistoletto installed the Minus Objects in his studio saw the publication, also in Turin, of Mario Tronti's *Operai e capitale* (*Workers and Capital*),[52] a landmark book on the theory and practice of Italian *operaismo* (workerism)[53] that argued that workers had no need to mediate with the hegemonic classes of the capital. Despite what the Marxist *doxa* maintained, workers embody the true force of human labor: it is they who can decide the destiny of capitalism and not vice versa. According to Tronti, the working class should abandon any plan of compromising with the ruling classes and instead pursue the "refusal of work" as a strategy to subtract itself from the alienating conditions of the factory and disrupt the dynamics of power that are the basis of social inequality. Pistoletto's Minus Objects are not exactly the artistic analogue of Tronti's paradigmatic thesis of the "refusal of work,"[54] but subtraction is paramount in Tronti's thinking as well as in the making of the Minus Objects, in the mirror paintings, and in the activities of

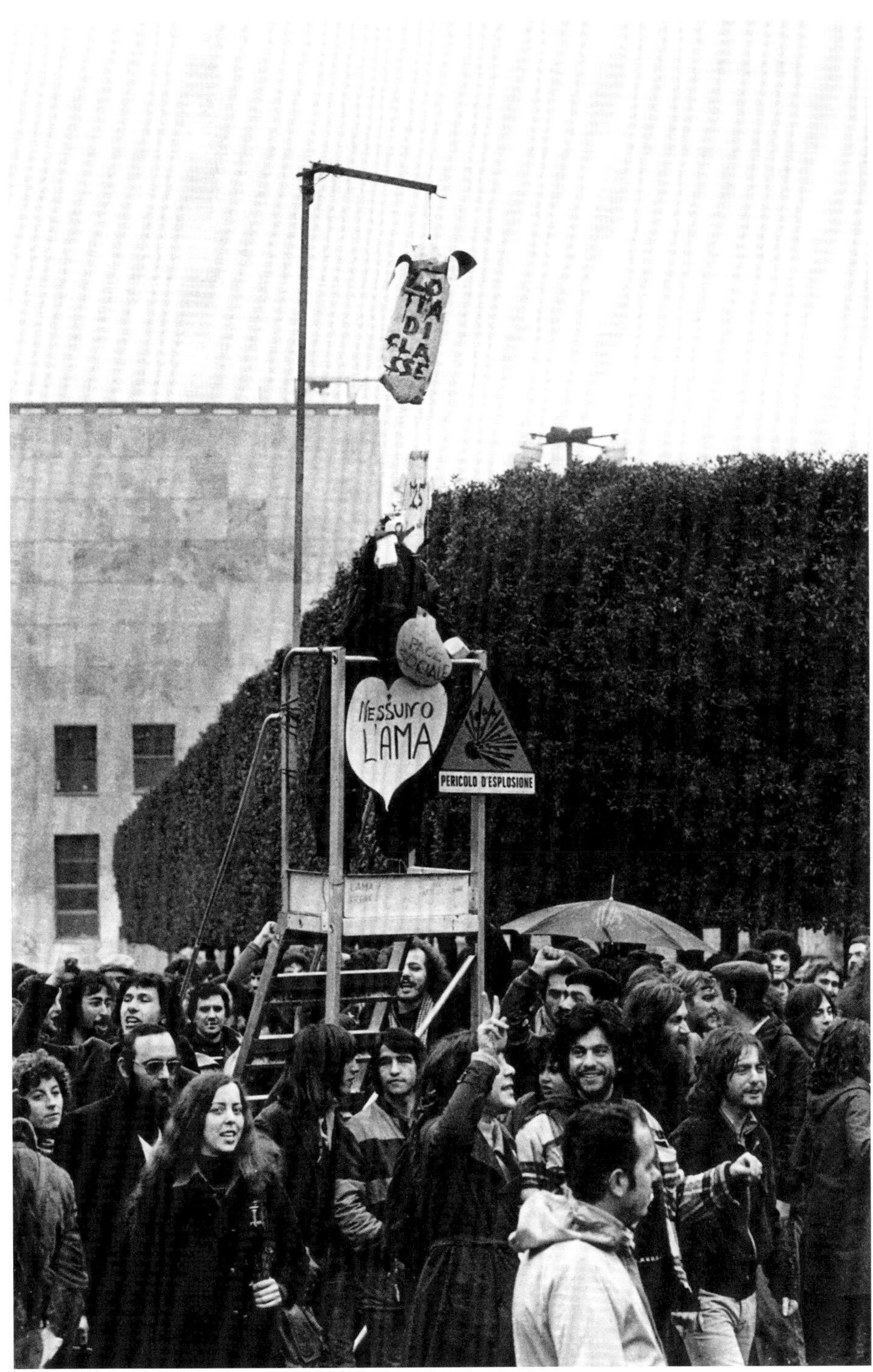

FIG. 114. The protest of the "Metropolitan Indians" during union leader Luciano Lama's assembly at the University of Rome, February 17, 1977. Photograph by Tano D'Amico. Courtesy of Tano D'Amico

Lo Zoo. Pistoletto's practice vindicates, as does Tronti's *operaismo*, the option of noncompliance with a given state of affairs. It positivizes subalternity, alienation, and distance by turning them into propellants for the creation of alternative modes of experience and knowledge.

Moreover, the community evoked by Pistoletto's work foreshadows in part the views of contemporary post-Marxist thinking—often inspired by the operaistic vision of the 1960s—which theorizes the forming of a multitude of singularities that does not require governing by a head because it is itself the living energy of the global system.[55] Disentangled from a prefixed domain of signs or powers, the multitude violates the hierarchical division of labor and realizes itself via the appropriation and public condivision of the "general intellect"—of those very cognitive and communicative resources that capitalism nourishes, objectifies, and exploits.[56] Similarly, Pistoletto's practice deprivatizes the artist's know-how and publicizes the mind that infringes disciplinary boundaries and externalizes itself through works in which some ordinary and readymade elements have been adapted and transformed into new forms. In these works, subtraction means rejecting institutionalized modes of artistic production while militating for an ever-growing consciousness of the differential space-times of a community of the non-All.

Arguably, even as it stands out as a crucial aspect of Pistoletto's stance in the 1960s, the advocacy of a community of the non-All is also what may make that stance appear rather opaque, even untimely, when viewed through the framework of the discourses and interests that currently prevail in artistic culture. Beginning with the 1980s, the last decades have witnessed a display of wealth and ostensible feelings of fulfillment in the increasingly globalized apparatus of institutions (art galleries, museums, mass media, auction houses, and so on) that supervises the production and reception of contemporary art. Eager to prove its planetary resonance, that apparatus has expanded itself at various levels. As segments of the art world have merged with the worlds of commerce, fashion, and advertising, and accordingly strengthened their ties with the realm of finance and speculative capitalism, the art world has tightened its embrace with the emerging field of creative industries.[57]

The resulting artistic culture can hardly tolerate the uncanny proposition of a non-All. Whether seeking the sensationalistic sanction of popular media or willing to criticize and reform the present social order, artistic practice today is often inclined to take for granted a totality that can be regarded as referencing the whole of the "given" interrelatedness of the world system in which we live. Even if only imaginatively, the figurability of the All becomes a priority. The All functions as a sort of big fantastical Other. It is the tacit referent for artistic practice that can therefore indifferently posit the totality of the extant as its more or less implicit object of reflection and negation as well as of deference and ratification. The end result of these appeals to the All is the removal of the sense of ontological incompleteness that may inhere to artistic practice as well as to human signification. While twentieth-century avant-garde and neo–avant-garde movements had delved into that incompleteness, the current lure of totalization and the ostentation of riches could be regarded as two facets of the same art-world hubris—of the same self-confident attempt to dispel any uncertainty about the work of art's position within the real.[58]

The dissonance between today's affluence and craving for mastery of the All and Pistoletto's stance in the 1960s cannot be explained away simply in terms of a rift between past and present orientations in artistic culture. It is therefore worth proposing that there be a confrontation: that the contending parties meet, and show themselves, right where they collide the most. In other words, the militancy for the idea of a non-All at the core of Pistoletto's stance in the 1960s may be viewed as the source of a collision that enlightens that stance not only as an object of the bygone past, but also in its capacity to transmigrate into the present and lay open some of today's contradictions. It is the very dissonance of Pistoletto's militancy for the non-All that exposes the flaws and the embarrassment of riches in the world of contemporary art as it has developed over the last decades. This paradox can be appreciated if we look at how and why today's art world pursues, sustains, and exploits some of the very demands and discoveries that have been associated here with a logic of the non-All, even though it does so from another perspective and with a different agenda.

Artistic culture today regards what is shared or in common as a natural and cultural wealth that can be privatized, as most often happens, or freely accessed and appropriated regardless of ownership and copyright. In both cases, community and the communal domain cease entailing the presence of a gap and take up the traits of an objective, underpinning ground of the All.[59] Thus artistic culture internalizes, albeit unwittingly, some implications of a non-All—the search for a communal domain, the genericness of the work of art, the blank of its origin and destination—and yet at the same time relies on the assuredness of the given and perpetuates a belief in a totalizing principle of reality. The recognition of the void or zero of an inconsistent multiplicity of being is blurred by a systematic relativization of artistic production, a dissemination of the many that hints at an undivided one as the substratum of the many's transcending unity.

A similar situation is noticeable apropos of the notion of poverty, which a community of the non-All posits in opposition to the notion of riches, linking poverty with the awareness of a nothing inextricable from being, and riches with the confidence in being per se. As the German philosopher Peter Sloterdijk has argued, there is no reason why the West should feel inhibited about its historically unprecedented affluence; it should, rather, make creative use of it (fig. 115).[60] For Sloterdijk, creative use of riches flows into a practice of widespread generosity molded upon the archetypal relationship between mother and infant, so as to orient civilization toward an ongoing clarification of the multidimensional faculties—biological and technological—correlated to the idea of "maternity."[61] But it is hard to argue that this has always been the case

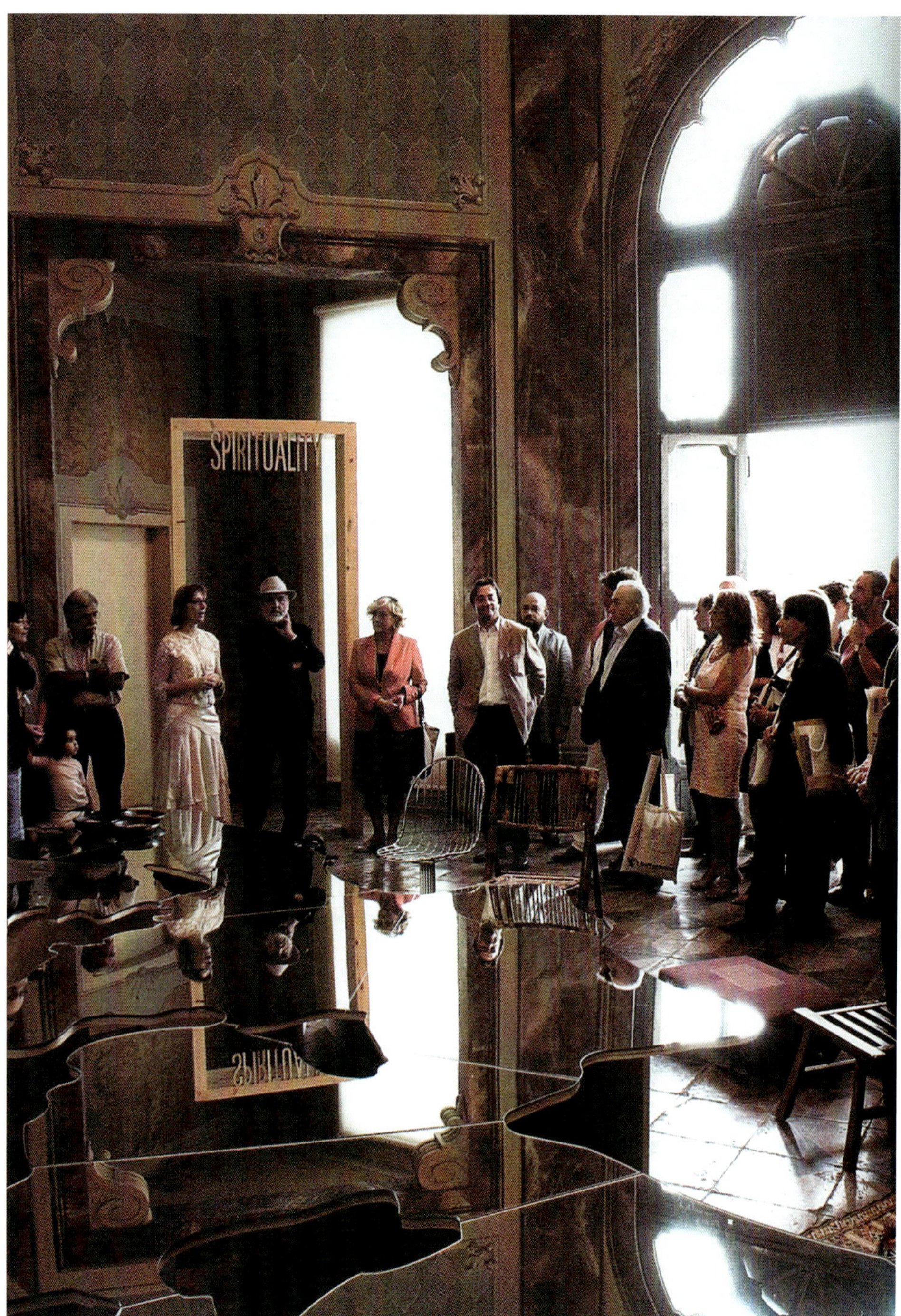

FIG. 115. The opening of the exhibition *Pistoletto e Cittadellarte: la mensa delle culture* (*Pistoletto and Cittadellarte: The Table of Culture*) at the Galleria Civica di Modena, Palazzina dei Giardini, Modena, September 16, 2005–January 8, 2006. Pistoletto is at center left. Photograph by M. Malagoli. Courtesy of Cittadellarte-Fondazione Pistoletto, Biella

in the world of contemporary art. Showing wealth, praising celebrity, maintaining that everything is possible in art while eulogizing its products for their monetary worth, the world of contemporary art is not necessarily involved in unrestricted giving. Rather, the more it depends on its own system of codes and discourses in order to justify its opulence, the less that world is able to find a purpose outside itself. In short, the riches of the art world may easily yield to the nihilistic belief that life is purposeless and that received values (in this case pertaining to art) can be kept only in their empty, vestigial forms because nothing is of importance anymore.

This means that the art world's confidence in being per se is something of a sham. Being is not severed from a quantum of nonbeing. Despite the pretense of nonbeing having been banned along with its associated taboos, such as negativity and death, nonbeing makes itself felt as soon as the art world is exposed to the lack upon which its apparatus unfolds. Poverty is not the opposite of riches but its disguised caretaker. The sense of a nothing can be regarded as the occult substratum (again, the undivided one) of the totalizing grip to which the art world seems so disposed to fall prey. If certain segments of today's art world are characterized by an embarrassment of riches, it is probably not because artistic culture has overcome its past tensions and, experiencing a moment of plenty, can now guarantee the ontological status of works of art. Rather, the excess of wealth is probably due to the fact that artistic culture has feared the implications of its past and capitalized on its legacy in ways that cover up the poverty of a void or nothing in common.

Far from being obsolete, Pistoletto's stance in the 1960s may therefore transmigrate to the present. This is no smooth passage, however. It provokes a collision of perspectives that illuminates both past and present as it shows how and why the hubris of today's art world simultaneously exploits and covers up what a militancy for the non-All had tried to confront in its compelling complexity. To some extent, the contemporary allure of the All cannot dispense with the legacy of a logic of the non-All. The new apparatus of the art world, for the sake of its own maintenance, must tame and reorient parts of that legacy while expunging its detotalizing message. And so it is paradoxically today's embarrassment of riches that may allow one to look at the mirror paintings, the Minus Objects, and Lo Zoo as works that continue to have a say precisely by virtue of the seeming obsolescence of their reclamation of a poverty in common.

The void or zero can become a source of inspiration and exploration as well as of removal and repression. As it tends toward the latter course, the hubris of riches predicts that the work of art will be a thing so resonant within the external world of reference as to be representative of the fabric of reality and have no dialectical ties with a "non-thing." Opting for the former course, the advocacy of a non-All demands that the work of art be unconcerned with this or that world of reference and expose the incompleteness of reality itself, not because there is a hidden core of reality that eludes it but because the work's emergence in the real is inextricable from the opening of a void.

A reconsideration of Pistoletto's works from the 1960s suggests that the sense of a communal plurality must be sought in the gap, in the tension of the one work divided within itself and vis-à-vis all the rest. Pistoletto's works are a cogent indication that there is no reason to mourn the loss of infinity, because infinity is not outside or inside the work of art. It corresponds to the lack: to the point of impossibility that the work of art epitomizes as soon as it acknowledges the problem of its ontological status.

1 The special nature of Pistoletto's installation is indirectly confirmed by the fact that in 1997, in the context of Documenta X, the artist realized an edition of clay tiles reproducing Bressano's photographs of the Minus Objects. The edition, entitled *Oggetti in meno—souvenir*, consisted of fifty-five sets of seven tiles (each $3\frac{1}{8}$ x $3\frac{15}{16}$ and $4\frac{5}{16}$ x $5\frac{7}{8}$ inches [8 x 10 and 11 x 15 cm]); one reproduces an overview of the Minus Objects as seen in the studio in 1965, and the other six are of individual works. It is as if Pistoletto (unwittingly? ironically?) wished to claim for these images a cult status like that ascribed to many artistic "masterpieces" that are reproduced on a variety of household keepsakes, such as plates, ashtrays, boxes, and so on.

2 For a recent account of the phenomenon, see Michael R. Taylor, "Bruce Nauman: Mapping the Studio, Changing the Field," in Carlos Basualdo and Michael R. Taylor, *Bruce Nauman: Topological Gardens*, exh. cat. (Philadelphia: Philadelphia Museum of Art, 2009), pp. 45–63.

3 As Taylor indicates (ibid., p. 51), the genre of documentary photography of artists' studios culminated in 1960 with the publication of Alexander Liberman's book *The Artist in His Studio*, which soon acquired a cult following among artists and students of art.

4 The idea of the inconsistent multiplicity of being is pivotal in Alain Badiou's endeavor to rethink Western ontology without reiterating the traditional dichotomies between identity and difference, the one and the many. See especially Badiou, *Being and Event* (1988), trans. Olivier Feltham (London: Continuum Press, 2005), and *Logiques des mondes: l'être et l'événement* (Paris: Seuil, 2006).

5 Alberto Boatto was probably the first to link Pistoletto's works with the idea of community, arguing, apropos of the Minus Objects, that the object no longer belonged to the private life of Pistoletto but to his life together with his associates, and so it implied the support of a "comunità minoritaria" (minority community). See Boatto, *Pistoletto: dentro / fuori lo specchio* (Rome: Fantini, 1970), p. 19.

6 Such a metamorphosis, as it reflects an attempt to counter the threat of isolation to which artists and works of art are exposed in modern society, can be traced back to the second half of the eighteenth century. For it was then that artists, beginning to produce works for the anonymous audience of public exhibitions, were increasingly creating isolated objects made by and for isolated subjects. See, among other sources, Oskar Bätschmann, *The Artist in the Modern World: A Conflict between Market and Self-Expression* (Cologne: Du Mont, 1997); and Thomas E. Crow, *Painters and Public Life in Eighteenth-Century Paris* (New Haven, Conn.: Yale University Press, 1985).

7 See Alfred Gell, *Art and Agency: An Anthropological Theory* (Oxford: Clarendon Press, 1998), for the crucial argument that, from an anthropological viewpoint, there is no need to separate actions and things because any artifact is a source and target of social forces and should be considered the same as a person or social agent.

8 Here and thoughout this essay I use the word *community* to refer to things as well as people, or to both.

9 These strikes were announced as early as 1962–63, when 90,000 workers rebelled against harsh factory discipline and poor pay. They culminated in the widespread protests of the *autunno caldo* (hot autumn) of 1969. The phenomenon saw the emergence of a new political subject, the "mass worker," or non-specialized worker, often an unskilled migrant from the south ready to do any kind of work. It was especially these workers' protests that, insofar as they were autonomous and scornful of union mediation, epitomized a desire to fight no longer for a better job but for the abolishment of labor *tout court*. During these years, two important journals provided a forum for analyses and political theories that exceeded the orthodoxy of the traditional Left: *Quaderni rossi*, founded in 1961 by Raniero Panzieri and Mario Tronti, and *Classe operaia*, founded in 1963 by Tronti, Alberto Asor Rosa, and Massimo Cacciari. See Steve Wright, *Storming Heaven: Class Composition and Struggle in Italian Autonomist Marxism* (London: Pluto, 2002); and Giuseppe Trotta and Fabio Milana, eds., *L'operaismo degli anni Sessanta: da "Quaderni rossi" a "Classe operaia"* (Rome: DeriveApprodi, 2008). See also Liliana Lanzardo, *Personalità operaia e coscienza di classe: comunisti e cattolici nelle fabbriche torinesi del dopoguerra* (Rome: Franco Angeli, 1989).

10 See Maurice Blanchot, *The Unavowable Community* (1983), trans. Pierre Joris (Barrytown, N.Y.: Station Hill Press, 1988); Jean-Luc Nancy, *The Inoperative Community* (1986), trans. and ed. Peter Connor, foreword by Christopher Fynsk (1991; Minneapolis: University of Minnesota Press, 2008); Giorgio Agamben, *The Coming Community* (1990), trans. Michael Hardt (Minneapolis: University of Minnesota Press, 2007); and Roberto Esposito, *Communitas: origine e destino della comunità* (1998; Turin: G. Einaudi, 2006).

11 Pistoletto, in conversation with the author, Biella, June 29, 2009.

12 See Jacques Lacan, *Le séminaire de Jacque Lacan, livre XX: encore*, 1972–1973, ed. Jacques-Alain Miller (Paris: Éditions du Seuil, 1975). On the cogent ontological implications of Lacan's "pas-toute," see Slavoj Žižek, *The Puppet and the Dwarf: The Perverse Core of Christianity* (Cambridge, Mass.: MIT Press, 2003), esp. chap. 3.

13 On Pistoletto's Minus Objects, see Michelangelo Pistoletto, "Oggetti in meno," in Galleria la Bertesca, Genoa, *Michelangelo Pistoletto*, exh. cat. (Genoa: Galleria la Bertesca, 1966), pp. 15–16; Germano Celant, "Arte Povera" (1968), in Celant, *Arte Povera / Art Povera* (Milan: Electa, 1985), pp. 49–57; Tommaso Trini, "Nuovo alfabeto per corpo e materia," *Domus* (Milan) 470 (January 1969), pp. 45–46, and "Michelangelo Pistoletto: il labirinto dell'individuazione," *Domus* 478 (September 1969), p. 55; Boatto, *Pistoletto: dentro / fuori lo specchio*, pp. 16–20; the artist's interviews with Celant in Forte di Belvedere, Florence, *Pistoletto*, ed. Germano Celant, exh. cat. (Milan: Electa Firenze, 1984), pp. 29–66; Bruno Corà, *Michelangelo Pistoletto: lo spazio della riflessione nell'arte* (Ravenna: Essegi, 1988); and the essays collected in *Michelangelo Pistoletto: Oggetti in meno, 1965–1966*, ed. Ulrich Loock and Edelbert Köb (Bern: Kunsthalle Bern, 1989).

14 Pistoletto associated the Minus Objects with the idea of an exhibition in which he would not be recognized "as protagonist, as individual, as a typical figure" because the outlook would be that of a "collective" or group show. See Pistoletto's interview with Germano Celant (Genoa, May 1971) in Forte di Belvedere, *Pistoletto*, p. 41 (my translation).

15 Agamben, *The Coming Community*, p. 1.

16 The idea of subtraction has acquired new philosophical worth and implications in Badiou's rethinking of ontology. For Badiou, something truly inventive would have to appear "subtracted" from the criteria of intelligibility that rule the dynamics of inclusion and exclusion within the context of its apparition. See "On Subtraction" (1991), in Badiou, *Theoretical Writings*, trans. and ed. Ray Brassier and Alberto Toscano (2004; London: Continuum Press, 2006), pp. 105–20.

17 Michelangelo Pistoletto, "The Minus Objects" (1966), here cited from *Michelangelo Pistoletto: A Minus Artist* (Florence: hopefulmonster, 1998), p. 14 (translation modified slightly).

18 See the artist's 1984 interview with Celant in Forte di Belvedere, *Pistoletto*, pp. 29–32 (my translation).

19 See the artist's 1971 interview with Celant in ibid., p. 52 (my translation).

20 I am adopting the suggestive and far more complex arguments of Slavoj Žižek, who takes Christ's words as an indication that in the Christian religion, with its concept of the Trinity, God is the gap between God and man. See Žižek, *The Puppet and the Dwarf*, esp. pp. 13–33. See also Slavoj Žižek and John Milbank, *The Monstrosity of Christ: Paradox or Dialectic?* ed. Creston Davis (Cambridge, Mass.: MIT Press, 2009).

21 It is possible, as Jean-François Chevrier has proposed, to regard the Minus Objects as the origins of Arte Povera—the group of Italian artists that includes, along with Pistoletto, Giovanni Anselmo, Alighiero Boetti, Pier Paolo Calzolari, Luciano Fabro, Piero Gilardi, Jannis Kounellis, Mario and Marisa Merz, Giulio Paolini, Pino Pascali, Giuseppe Penone, Emilio Prini, and Gilberto Zorio. See Jean-François Chevrier, Benjamin H. D. Buchloh, and Catherine David, "The Political Potential of Art 2," in *Politics-Poetics: Documenta X—The Book* (Ostfildern-Ruit: Cantz, 1997), p. 628. However, whether my remarks on poverty and Franciscanism may shed fresh light on the Arte Povera movement is a question extraneous to the scope of the present essay. My use of the term *poverty* is specifically meant to explore the idea of community in Pistoletto's practice in the 1960s, and it inspires a course of speculations that do not entirely coincide with the understanding of *arte povera* as originally formulated by Germano Celant in 1967. That year, referring to the "poor theatre" theorized by Jerzy Grotowski in 1965, Celant introduced the term *arte povera* to qualify a new artistic practice open to contingency and determined to overcome the limitations of language while reducing its materials to the barest and most essential. In an overtly politicized mode, Celant endorsed Arte Povera for its attack on consumerism and its pursuit of a thorough osmosis of life and art, individual and world. See Germano Celant, "Arte povera—im spazio" (1967), in *Arte Povera*, ed. Carolyn Christov-Bakargiev (Phaidon: London, 1999), pp. 220–21; and Celant, "Arte Povera: appunti per una guerriglia," *Flash Art* 5 (November–December 1967), p. 3. Celant's interpretation surely tended to construe Arte Povera as a practice that defied the status quo—artistic, social, or existential—through a process of radical reduction of its forms and subsequent withdrawal from the conventional modes of artistic production and reception. But it would be hard to say that reduction and withdrawal suffice to account for the dynamic of subtraction and the logic of the non-All that I associate with the "poverty" characterizing the communal nature of Pistoletto's works. Finally, it is worth noticing that a link between art, poverty, and Franciscanism can be traced in the literature on Alberto Burri. His *sacchi*, consisting of ripped and stitched sackcloth often covered with daubs of red paint, could easily evoke the cowl of Saint Francis and the artist's upbringing in an Umbrian village near Assisi, as well as a sense of wounds and stigmata that resonate with both the life of Francis and the recent traumas of World War II. In the

catalogue essay for Burri's exhibition at Galleria Marlborough in Rome in December 1962, Cesare Brandi emphasized the poor material of Burri's *sacchi* and pioneered an understanding of poverty in both its formal and conceptual implications. For the link between poverty and Franciscanism in Burri's literature and its subsequent resonance in Italian art, see Nicholas Cullinan, "Made in Italy: fatto a mano, fatto a macchina, già fatto, rifatto," in *Il confine evanescente: arte italiana, 1960–2010*, ed. Gabriele Guercio and Anna Mattirolo (Rome: Electa, 2010), pp. 225–61, esp. pp. 232–33.

22 See Esposito, *Communitas*, esp. pp. xiii–xiv, 148–50.

23 This is a key point in Esposito's *Communitas*. On the need to rethink the "nothing" in its connections with community and worldliness, see also Jean-Luc Nancy, *The Sense of the World* (1983), trans. and with a foreword by Jeffrey S. Librett (Minneapolis: University of Minnesota Press, 1997).

24 On Pistoletto's mirror paintings, see, among other treatments, the essays in Galleria la Bertesca, *Michelangelo Pistoletto*; Martin Friedman, *Michelangelo Pistoletto: A Reflected World*, exh. cat. (Minneapolis: Walker Art Center, 1966) n.p. ; Boatto, *Pistoletto: dentro / fuori lo specchio*; Corà, *Michelangelo Pistoletto: lo spazio della riflessione nell'arte*; Germano Celant and Alanna Heiss, eds., *Pistoletto: Division and Multiplication of the Mirror* (Milan: Fabbri, 1988); and Claire Gilman, "Pistoletto's Staged Subjects," *October* 124 (Spring 2008), pp. 53–74.

25 For more on Pistoletto's method of creating the mirror paintings, see Suzanne Penn's essay in this volume, pp. 143–67 below.

26 In his untitled text for the catalogue of the 1964 exhibition of the mirror paintings at the Ileana Sonnabend Gallery in Paris, Tommaso Trini remarked that Pistoletto worked "by means of transparency"; here cited from Forte di Belvedere, *Pistoletto*, p. 30 (my translation).

27 In the 1960s, this was clearly noted by Martin Friedman, who spoke of the "apotheosis of the ordinary" apropos of the mirror paintings; see Friedman, *Michelangelo Pistoletto: A Reflected World.*

28 Underscoring the rootedness of Pistoletto's work in its geocultural context of Turin, Ettore Sottsass was one of the first to object to the tendency, widespread in the art literature of the period, to associate the mirror paintings with the Pop imagery of Roy Lichtenstein, James Rosenquist, Claes Oldenburg, and others. See Ettore Sottsass Jr., "Pop e non pop: a proposito di Michelangelo Pistoletto," *Domus* 414 (May 1964), pp. 32–35. On Pistoletto's mirror paintings vis-à-vis Pop imagery, see also Boatto, *Pistoletto: dentro / fuori lo specchio*, and Gilman, "Pistoletto's Staged Subjects."

29 Gillman, "Pistoletto's Staged Subjects," p. 64.

30 See ibid., p. 69.

31 Umberto Eco, *The Open Work*, trans. Anna Concogni, introduction by David Robey (Cambridge, Mass.: Harvard University Press, 1989).

32 See Trini's 1964 text for the Sonnabend Gallery, Paris, here cited from Forte di Belvedere, *Pistoletto*, p. 30.

33 See Boatto, *Pistoletto: dentro / fuori lo specchio*, p. 9.

34 Claire Gilman, in "Pistoletto's Staged Subjects," p. 64 n. 17, indicates that there is a "fundamental disjunction" between the domain of the cutout photographs and that of the beholder's reality.

35 That temporal duration can be conceived as a space in which one "dwells within time itself" is a key notion in Francisco J. Varela's radical attempt to bridge the gap between cognitive science, Buddhist meditative psychology, and philosophical traditions of phenomenology. See Varela, "The Specious Present: A Neurophenomenology of Time Consciousness," in *Naturalizing Phenomenology: Issues in Contemporary Phenomenology and Cognitive Science*, ed. Jean Petitot et al. (Stanford, Calif.: Stanford University Press, 1999), pp. 266–314. See also Varela, Evan Thompson, and Eleanor Rosch, *The Embodied Mind: Cognitive Science and Human Experience* (Cambridge, Mass.: MIT Press, 1991).

36 Michelangelo Pistoletto, in conversation with the author, Biella, June 29, 2009.

37 Michelangelo Pistoletto, "Between" (1968), in Pistoletto, *A Minus Artist*, p. 22.

38 During the month of the exhibition, three cameramen walked the rooms with Pistoletto, helping him to make films (screened on the closing night of the exhibition) featuring himself as the protagonist. For Pistoletto, these films were "creative convergences" between the director's work and his own work. See Marcello Venturoli, "Dialogo con Pistoletto," in *Tutti gli uomini dell'arte* (Milan: Rizzoli, 1968), here cited from Corà, *Michelangelo Pistoletto: lo spazio della riflessione nell'arte,* p. 85 (my translation). The films included Antonio De Bernardi's *La vestizione* (*The Rite of Dressing*); Renato Dogliani's *Il giornale* (*The Newspaper*); Pia Epremiam's *Pistoletto & Sotheby*; Renato Ferraro's *Comunicato speciale* (*Special Announcement*); Mario Ferrero's *Michelangelo andrà all'inferno* (*Michelangelo Will Go to Hell*); Plinio Martelli's *Maria Fotografia* (*Maria Photography*); Paolo Menzio's *Frankenstein prossimamente* (*Coming Soon: Frankenstein*); Marisa Merz's untitled film; Ugo Nespolo's *Buongiorno, Michelangelo* (*Good Morning, Michelangelo*); and Franco Giachino Nichot and Cesare Tacchi's *Vernissage* (*Preview / Opening*).

39 The four works were *Lo sgabello* (*The Stool*, 1962–66); *Donna nuda di schiena* (*Nude Woman from the Back*, 1962–66); *Lui e lei abbracciati di schiena* (*He and She Embracing from the Back,* 1962–68); and *Lui e lei—Maria e Michelangelo* (*He and She—Maria and Michelangelo,* 1962–68).

40 See Alberto Boatto, "Pistoletto: dissipazione come procedimento," *Cartabianca* (Locarno), March 1968, pp. 9–12.

41 Giulio Carlo Argan, *Michelangelo Pistoletto*, exh. cat. (Rome: Galleria L'Attico, 1968), here cited from Forte di Belvedere, *Pistoletto*, p. 66.

42 See ibid., pp. 65–71.

43 See Georges Bataille, "La limite de l'utile", in *Oeuvres complètes* 7 (Paris: Gallimard, 1976), pp. 245–46.

44 Nancy, *The Inoperative Community,* p. 15.

45 Ibid., p. 19. For Bataille's role in the modern thinking about community, see also Esposito, *Communitas*, pp. 115–42.

46 On the Zoo, see Matthias Dusini, "Theatre, Art, Politics, and the 'Zoo'—The Performative Traits in Michelangelo Pistoletto's Work," in *Michelangelo Pistoletto: azioni materiali*, ed. Matthias Dusini and Silvia Eiblmayr (Cologne: Walter König, 1999), pp. 115–26; and Marco Farano, Maria Cristina Mundici, and Maria Teresa Roberto, *Michelangelo Pistoletto: il varco dello specchio; azioni e collaborazioni* (Turin: Edizioni Fondazione Torino Musei, 2005). Pistoletto's book *L'uomo nero: il lato insopportabile* (Salerno: Rumma Editore, 1970)—or *The Minus Man: The Unbearable Side*—is a vivid autobiographical account of the Zoo's activities.

47 For further discussion of Lo Zoo's activities, see Claire Gilman's essay in this volume, pp. 81–107 above.

48 Cited from Maria Teresa Roberto, "Davanti allo specchio, al di qua delle sbarre: lo Zoo dagli antefatti a *L'uomo nero*, 1966/1970," in *Michelangelo Pistoletto: il varco dello specchio*, p. 21 (my translation). In *L'uomo nero* (p. 79), Pistoletto wrote that the "Zoo" referred to that state of imprisonment in which the human animal finds itself as soon as it becomes aware of its vital need for creative expansion.

49 See, for instance, Gillo Dorfles, "The Meetings of Amalfi," in *Arte Povera e Azioni Povere*, here cited from the English translation in *Michelangelo Pistoletto: azioni materiali*, p. 73; and Germano Celant, "Zoo," *Sipario* 291 (July 1970), p. 19. Grotowski was also Celant's reference in inventing the term *arte povera* in 1967; see Celant, "Arte Povera—im spazio" and "Arte Povera: appunti per una guerriglia."

50 In particular, Pistoletto criticized Grotowsky's theater, arguing that, despite its seeming desire to establish a direct relationship between people, it remained elitist. See Pistoletto, "Il momento della negazione?" *Sipario* 268–69 (August–September 1968), pp. 16–17.

51 Henry Martin, "Uno Zoo non è una balia," *Data* 1 (1971), n.p.

52 Mario Tronti, *Operai e capitale* (Turin: Einaudi, 1966).

53 See Guido Borio, Francesca Pozzi, and Gigi Roggero, eds., *Gli operaisti* (Rome: DeriveApprodi, 2005). See also Steve Wright, *Storming Heaven*, and *L'operaismo degli anni Sessanta.*

54 Tronti's thesis finds its artistic analogue in the practice of nonwork (or "work in struggle") pursued by the Italian artist Francesco Matarrese since 1978, when he announced with a telegram his refusal of "abstract work" in art and his subsequent research for "what comes after art." See Gabriele Guercio, "Rifiuto," in *Anni Settanta,* eds. Marco Belpoliti, Gianni Canova, and Stefano Chiodi (Milan: Skyra, 2007), p. 419.

55 See Antonio Negri and Michael Hardt, *Empire* (Cambridge, Mass.: Harvard University Press, 2000); and Paolo Virno, *A Grammar of the Multitude: For an Analysis of Contemporary Forms of Life* (2002), trans. Isabella Bertoletti, James Cascaito, and Andrea Casson, foreword by Sylvère Lotriger (Cambridge, Mass.: Semiotexte, 2004).

56 In the famous "fragment on machines" in his *Grundisse* (1857–58), Karl Marx meant by "general intellect" the forming of an abstract knowledge, independent from production, that constitutes the chief productive force of the capitalistic system. Here cited from Marx, *Grundisse: Foundations of the Critique of Political Economy (Rough Draft)*, trans. and with a foreword by Martin Nicolaus (London: Penguin Books, 1993), pp. 690–712.

57 The new "creative" industries seek to maximize the inventiveness of producers and consumers in myriad converging fields of media: cinema, television, communications technology, fashion, video games, and advertising. See, among other treatments of this topic, John Hartley, ed., *Creative Industries* (Malden, Mass.: Blackwell, 2005); Henry Jenkins, *Convergence Culture: Where Old and New Media Collide* (New York: New York University Press, 2006); and Nigel J. Thrift, *Non-Representational Theory: Space/Politics/Affect* (New York: Routledge, 2007), pp. 29–55.

58 It is too early to claim that the recent global economic crisis will halt this hubris of the art world. Even if that were to be the case, the understanding of artistic phenomena may well continue to avoid the issue of their ontological incompleteness.

59 This view of the All may also characterize post-Marxist thinking when it theorizes an ethics of political democracy within and against the Empire. See, for example, Michael Hardt and Antonio Negri, *Commonwealth* (Cambridge, Mass.: Belknap Press of Harvard University Press, 2009).

60 See Peter Sloterdijk, *Sphären*, vol. 3, *Schäume* (Frankfurt am Main: Suhrkamp, 2004) pp. 671–711.

61 Ibid., pp. 754–55.

"THE COMPLICITY OF THE MATERIALS" IN PISTOLETTO'S PAINTINGS AND MIRROR PAINTINGS

SUZANNE PENN

Hindsight affords an advantageous perch from which to trace an artist's trajectory. It is all too tempting to say that mirrors were a seminal part of Pistoletto's art-making from the very beginning, when he looked into one to draw his first self-portrait at age fourteen. But using a mirror as a tool to help render his own image as a teenager did not lead Pistoletto as directly as one might suppose to incorporating the element of reflection into his work.

Pistoletto has repeatedly recounted the revelatory moment that led to the mirror paintings, which occurred in 1961 when he saw his own reflection in the glossy black background of the canvas painting *Il presente* (*The Present*):

> In 1961, on a black background that had been varnished to the point that it reflected, I began to paint my face. I saw it come toward me, detaching itself from the space of an environment in which all things moved, and I was astonished. I realized that I no longer had to look at myself in another mirror, that I could copy myself while looking at myself directly in the canvas. In the next painting I turned the figure around, because the painted eyes were still artificial, whereas those of the reflection could be as real as those of the figure that now was on the surface of the painting looking into the painting.[1]

This story suggests a happy accident, but a detailed consideration of the paintings that preceded *Il presente* reveals the early explorations that led more methodically to that transformative moment than this condensed, oft-repeated explanation implies. Pistoletto has emphatically stated: "The materials were important in the evolution of my work. It is not that I arrived at the mirror for a conceptual reason; I arrived at the mirror through a material evolution. I did not arrive through the representation of the figure alone, but with the complicity of the materials, from the beginning."[2] The beginning to which he refers is the point in his life, around age twenty, when he gained financial independence from his parents and rented his first studio space.[3]

From the outset, Pistoletto established finite parameters to help him determine what he might create as a contemporary artist, or, more specifically, as a contemporary Italian artist, as indicated by his comment "I had to begin where all Italian art began, with the icon. For me, the icon was always there as the basic problem of the spirituality I had to develop through art."[4] It was a form that Pistoletto felt he could harness to assist him in creating meaningful contemporary art: "The icon was the place of the fascination and the problem at the same time. I had to find the solution to the problem through something that came from the past, the icon."[5] In many instances throughout his career, Pistoletto would invoke art forms or materials with potent associations in order to advance his work. It was not an act of hubris that his first works of art were self-portraits modeled after religious icons. Rather, these works represented the coalescence of a traditional form with gravity and meaning for Pistoletto—the icon—and the most readily available subject—himself. From this starting point, Pistoletto embarked on his lifelong practices of self-portraiture and of referencing the subjects of religious and old master paintings. From the very beginning, the art of the past fueled his intention to make contemporary art.

There is a sense of urgency and immediacy in the earliest surviving work by Pistoletto, a small *autoritratto* (self-portrait) from 1955, which he modeled after an icon and painted on a piece of discarded wood (the shoulders of the half-length frontal figure are truncated by the narrow width of the board [see figs. 38, 116]). More likely than not, the board came from his father's art-restoration studio, the source for many of his art-making materials and the place where in his youth he had honed his artistic hand skills by assisting his father with the restoration of paintings.[6]

Even now, a half century after he last worked there, Pistoletto can describe in vivid detail the array of paintings that passed through his father's studio.[7] Many of them came from castles and villas in northern Italy, as aristocratic families—no longer affluent—divested their assets. Various works of art made their way to Turin for restoration and resale to a new generation of collectors made wealthy by the industrial enterprises of the twentieth century. The many hours Pistoletto spent in the studio assisting in the treatment of paintings, and the visits he made with his father to churches and villas to examine works of art in need of restoration, afforded a particularly rich art education. In those formative years he acquired a deep admiration for paintings of the past and a thorough understanding of their materials and techniques. He would continue to mine these experiences throughout his career, both in the subjects he depicted and in his choice and use of materials.

While Pistoletto's earliest paintings, those created in the years 1955–59 (fig. 116), were inspired by icons and made with materials and processes he had used in the course of restoring old master paintings, they were also greatly influenced by the work of his contemporaries. Pistoletto was well aware of the abstract and non-representational paintings by artists such as Jackson Pollock and Emilio Vedova: "Pollock was the protagonist of the *informale* or no-form, but the no-form for me had to be included in the form. I could not make something like Vedova did. I couldn't make something like that alone; it had to be circumscribed by my face, and there also had to be something flat behind, limiting the figure."[8]

In 1956–57, Pistoletto made a foray into abstraction with several self-portraits in which the head fills the entire canvas and the face is created with gestural brushstrokes and multiple layers of paint. In one of these (see fig. 33), he built up the paint and selectively wiped it away with a rag as he swept his arm like a window washer to expose broad swathes of a multicolored underlying paint layer during his rendering of the face. In another self-portrait (plate 1), the canvas is not painted with artists' commercial tube colors but with dry pigments and mastic varnish,

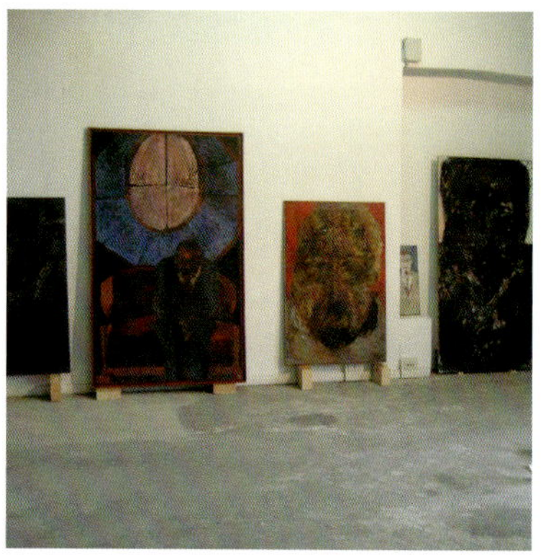

FIG. 116. Interior of Cittadellarte, Biella, 2009. Displayed against the wall, from left to right, are *La folla ingrata* (*The Thankless Crowd*, 1958–59; fig. 34), *Uomo sul sofà* (*Man on the Sofa*, 1958; fig. 117), *Autoritratto* (*Self-Portrait*, 1956; plate 1), *Autoritratto* (*Self-Portrait*, 1955; fig. 38), and *Autoritratto* (*Self-Portrait*, 1957; fig. 33). Photograph by Suzanne Penn

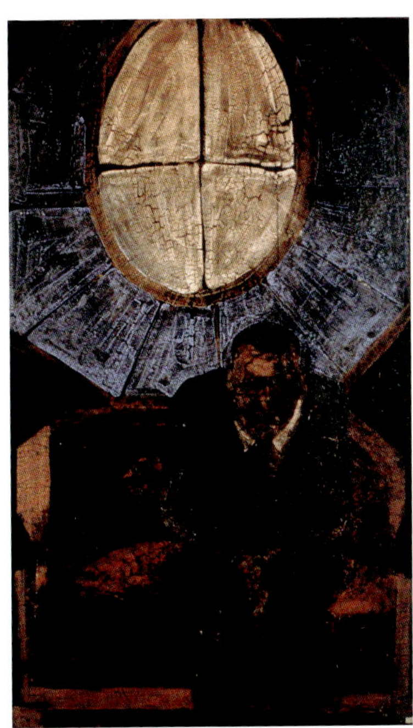

FIG. 117. Michelangelo Pistoletto. *Uomo sul sofà* (*Man on the Sofa*), 1958. Oil and acrylic on canvas, 78¾ x 47¼ inches (200 x 120 cm). Collection of the artist

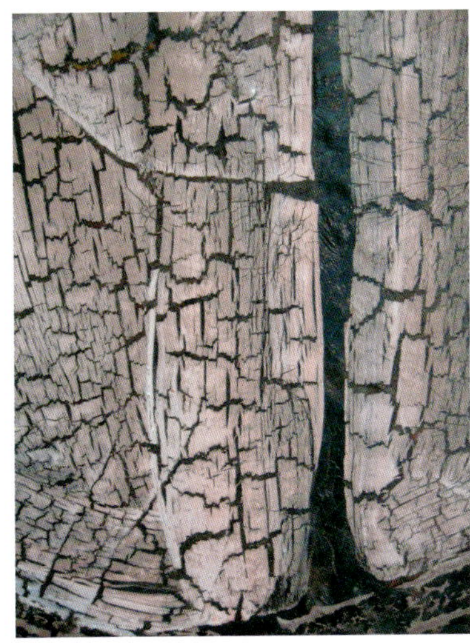

FIG. 118. Detail of intentionally induced craquelure in Pistoletto's painting *Uomo sul sofà* (*Man on the Sofa*, 1958; see fig. 117). Photograph by Suzanne Penn

materials Pistoletto had used in his father's restoration studio for retouching losses in damaged paintings. In making this portrait, Pistoletto used the mastic varnish to bind the dry pigments in clumps, creating a series of craggy layers. He also applied the varnish with broad swipes of his brush, interspersing the syrupy medium amid the paint layers as well as on the painting's surface.[9]

As he did for the majority of his paintings on canvas, Pistoletto created this self-portrait on a type of open-weave fabric that his father used in the restoration studio for lining paintings. The fabric was favored for this use as it readily conformed to the reverse of old canvases and over time could be removed and replaced as needed. It was somewhat more challenging to use as a support on which to *make* a painting, however, as it required a heavy priming layer to fill in the interstices of the open weave. Here, as in many similar instances throughout his career, Pistoletto's skill and inherent understanding of materials allowed him to seize readily available or unconventional materials and adapt them for his purposes.

In another nod to his time spent in the restoration studio, and to his technical expertise, Pistoletto induced the paint layers in *Uomo sul sofà* (*Man on the Sofa*, 1958; fig. 117) to crack and contract by applying lean paint over a more medium-rich and unctuous black paint, so that the underlying black color would be revealed in the broad cracks formed as the uppermost paint layer dried and contracted (fig. 118). He used the materials here as a conduit to the past and as an active agent in problem solving. As he explained: "Craquelure, coming from restoration, is something I appreciated. I like the idea that through this system the materials are not static, that the materials are reactive. Making the craquelure was using something familiar that was helping me to solve the work. It couldn't be solved with something flat."[10] In allowing the black underlayer to be seen within the cracks, Pistoletto was using craquelure as a means of linking figure and ground. He continued this exploration in *La folla ingrata* (*The Thankless Crowd*, 1958–59; see fig. 34), in which the black background layer asserts itself in between small blocks of color applied over it with a brush (fig. 119), the entire composition resembling an exploded view of the craquelure in *Uomo sul sofà*. In *La folla* (*The Crowd*, 1959; plate 2), the abstract pattern over the canvas is made up of multiple faces whose linear delineations nest within the black background.

When Pistoletto prepared his next canvas, *Esperimento* (*Experiment*, 1959; plate 3), with a black priming layer, he noticed the shadow cast on its surface by his head and shoulders as he worked, and he decided to "leave the shadow black and cover everything else in silver paint." In doing so, the surface phenomenon of the shadow was transformed into an image embedded in the painting. "But that was not enough for me," he recalled. "I was looking for space, trying something . . . I wanted to create some space on the painting, so I put on these boards and added some strings."[11] The wood boards Pistoletto attached to the top and bottom edges of the canvas project beyond the surface of the painting (fig. 120). Between these, and suspended above the painting's surface, he inserted a wood dowel, also bridging the two boards with strings. The dowel and the suspended strings can cast shadows on the surface of the painting, depending on lighting, but Pistoletto also painted shadows for some of the strings, so that the depth they emphasize would be represented regardless of the lighting conditions. He recalls that "this was the first painting where I used silver paint."[12]

It is important to understand that the metallic paint the artist used does not produce a reflected image. Quite the contrary, it produces a slightly granular surface that diffuses and scatters reflected light in a manner akin to the gilded backgrounds of icon paintings. The metallic backgrounds in Pistoletto's paintings transform the picture plane into a nebulous space with an ethereal glow within which the figure resides. As he would in his mirror paintings, Pistoletto was already, at this point in his work, striving to fuse figure and ground in a uniquely expressive way.

In the nonfigurative painting *Linoleum* (1960; see fig. 44), he continued his exploration of how to introduce a third dimension into the two-dimensional picture plane while also enhancing the atmospheric effects of the silver paint. Here, he built up a highly textured gesso layer prior to the application of successive layers of black and silver metallic paint. Not only does the texture provided by the gesso further fracture the reflected light, but the gesso's dimensionality also creates space within the background. This system of combining textured gesso with metallic paint provided Pistoletto with the type of "anonymous decorative background"[13] and spatial ambiguity he was seeking in his self-portraits. With his self-portrait of 1960 (see fig. 42), he embarked on a series of self-portraits made on textured gesso grounds covered with an intermediary layer of black paint topped with silver or gold (fig. 121).

Pistoletto has described many times how the paintings of Francis Bacon served as a springboard for refocusing his own endeavors.[14] In 1960, he abandoned abstraction and returned to painting variations of the self-portrait he had made in 1955, with the figure now placed not on a narrow board but engulfed by an expansive metallic ground. The self-portraits in these works, which include *Autoritratto argento* (*Silver Self-Portrait*, 1960; plate 4), *Autoritratto oro* (*Gold Self-Portrait*, 1960; plate 5), and *Autoritratto bronzo* (*Bronze Self-Portrait*, 1961; plate 6), are full-length standing figures approaching life-size and are rendered with as few brushstrokes as possible. As he recalled of them: "I wanted the figure always to not be dramatic—to be like an object, a piece of existence, without any expression: an unexpressive situation. And it is why the figure is so simple and flat, without any elaboration."[15]

Pistoletto had used black paint as an underlayer in all of his prior paintings. But in 1961, when making the painting *Il presente*, he decided to cover the black paint with what he calls "a plastic boat varnish" to create a glossy surface, as an alternative to the metallic pigmented surfaces he had been making in his self-portraits. Although he noticed that the varnished

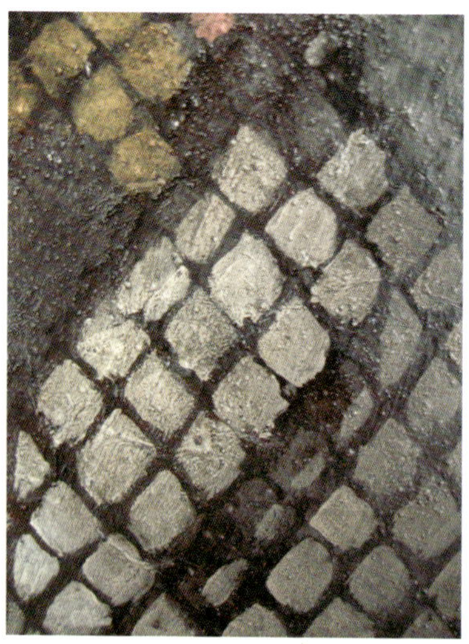

FIG. 119. Detail of *La folla ingrata* (*The Thankless Crowd*, 1958–59; fig. 34) showing small blocks of color applied over the black background. Photograph by Suzanne Penn

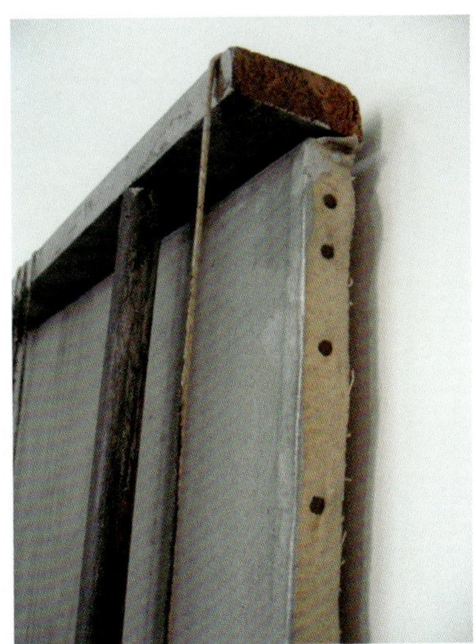

FIG. 120. Detail of *Esperimento* (*Experiment*, 1959; plate 3) showing the wood board affixed to the top of the canvas, and the strings and wood dowel affixed to the board. Photograph by Suzanne Penn

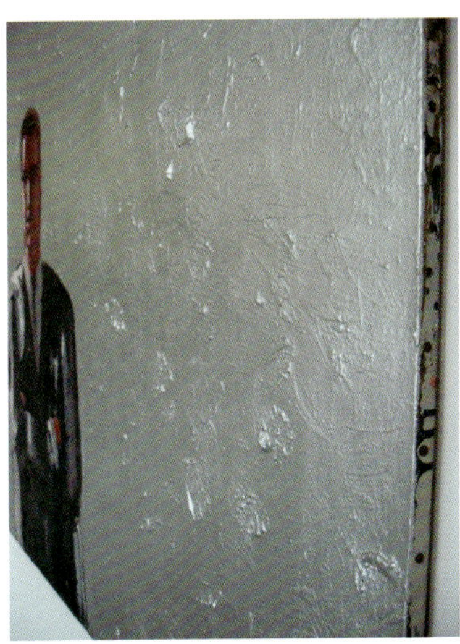

FIG. 121. Detail of *Autoritratto* (*Self-Portrait*, 1960; fig. 42), shot at an oblique angle to show the highly textured gesso ground covered with black and then silver paint. Photograph by Suzanne Penn

black paint produced enough of a reflection to aid him in rendering his own image, he did not immediately seek a more reflective, ready-made support on which to paint. During this year he made a series of self-portraits on glossy black backgrounds, depicting himself in a variety of seated and standing poses (see fig. 46; plates 7–9). It is the array of poses in these works, and the reflective nature of the glossy black support, that led him to extend his figurative art beyond the self-portrait and to seek a ready-made support that would produce a reflection of even greater clarity than did the varnished black ground.

One of Pistoletto's paramount concerns from the outset was to ensure that the composition he was creating on the surface of the support appear to reside as closely as possible on the same plane as the reflection. He ruled out mirrored glass as a support not merely because of its fragility, but because of how and where the reflection is created in it. Because the mirroring is applied to the back of the glass, the reflection is created within, and read beneath, the thickness of the glass. This difference in plane between an image placed on the surface of the mirrored glass and the relatively deeper plane where the reflection actually occurs created a disjunction that Pistoletto did not desire.

In 1961, Pistoletto glued a piece of aluminum sheet metal to a stretched canvas to make *Uomo grigio di schiena* (*Gray Man from the Back*; see fig. 48) and coated it with the same varnish he had used on the black-ground paintings. The varnish imparted both an amber tone to the white metal and a striated pattern of brush marks on the background, qualities that Pistoletto thought helped to create a visual compatibility between the painted figure and the reflective metal support. The aluminum sheet he used for *Uomo grigio di schiena* was readily available, easy to cut, and lightweight, but the dull metal did not reflect a sharp image. In discussing with a friend the effect he was trying to achieve, Pistoletto was directed to a local industrial shop that made polished steel sheets for decorative and architectural purposes. He was able to purchase some scraps, which he used for making the first of what have become known as his mirror paintings.

The clarity of the reflections produced by the polished steel support prompted Pistoletto to make changes in the way he was making the figures. The painted self-portraits had become increasingly abbreviated, comprising only the minimum number of paint strokes needed to render the figure or, as in *Autoritratto oro* of 1960 (plate 5), to create a featureless silhouette. With the adoption of the polished stainless-steel support, a greater degree of realism was required in order for the composed figure to be visually compatible with the reflections in the polished steel. Pistoletto explained: "I couldn't make something like this [a painted self-portrait] on the real reflection. That was good with a painted background but not with an objective representation. It is why I had to go find something that was objective, like the reflection, to be used for the figure. It is why I couldn't escape photography."[16]

Once again, it was his father's restoration studio that served as a resource. For assistance, Pistoletto called on Paolo Bressano, the professional portrait photographer his father employed to document paintings during the course of their restoration. Working in Bressano's photography studio, Pistoletto posed himself and various friends and family members against the studio's mottled paper backdrops (see figs. 5, 129, 130, 133). Bressano then shot the photographs using a 5 x 7–inch (13 x 18–cm) view camera set on a tripod.[17] Although Bressano pressed the shutter, Pistoletto directed the shots, staging the poses and groupings as well as determining the camera framing and lighting. The subjects were lit from the front in order to minimize shadows and any angle of light that could be associated with a particular time of day or a specific place, thus allowing the final form of the figures on the polished stainless steel to mesh better with whatever reflections are created by any given viewing circumstance.

The poses and groupings of the figures were worked out in the studio with great deliberation before being captured by the camera. There are not multiple shots of a given grouping of figures, nor are there variations in the pose of each figure. Although there are some photographs of subjects that were never realized as mirror paintings, most of the photographs shot by Pistoletto and Bressano ended up being used in one form or another. In part, this is a consequence of the amount of labor involved in the process, which entailed lighting the figures, loading each sheet of film (or glass-plate negative, as was used in the beginning), and developing and printing the images. But it is also an indication of how Pistoletto regards photography. He does not think of the camera as a means of capturing a fleeting moment but as a tool to provide a record of his "putting figures in a theoretical situation." The photographs document "classical conceptions of the figure in space," which the artist had carefully composed.[18]

Pistoletto and Bressano worked together to enlarge the negatives and print the large-scale photographs that are the basis of the mirror paintings. The enlarger was set up to project the 5 x 7–inch negative onto the wall of the photography studio, so that the figures or objects could be printed life-size, a determination that was done by eye. It was at this point that a decision had to be reached about the orientation of the figures in the finished work and whether the negative needed to be reversed for printing the enlargement. Once the desired size and orientation had been determined, large sheets of photographic printing paper were pinned to the wall of Bressano's studio and the exposure was made. It was often necessary to make more than one print in order to achieve the desired degree of contrast and saturation of the darks in the figures. When he was satisfied with the results, Pistoletto took the enlargements to his studio, where he continued the processes involved in making the mirror paintings.

Initially, Pistoletto cut out the figures or objects in the photographs and glued them directly onto the polished stainless-steel panels. He felt that this method was successful for his compositions of objects, such as *Bottiglia per terra* (*Bottle on the Floor*, 1963; plate 19), but he rejected it for figures, feeling that it did not achieve a suitable fusion of the figure and the reflections, as the photograph too obviously appeared to be stuck atop the surface of the steel and to be residing slightly in front of the reflection. This method worked for compositions of objects such as the bottle, lamp, and frame because, according to the artist, "the objects need more physicality, as they are neutral . . . while the figure needs to live inside the surface. The consistency of the photograph took it totally away from the penetration."[19]

Still seeking a greater visual fusion of the figures and the reflections on the polished steel surfaces, Pistoletto experimented with gelatin transfer prints, which use a special type of photographic paper from which the image-bearing gelatin layer can be separated from the paper substrate. He recollects working at home in his bathtub, and heating the water to 50°C (122°F), at which point the gelatin image could be floated off the paper and, with great care, laid atop the polished steel.[20] This method proved difficult to execute without flaws, and the gelatin remained extremely fragile and reactive to any increase in humidity, which inevitably caused the image to wither and melt and eventually become illegible.

Pistoletto believes that most of these gelatin-print works no longer exist. One extant mirror painting that used this technique in part is *Alighiero Boetti che guarda un negativo* (*Alighiero Boetti Looking at a Negative*, 1967; figs. 122, 123; plate 44), in which the negative held by Boetti is a gelatin print made directly on the steel (figs. 124, 125). The source photograph for this component of the composition was selected from Bressano's cache of client portrait photographs and was rephotographed by him in order to create a negative from which Pistoletto then created the gelatin transfer print on the steel.

Pistoletto's desire for a more visually harmonious relationship between depicted subject and the reflections in the polished steel led him to translate the black-and-white photographs into monochromatic renderings on tissue paper (*velina*), which he then adhered to the steel surface. The thinness of the tissue paper solved the problem of the image seeming to rest above and separate from the plane of the reflecting surface. Tissue paper also had the advantage of becoming translucent when wetted with turpentine, which helped greatly in the process of tracing the details of the photographs onto the tissue paper, and it remained translucent when saturated with the adhesive used to glue the tissue-paper figures to the polished steel.

To create the renderings on tissue paper, Pistoletto pinned the large, full-sheet photographs (fig. 126) onto a plywood wall that he had installed in his studio expressly for that purpose. The tissue paper was then placed atop the photograph and pinned in place. Next it was saturated with turpentine in order to make it temporarily transparent, allowing the details of the underlying photograph to show through. Using a pencil to trace the outline of the figure and delineate facial features, as well as to do some shading, and a brush for broad applications of black oil paint

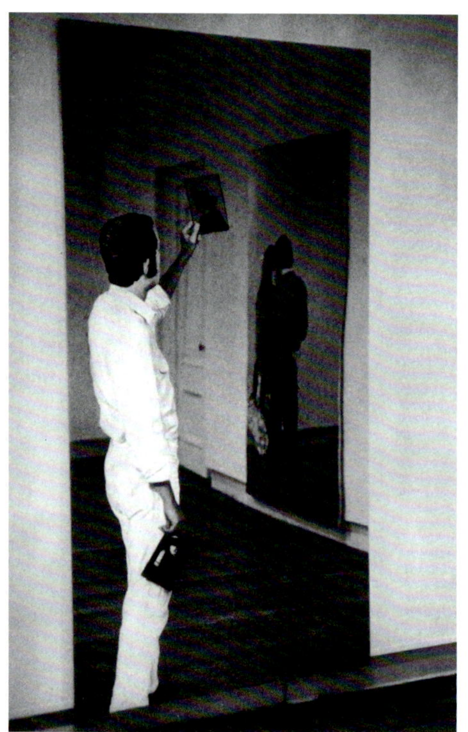

FIG. 122. Pistoletto's mirror painting *Alighiero Boetti che guarda un negativo* (*Alighiero Boetti Looking at a Negative*, 1967; plate 44) as photographed in his solo exhibition at the Kornblee Gallery, New York, 1967. Courtesy of Cittadellarte-Fondazione Pistoletto, Biella

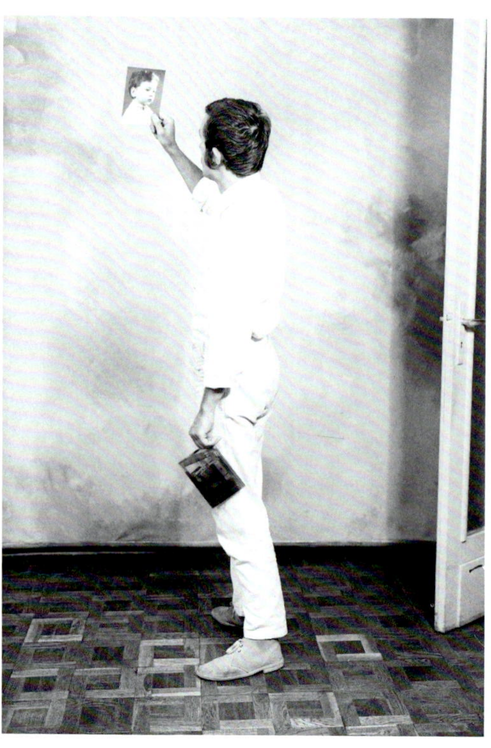

FIG. 123. The source photograph for *Alighiero Boetti che guarda un negativo* (*Alighiero Boetti Looking at a Negative*, 1967; plate 44). Courtesy of Cittadellarte-Fondazione Pistoletto, Biella

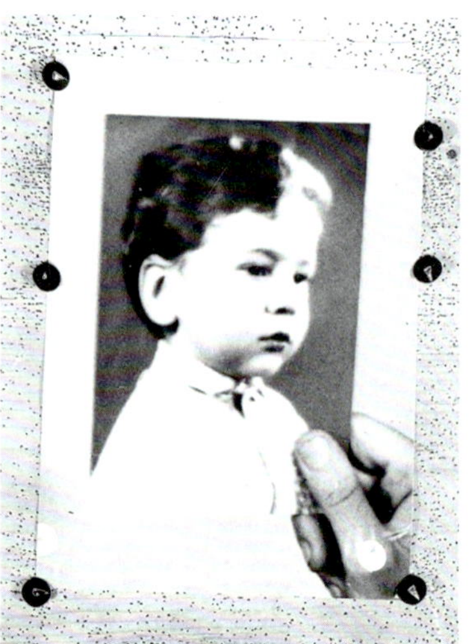

FIG. 124. The photograph used to create the negative gelatin transfer print that Boetti holds in his raised hand in the finished mirror painting *Alighiero Boetti che guarda un negativo* (fig. 122; plate 44). Courtesy of Cittadellarte-Fondazione Pistoletto, Biella

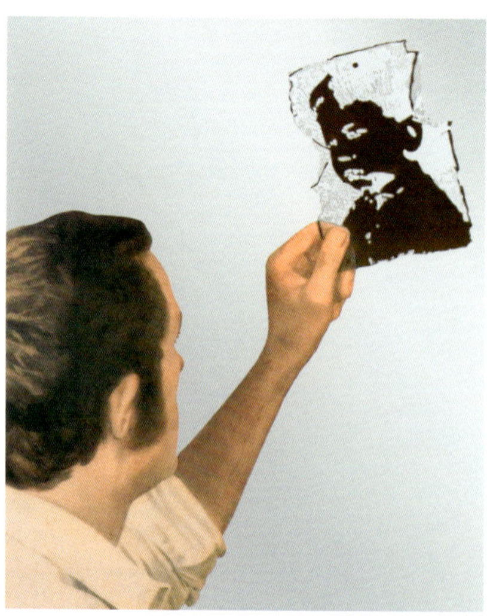

FIG. 125. Detail of *Alighiero Boetti che guarda un negativo* (fig. 122; plate 44) showing the "negative" held by Boetti, made by the gelatin transfer print technique

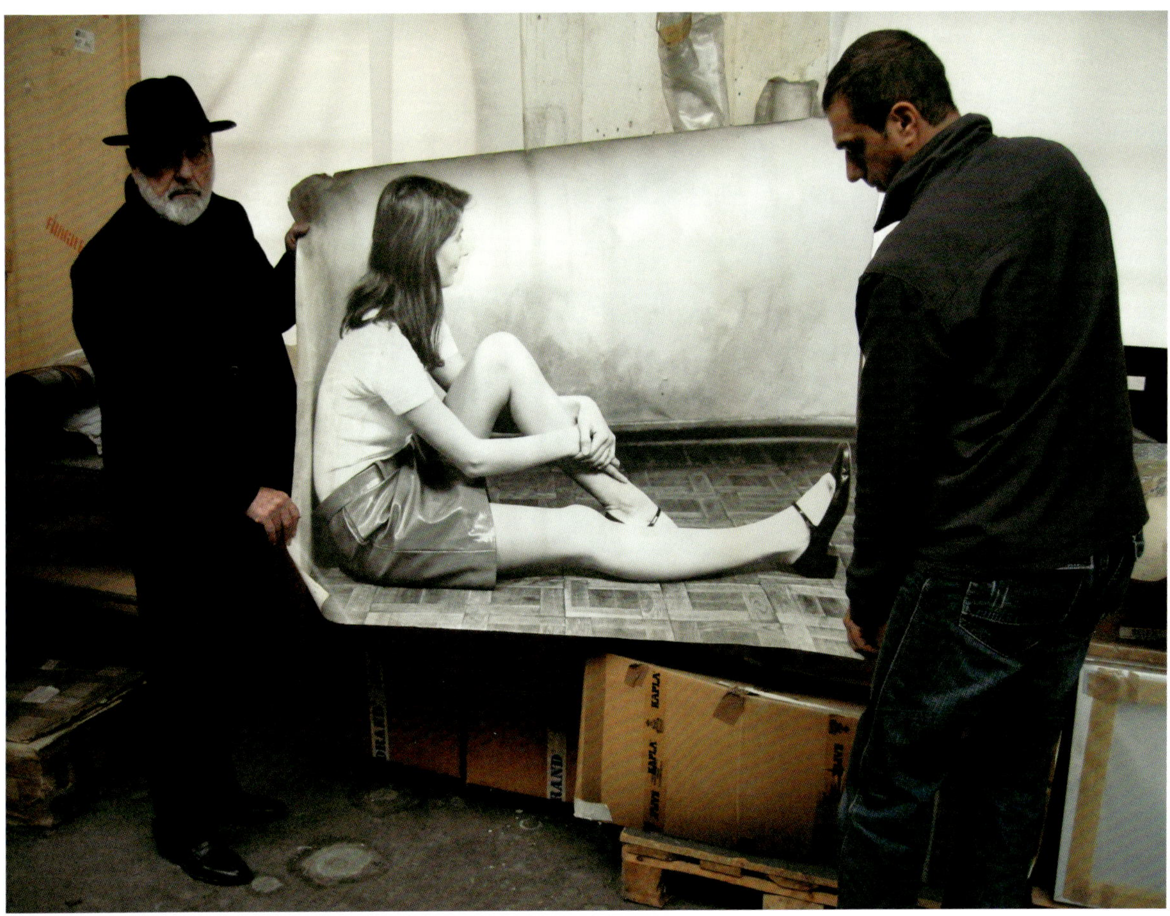

FIG. 126. Pistoletto and Alessandro Lacirasella holding the photographic enlargement used for making the *velina* (tissue paper) figure for *Ragazza seduta per terra* (*Girl Sitting on the Floor*, 1967; plate 46), Cittadellarte-Fondazione Pistoletto, Biella, 2009. The tissue paper was laid over this photograph and the image rendered in black paint and pencil. The tissue-paper figure was then flipped over before it was adhered to the stainless-steel panel, resulting in an orientation opposite to that of the enlarged photograph. Color was added to the tissue-paper figure after it was adhered. Photograph by Suzanne Penn

to render other elements, such as clothing, Pistoletto re-created the photographic figure on the tissue paper. When his rendering was complete and the turpentine had evaporated from the tissue, he carried the full sheet of paper over to the polished steel panel, where he flipped it over so that the drawing layer was in direct contact with the surface of the steel. Connecting the drawing side directly with the support was a means of further fusing the figure with the reflective steel. Before making a final decision about the placement of the tissue-paper figure, Pistoletto moved it around on the polished steel panel to test various positions. Once the position was determined, he fastened the tissue in place at its top edge with a couple of daubs of "boat varnish" adhesive and then flipped the tissue up, out of the way, so that an ample amount of the varnish could be applied to the surface of the steel. The tissue was then laid down over the varnish and smoothed out, and the outline of the figure was cut with a razor blade and the excess paper removed. Any varnish adhesive on the steel surrounding the figure was wiped off. The tiny incised lines that can be seen on some of the mirror paintings, adjacent to the edge of the figure, are remnants of this process and the several passes of the razor blade required to cut the figure from the full sheet of tissue paper.

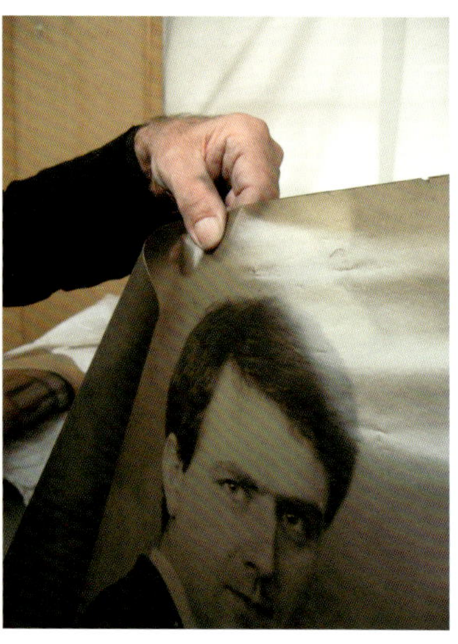

FIG. 127. Pistoletto holding one of his early photographic enlargements printed on translucent paper, Cittadellarte-Fondazione Pistoletto, Biella, 2009. Photograph by Suzanne Penn

The adhesive used for adhering the monochromatic tissue-paper figures to the polished steel panels was the same "boat varnish" that Pistoletto had used in creating the glossy black grounds on *Il presente* and the subsequent works in that series (see fig. 46; plates 7–9). The pale, amber-colored varnish penetrated the tissue paper, giving it a degree of permanent translucency that made the drawing on the underside more readily visible and lent the figures a subtle sepia tonality that over time has continued to darken. The wrinkling of the tissue that can be seen in some works was caused by the drying of the varnish. The quantity of varnish, and hence the degree of saturation, translucency, and wrinkling of the tissue paper, varies from work to work.

Pistoletto eventually switched to using white enamel paint rather than varnish to adhere the tissue paper to the polished steel. This resulted in a number of subtle differences in the appearance of the adhered image. The paper was not made as translucent by the enamel paint as it had been by the varnish, although some of the medium in the enamel did penetrate the paper to impart an amber tone. The wrinkling of the paper was also much reduced, and the continuous layer of white paint beneath the paper gives it a denser, more substantial appearance.

When Pistoletto began to add colored paint to the tissue-paper figures, he did so after they had already been adhered to the polished steel. The drawing and the preliminary rendering of the figures were still done with pencil and black paint. The color paint was added to the figure's skin and garments after the tissue was adhered to the steel panel with the white enamel paint. For the color, Pistoletto used oil paint thinned to a consistency that penetrated the tissue paper, thereby imbuing it with color rather than depositing a skin or layer of paint on the surface of the

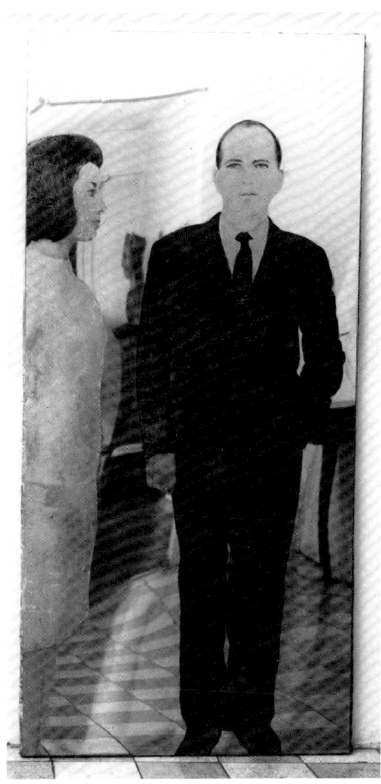

FIG. 128. Michelangelo Pistoletto, *Uomo e donna* (*Man and Woman*), 1962. Painted tissue paper on polished stainless steel, 70 ⅞ x 35 ⅜ inches (180 x 90 cm). Private collection

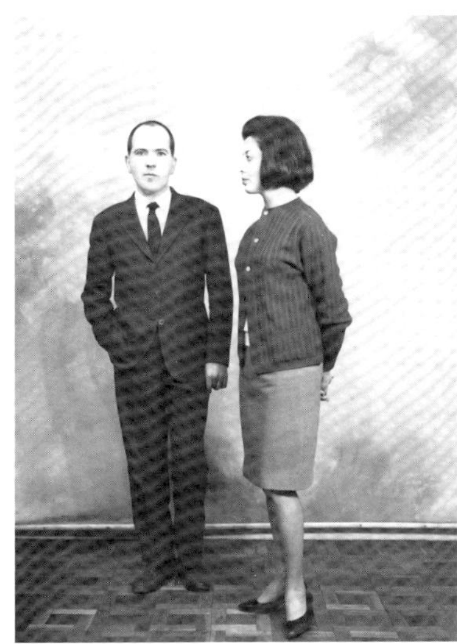

FIG. 129. The source photograph for *Uomo e donna* (*Man and Woman*, 1962; fig. 128). Courtesy of Cittadellarte-Fondazione Pistoletto, Biella

paper. The white enamel paint under the tissue paper provides a luminous base that gives the colors greater intensity. Pistoletto likens his addition of color at the end, after the black-and-white figures had been made and adhered to the steel, to the technique of Titian and other Venetian Renaissance painters, who added their luminous colors in final glazes atop monochromatic underpaintings.[21] The colored mirror paintings were still based on black-and-white photographs. The color added by Pistoletto was of his own choosing and does not necessarily re-create the actual colors of the clothing worn by the people when they posed for him.

The staging of figures and objects in Bressano's studio and the shooting and printing of the photographs were just the first steps of composing for Pistoletto. From the photographic enlargements he made decisions about how he wished to use the figures to create a particular mirror painting. The earliest enlargements were actually printed on translucent paper (fig. 127) because Pistoletto thought that being able to see the steel surface beneath as he moved the large-scale photographs around on the panels, even in advance of transforming them into tissue-paper paintings, would be advantageous in making decisions about their eventual positioning and cropping. He soon deemed the translucent paper unnecessary, however, and he and Bressano made all subsequent prints on large sheets of standard photographic paper.

In transforming the photographs into mirror paintings, some of the figures or groups of figures remained as originally staged, although their positioning on the mirror might crop them, as in *Uomo e donna* (*Man and Woman*, 1962; figs. 128, 129). In other instances, Pistoletto chose to omit several figures present in the source photograph, as in a self-portrait from 1962 (see fig. 4), a work based on a photograph that included a trio of figures (see fig. 5). Sometimes, figures from a single photograph were used to make more than one mirror painting. For example, in *Annina* (1964; fig. 131) the figure of Annina Nosei was extracted from a photograph that also included Pistoletto and his parents (fig. 130). This same photograph was used, in part, for *Due persone in coda* (*Two People in Line*, 1964; fig. 132; plate 28), for which Pistoletto combined the image of his mother with that of Clino Trini Castelli, extracted from a double-figure photograph (fig. 133) whose second figure, Gian Enzo Sperone, was in turn used for another single-figure mirror painting, *Uomo con pantaloni gialli* (*Man with Yellow Pants*, 1964; fig. 134).

In some cases, Pistoletto had the composition of the mirror painting in mind before the photographs were taken, as in *Quattro persone alla balconata* (*Four People on a Balcony*, 1964; figs. 135, 136; plate 26). For this composition, he posed each person separately, having them lean on a chair or in space in anticipation of placing them collectively along a balcony rail. The balcony rail itself was entirely crafted by Pistoletto from pieces of colored tissue paper that he adhered to the steel, conjoining the figures to complete the illusion of four people standing on an upper-story balcony and leaning on the rail as they look down at the street below. In order to

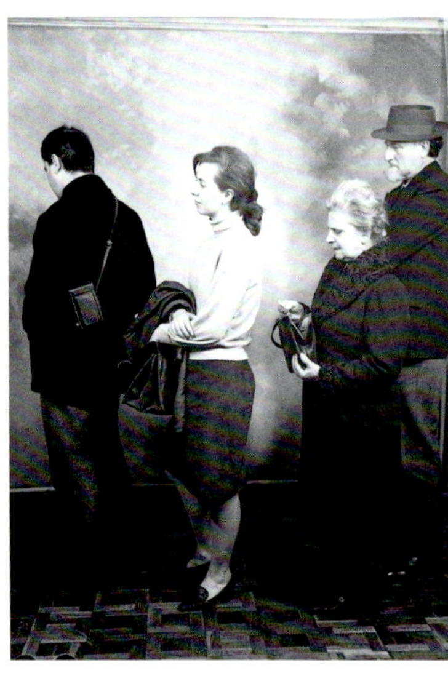

FIG. 130. The source photograph for *Annina* (1964; fig. 131) and *Due persone in coda* (*Two People in Line*, 1964; plate 28). From left to right are Pistoletto, Annina, and Pistoletto's mother and father. Courtesy of Cittadellarte-Fondazione Pistoletto, Biella

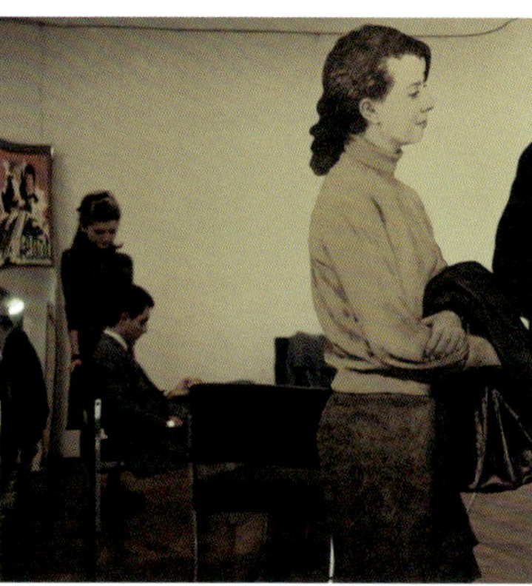

FIG. 131. Michelangelo Pistoletto, *Annina*, 1964. Painted tissue paper on polished stainless steel, 47¼ x 47¼ inches (120 x 120 cm). Private collection

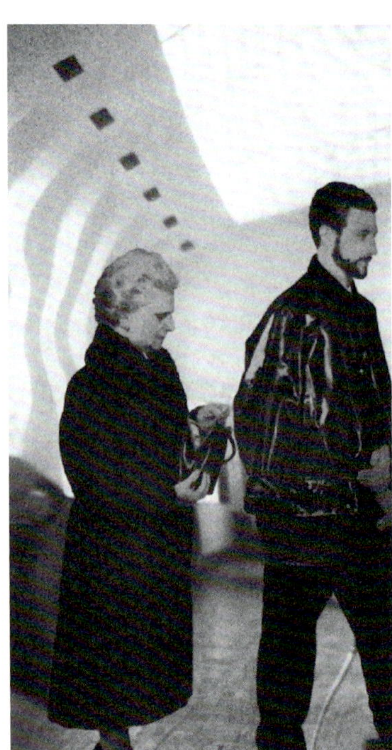

FIG. 132. Michelangelo Pistoletto, *Due persone in coda* (*Two People in Line*, 1964; plate 28) in Pistoletto's solo exhibition at the Museum Boijmans Van Beuningen, Rotterdam, 1969

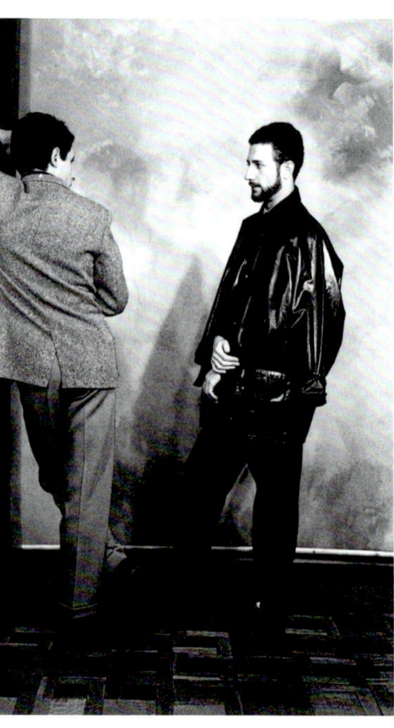

FIG. 133. The source photograph for *Uomo con pantaloni gialli* (*Man with Yellow Pants*, 1964; fig. 134) and *Due persone in coda* (*Two People in Line*, 1964; plate 28). Courtesy of Cittadellarte-Fondazione Pistoletto, Biella

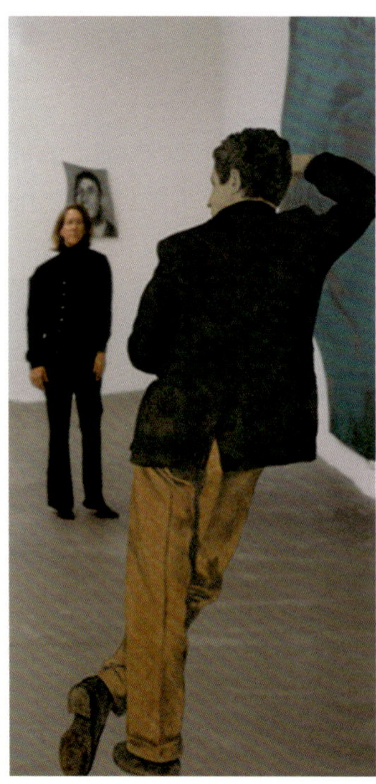

FIG. 134. Michelangelo Pistoletto, *Uomo con pantaloni gialli* (*Man with Yellow Pants*), 1964. Painted tissue paper on polished stainless steel, 78⅞ inches x 39⅜ inches (200.3 x 100 cm). The Museum of Modern Art, New York. Blanchette Hooker Rockefeller Fund, 1965

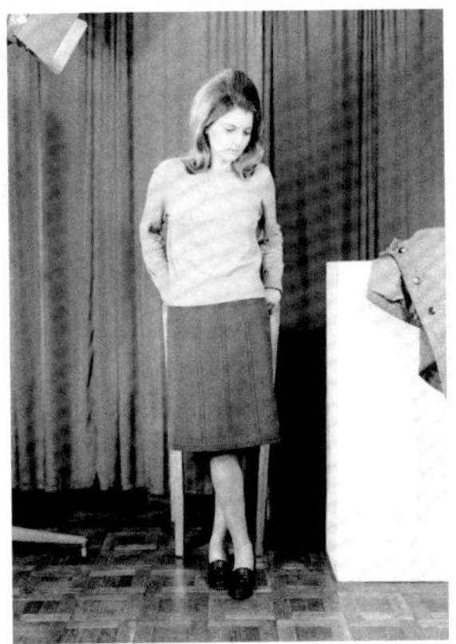
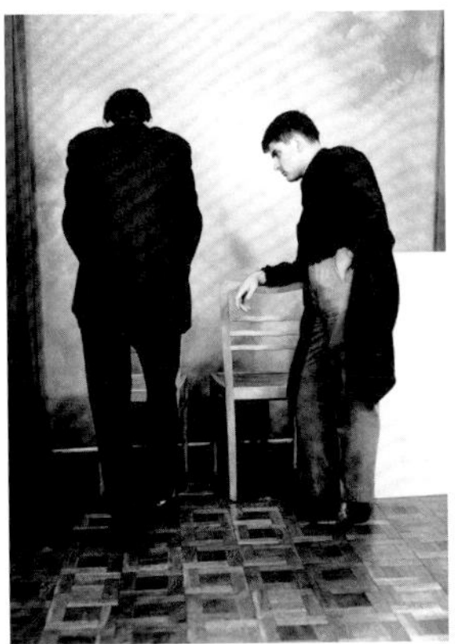
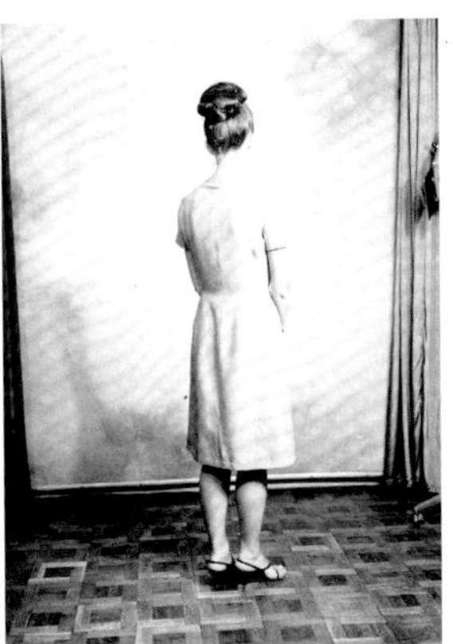
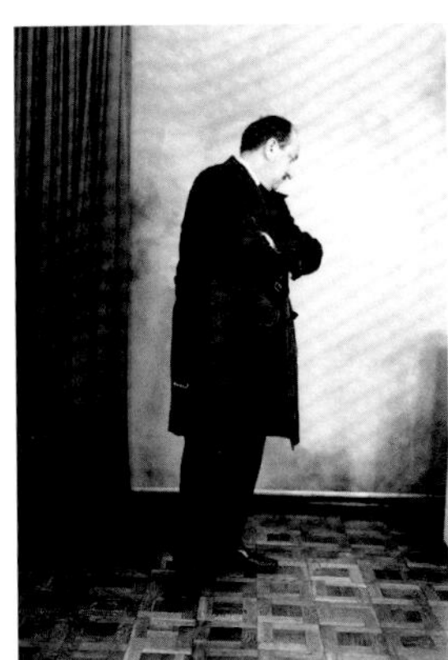

FIG. 135. The source photographs for *Quattro persone alla balconata* (*Four People on a Balcony*, 1964; plate 26). Courtesy of Cittadellarte-Fondazione Pistoletto, Biella

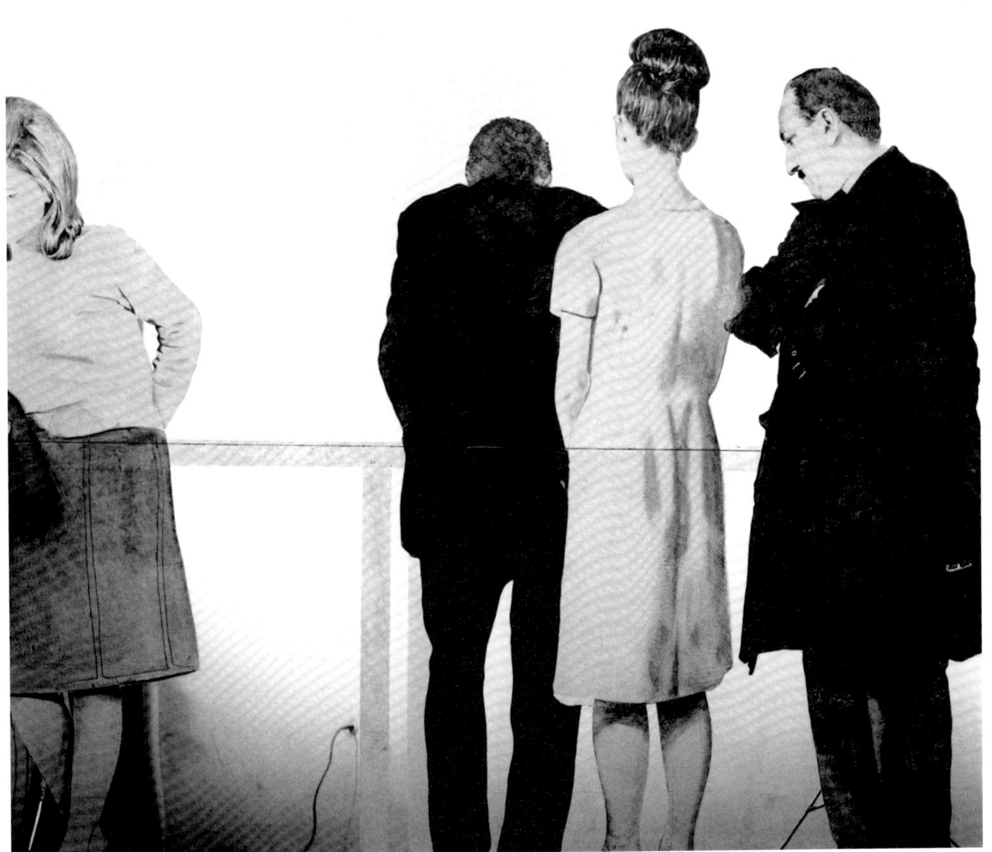

FIG. 136. Michelangelo Pistoletto, *Quattro persone alla balconata* (*Four People on a Balcony*, 1964; plate 26)

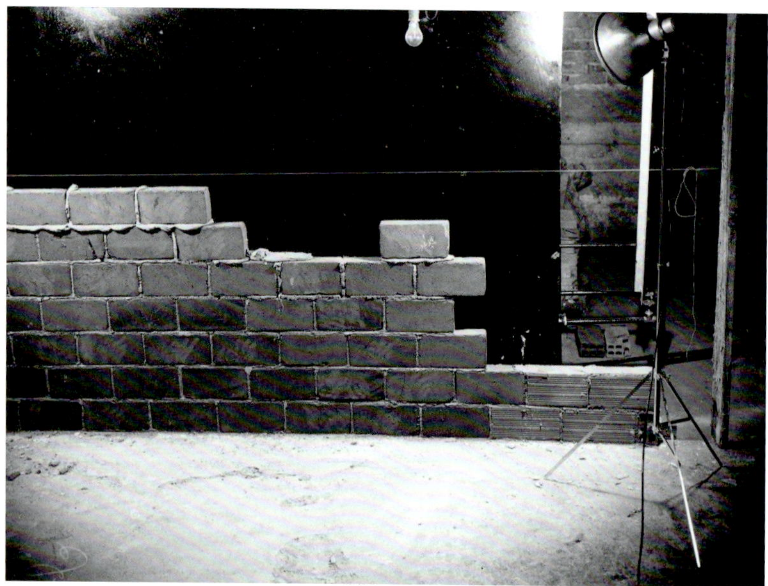

FIG. 137. The source photograph for *Muro di mattoni* (*Wall of Bricks*, 1967; fig. 138) and *Muretto di mattoni* (*Small Wall of Bricks*, 1970; plate 53). Courtesy of Cittadellarte-Fondazione Pistoletto, Biella

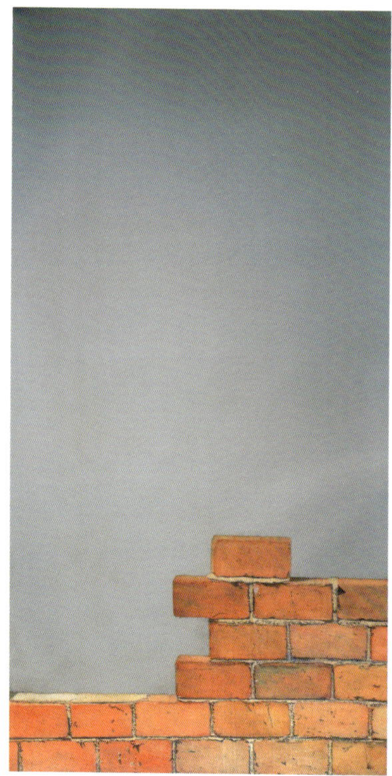

FIG. 138. Michelangelo Pistoletto, *Muro di mattoni* (*Wall of Bricks*), 1967. Painted tissue paper on polished stainless steel, 90 9/16 x 47 1/4 inches (230 x 120 cm). Private collection © Christie's Images Limited 2010

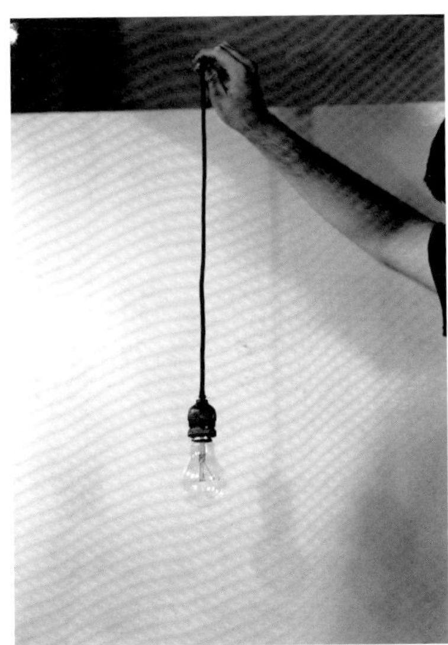

FIG. 139. The source photograph for *Lampadina* (*Lightbulb*, 1964; plate 22). Courtesy of Cittadellarte-Fondazione Pistoletto, Biella

have a stainless-steel support of adequate size to accommodate so many life-size figures and provide adequate air space above them for a convincing illusion of their positioning on an outside balcony, Pistoletto had to use two maximum-size polished steel panels, which he abutted. He made the horizontal join of the two panels as unobtrusive as possible by having it coincide with the top of the balcony rail and the waistline of the figures.

The first mirror paintings were made on random sizes of polished steel that Pistoletto found precut at the supplier. Initially, he glued the polished steel sheets to stretched canvases. This step, along with the fact that Pistoletto himself calls the works in this medium mirror "paintings" when he is speaking in English, is an indication that he regards them as part of the painting tradition. He explained that, for him, the process involved in making the mirror paintings "was not jumping out of the traditional material of painting. I was forced to do it. I was very unhappy to go away from painting. I wanted to keep the idea of the stainless steel like it was a painting; it is why canvas was important as a support. After two or three works, I realized it was a crazy idea to keep the canvas. The passage was very slow."[22]

Pistoletto replaced the stretched canvases with a metal stretcher that he glued to the reverse of the stainless-steel panels, a system that he would continue to use for all subsequent mirror paintings as well as for his serigraphs on polished steel. By 1964, he was availing himself of the maximum size of steel sheet available from the manufacturer—230 x 120 cm—instead of buying scraps. Although these full-size sheets were used for many of his mirror paintings, in others he chose to reduce one or both dimensions of the sheet as needed for a particular composition. The works on the maximum-size panels bear the marks of the manufacturing process in the form of screw holes and a discolored band along one short side where the panel was held in the machine during the polishing of its surface.

The tissue paper used for the figures also had a size limitation. It came in sheets, not as a roll of paper, and Pistoletto often had to piece together the figures from more than one sheet of paper, hiding the juncture of the pieces along a neckline, shoulder seam, or elsewhere in the figure.

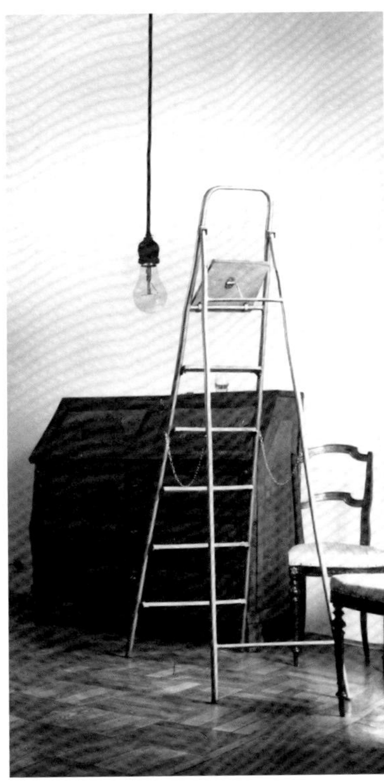

FIG. 140. Michelangelo Pistoletto, *Lampadina* (*Lightbulb*, 1964; plate 22) in Pistoletto's studio, Turin, 1964. Photograph by Paolo Bressano. Courtesy of Cittadellarte-Fondazione Pistoletto, Biella

The vast majority of mirror paintings, whether of figures or objects, are based on photographs that Pistoletto staged. Even subjects as elementary as a lightbulb or as elaborate as a brick wall were staged indoors, as indicated by the source photographs (figs. 137–40; plates 22, 53). Among the exceptions are the numerous examples that make use of a series of parade photographs taken by Pistoletto's friend Renato Rinaldi.[23] Pistoletto excerpted and combined figures from this series to create the 1965–66 mirror paintings *Ragazzo* and *Comizio n. 2* (*Boy* and *Demonstration no. 2*; figs. 141–44; plate 33), *Biennale 66* (*Biennial 66*; plate 39),[24] *Bandiera rossa* (*Red Flag*; plate 37), *No all'aumento del tram* (*No to the Raise of the Tram Fare*; plate 34), and *Vietnam* (plate 32). The latter work is based on a photograph of people in the parade holding a banner spelling *Giovanni*, a political candidate (fig. 145). The type style of the banner was mimicked by Pistoletto as he transformed the scene into a more globally topical subject,

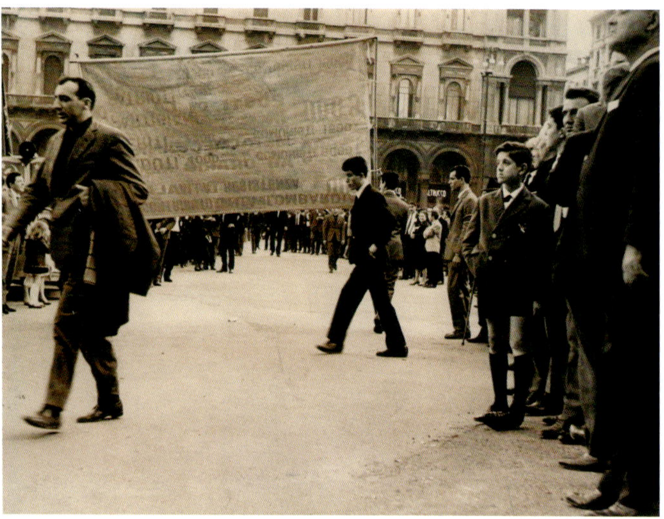

FIG. 141. The source photograph for *Ragazzo* (*Boy*, 1965; plate 33) and *Biennale 66* (*Biennial 66*, 1966; plate 39). Photograph by Renato Rinaldi. Courtesy of Cittadellarte-Fondazione Pistoletto, Biella. Rinaldi's photographs were shot by Paolo Bressano so they could be enlarged; thus the final orientation of the figures in the mirror paintings is the same as that of the figures in the original photographs rather than reversed.

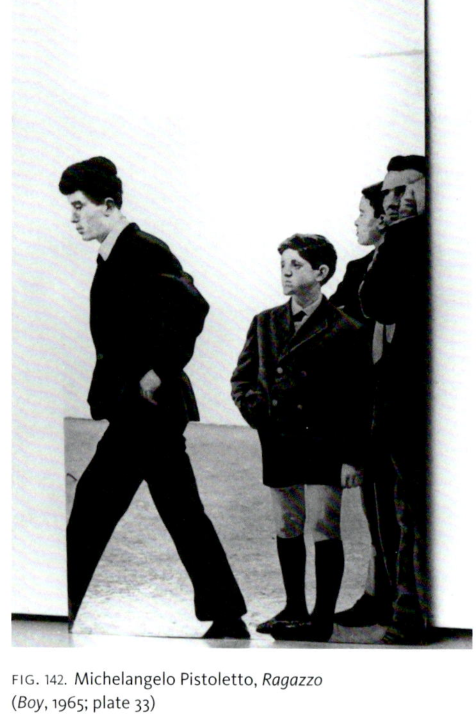

FIG. 142. Michelangelo Pistoletto, *Ragazzo* (*Boy*, 1965; plate 33)

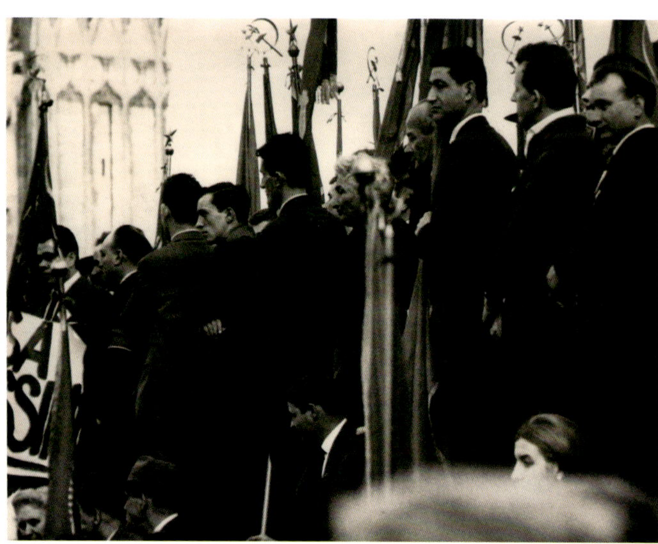

FIG. 143. The source photograph for *Comizio n. 2* (*Demonstration no. 2*, 1965; fig. 144). Photograph by Renato Rinaldi. Courtesy of Cittadellarte-Fondazione Pistoletto, Biella

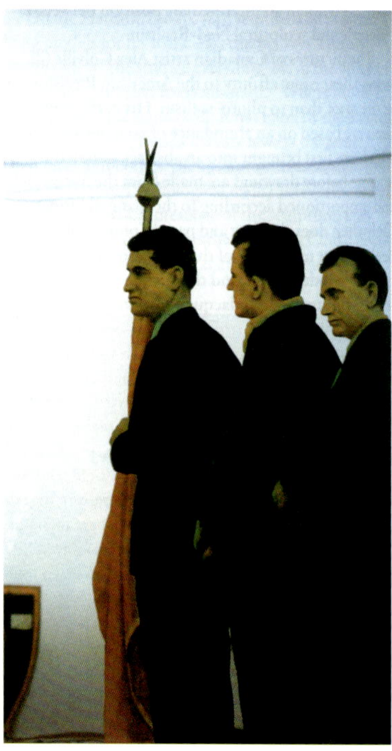

FIG. 144. Michelangelo Pistoletto, *Comizio n. 2* (*Demonstration no. 2*), 1965. Painted tissue paper on polished stainless steel, 84⅝ x 47¼ inches (215 x 120 cm). Ludwig Museum, Cologne

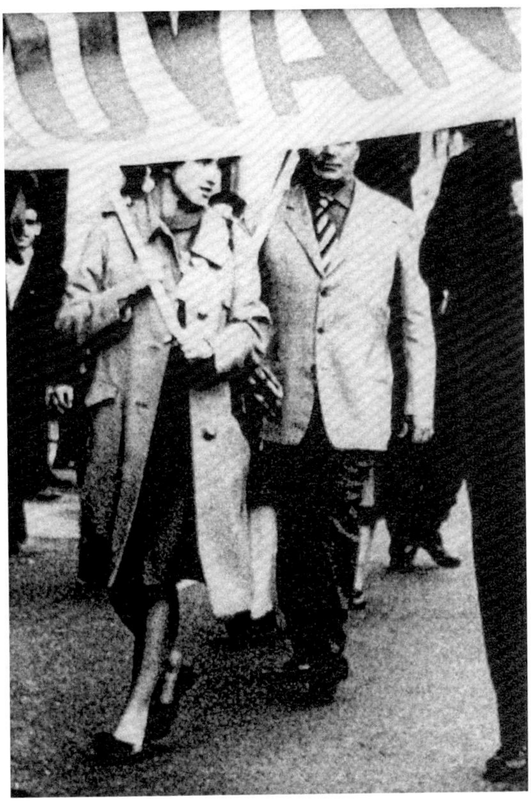

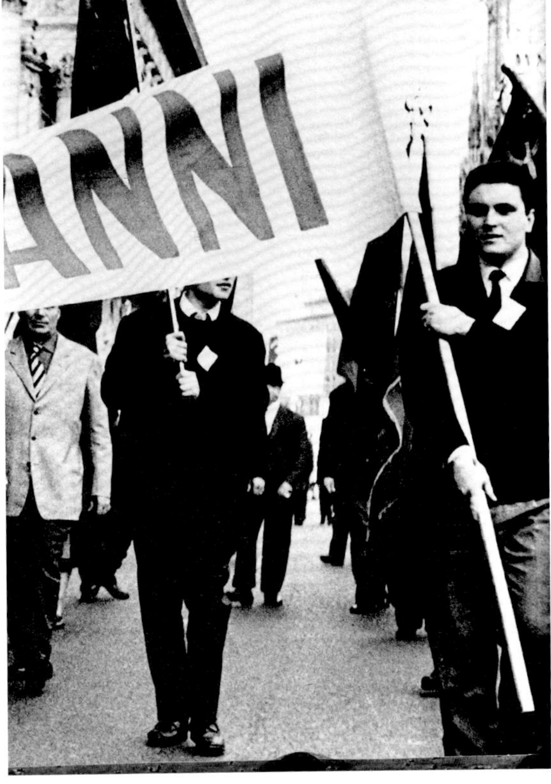

FIG. 145. The source photographs for *Vietnam* (1965; plate 32). Courtesy of Cittadellarte-Fondazione Pistoletto, Biella

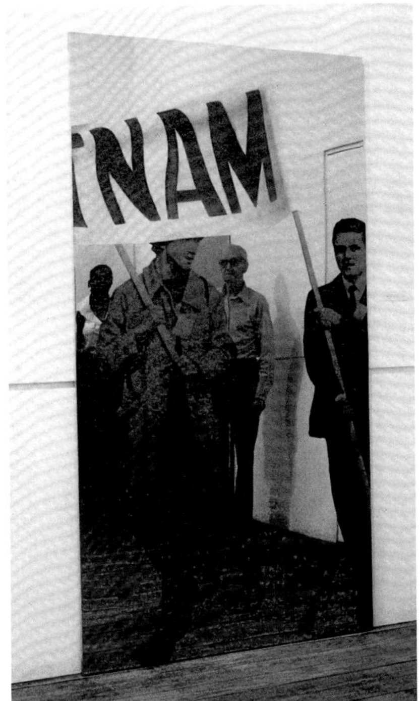

FIG. 146. Michelangelo Pistoletto, *Vietnam* (1965; plate 32)

the protests against the war in Vietnam. Pistoletto recounted: "Through Rinaldi, I started to use . . . images from the social world from outside the family and friends. He was a kind of an eye that went on the street."[25]

There are also some mirror paintings based on photographs taken by Bressano without Pistoletto's involvement. After they had worked together for a number of years, Pistoletto implored Bressano to look for possible subjects, asking him: "'Why don't you go around with your camera and when you look at a situation that will be interesting for me, take a picture?' . . . and he did sometimes bring me pictures—people waiting for the tram, etc."[26] Works based on Bressano's snapshots include *Ragazzo con la visiera* (*Boy with the Visor*, 1970; figs. 147, 148), *Uomo che aggiusta un camion* (*Man Fixing a Van*, 1967; fig. 149), and *Uomo e donna con occhiali neri* (*Man and Woman with Dark Glasses*, 1970; figs. 150, 151).

Pistoletto created only two of his mirror paintings on commission. For the first, Prince Aldobrandini asked him to make a portrait of his fiancée, Graziella Lonardi Buontempo. Pistoletto initially hesitated to accept, but then the photograph of the nude Graziella on which the work was to be based fell out of the prince's wallet, and Pistoletto realized that it would indeed make a beautiful mirror painting (intended as a gift to the bride-to-be), so he agreed to the commission (plate 57). The second, titled *Art International* (1968) after the journal, was commissioned by Christian Stein, the founder of the Milan gallery of the same name; it is a portrait of her son holding an issue of the journal.

A few mirror paintings were created from images obtained from other sources, including *Marcel Duchamp seduto su un Brancusi* (*Marcel Duchamp Sitting on a Brancusi*, 1974), based on a photograph given to him by Ugo Mulas, a close friend, and *La stufa di Oldenburg* (*Oldenburg's Stove*, 1965) and *Scultura di Chamberlain* (*Chamberlain's Sculpture*, 1966), both based on images in publications. For each of the works based on preexisting photographs, Pistoletto had the source image rephotographed by Bressano so that full-size enlargements could be made and transformed into tissue-paper renderings.

The first instance of Pistoletto using a photograph by someone other than Bressano and himself is *Due donne nude che ballano* (*Two Nude Women Dancing*, 1964; plate 23), a work based on a photograph by Eadweard Muybridge that the artist found in a book. Pistoletto chose this particular Muybridge image "because it was a nude" and because, taken out of context, it conveys "the idea of provocation." Pistoletto was drawn to Muybridge's work because, he said, "this photographer was very important . . . he was part of the history of photography." Having employed photography in the service of his own work for two years, he felt that "it was very interesting . . . to turn around the fact that Muybridge was trying to move the photography, and I was trying to fix the photography and move the world around."[27]

Muybridge used photography to re-create movement, taking sequential still photographs of subjects in motion and subsequently animating them with the zoopraxiscope, a device of his own invention. While it is true that Pistoletto used the camera to capture himself, his friends, and his family, whom he posed in Bressano's studio, there was no real action to be stopped by the camera. The figures were already fixed in a solemn quiescence in the poses he devised. They are invariably static and rigid, even in their nonchalance. Figures face one another, but there is no sense that the camera has silenced them, as no words appear to have been exchanged. It was in his initial step of making the photographic figure studies, and conceiving their poses and placement in his compositions, that Pistoletto accomplished his desire to "cool the drama" in the figures.[28]

The figures in Pistoletto's photographic *tableaux vivants*, and their final incarnations in the mirror paintings, owe much to the work of Titian, Giovanni Bellini, and Piero della Francesca, the latter of whom has often been spoken of and written about admiringly by Pistoletto.[29] Like the figures in the foreground of Piero's *Flagellation of Christ* (see fig. 56), who invite us to join them in bearing witness to the event transpiring, it is the nonconfrontational demeanor, poise, and detachment of Pistoletto's figures, whom we happen upon and join via the mirror, that in large measure allow our encounter with them to occur with such ease.

Pistoletto admires the beauty of how Piero employed perspective to unify the posed figures in the foreground with the dramatic scene of the Flagellation of Christ in the near distance, and he has compared Piero's use of perspective to how the mirror functions in his own work.[30] While Piero's perspective effectively pierces the picture plane, creating a world within, the polished steel used by Pistoletto goes even further in its dimensional expansion and effect on the viewer. Pistoletto has said that in paintings by Piero "the perspective is phenomenological, it is not invented, it is true. It is scientific. The mirror is scientific, too. But the perspective in the Piero painting was going from the window to the street, while the mirror goes from the window to the street and back again."[31] It is this visual reverberation, made possible by the mirror, that not only pierces the picture plane but also explodes it in all directions, and it is the mirror that gives the work the ability to reinvent itself continually through the ever-changing, shifting reflections of its viewing circumstances.

Pistoletto made a number of works whose titles reference traditional religious subjects, including *Sacra conversazione* (1963; plate 16), *Annunciazione* (1968), *Sacra conversazione (Anselmo, Zorio, Penone)* (1973; plate 60), and *Deposizione* (1973; plate 61). When asked about this, he said that he was not quoting or thinking of specific paintings when making these works, but was referencing these traditional subjects in a general way, with a "sense of humor or irony that there is something happening today just like yesterday. We know that we can have a figure coming from the time of the religious traditions but also have the same thing happening today. A boy and girl can be a Deposition but in a completely different time situation. A woman waiting with a man on the telephone can be the Annunciation. In the story of religious paintings there are many, many stories."[32] Although

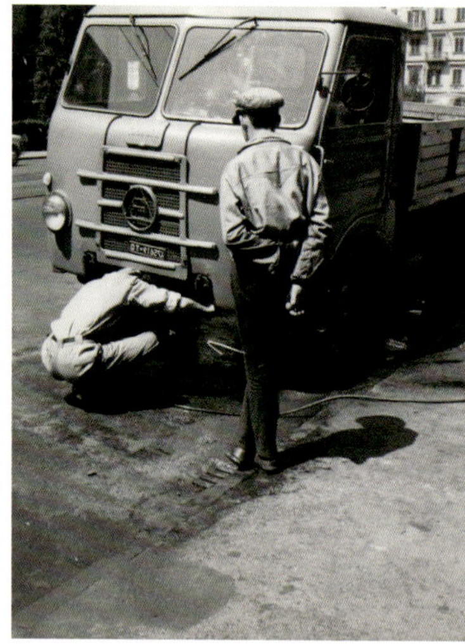

FIG. 147. The source photograph for *Ragazzo con la visiera* (*Boy with the Visor*, 1970; fig. 148), and *Uomo che aggiusta un camion* (*Man Fixing a Van*, 1967; fig. 149). Courtesy of Cittadellarte-Fondazione Pistoletto, Biella

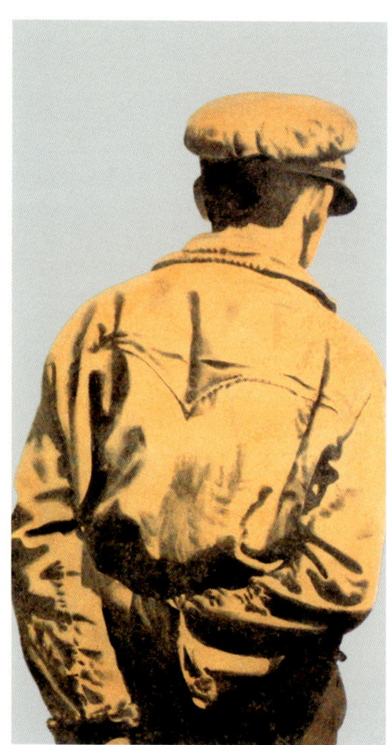

FIG. 148. Michelangelo Pistoletto, *Ragazzo con la visiera* (*Boy with the Visor*), 1970. Painted tissue paper on polished stainless steel, 41⅜ x 21⅝ inches (105 x 55 cm). Private collection

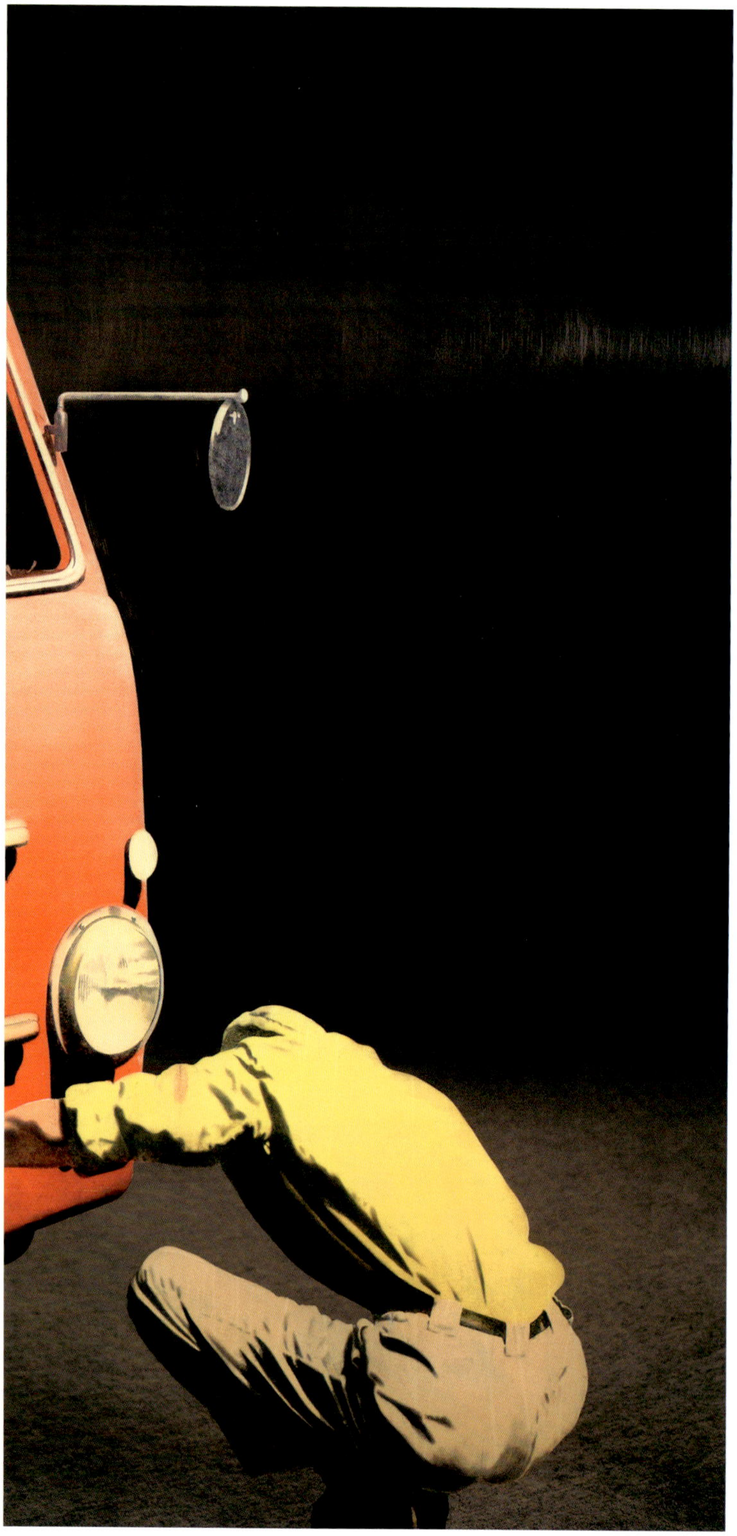

FIG. 149. Michelangelo Pistoletto, *Uomo che aggiusta un camion* (*Man Fixing a Van*), 1967. Painted tissue paper on polished stainless steel, 90½ x 47¼ inches (230 x 120 cm). Private collection

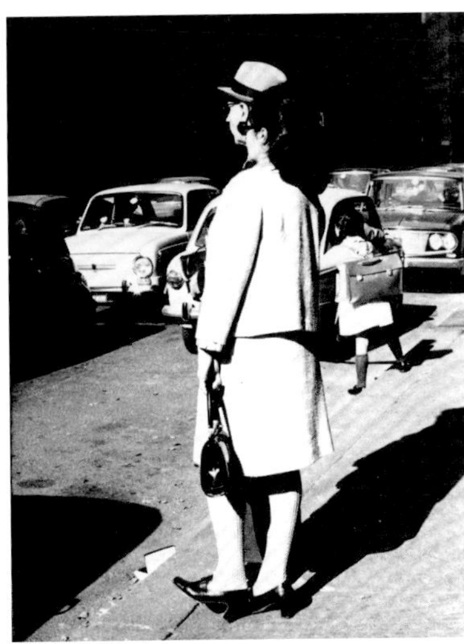

FIG. 150. The source photograph for *Uomo e donna con occhiali neri* (*Man and Woman with Dark Glasses*, 1970; fig. 151). Courtesy of Cittadellarte-Fondazione Pistoletto, Biella

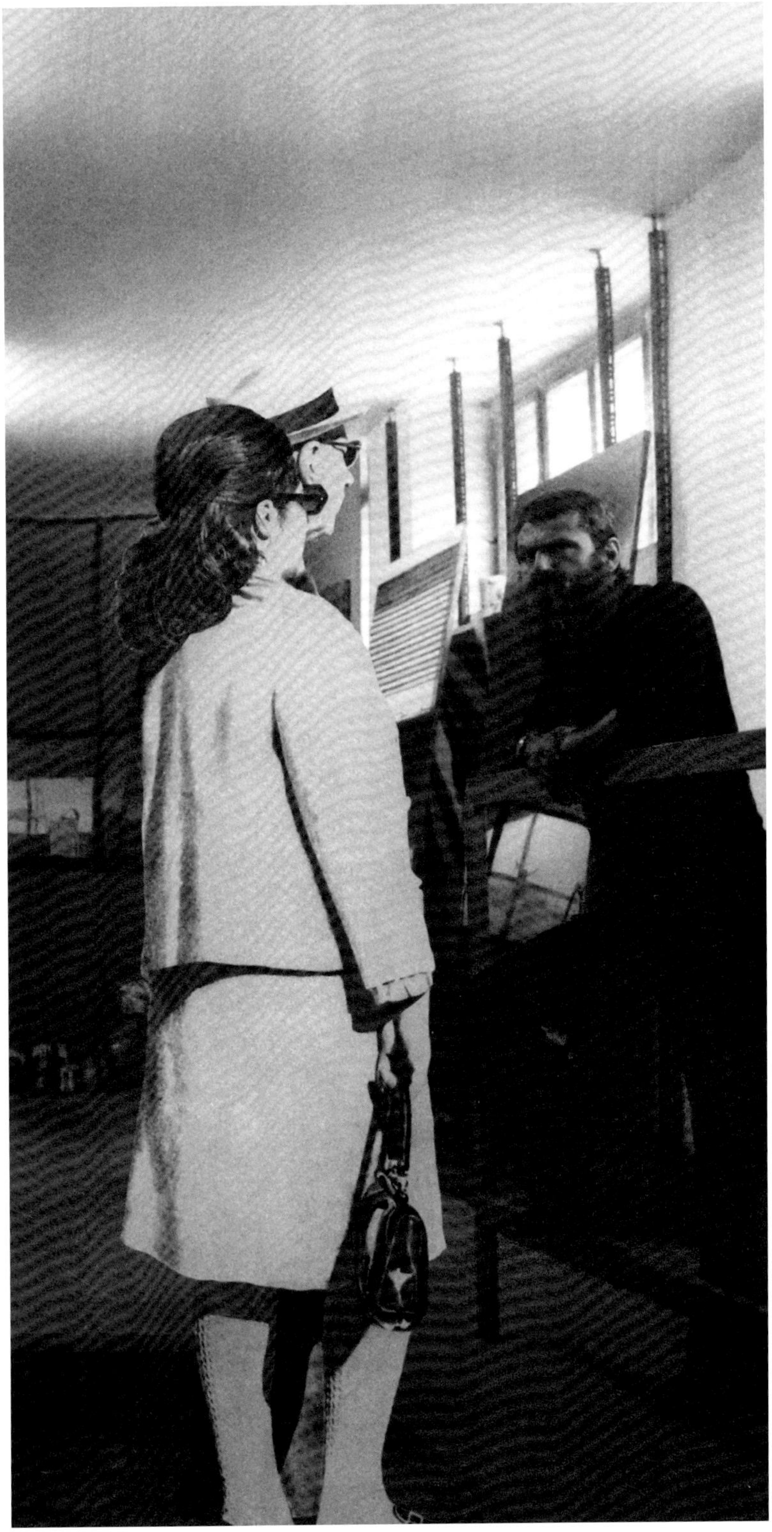

FIG. 151. Michelangelo Pistoletto, *Uomo e donna con occhiali neri* (*Man and Woman with Dark Glasses*), 1970. Painted tissue paper on polished stainless steel, 90½ x 47¼ inches (230 x 120 cm). Private collection. Pistoletto is reflected in the painting, leaning on *Struttura per parlare in piedi* (*Structure for Talking while Standing*, 1965–66; plate 87), one of his Minus Objects.

Pistoletto used the word *irony* in describing his adoption of traditional religious subjects, it is clear when speaking with him that in these works, and in all his work, he finds delight in traversing the history of art and in the ways in which art and life can reciprocally reflect one another.

This concept is well exemplified by a work from 1973 that references a specific old master painting as well as a memory from Pistoletto's youth. *Donna che fa la cacca* (*Woman Defecating*; figs. 152, 153; plate 62) is based on a detail in a painting by Pietro Domenico Olivero, an eighteenth-century Piedmontese genre painter. Pistoletto had worked on this particular painting by Olivero (whose title he does not recall) in his father's restoration studio, and he remembers with amusement how Olivero populated his genre scenes with all sorts of scatological details, such as people defecating off balconies or in the street. Pistoletto posed the wife of Paolo Mussat Sartor, the photographer who took the source photo for *Donna che fa la cacca*, to re-create just such a detail, enlarging the figure to fill the lower half of the polished steel panel. This work also references a memory of a day spent working with his father on a mural when the weather was brutally cold. When Pistoletto opened the door of the building to leave, he saw women squatting outside, "just like the women in the painting by Olivero," peeing as quickly (and nearby) as possible in order to get back inside out of the cold.[33]

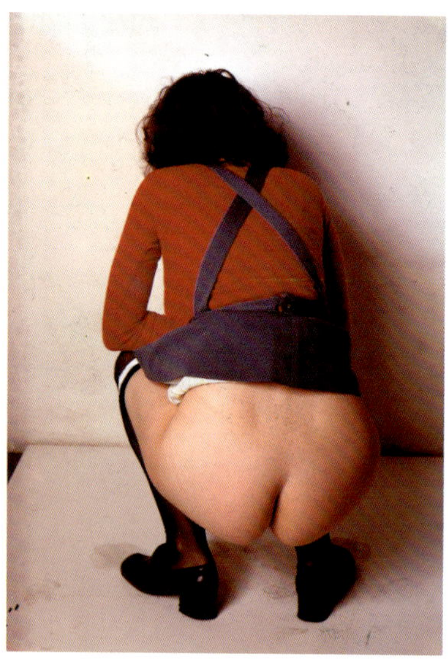

FIG. 152. The source photograph for *Donna che fa la cacca* (*Woman Defecating*, 1973; plate 62). Courtesy of Cittadellarte-Fondazione Pistoletto, Biella

Donna che fa la cacca is a serigraphic (or silkscreen) print on stainless steel. Pistoletto began to use serigraphy in 1969 to make editions of prints on the polished steel panels, at the suggestion of his dealer, Gian Enzo Sperone, who felt that these "multiples" would provide young collectors with an opportunity to acquire the artist's work at an affordable price. The color transparencies that are the basis of the early serigraphs were shot by Mussat, who had been documenting Pistoletto's work for the gallery, taking photographs of the artist and his paintings in the studio and in gallery installations. It was an easy transition for the two men to begin working collaboratively to produce photographs for the serigraphs. Initially the process was not dissimilar to the way Pistoletto and Bressano had worked: Pistoletto would provide Mussat with the ideas and stage the subjects in Mussat's studio. The two would also go to the zoo or other locations to capture images that Pistoletto wanted for the serigraphs. Mussat shot color transparencies, as this format was the basis of the color separations needed for printing the serigraphs. For the early serigraphs, Mussat and Pistoletto worked together with the printer to produce full-scale proofs that were used to make decisions about the scale and placement of the images on the steel panels, in advance of the printer making the color separations and printing the images on the panels.

When the serigraphs began to be sold by Galleria Persano, Paolo Pellion—the brother of the gallery owner, Giorgio Persano—replaced Mussat as the photographer taking the source images. Over time, the process for making the serigraphs also evolved, in conjunction with changes in photography and commercial printing. In the 1970s, Polaroid cameras were sometimes used to capture subjects for the multiples (fig. 154). The

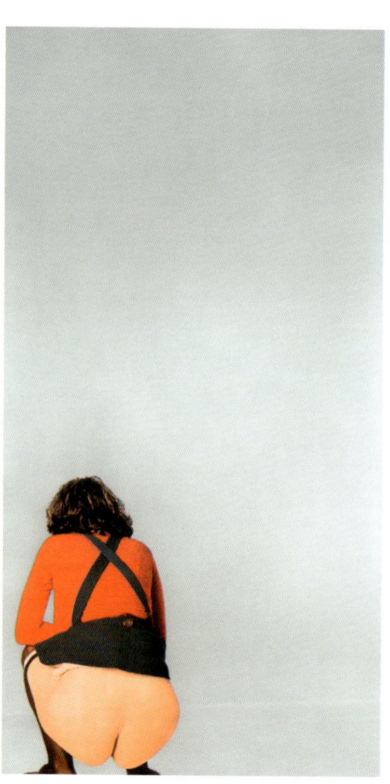

FIG. 153. Michelangelo Pistoletto, *Donna che fa la cacca* (*Woman Defecating*, 1973; plate 62)

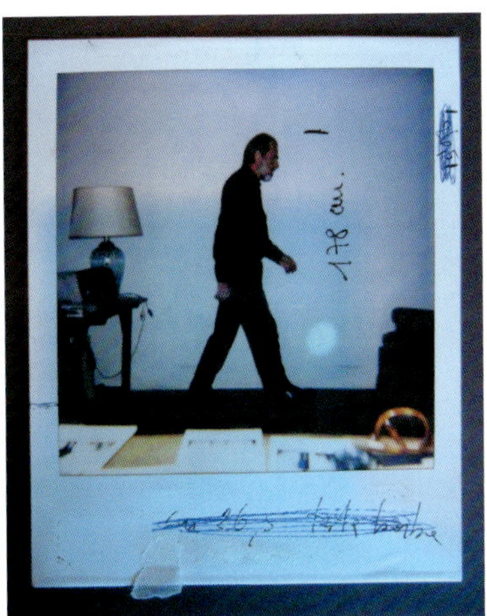

FIG. 154. Polaroid used by Pistoletto as the source for one of his mirror paintings, Cittadellarte-Fondazione Pistoletto, Biella. Photograph by Suzanne Penn

relatively poor resolution of the Polaroid photographs was a feature that appealed to Pistoletto: "When the Polaroids were blown up for the serigraphs they were very imprecise, and I liked the fact that they were not perfect."[34] Eventually, digital cameras and the computer began to be used to capture, manipulate, and transmit the images to the printer.

Concurrent with the production of serigraphic multiples, Pistoletto continued to make unique works in tissue paper on steel panels until about 1972, when he adopted serigraphy as his sole means of making both multiples and unique works. Some of the unique works in serigraphy have variants in which the same image is used in more than one mirror painting, but with changes in the positioning. Other works have "twins," as Pistoletto sometimes made two of a work so that he could retain ownership of one for use in mounting exhibitions. Pistoletto considers these "twins" to be unique works, as opposed to the multiples, which were produced in large print editions.

There are two versions of *Donna che fa la cacca*. Pistoletto has retained ownership of one of them, but the other was inscribed sometime after 1973 on the reverse of the steel with the following:

> I am very satisfied with the result. I put in the foreground a detail of a painting by Olivero, a Piedmontese artist from the eighteenth century, obviously with the use of the camera lens. The photograph for this painting was shot by Mussat in his studio in Turin. Since I use serigraphy, I no longer work in my studio but use various studios or laboratories that are already equipped. And I benefit from the collaboration of technical experts, each one with his own expertise. I would say that mine is the role of director.[35]

Pistoletto had been acting in the role of director from the time of his initial employment of photography in 1962, in that he conceived of the compositions, assembled and posed the subjects, and directed the use of the camera in capturing them. But the inscription on *Donna che fa la cacca* is telling of a fundamental shift from the early mirror paintings and their handcrafted tissue-paper figures to the subsequent adoption of serigraphy as a means of creating unique works: Pistoletto's role as director went from being one of many roles he played in creating the works to being solely a director with numerous collaborators. While it is true that Pistoletto's initial employment of photography necessitated a collaboration with another person, namely Bressano, whose expertise, equipment, and studio facility were essential for the staging, photographing, and creation of the photo enlargements that were used in making the tissue-paper cutouts, none of these activities were undertaken without Pistoletto's direct participation and overseeing aesthetic judgment. After the photographic enlargements were made, Pistoletto took them to his own studio, where he worked independently to create the tissue-paper cutouts that were then affixed to the steel supports. At no point in the labor-intensive process did he relinquish a step to anyone else.

After he adopted serigraphy as the means of both transforming his source photographs and affixing his compositions to the polished steel, his role was indeed very different, as the entire process of producing the serigraphic works was a collaborative effort, with much of the work taking place out of the artist's hands. It is noteworthy that Pistoletto felt compelled to communicate such specific information about what is old and what is new in the processes involved in making *Donna che fa la cacca*. The inscription informs us that although the processes for transforming the source photograph and placing the figurative image on the steel panel had changed, the conceptual process had not. Working with Mussat, Pistoletto used the camera to capture a figure that he posed, in this case in reference to his memory of a detail in a specific old master painting as well as an event of his youth. He also lets us know that this was the end of his direct involvement in the process and that at no point did the panel, the transformation of the source photograph, or the placement of the composition on the steel surface involve him or take place at his studio.

The early mirror paintings, in their materials and technique, encompass many art forms, including photography, drawing, collage, and assemblage, and the later works, with the switch to serigraphy, relate to printmaking and commercial art, but it is important to remember that Pistoletto considers all forms of the mirror paintings to be direct descendants of his painting practice, because it was the materials and techniques of those early paintings, rather than a conceptual leap, that led him to use the reflective stainless-steel supports and to employ photography. Pistoletto has stated that over time the "materiality of these works became less and less."[36] From the heavily textured and painted figurative works, where he first attempted to merge figure and ground, to the experiments with various reflective surfaces and different means of creating the figures in gelatin, in tissue paper with different adhesives, and ultimately in serigraphy, the materiality of Pistoletto's compositions has indeed decreased, with the images becoming more and more ethereal. The serigraphic process renders the images with just a whisper of colored inks on the surface of the steel, allowing the figures to supremely inhabit the reflective surface. The direct action of Pistoletto's hand in rendering the figure is no longer a necessity.

1 Michelangelo Pistoletto, "Il rinascimento dell'arte," 1979, unpublished manuscript, Cittadellarte-Fondazione Pistoletto, Biella. See also Pistoletto's Web site, at www.pistoletto.it/eng/crono03.htm, and his interview with Martin Friedman (1966); as cited in Palazzo Grassi, Venice, *Pistoletto*, exh. cat. (Milan: Electa, 1976), p. 5, for similar recountings.

2 Michelangelo Pistoletto, in conversation with the author, October 20, 2009, Cittadellarte-Fondazione Pistoletto, Biella. Much of the information presented in this essay was gathered from a series of conversations I had with the artist in October 2009 and on January 25, 2010, at Cittadellarte. The great majority of these were conducted in English.

3 At age twenty, having completed his training at the advertising school run by Armando Testa, Pistoletto was given the opportunity to take over a small advertising business from a man who was taking a job in a large firm and seeking someone to carry on with his roster of clients. Pistoletto kept this business going for only a few years, and he recounts that the decision to give it up "was made for him" in 1958 by his exhibition and contract with Galleria Galatea in Turin. Pistoletto, in conversation with the author, Cittadellarte-Fondazione Pistoletto, Biella, October 22, 2009.

4 Ibid., October 20, 2009.

5 Ibid.

6 Pistoletto worked with his father restoring paintings from age fourteen until approximately age

nineteen, when his mother urged him to enroll in Armando Testa's advertising school so that he might have an alternative means of earning a living.

7 Pistoletto, in conversation with the author, October 22, 2009, Cittadellarte-Fondazione Pistoletto, Biella, October 20, 2009.

8 Ibid., October 20, 2009.

9 Ibid.

10 Ibid.

11 Ibid.

12 Ibid.

13 Michelangelo Pistoletto, interview with Germano Celant, in *Pistoletto*, ed. Germano Celant, exh. cat. (Milan: Electa, 1984), p. 23 (my translation).

14 "In this reduction of the figure to life-size I was helped a lot by Bacon's show at Galatea. Seeing Bacon I perceived that my problem and my drama were there already, made explicit, in a man in search of his own dimension and his own space, an impenetrable glass cage, in which the man lived in a state so dramatic it suffocated him, deprived him of voice and space. . . . I continued my inquiry, honing my work in on man, but seeking to do just the opposite of what Bacon did: to remove all expression and all movement from the figures in order to cool their drama." The translation is from Pistoletto's Web site, www.pistoletto.it/eng/crono02.htm. See also Claire Gilman, "Pistoletto's Staged Subjects," *October* 124 (Spring 2008), pp. 53–74, for a description of the contemporary art scene in Turin and the many showings there of Bacon's work.

15 Pistoletto, in conversation with the author, Cittadellarte-Fondazione Pistoletto, Biella, October 20, 2009.

16 Ibid., October 22, 2009.

17 Although film negatives had long been available, Bressano used glass-plate negatives for the first two or three years that he took photographs with Pistoletto, as indicated by the collection of negatives in the artist's archives at Cittadellarte-Fondazione Pistoletto, Biella.

18 Pistoletto, in conversation with the author, Cittadellarte-Fondazione Pistoletto, Biella, October 23, 2009.

19 Ibid., October 22, 2009. *Lampadina* (*Lightbulb*, 1964; plate 22), however, comprises a combination of cutout photographs and tissue paper: the cord, socket, and bulb filament are actual photographs glued to the steel; and the glass of the bulb is created from tissue paper adhered atop the photographic filament and made transparent with the adhesive.

20 Ibid., January 25, 2010.

21 Ibid., October 22, 2009.

22 Ibid., October 23, 2009. *Lampadina* is a transitional work in terms of auxiliary support. Here Pistoletto eliminated the stretched canvas and adhered the mirror painting directly to the wood stretcher. In subsequent works he abandoned the use of traditional wood stretchers in favor of metal stretchers.

23 Pistoletto and Rinaldi met and became close friends as students at Armando Testa's advertising school. Rinaldi collaborated with Pistoletto on the short-lived journal *Presenze* and posed for him in many of the photographs used for his early drawings and mirror paintings. When Rinaldi shot the parade photographs, he was just beginning to explore what would be his eventual career as a professional photographer.

24 The enlarging process allowed a change in scale in the figures. In *Ragazzo* (*Boy*, 1965; plate 33), the young boy in the far middle ground and the man in the nearer middle ground of the source photograph were able to be resized in the enlarging process so that they would be in scale, standing side by side, in the mirror painting.

25 Pistoletto, in conversation with the author, Cittadellarte-Fondazione Pistoletto, Biella, October 22, 2009.

26 Ibid., October 23, 2009.

27 Pistoletto, in conversation with Carlos Basualdo, Erica Battle, and the author, Cittadellarte-Fondazione Pistoletto, Biella, October 21, 2009.

28 See note 14 above.

29 Michelangelo Pistoletto, interview with Giovanni Lista, in *Ligeia* (Paris) 25–28 (1999), and in conversation with the author, Cittadellarte-Fondazione Pistoletto, Biella, October 23, 2009.

30 Pistoletto, in conversation with the author, Cittadellarte-Fondazione Pistoletto, Biella, October 23, 2009.

31 Ibid.

32 Ibid.

33 Pistoletto, in conversation with Carlos Basualdo, Erica Battle, and the author, Cittaellarte-Fondazione Pistoletto, Biella, October 21, 2009.

34 Pistoletto, in conversation with the author, Cittadellarte-Fondazione Pistoletto, Biella, January 25, 2010.

35 The inscription, in Italian, reads: "Sono molto soddisfatto del risultato, ho portato in primo piano un particolare di un quadro di Olivero, artista piemontese del 1700 naturalmente con l'intervento dell'occhio fotografico. . . . La fotografia di questo quadro è stata fatta da Mussat nel suo studio di Torino, da quando uso la serigrafia non lavoro più in un mio studio ma uso vari studi o laboratori già attrezzati. E mi avvalgo della collaborazione di tecnici esperti, ognuno nel suo ambito. Direi che la mia è un'operazione di regia." I thank Roberta Nuzzaci for her help with the translation of this inscription.

36 Pistoletto, in conversation with the author, Cittadellarte-Fondazione Pistoletto, Biella, October 23, 2009.

PLATES

1
Autoritratto **(*****Self-Portrait*****), 1956**
Oil and acrylic on canvas
55⅛ x 35 7/16 inches (140 x 90 cm)
Collection of the artist

2
La folla **(*****The Crowd*****), 1959**
Oil and acrylic on canvas
78¾ x 47¼ inches (200 x 120 cm)
Private collection

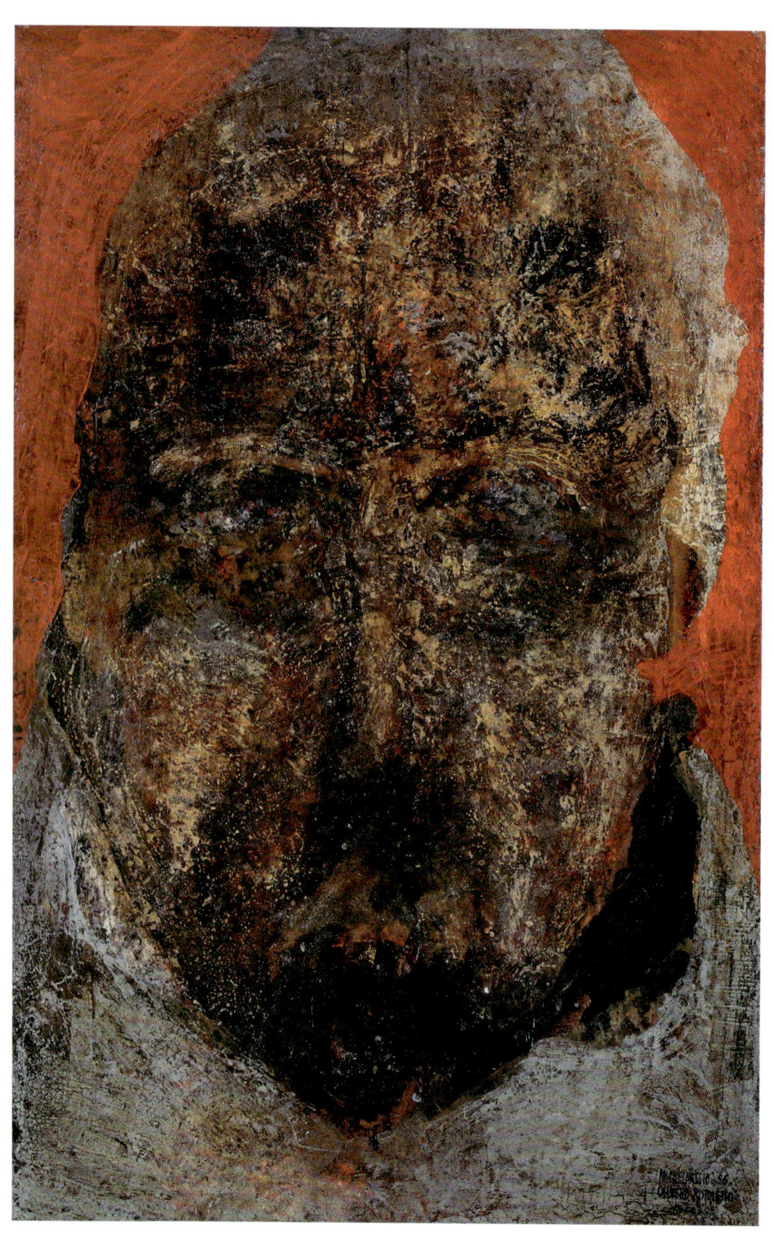

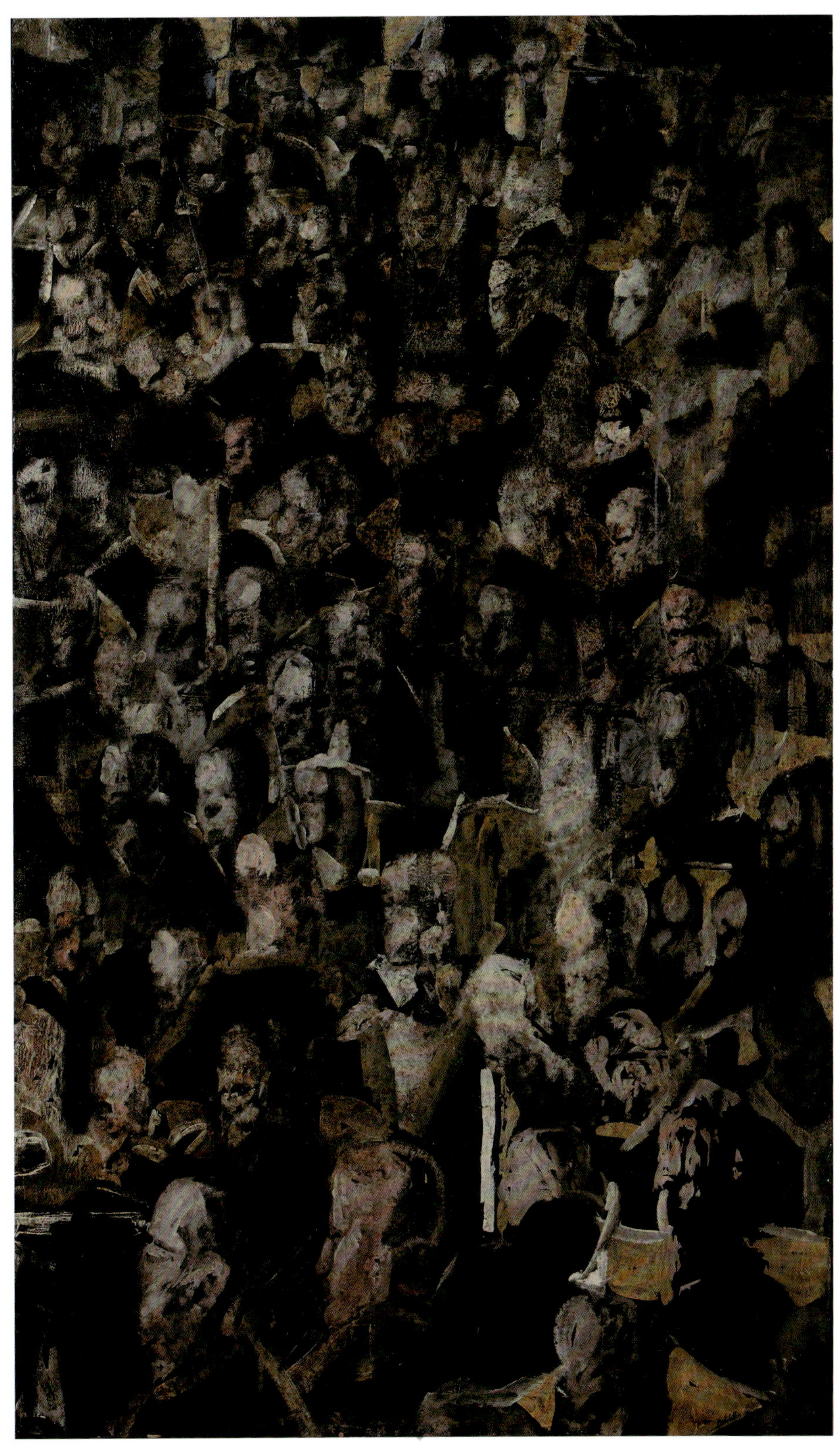

3
***Esperimento* (*Experiment*), 1959**
Silver, acrylic, rope, wood, and canvas
29⅛ x 23⅝ inches (74 x 60 cm)
Collection of the artist

4
***Autoritratto argento* (*Silver Self-Portrait*), 1960**
Oil, acrylic, and silver on wood
78¾ x 78¾ inches (200 x 200 cm)
Collection of the artist

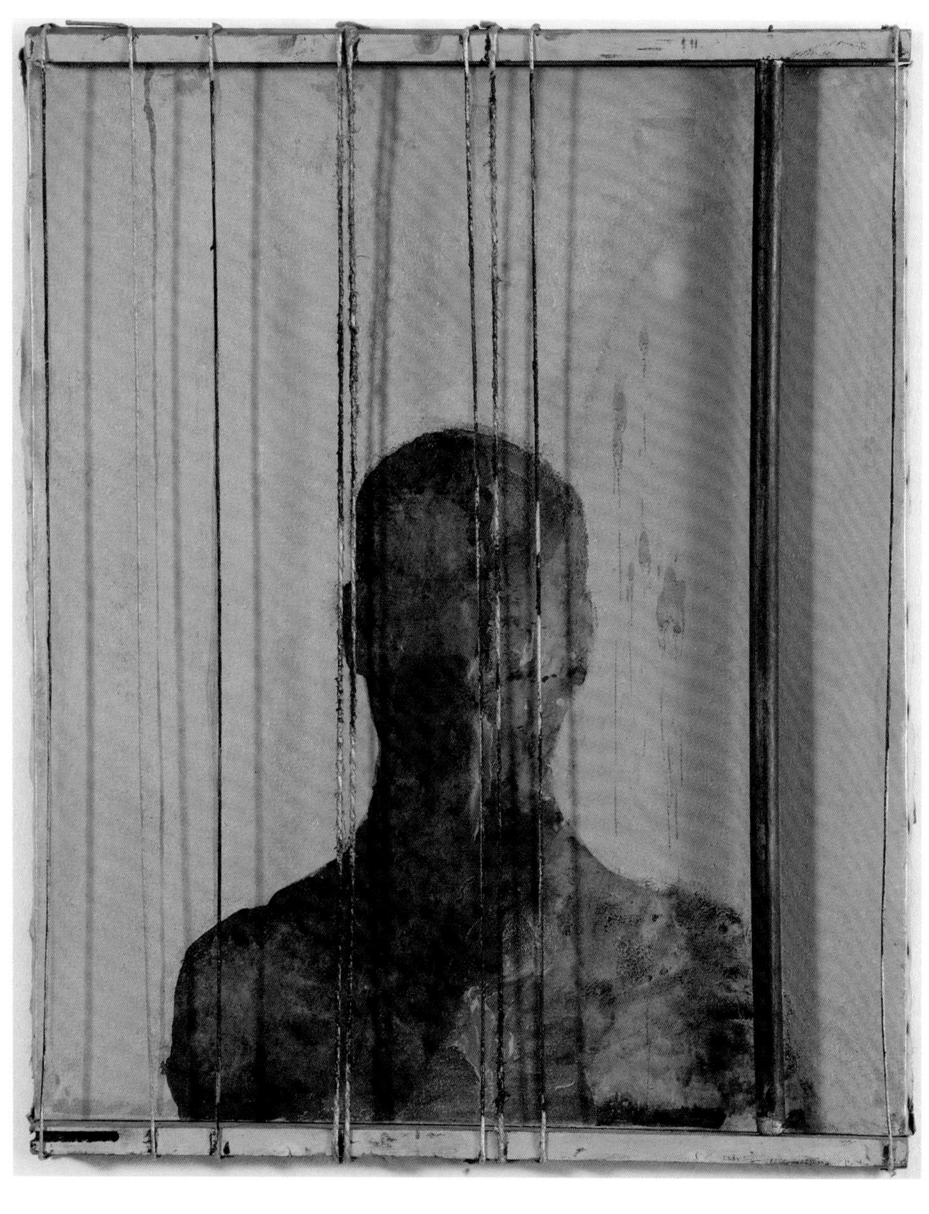

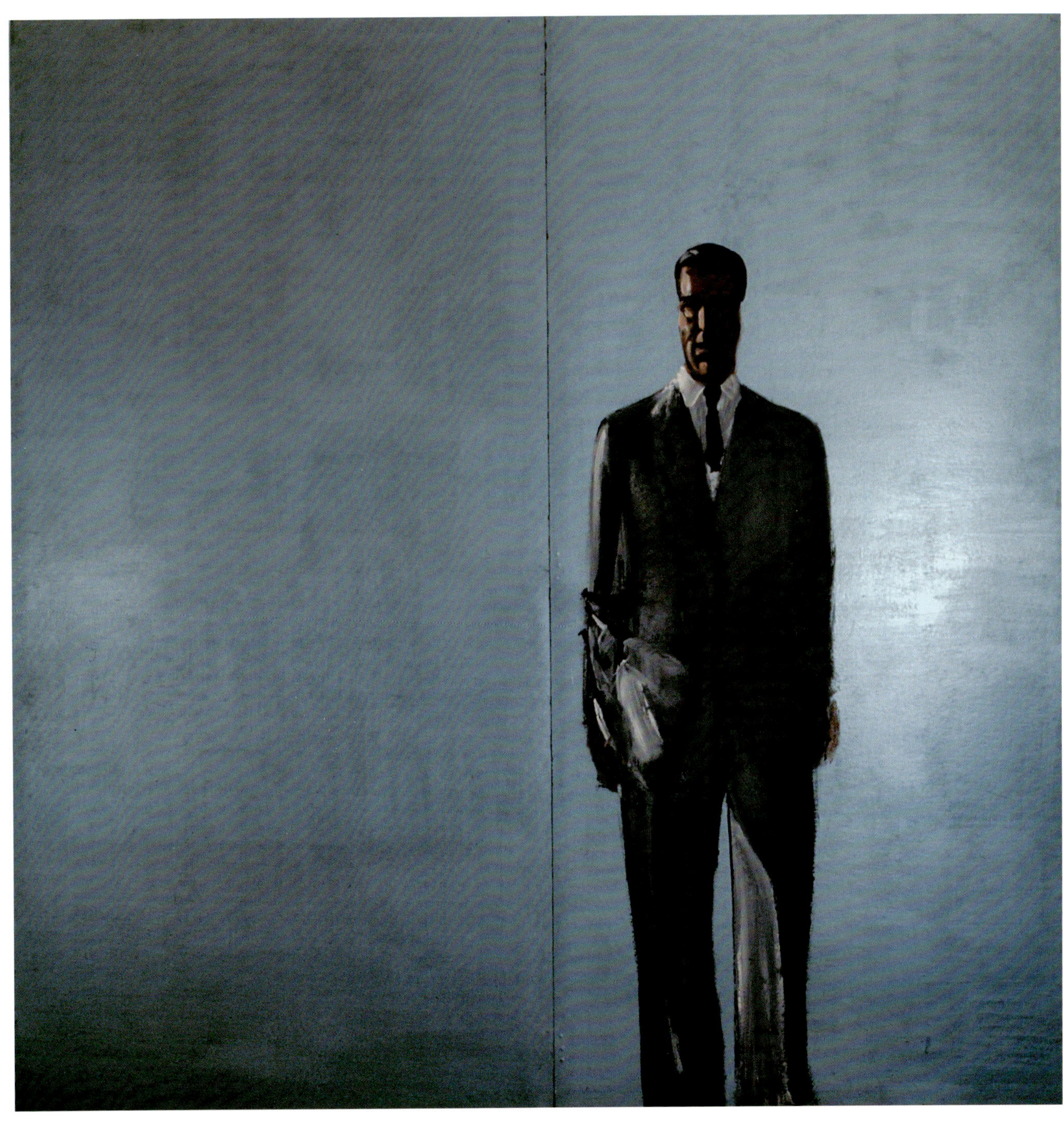

5
Autoritratto oro **(*Gold Self-Portrait*), 1960**
Oil, acrylic, and gold on canvas
78¾ x 59 1/16 inches (200 x 150 cm)
Collection of the artist

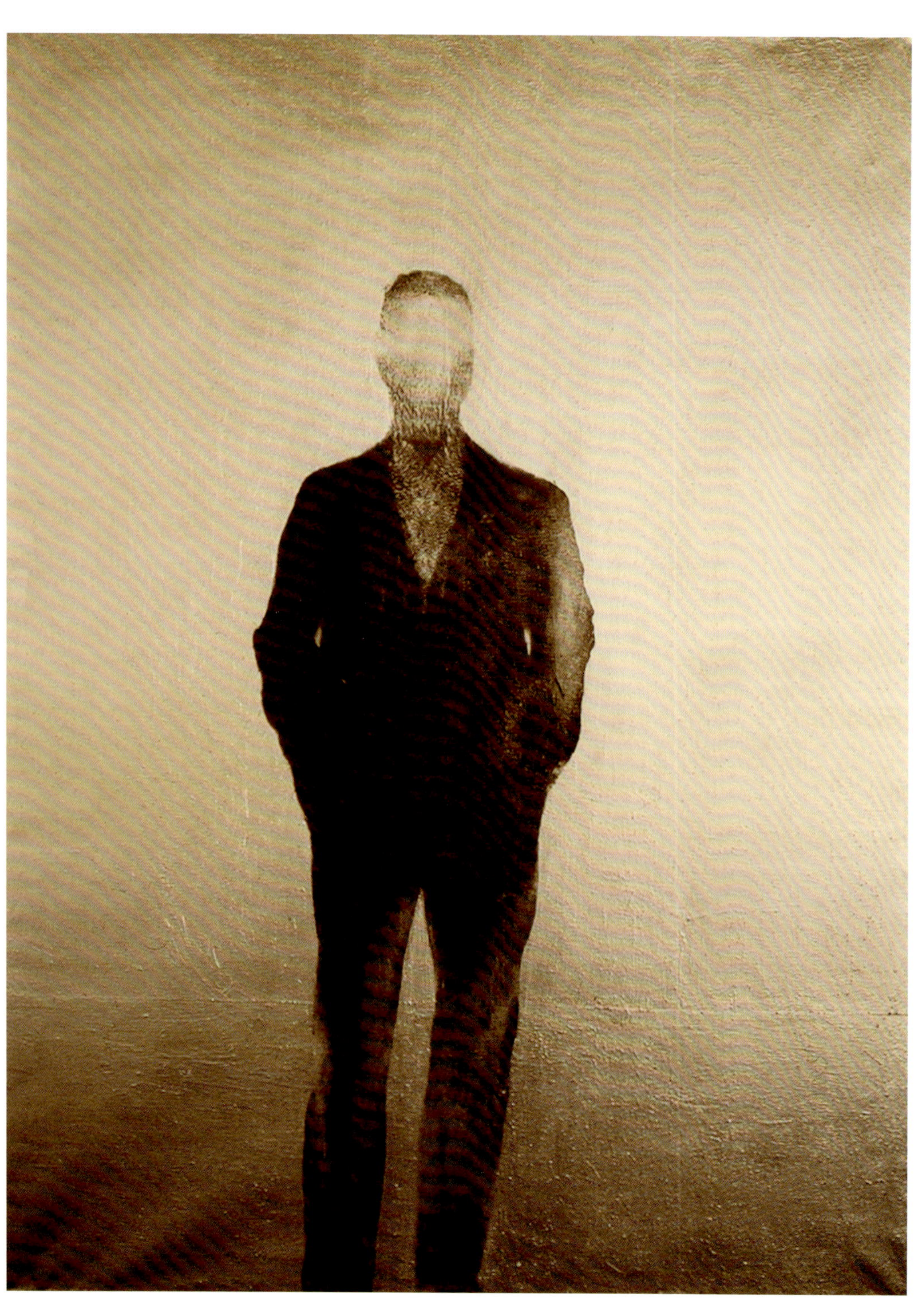

6
Autoritratto bronzo
(Bronze Self-Portrait), 1961
Oil, acrylic, and bronze on canvas
78¾ x 47¼ inches (200 x 120 cm)
Private collection

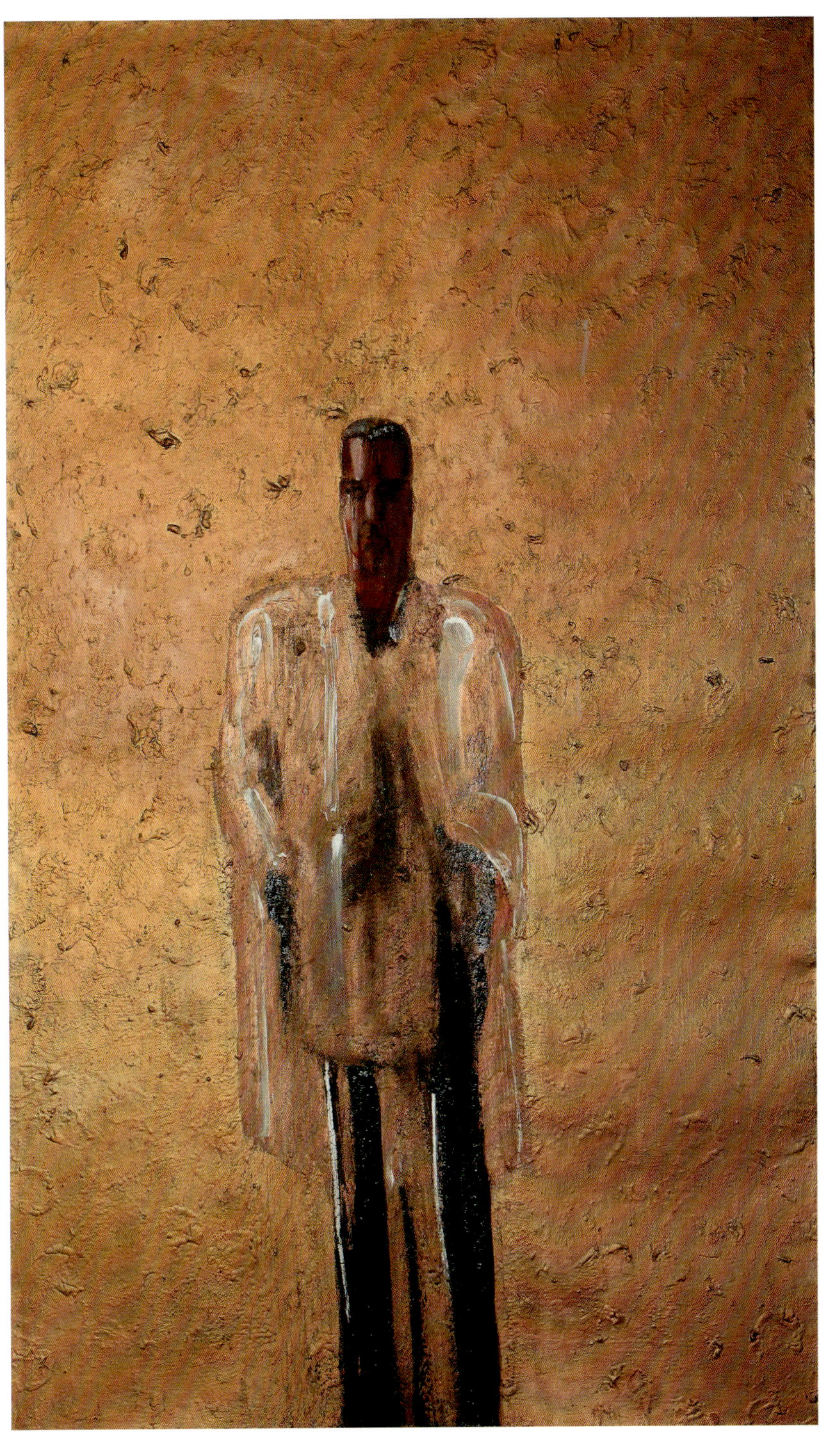

7
Verso il presente **(*Toward the Present*), 1961**
Acrylic and plastic varnish on canvas
59 1/16 x 59 1/16 inches (150 x 150 cm)
Collezione La Gaia, Busca, Italy

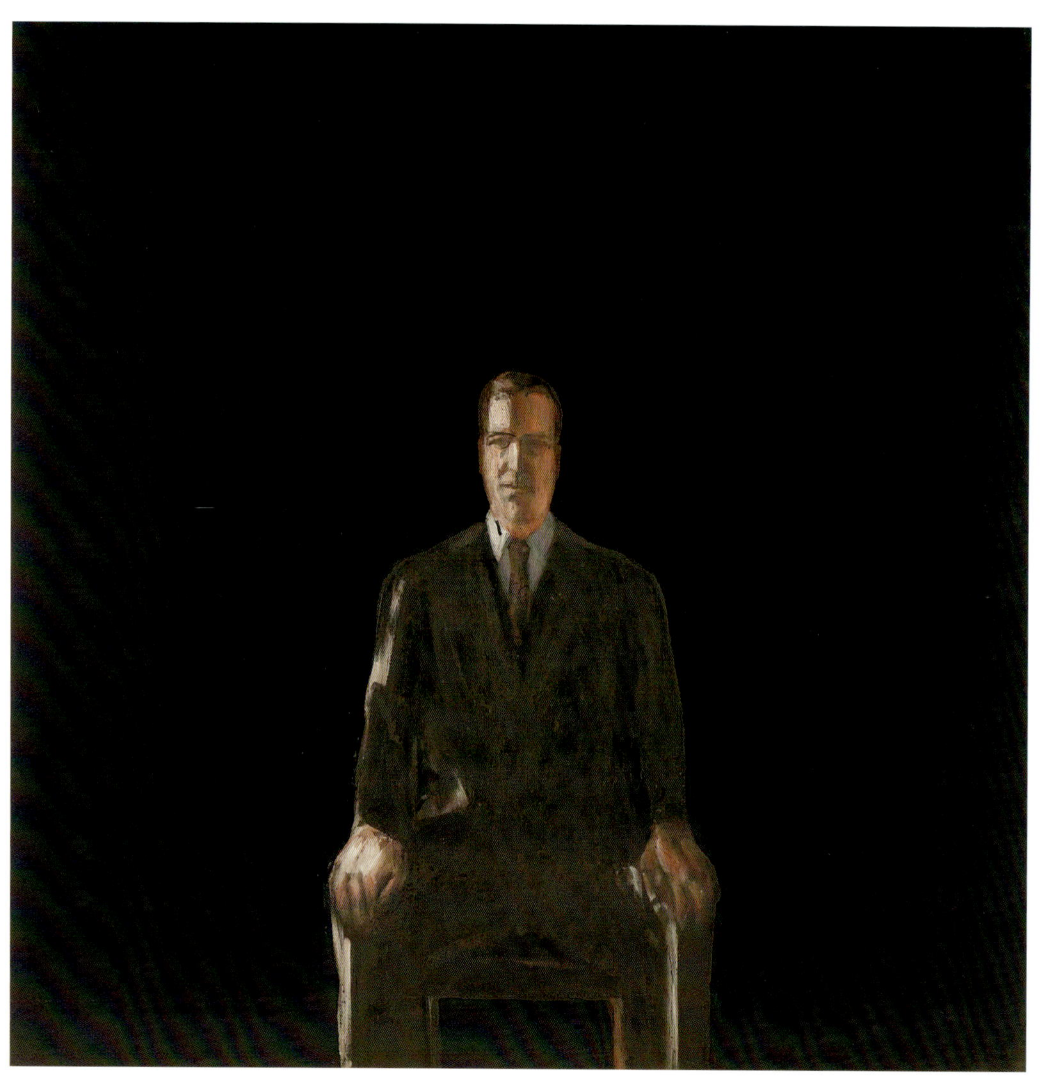

8
Il presente—Autoritratto in camicia
(*The Present—Self-Portrait in Shirt*), 1961
Acrylic and plastic varnish on canvas
78¾ x 59$^{1}/_{16}$ inches (200 x 150 cm)
Collection of the artist

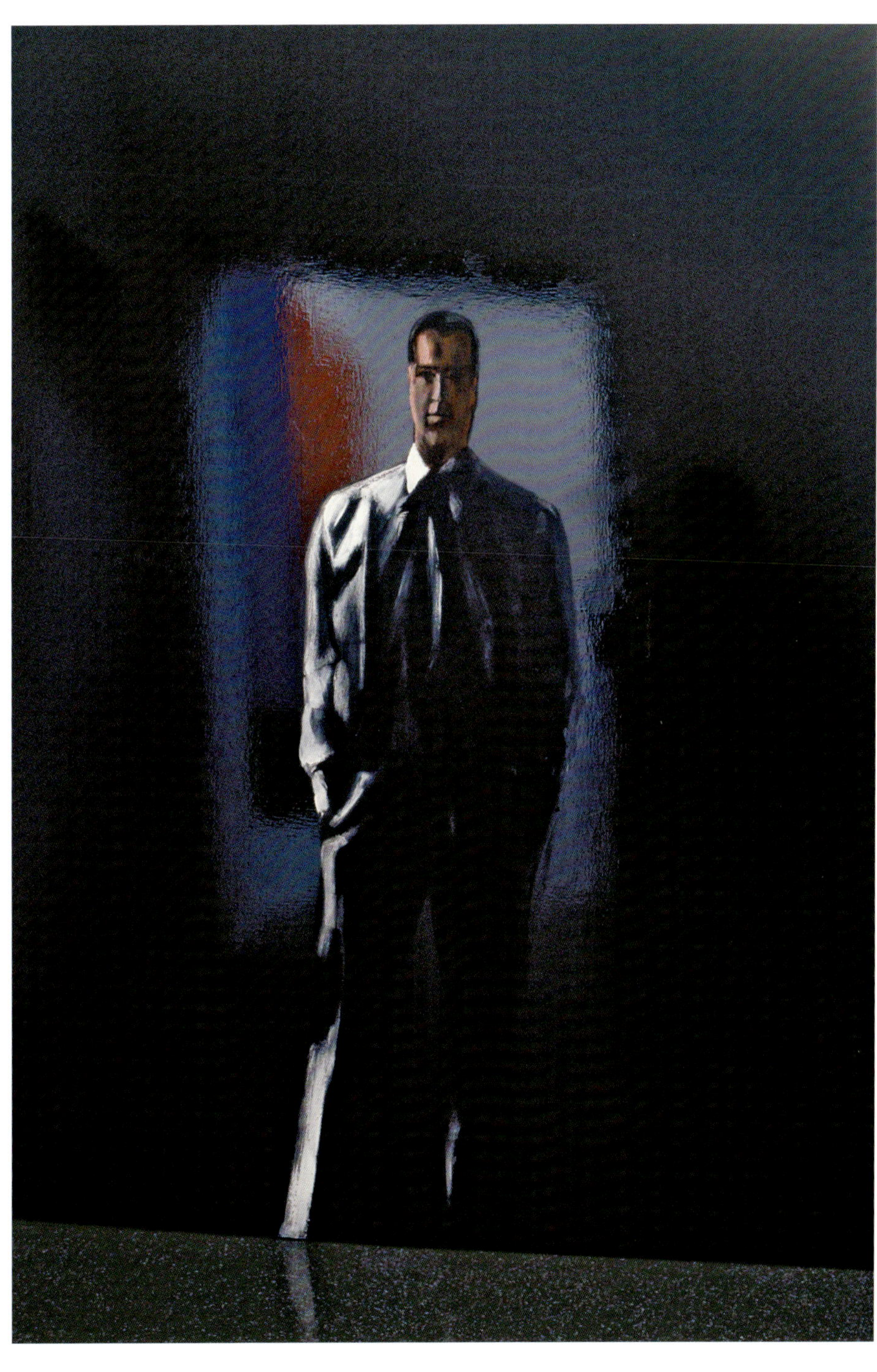

9
Il presente—Uomo di schiena
(*The Present—Man from the Back*), 1961
Acrylic and plastic varnish on canvas
78¾ x 59$^{1}/_{16}$ inches (200 x 150 cm)
Collection of the artist

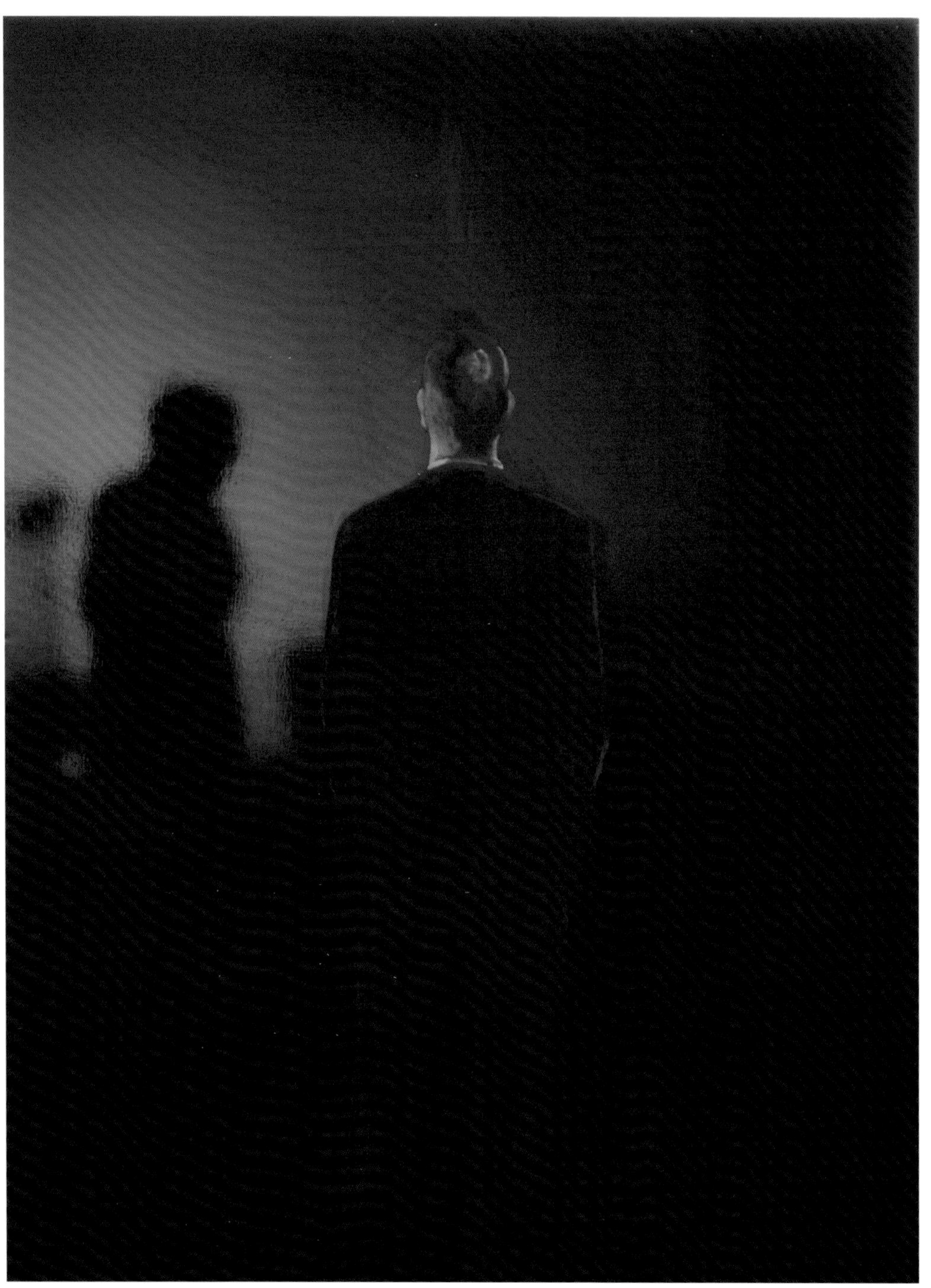

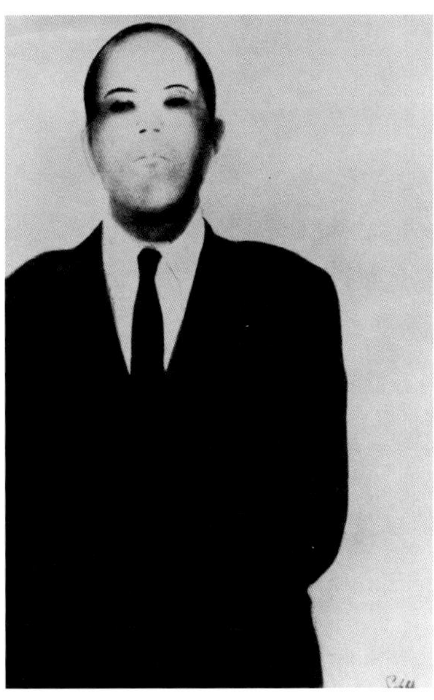

10
***Disegno 5* (*Drawing 5*), 1962**
Pencil on paper
25 13/16 x 18 11/16 inches (65.5 x 47.5 cm)
Private collection

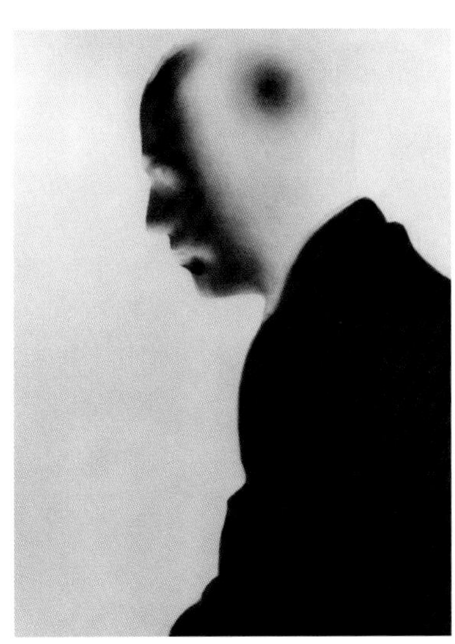

11
***Disegno* (*Drawing*), 1962**
Pencil on paper
23 5/8 x 17 3/4 inches (60 x 45 cm)
Private collection

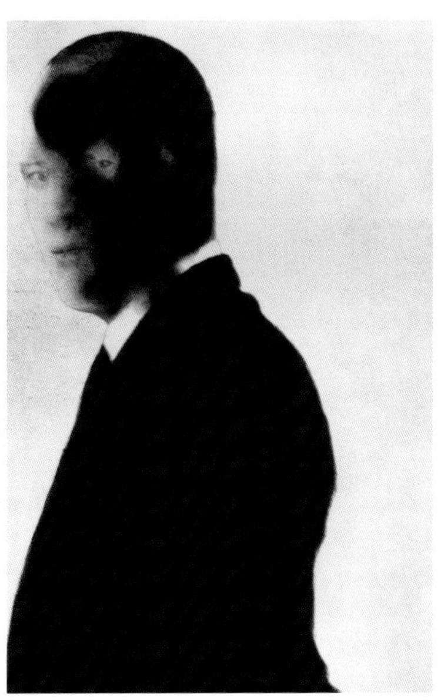

12
***Disegno 1* (*Drawing 1*), 1962**
Pencil on paper
26 3/8 x 18 7/8 inches (67 x 48 cm)
Collection of Giorgio and Giorgiana Persano

13
***Figura di profilo* (*Figure in Profile*), 1962**
Painted tissue paper on polished stainless steel
$24\frac{7}{16}$ x $20\frac{1}{2}$ inches (62 x 52 cm)
François Pinault Foundation

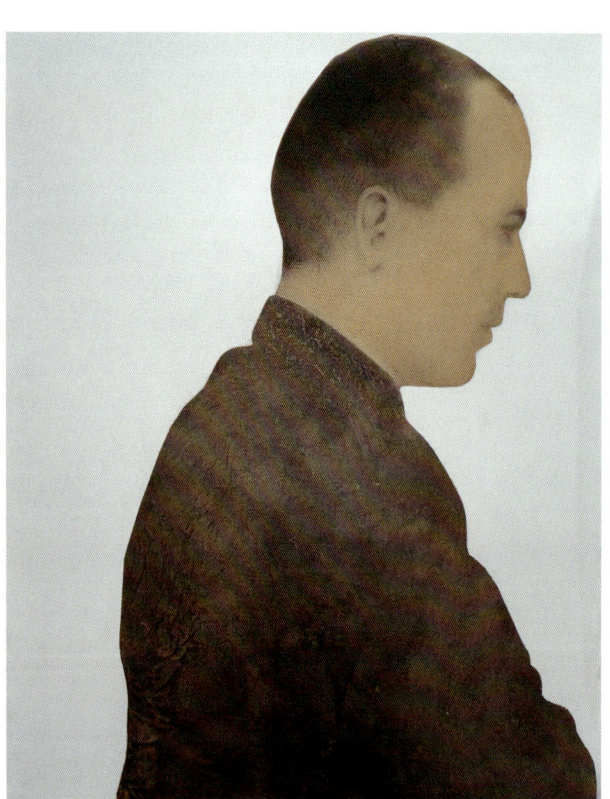

14
***Particolari di persone* (*Details of People*), 1962**
Painted tissue paper on polished stainless steel
49 3/16 x 48 13/16 inches (125 x 124 cm)
San Francisco Museum of Modern Art. Gift of
Edwin Janss, 1978

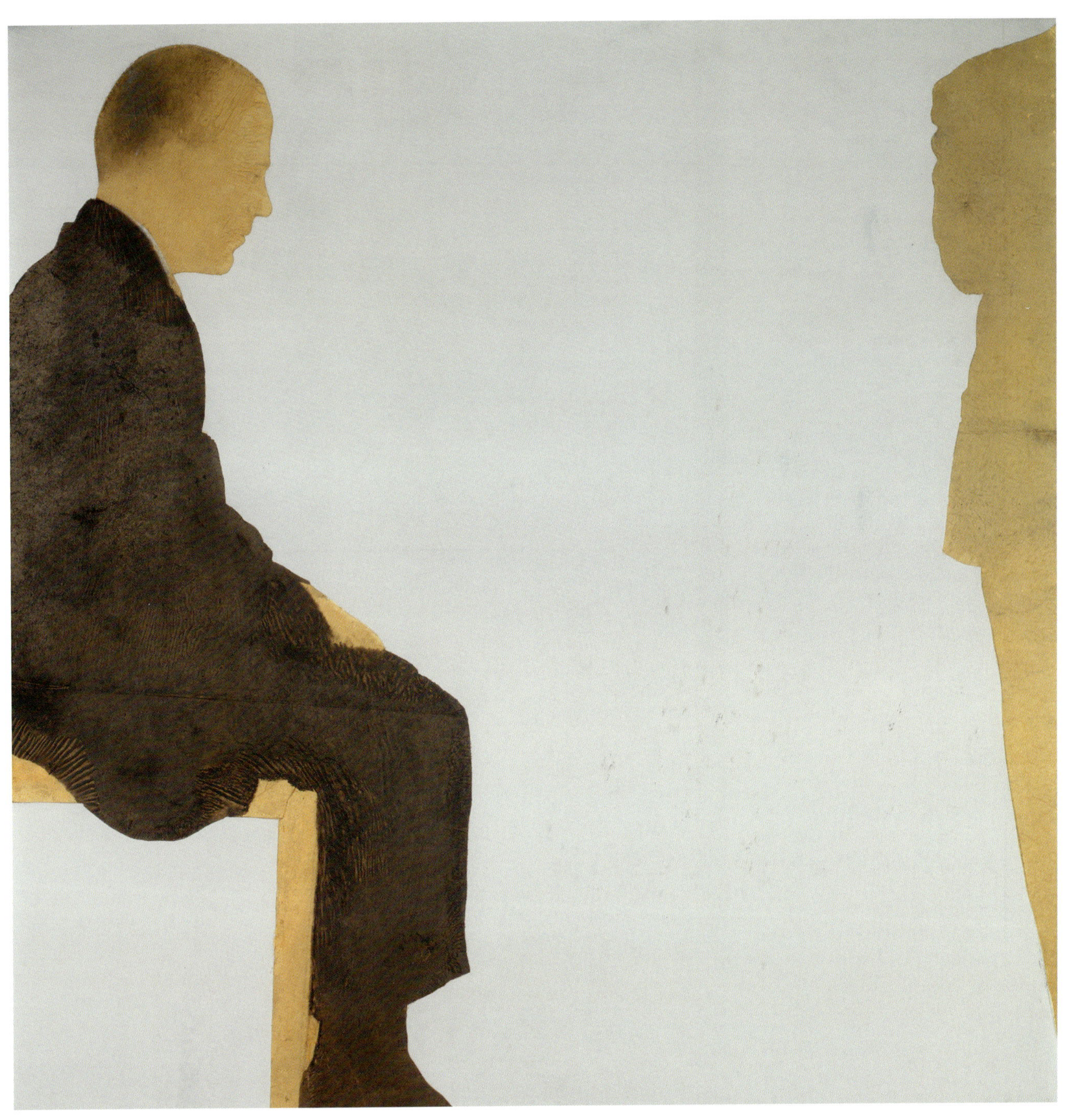

15
Ritratto di Clino (*Portrait of Clino*), 1963
Painted tissue paper on polished stainless steel
31½ x 21¹¹⁄₁₆ inches (80 x 55 cm)
Private collection

16
Sacra conversazione, 1963
Painted tissue paper on polished stainless steel
67 x 39⅜ inches (170 x 100 cm)
Albright-Knox Art Gallery, Buffalo.
Gift of Seymour H. Knox, Jr., 1964

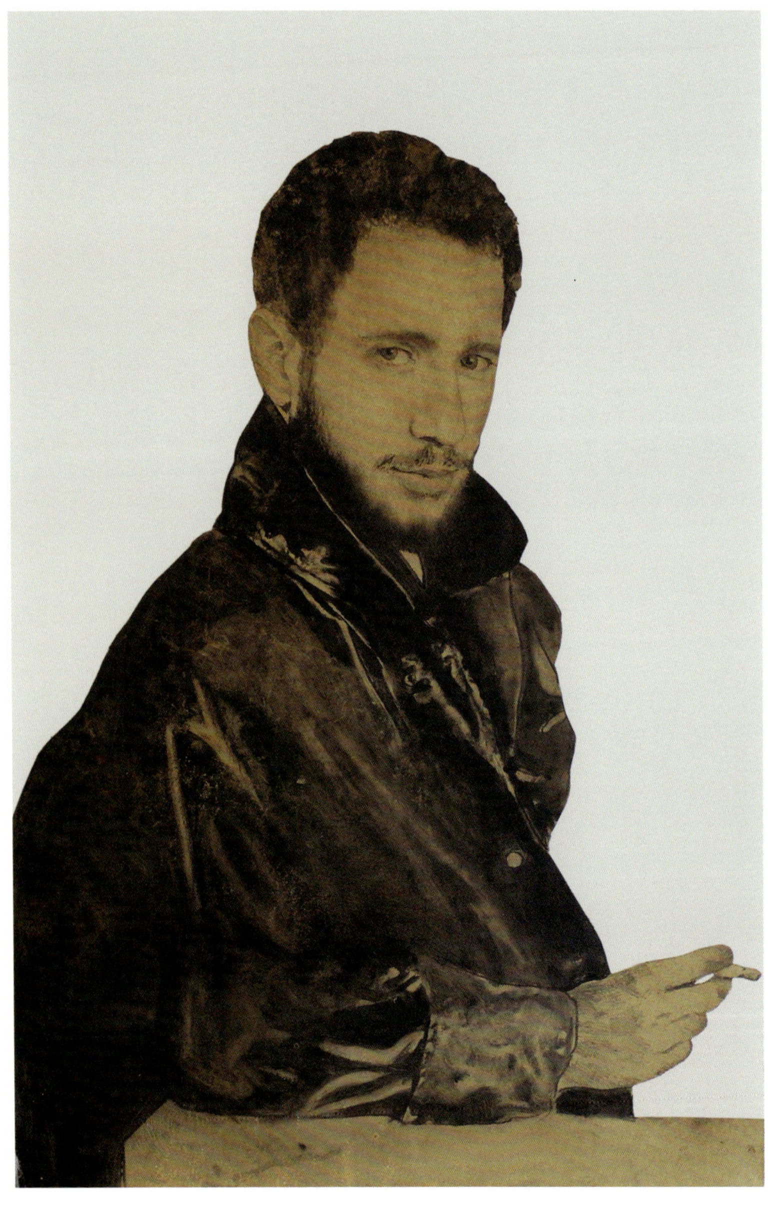

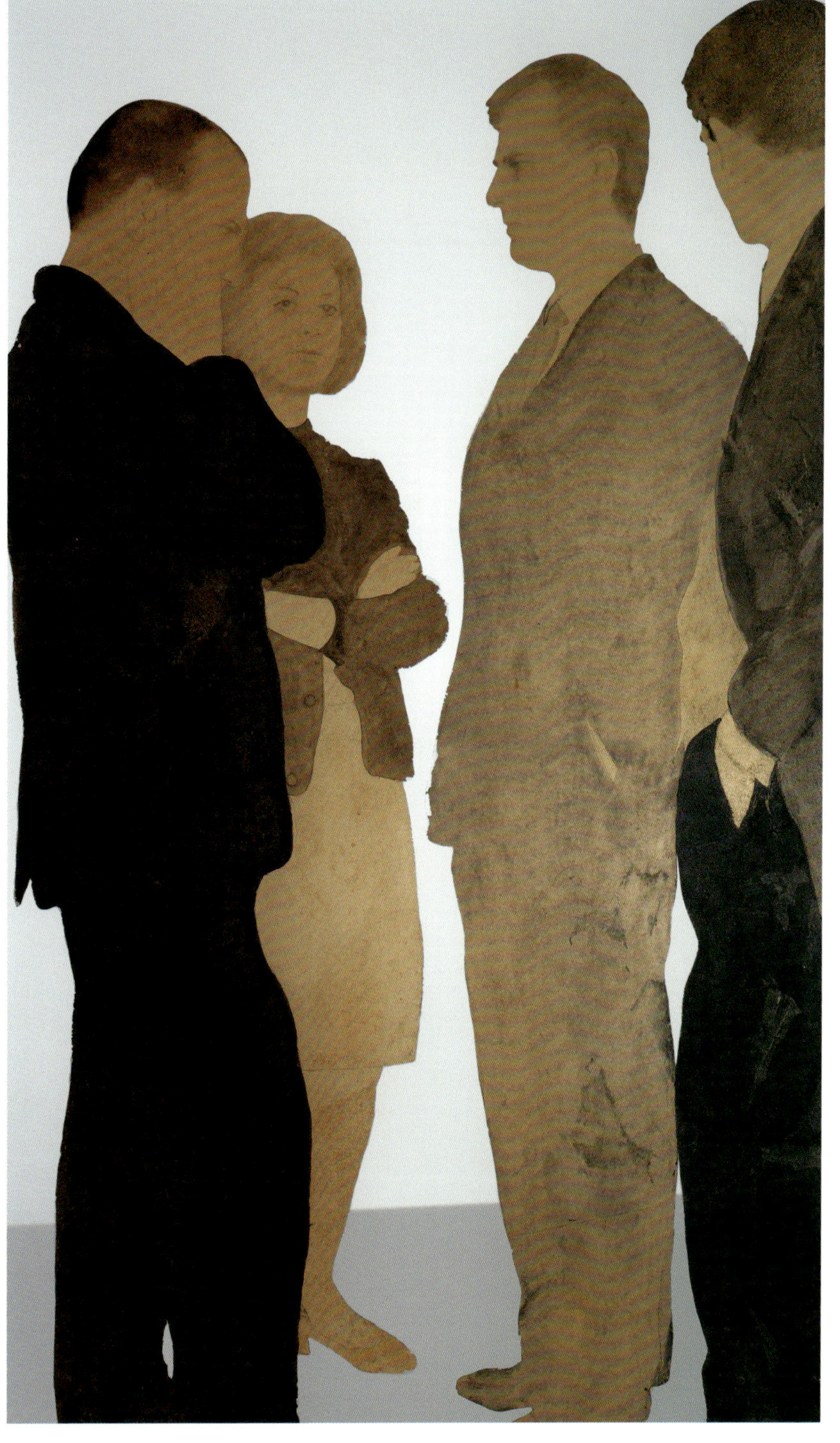

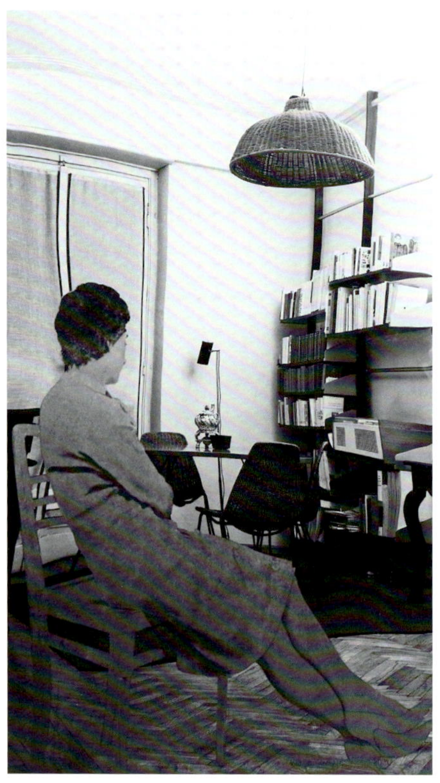

FIG. 155. *Donna seduta di spalle* in Pistoletto's house on via Cibrario in Turin, 1963. Photograph by Paolo Bressano. Courtesy of Cittadellarte-Fondazione Pistoletto, Biella

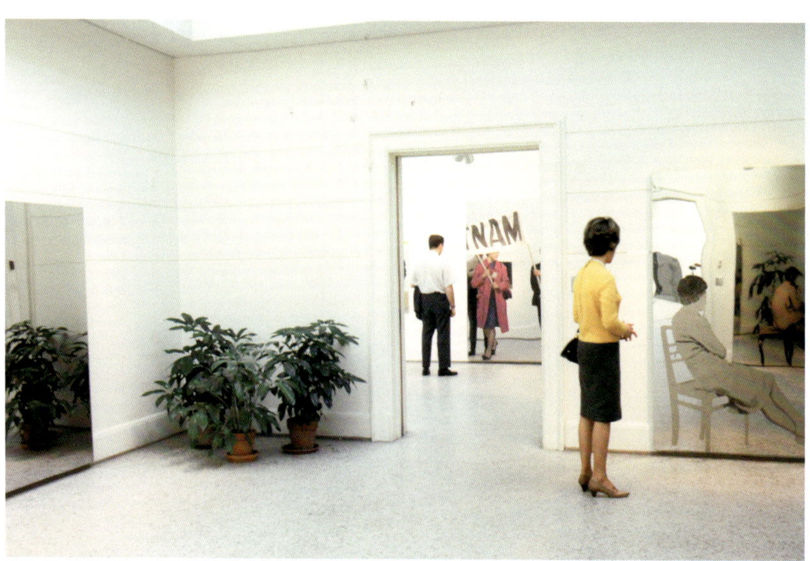

FIG. 156. The exhibition *Michelangelo Pistoletto: A Reflected World* at the Walker Art Center, Minneapolis, with *Donna seduta di spalle* on the right, 1966. Courtesy of the Walker Art Center, Minneapolis

17
Donna seduta di spalle
***(Seated Woman from Behind*), 1963**
Painted tissue paper on polished stainless steel
78¾ x 47¼ inches (200 x 120 cm)
The Sonnabend Collection

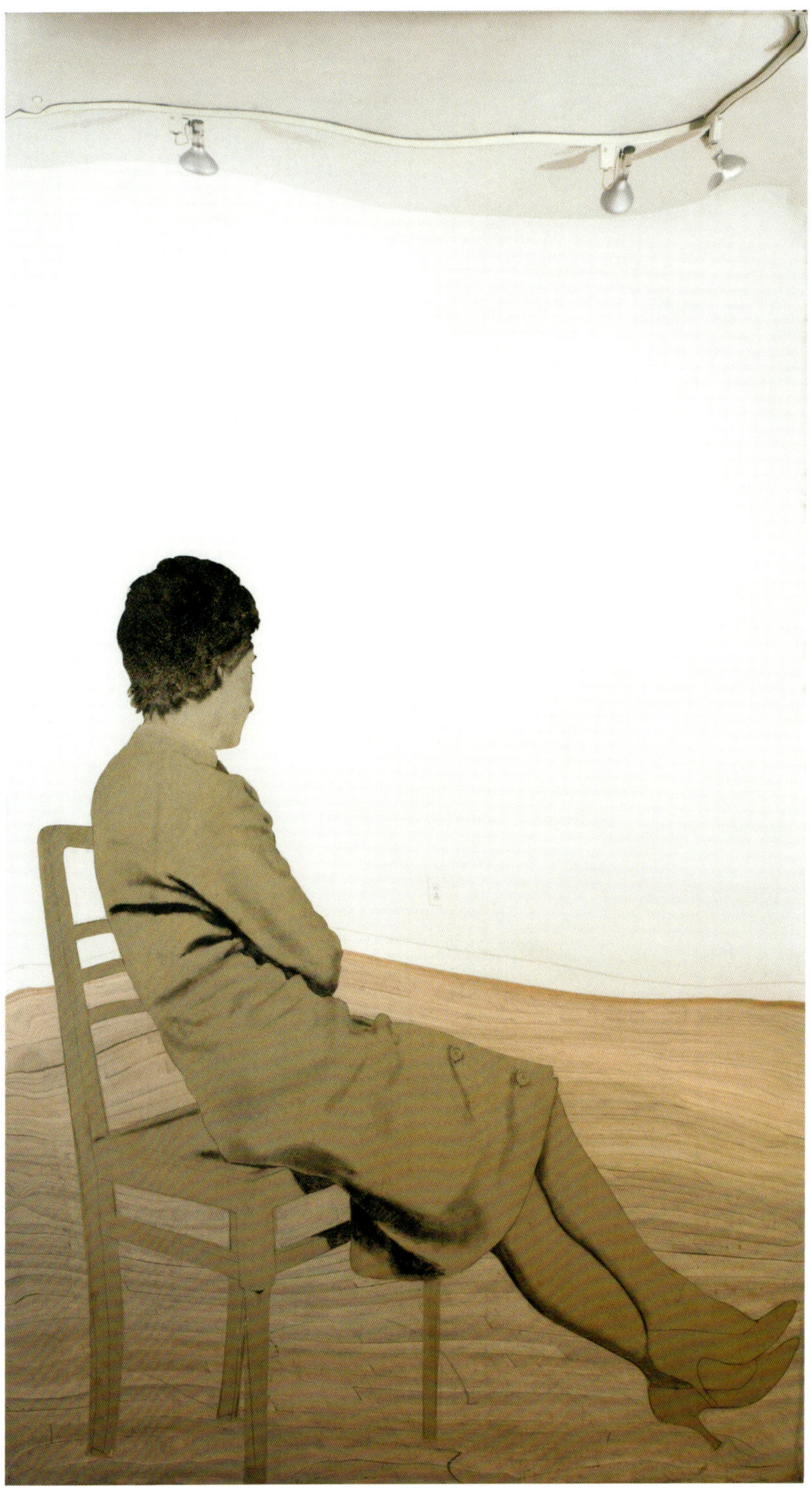

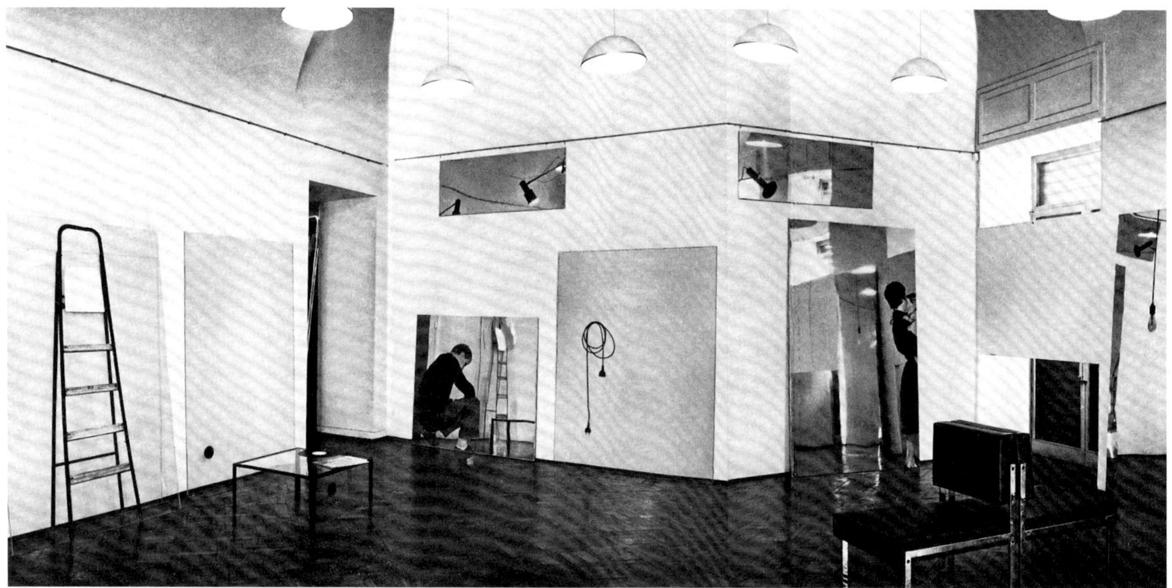

FIG. 157. The exhibition *Michelangelo Pistoletto: I plexiglass* at Galleria Sperone, Turin, with *Autoritratto* at center left, October 2, 1964. Photograph by Paolo Bressano. Courtesy of Cittadellarte-Fondazione Pistoletto, Biella

FIG. 158. *Autoritratto* at Galleria Sperone, Turin, 1964. Photograph by Paolo Bressano. Courtesy of Cittadellarte-Fondazione Pistoletto, Biella

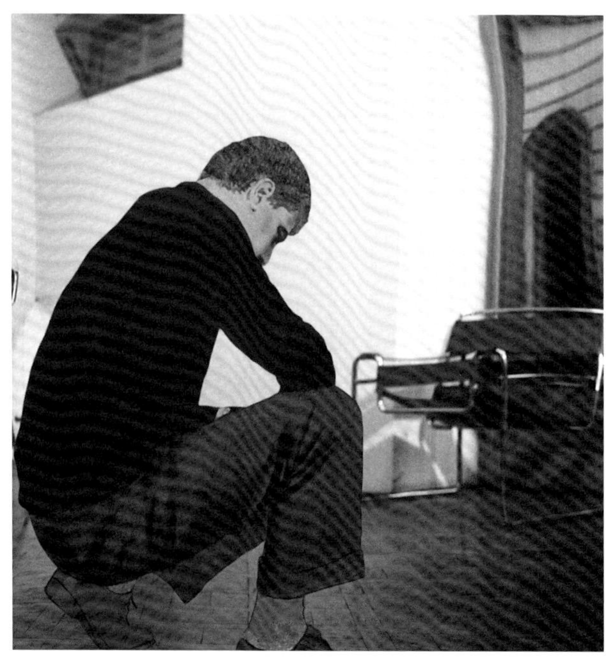

18
***Autoritratto* (*Self-Portrait*), 1963**
Painted tissue paper on polished stainless steel
47¼ x 47¼ inches (120 x 120 cm)
Private collection. On long-term loan to MART—Museo di Arte Moderna e Contemporanea di Trento e Rovereto, Rovereto, Italy

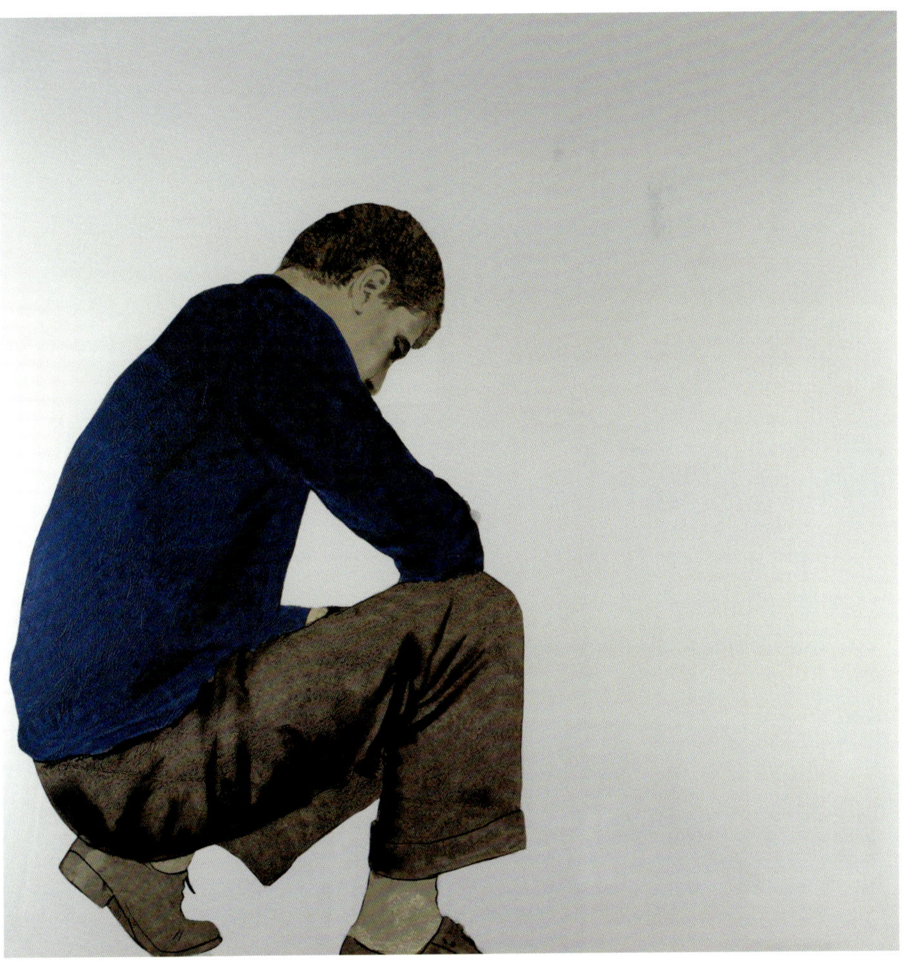

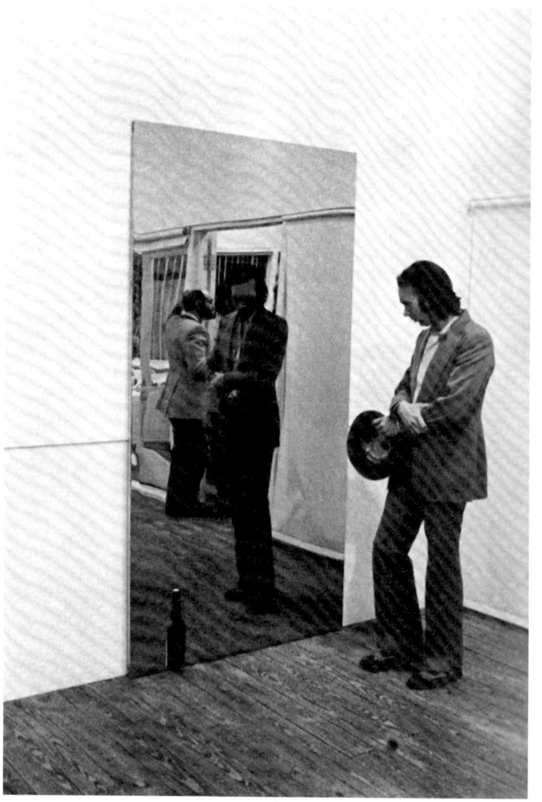

FIG. 159. *Bottiglia per terra* in the exhibition *Michelangelo Pistoletto: Mirror-Works* at the Institute for the Arts, Rice University, Houston, 1979. Courtesy of Cittadellarte-Fondazione Pistoletto, Biella

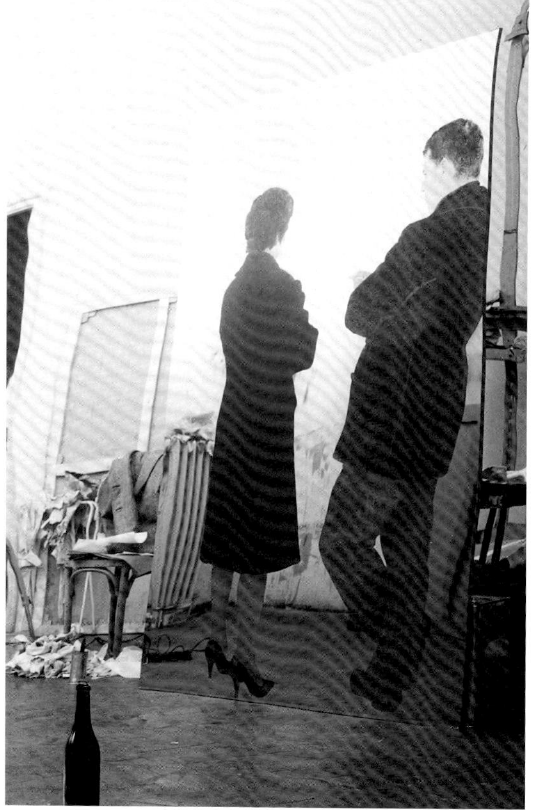

FIG. 160. *Bottiglia per terra* in Pistoletto's house on via Cibrario in Turin, 1964. *Due persone* (*Two People*; plate 20) is reflected in its surface. Photograph by Paolo Bressano. Courtesy of Cittadellarte-Fondazione Pistoletto, Biella

19
Bottiglia per terra **(*Bottle on the Floor*), 1963**
Photographic paper on polished stainless steel
90 9/16 x 47 1/4 inches (230 x 120 cm)
The Sonnabend Collection

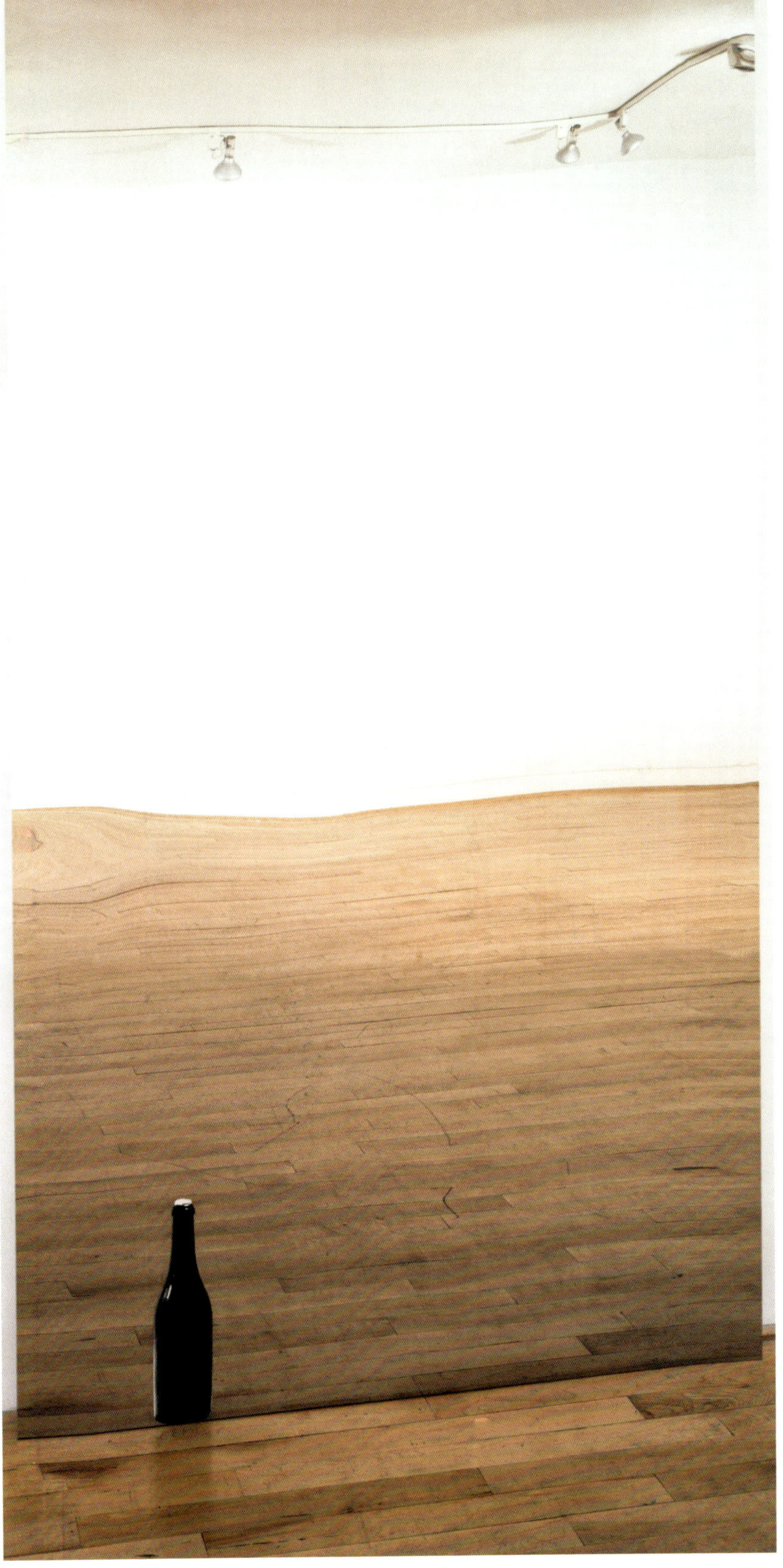

FIG. 161. *Due persone* in John and Dominique de Menil's house. Courtesy of Cittadellarte-Fondazione Pistoletto, Biella

20

***Due persone* (*Two People*), 1963–64**

Painted tissue paper on polished stainless steel
78¾ x 47¼ inches (200 x 120 cm)
The Menil Collection, Houston

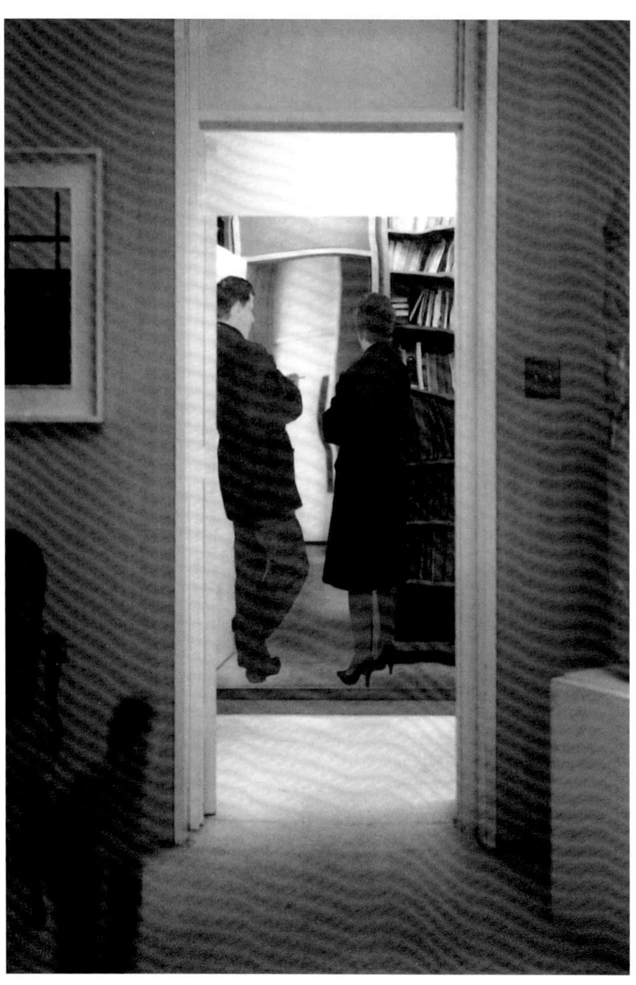

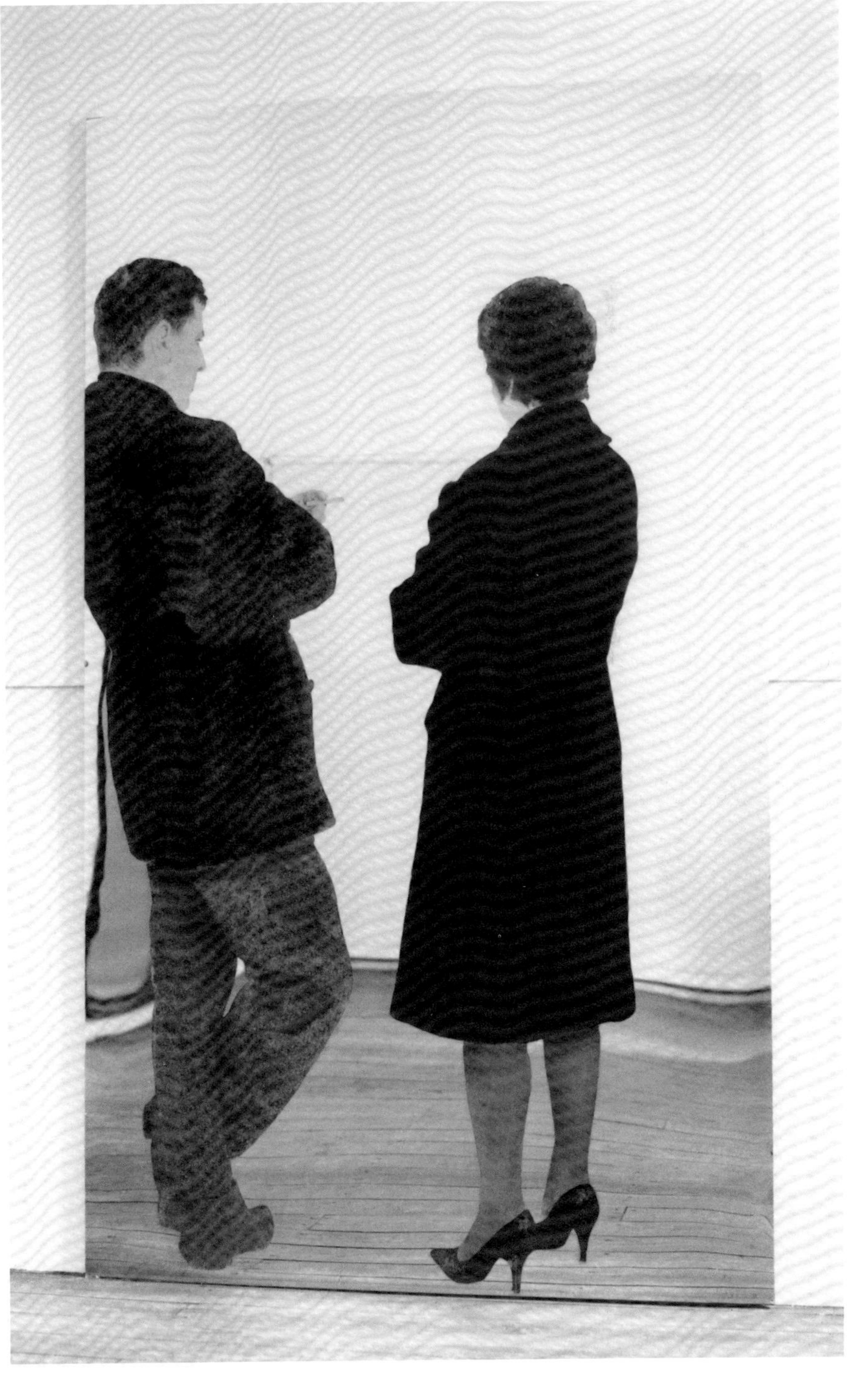

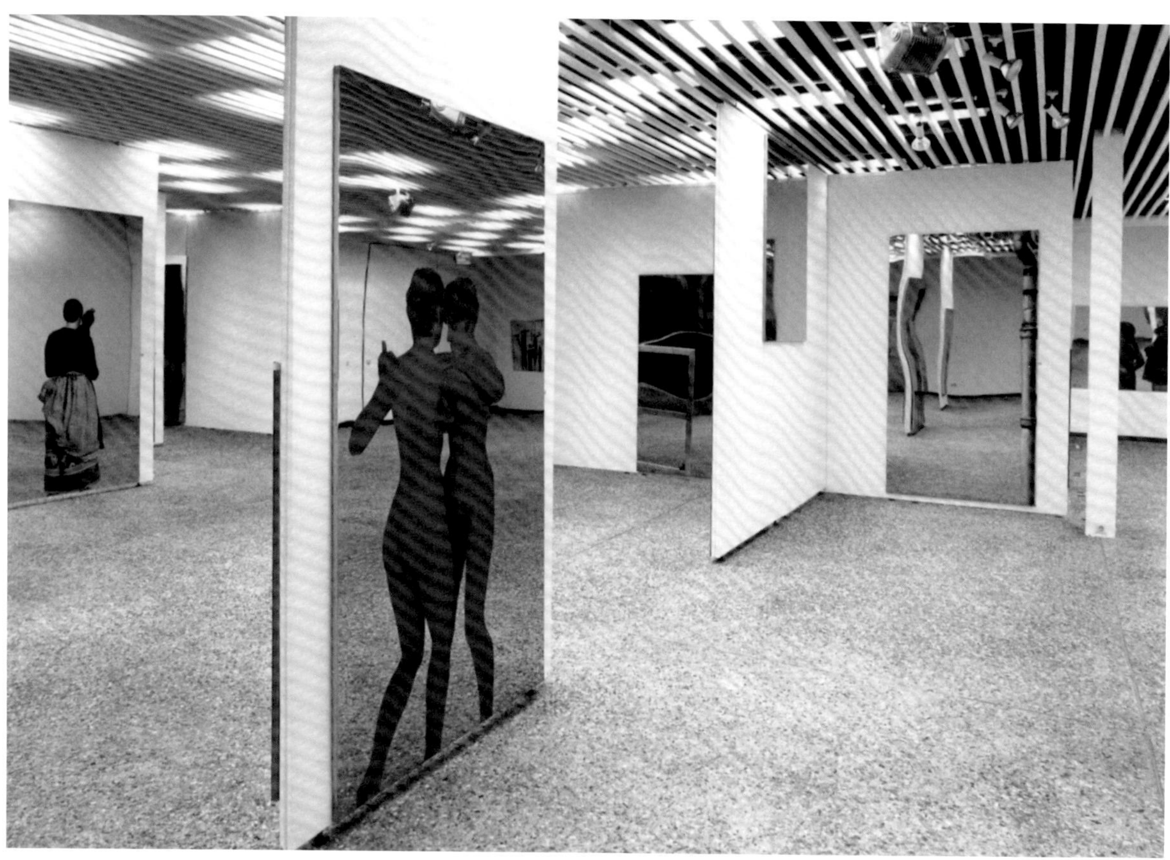

FIG. 162. The exhibition *Michelangelo Pistoletto* at the Kestner Gesellschaft, Hanover, Germany, with *Chassis* in the background at center, 1973. Photograph by Angelika Platen. Courtesy of Cittadellarte-Fondazione Pistoletto, Biella

21
Chassis **(*Frame*), 1964**
Photography on polished stainless steel
78¾ x 39⅜ inches (200 x 100 cm)
Private collection

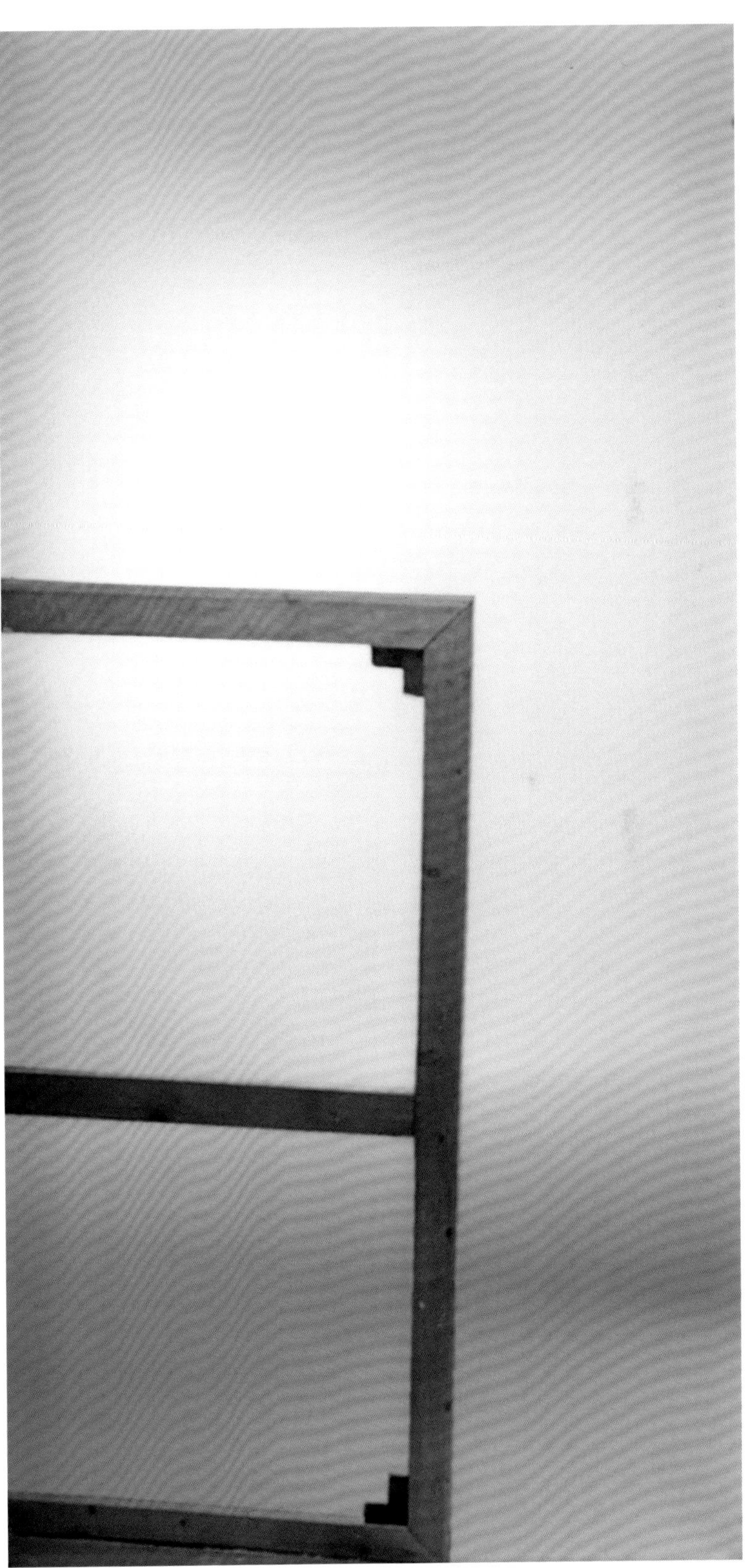

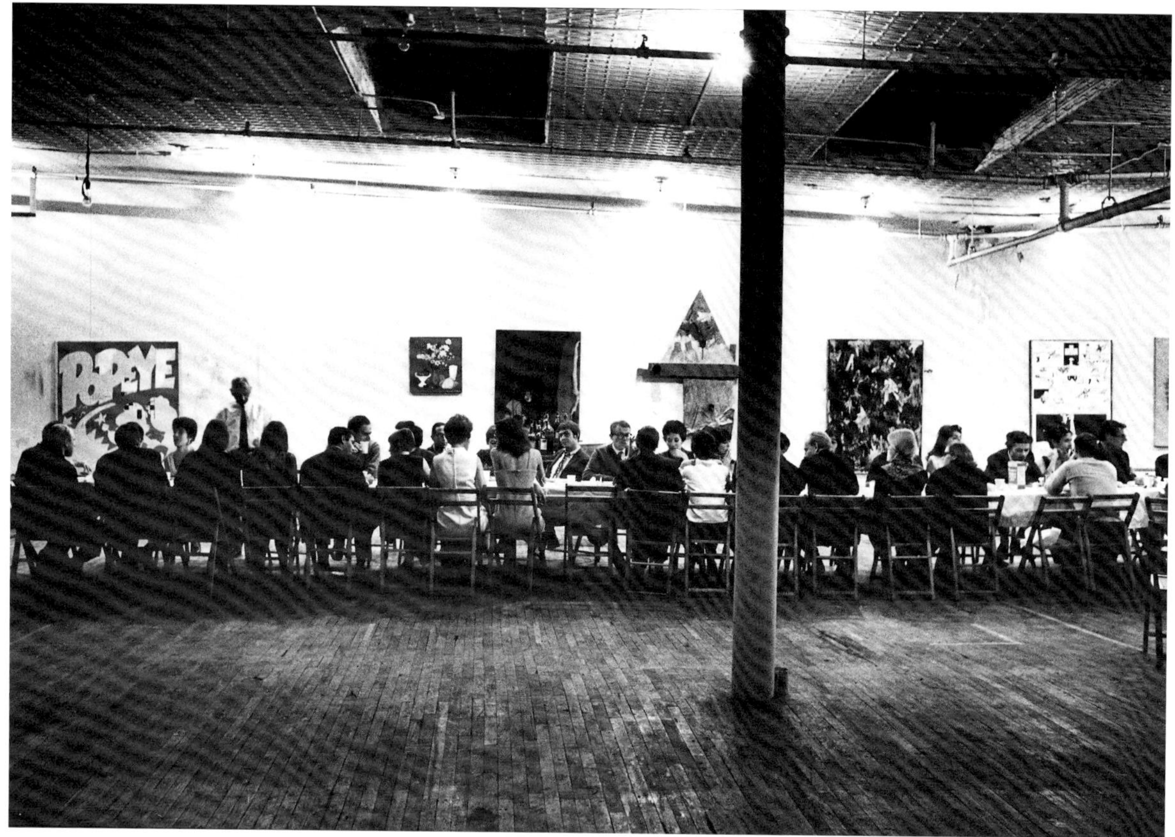

FIG. 163. Thanksgiving dinner at Robert Rauschenberg's New York loft, November 1964. *Lampadina* hangs on the wall behind the table at center. Photograph by Ugo Mulas. Courtesy of the Ugo Mulas Archive. © Ugo Mulas Heirs, All rights reserved

22
***Lampadina* (*Lightbulb*), 1964**
Painted tissue paper and photograph on polished stainless steel
78¾ x 39⅜ inches (200 x 100 cm)
Estate of Robert Rauschenberg

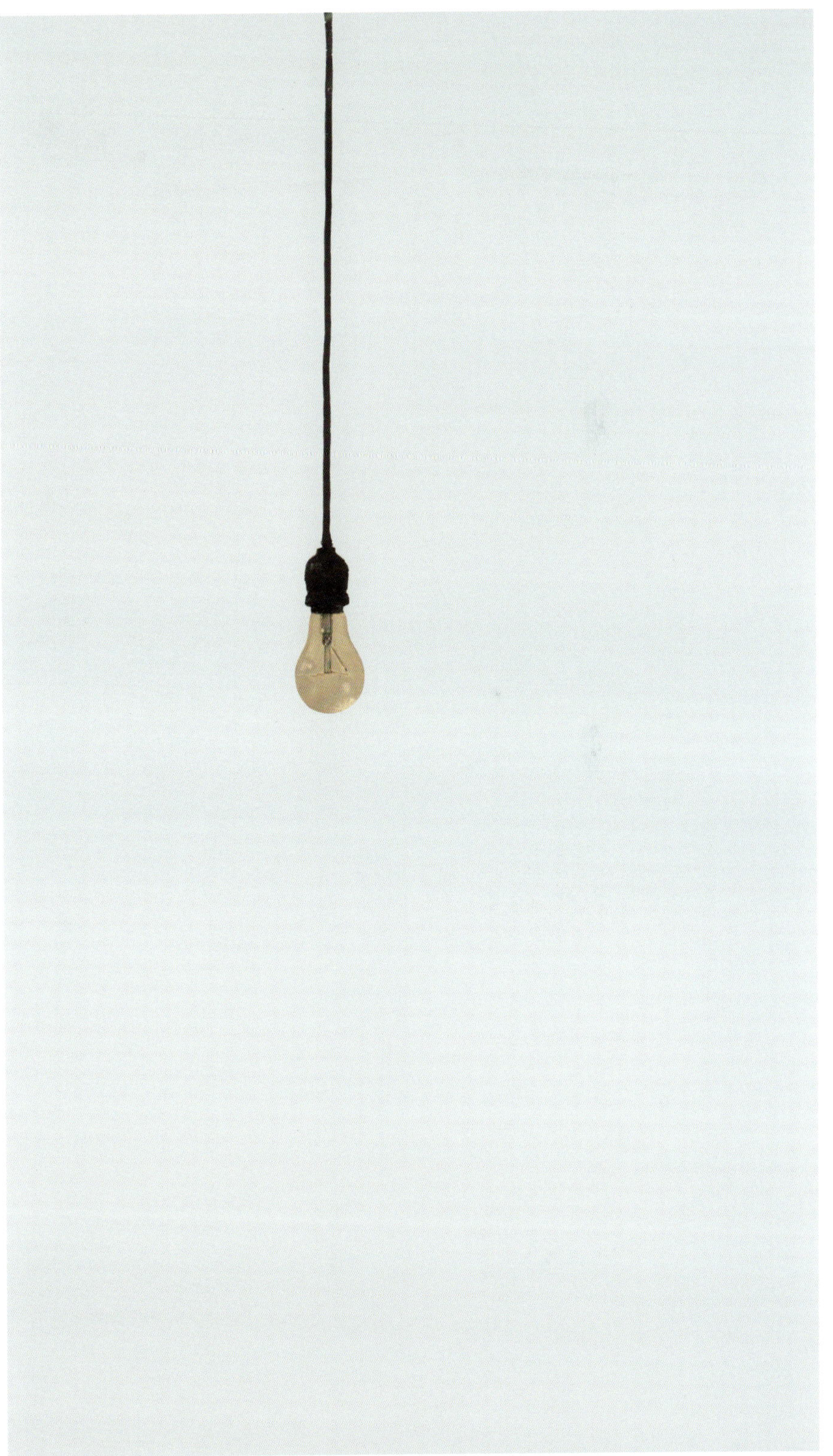

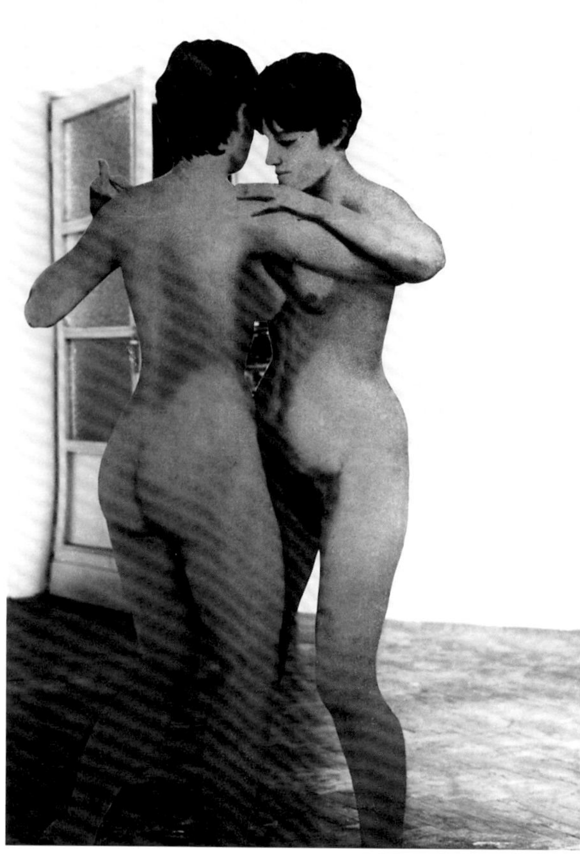

FIG. 164. *Due donne nude che ballano* in Pistoletto's house on via Cibrario in Turin, 1964. Photograph by Paolo Bressano. Courtesy of Cittadellarte-Fondazione Pistoletto, Biella

23
Due donne nude che ballano
(*Two Nude Women Dancing*), 1964
Painted tissue paper on polished stainless steel
86⅝ x 47¼ inches (220 x 120 cm)
Collection of Beatrice Monti della Corte von Rezzori

In Pistoletto's solo exhibition at GNAM, Galleria Nazionale d'Arte Moderna e Contemporanea, Rome, 1990. Photograph by Attilio Maranzano. Courtesy of Cittadellarte-Fondazione Pistoletto, Biella

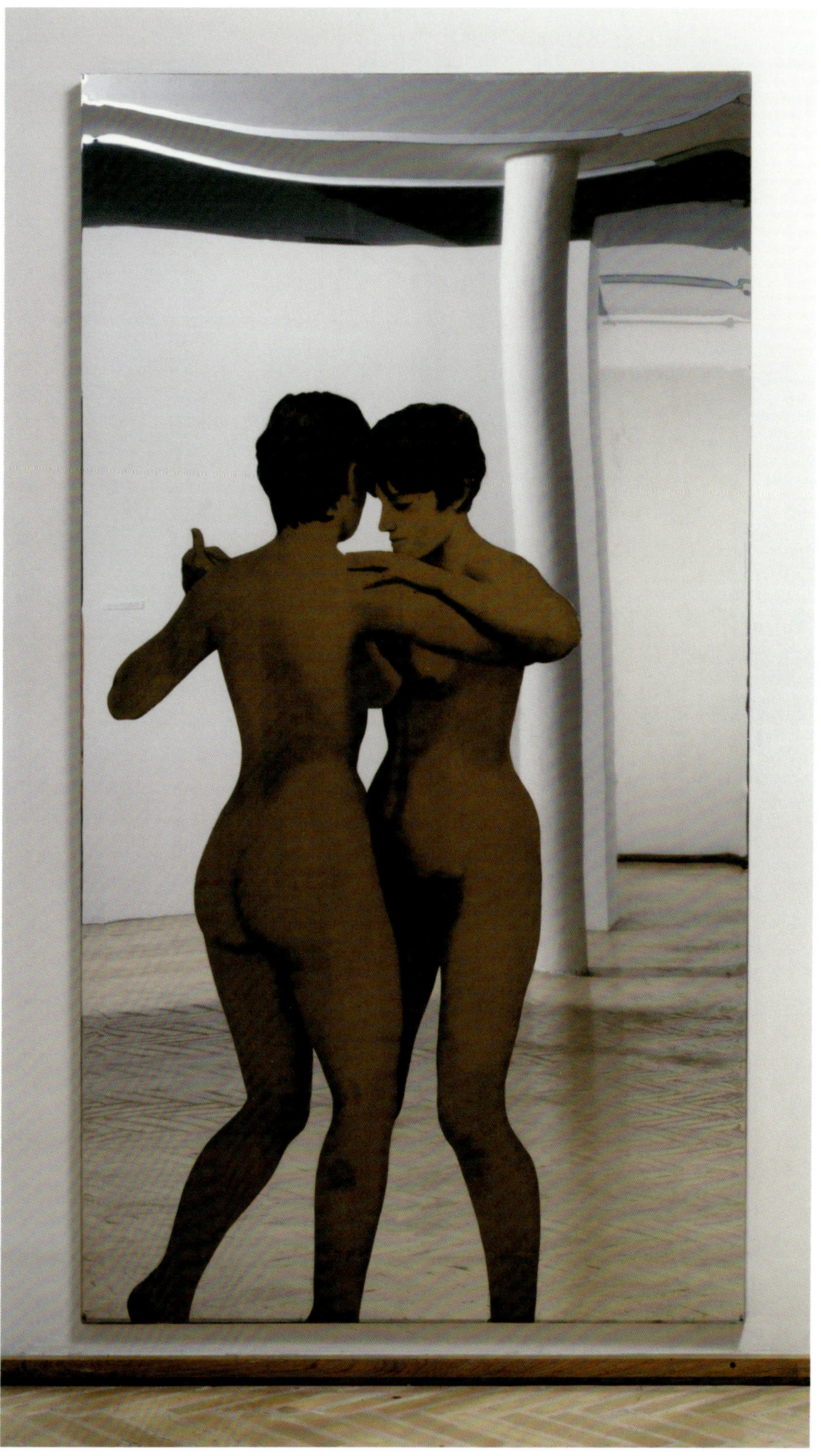

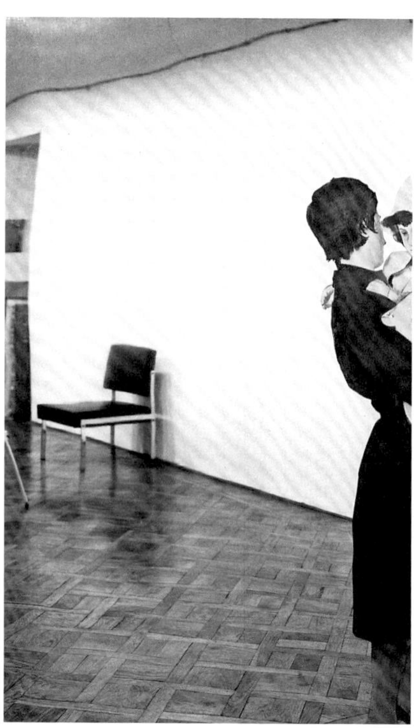

FIG. 166. *Marzia con la bambina* in the exhibition *Michelangelo Pistoletto: I plexiglass* at Galleria Sperone, Turin, October 2, 1964. Photograph by Paolo Bressano. Courtesy of Cittadellarte-Fondazione Pistoletto, Biella

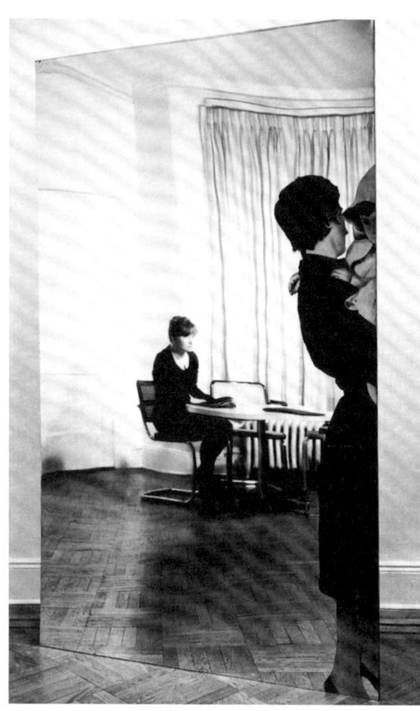

FIG. 165. *Marzia con la bambina* as reproduced in the catalogue of the exhibition *Michelangelo Pistoletto: A Reflected World* at the Walker Art Center, Minneapolis, 1966. Courtesy of Cittadellarte-Fondazione Pistoletto, Biella

24
Marzia con la bambina
(*Marzia with the Baby*), 1964
Painted tissue paper on polished stainless steel
78¾ x 47¼ inches (200 x 120 cm)
The Sonnabend Collection

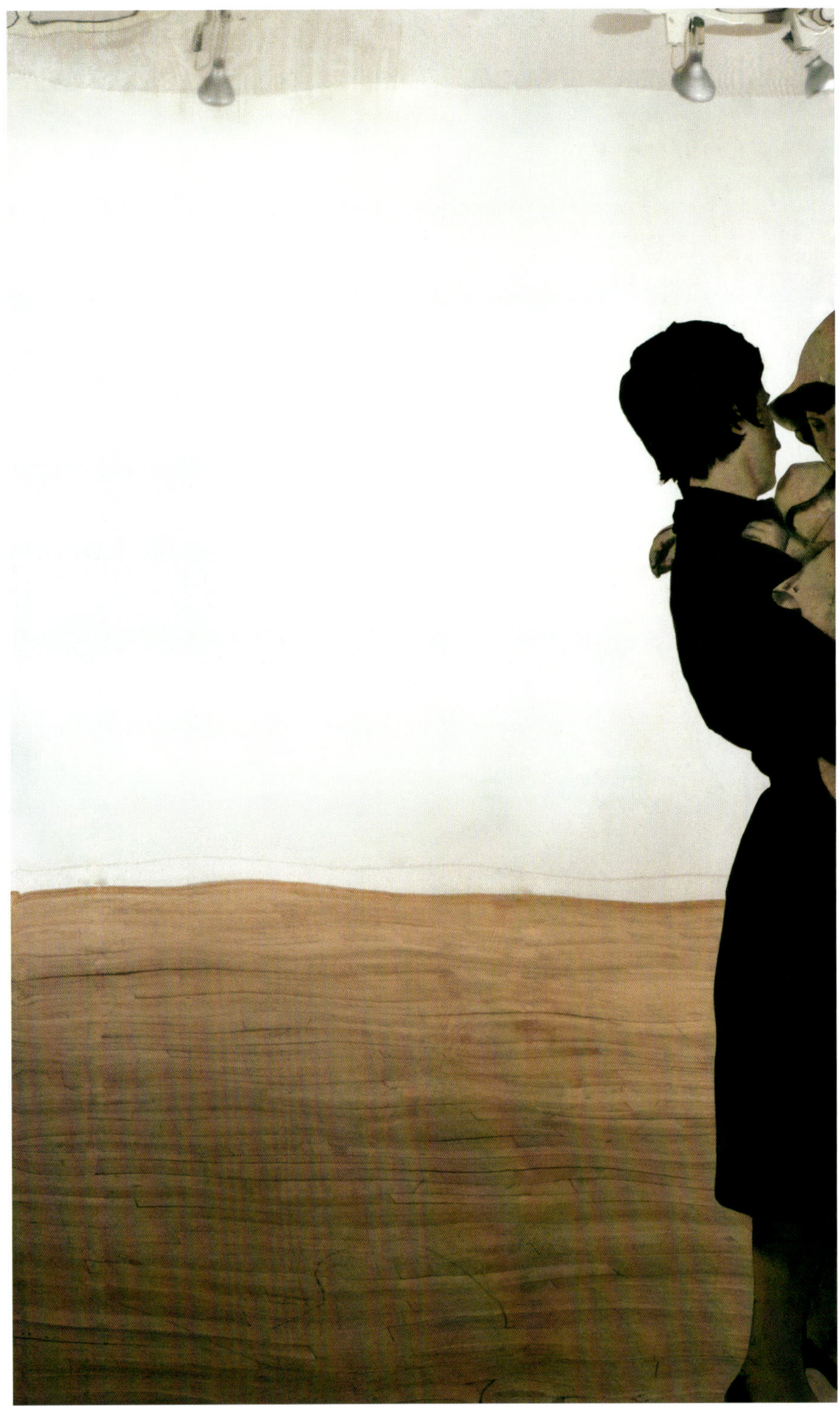

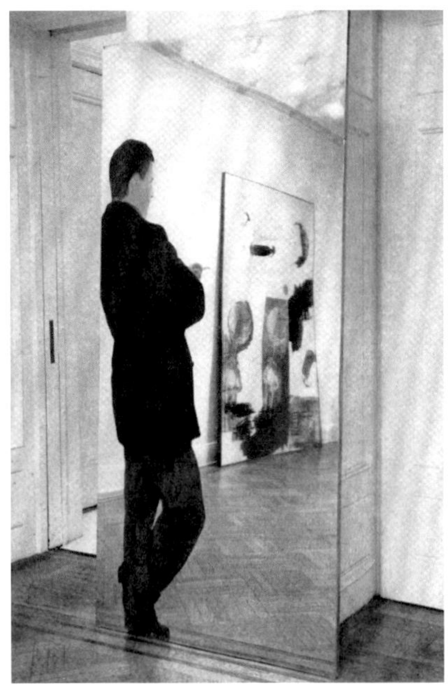

FIG. 167. *Persona appoggiata* at the Leo Castelli Gallery, New York, 1966. A painting by Robert Rauschenberg is reflected in the background. Courtesy of Cittadellarte-Fondazione Pistoletto, Biella

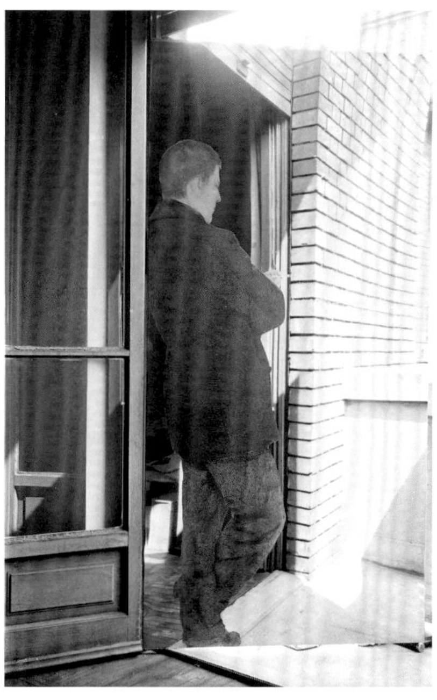

FIG. 168. *Persona appoggiata* in Pistoletto's house on via Cibrario in Turin, 1964. Photograph by Paolo Bressano. Courtesy of Cittadellarte-Fondazione Pistoletto, Biella

25
***Persona appoggiata* (*Person Leaning*), 1964**
Painted tissue paper on polished stainless steel
78¾ x 39⅜ inches (200 x 100 cm)
Collection of Keith L. and Katherine Sachs

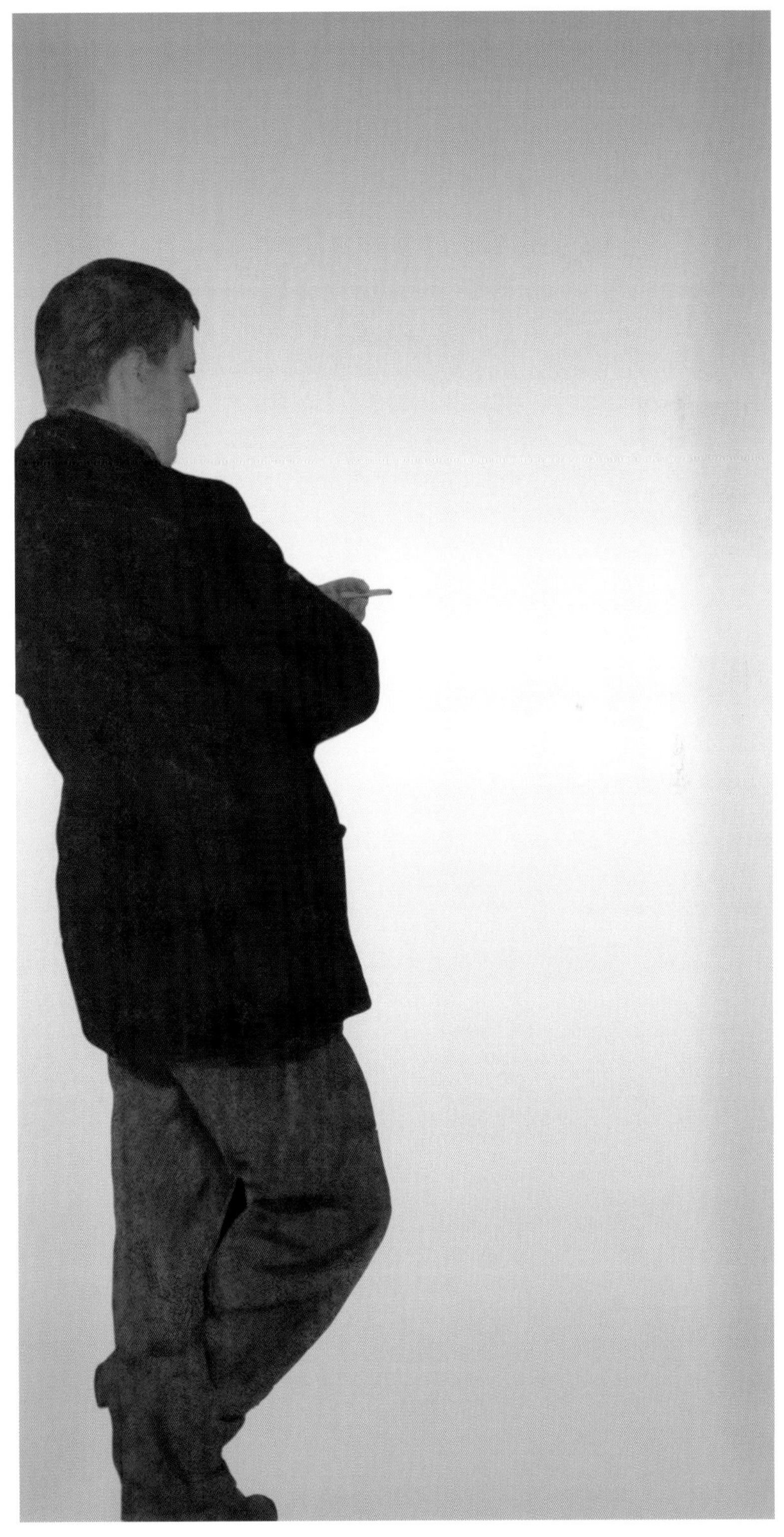

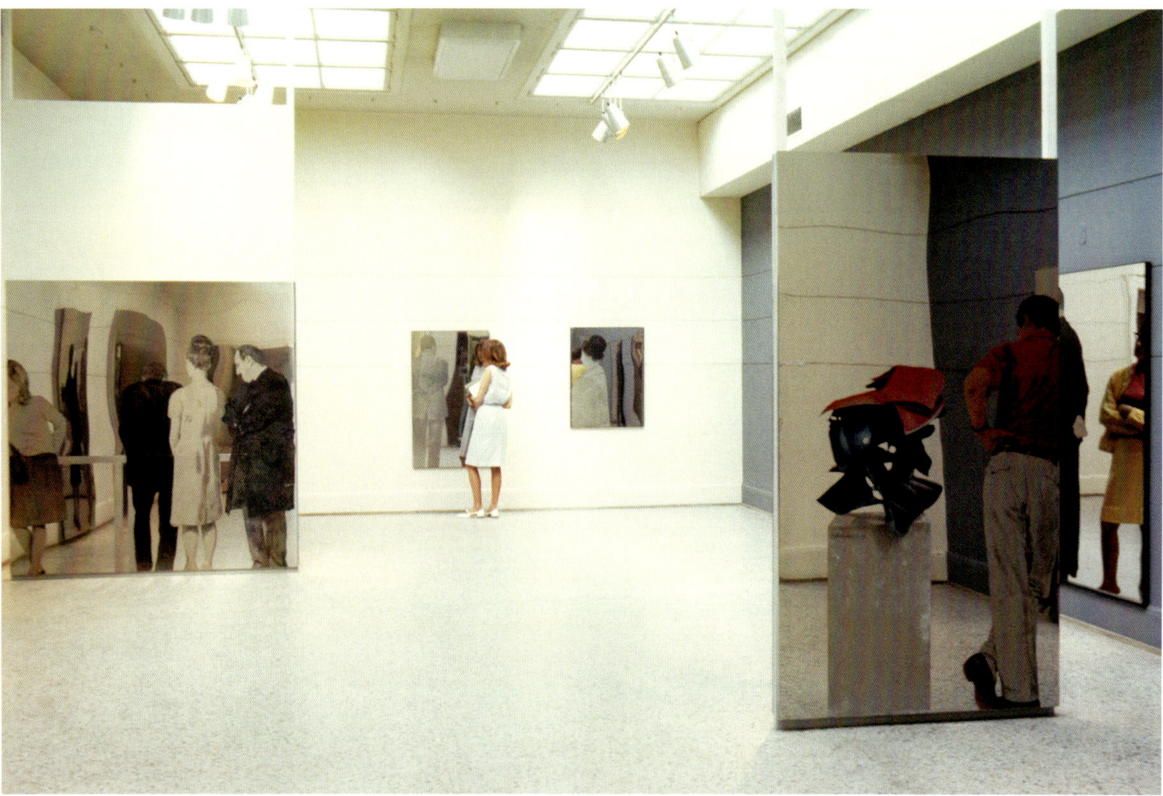

FIG. 169. The exhibition *Michelangelo Pistoletto: A Reflected World* at the Walker Art Center, Minneapolis, with *Quattro persone alla balconata* on the left, 1966. Courtesy of the Walker Art Center, Minneapolis

26
Quattro persone alla balconata
***(Four People on a Balcony)*, 1964**
Painted tissue paper on polished stainless steel
78¾ x 78¾ inches (200 x 200 cm)
Collection of Martin Z. Margulies, Miami

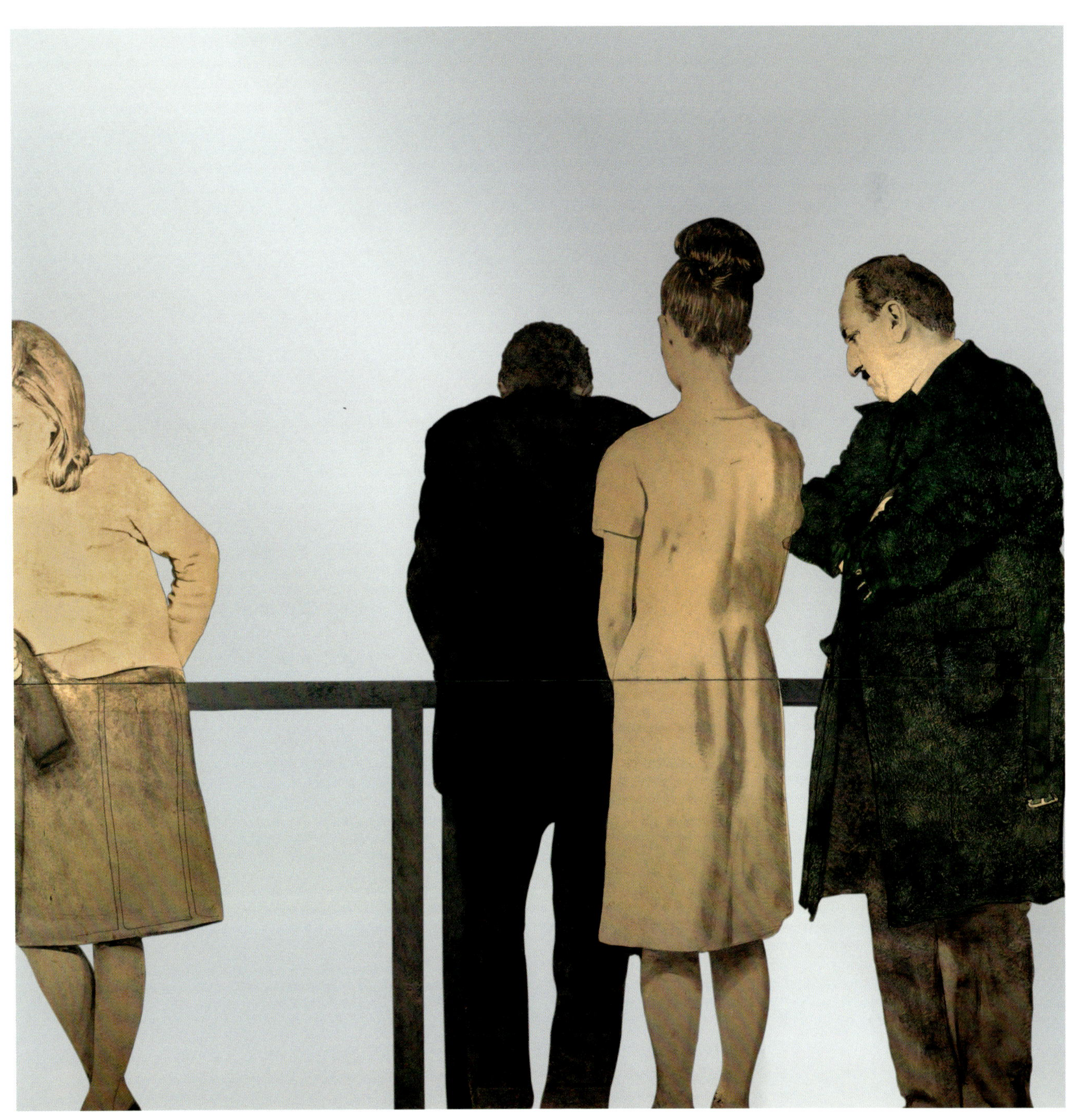

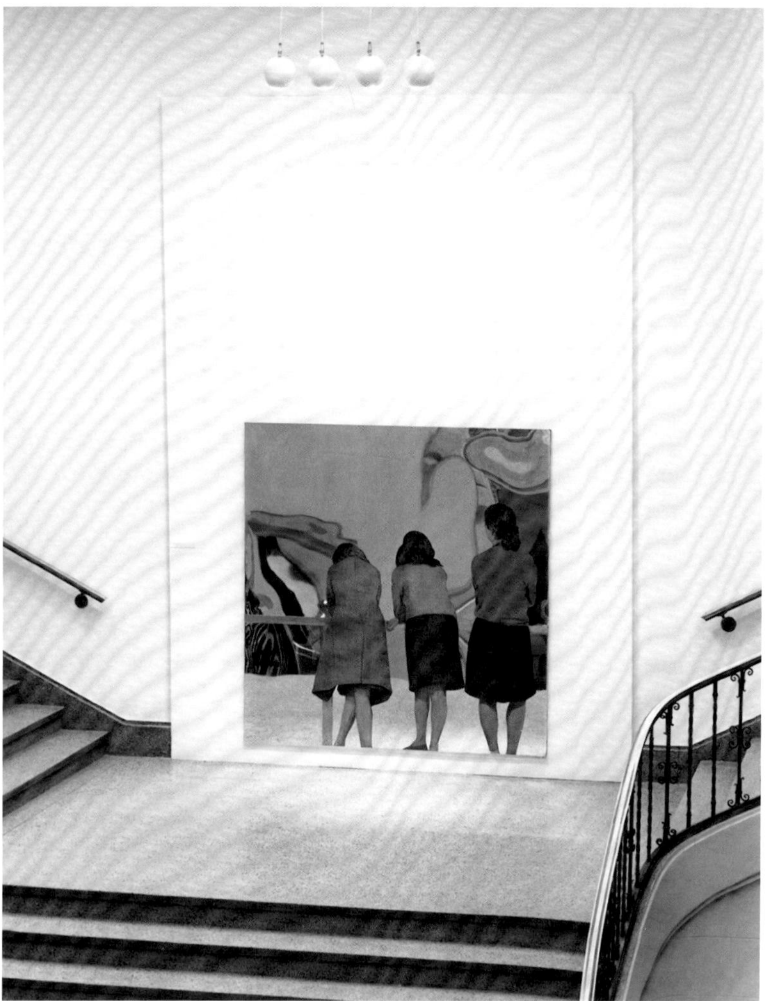

FIG. 170. *Tre ragazze alla balconata* in the exhibition *Michelangelo Pistoletto: A Reflected World* at the Walker Art Center, Minneapolis, 1966. Courtesy of the Walker Art Center, Minneapolis

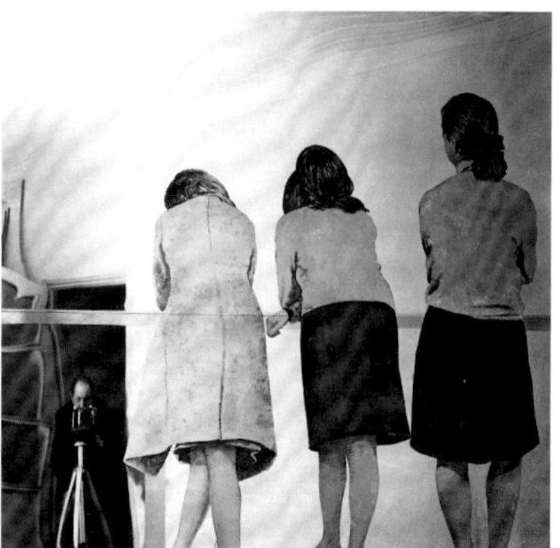

FIG. 171. *Tre ragazze alla balconata* in Pistoletto's house on via Cibrario in Turin, 1964. Photograph by Paolo Bressano. Courtesy of Cittadellarte-Fondazione Pistoletto, Biella

27
Tre ragazze alla balconata
(*Three Girls on a Balcony*), 1964
Painted tissue paper on polished stainless steel
78¾ x 78¾ inches (200 x 200 cm)
Walker Art Center, Minneapolis.
Gift of Mrs. Julius E. Davis, 1999

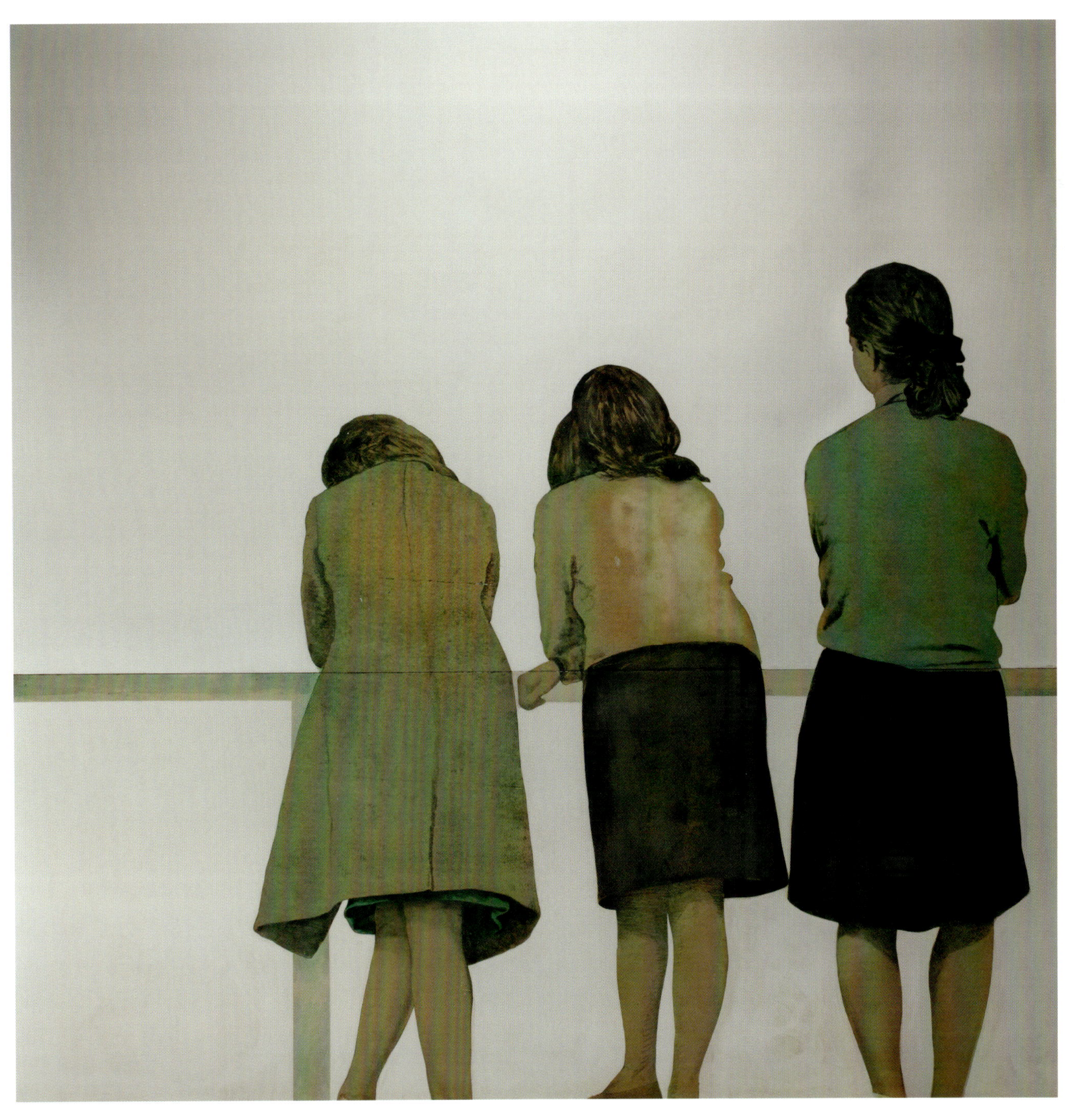

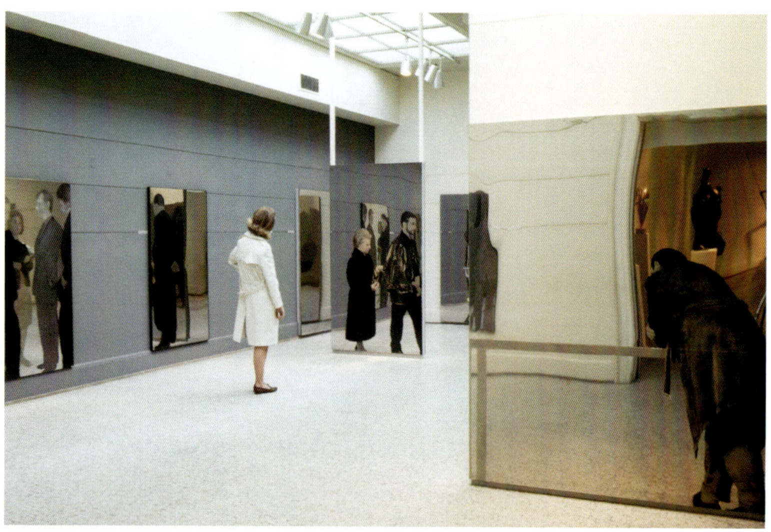

FIG. 172. The exhibition *Michelangelo Pistoletto: A Reflected World* at the Walker Art Center, Minneapolis, with *Due persone in coda* in the background at center, 1966. Courtesy of the Walker Art Center, Minneapolis

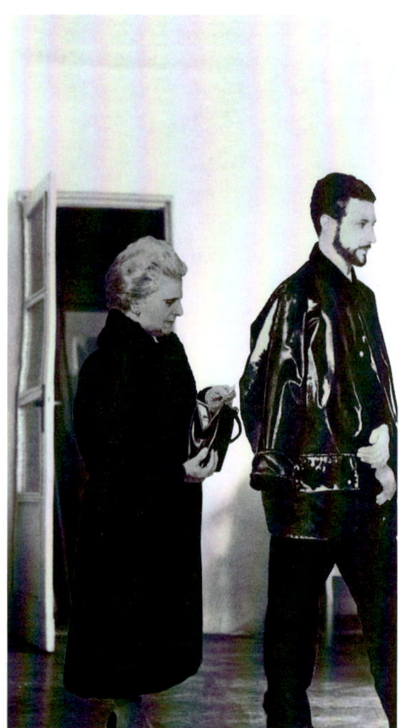

FIG. 173. *Due persone in coda* in Pistoletto's house on via Cibrario in Turin, 1964. Photograph by Paolo Bressano. Courtesy of Cittadellarte-Fondazione Pistoletto, Biella

28
Due persone in coda
(*Two People in Line*), 1964
Painted tissue paper on polished stainless steel
86 13/16 x 47 1/4 inches (220.5 x 120 cm)
Museum Boijmans Van Beuningen, Rotterdam

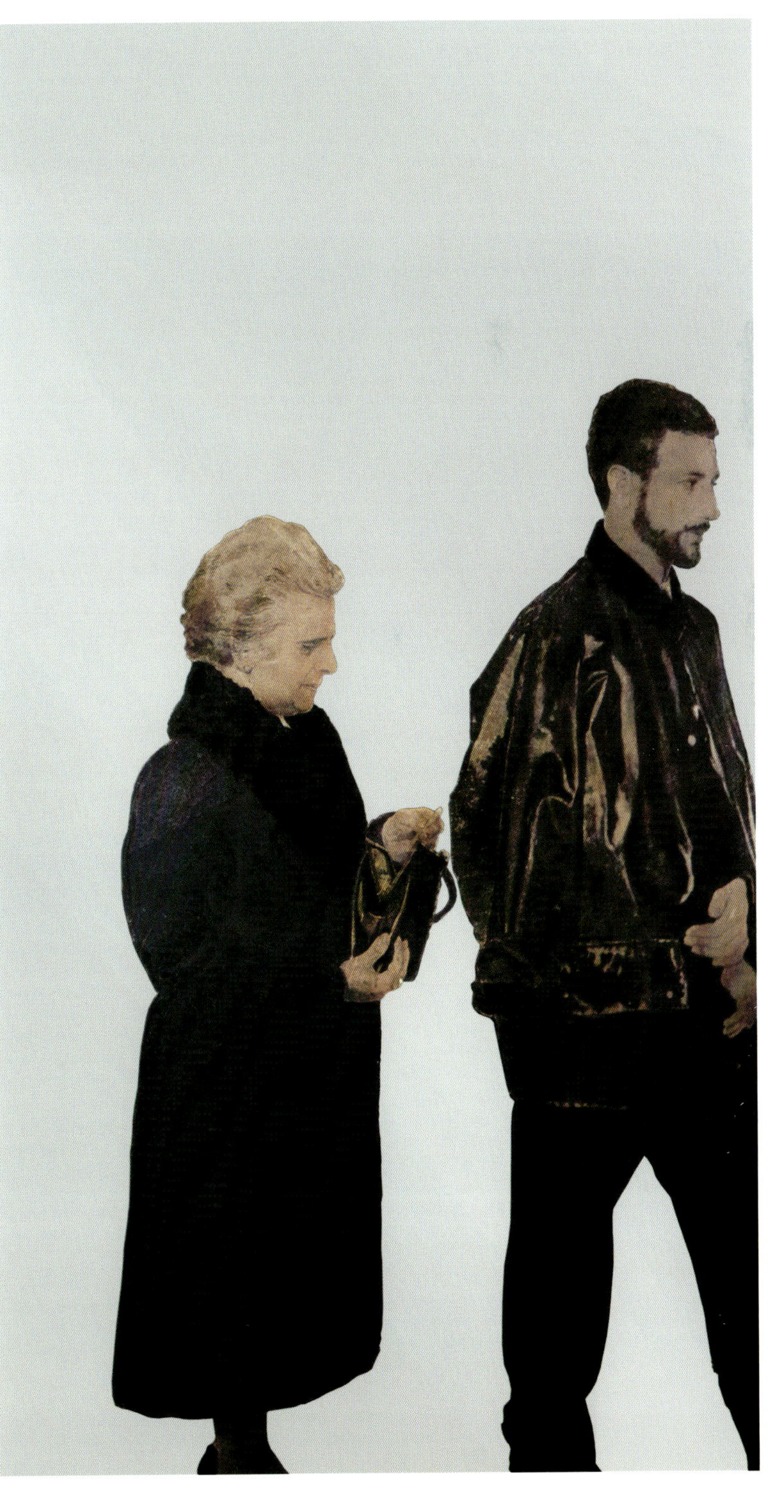

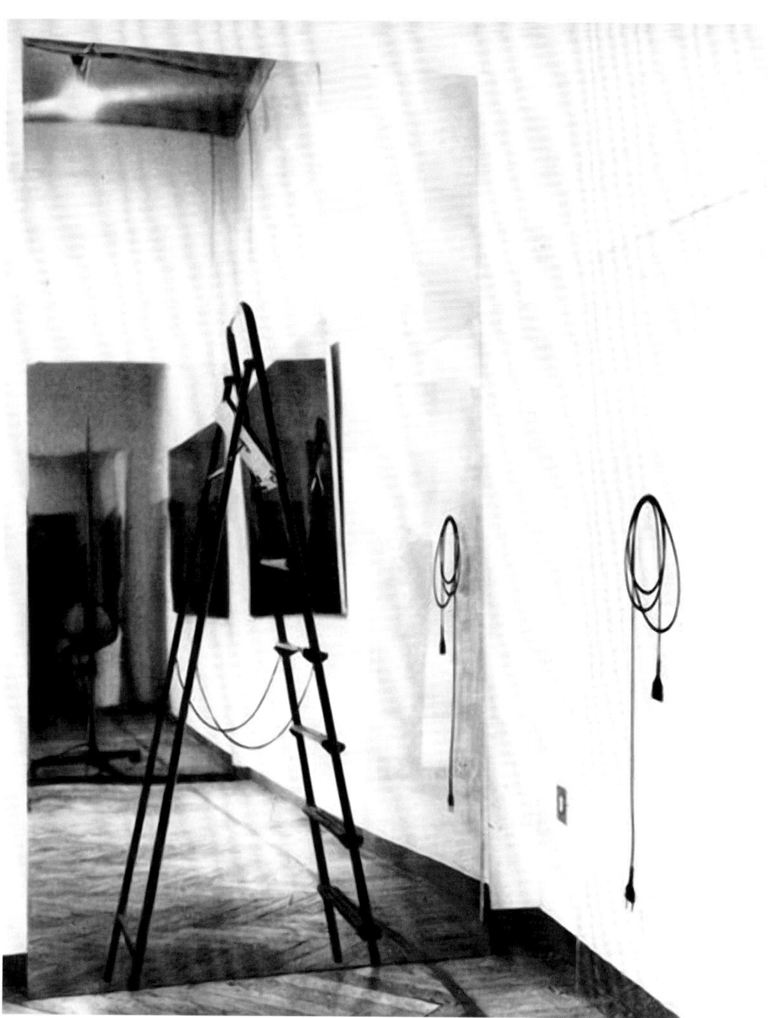

FIG. 174. *Scala* in Pistoletto's solo exhibition at Galleria Sperone, Milan, 1966. To the right is one of Pistoletto's Plexiglas works (see plate 69). Photograph by Paolo Bressano. Courtesy of Cittadellarte-Fondazione Pistoletto, Biella

29
***Scala* (*Ladder*), 1964**
Painted tissue paper on polished stainless steel
90 9/16 x 47 1/4 inches (230 x 120 cm)
Courtesy of Fondazione Marconi, Milan

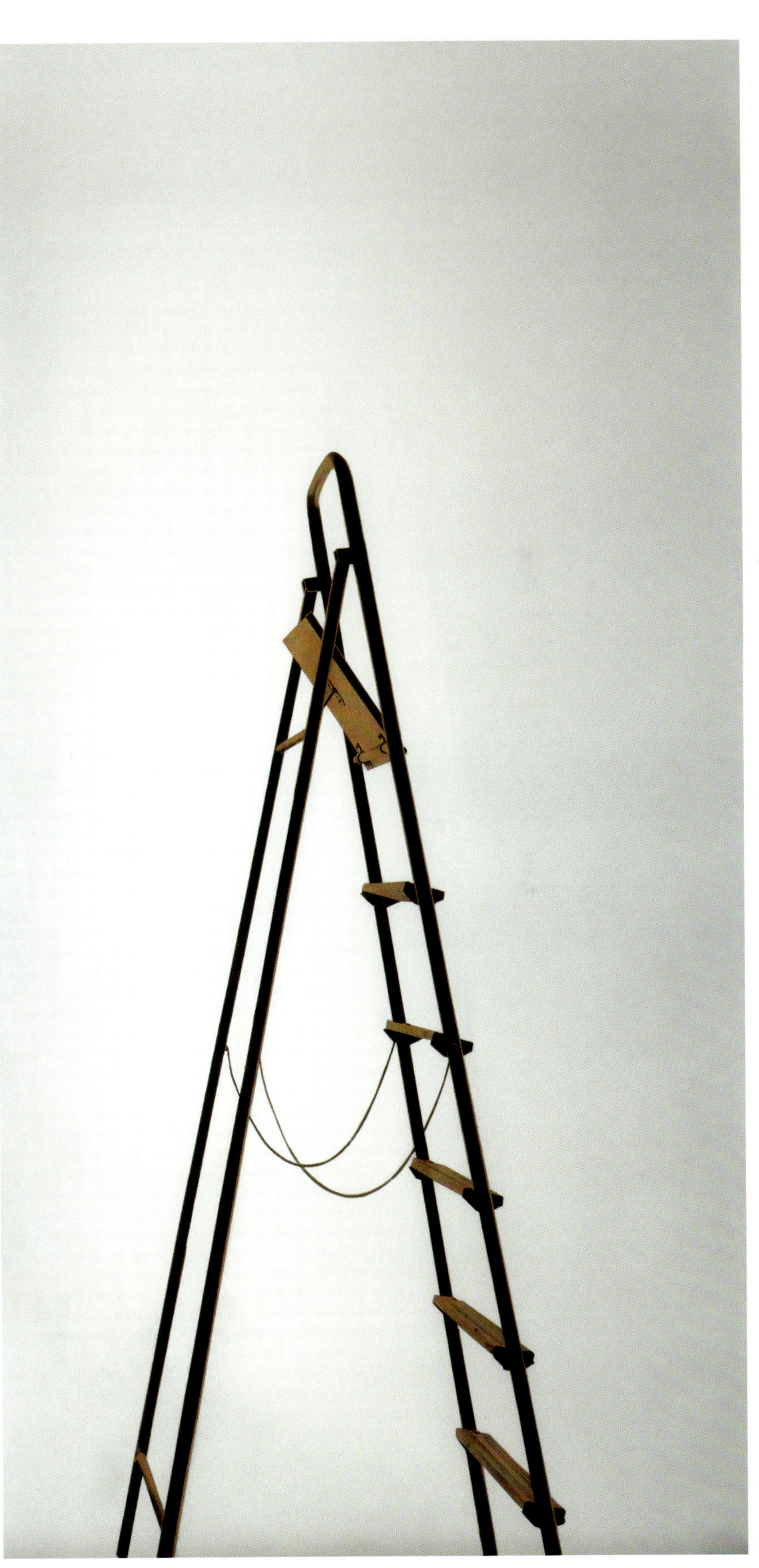

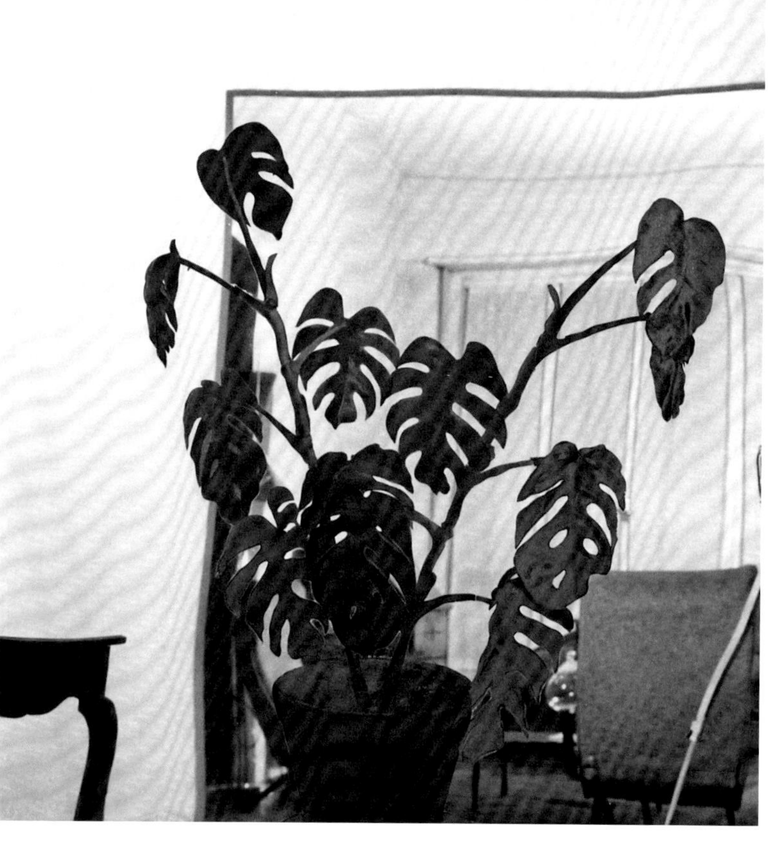

FIG. 175. *Filodendro* in Pistoletto's house on via Cibrario in Turin, 1965. Photograph by Paolo Bressano. Courtesy of Cittadellarte-Fondazione Pistoletto, Biella

30
***Filodendro* (*Philodendron*), 1965**
Painted tissue paper on polished stainless steel
47¼ x 47¼ inches (120 x 120 cm)
Albright-Knox Art Gallery, Buffalo. Gift of
The Seymour H. Knox Foundation, Inc., 1971

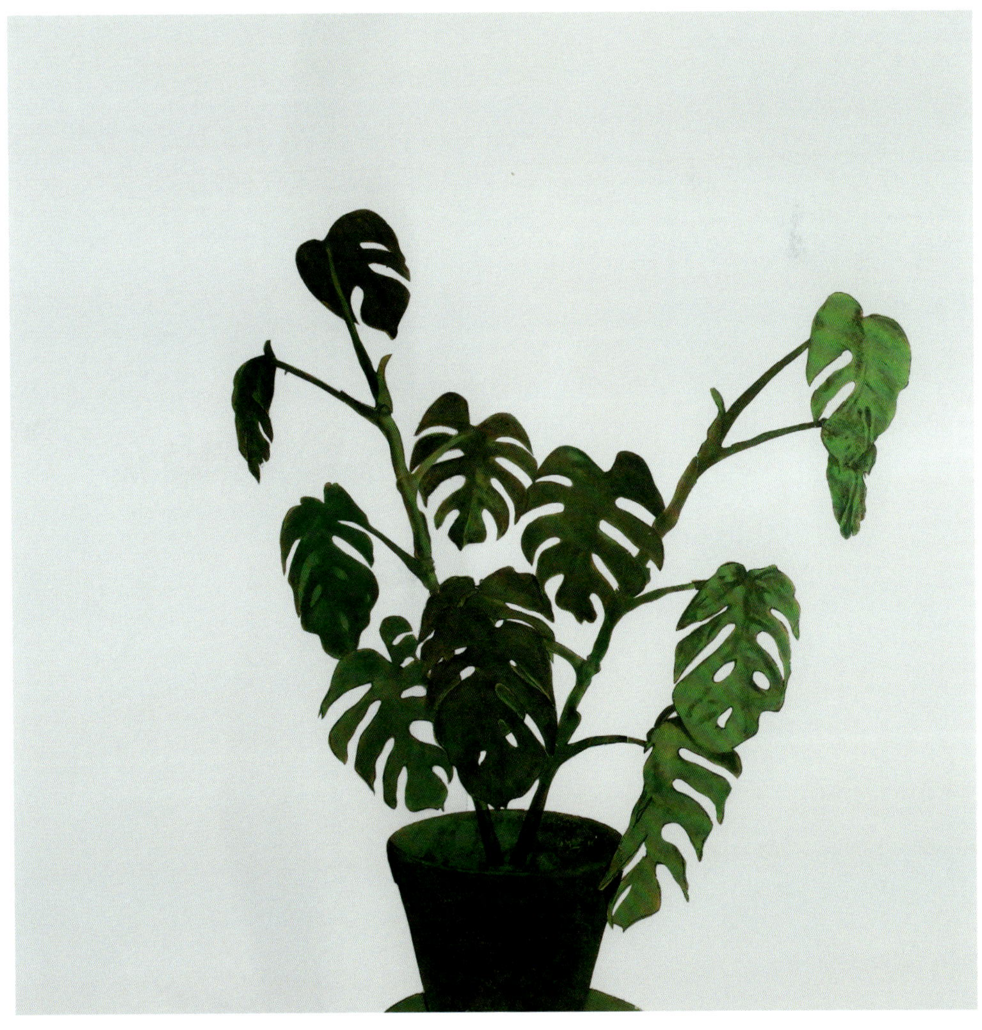

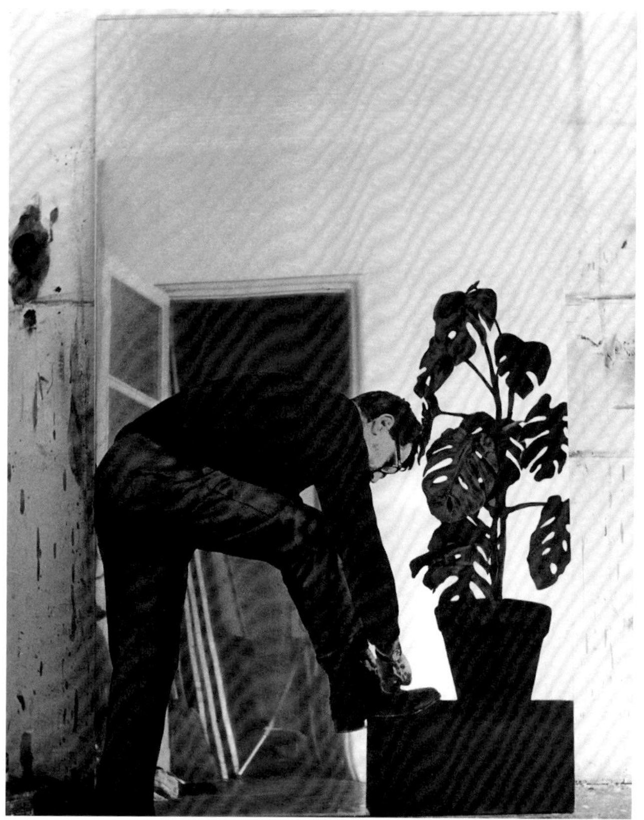

FIG. 176. *Autoritratto con pianta* in Pistoletto's house on via Cibrario in Turin. Photograph by Renato Rinaldi. Courtesy of Cittadellarte-Fondazione Pistoletto, Biella

31
Autoritratto con pianta
(*Self-Portrait with Plant*), 1965
Painted tissue paper on polished stainless steel
77 15/16 x 47 1/4 inches (198 x 120 cm)
Private collection

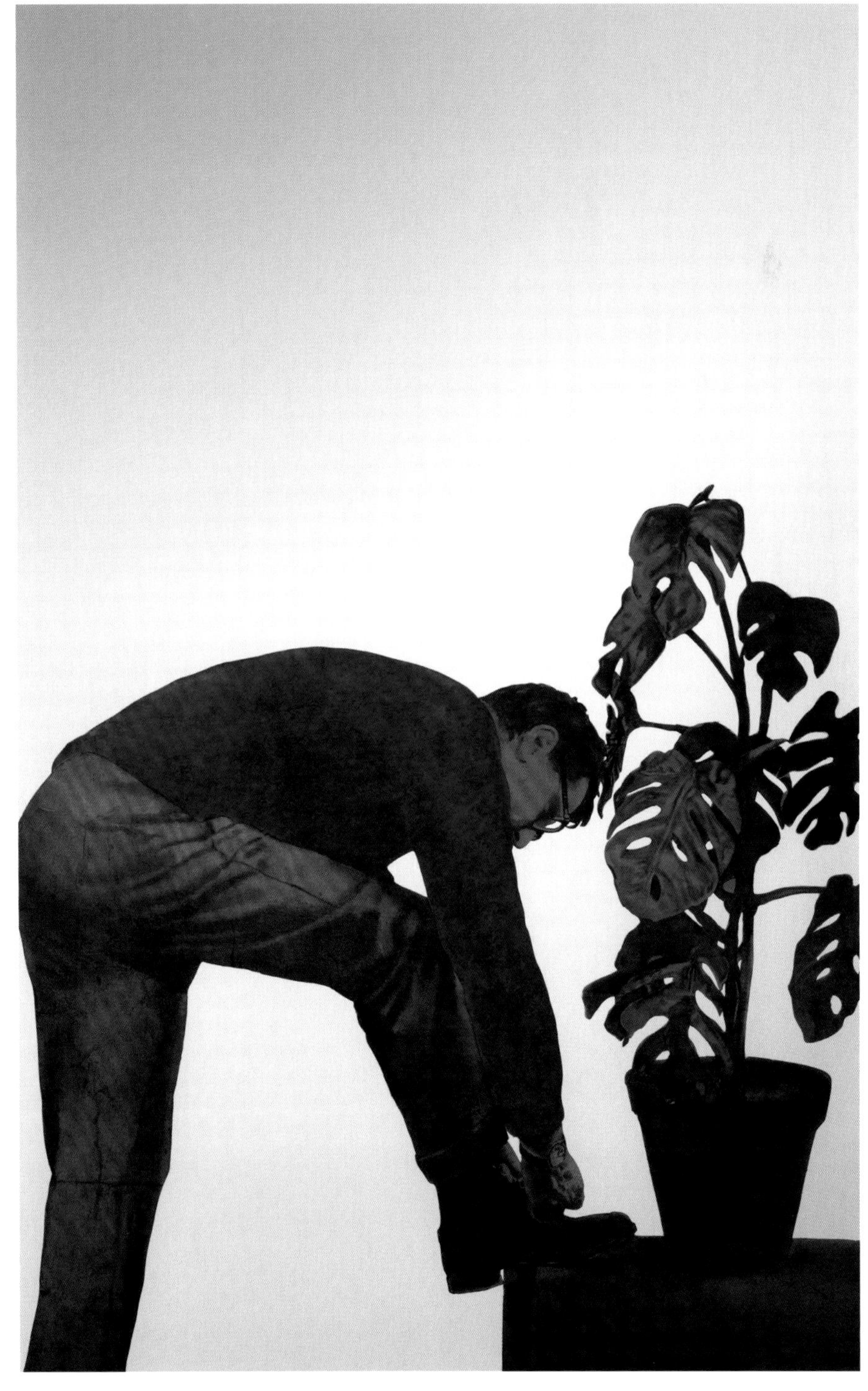

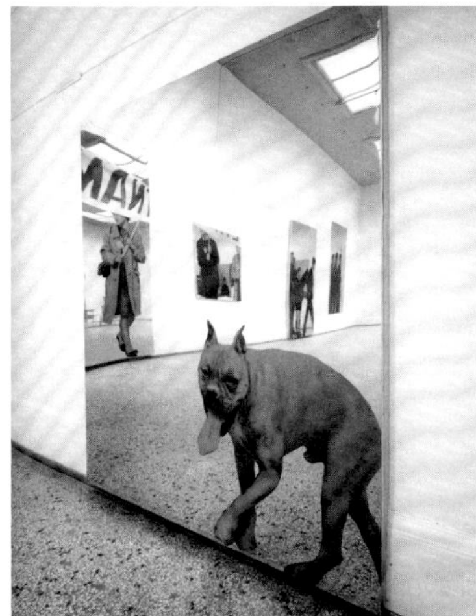

FIG. 177. *Vietnam* reflected in the mirror painting *Cane* (*Dog*, 1965) in Pistoletto's solo exhibition at the Kornblee Gallery, New York, 1967. Courtesy of Cittadellarte-Fondazione Pistoletto, Biella

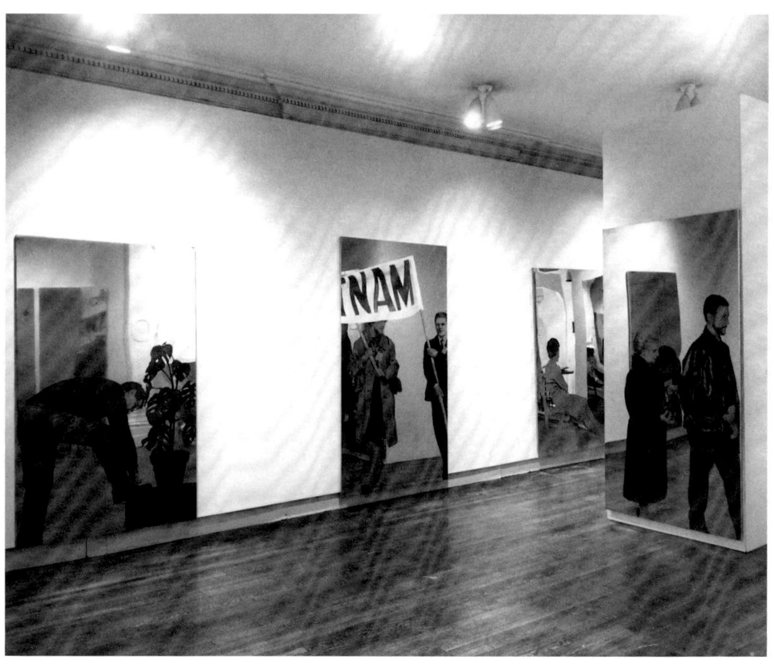

FIG. 178. The exhibition *Michelangelo Pistoletto: A Reflected World* at the Walker Art Center, Minneapolis, with *Vietnam* at center, 1966. Courtesy of the Walker Art Center, Minneapolis

32
***Vietnam*, 1965**
Painted tissue paper on polished stainless steel
86⅝ x 47¼ inches (220 x 120 cm)
The Menil Collection, Houston

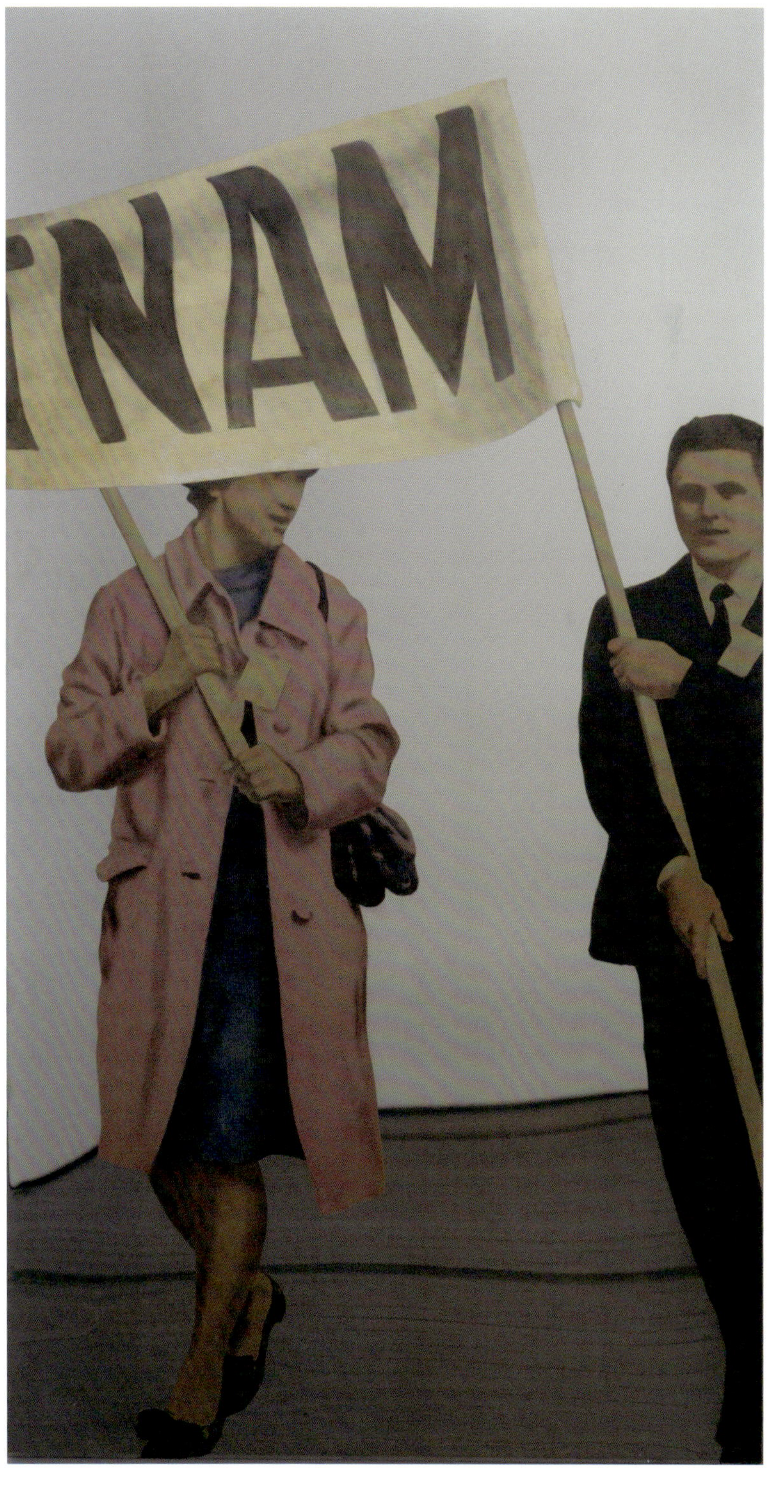

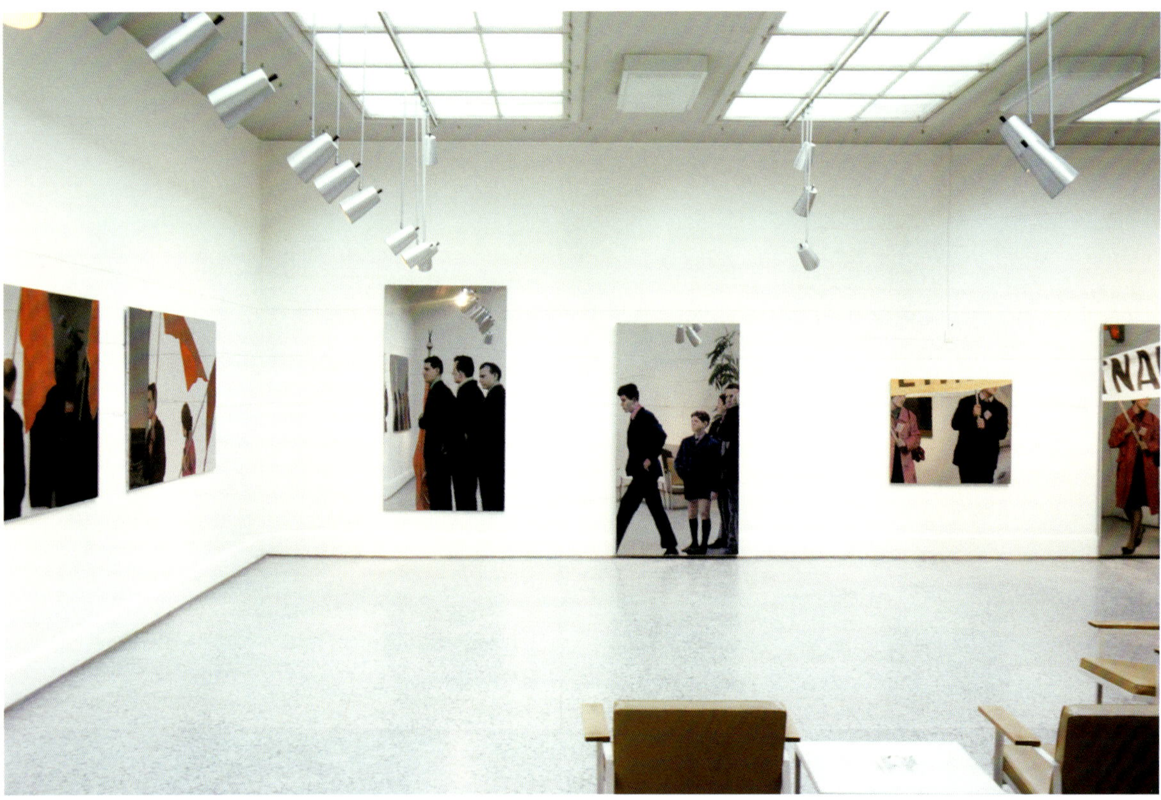

FIG. 179. The exhibition *Michelangelo Pistoletto: A Reflected World* at the Walker Art Center, Minneapolis, with *Ragazzo* at center, 1966. Courtesy of the Walker Art Center, Minneapolis

33
***Ragazzo* (*Boy*), 1965**
Painted tissue paper on polished stainless steel
86⅝ x 47¼ inches (220 x 120 cm)
The Robert B. Mayer Family Collection, Chicago

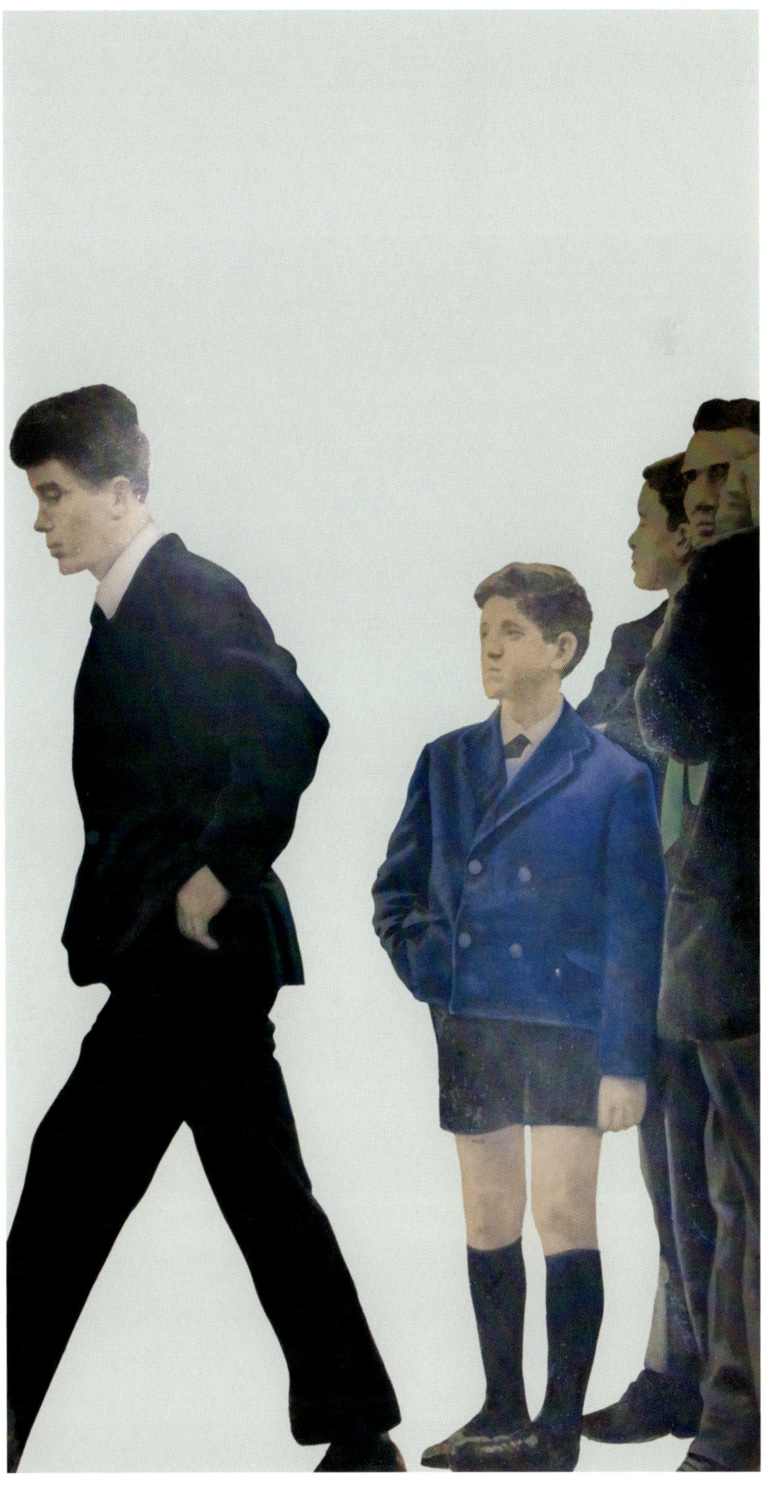

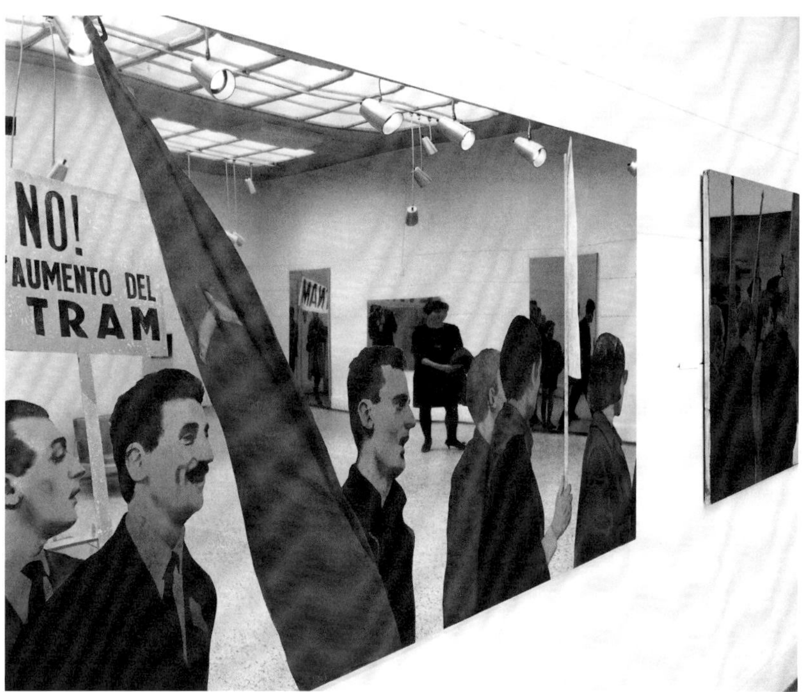

FIG. 180. *No all'aumento del tram* in the exhibition *Michelangelo Pistoletto: A Reflected World* at the Walker Art Center, Minneapolis, 1966. Courtesy of the Walker Art Center, Minneapolis

34
No all'aumento del tram
***(No to the Raise of the Tram Fare)*, 1965**
Painted tissue paper on polished stainless steel
47¼ x 86⅝ inches (120 x 220 cm)
The Detroit Institute of Arts. Gift of Mr. and Mrs.
Richard A. Manoogian

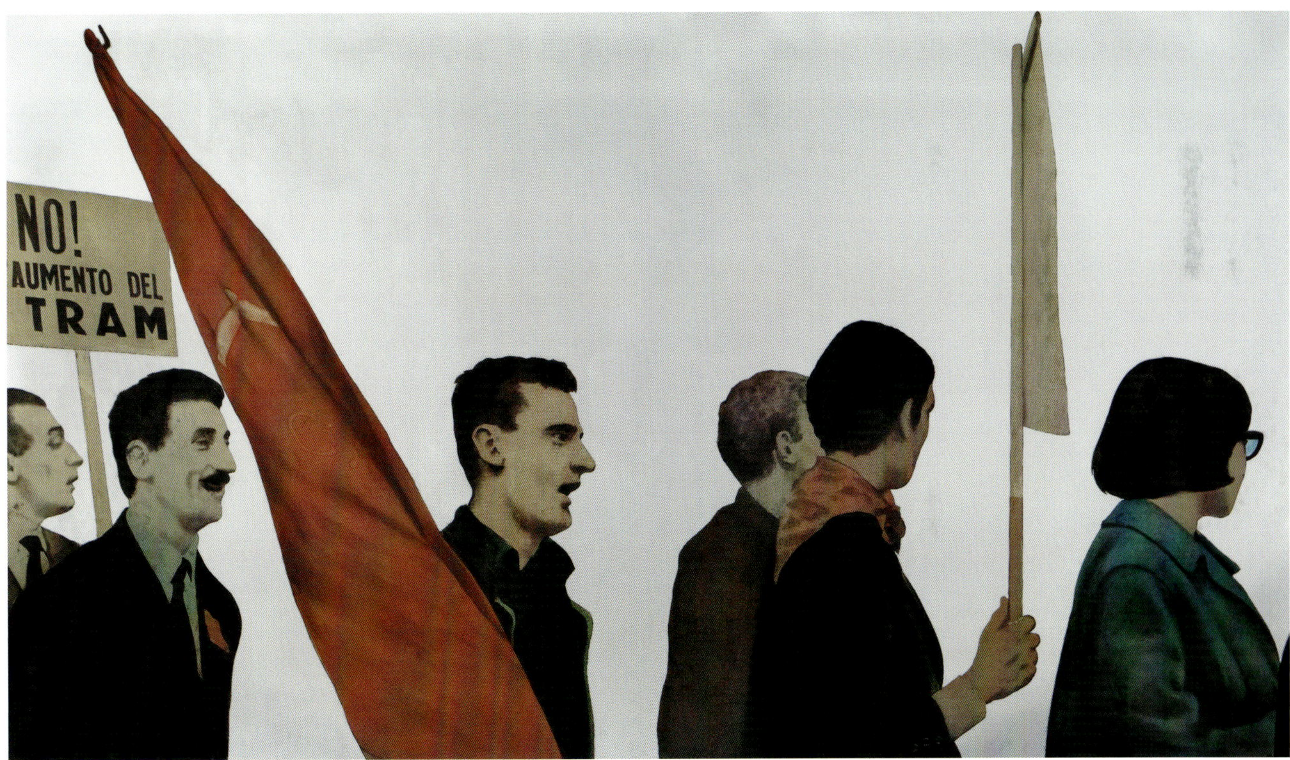

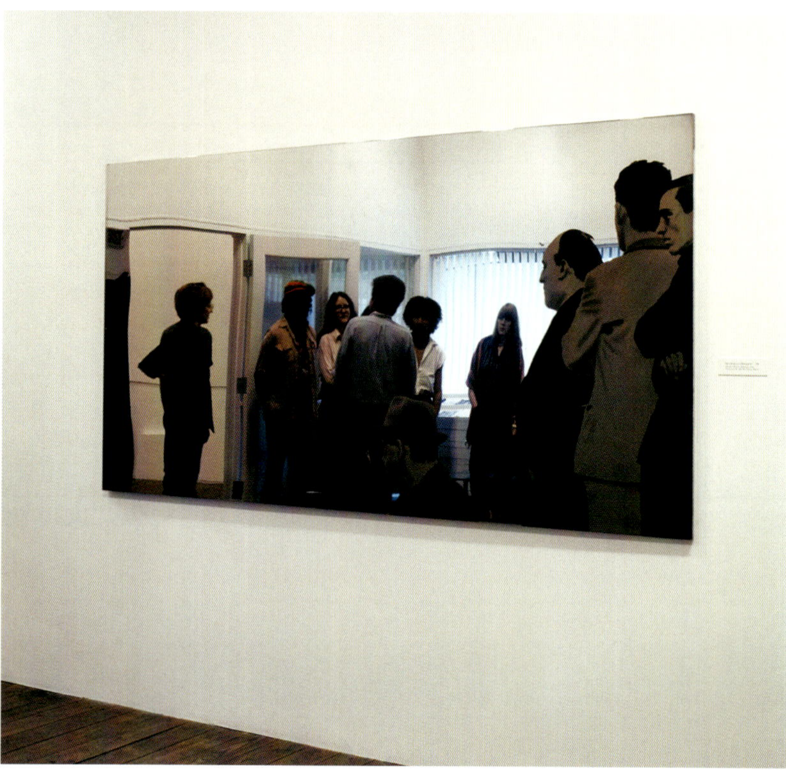

FIG. 181. *Persone che guardano* in the exhibition *Michelangelo Pistoletto: Mirror-Works* at the Institute for the Arts, Rice University, Houston, 1979. Courtesy of Cittadellarte-Fondazione Pistoletto, Biella

35
***Persone che guardano* (*People Looking*), 1965**
Painted tissue paper on polished stainless steel
47¼ x 86⅝ inches (120 x 220 cm)
Private collection

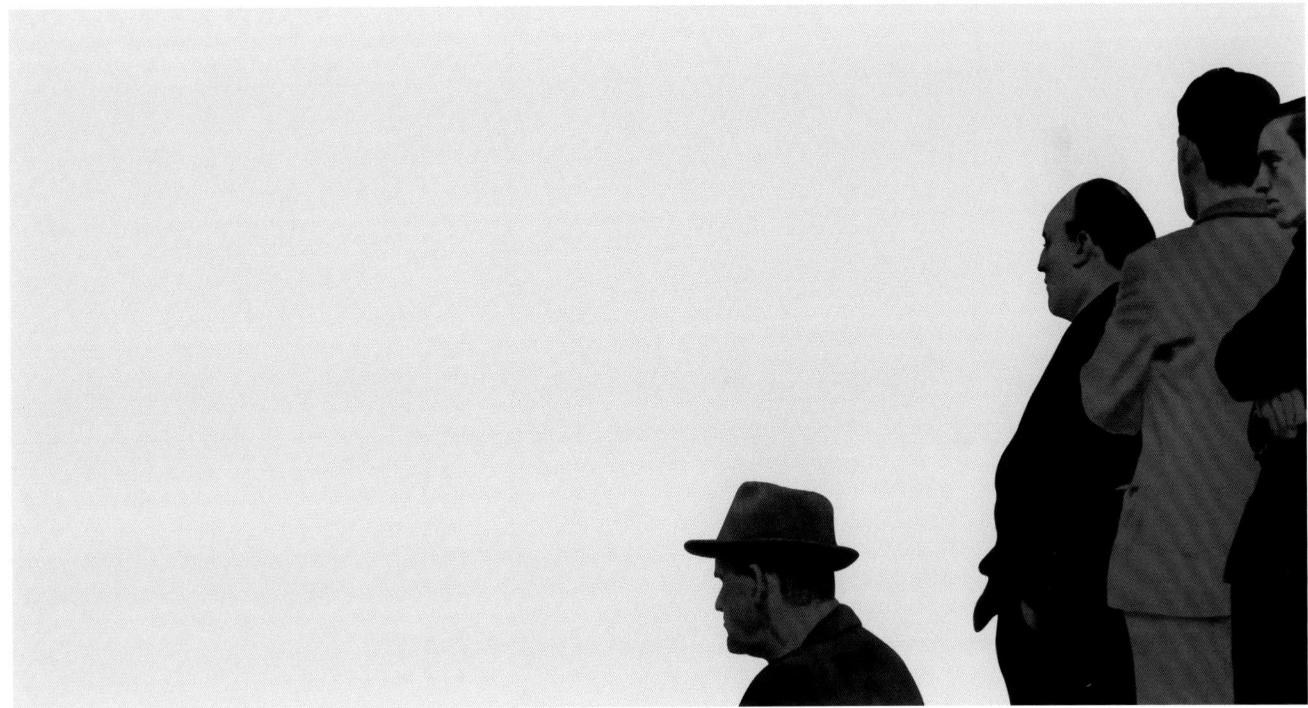

36
***Person—Back View*, 1965**
Painted tissue paper on polished stainless steel
22½ x 16¼ inches (57.2 x 41.3 cm)
Collection of Suzanne Weil, New York

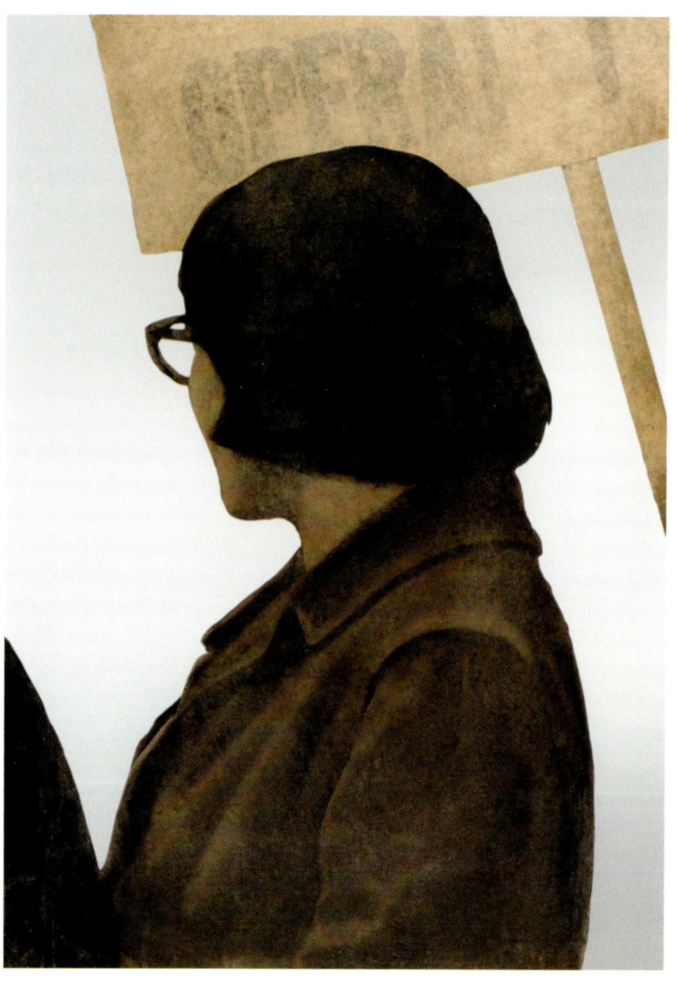

37
***Bandiera rossa* (*Comizio I*)**
(*Red Flag [Demonstration I]*), 1966
Painted tissue paper on polished stainless steel
47¼ x 39⅜ inches (120 x 100 cm)
François Pinault Foundation

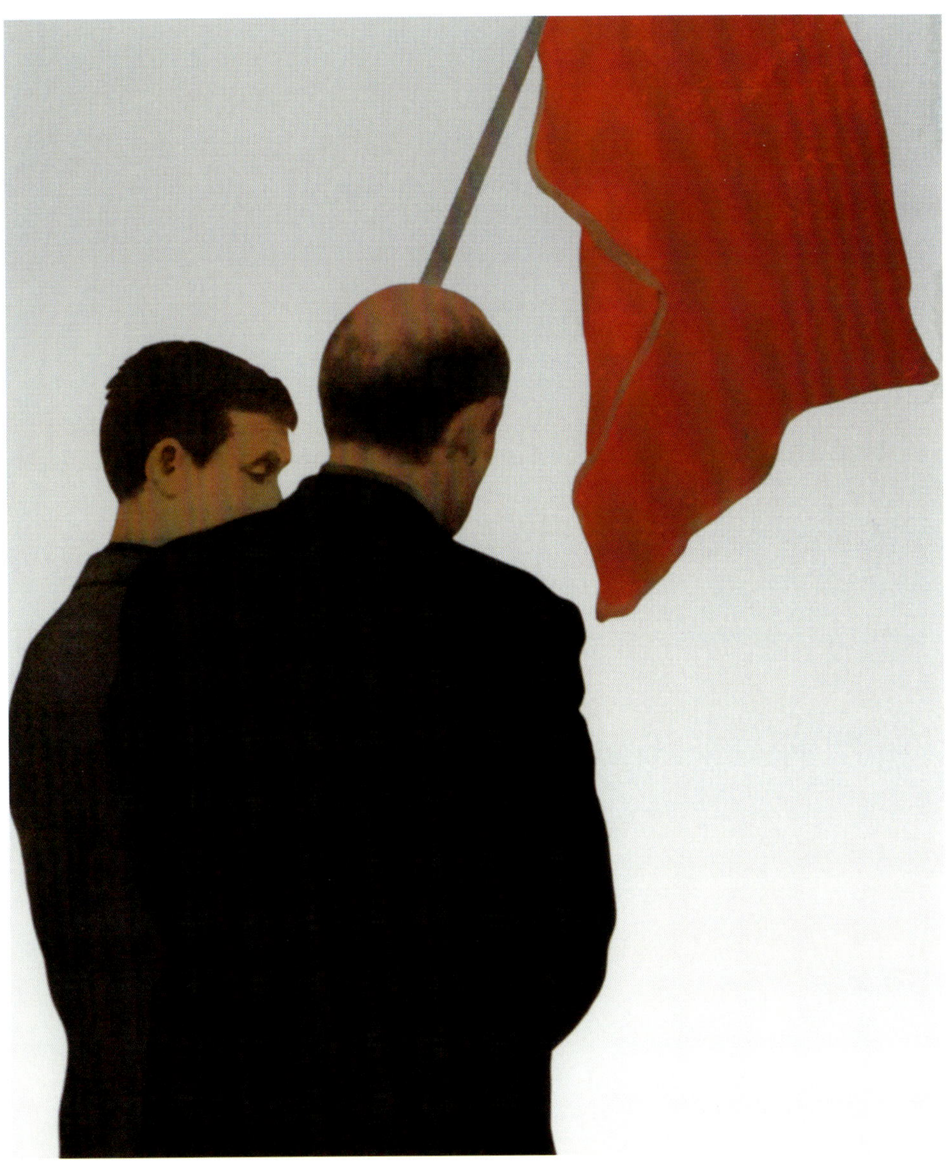

FIG. 182. *Due persone che passano* in Pistoletto's solo exhibition at Galleria Sperone, Milan, 1966. Gian Enzo Sperone is reflected in the painting. Photograph by Paolo Bressano. Courtesy of a private collection

38
Due persone che passano
(*Two People Passing By*), 1966
Painted tissue paper on polished stainless steel
47 ¼ x 90 9/16 inches (120 x 230 cm)
Private collection

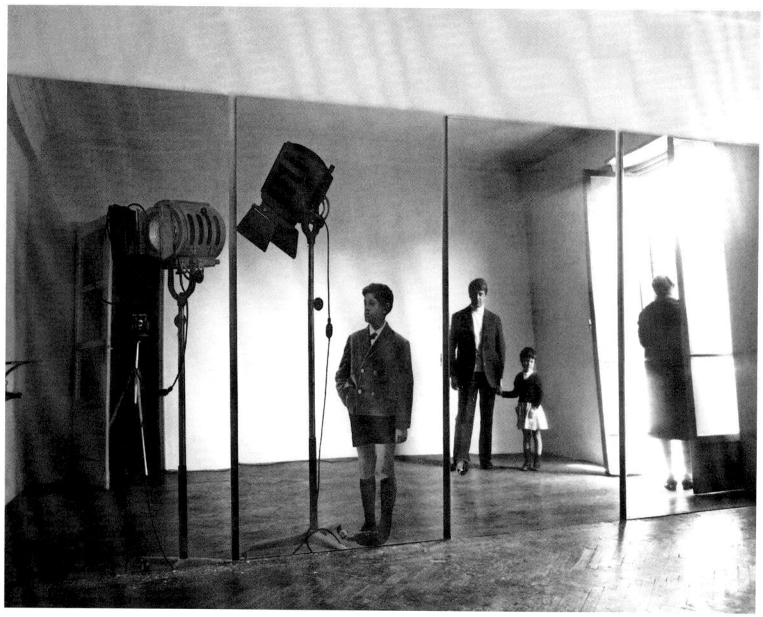

FIG. 183. *Biennale 66* in Pistoletto's house on via Cibrario in Turin, 1966. Pistoletto, his daughter Cristina, and another family member are reflected in the painting. Photograph by Paolo Bressano. Courtesy of Cittadellarte-Fondazione Pistoletto, Biella

39
***Biennale 66* (*Biennial 66*), 1966**
Painted tissue paper on polished stainless steel, four panels
Overall 90 9/16 x 189 inches (230 x 480 cm)
The Sonnabend Collection

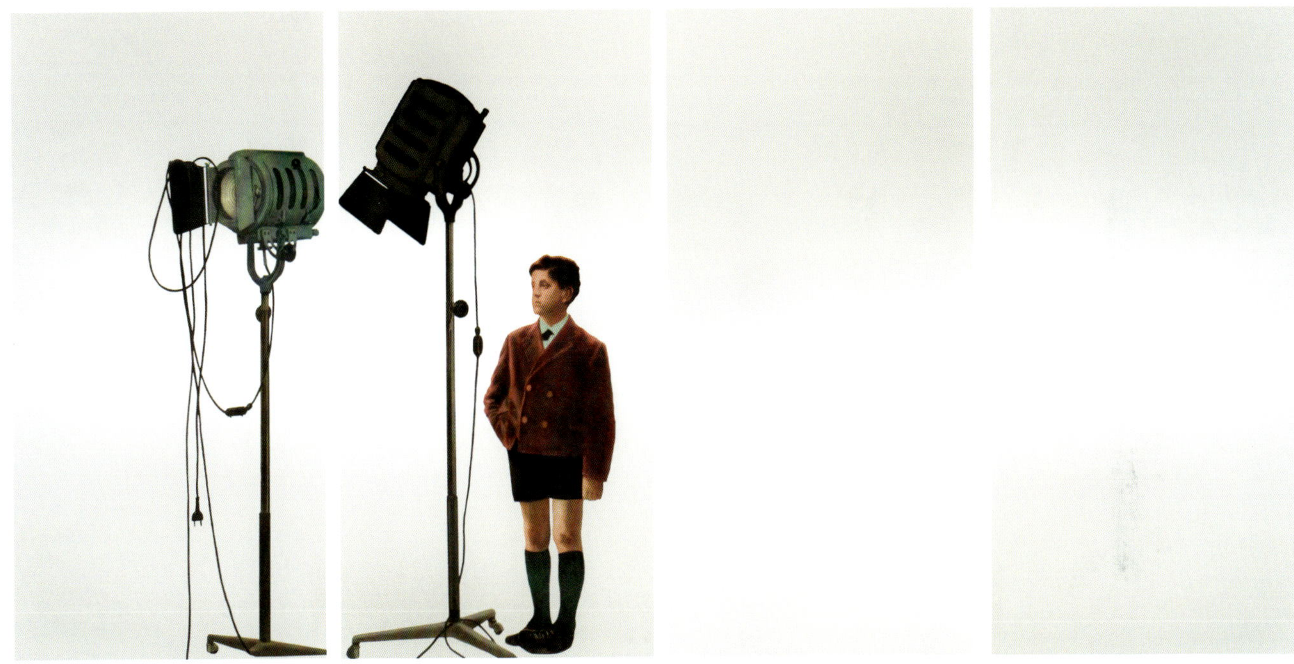

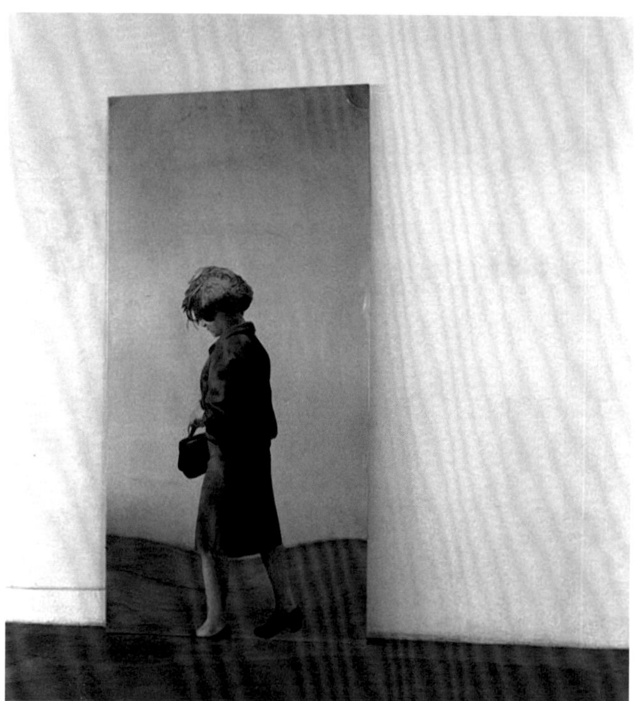

FIG. 184. *Ragazzo che cammina* at Galleria Sperone, Turin, 1968. Photograph by Paolo Mussat Sartor. Courtesy of Cittadellarte-Fondazione Pistoletto, Biella

40
Ragazza che cammina **(*Girl Walking*), 1966**
Painted tissue paper on polished stainless steel
90 9/16 x 47 1/4 inches (230 x 120 cm)
Fondazione per l'Arte Moderna e Contemporanea —CRT, on loan to Castello di Rivoli Museo d'Arte Contemporanea, Rivoli-Turin; GAM—Galleria Civica d'Arte Moderna e Contemporanea, Turin

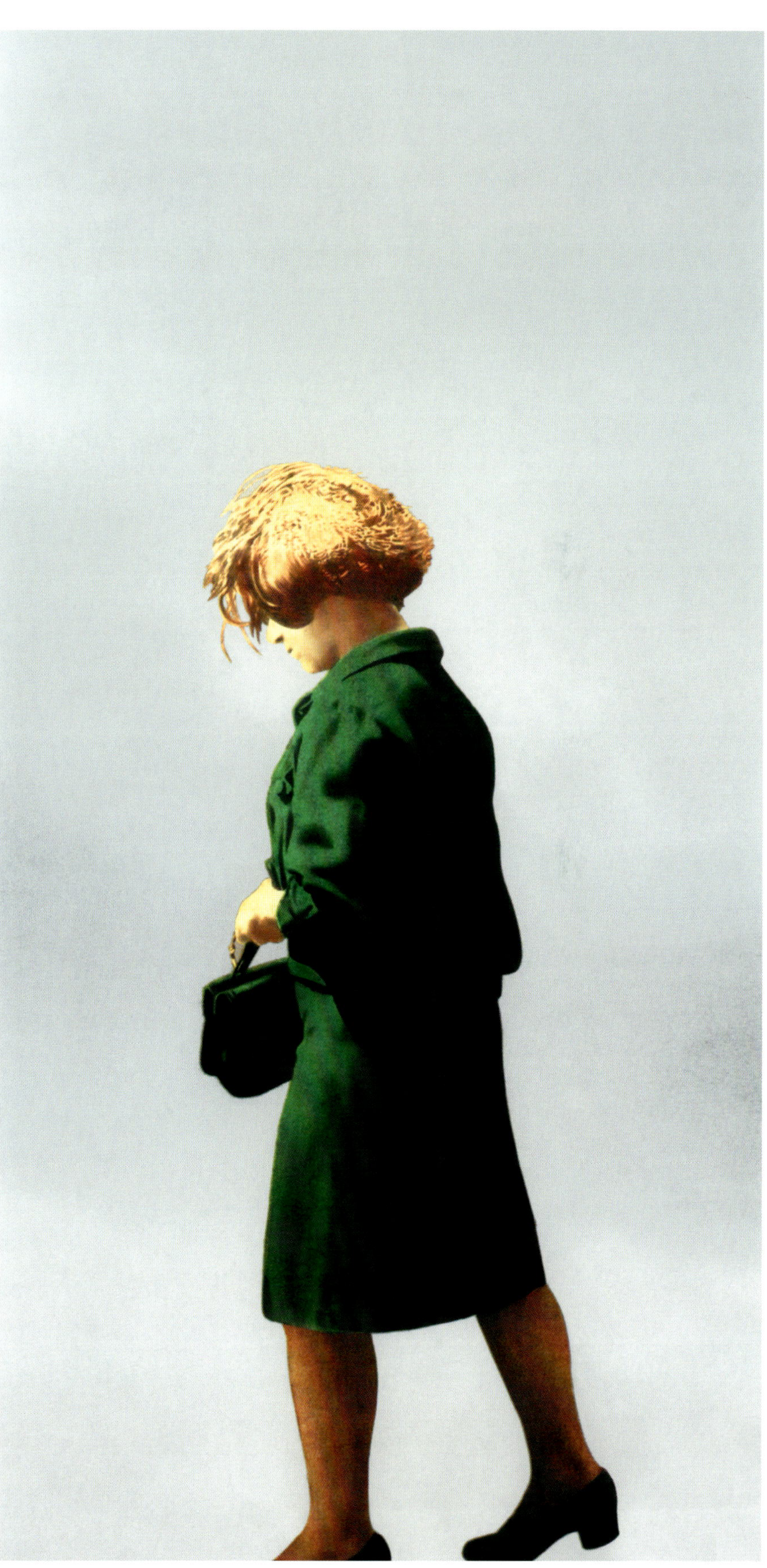

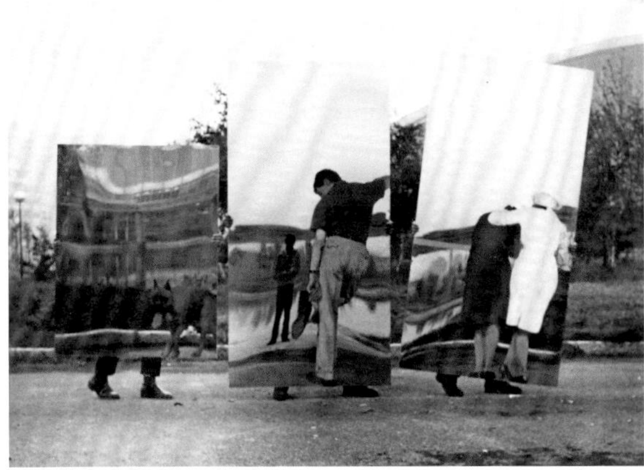

FIG. 185. Mirror paintings being transported to Galleria Sperone, Milan, on the occasion of Pistoletto's solo exhibition there in 1966. *Uomo che si tocca il piede* is flanked by *Cane* (*Dog*, 1965) and *Infermiera con ragazza* (*Nurse with Girl*, 1965). Courtesy of a private collection

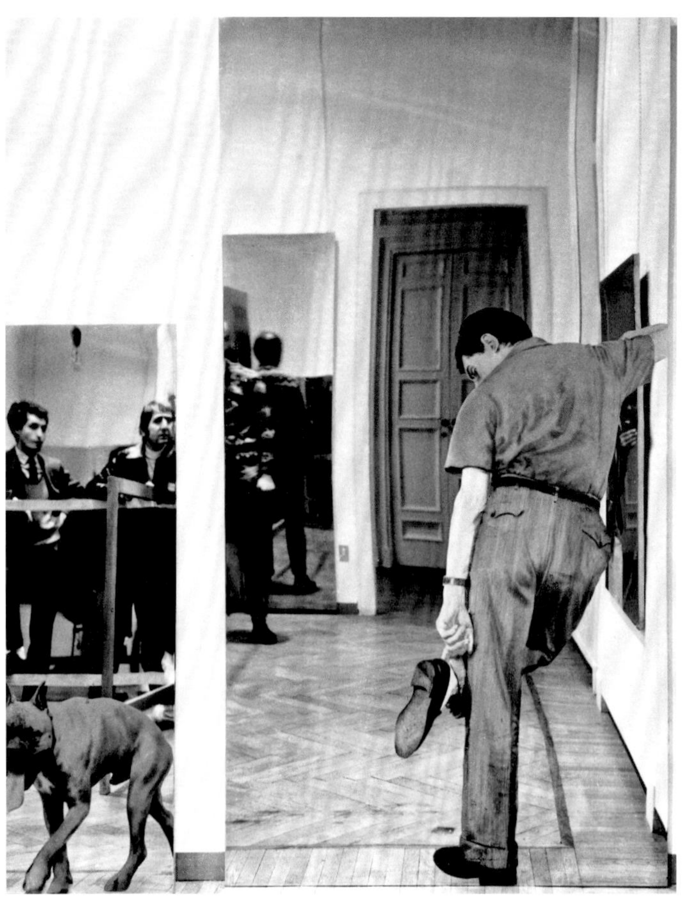

FIG. 186. *Uomo che si tocca il piede* in Pistoletto's solo exhibition at Galleria Sperone, Milan, 1966. Photograph by Paolo Bressano. Courtesy of Cittadellarte-Fondazione Pistoletto, Biella

41
Uomo che si tocca il piede
(*Man Touching His Foot*), 1966
Painted tissue paper on polished stainless steel
90 9/16 x 47 1/4 inches (230 x 120 cm)
Private collection

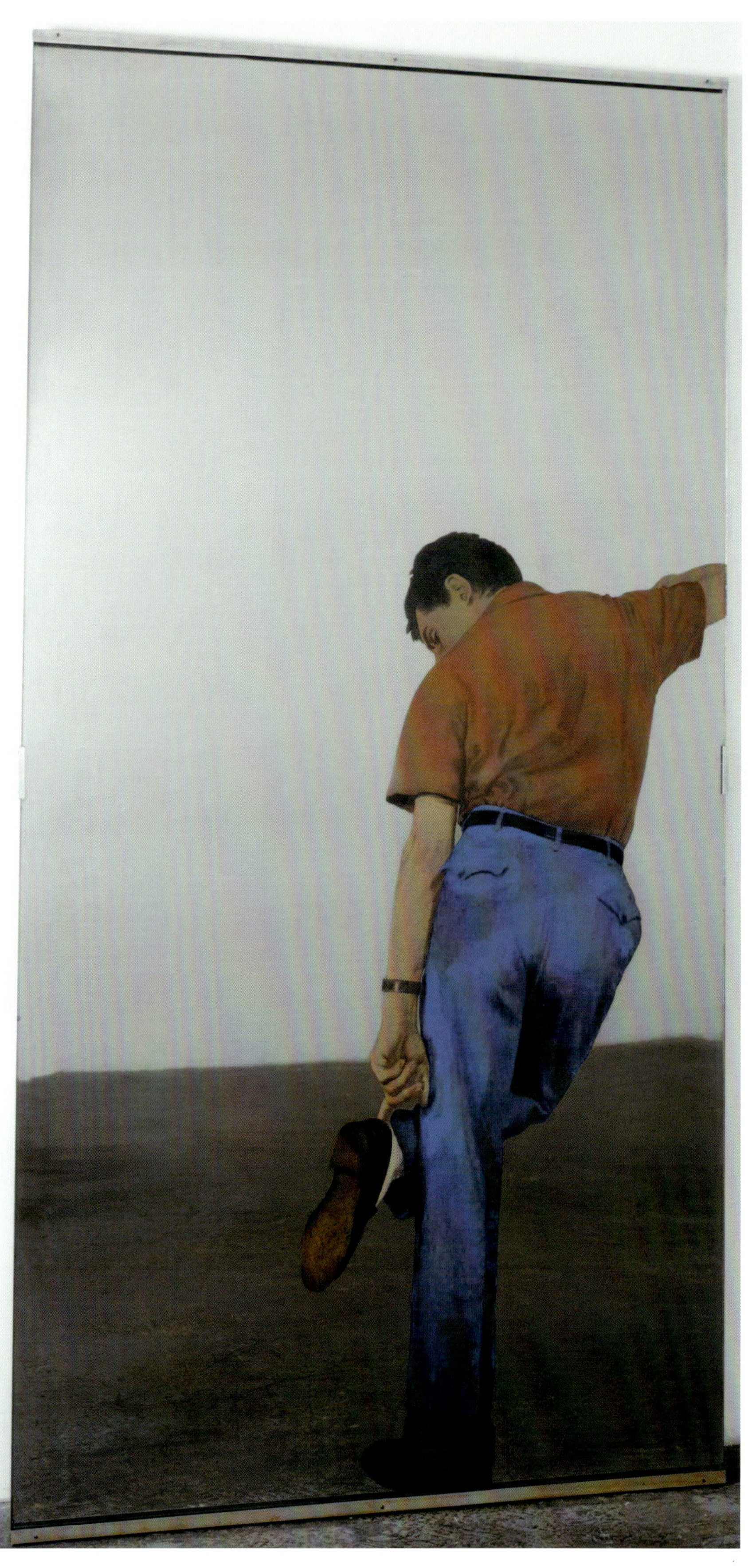

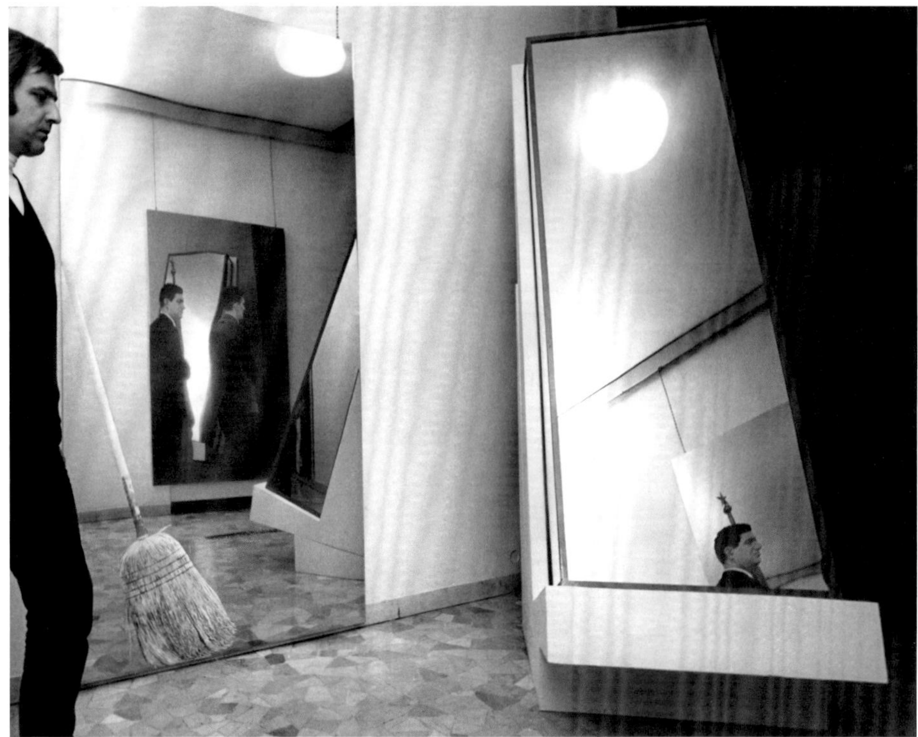

FIG. 187. *La scopa* (*The Broom*) of 1966 in the exhibition *Michelangelo Pistoletto* at Galleria Il Naviglio, Milan, 1966. Pistoletto, at the far left, would re-create this image for his 1967 *Scopa*. Photograph by Renato Rinaldi. Courtesy of Cittadellarte-Fondazione Pistoletto, Biella

42
***Scopa* (*Broom*), 1967**
Painted tissue paper on polished stainless steel
90 9/16 x 47 1/4 inches (230 x 120 cm)
Private collection

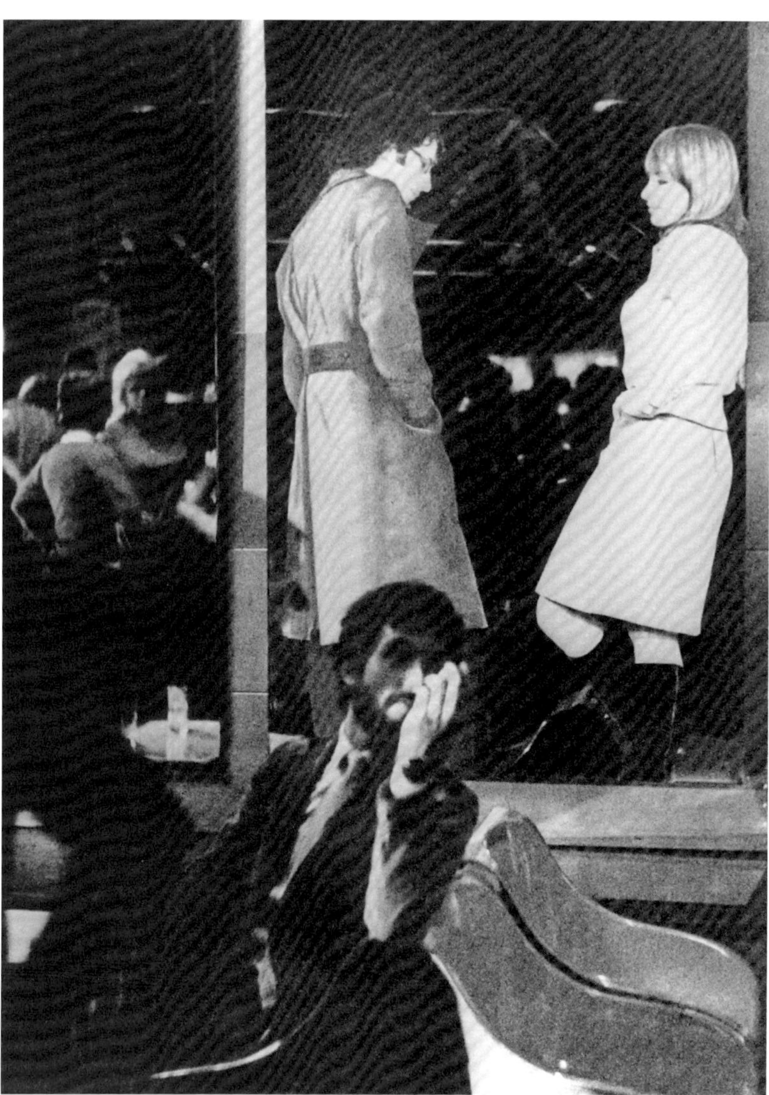

FIG. 188. The interior of the Piper Pluriclub during the action *La fine di Pistoletto* (*The End of Pistoletto*), Turin, March 6, 1967. *Lui e lei che parlano* is in the background; the figure in the foreground is Gian Enzo Sperone. Photograph by Renato Rinaldi. Courtesy of Cittadellarte-Fondazione Pistoletto, Biella

43
Lui e lei che parlano
(*He and She Talking*), 1967
Painted tissue paper on polished stainless steel
90 9/16 x 47 1/4 inches (230 x 120 cm)
Private collection

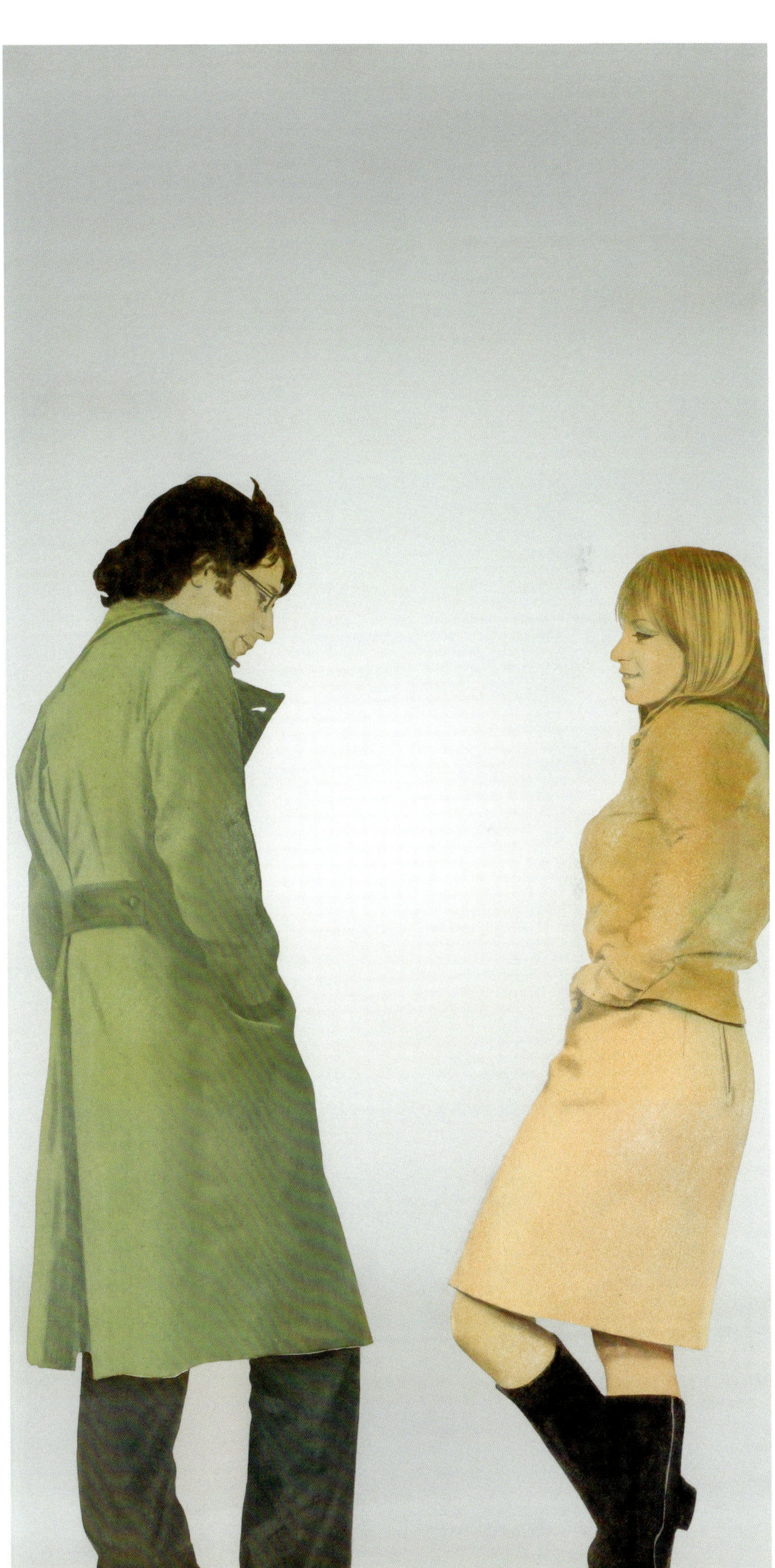

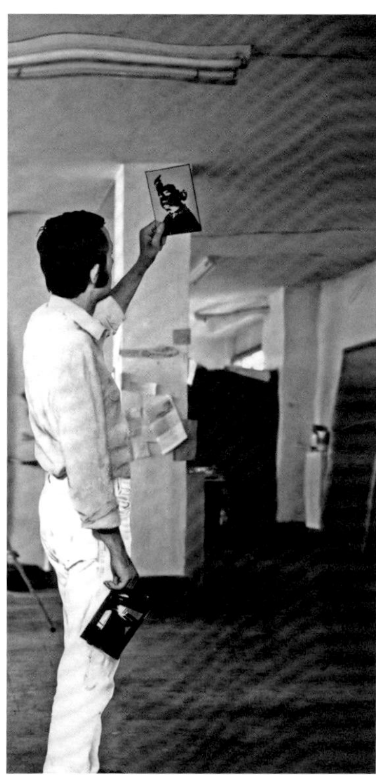

FIG. 189. *Alighiero Boetti che guarda un negativo* in Pistoletto's studio on via Reymond in Turin, 1967. Photograph by Paolo Bressano. Courtesy of Cittadellarte-Fondazione Pistoletto, Biella

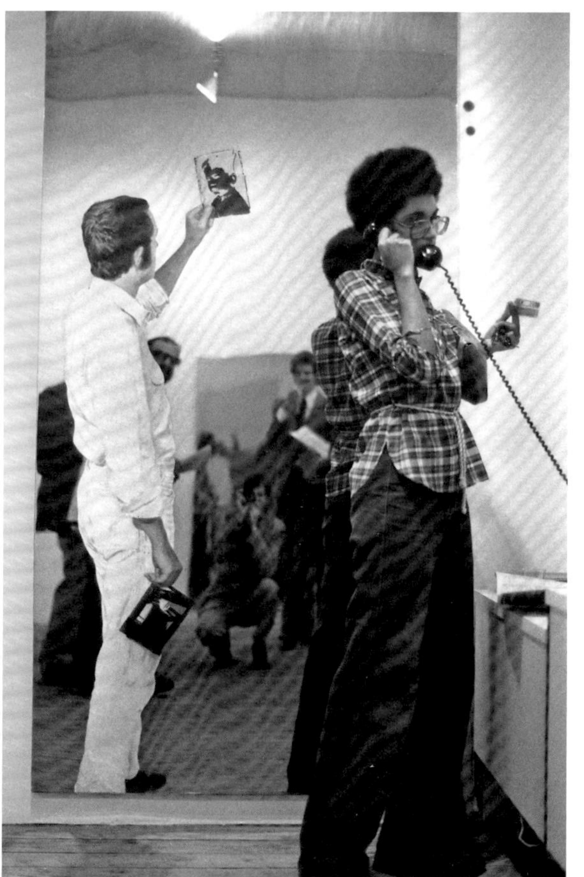

FIG. 190. *Alighiero Boetti che guarda un negativo* in the exhibition *Michelangelo Pistoletto: Mirror-Works* at the Institute for the Arts, Rice University, Houston, 1979. Courtesy of Cittadellarte-Fondazione Pistoletto, Biella

44
Alighiero Boetti che guarda un negativo
(*Alighiero Boetti Looking at a Negative*), 1967
Painted tissue paper on polished stainless steel
90 9/16 x 47 1/4 inches (230 x 120 cm)
Abrams Family Collection

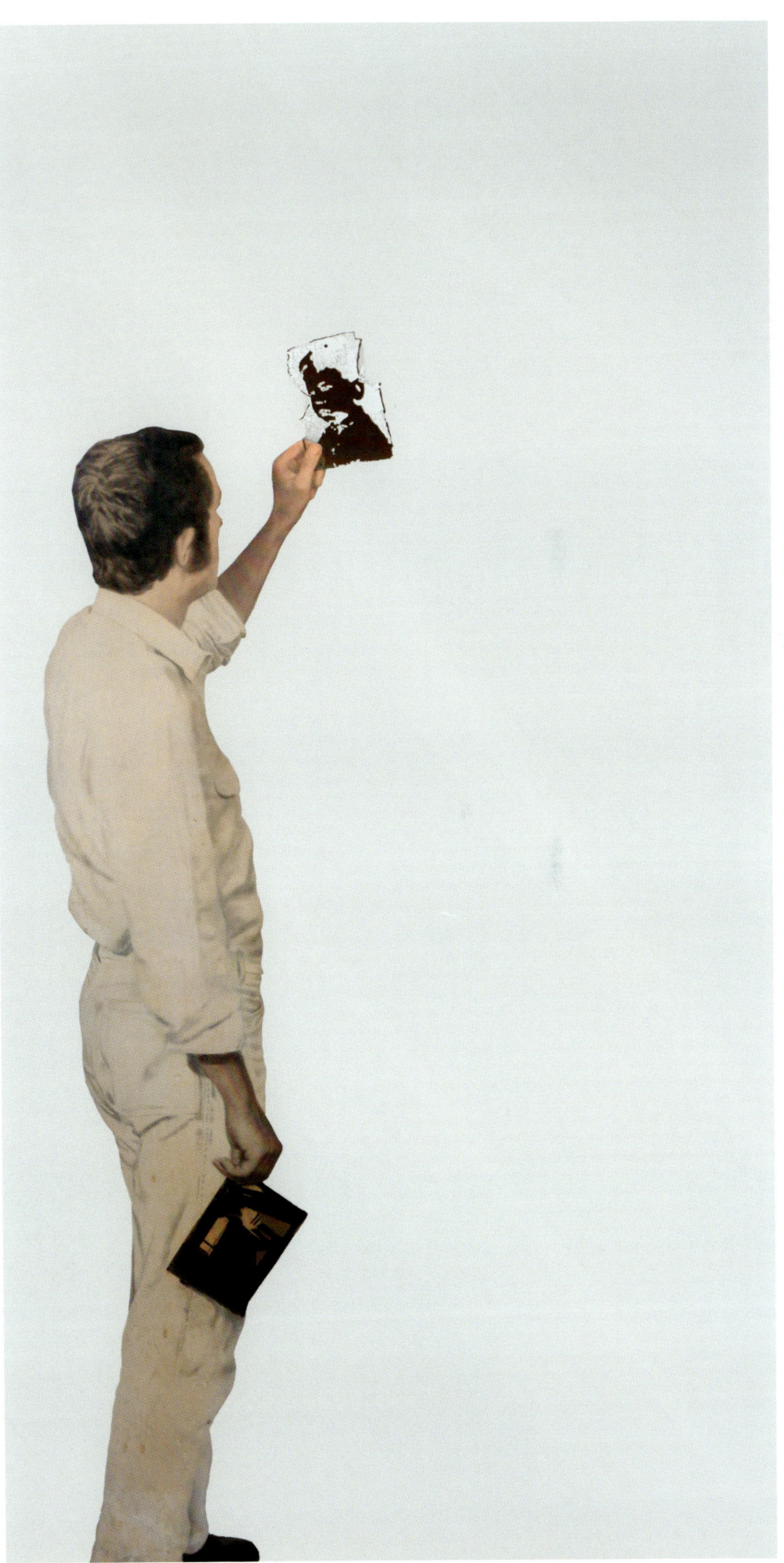

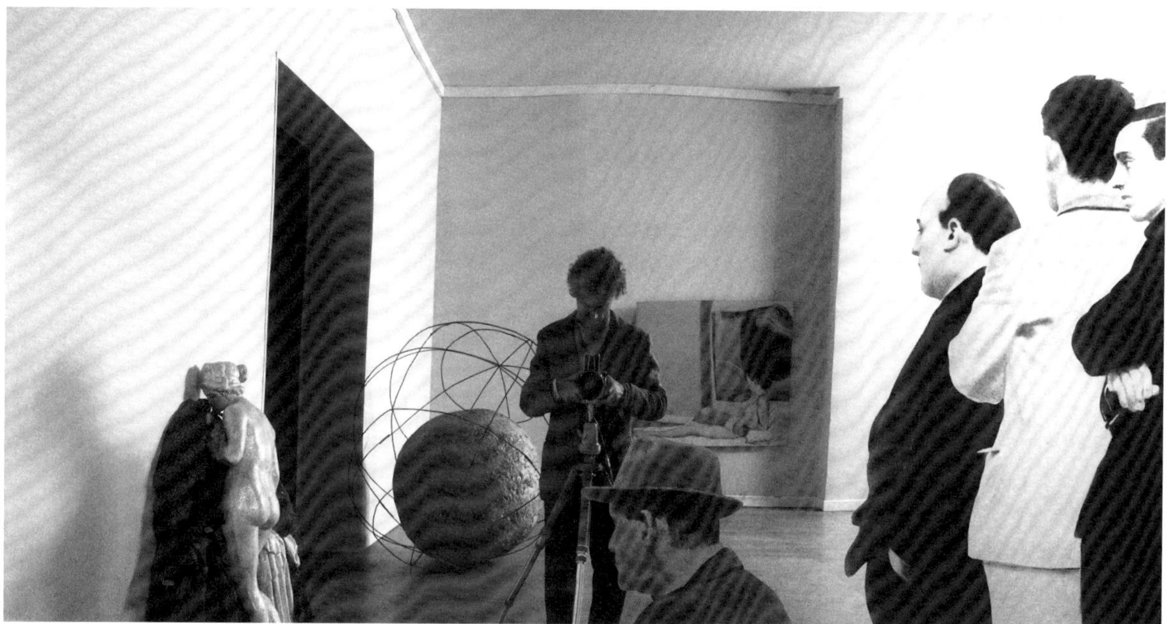

FIG. 191. *Maria nuda* reflected in the mirror painting *Persone che guardano* (plate 35) in the Pistoletto room of the exhibition *Vitalità del negativo* (*Vitality of the Negative*) at the Palazzo delle Esposizioni, Rome, 1970. The photographer is reflected at the center of the painting. Photograph by Ugo Mulas © Ugo Mulas Heirs.

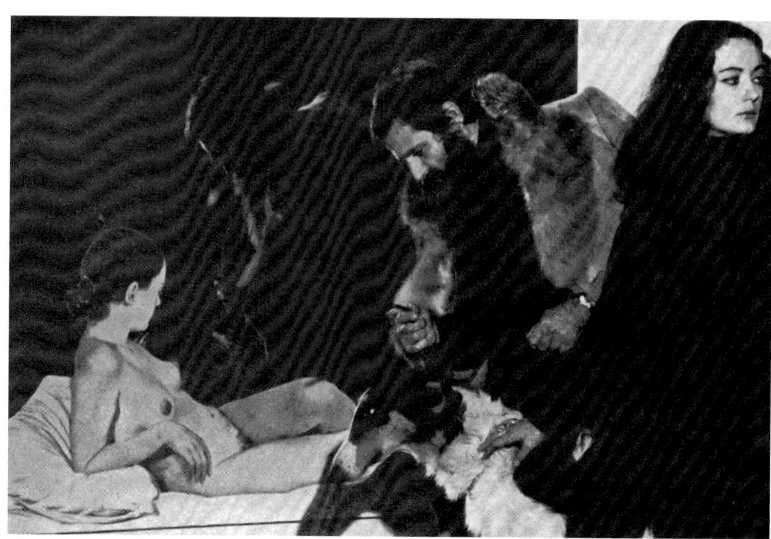

FIG. 192. *Maria nuda* in the Pistoletto room of the exhibition *Vitalità del negativo* (*Vitality of the Negative*) at the Palazzo delle Esposizioni, Rome, 1970. Pistoletto and Maria Pioppi are standing in front of the painting. Published in Italian *Vogue*, January 1971, p. 75.

45
***Maria nuda* (*Maria Nude*), 1967**
Painted tissue paper on polished stainless steel
47¼ x 59¹⁄₁₆ inches (120 x 150 cm)
Private collection

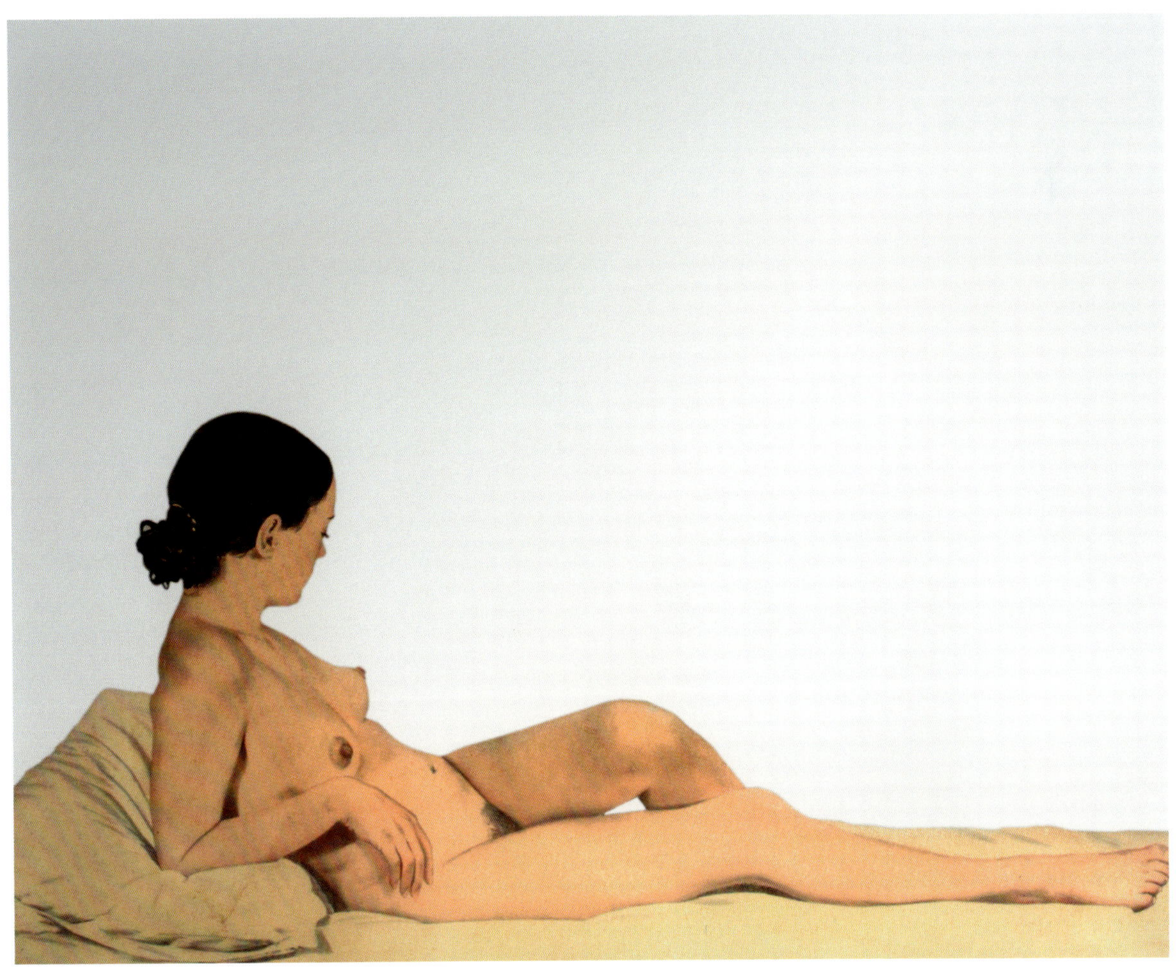

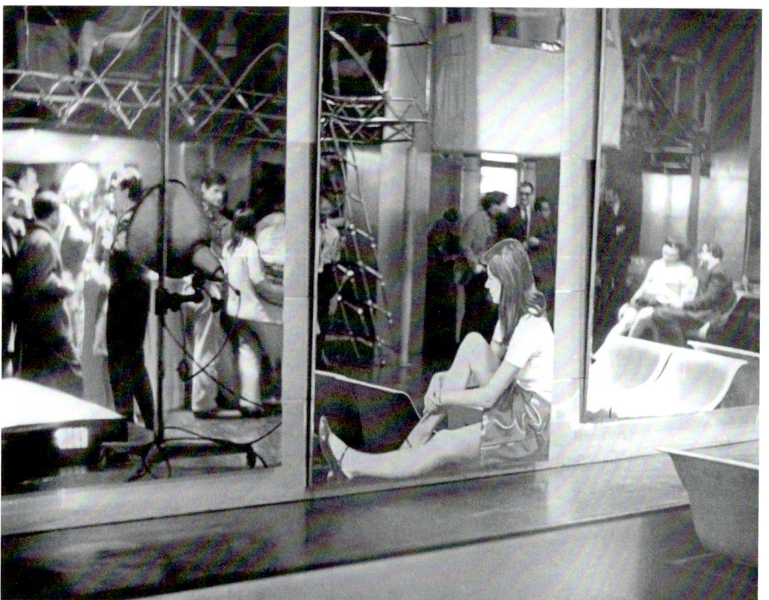

FIG. 193. *Ragazza seduta per terra* at the Piper Pluriclub during the action *La fine di Pistoletto* (*The End of Pistoletto*), Turin, March 6, 1967. Photograph by Renato Rinaldi. Courtesy of Derossi Associati, Turin

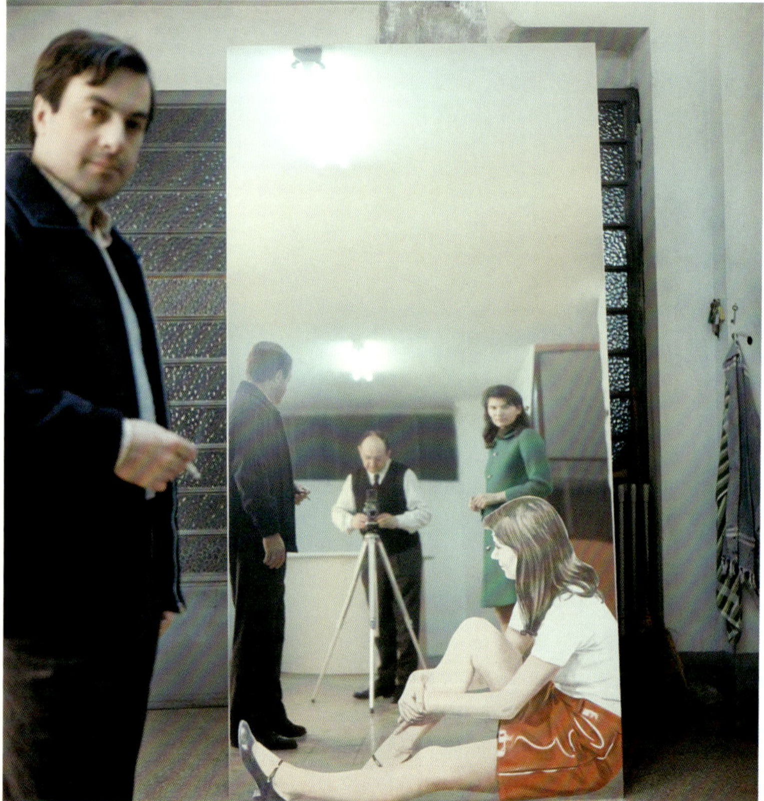

FIG. 194. *Ragazza seduta per terra* in Pistoletto's studio on via Reymond in Turin, 1967. Standing to the left is the architect of the Piper Pluriclub, Piero Derossi. Also reflected in the painting are Paolo Bressano and Graziella Derossi (the painting's subject). Photograph by Paolo Bressano. Courtesy of Cittadellarte-Fondazione Pistoletto, Biella

46
Ragazza seduta per terra
(*Girl Sitting on the Floor*), 1967
Painted tissue paper on polished stainless steel
90 9/16 x 47 1/4 inches (230 x 120 cm)
Private collection

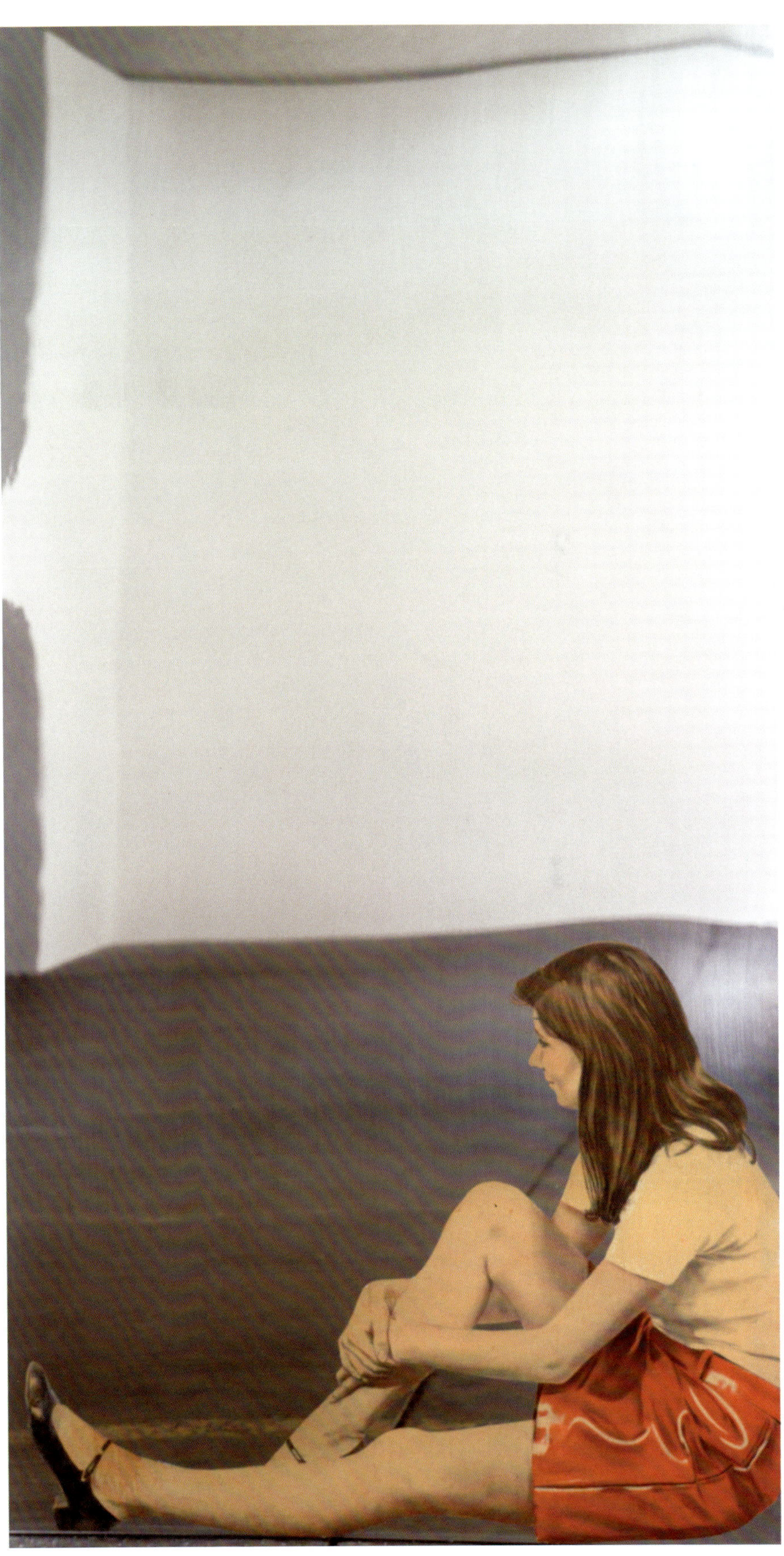

47
Lui e lei abbracciati
(*He and She Embracing*), 1968
Painted tissue paper on polished stainless steel
47¼ x 39⅜ inches (120 x 100 cm)
Collezione Maramotti, Reggio Emilia

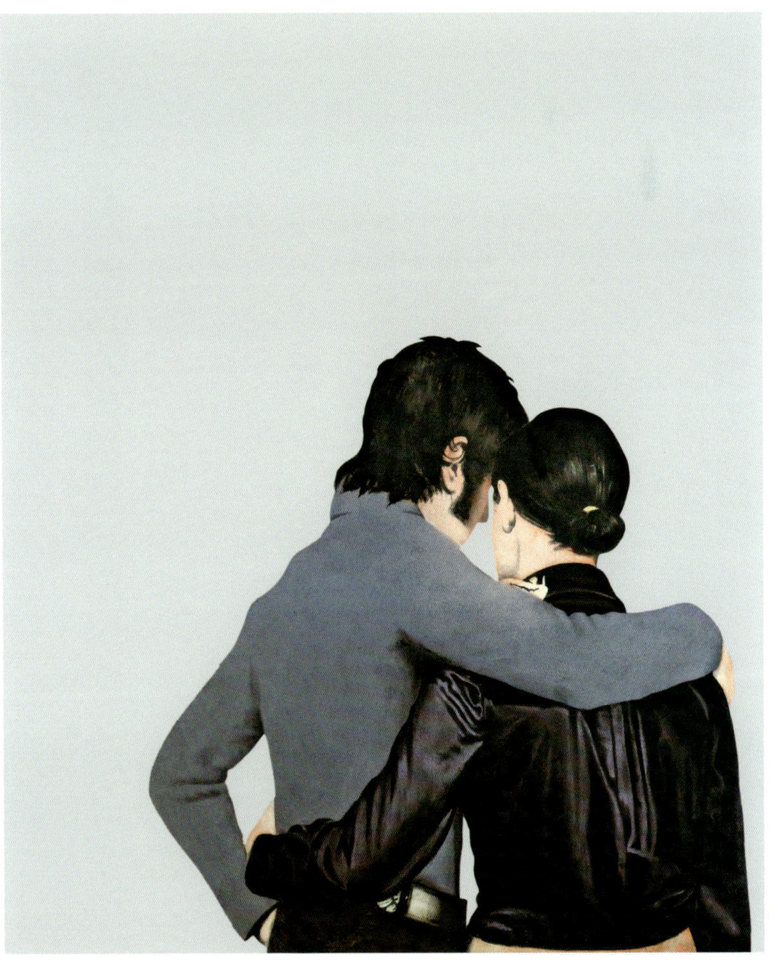

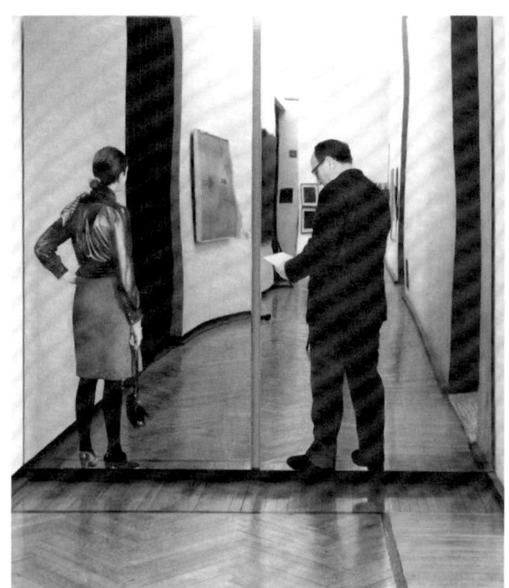

FIG. 195. *I visitatori* at GNAM—Galleria Nazionale d'Arte Moderna e Contemporanea, Rome, c. 1968. Courtesy of Cittadellarte-Fondazione Pistoletto, Biella

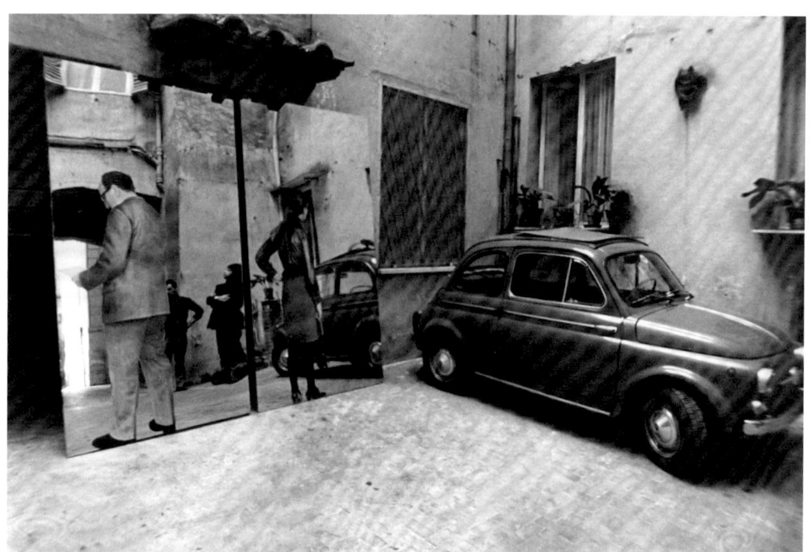

FIG. 196. *I visitatori* in the courtyard of Maria Pioppi's house on Ripretta alley, Rome, 1968. Courtesy of Cittadellarte-Fondazione Pistoletto, Biella

48
***I visitatori* (*The Visitors*), 1968**
Painted tissue paper on polished stainless steel
90 9/16 x 94 ½ inches (230 x 240 cm)
GNAM—Galleria Nazionale d'Arte Moderna e Contemporanea, Rome. Courtesy of the Italian Ministry of Cultural Heritage and Activities

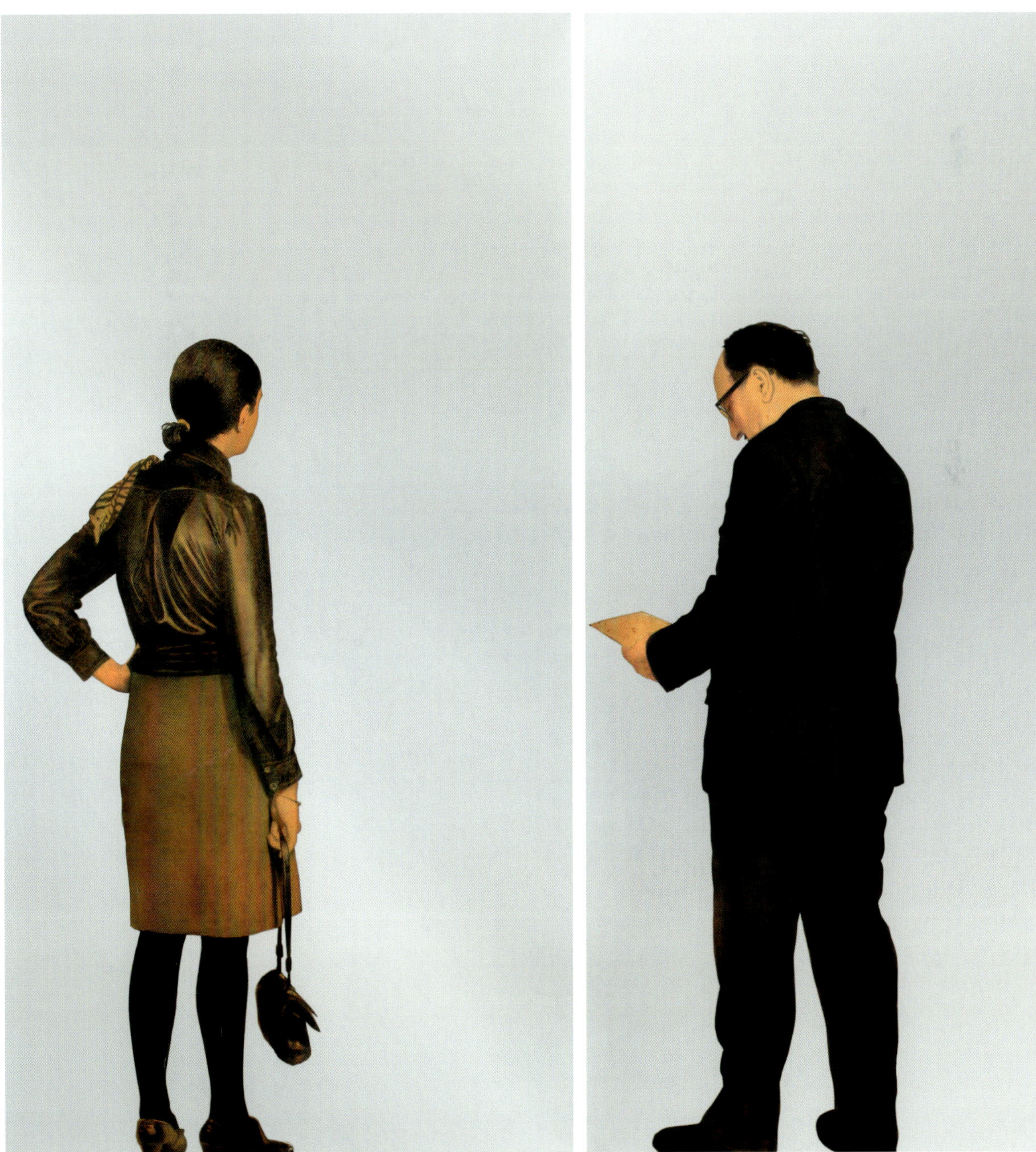

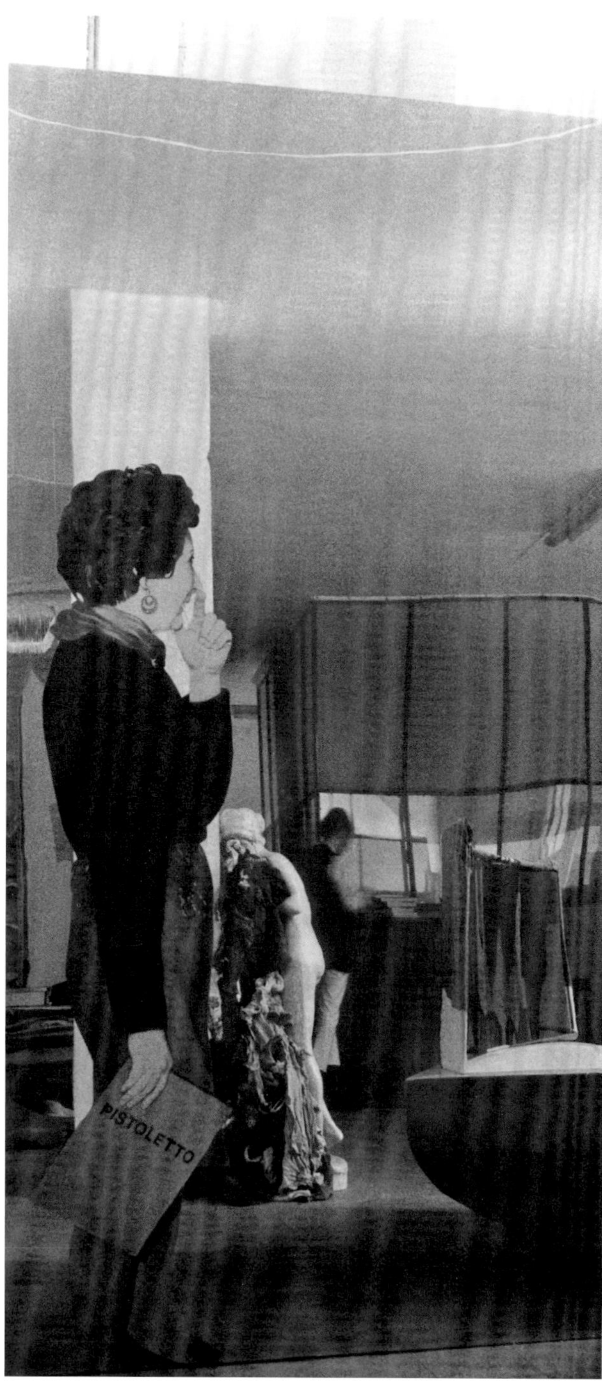

FIG. 197. *Visitatrice con catalogo* in Pistoletto's studio on via Reymond in Turin, 1969. Photograph by Paolo Mussat Sartor. Courtesy of Cittadellarte-Fondazione Pistoletto, Biella

49
Visitatrice con catalogo
(Visitor with Catalogue), 1969
Painted tissue paper on polished stainless steel
90 9/16 x 47 1/4 inches (230 x 120 cm)
Collection of Pietro Valsecchi

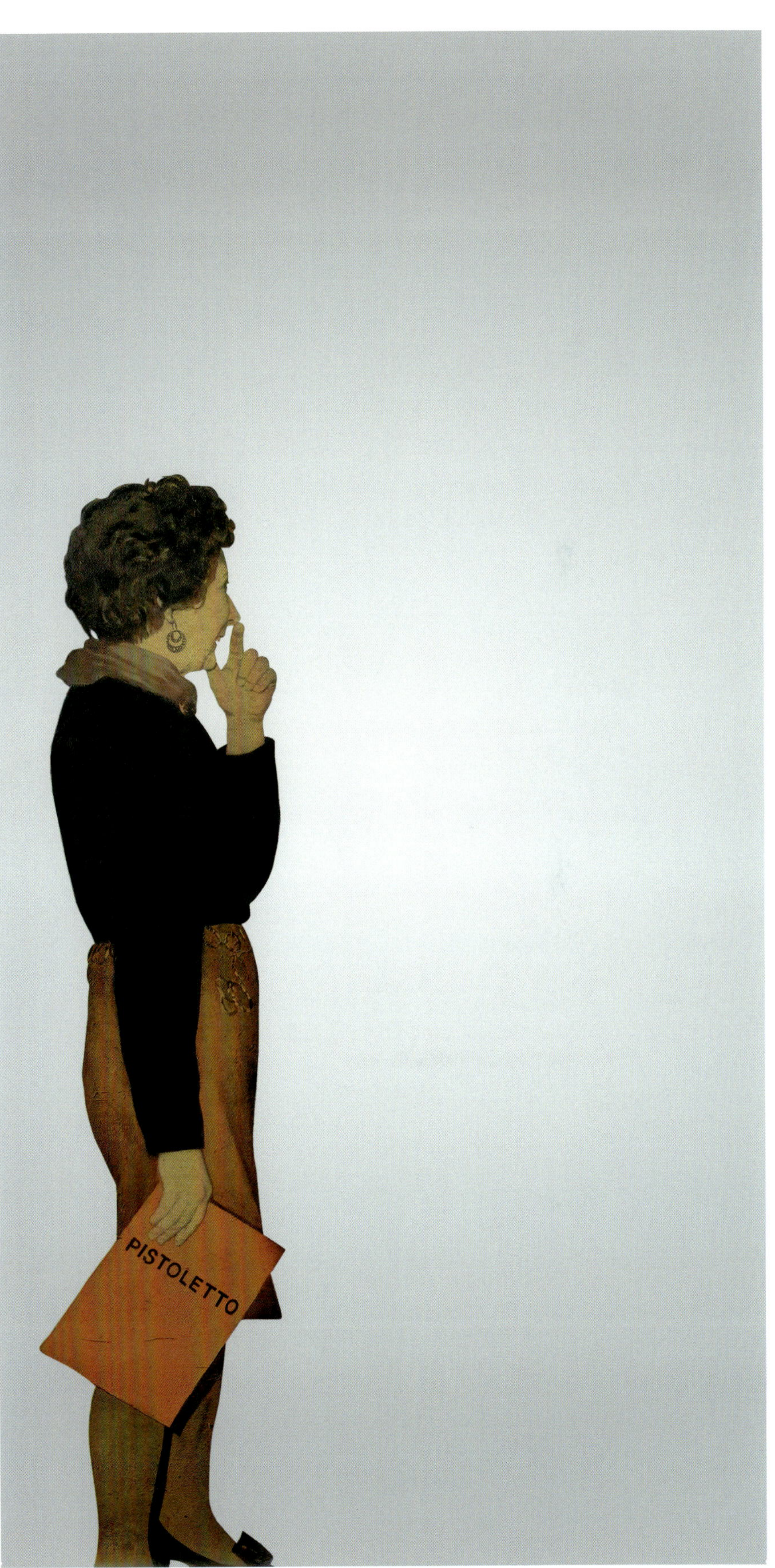

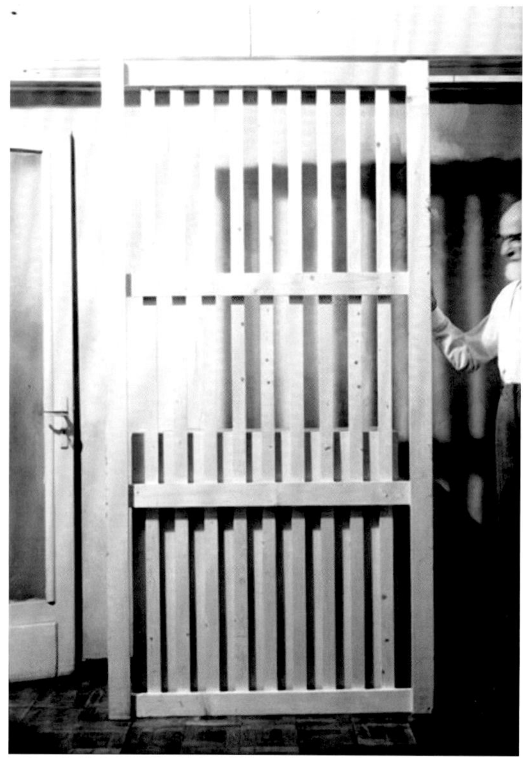

FIG. 198. Pistoletto's father, Ettore Olivero Pistoletto, holding the wood construction that is the subject of *Gabbia*, Turin, 1969. Photograph by Paolo Bressano. Courtesy of Cittadellarte-Fondazione Pistoletto, Biella

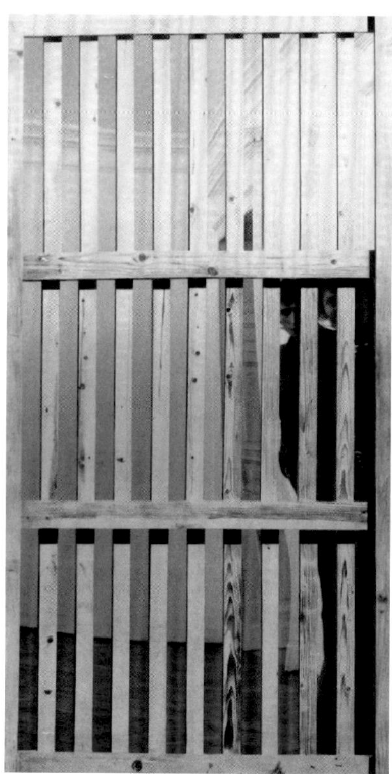

FIG. 199. *Gabbia* in Pistoletto's studio on via Reymond in Turin, 1969. The reflected figures are Giuseppe Penone and Pier Luigi Pero. Photograph by Paolo Mussat Sartor. Courtesy of Cittadellarte-Fondazione Pistoletto, Biella

50
***Gabbia* (*Cage*), 1969**
Painted tissue paper on polished stainless steel
90 9/16 x 47 1/4 inches (230 x 120 cm)
Collection of the artist

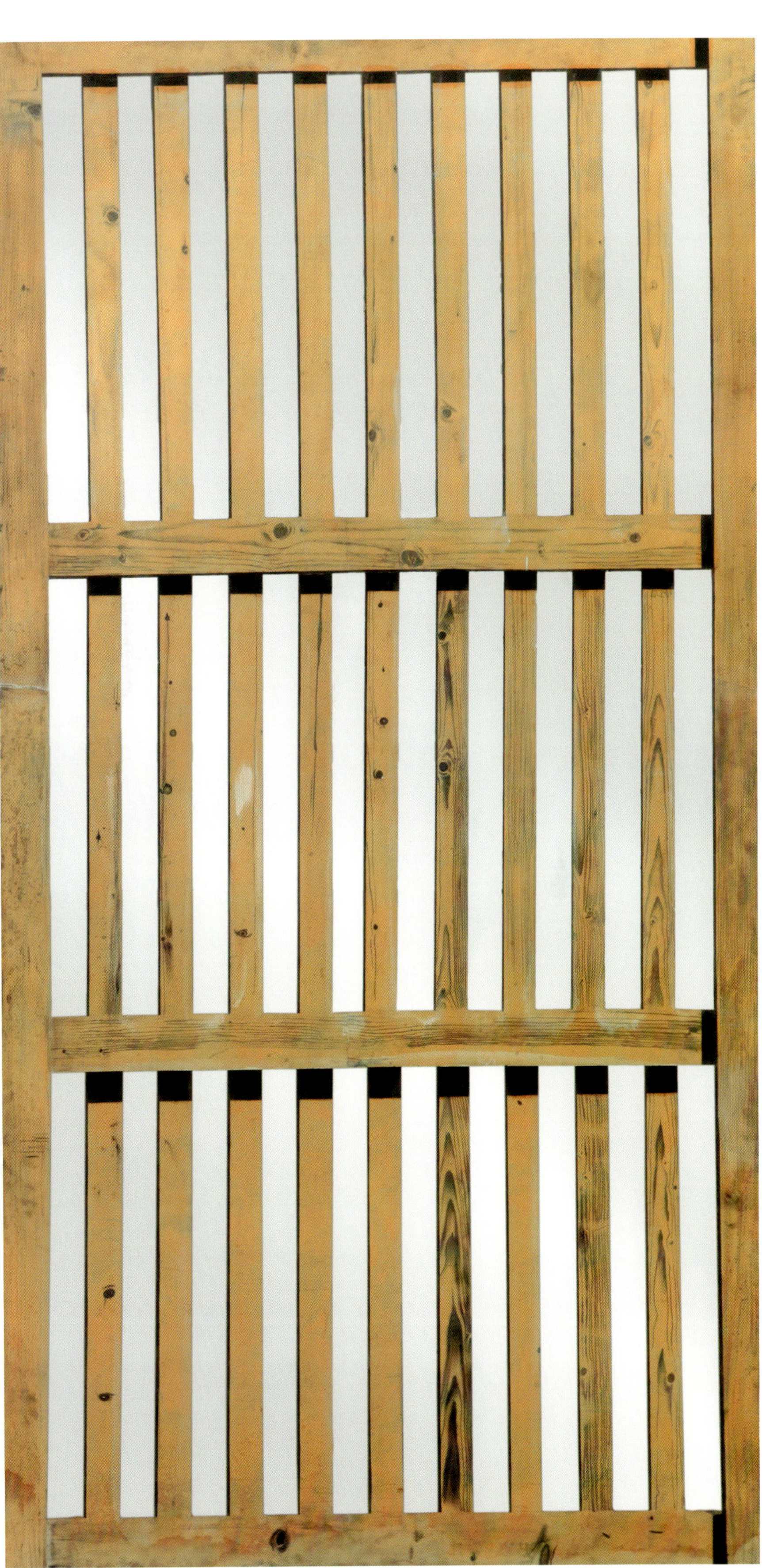

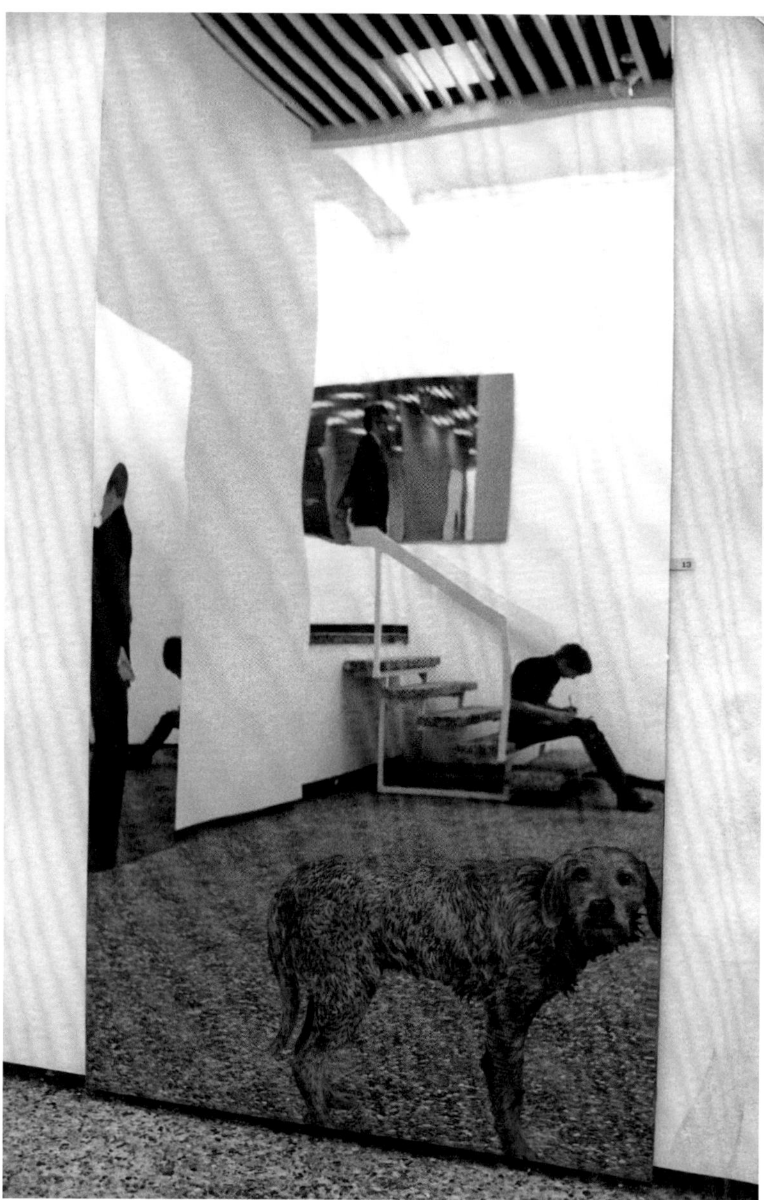

FIG. 200. *Il cane con la coda giù* in the exhibition *Michelangelo Pistoletto* at the Kestner Gesellschaft, Hanover, Germany, 1973. Photograph by Angelika Platen. Courtesy of Cittadellarte-Fondazione Pistoletto, Biella

51
Il cane con la coda giù
(*The Dog with Its Tail between Its Legs*), 1969
Painted tissue paper on polished stainless steel
90 9/16 x 47 1/4 inches (230 x 120 cm)
Courtesy of Fondazione Marconi, Milan

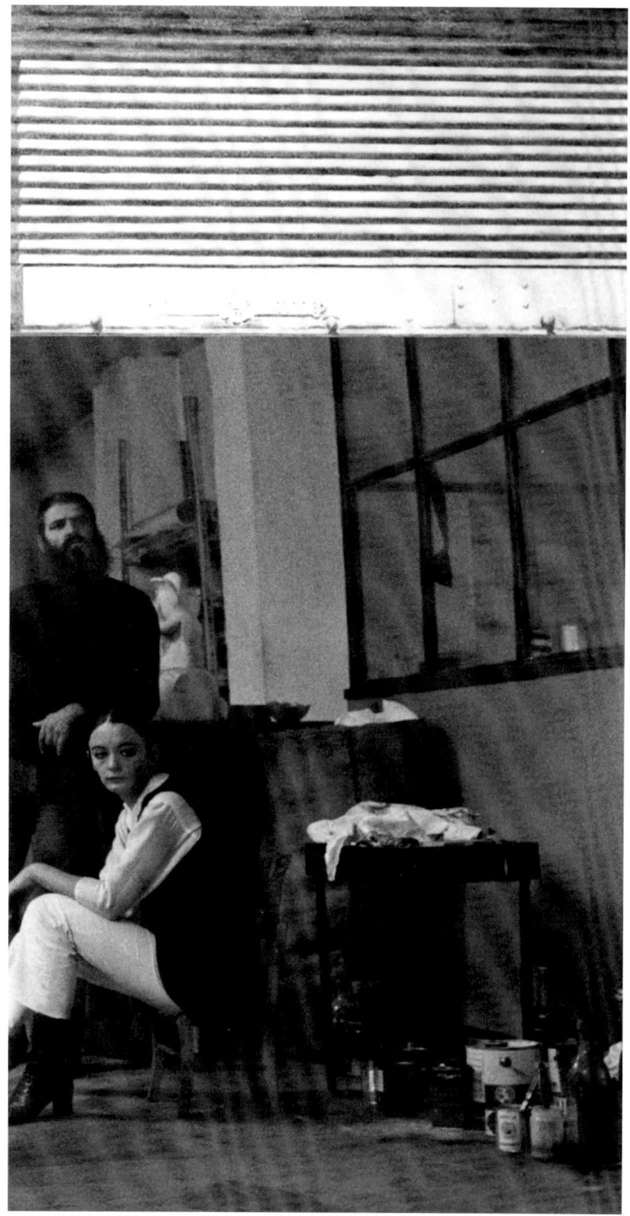

FIG. 201. *Saracinesca* in Pistoletto's studio on via Reymond in Turin, 1971. Pistoletto and Maria Pioppi are reflected in the painting. Photograph by Paolo Mussat Sartor. Courtesy of Cittadellarte-Fondazione Pistoletto, Biella

52
***Saracinesca* (*Iron Gate*), 1970**
Painted tissue paper on polished stainless steel
90 9/16 x 47 1/4 inches (230 x 120 cm)
Private collection

53
Muretto di mattoni
(*Small Wall of Bricks*), 1970
Painted tissue paper on polished stainless steel
90 9/16 x 47 1/4 inches (230 x 120 cm)
Private collection

54
***Donna che fugge* (*Woman Escaping*), 1971**
Painted tissue paper on polished stainless steel
90 9/16 x 47 1/4 inches (230 x 120 cm)
Private collection. Courtesy of Lia Rumma

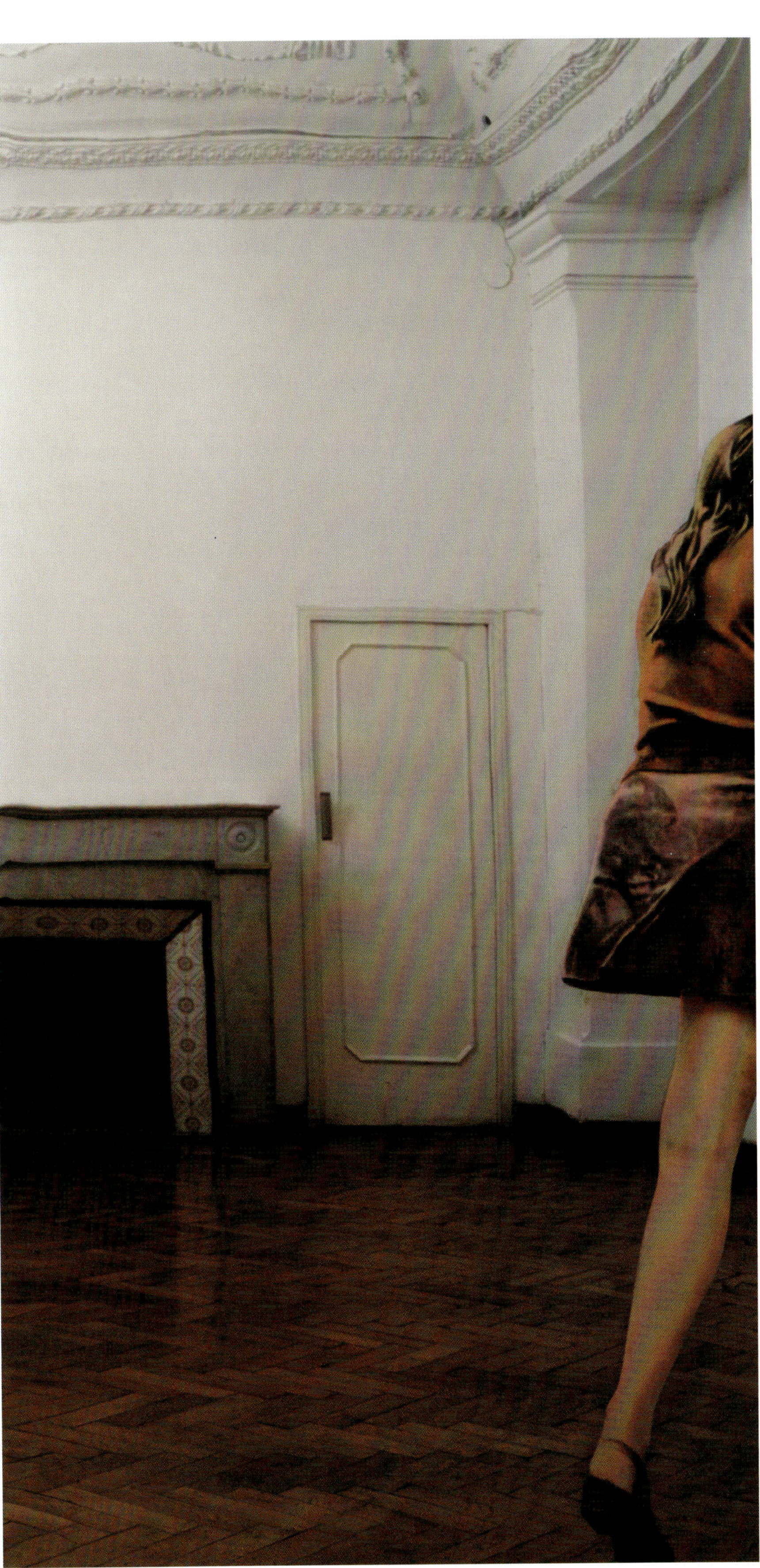

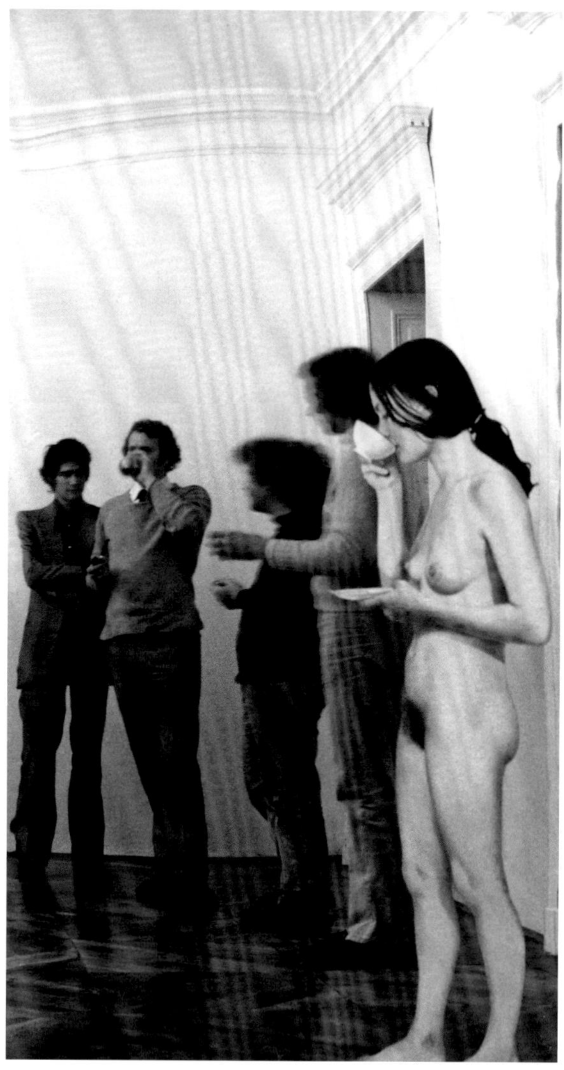

FIG. 202. *Donna nuda che beve il tè* in Giorgio Persano's house in Turin, 1971. Giuseppe Penone, Gian Maria Persano, Pier Luigi Pero, and Giorgio Persano are reflected in the painting. Photograph by Paolo Mussat Sartor. Courtesy of Cittadellarte-Fondazione Pistoletto, Biella

55
Donna nuda che beve il tè
(*Nude Woman Drinking Tea*), 1971
Painted tissue paper on polished stainless steel
90 9/16 x 47 1/4 inches (230 x 120 cm)
Private collection

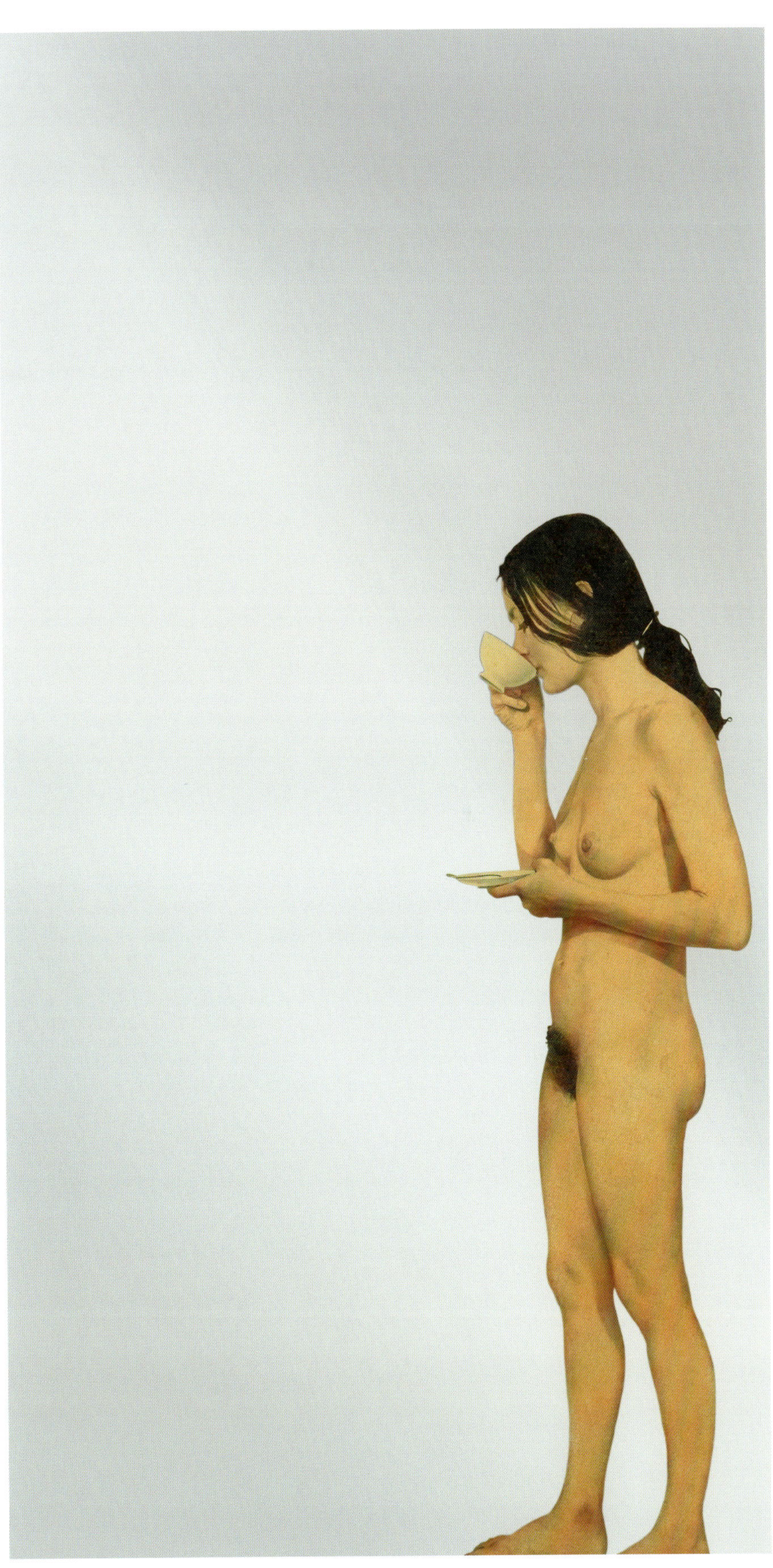

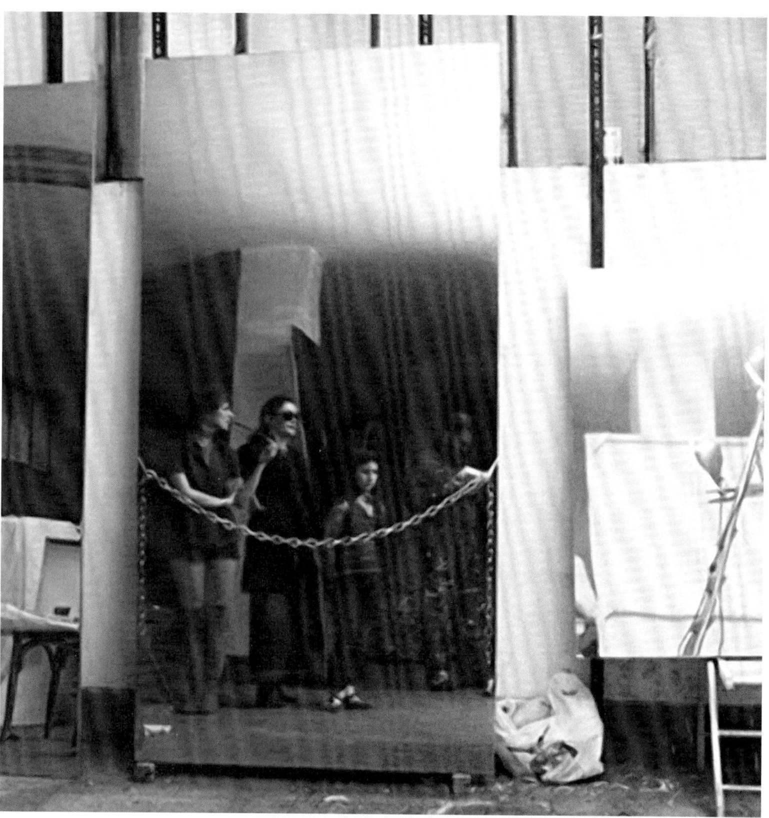

FIG. 203. *Catena* in Pistoletto's studio on via Reymond in Turin, 1971. Photograph by Paolo Mussat Sartor. Courtesy of Paolo Mussat Sartor

56
Catena (Chain), 1971
Painted tissue paper on polished stainless steel
90 9/16 x 47 1/4 inches (230 x 120 cm)
Private collection

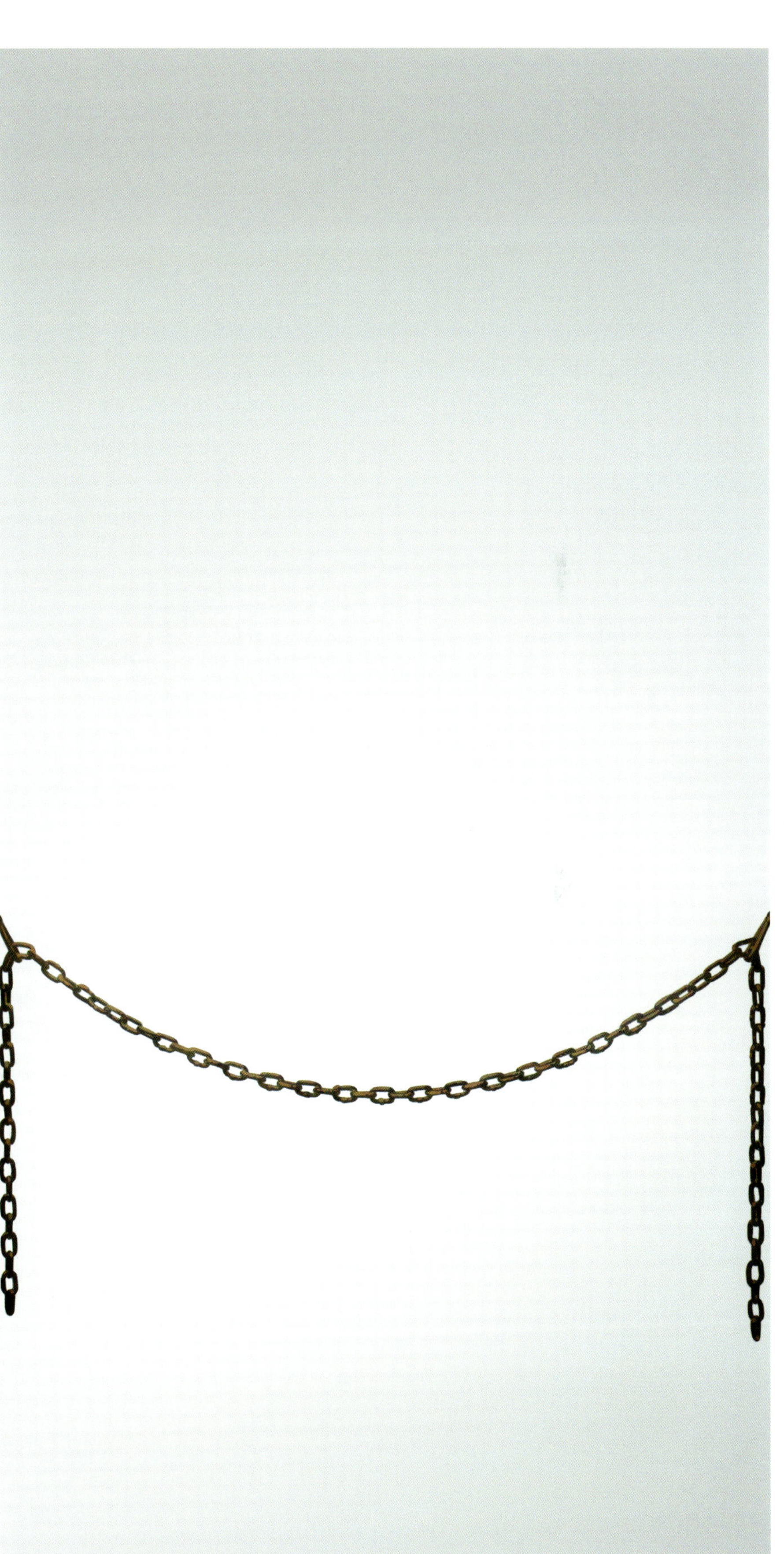

57
Graziella, 1971
Painted tissue paper on polished stainless steel
59 1/16 x 47 1/4 inches (150 x 120 cm)
Private collection

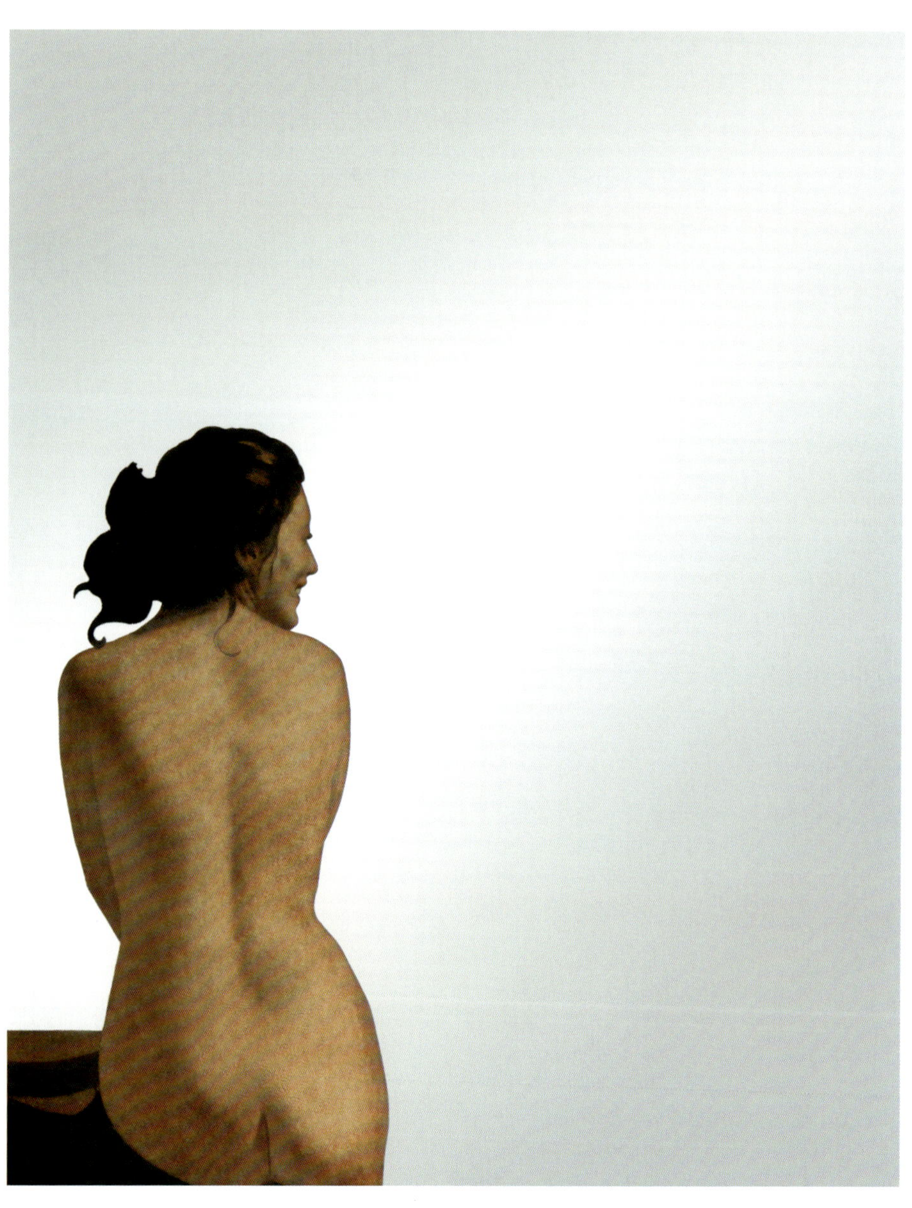

58
***Senza titolo* (*Untitled*), 1972**
Painted tissue paper on polished stainless steel
90 9/16 x 47 1/4 inches (230 x 120 cm)
Collection of Marco and Franca Brignone

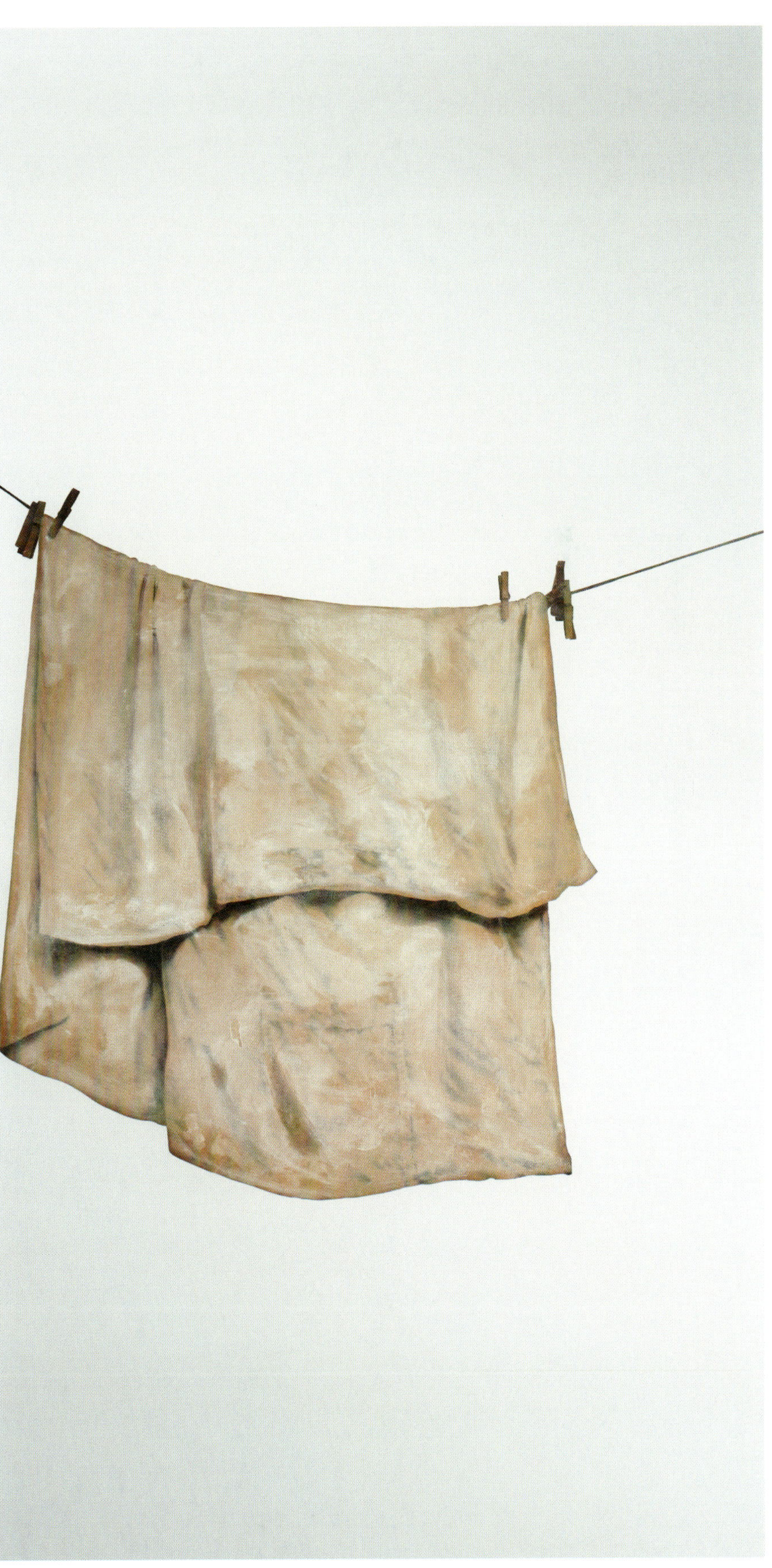

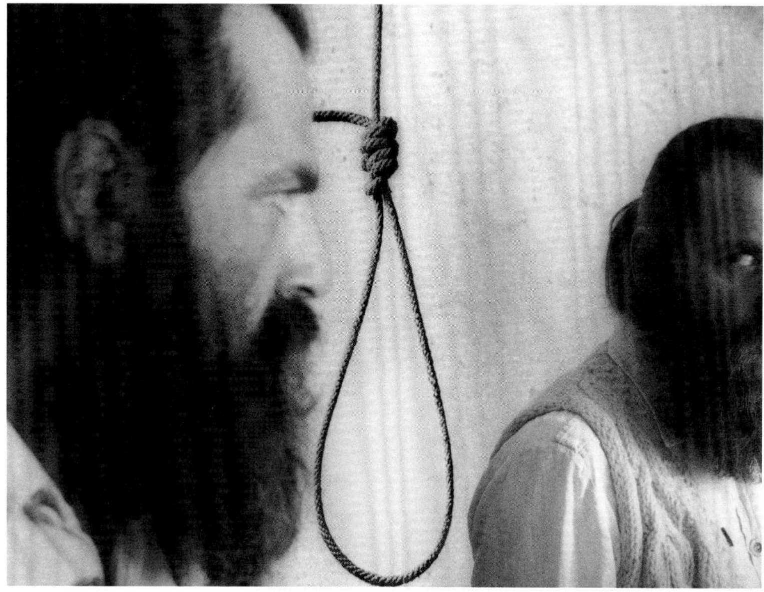

FIG. 204. Pistoletto reflected in *Cappio* at his house in San Sicario, 1973. Photograph by Paolo Mussat Sartor. Courtesy of Paolo Mussat Sartor

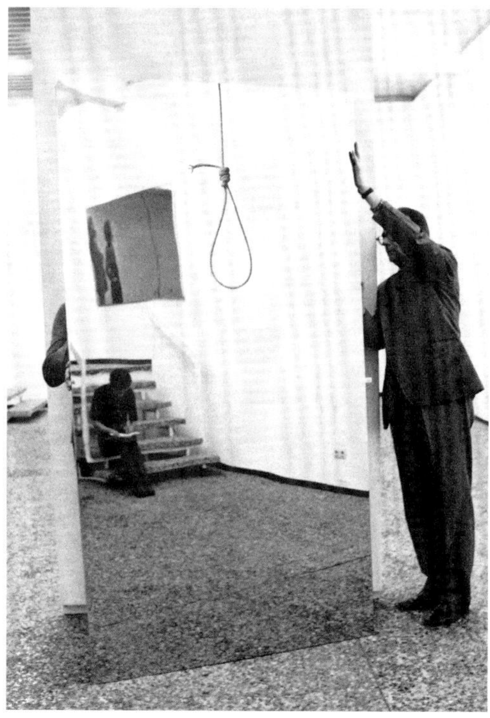

FIG. 205. *Cappio* being installed in the exhibition *Michelangelo Pistoletto* at the Kestner Gesellschaft, Hanover, Germany, 1973. Courtesy of Cittadellarte-Fondazione Pistoletto, Biella

59
***Cappio (Noose)*, 1973**
Silkscreen on polished stainless steel
$90^{9}/_{16}$ x $47^{1}/_{4}$ inches (230 x 120 cm)
Collection of the artist

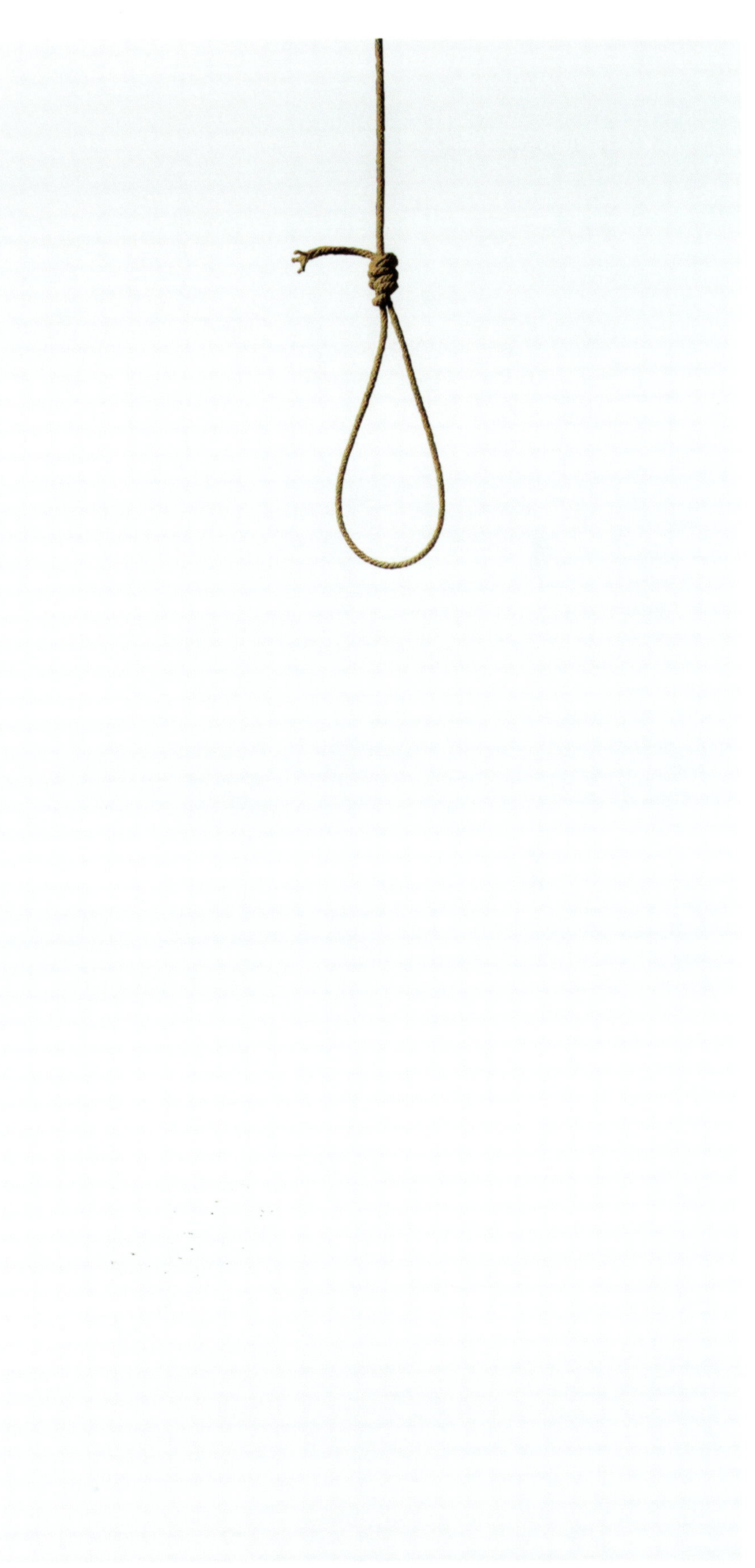

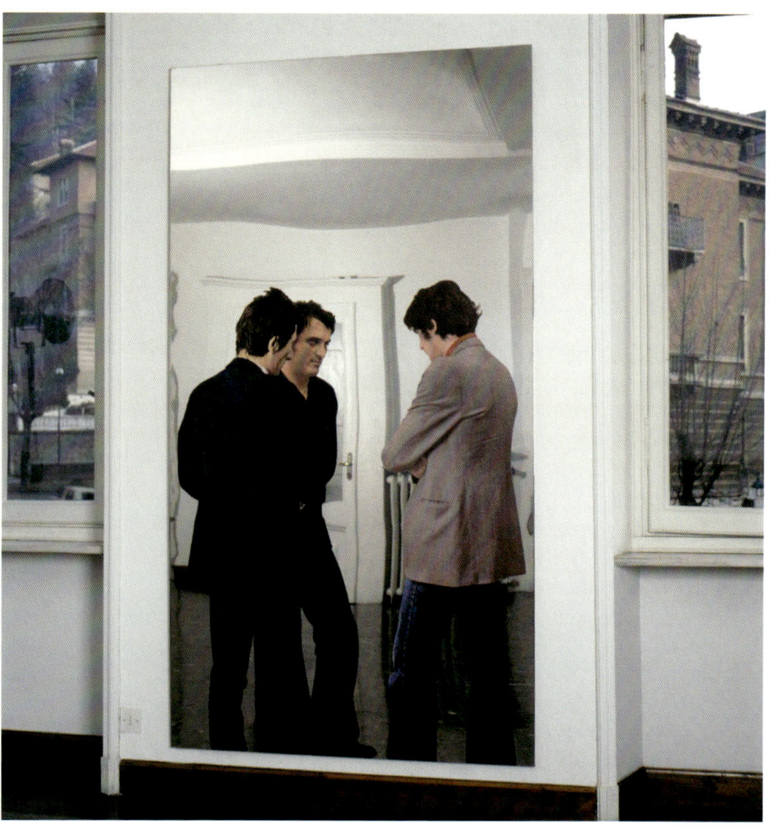

FIG. 206. *Sacra conversazione (Anselmo, Zorio, Penone)* in Pistoletto's house on via Cibrario in Turin. Courtesy of Cittadellarte-Fondazione Pistoletto, Biella

60
***Sacra conversazione* (*Anselmo, Zorio, Penone*), 1973**
Silkscreen on polished stainless steel
90 9/16 x 47 1/4 inches (230 x 120 cm)
Collection of the artist

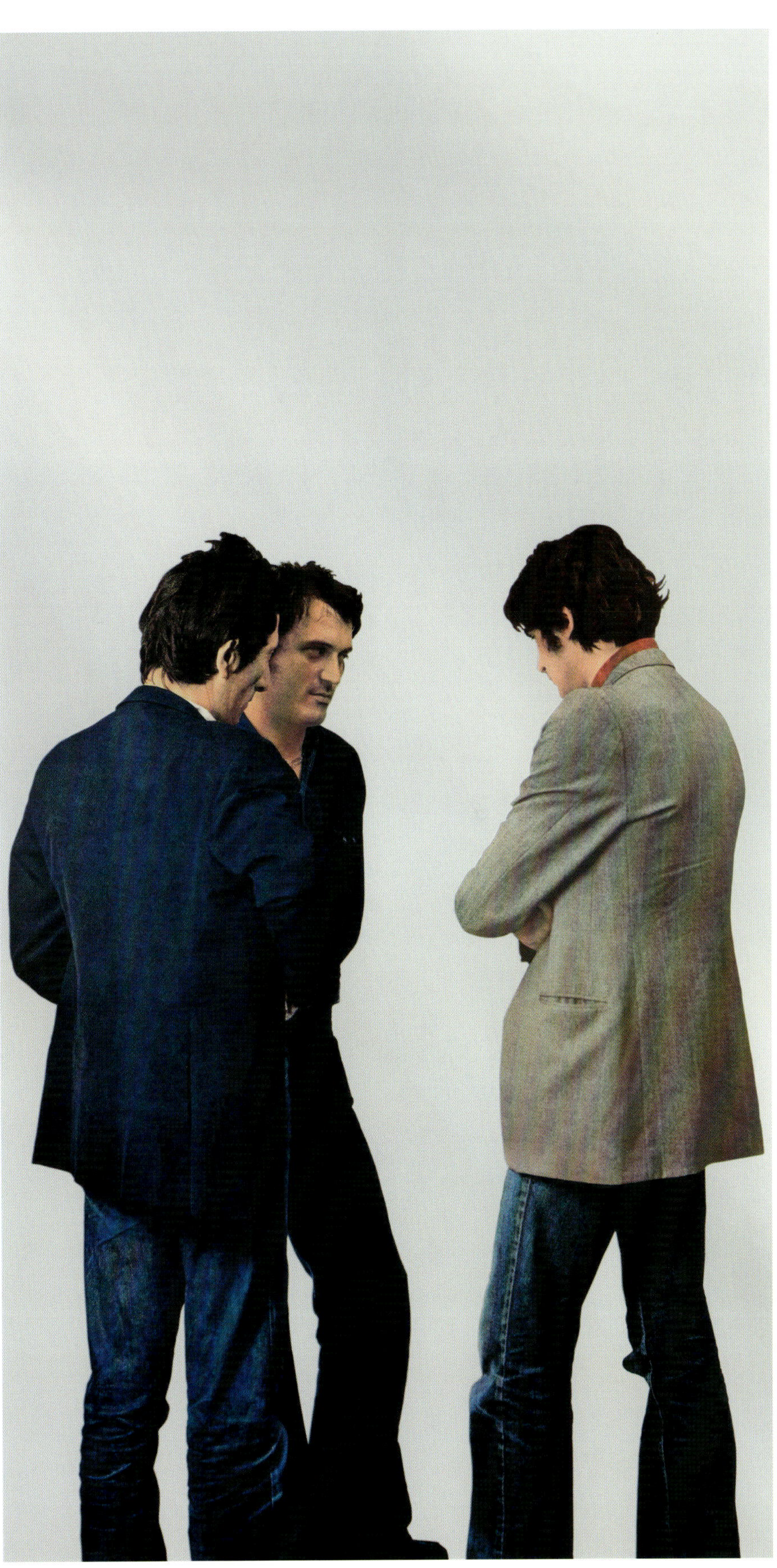

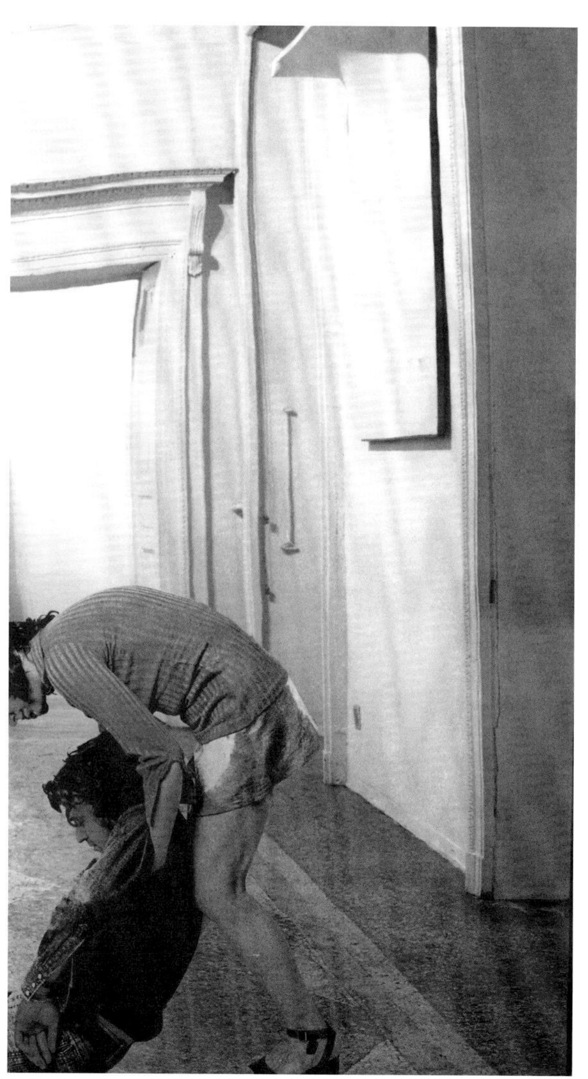

FIG. 207. *Deposizione in bianco e nero* (*Deposition in Black and White*), 1979, in the Persano Gallery, Turin. Photograph by Paolo Pellion di Persano. Courtesy of Cittadellarte-Fondazione Pistoletto, Biella

61
***Deposizione* (*Deposition*), 1973**
Silkscreen on polished stainless steel
90 9/16 x 47 1/4 inches (230 x 120 cm)
Collection of the artist

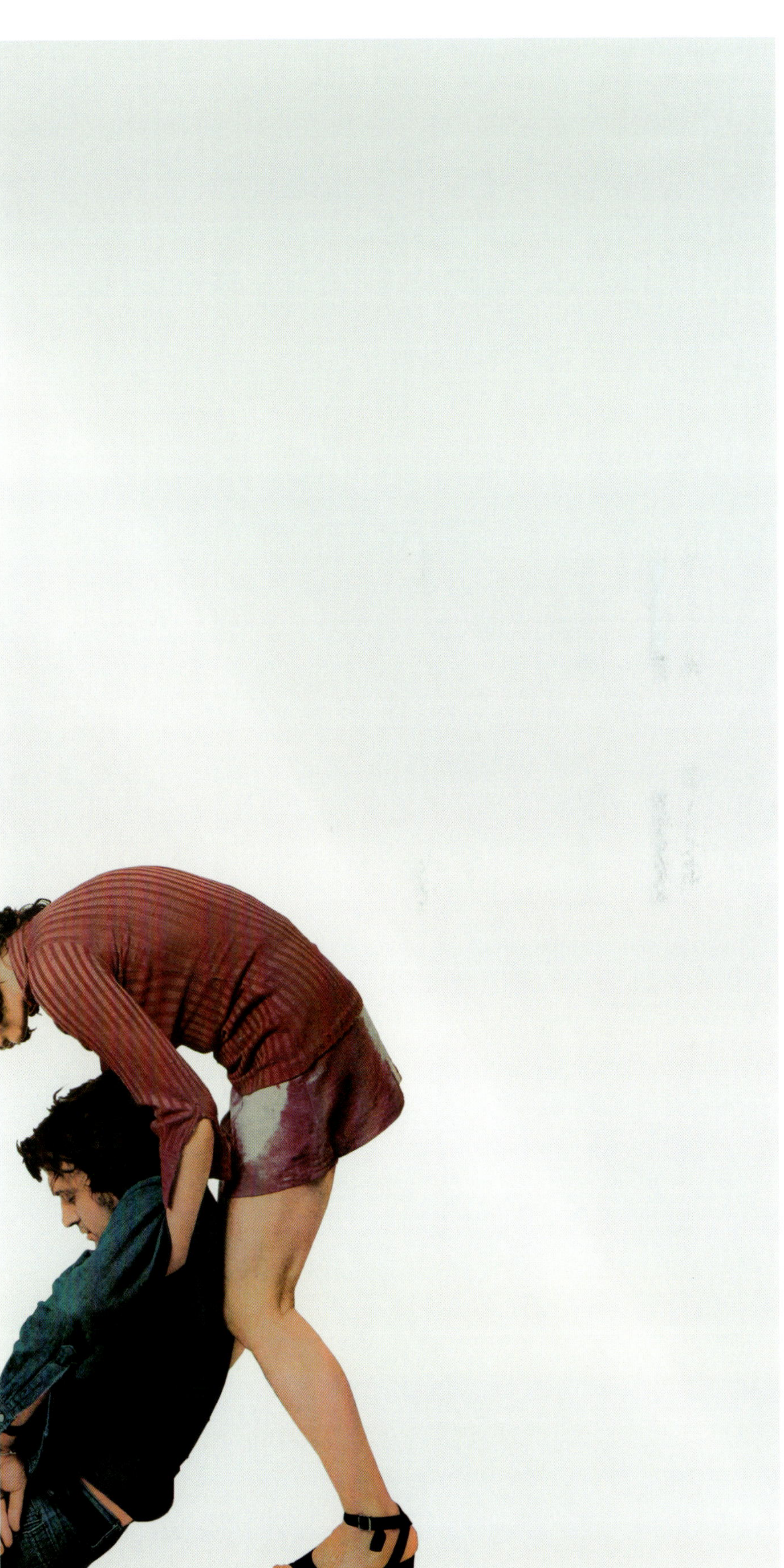

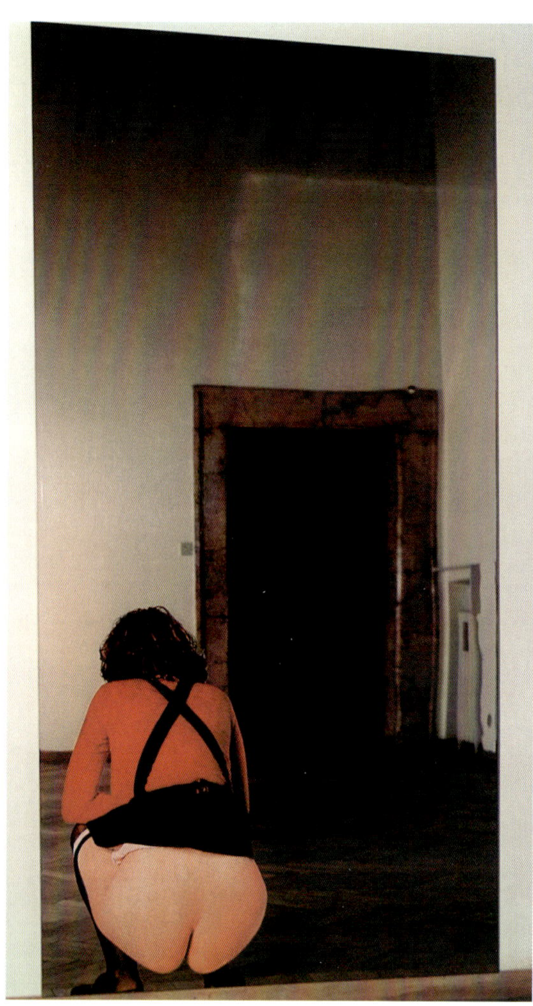

FIG. 208. *Donna che fa la cacca* at Galleria Sperone, Rome, 1974. Courtesy of Cittadellarte-Fondazione Pistoletto, Biella

62
Donna che fa la cacca
(*Woman Defecating*), 1973
Silkscreen on polished stainless steel
90 9/16 x 47 1/4 inches (230 x 120 cm)
Collection of Constance R. Caplan

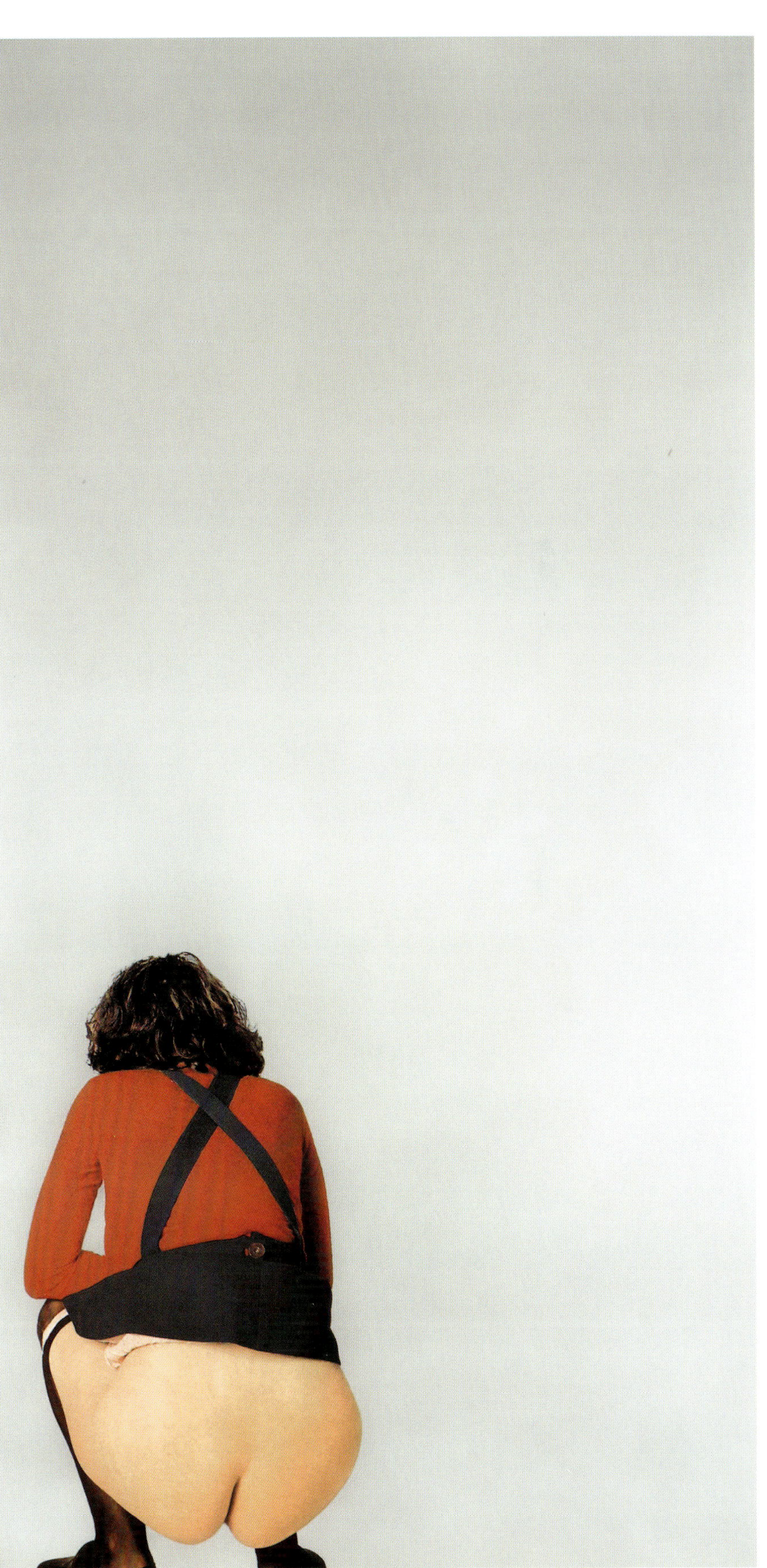

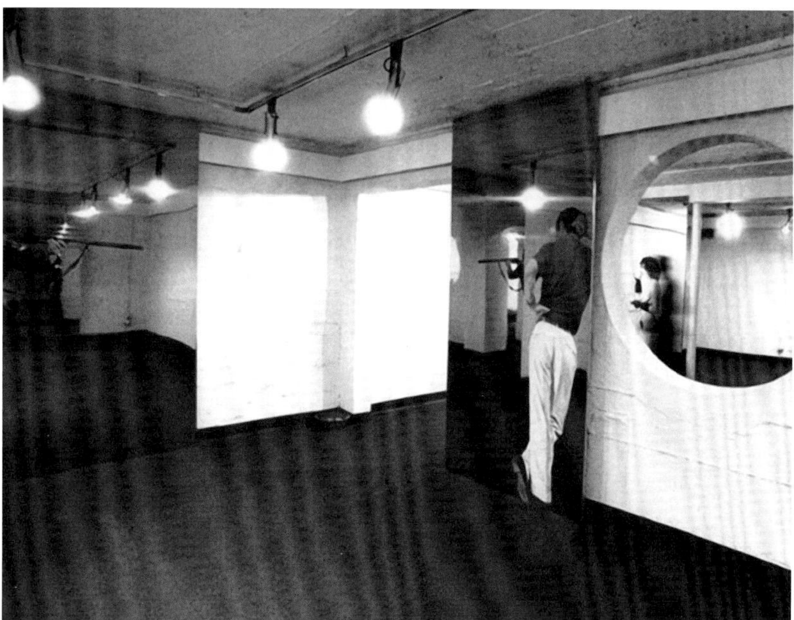

FIG. 209. *Uomo che spara* in Pistoletto's solo exhibition at Galleria Il Centro, Naples, 1975. *Uomo che spara*, on the left, is also reflected in the mirror painting *Uomo appoggiato* (*Man Leaning*, 1966) at center right.

63
Uomo che spara (Man Shooting), 1973
Silkscreen on polished stainless steel
90 9/16 x 47 1/4 inches (230 x 120 cm)
Private collection. Courtesy of Rory Howard

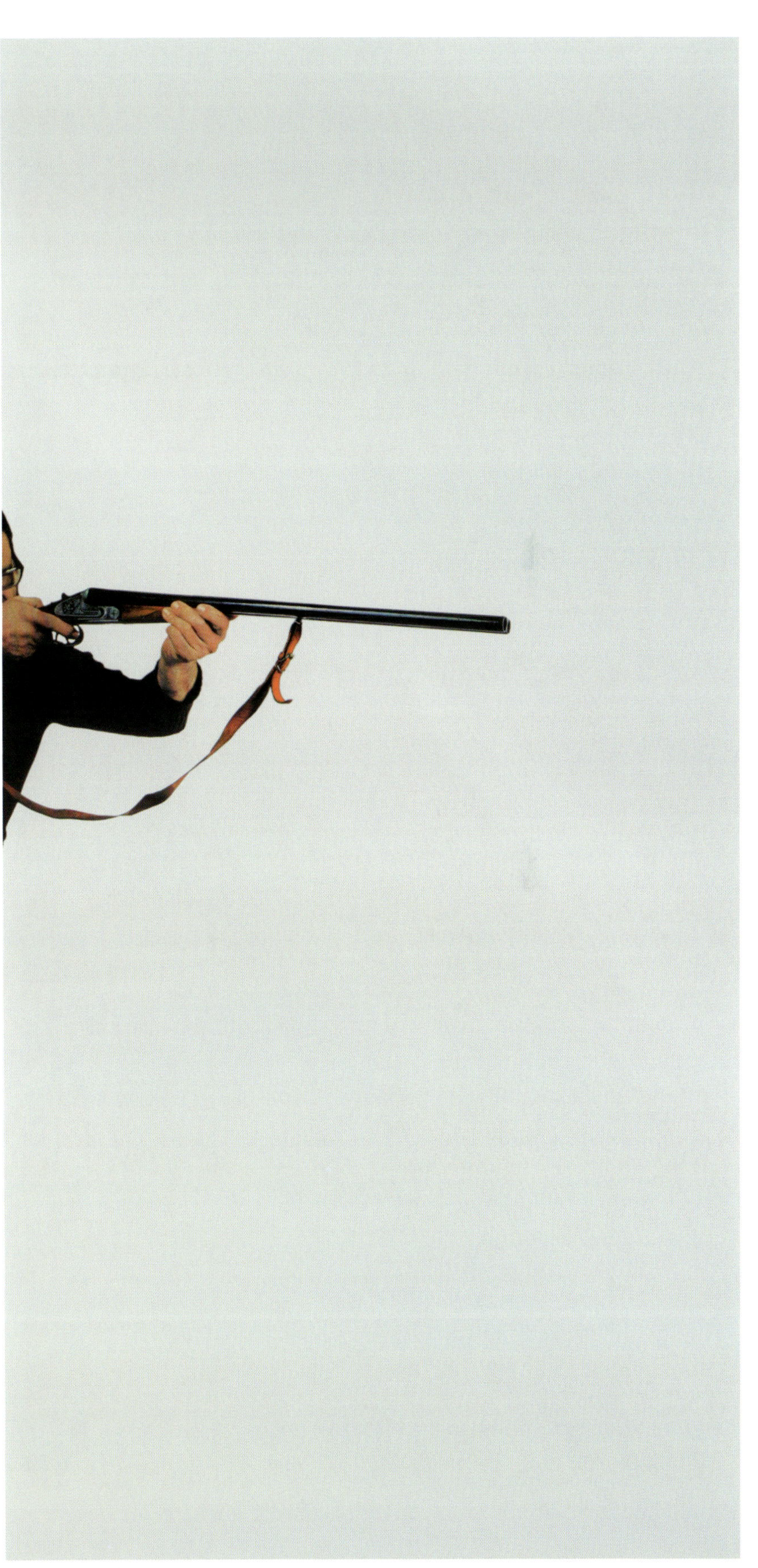

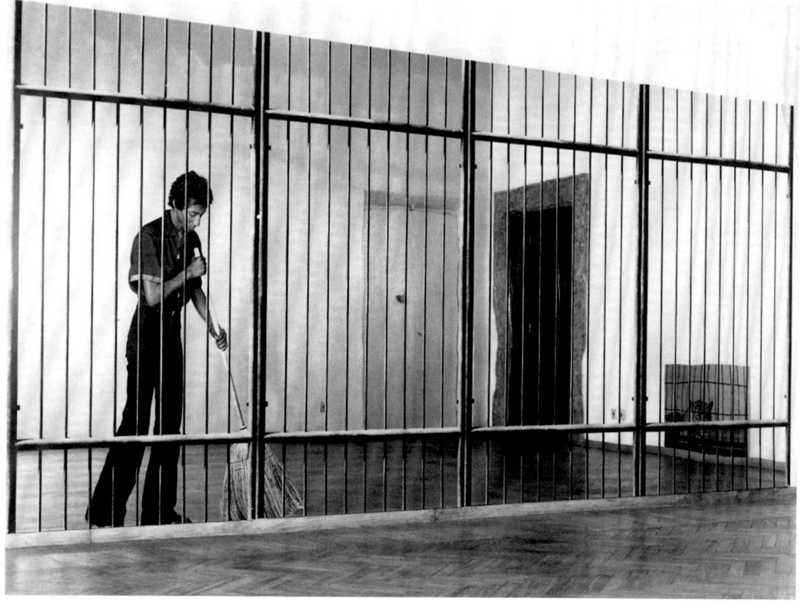

FIG. 210. *Cage* at Galleria Sperone, Rome, 1975. Photograph by Paolo Mussat Sartor. Marco Maò, who was then Mussat Sartor's assistant, is the subject of the painting. Courtesy of Cittadellarte-Fondazione Pistoletto, Biella

64
***Cage*, 1973**
Silkscreen on polished stainless steel
90 9/16 x 228 3/8 inches (230 x 580 cm)
Collection of the artist

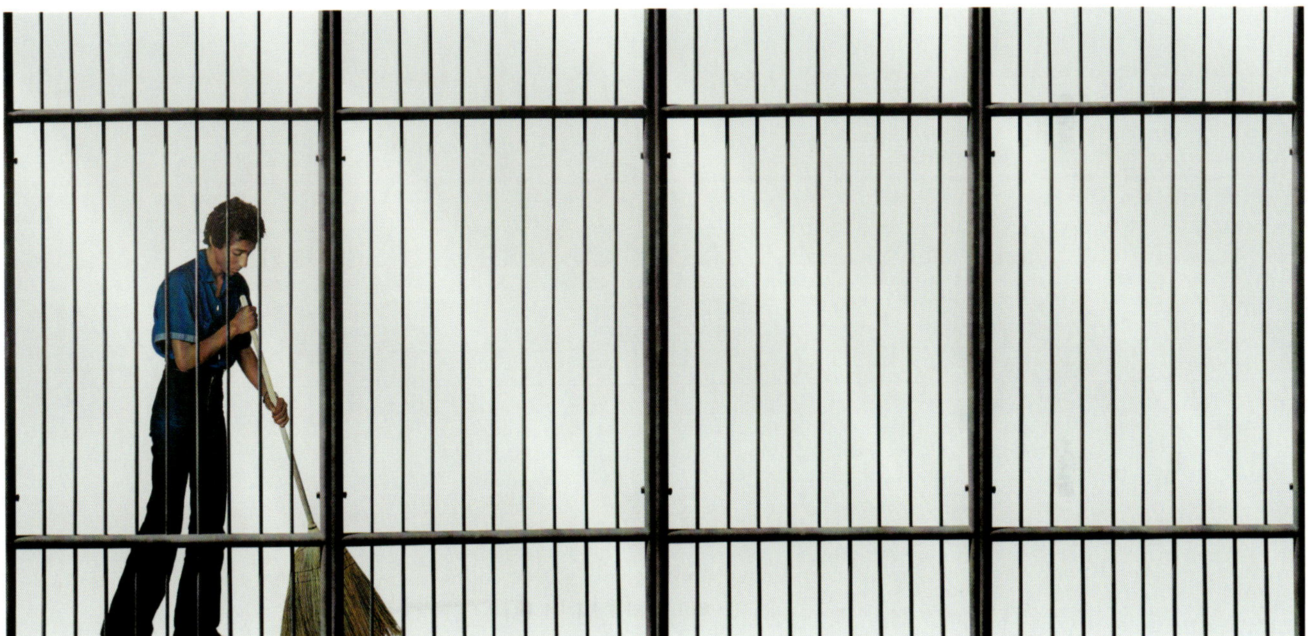

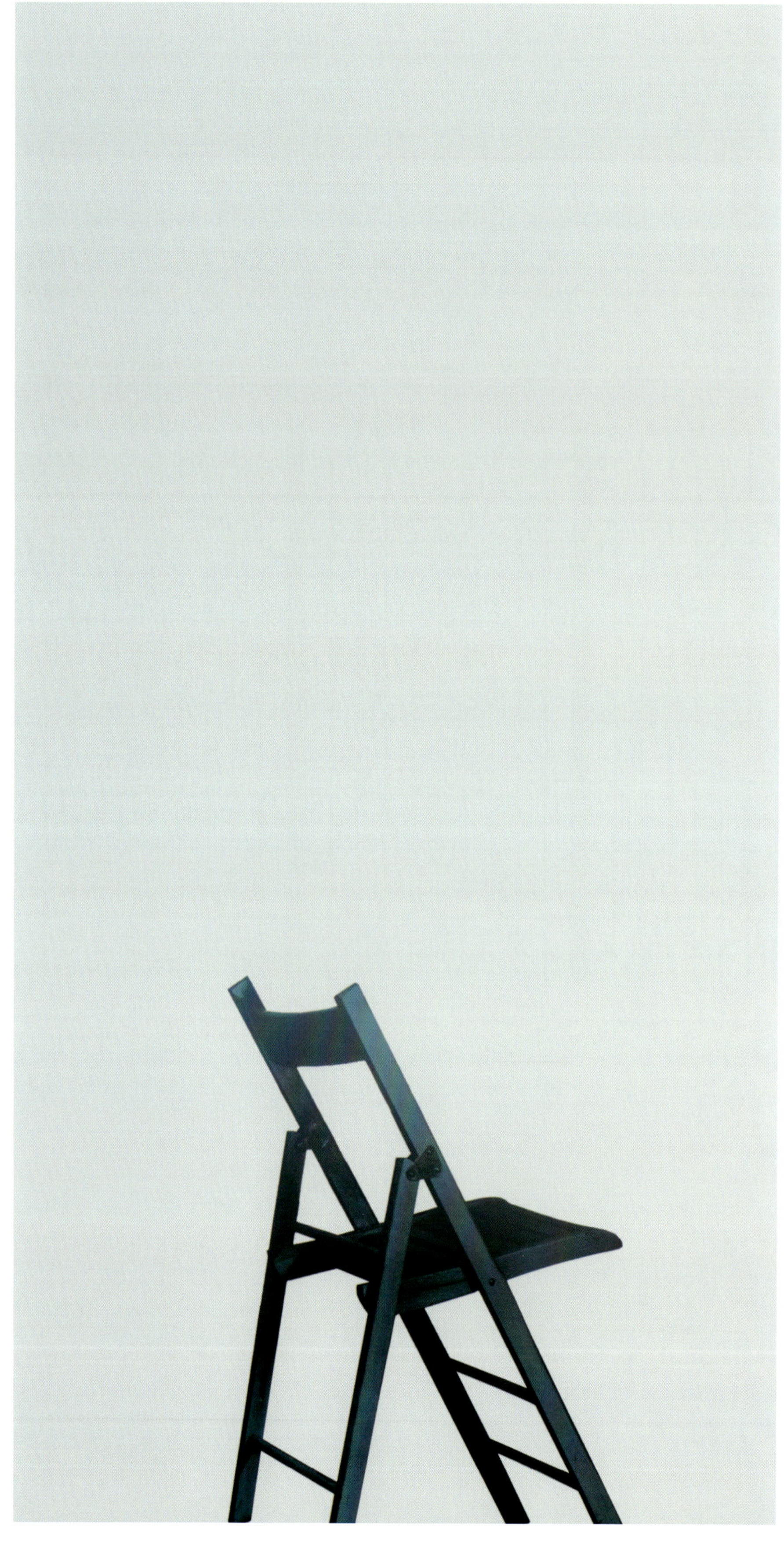

65
***Sedia* (*Chair*), 1974**
Silkscreen on polished stainless steel
$90\frac{9}{16}$ x $49\frac{3}{16}$ inches (230 x 125 cm)
Collection of the artist

66
***Pericolo di morte* (*Danger of Death*), 1974**
Silkscreen on polished stainless steel
$49\frac{3}{16}$ x $90\frac{9}{16}$ inches (125 x 230 cm)
Private collection

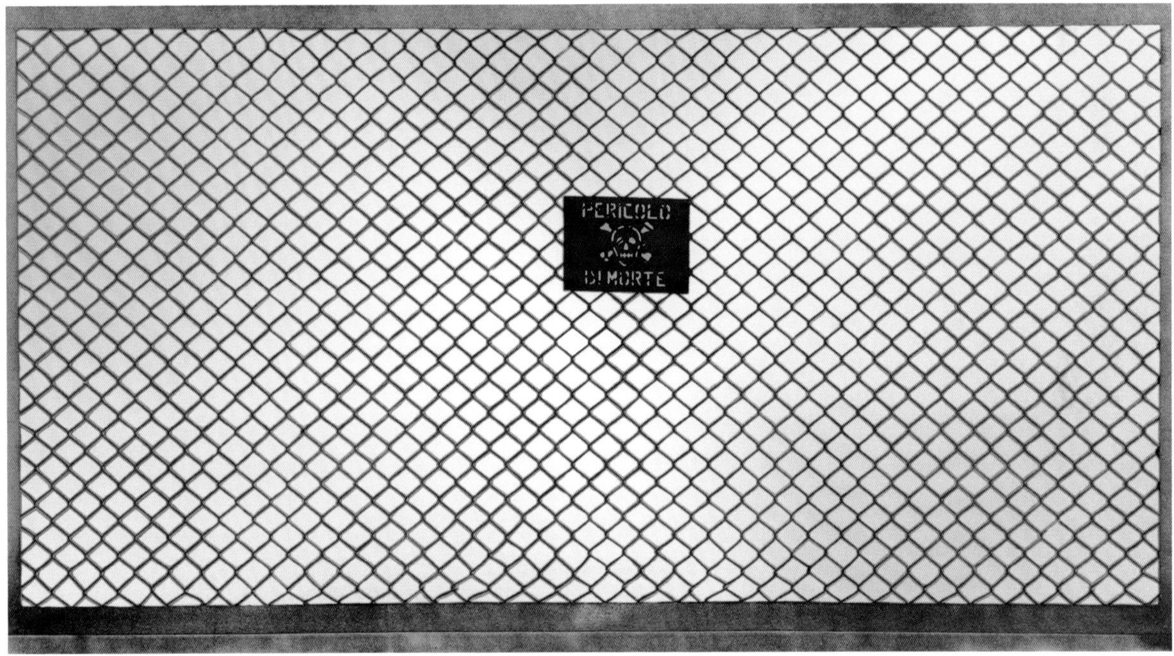

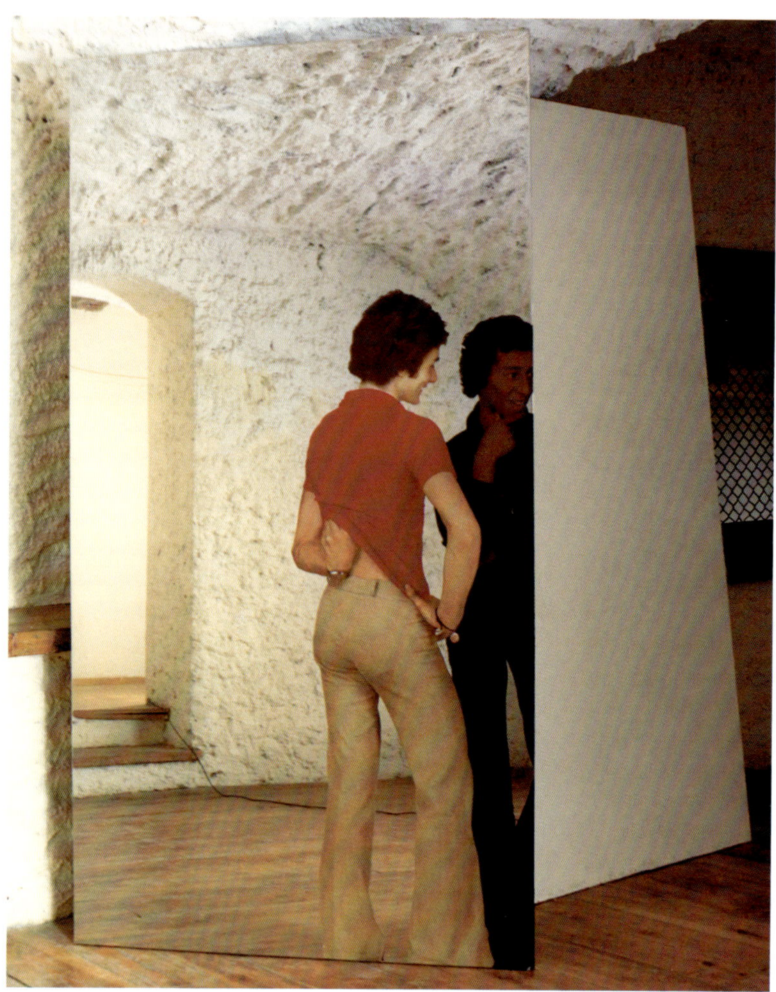

FIG. 211. *Ragazzo che si gratta la schiena* in Pistoletto's house in San Sicario, 1974. The right-hand figure in the painting is Marco Maò. Courtesy of Cittadellarte-Fondazione Pistoletto, Biella

67
***Ragazzo che si gratta la schiena* (*Boy Scratching His Back*), 1974**
Silkscreen on polished stainless steel
90 9/16 x 49 3/16 inches (230 x 125 cm)
Collection of the artist

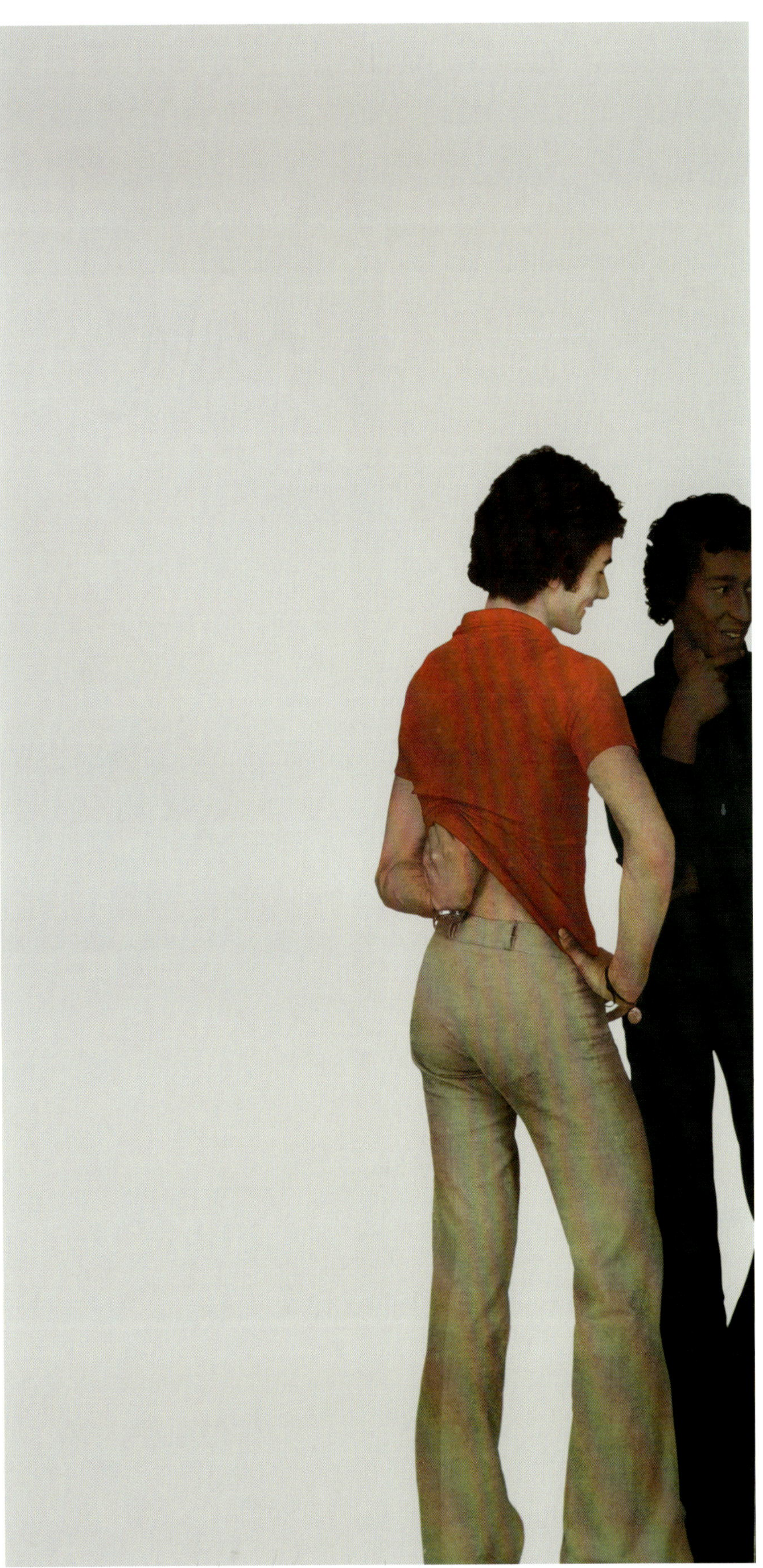

68
Il muro (*The Wall*), 1964
Transparent Plexiglas
70 ⅞ x 47¼ inches (180 x 120 cm)
Cittadellarte-Fondazione Pistoletto, Biella

69
Filo elettrico appeso al muro
(*Electric Cord Hanging on the Wall*), 1964
Photograph on transparent Plexiglas
70 ⅞ x 47¼ inches (180 x 120 cm)
Cittadellarte-Fondazione Pistoletto, Biella

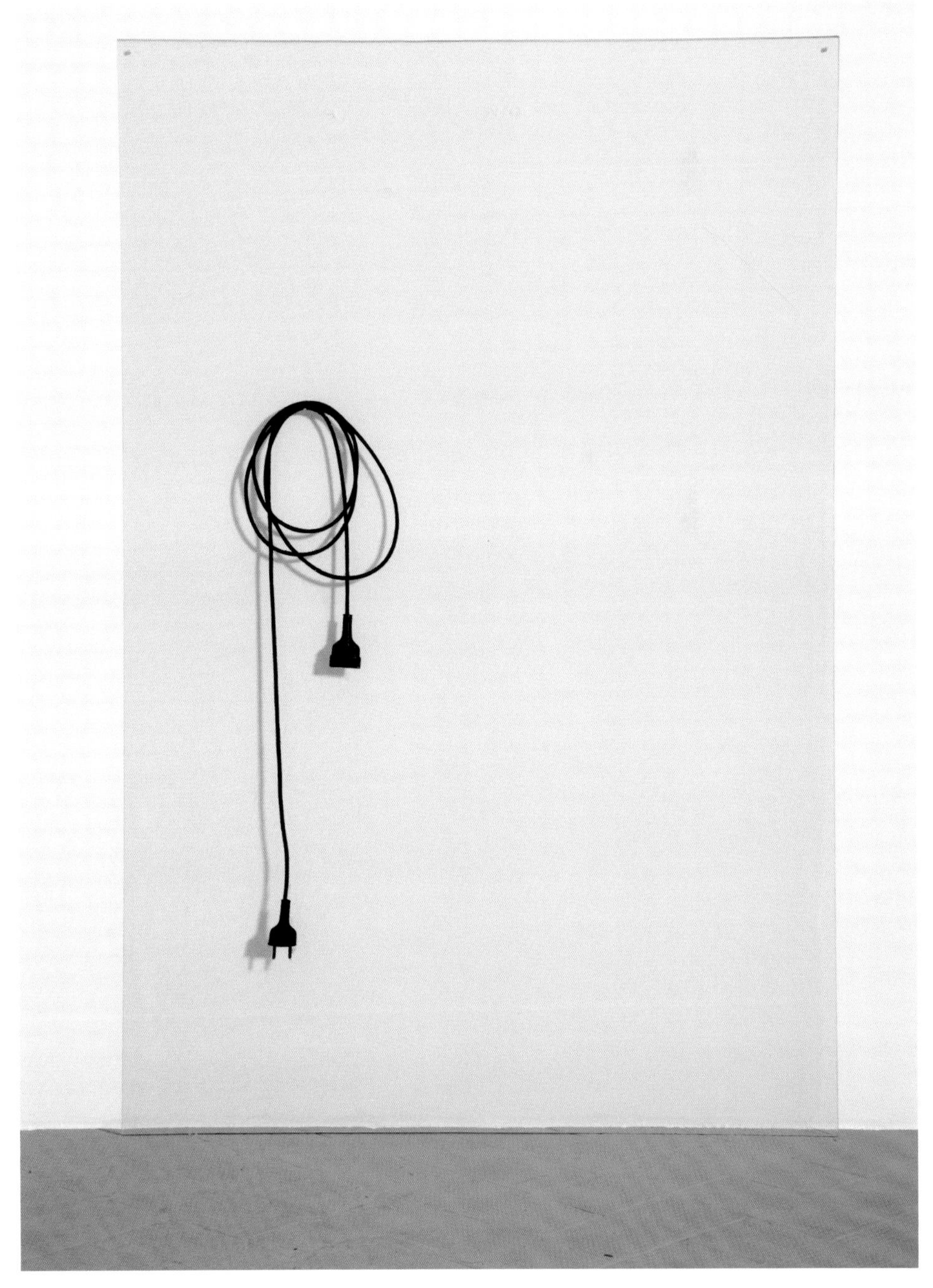

70
Filo elettrico caduto
***(Fallen Electric Cord*), 1964**
Photograph on transparent Plexiglas
70 7/8 x 47 1/4 x 15 3/4 inches (180 x 120 x 40 cm)
Cittadellarte-Fondazione Pistoletto, Biella

71
Scala doppia appoggiata al muro
(Double Ladder Leaning against
***the Wall*), 1964**
Photograph on two sheets of
transparent Plexiglas
70 7/8 x 47 1/4 inches (180 x 120 cm)
59 1/16 x 47 1/4 inches (150 x 120 cm)
Cittadellarte-Fondazione Pistoletto, Biella

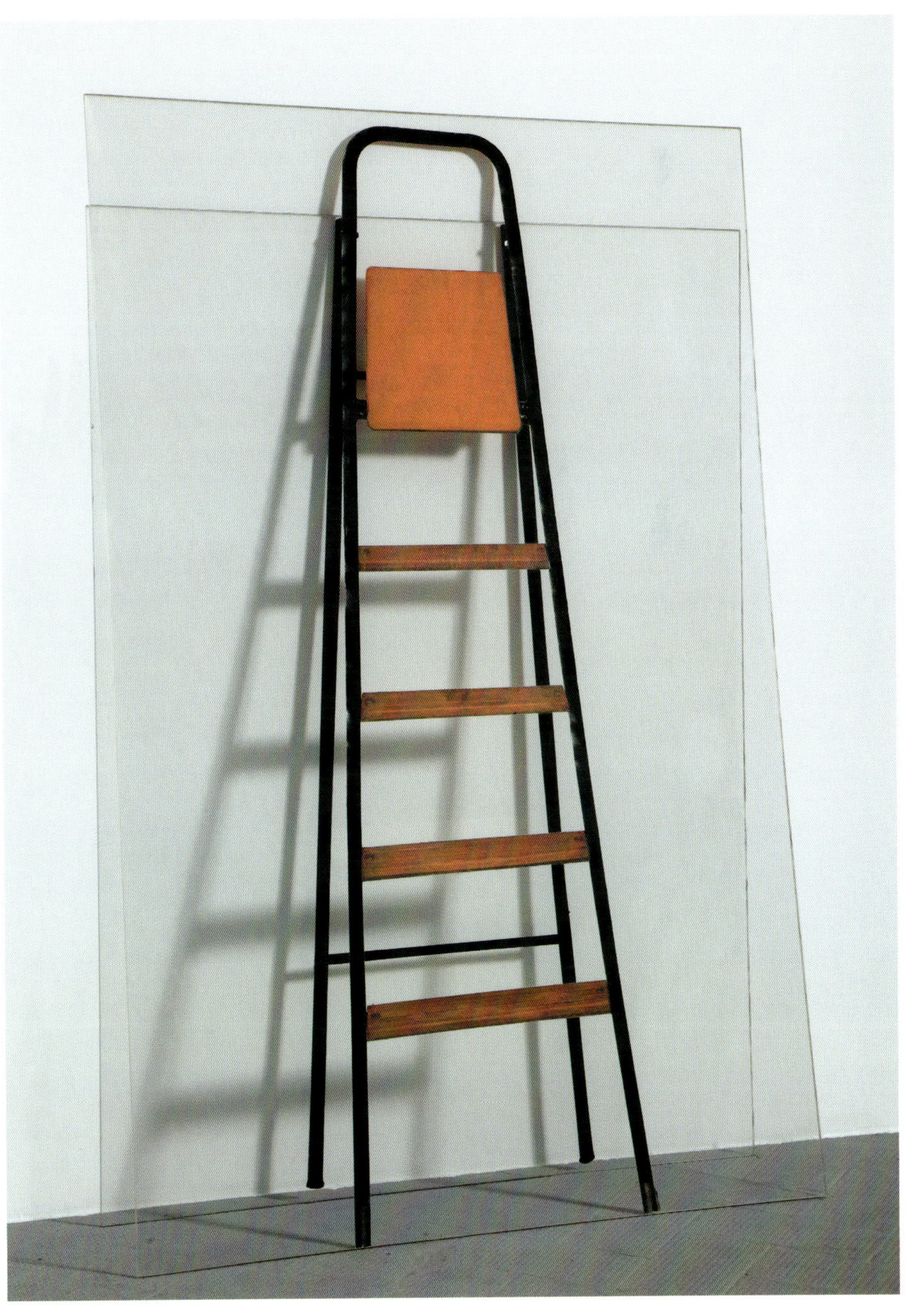

72
Segnale rosso su plexiglass
(*Red Signal on Plexiglas*), 1964
Red Plexiglas disc on transparent Plexiglas
70⅞ x 47¼ inches (180 x 120 cm)
Cittadellarte-Fondazione Pistoletto, Biella

73
***Tavolino con disco e giornale* (*Small Table with Record and Newspaper*), 1964**
Photographs and paint on transparent Plexiglas
13¾ x 23⅝ x 23⅝ inches (35 x 60 x 60 cm)
Cittadellarte-Fondazione Pistoletto, Biella

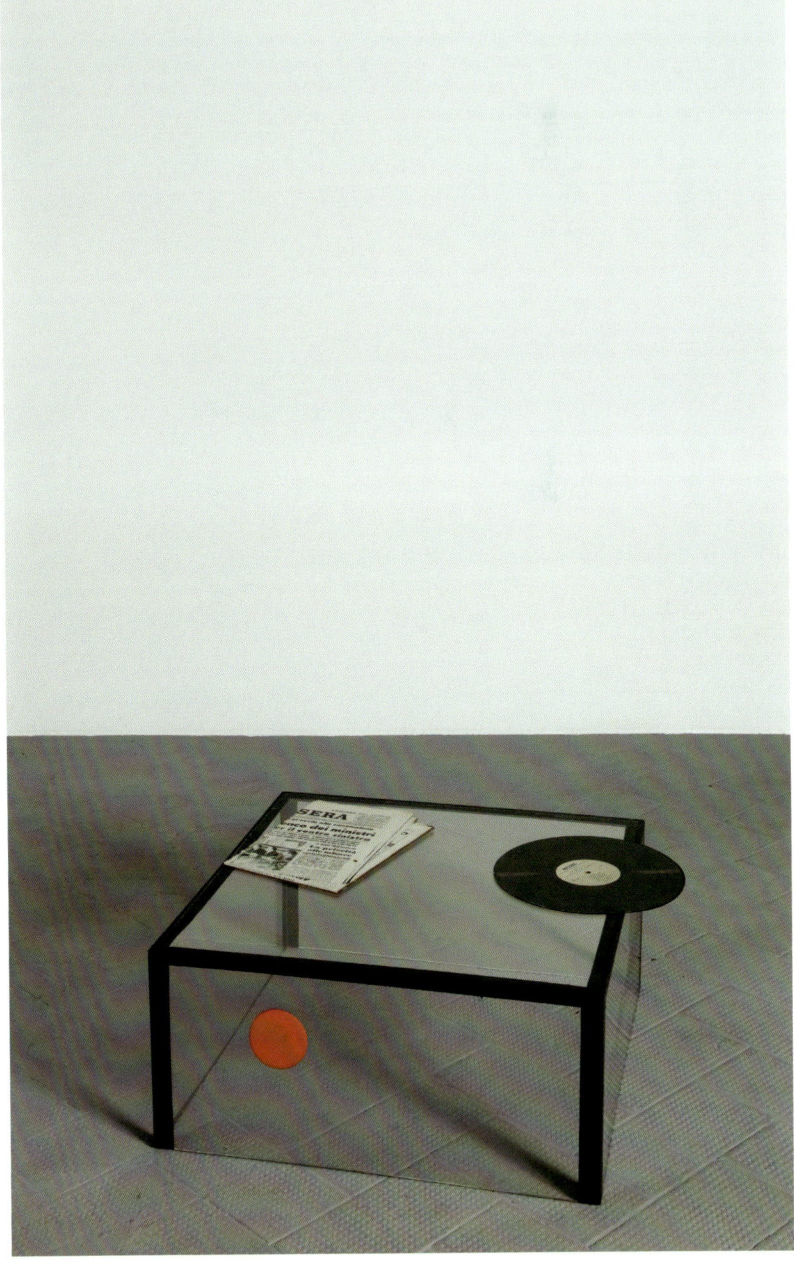

74
***Pila di dischi* (*Pile of Records*), 1964**
Photograph on transparent Plexiglas,
eleven elements
Each 15¾ x 15¾ inches (40 x 40 cm)
Cittadellarte-Fondazione Pistoletto, Biella

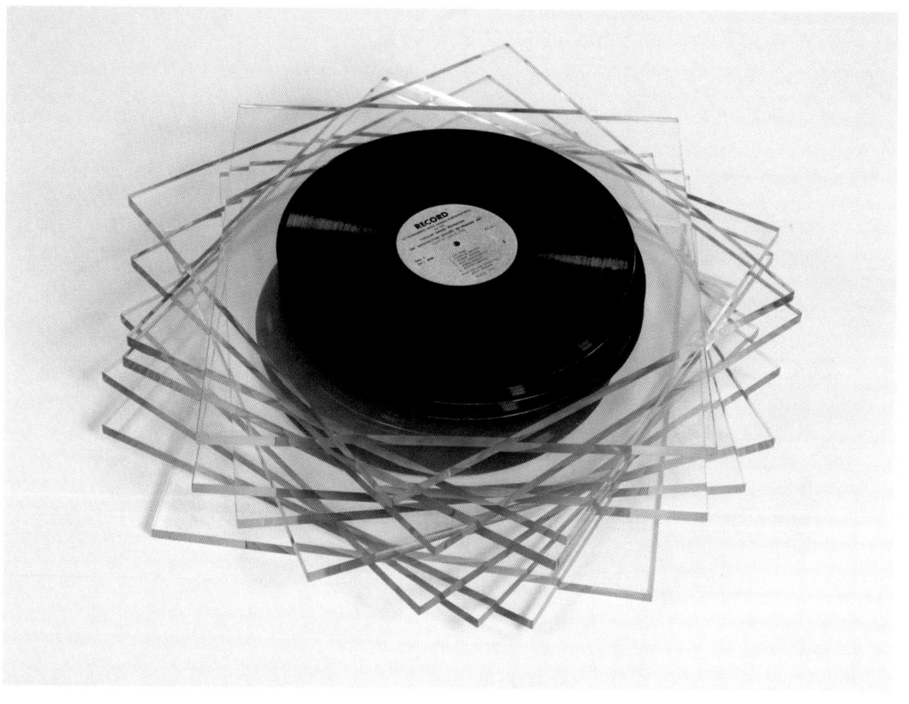

75
Quadro da pranzo
(*Lunch Painting*), 1965
Wood
78¾ x 81¼ x 17⅜ inches
(200 x 207.6 x 44.1 cm)
Walker Art Center, Minneapolis. T. B. Walker
Acquisition Fund, 2002

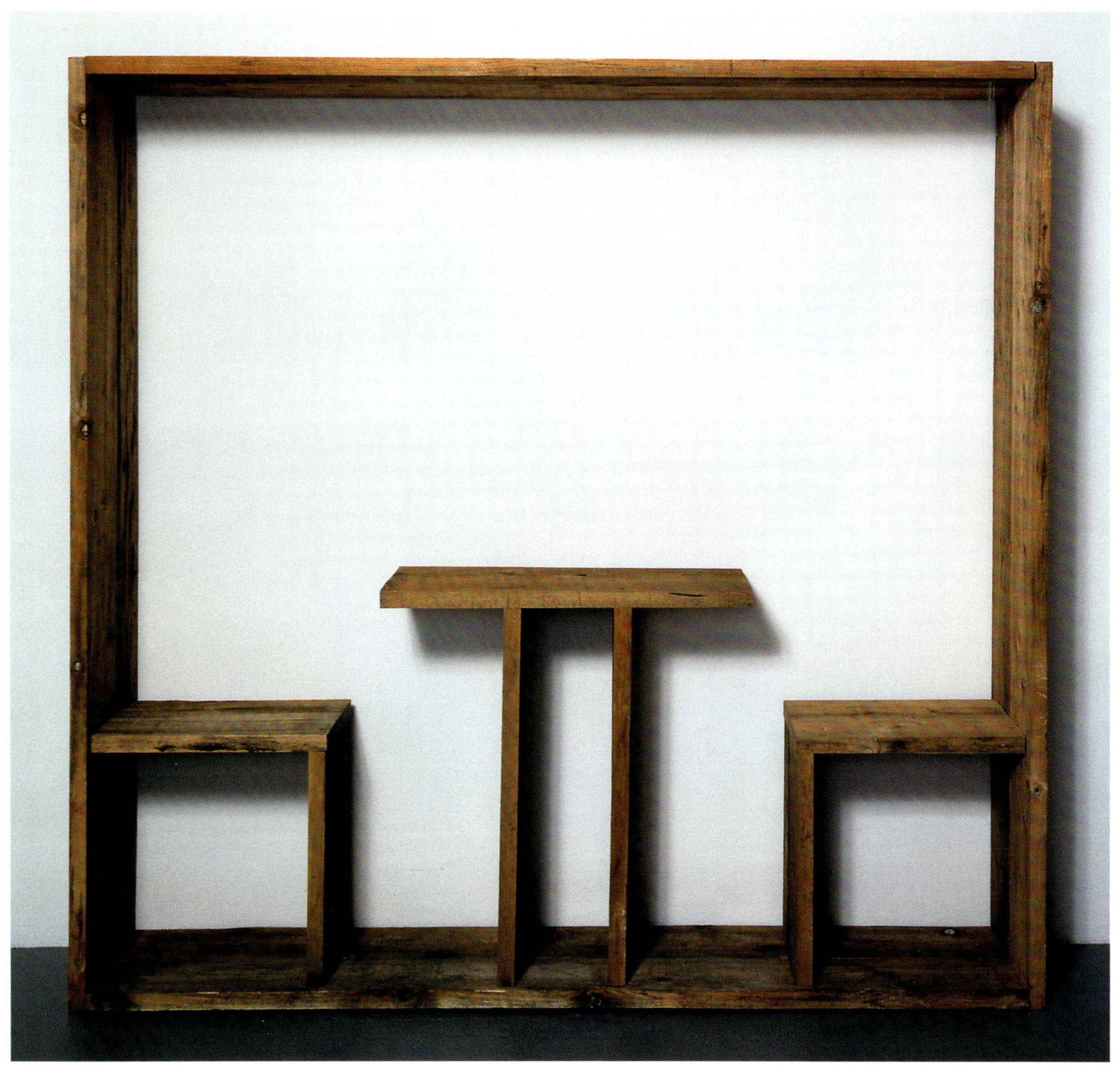

76
***Rosa bruciata* (*Burnt Rose*), 1965**
Corrugated cardboard and spray paint
55 1/8 x 55 1/8 x 39 3/8 inches
(140 x 140 x 100 cm)
Cittadellarte-Fondazione Pistoletto, Biella

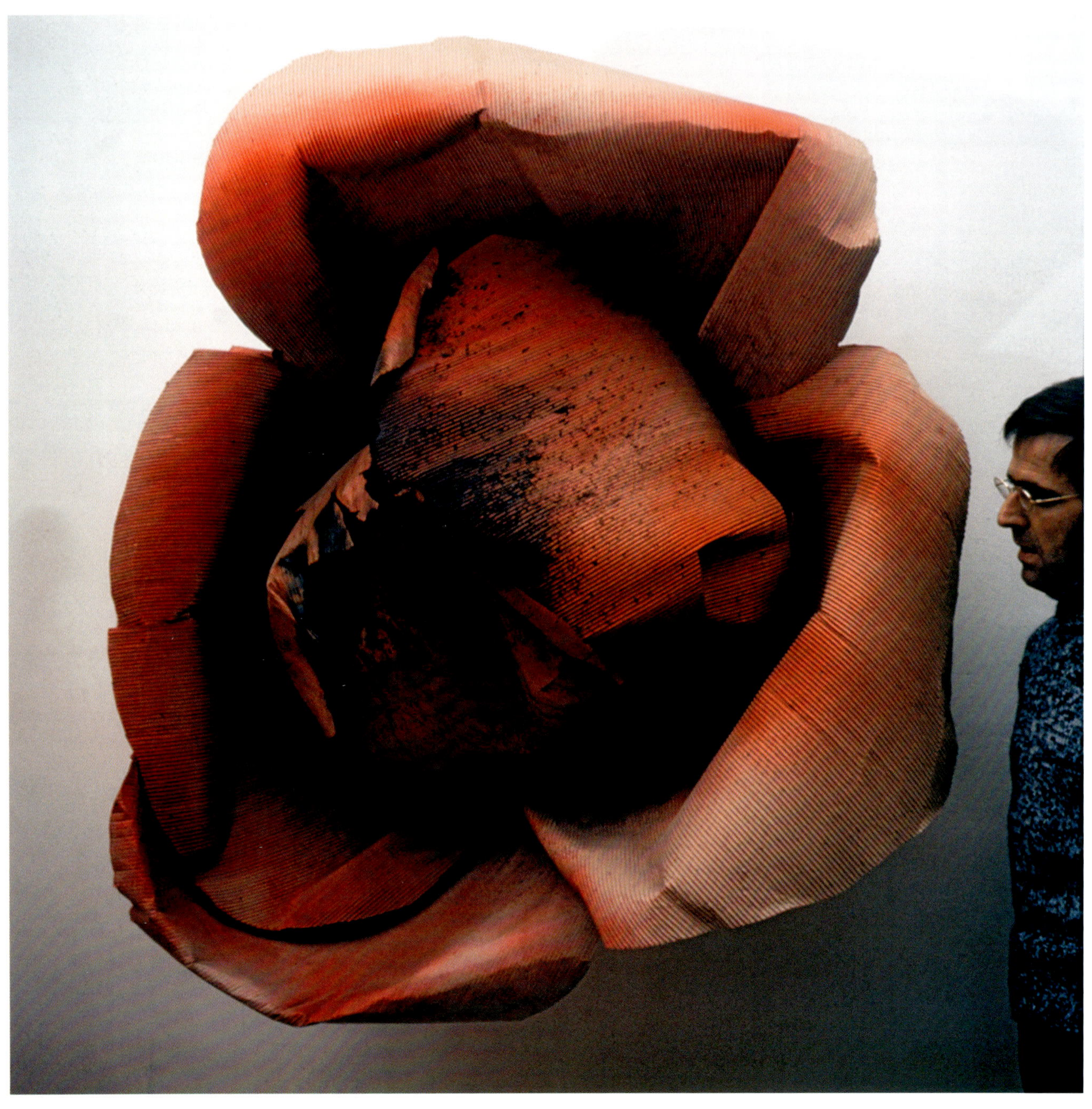

77
Paesaggio **(*Landscape*), 1965**
Cardboard, tissue paper, rags, and clay figures
27 9/16 x 15 3/4 x 7 7/8 inches (70 x 40 x 20 cm)
Cittadellarte-Fondazione Pistoletto, Biella

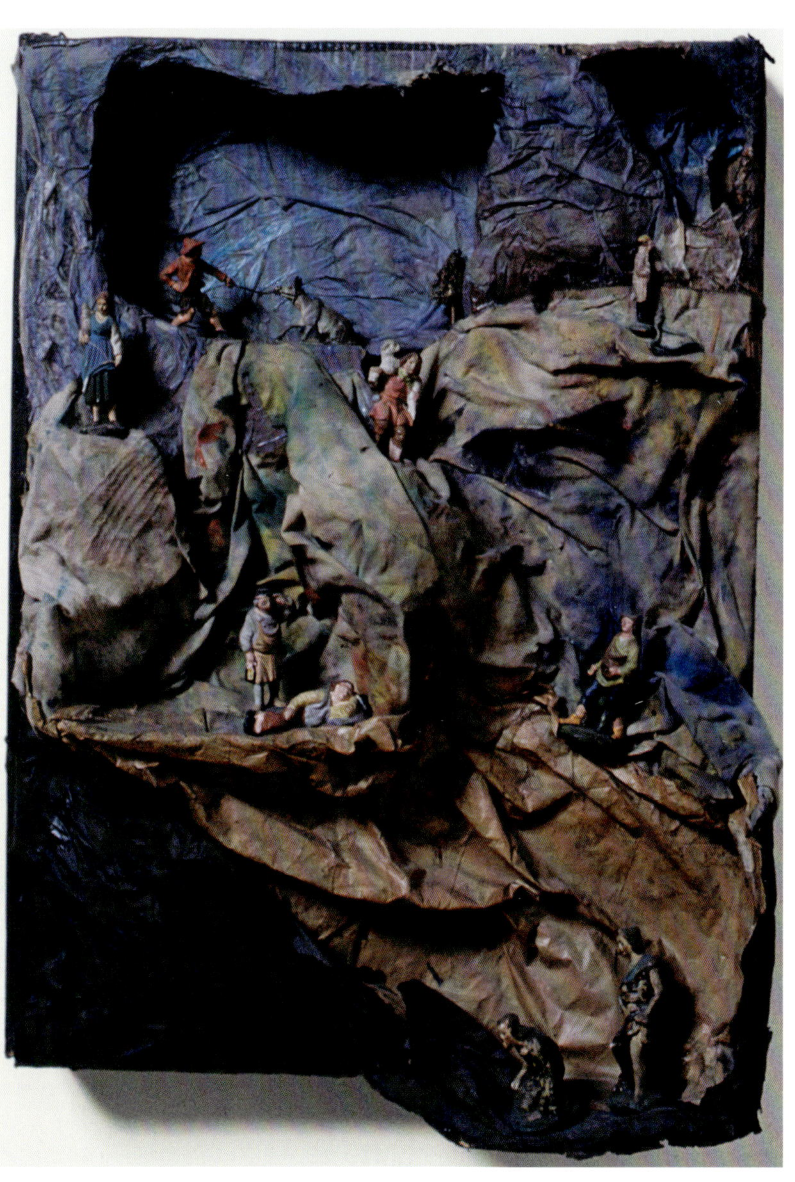

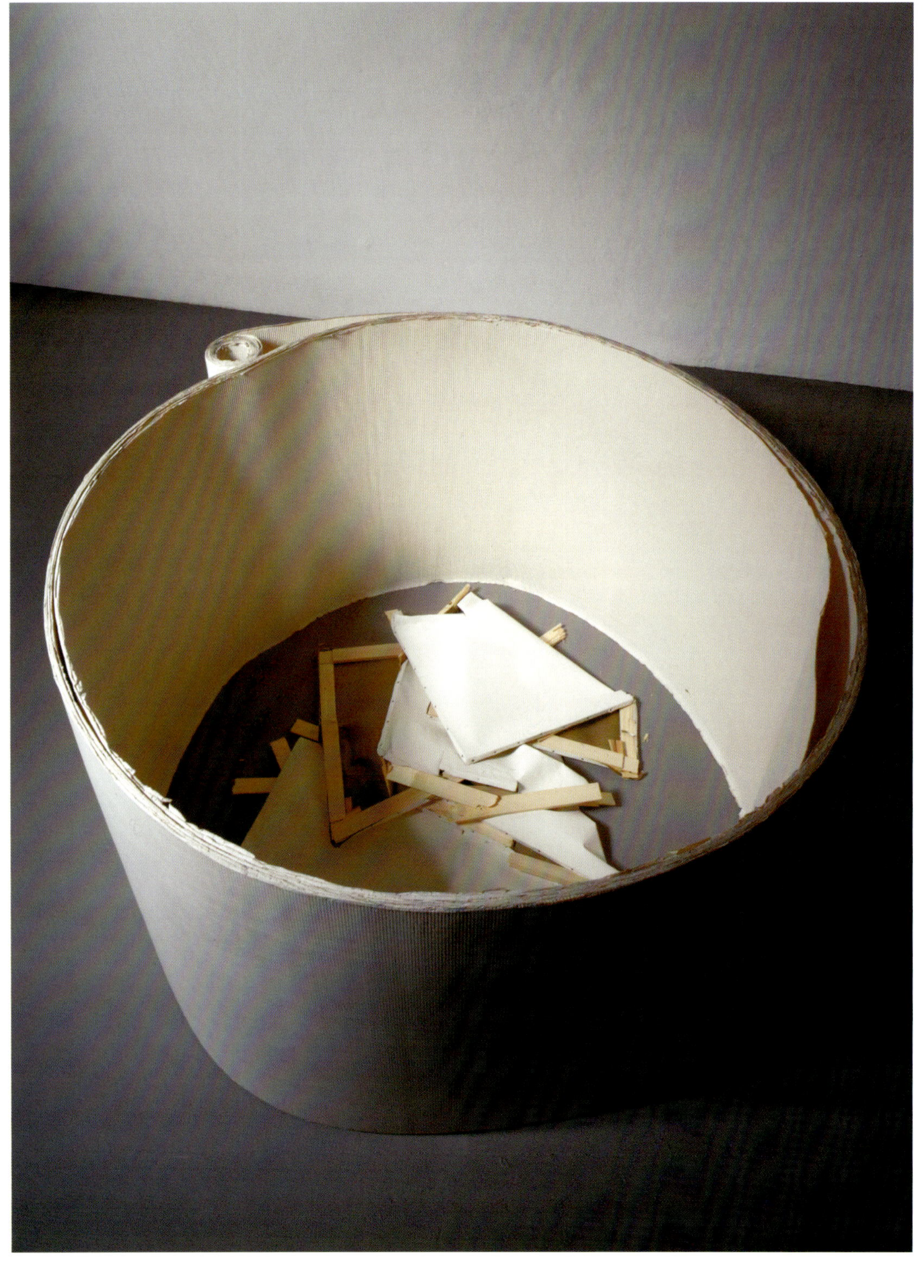

78
***Pozzo* (*Well*), 1965**
Corrugated cardboard, canvases,
and broken frames
H. 39⅜ (100 cm); diam. 55⅛ inches (140 cm)
Cittadellarte-Fondazione Pistoletto, Biella

79
***Lampada a mercurio* (*Mercury Lamp*), 1965**
Aluminum, iron, and lightbulbs
H. 31½ (80 cm); diam. 17 11/16 inches (45 cm)
Cittadellarte-Fondazione Pistoletto, Biella

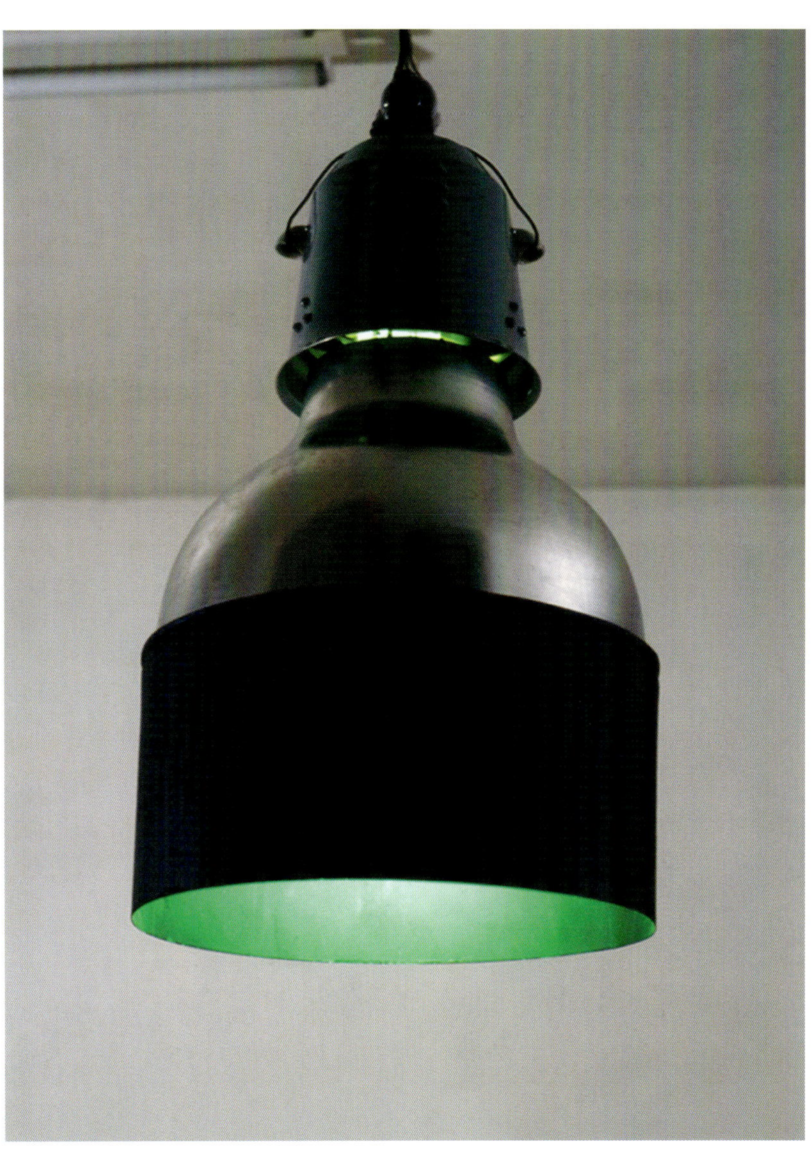

80
Piramide verde **(*Green Pyramid*), 1965**
Wood table and chairs
$51\frac{3}{16}$ x $59\frac{1}{16}$ x $59\frac{1}{16}$ inches
(130 x 150 x 150 cm)
Cittadellarte-Fondazione Pistoletto, Biella

81
***Colonne di cemento (Concrete Columns)*, 1965**
Concrete, four elements
Each $94\frac{1}{2}$ x $17\frac{11}{16}$ x $17\frac{11}{16}$ inches (240 x 45 x 45 cm)
Cittadellarte-Fondazione Pistoletto, Biella

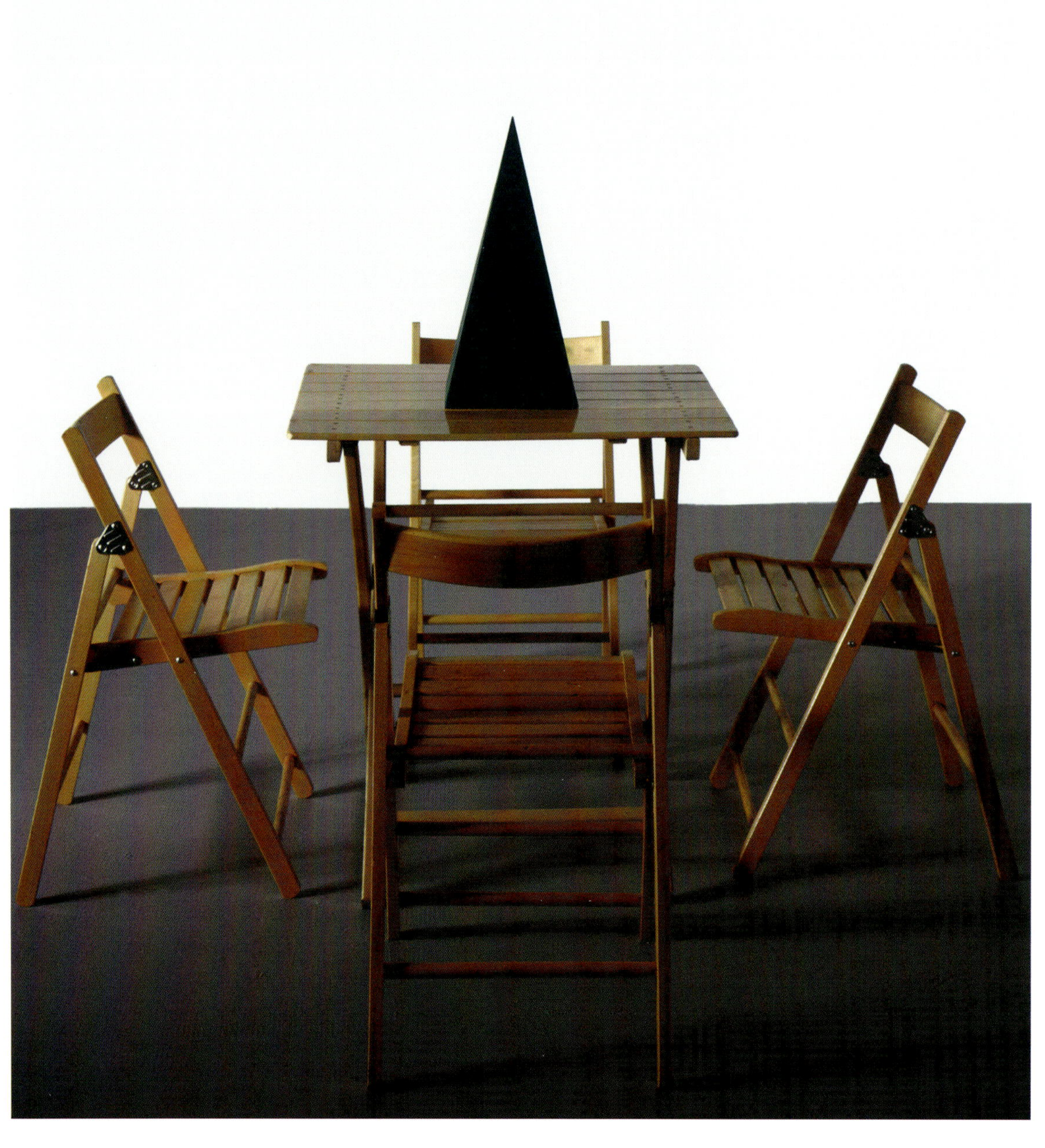

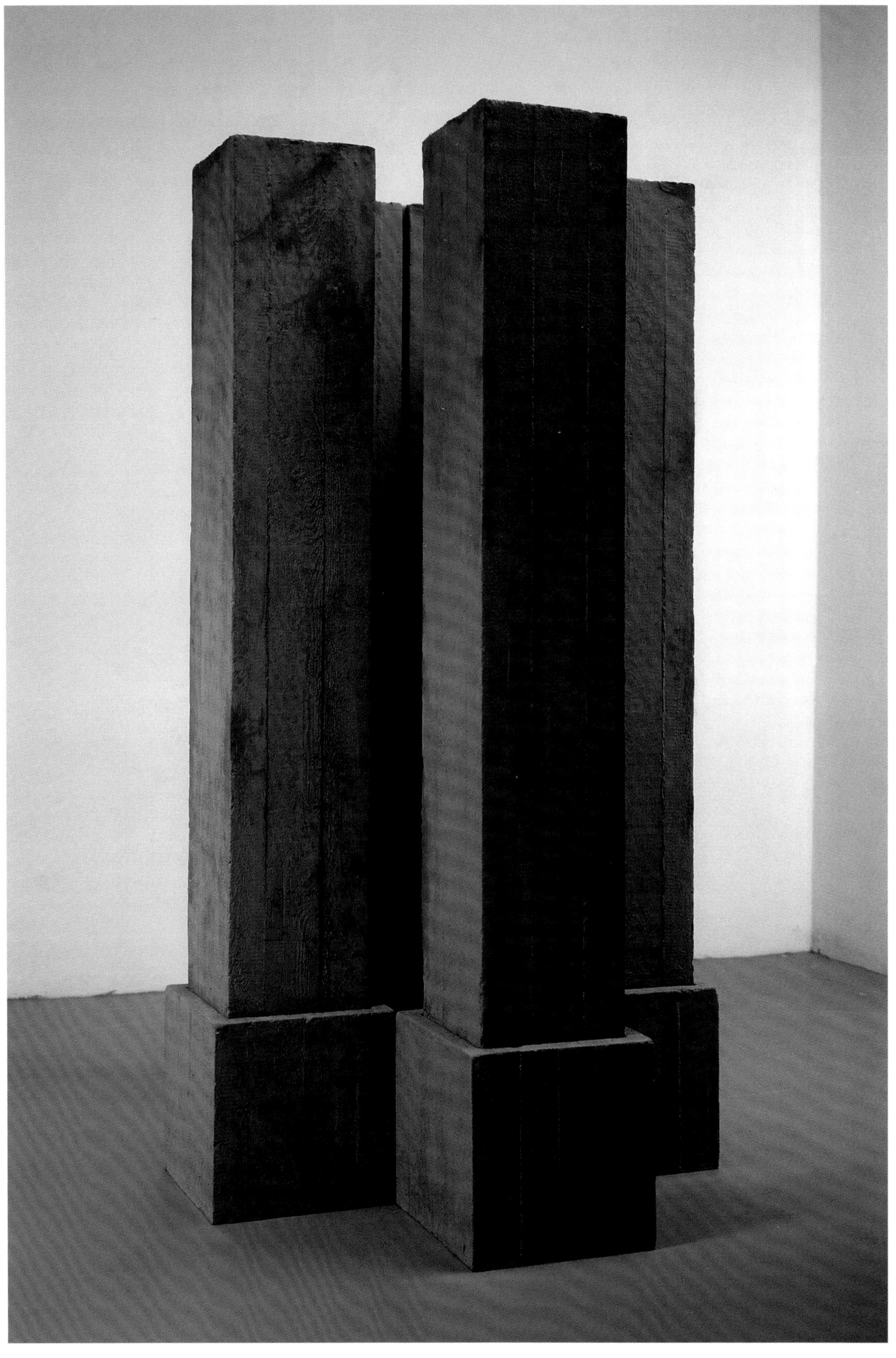

82
Semisfere decorative
(*Decorative Semispheres*), 1965–66
Colored plastic semispheres, nine elements
Overall 84¼ x 92⅛ inches (214 x 234 cm)
Cittadellarte-Fondazione Pistoletto, Biella

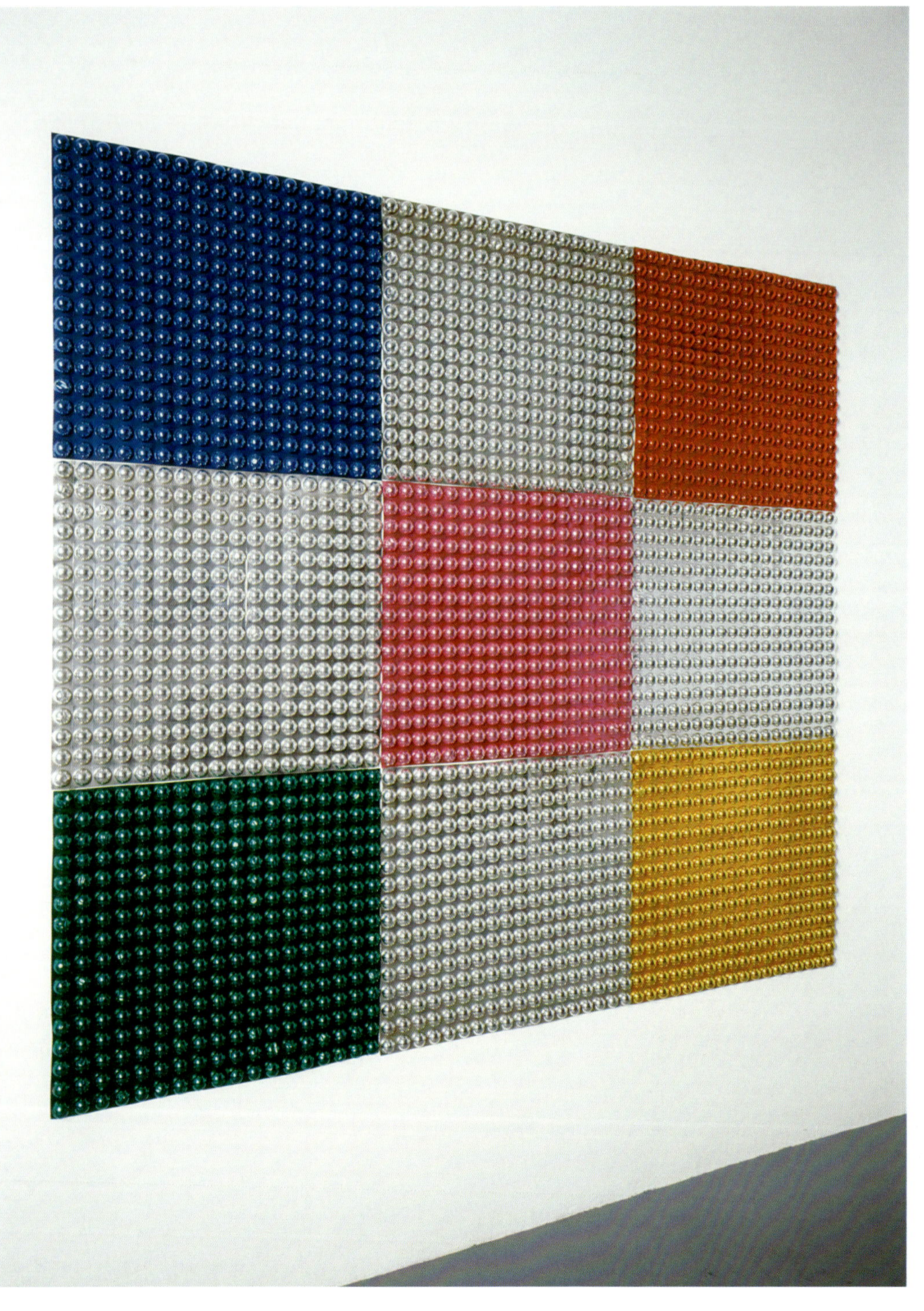

83
***Teletorte* (*Twisted Canvases*), 1965–66**
Tempera on canvas, three elements
Each 90 9/16 x 47 1/4 inches (230 x 120 cm)
Cittadellarte-Fondazione Pistoletto, Biella

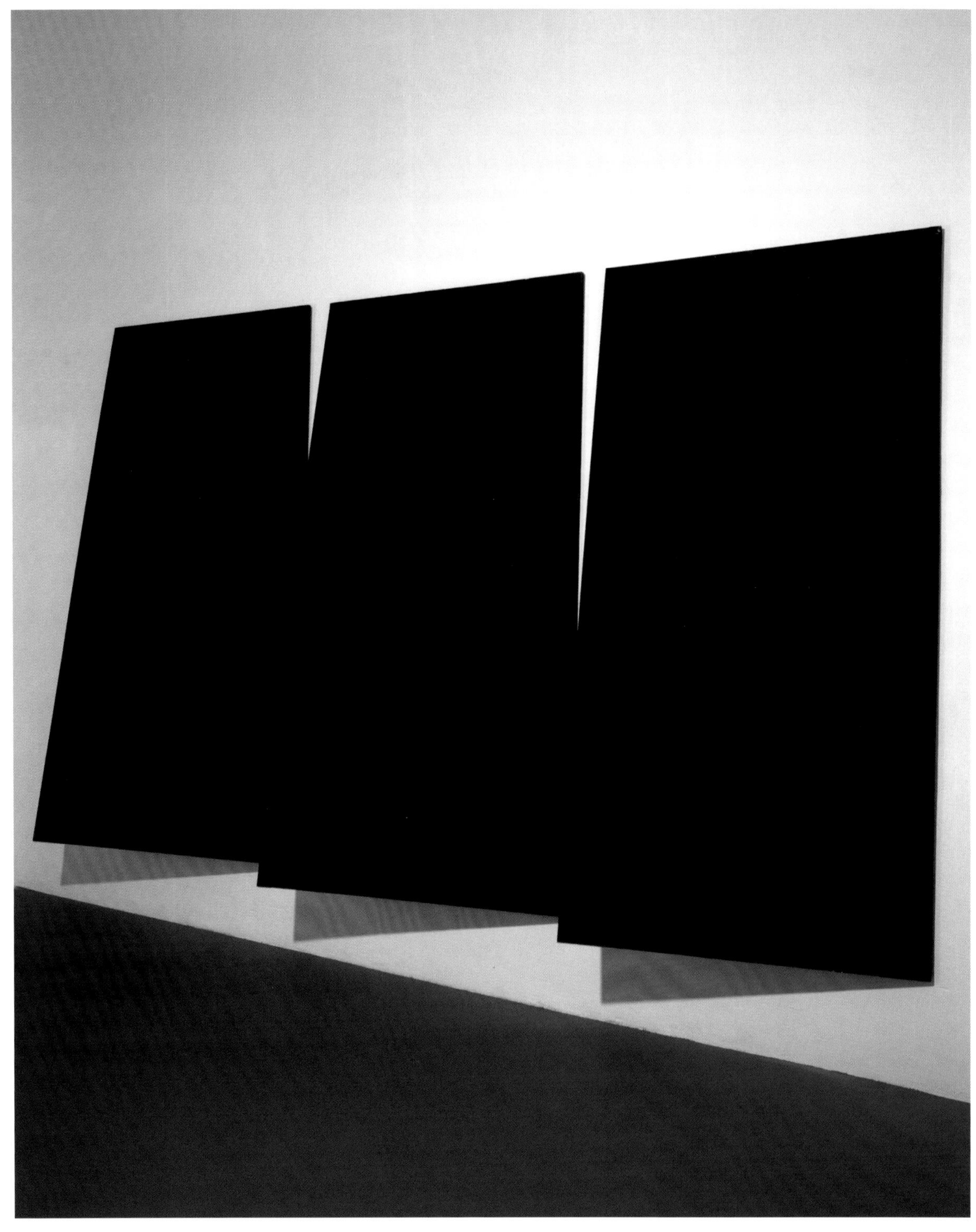

84
Mobile (*Furniture*), 1965–66
Wood, canvas, and velvet
33⅞ x 33⅞ x 33⅞ inches
(86 x 86 x 86 cm)
Cittadellarte-Fondazione Pistoletto, Biella

85
Bagno (*Bath*), 1965–66
Fiberglass
23⅝ x 78¾ x 39⅜ inches
(60 x 200 x 100 cm)
Cittadellarte-Fondazione Pistoletto, Biella

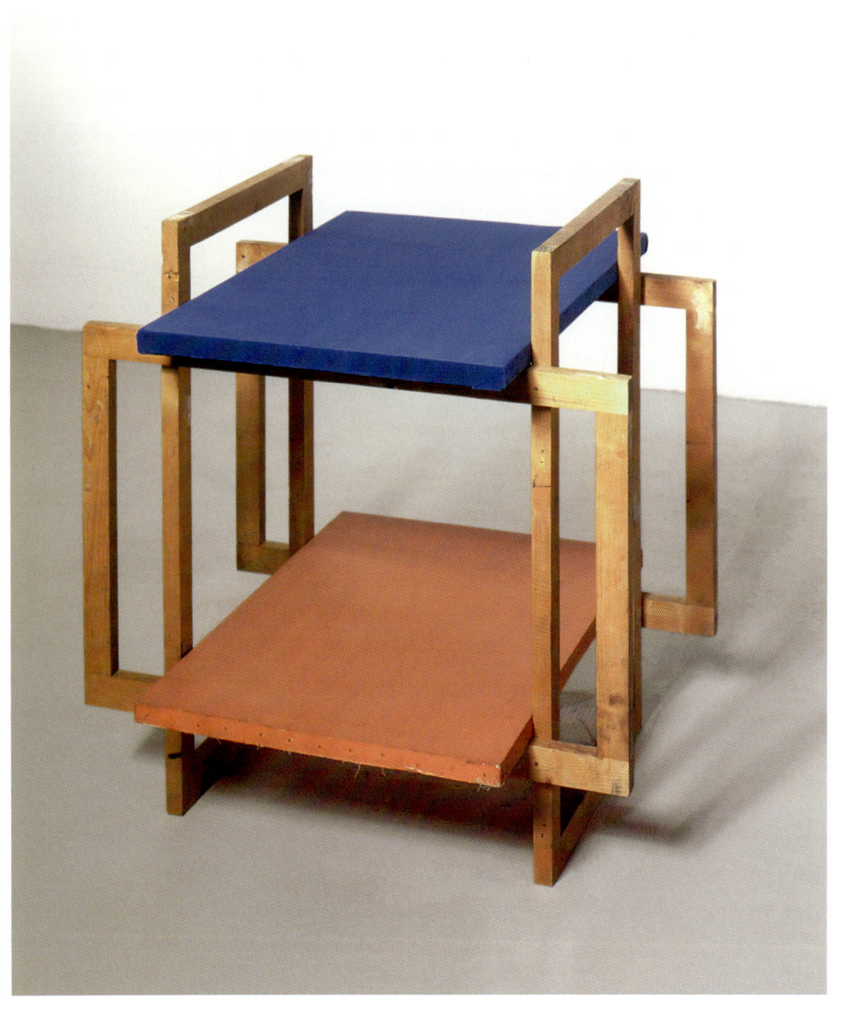

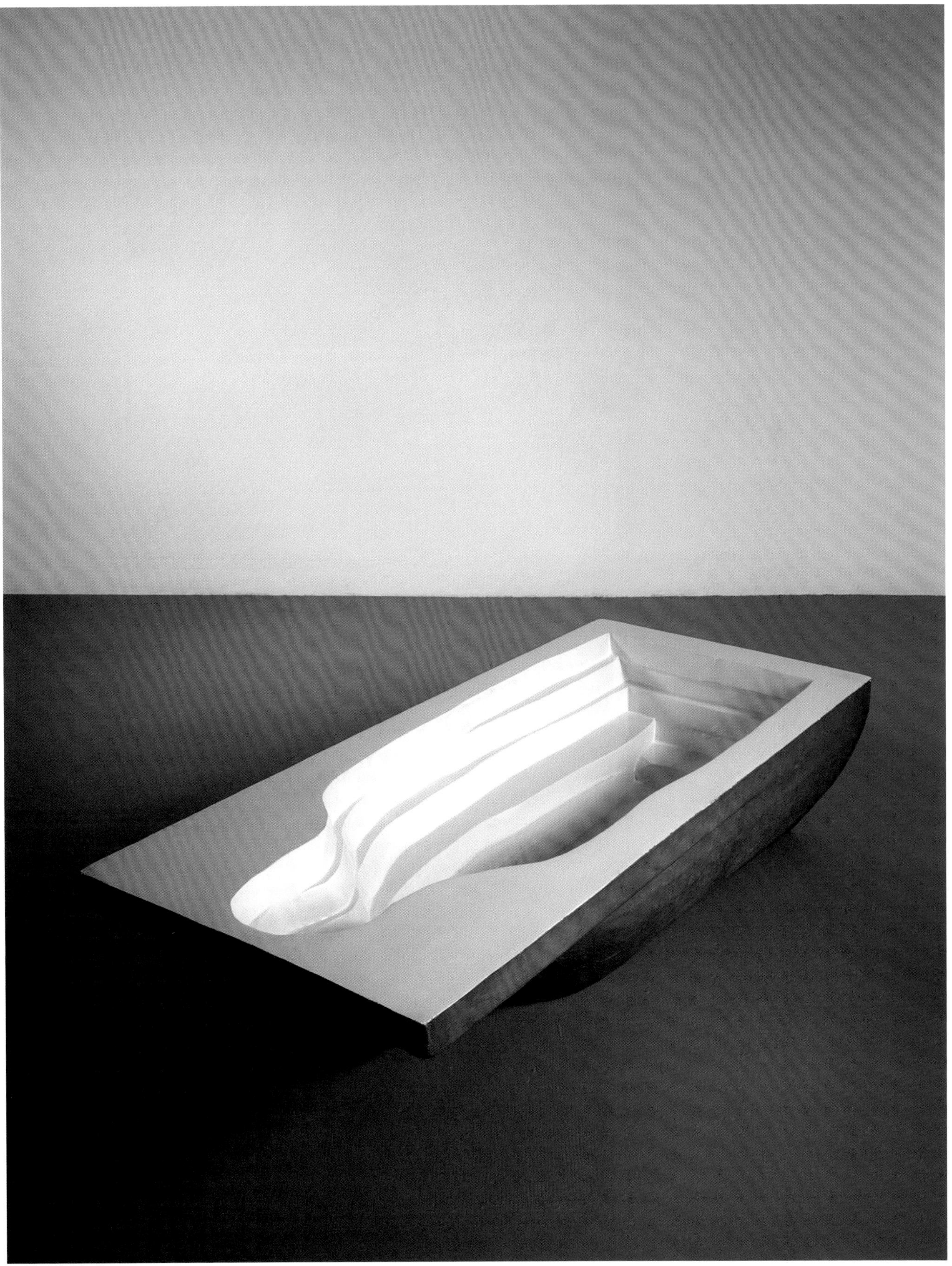

86
***Mica*, 1965–66**
Mica on canvas
47¼ x 47¼ inches (120 x 120 cm)
Cittadellarte-Fondazione Pistoletto, Biella

87
***Struttura per parlare in piedi* (*Structure for Talking while Standing*), 1965–66**
Welded and painted iron pipe
47¼ x 78¾ x 78¾ inches
(120 x 200 x 200 cm)
Cittadellarte-Fondazione Pistoletto, Biella

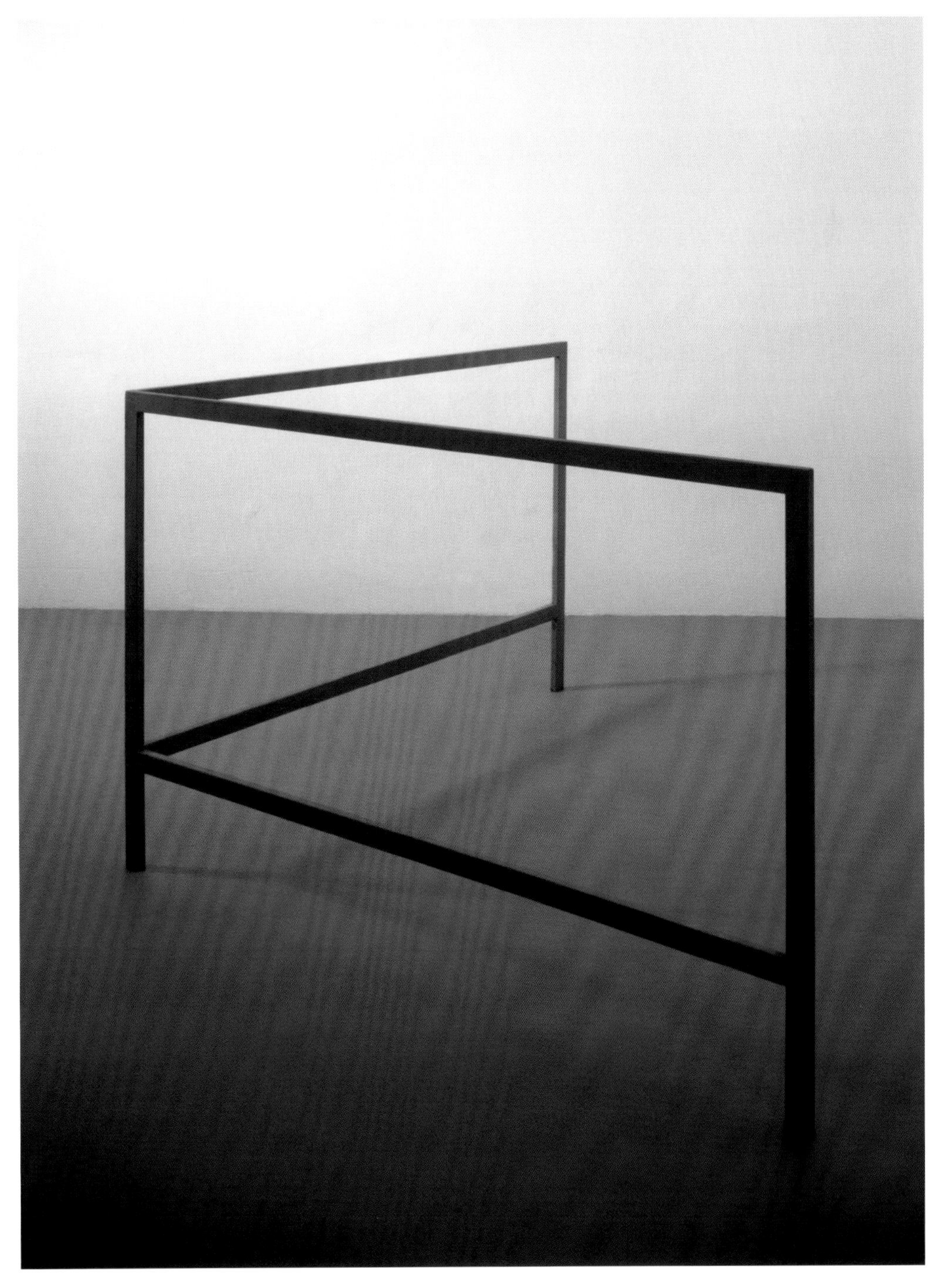

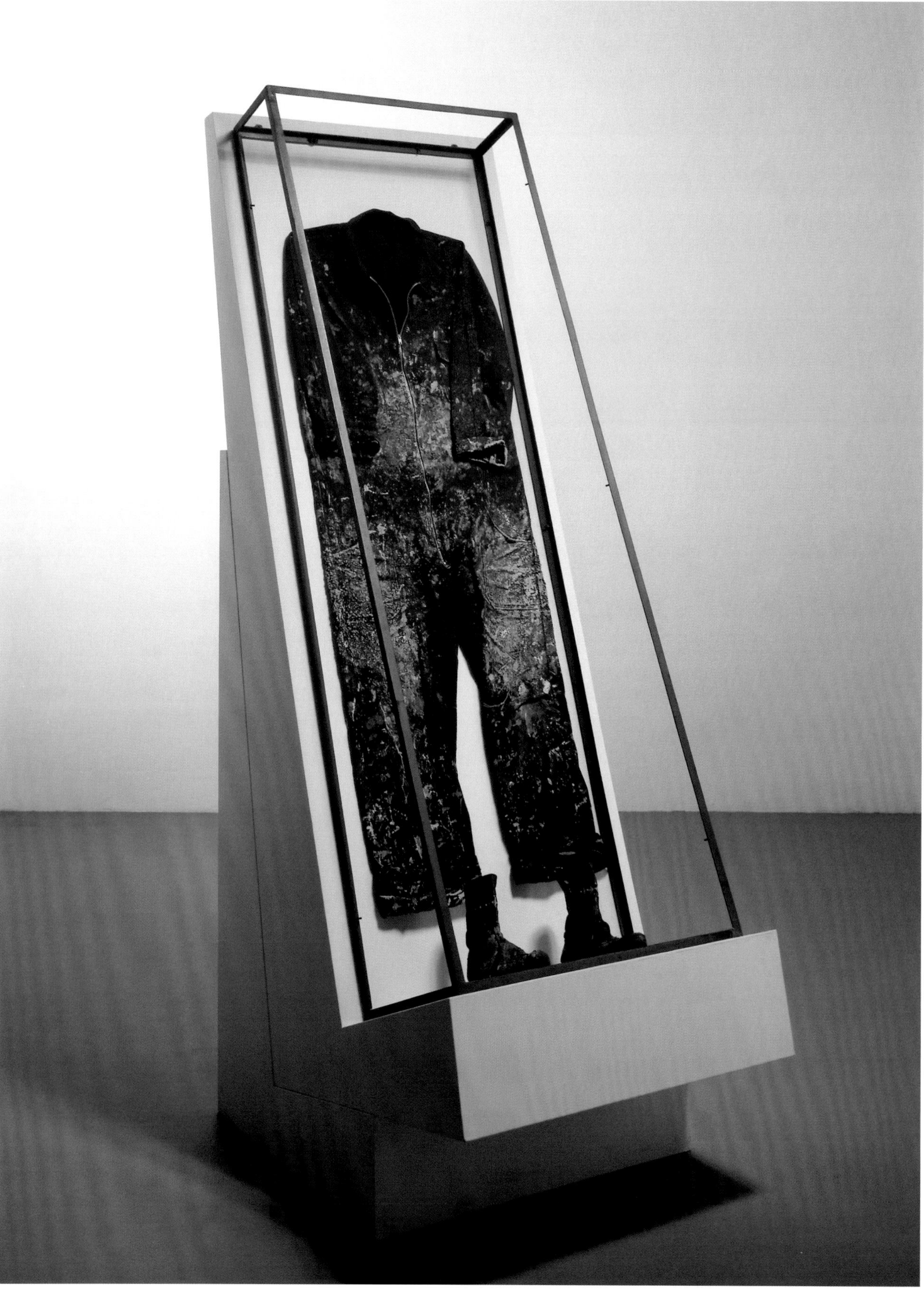

88
***Vetrina* (*Display Case*), 1965–66**
Wood, iron, mirror, and clothes
92½ x 39⅜ x 31½ inches (235 x 100 x 80 cm)
Cittadellarte-Fondazione Pistoletto, Biella

89
***Fontana luminosa* (*Luminous Fountain*), 1965–66**
Oil on canvas
31½ x 39⅜ inches (80 x 100 cm)
Cittadellarte-Fondazione Pistoletto, Biella

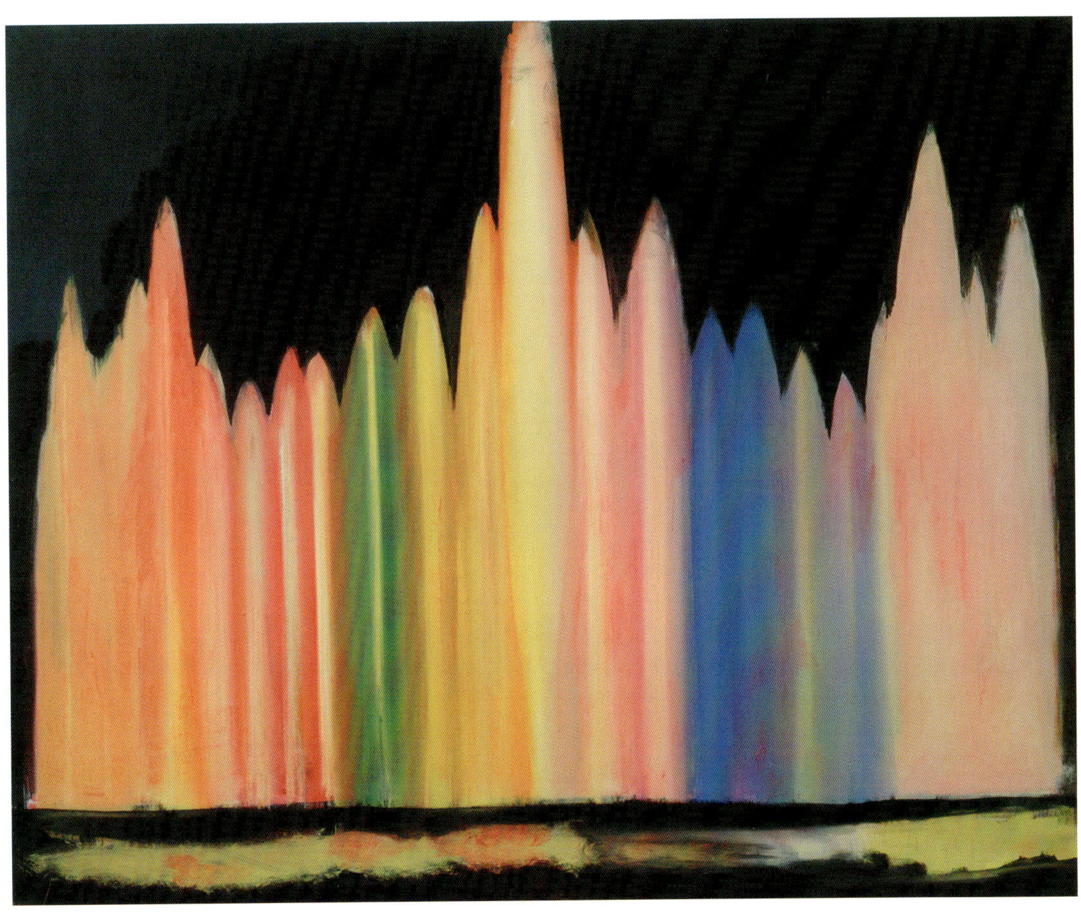

90
***Ti amo** (**I Love You**)*, 1965–66
Acrylic on canvas
23 5/8 x 27 9/16 inches (60 x 70 cm)
Cittadellarte-Fondazione Pistoletto, Biella

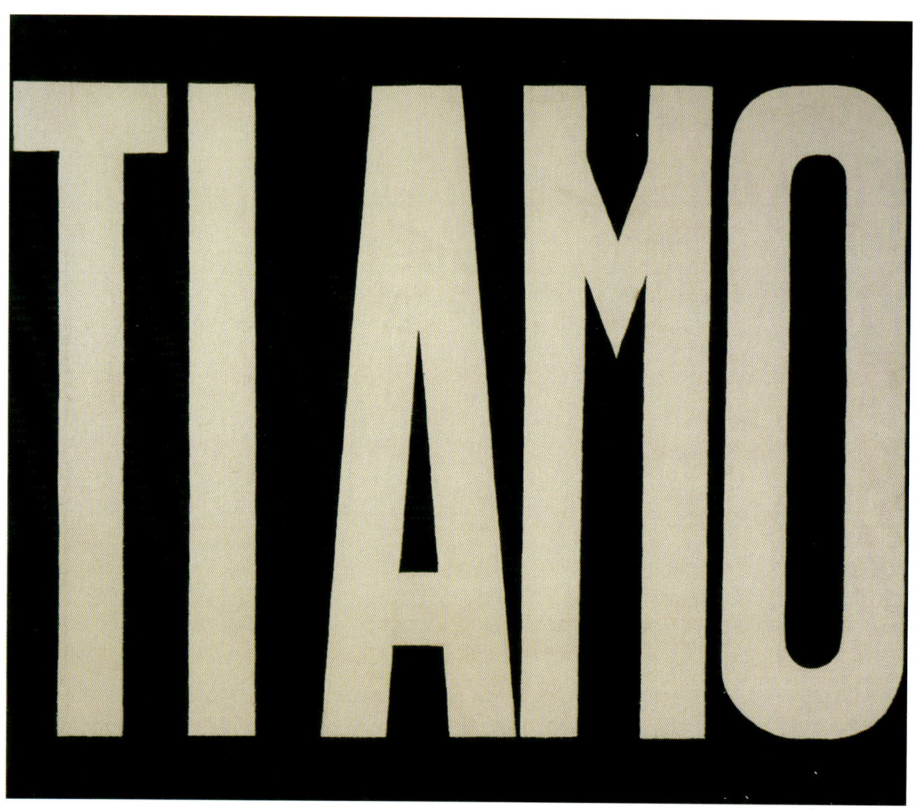

91
Scultura lignea
(*Wood Sculpture*), 1965–66
Antique wood sculpture encircled by orange Plexiglas on a wood stand
39 3/8 x 11 13/16 x 9 13/16 inches
(100 x 30 x 25 cm)
Cittadellarte-Fondazione Pistoletto, Biella

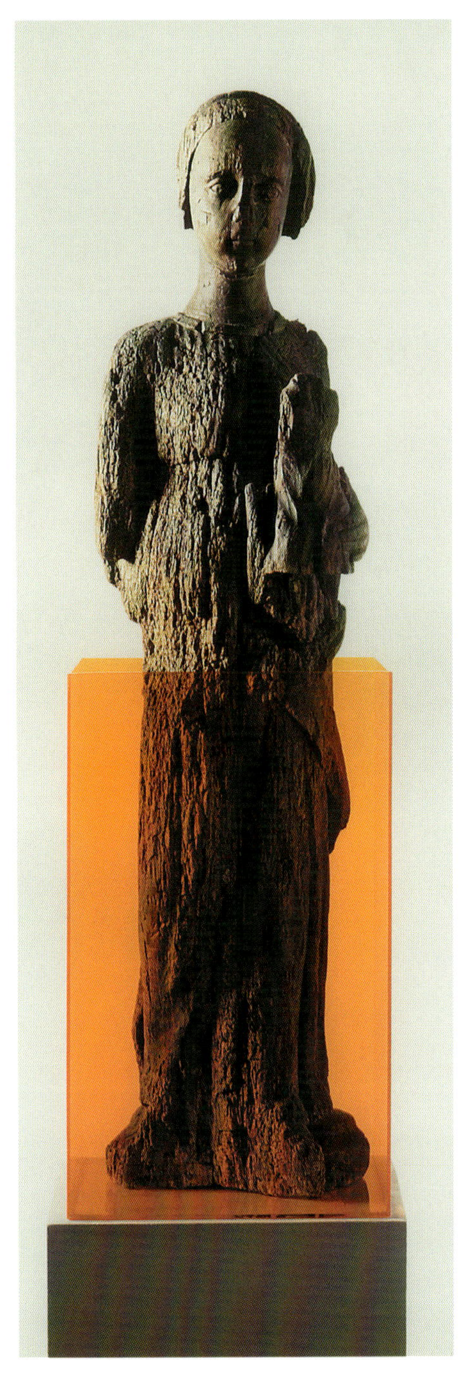

92
Sfera sotto il letto
(*Sphere under the Bed*), 1965–66
Wood, canvas, polyurethane, lightbulb, and pressed newspaper
Overall 17 x 78¾ x 40⅛ inches (43 x 200 x 102 cm); sphere 13⅜ inches (34 cm)
Private collection

93
Casa a misura d'uomo
(*House on a Human Scale*), 1965–66
Wood and enamel
78¾ x 39⅜ x 47¼ inches
(200 x 100 x 120 cm)
Cittadellarte-Fondazione Pistoletto, Biella

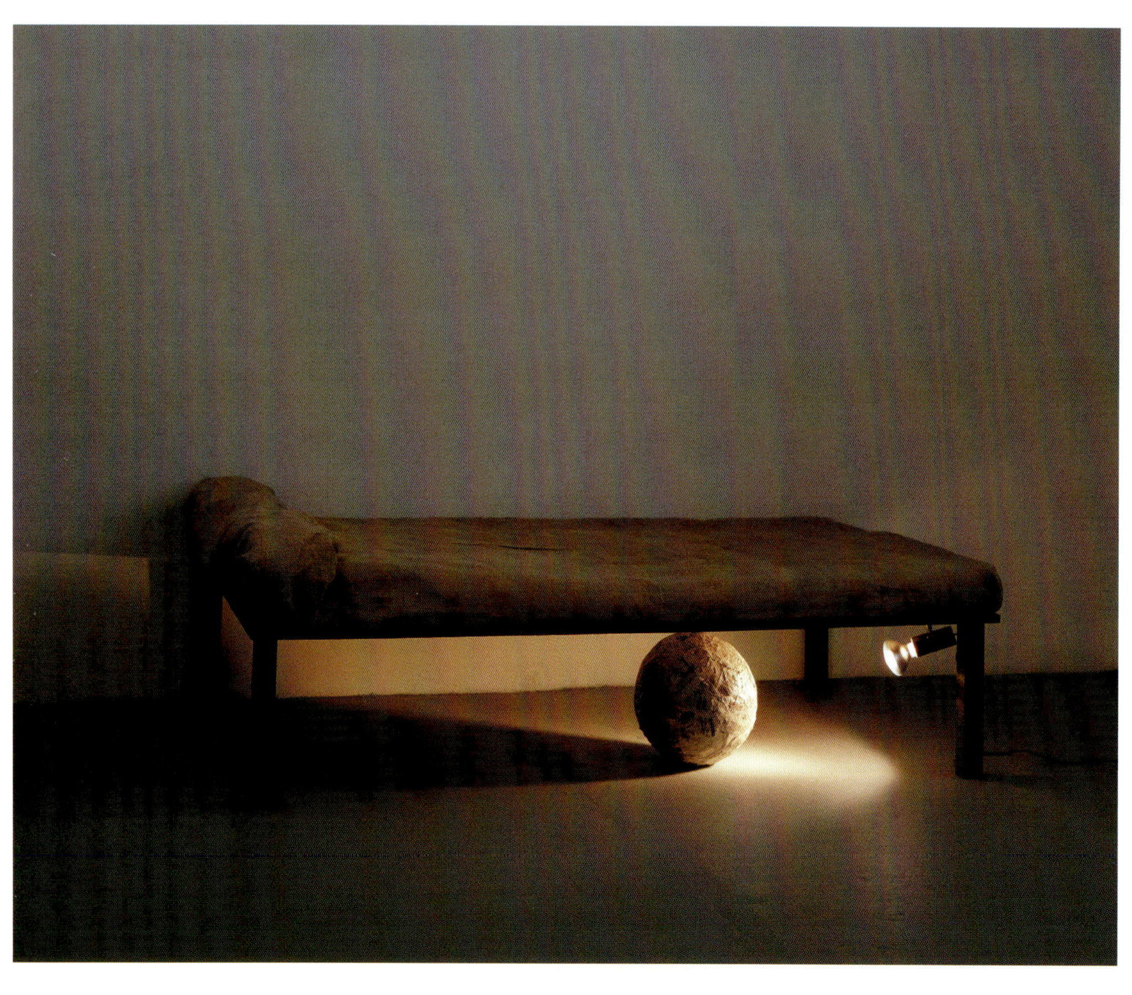

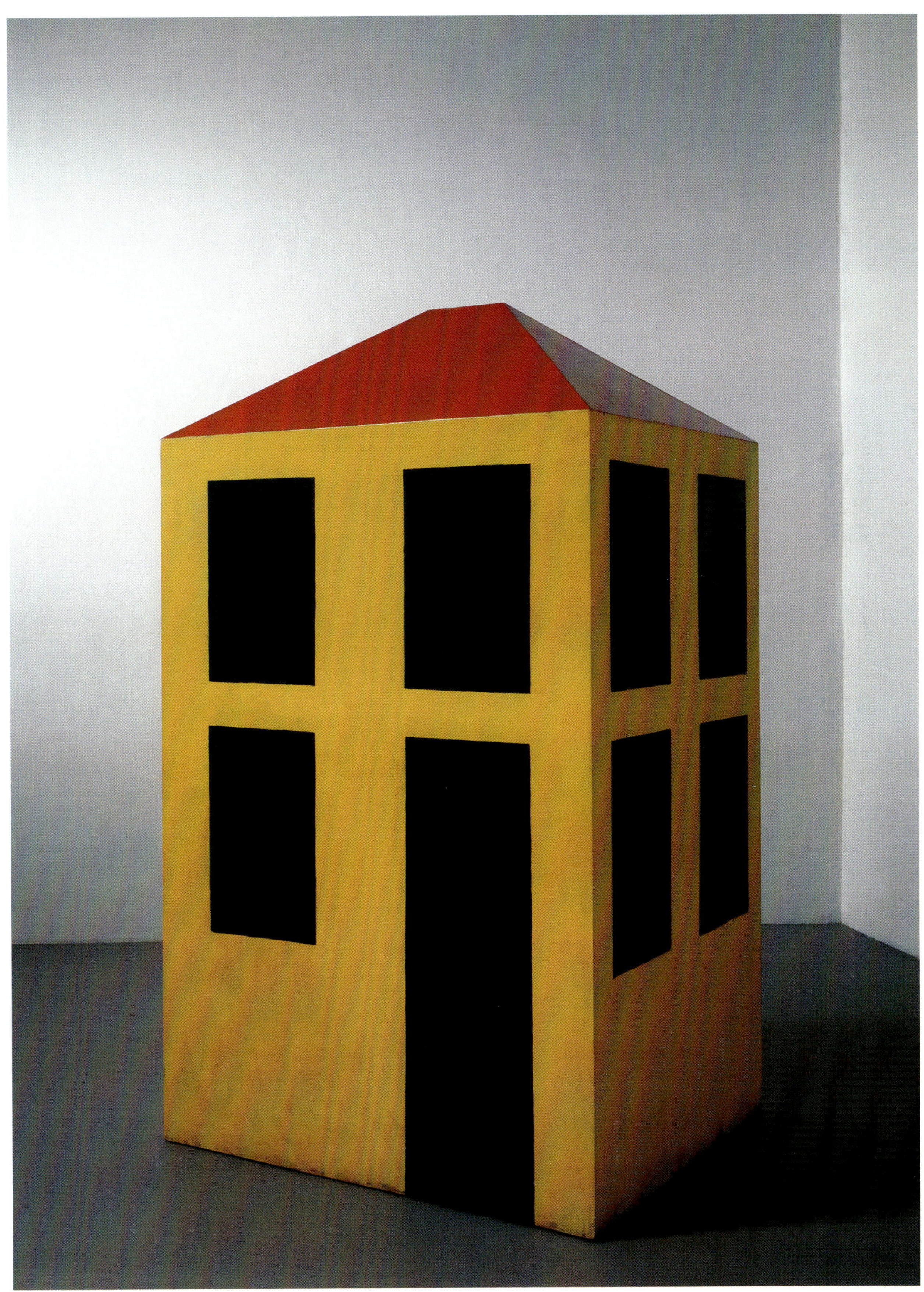

94
***Sarcofago* (*Sarcophagus*), 1966**
Wood, cement, and mica
60 5/8 x 78 3/4 x 29 15/16 inches
(154 x 200 x 76 cm)
Cittadellarte-Fondazione Pistoletto, Biella

95
Foto di Jasper Johns
(*Photograph of Jasper Johns*), 1966
Photograph on paper
98 7/16 x 39 3/8 inches (250 x 100 cm)
Cittadellarte-Fondazione Pistoletto, Biella

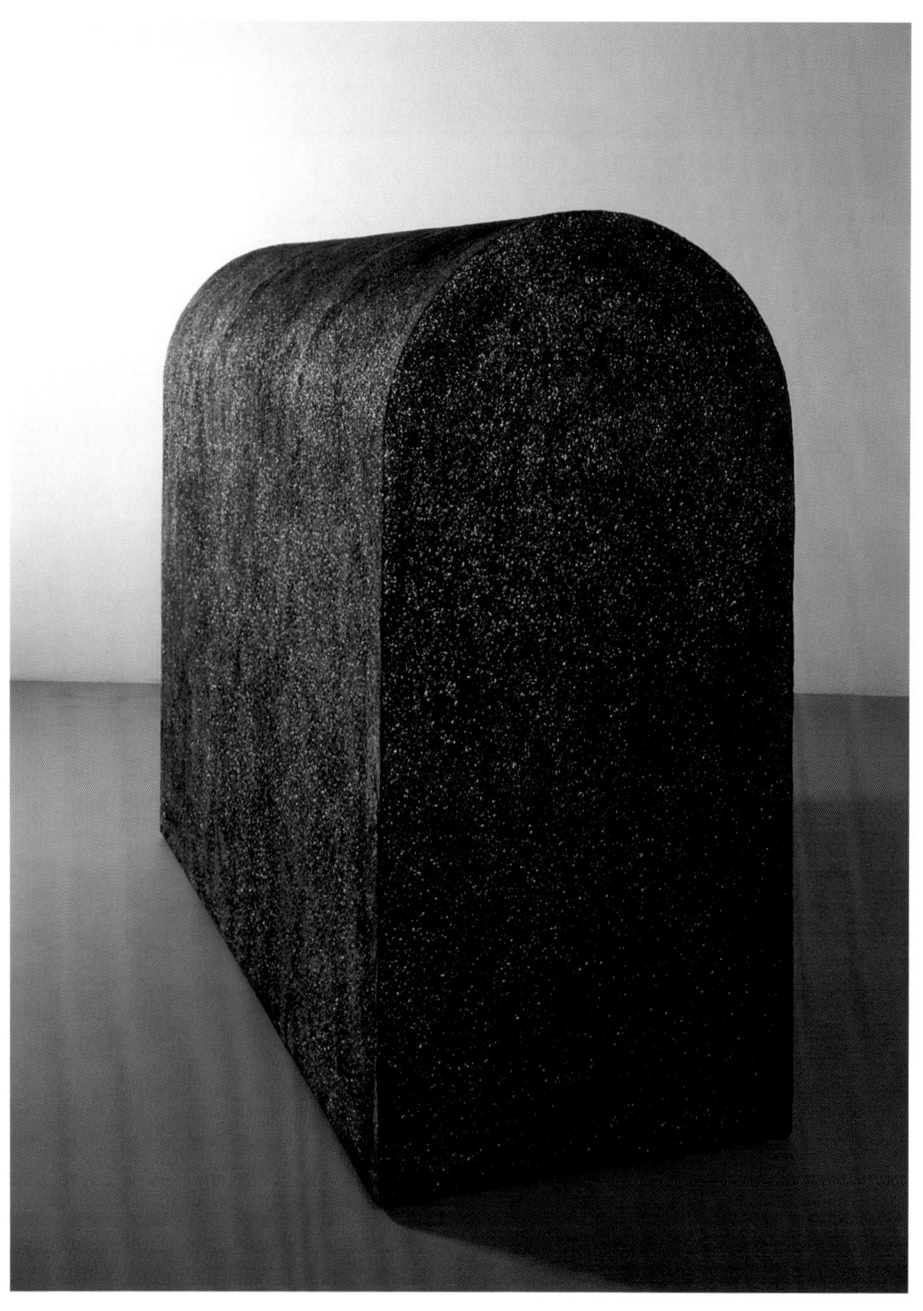

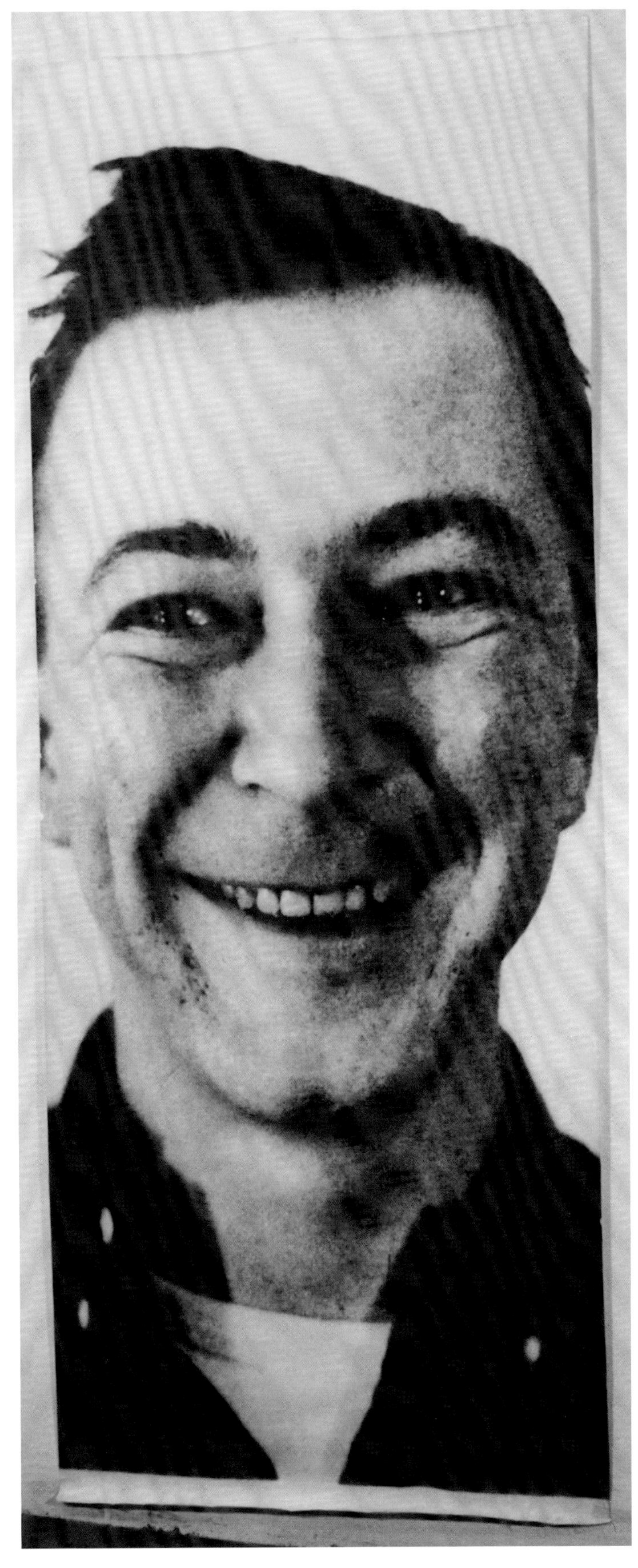

96
Metrocubo d'infinito
(*Cubic Meter of Infinity*), 1966
Six mirrors turned inward and tied with string
47¼ x 47¼ x 47¼ inches
(120 x 120 x 120 cm)
Cittadellarte-Fondazione Pistoletto, Biella

97
Mappamondo (_Globe_), 1966–68
Newspaper and wire
Wire ball: diam. 70⅞ inches (180 cm)
Newspaper ball: diam. 39⅜ inches (100 cm)
Collection of Lia Rumma

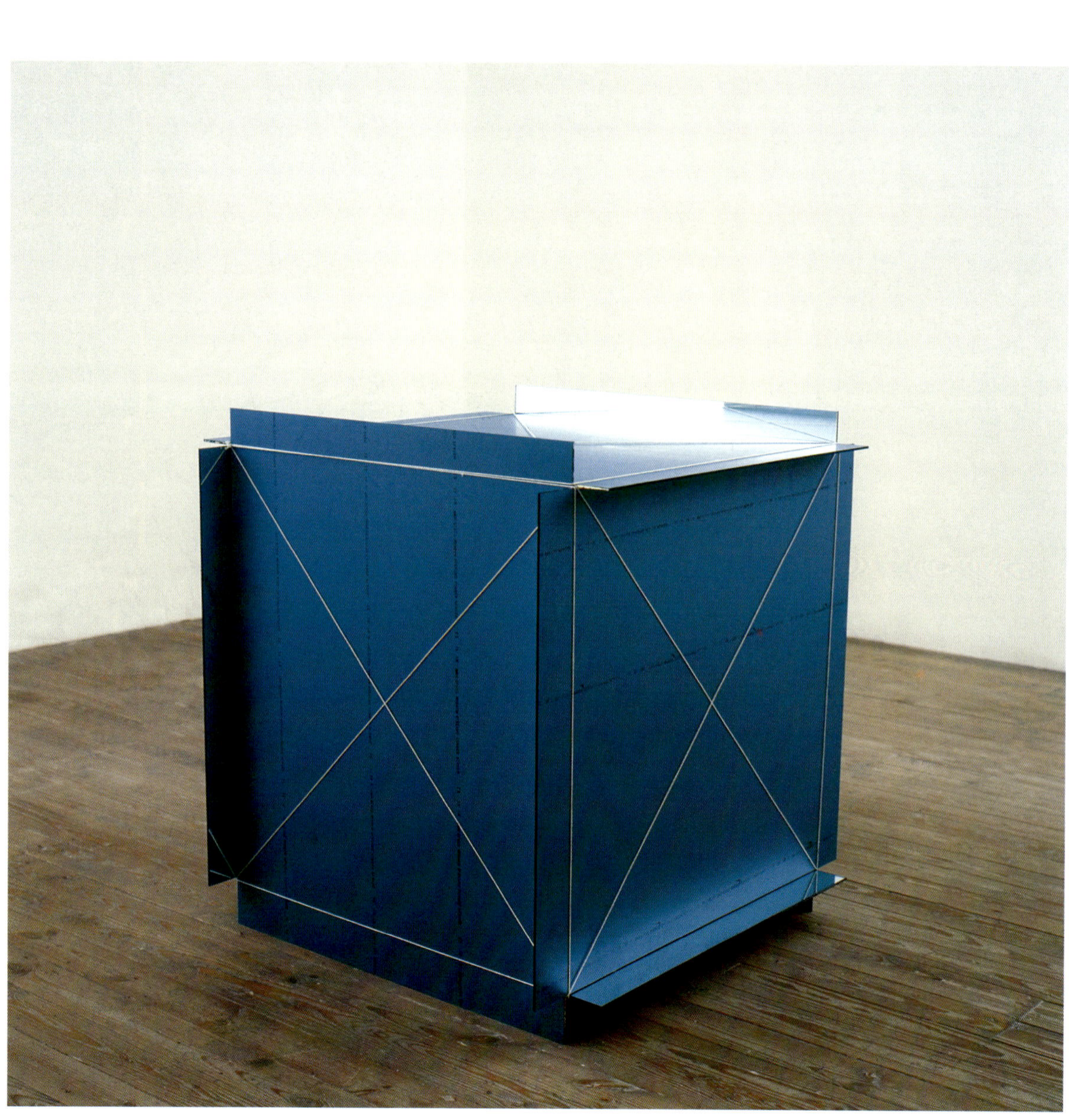

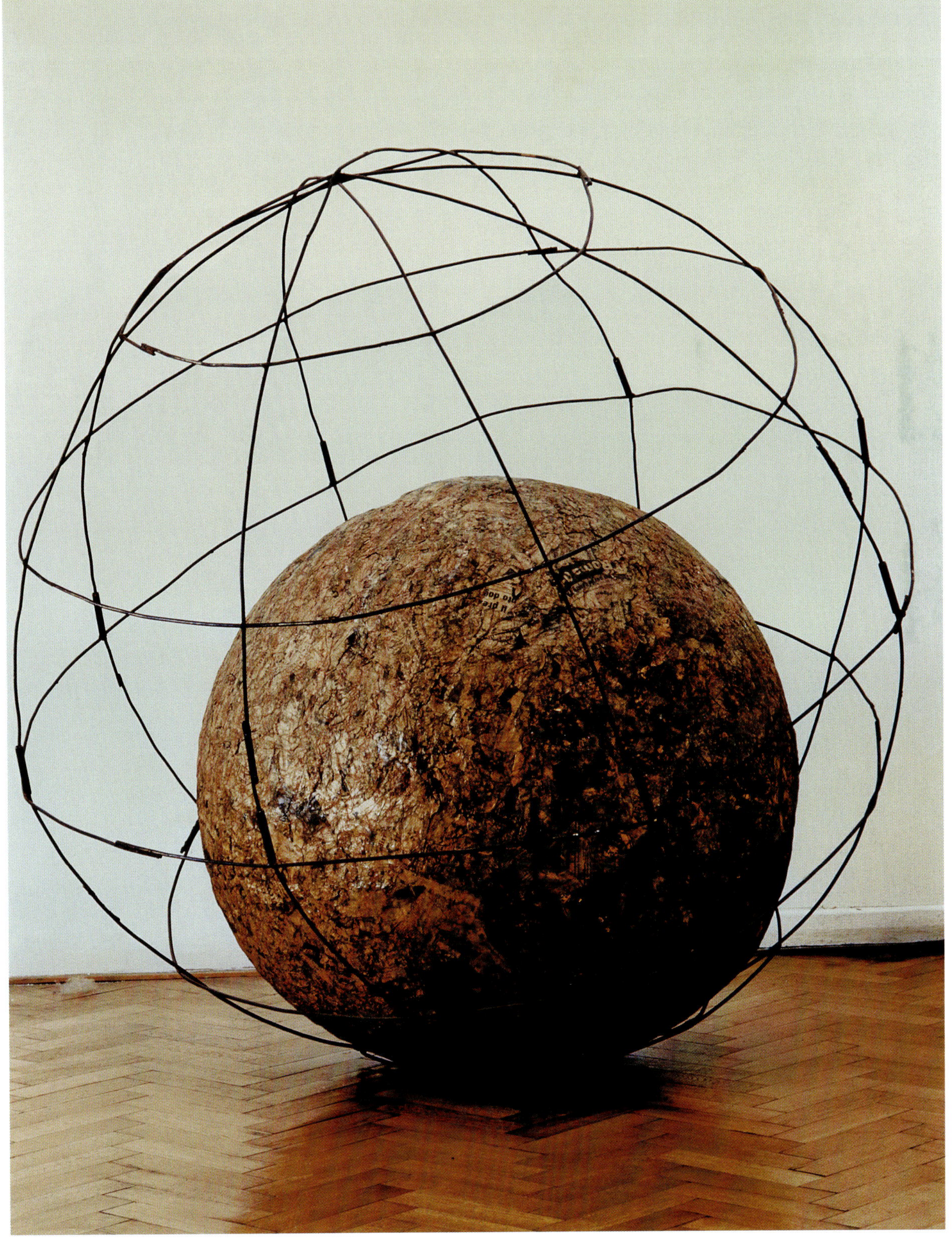

98
***Pietra miliare (Milestone)*, 1967**
Roadside post with mica, engraved "1967"
H. 31½ inches (80 cm);
diam. 15¾ inches (40 cm)
Cittadellarte-Fondazione Pistoletto, Biella

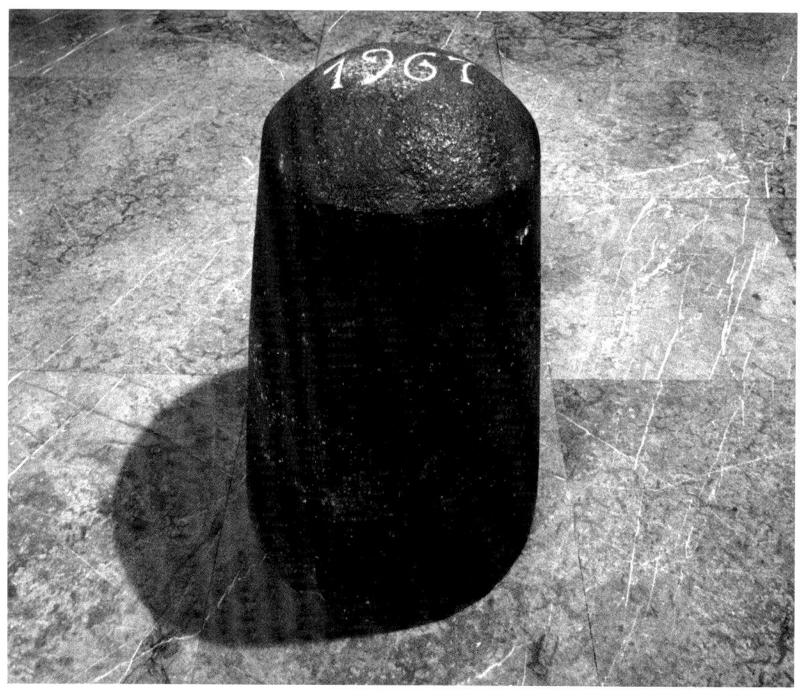

99
Venere degli stracci
(*Venus of the Rags*), 1967
Marble and rags
Statue: 65¾ x 23⅝ x 19¹¹⁄₁₆ inches (167 x 60 x 50 cm)
Overall: 74¾ x 98⅜ x 55⅛ inches (190 x 250 x 140 cm)
Cittadellarte-Fondazione Pistoletto, Biella

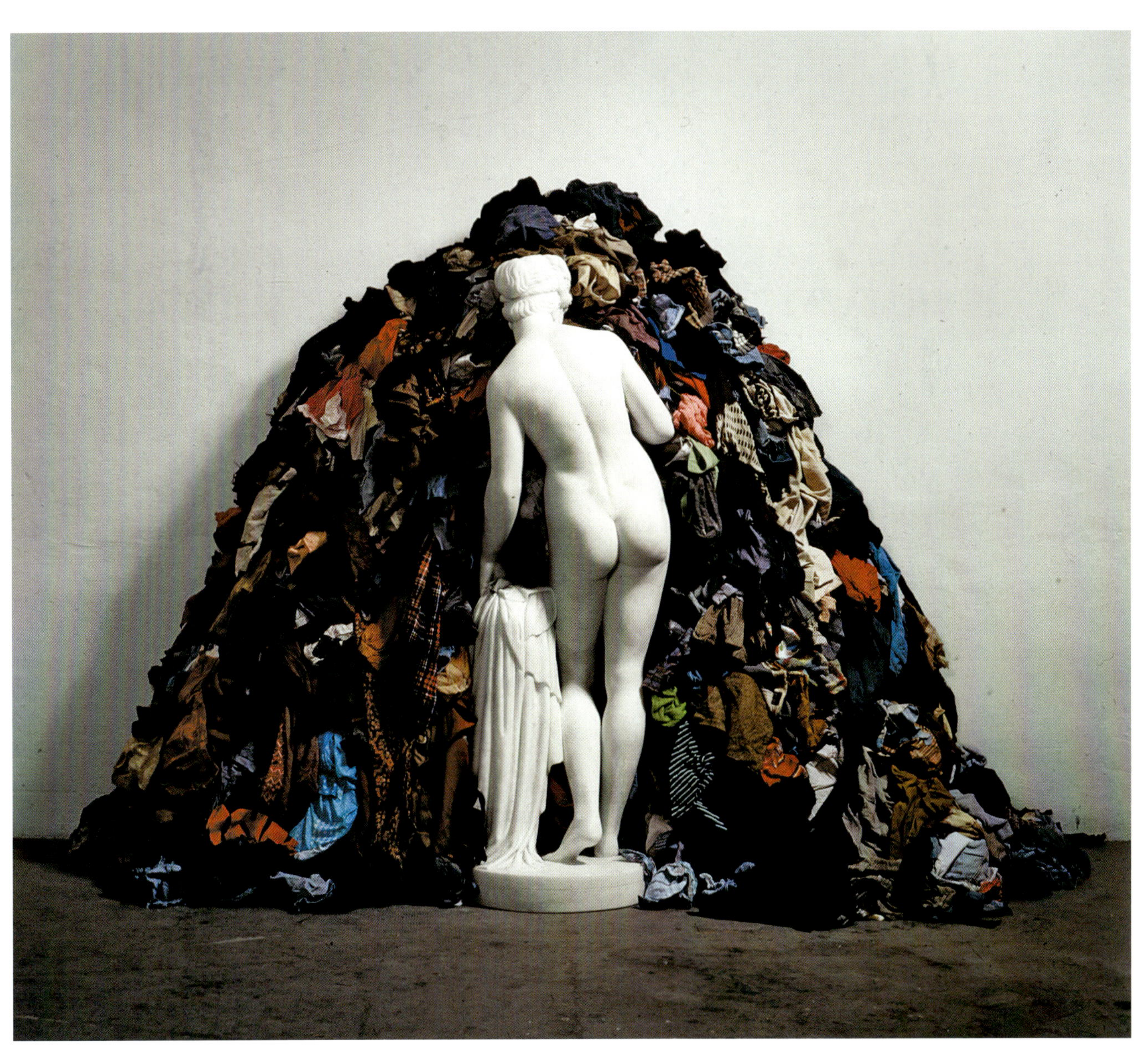

100
***Orchestra di stracci—quartetto* (*Orchestra of Rags—Quartet*), 1968**
Rags, glass, teakettles, steam, and electric circuit; four elements
Dimensions variable
MART—Museo per l'Arte Contemporanea di Trento e Rovereto, Rovereto, Italy

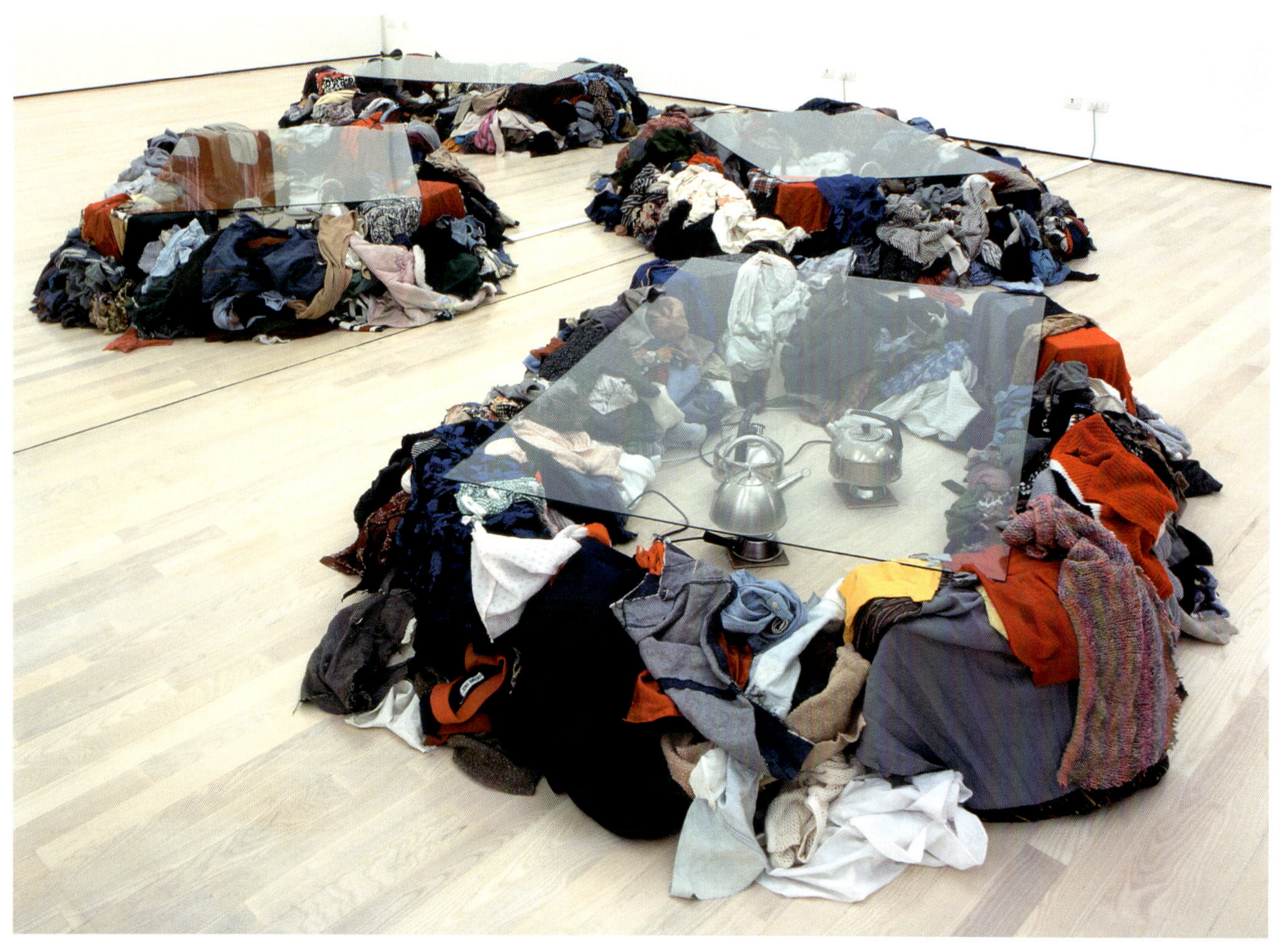

101
***Monumentino* (*Little Monument*), 1968**
Bricks, rags, and shoe
37 x 17¾ x 8⅝ inches (94 x 45 x 22 cm)
Private collection

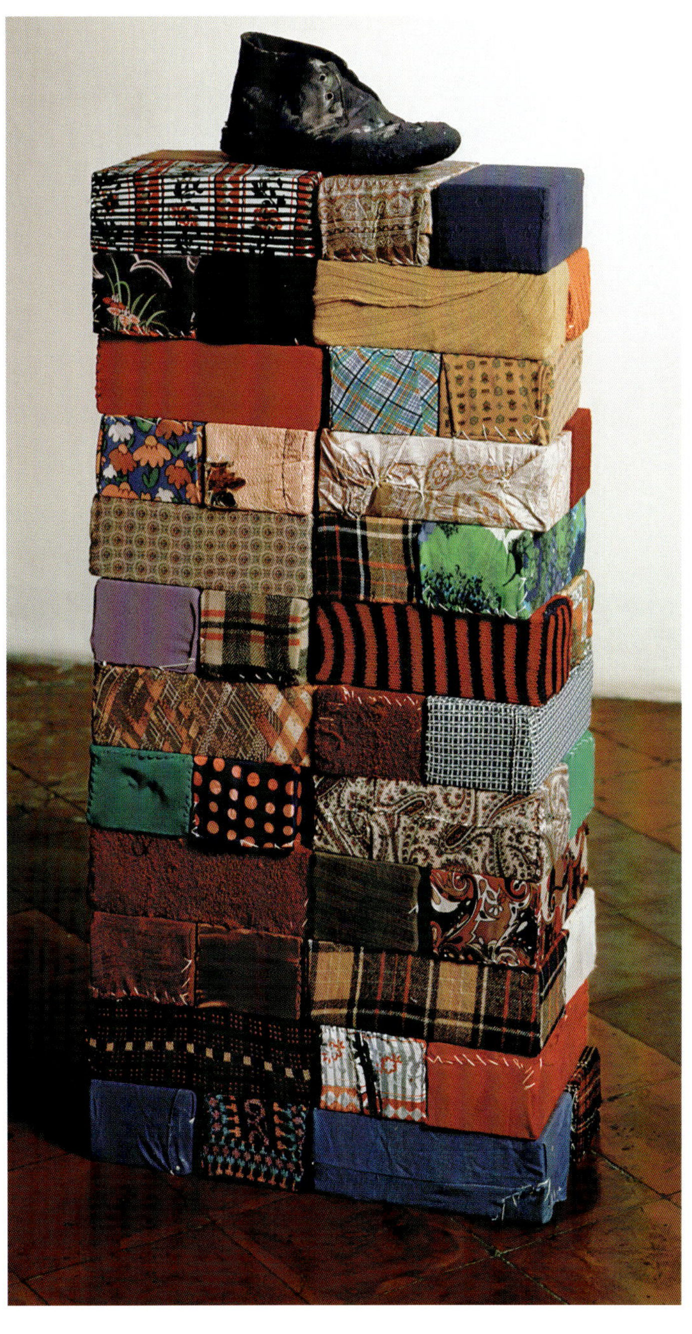

102
Muretto di stracci
(*Small Wall of Rags*), 1968
Bricks and rags
47¼ x 71⅞ x 9¼ inches
(120 x 182.5 x 23.5 cm)
Fundação de Serralves—Museu de Arte
Contemporânea, Porto, Portugal

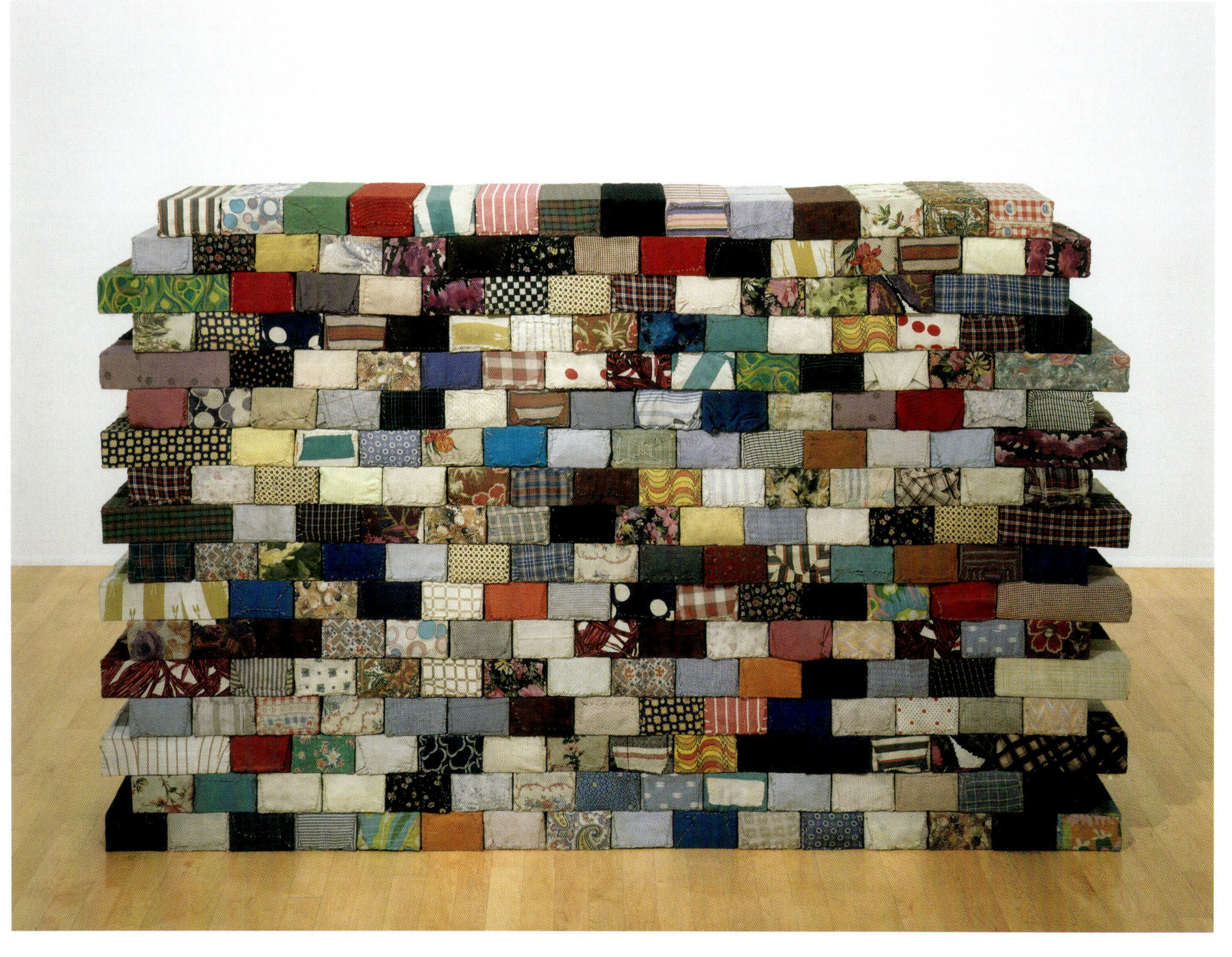

103
***Candele* (*Candles*), 1967**
Candles on mirroring Mylar foil
Dimensions variable
Cittadellarte-Fondazione Pistoletto, Biella

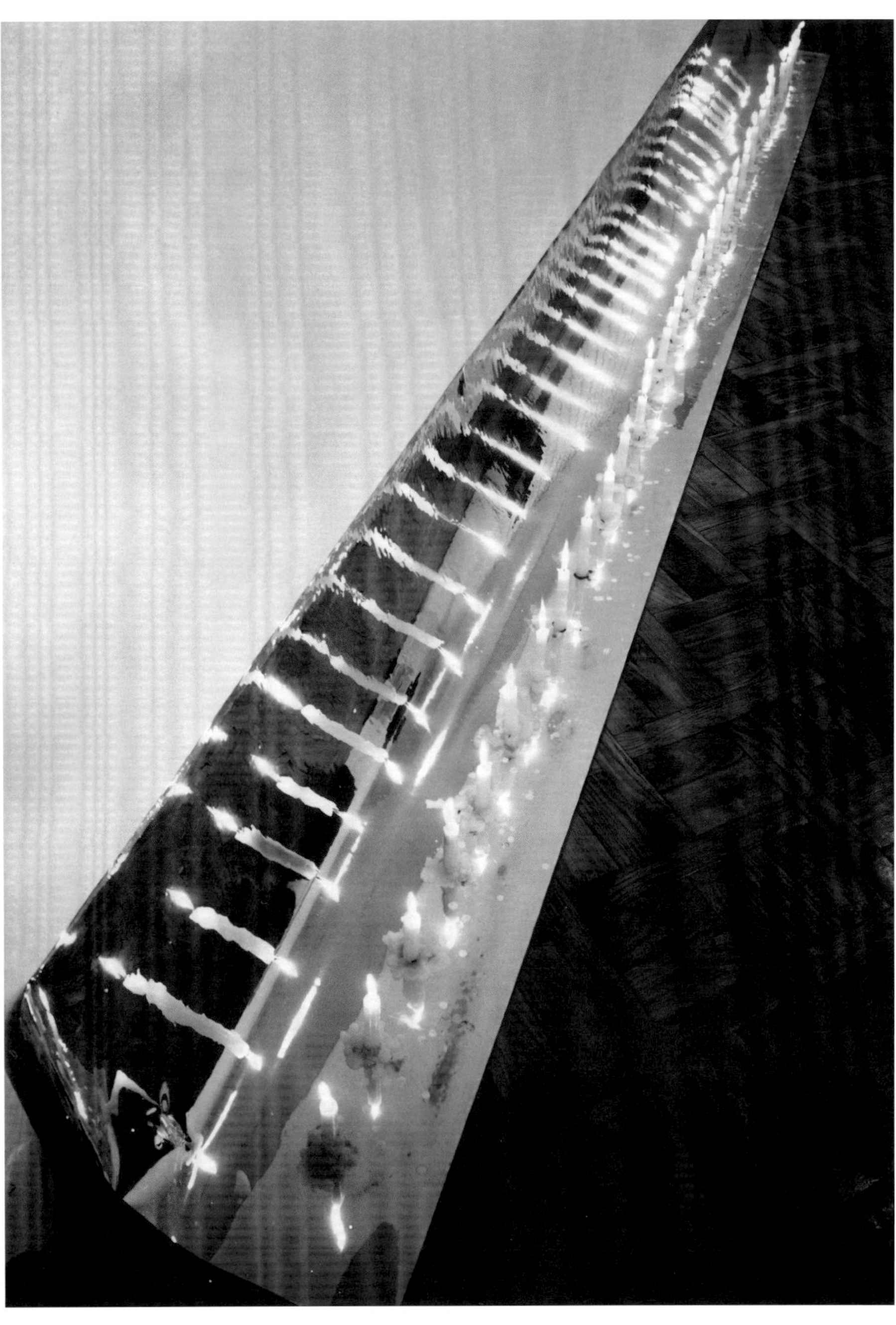

104
Riflessi sul muro
(*Reflections on the Wall*), 1967
Mirroring Mylar foil
Dimensions variable
Cittadellarte-Fondazione Pistoletto, Biella

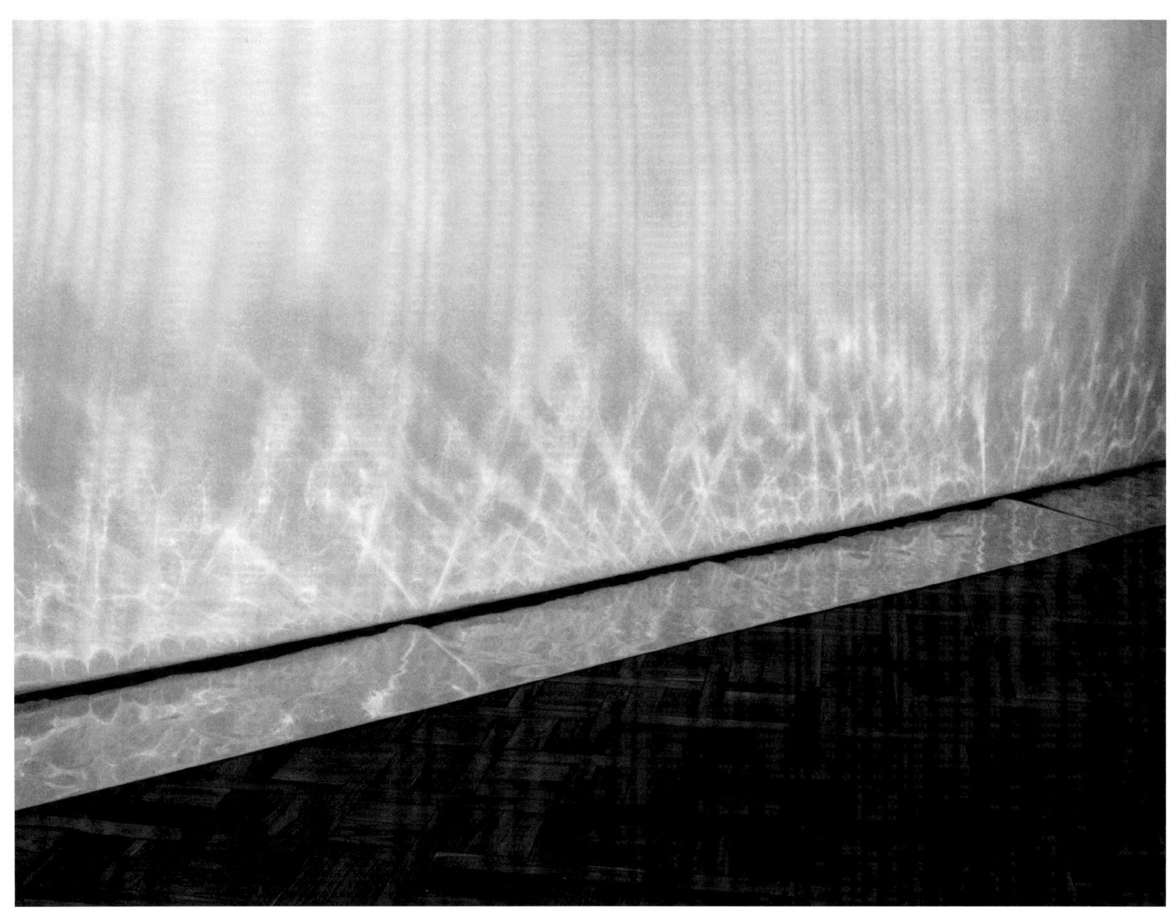

105
Quadro di fili elettrici
(*Painting of Electric Wires*), 1967
Twenty-one electric wires and lightbulbs
105½ x 173¼ x 315/16 inches (268 x 440 x 10 cm)
MAXXI—Museo Nazionale delle Arti del XXI Secolo, Rome. Courtesy of the Italian Ministry of Cultural Heritage and Activities

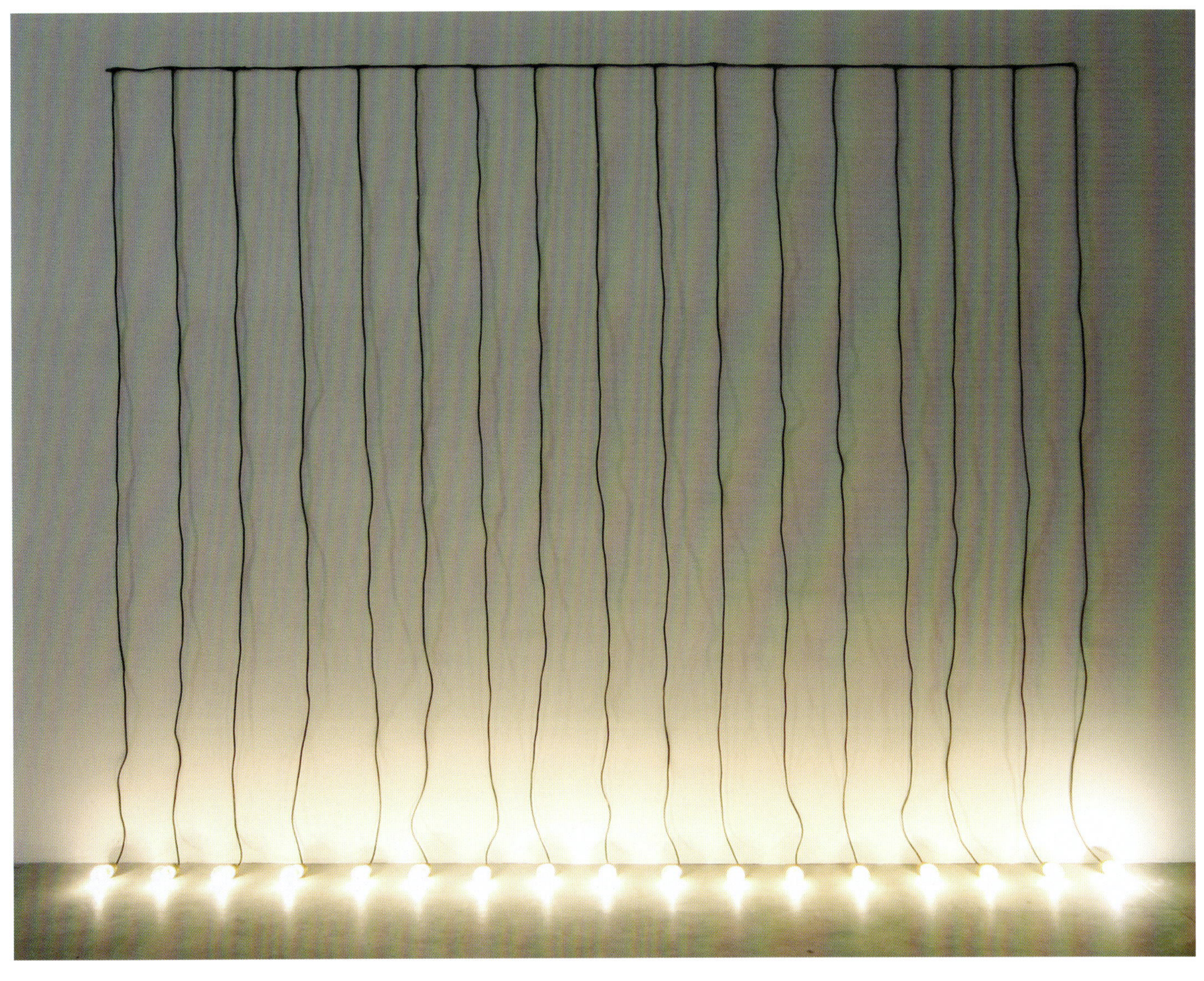

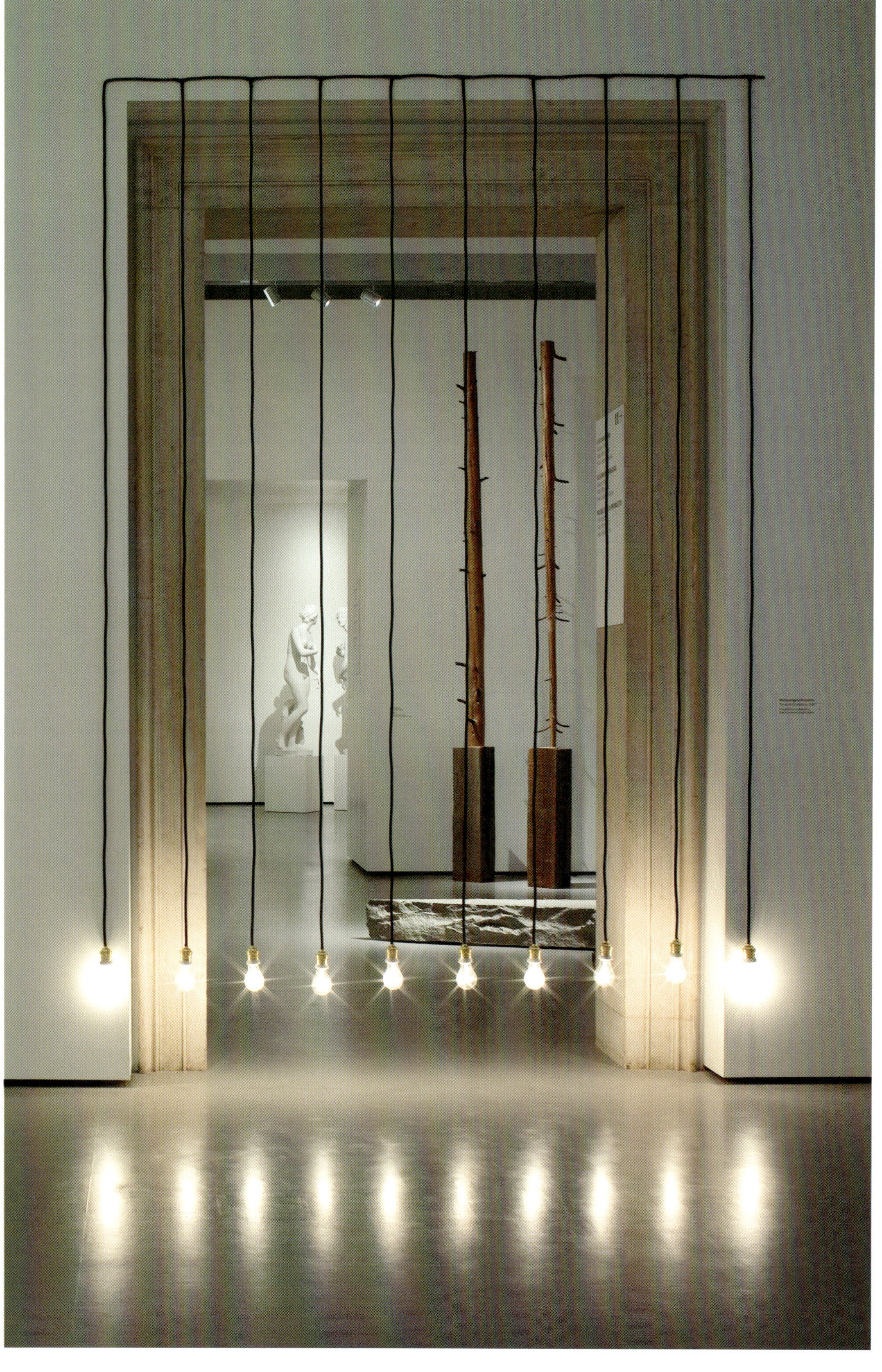

106
Tenda di fili elettrici
(Curtain of Electric Wires), 1967
Electric wire and lightbulbs
Dimensions variable, approx. 149½ x 157½ inches (379.7 x 400.1 cm)
Private collection

As installed in the exhibition *Where Are We Going?* at the Palazzo Grassi, Venice, 2006. Photograph by Santi Caleca

107
Slitta di acqua e sapone
(Sled of Water and Soap), 1968
Frosted glass, soap, water, and aluminum
11$^{13}/_{16}$ x 78¾ x 39⅜ inches
(30 x 200 x 100 cm)
Cittadellarte-Fondazione Pistoletto, Biella

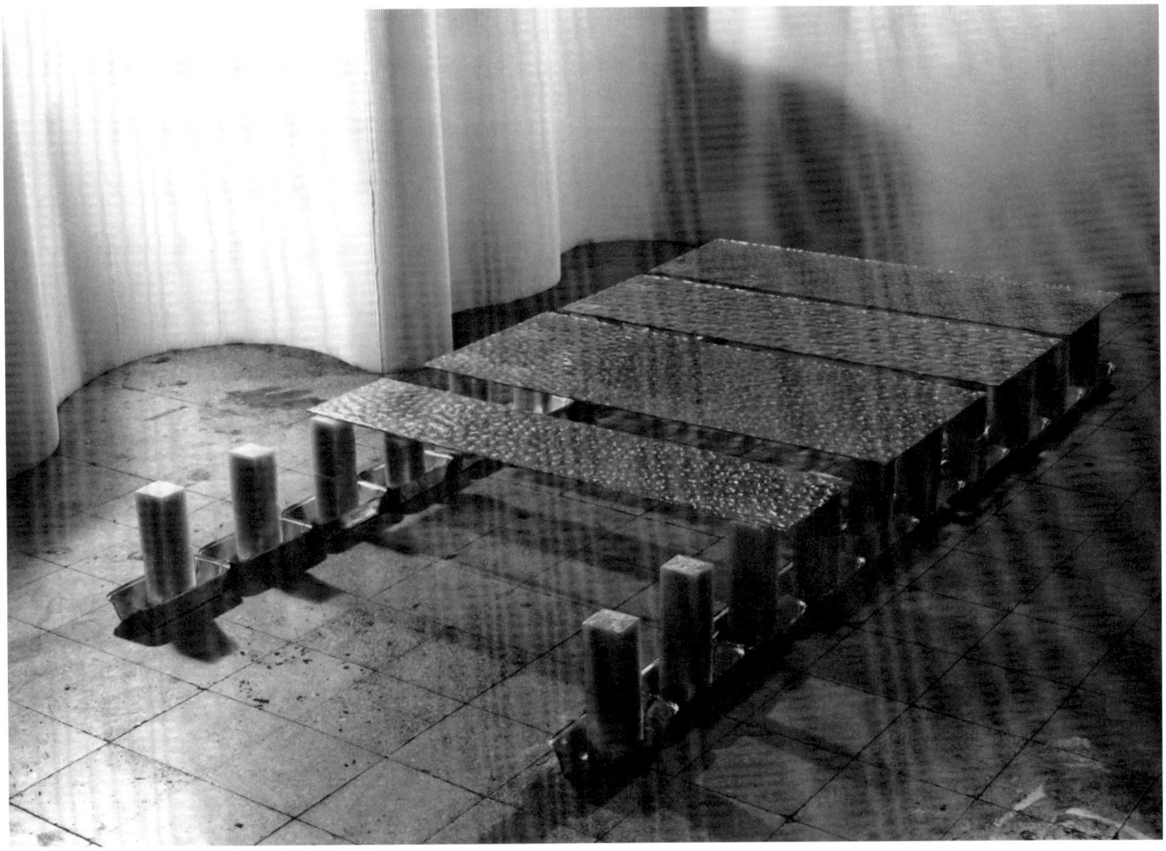

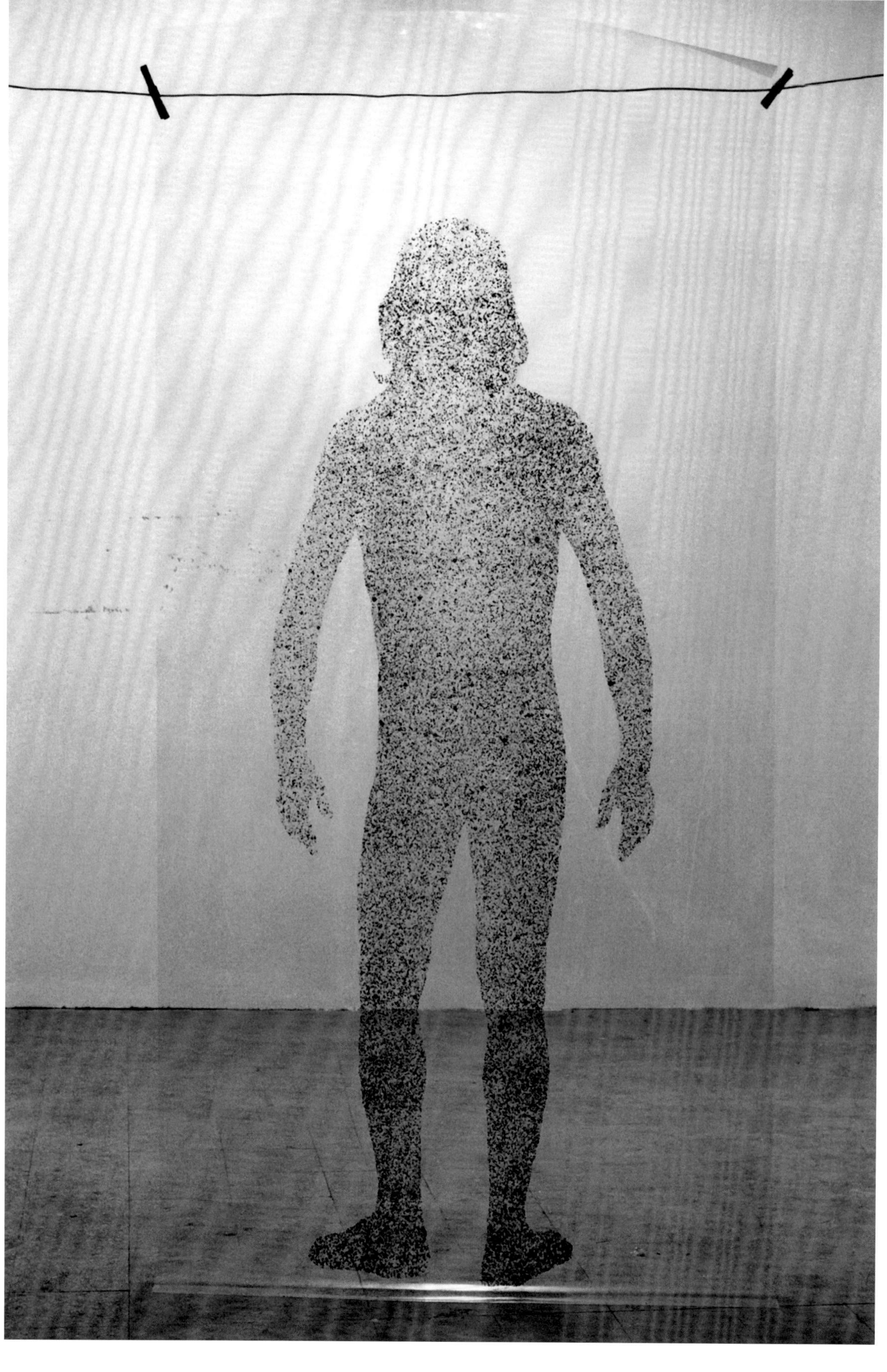

108
Autoritratto di stelle
***(Self-Portrait of Stars)*, 1973**
Photograph on transparent plastic
78¾ x 41$^{5}/_{16}$ inches (200 x 105 cm)
Cittadellarte-Fondazione Pistoletto, Biella

TEXTS BY MICHELANGELO PISTOLETTO

SELECTED BY CARLOS BASUALDO

ON THE ONE HAND
1962

On the one hand the canvas, in the other the mirror—with myself in between. One eye staring at the canvas, the other at the mirror. If you gaze at them intensely enough the objects gradually become superimposed: my mirror portrait transfers itself onto the canvas while remaining in the mirror, and the canvas transfers itself to the mirror, becoming one with it.

PLEXIGLAS
1964

The beginning and the end of this story is the wall. For it is on the wall that pictures are hung; but mirrors are fixed there too. I believe that man's first real figurative experience is the recognition of his own image in the mirror: the fiction which comes closest to reality. But it is not long before the reflection begins to send back the same unknowns, the same questions, the same problems, as reality itself: unknowns and questions which man is driven to re-propose in the form of pictures.

My first "question" on canvas was the reproduction of my own image: art was only barely accepted as a second reality. For some time my work went ahead intuitively in the attempt to bring closer together the two images—the one offered by the mirror and the one I myself proposed.

The conclusion was the superimposition of the picture directly on the mirror image.

The figurative object born of this action allows me to pursue my inquiry within the picture as within life, given that the two entities are figuratively connected. I do indeed find myself inside the picture, beyond the wall which is perforated (though not, of course, in a material sense) by the mirror. On the contrary, since I cannot enter it physically, if I am to inquire into the structure of art I must make the picture move outward into reality, creating the "fiction" of being myself beyond the mirror.

At the present time it is easy to play on the identity between reality-object and the art-object. A "thing" is not art: but the idea expressed by the same "thing" may be. Aesthetics and reality may be mutually identified; but each remains within its own autonomous life. The one cannot replace the other unless one or the other gives up its need to exist. This is why I wish to conclude this presentation of my work by returning ideally to the wall. For it is on this idea of the wall that we may conveniently "hang" the idea of the picture, and to the latter that we may link the idea of the subject.

For me at this time the "thing" is the structure of figurative expression, which I have accepted as reality. The physical invasion of the picture in the real environment (bringing with it the representation of the mirror) gives me the chance to introduce myself among the broken-down elements of figuration.

THE MINUS OBJECTS
1966

In March 1962 at the Promotrice in Turin I exhibited my first mirror painting, entitled *Il presente* (*The Present*). The figure of a man seemed to come forward, as if alive, in the space of the gallery; but the true protagonist was the relationship of instantaneousness which was created between the spectator, his own reflection, and the painted figure, in an ever-present movement which concentrated the past and the future in itself to such an extent as to cause one to call their very existence into doubt: it was the dimension of time itself. I feel that in my recent works I have entered the mirror and actively penetrated that dimension of time which was merely represented in the mirror paintings. These recent works bear witness to the need to live and act in accordance with this dimension, i.e. in the light of the unrepeatable quality of each instant of time, each place, and thus of each "present" action.

In the introduction I wrote for the exhibition of Plexiglas works at Galleria Sperone in Turin in 1964, I spoke of my intention to bring the meaning of the mirror out into the inhabited space around it. The new dimension of the mirror paintings is revealed by virtue of the simultaneous representation of the three traditional dimensions and of reality in movement, reproduced literally.

All the elements in the picture are of such a degree of reality that the result cannot be a mere hypothesis. The result is real. One has to seek out the point where the three dimensions, and stability and movement, converge—it is to be found in the contour which marks the interface between the silhouettes and the mirror surface. This line is at once immobile, like the silhouette, and mobile, like the background: it is drawn on a planar surface which includes the silhouettes and the background, and is thus the real outline of the two-dimensional figures, given that the background is also tipped up onto a planar surface. The third dimension is revealed in this very line, through the sense of distance which we feel between ourselves, the silhouette, and our own reflected image: all is focused on this line, in fact.

The line, which is partly mobile and partly static, and which is not only one-dimensional but also two- and three-dimensional, is contemporaneity, and is represented in my picture.

What interests me today is the possibility of introducing myself physically into this line of convergence of the four dimensions—as if I could inhabit the space between the silhouette and the mirror background.

One must bear in mind that every place is created by virtue of a movement: to put it another way, every distance is measurable in relation to the speed at which it is covered. In my mirror paintings the dynamic reflection does not create a place, because it only reflects a place which already exists—the static silhouette does no more than re-propose an already existing place. But I can create a place by bringing about a passage between the photograph and the mirror: this place is whole time.

If the film frame could carry out another movement in addition to its interrupted gesture, there would be a new time between the two movements; but this does not come about, so the film frame represents a maximum of slowness. The reflection is simultaneous with the real image—there is no time between a body and its reflection in a mirror: if the reflection occurred an instant before or after the presence of the body, it would be possible to measure the velocity of the image in becoming a reflection, but this does not happen. In the case of a mirror the image is so fast as to be body and reflection simultaneously, thus representing a maximum of speed.

In the distance-in-time between the film frame (minimum velocity) and the reflection (maximum velocity), all possible places and all possible times exist. But because the two extremes coincide in the picture, we perceive, simultaneously, the canceling of all created places and times at the moment of their creation. Past and future simply do not come into this process.

All that remains of my action in any given moment are the materials and the language; but if I limit myself to repeating the same action in time, I do not succeed in realizing that meaning of a conclusive instant which is always new and always somehow upset, totally open and yet fixed, as in the action of the mirror paintings; while their meaning suggests actions which are free to manifest themselves in any time and any space. Indeed, my works are not intended to occupy space of time: they begin and end their story in contingency. Just as no space is occupied by the relationship between the silhouette and the mirror (although the entirety of existing time is suggested) so each new work comes about as though it were inside the space between the paper of the film frame and the mirror of the previous pictures.

The artistic act must contain an individual dynamic system. My idea of "actuality" is at the opposite pole from a mere sense of timing, by which in this context I mean an action (even an original, absolutely new action) which is intended to meet society's need for the continuous renewal of the artistic panorama, especially when such a need, otherwise perfectly legitimate, becomes as automatic as a bad habit.

The individual who accepts this automatic mechanism of the social desire for evolution runs the risk of binding himself inextricably to a single moment in time. For whether he reinforces and builds consensus around his idea, or fulfils his desire to be recognizable (and at the same time society's desire to transform everything into a myth), he is forced to repeat himself and to leave topicality to others. If the individual does not encourage in his own system the dynamic side of the transformation and the non-repeatability of each action, he will have to witness topicality working itself out in other hands than his. I have myself seen the actuality of a good number of interesting artistic situations pass, and even if they now have a residual historic value, I cannot help thinking of the grim position of those who at the time were fully involved in the current situation and are now excluded from topicality.

I do not feel able to subscribe to any pre-determined concept of topicality: in the best of cases, any such predetermination dramatizes the present in the tension of breaking with the past and the hope of a fuller realization in the future. What I am interested in is situating my own action outside of time as conventionally defined. It is of no importance to me whether or not a work of mine answers the current general need, but what I strive for in each work is the expression of a real contingent perception, which will anyway always be different from the previous expression. If my action is perpetually authentic, it will not need to be repeated, for its very accomplishment will have effectively exhausted the possibilities it contains.

The relationship with external, social topicality should, however, be implicit, in that it is the combination of the experience of my previous actions and those supplied by external awareness which determines each new perception.

I should like the result to tranquilize rather than dramatize my relationship with the outside world.

My works are not constructions or fabrications of new ideas, any more than they are objects which represent me, intended to be imposed and to impose me on others. Rather, they are objects through whose agency I free myself from something—not constructions, then, but liberations. I do not consider them more but less, not pluses but minuses, in that they bring with them a sense of a perceptual experience which has been definitively manifested once and for all.

According to my idea of time, one must learn how to free oneself from a position even while one is engaged in conquering it. It is perhaps more consistent with reality that others should change it—instead of evolving an opinion on me. I believe that if I act according to the dimension of time, it will be difficult for others to catch me in the exact spot where they are lying in wait.

My idea of evolution is also anti-evolutionary (like walking forward on a moving sidewalk that is going backward). Unlike the mirror paintings, my new objects do not represent: they are. Each individual work is a single word in a discussion which could last a lifetime and which is also a language closed in upon itself. In this sense I tend to consider the duration of my life as a picture which is free for any place.

Every object, from the moment of its creation, can enter into and partake of the inertia of consumed energy without dragging me with it—provided I am already active in another place. The materials are chosen separately each time according to this or that particular perceptual need—for me all materials are suitable, and the idea of modern or less modern does not exist: an object which is extremely complicated from the point of view of materials and ideas can have a primary sense exactly as a very simple object which fulfils an elementary need, as it must be considered as an isolated self-contained unit. One element—such as the mirror in many of my recent works—can be kept constant in a number of objects, provided it is always linked to a diversity of situations, thus taking on a new meaning with each new combination. Other objects may even be determined by a purely practical consumer need, such as the *Structure for Talking while Standing*.

FAMOUS LAST WORDS
1967

Speculation

When a person realizes he has two lives—an abstract one for his mind and a concrete one, also for his mind—he ends up either as a madman, who, out of fear, hides one of his lives and plays the other as a role, or as an artist, who has no fear and who is willing to risk both lives.

Man has always attempted to double himself as a means of attaining self-knowledge. The recognition of one's own image in a pool of water—like recognizing oneself in a mirror—was perhaps one of the first real hallucinations that man experienced. Part of man's mind has always remained attached to that reproduction of himself. With the passage of time, this doubling, this process of duplication, came to be used in ways that were ever more systematic and convincing. The mind created representation on the basis of the reflection of the self; and art has become one form of this representation.

Man began to use reflection as a strategic point for measuring the universe. No longer content with the first hallucination of himself, he convinced himself that he could double the whole universe. This was his way of trying to understand it.

Mathematics was constructed out of the realization that oneself plus another could make two and that oneself minus another was one. In the beginning the lesson was rather brutal. It wasn't simply a matter of what happens today when we hide one of two apples behind our backs to show baby that there is only one. At the beginning "minus one" meant that one of the two was dead—that the beloved mother or father or brother, who when added to the self had made two, was no longer among the living. Thus the experience of life and death was made abstract; addition became a positive sign and subtraction became a negative sign. The complicating intelligence elaborated these signs into multiplications and divisions, creating an increasingly majestic series of hallucinations; and everything in life ordered itself in the mind in terms of two extreme and contrary, positive and negative possibilities.

It seems paradoxical that drugs today should be prohibited when one stops to think that our civilization itself is the fruit of one mammoth mind-shaking hallucination. But perhaps it is feared that drugs constitute a kind of inverse reflection that could dismantle the whole set-up.
Man began to measure the universe in terms of his own direct experience of life and death, then went on to the great task of creating good and evil. In the light of the day he said "white" and in the darkness of the night he said "black." And always remaining at the center of things he created perspective. The world was seen in terms of vanishing points and points of view with respect to the position of man's eye at about five feet above ground level, and from that point he created high and low.
Past and future, near and distant, profound and superficial, true and false, single and multiple, subjective and objective, static and dynamic. These are a few examples of the complex of antinomies that has grown up around the human being as the fruit of his mind. In constant expansion, the process began with the first man who walked the earth, and it has continued until today. The world that we daily inhabit both physically and mentally is made up of the conflict between the two extreme halves of every proposition and every judgment.
When my need to understand things came to include the consideration of life itself, I instinctively understood all of the conflicts in the system of doubling all things of the universe. Looking at works of art, I felt the force with which I was compelled to oscillate between one dimension of experience that was abstract and mental and another dimension of experience that was concrete and physical. And it was in the fact of representation that I discovered the poles that were in simultaneous attraction and repulsion—my literal presence as proposed by the mirror, and my intellectual presence as proposed by my painting. These two presences of myself were the two lives that were simultaneously tearing me in two and calling me with urgency to the task of their unification.
When I first began to paint, the art of the avant-garde was abstract. It was directing its attention only to the second life—the reflected life. This reflected life seemed to have become so true as to convince us that it was now the only life that was livable. And Pollock had truly attempted to live it. In every moment and with all of the will of living, his every gesture violently transferred itself to the canvas—and to such an extent that he no longer knew what to do with physical life. Not even madness could save him, since, as an artist, he was incapable of play-acting. There was nothing left but death.
My way of risking both of my two lives has been to superimpose my painted image upon my reflected image. By becoming one single thing, my two "characters" have ceased acting out the drama of the death of one of them for the benefit of the other. And thus, being and non-being, question and answer, doubt and certainty, and all of the other antinomies have unified their terms into one single element. The culture projected by

the mirror is thrown back upon the mirror and we stand in front of a new hallucination—the hallucination of reflection in reverse. The entire system of representation has been flipped over—like turning a sleeve inside out. By means of the arc of reverberations that is literally pertinent to these paintings (the abstract reflected by life, and life reflected by the abstract), the system has arrived at a reflection of itself, like a dog that chases its own tail. The experience that these paintings offer is that of finding oneself in a vehicle of extraordinary speed that is capable in a single instant of making a round trip from today to the remotest past and back again.

Being

The purpose and result of my mirror paintings was to carry art to the edges of life in order to verify the entire system in which both of them function. After this, there remains only one choice. On one hand there is the possibility of a monstrous involution and a return into the system of doubling and conflict; on the other hand there is the possibility of revolution and leaving the system altogether. One can bring life to art, as Pollock did, or one can choose to bring art into life—but no longer in terms of metaphor.

I don't want to talk, now, about my new works one at a time. Because they are each different from the other, that would require numerous descriptions of the various contingent factors and motivations that went into their making. I want to talk about the vision that I have had as a result of the mirror paintings since 1964.

Some time ago, I wrote this sentence on the wall of my studio: "One must prepare oneself for being." My every action is in this direction. Nothing is more opposed to being than the beloved ambiguity of art. The ambiguity of art is simply a matter of putting two things in relationship in order to observe the representation of their conflict; it's what the Romans were doing when they put the lions and the Christians in the arena so as to be able to enjoy the spectacle. The discovery that flint can make fire is a very primitive hallucination, and a new civilization cannot be organized by using the two halves of man's mind like two pieces of flint. There must be no spark between the two things—no spark between us and ourselves. If we remain suspended between ourselves and our representation, we ourselves are the spark and the conflict.

The error was all a matter of giving two functions to the intellect. The intellect is capable of raising questions, but it can't give answers. Nonetheless, we have always attempted to make it give answers, as if the middle of the day could create the heart of night, or vice versa. The day and the night follow upon one another, but they are two separate things with two different natures. We believed that day and night, life and death, were a single thing with two possibilities, that the intellect was a single thing with two possibilities. Yes, the intellect is a single thing, but it has only one possibility. If the intellect raises the questions, we must outflank it, step to one side, and use another mechanism for the answers. The intellect now is frustrated since it has continuously failed to do two tasks, and the other mechanisms have atrophied.

In my new work, every piece grows out of an immediate stimulus of the intellect, but the pieces in no way function as definitions, justifications, or answers. They do not represent me. Each successive work or action is the product of the contingent and isolated intellectual or perceptual stimulus that belongs to one moment only. After every action, I step to one side, and proceed in a direction different from the direction formulated by my object, since I refuse to accept it as an answer. Predetermined directions are contrary to man's liberty. To predetermine something means to make a commitment for tomorrow; it means that tomorrow I will no longer be free. To adhere to a predetermined idea means to reflect oneself in the past and to deprive oneself of free will. Unity of language must be predetermined and it demands that we adhere to it. To believe in one's own language means to play one's own role. Languages are posited as fictions between us and the others in the midst of a mass of individuals who play-act themselves and who are always ready to be manipulated by the directors. There are certain people of extraordinary intelligence who are frustrated by some kind of a personal complex or another, and they have turned themselves into theatrical characters on the basis of it, they believe in the character so thoroughly that they presume to make even the others play it. These are society's directors—the ones who send the actors to kill and be killed by the evil that they, they directors, have perceived in themselves. And all of this happens when it would have been sufficient to take a little step to one side, proceed on one's own way and abandon the complexes without instrumentalizing them.

The way I move now is by stepping to one side. Every piece I make is a liberation and not a construction that is intended to represent me. I am not reflected in them, and the others cannot reflect upon me by means of them. Every piece I make is destined to proceed on its own way by itself without dragging me along behind it, since I am already somewhere else and doing something different. There is no longer any sense in the problem of being up to date in form. The problem is not to change the forms and leave the system intact, but rather to take the forms, intact, out of the system. In order to do this it's necessary to be absolutely free. And worrying about whether or not the forms are up to date means not being free to consider the forms of the past. And as we do not yet possess the forms of the future, liberty within the system means liberty to do only one thing.

As far as I am concerned, there are no such things as forms that are more or less up to date. All forms, materials, ideas, and means are available and to be used. Walking by means of stepping to one side takes us out of the system that goes straight ahead. There is no goal before us with laurels for the first to arrive and ashes for the last. The wild race for this abstract point structures itself into a system of battles between both individuals and masses. When we move ahead by stepping to one side, the race between individuals becomes a series of parallels, as every individual proceeds individually, without projecting himself out of himself onto abstract points or onto other individuals. When we move in this way there are no such things as the better and the worse, as everybody is what he is and does what he does. Nobody has a need to pretend in order to prove that he is the better, and communication becomes very easy without the structures of language, as it is easy to understand who everybody is and what he is like. By communication and understanding, we will finally be able to develop all of the possibilities of the mechanism of perception.

BETWEEN
1968

I am interested in the passage between objects more than in the objects themselves. I am interested in the perceptive faculty, in the sensitization of the individual.

Objects, the state of things, human movements accepted in their conventional appearance, do not contribute in any way to the profound stimulus of man, the full use of his cerebral capacities.

The passage continues from one thing to another without any perception of the deep gulf between the two—or the gulf which separates two moments, mingles and confounds the perceptive faculties. Life becomes like a sea, gray with pollution, colorless and shallow.

The vice of considering things only in their fullness does not leave us enough time to consider that in actual fact we can only circulate in the physical channels which are left open to us by objects. We move around a room, amid a variety of objects, along paths which are conventional or in some way vitiated because we consider only the presence of the objects and not the empty space in which we actually live. For example, two individuals live and move considering as real their own bodies, instead of the bodiless space which lies between them; yet it is only in this space that they can really meet and communicate.

The active experience of life lived in empty space began with an exhibition in my studio in the spring of 1966.

In the objects shown I abolish the continuity that derives from a personal style. Each object was defined materially and mentally by the contingency of its execution. My effective, unitary presence was manifested not in the space and time of the objects, but in the invisibility of their non-presence. The absence of any apparent link between these objects was a demonstration of the will to feel and experience the distance between them. The works

which followed this exhibition—such as the show at L'Attico in Rome or at Galleria Sperone in Turin—are really deconditioning environments. They are like decompression chambers for sensitizing the moment of passage from one state to another: like the airlocks in a spaceship.
During the exhibition at L'Attico (the most recent) ten people accepted my invitation to enter the decompression chamber.
The jointly executed ten films were created in a space which was halfway between me and each of these ten people. The real meaning of each film is creation in empty space (the space between two people). As far as the exhibition is concerned, for me it became more than a mere one-man show; for others it offered an opportunity to penetrate actively into a precluded space.

THE GOLD MONUMENT
1968

By the time I reached Almafi, all the space available in the vast underground hall was already occupied by the works of the artists who had been invited. I hadn't been in a hurry, and indeed there was no problem; for there was, at the very back, a space left for those who sent objects to put in the show—a completely useless space, already occupied by some Roman remains.
It so happened that I had brought with me (together with the sacks, old shoes, and so on needed for the spectacle entitled *L'Uomo ammaestrato*) two bales of rags.
These rags took to the ruins like ducks to water, immediately recognizing them as comrades in misfortune—indeed, sensing the noble origins of the ruins, the rags even felt somewhat ennobled by their new job. Then there was that ball I had taken for walks around the streets before eventually selling it to Rumma (the organizer of the festival)—I had encaged it in welded iron-rod meridians and parallels.
And now it was rolling around somewhat heavily—the fault of the weight of all that culture. Anyway, Rumma had already sent it there.
I had made another small monument to add to the Roman ones, using a handful of bricks, rags and a broken shoe. But, because of a sort of premonition, I had encircled it with insecticide, as if to protect it against attacks from insects.
When I returned, after spending a few hours in the hotel, I saw the monument had disappeared; it was not the work of insects, but of my artist friends who were playing ball, having moved from the more comfortable square where they had previously played down to the more limited space of the exhibition. I didn't say a word, but the actor Carlo Colnaghi, a member of Lo Zoo, began to argue that if one can move the

work of an artist to play ball, then one can also move an actor while he's at work, simply to play ball. I still didn't say a word, for the space and the little monument I had made were no problem of mine: what counted was the experience.
If the monument had been made of gold they would have gone off to play ball somewhere else.

THE MINUS MAN

The Unbearable Side

Preface

On December 15, 1969, in Catania, I bought a notepad of 365 pages, as many pages as there are days in the year, bound in brown leather on which were impressed the initials V.I.P. I paid 6,000 liras for it. I decided to fill the 365 pages in a month without second thoughts, that is, in the final draft from the beginning.
The need to write a book was a question of contingency as are all the other works and actions I have done.
The reasons and motives behind this book are part of the text itself.
The book, the person who writes it, and the one who reads it are sensitive strings of this instrument.
You could say it's a story with three protagonists, a writer, a book, and a reader. Among these characters are intertwined: poetry, art, economics, madness, prose, the nervous system, rhythm, and surprise just like in real literary work.
I Pistoletto am not a specialist but in 1967 I wrote also "Famous Last Words".
I was born in Biella in 1933.
I live in Turin.
I have experience in making dentures, cultivating fields, designing ads, restoring paintings, marriage, painting, cinema, theater, and literature.

Writing is good for accomplishing all those things that for some reason can't be accomplished (explain fully) it's good for fixing thought, an active or creative need (there is no light without something for it to fall on or to put it another way light suffers if there is no place for it to fall and make itself manifest). The dream was of a book, at least the part I'm able to remember—with that slight distortion that comes from translating it into a waking image. A book measuring 40 x 60 cm I think made entirely by hand by cutting columns out of the newspaper: I broke it off because I had direct dealings with the waiter who brought me bread and salami and talked to me.
Dog collection.
Teatrino Taormina.
My mother used to tell me . . . no, we give some serious thought to beginning this book.

PAUSE

Look up.

Think about whether or not to read this book, maybe you have something better to do.

Take a moment to think.

Think it over.

If you truly decide to go on reading, don't expect anything from me, I have absolutely nothing to do with the present you're living in.

(Don't confuse the game with the player.)

Do you want to go on reading? If you do, you have to do the exercises I tell you to do. If you don't you're a pig, a bastard, a turd.

Personally, I don't read, I almost never read anything, I never want to. One day with an air of defiance I told a person who evidently wanted to test my culture and asked me if I had read some book or another: I don't read, I write.

Now pay attention, don't let your mind wander, don't think of anything else, think only, exclusively of the words you're about to read.

Don't think of these words, think of the ones you'll read in the next few lines. The words you're reading now are important, very important, the words you'll read in a little while are decisive for you.

Watch out, they're waiting for you, waiting inexorably for you, so be careful. You can still escape from the words that are waiting for you, I'm warning you think it over don't go on if you're not absolutely sure you have to, it's at your own risk, don't do it, on the contrary forget it, relax, the words you'll read are very important for you because if you read them they'll be words that you've absolutely decided to read.

Put the book down, start walking and get as far away as you can and come back only when you can't help it, when you can't do anything else.

Look really you can't get out of doing this if you try it's no use reading further.

My mother taught me that a real gentleman always has shiny shoes. Nowadays everyone has shiny shoes. All the asphalted, paved streets are a carpet for people. In the old days the poor wretched workers and peasants went around on foot and the roads were made of dust and mud. Gentlemen traveled in carriages and got out and walked up to their mansions on carpets.

If you want to know more—this is optional—you can go up to the maître of some fancy Hotel, one of those hotels in which you think you'll set foot one day if you get really rich, one of those refined expensive superluxurious hotels. Those who habitually stay in such places are dispensed from this exercise. Ask the maître d' if he can still tell a real gentleman by his shoes and then, since they're all shiny nowadays, what attribute the shoe of a gentleman must have, according to his experience.

PAUSE

Look slowly all around, very slowly, and try to discover a truly useless object.

I write because it's a way of accomplishing things. Writing helps me accomplish right away all the things I can't accomplish otherwise because it's too hard or impossible or better not to accomplish them. Let me explain: there's something I've enjoyed thinking about from time to time. A collection of majolica dogs. I'm writing a book above all because it's a means that's been given to me to use right this moment. I was saying, a collection of majolica dogs, more or less life-size or even bigger, but lots and lots of dogs of all kinds and all colors, standing, sitting or crouching or lying down. Enough dogs to cover the floor of every room of an entire castle leaving only room enough to walk all around each dog. This could be the goal of a lifetime, I thought, it could be my goal.
What do I have to do to get started? I have enough money to buy those two dogs I saw in an antique shop in via dei Coronari in Rome and even for this dog here, but I have to go to work and make money, make a lot of money, stash it away to buy the castle and have it cleaned from top to bottom and then start to pile up money to buy the dogs, to run around the world looking for dogs. I'm writing it down. Just like so many other things; for instance there are things that have never been done even if they're just the opposite of the thing of the dogs, which for the time being isn't costing me anything except the time to write about it.
There are things that have never been accomplished even if we've worked many months on them, for instance the stage version of *The Minus Man*. Maybe for me this is the way to accomplish it no matter what. I don't feel like talking about it now but I absolutely must talk about it, in fact it's exactly because of the desire to talk about this, to give reason and meaning to my life somehow after this unaccomplished play that I jumped at the opportunity to write a book. But I'll talk about that later.

. . .

Title of the book *The Minus Man* an unbearable side. Yes, because there is an unbearable side that is the height of immediacy. Last night's nightclub made me think of that kind of writing or painting or theater or music in which all the phenomena of life, the scenes, words, colors, and sounds, are plundered and recorded in the most minute detail. Attitudes, psychological relationships, all to be exploited in a faithful reproduction. This makes traditional writing, painting painting, narrative theater, music composed on tried-and-true notes, unbearable for me.
Our western civilization's tendency toward reproduction, the tendency to find interest and peace in the mechanical ability to reproduce a phenomenon with the means of the intellect has lost its power to stimulate.
People like us have perfected this system of reproduction by building machines that carry out this task perfectly.

. . .

I'm writing.

And I wrote: a man dressed in a black cloak comes onto the scene. With a piece of chalk he has in his hand he draws a large circle on the ground. The others come onto the stage, they line up along the radius of the circle in a starting position, then they each trace a circle of their own inside the larger one, each person with his own chalk. But they all try to complete the circle before the others, as in a race.

The first to finish wins.

All the others jump on him and beat him up, there's a big brawl. Then everybody goes to sleep and the winner remains where he is stretched out on the ground.

While the others sleep he gets up and performs an individual action of his own, until the others get up and with no memory whatsoever of the earlier event, begin a totally different group action, until one remains stretched out on the ground. Everyone goes to sleep in a line downstage. The new (black) man gets up and performs his individual action until the others get up for a new action or day and so on.

After which we all got together and took off for Corniglia. Lionello Gennero left the group at this point. Lionello was the orchestra conductor with the curly wig and bare feet who played the keys of the dismantled xylophone and threw the balls of tinfoil at me in the "rattibaratti" in Rotterdam. He wasn't happy with the state of dependency in which many members of the group continuously found themselves.

We found ourselves in Corniglia sitting around a table and everybody expressed their views and their ideas for the new play to put on in the fall. It was the beginning of June.

Everybody had their say and I had mine. Everyone felt it was a good idea to do "The minus man."

Everyone found, or if they didn't they didn't express this opinion that the minus man allowed each person to put his own idea in the play. So everyone could be the director of the group action that he liked most and could act freely in every individual action.

I have to apologize but the film of the movie of Corniglia, summer '69, broke and it'll take a while to put it back together again.

. . .

Today there's a possibility of glimpsing an interval in the disease of power. There's a possibility of launching antibodies against the influenza that fogs the vision of the body and breaks the joints. For instance with a little attention an artist can do his little thing. With a little observation he can realize that power is a question of space.

Power is a space occupied by a person or thing.

It can be a famous painter or a thunderstorm, for instance.
The famous painter is a guy who paints little squares, another stupid painter believes that the importance lies in the little squares, so he too starts making little squares. Then he complains that the other guy's fame grows and he's unsuccessful. An artist instead starts drawing little lines, or does the little squares knowing that the power is in his will and doesn't complain.
If I believe that power is occupied by a person I have no space for myself. The art lies in finding the space free. If I believe that power is occupied by a person I automatically give that person the power to occupy my space. This is the goal: to free the space of our power. To liberate our person from the power of another. To liberate our inner space, the space inside our brain.
I don't believe in power, but in my power. You're silly if you believe in my power.
A little antiquity.
Do you still believe in oracles? But oracles didn't make house calls, it was the people who went to the oracles. If nobody ever went to oracles they wouldn't have existed. Can you see an oracle going to another oracle?
A name for a pop band "The Oracles."

. . .

Lo Zoo. Four months in Corniglia.
Meanwhile Carlo was in jail. He wrote us long letters. In October we all went to Fondi to the district prison. We stayed with him for an hour. The others were anxiously silent sitting on the benches and on the steps. Maria and I talked to Carlo. Dennis waved goodbye and left.
He wasn't outside.
He came back in smiling.
Later on, in the car, I was going crazy. Dennis told me: it was horrible to see Carlo in jail, to see us in jail, it occurred to me that we were all in jail. He said: the first thing to do is take "The Zoo" off the van.
In Marcerata the three Americans received an injunction from the police to leave the country because they didn't have the proper papers.
Maybe if you use a microscope to read you'd be able to see what's between the lines a lot better. Or else you could hold the book out at a distance. Ask permission from the people in the apartment in the building across the street, put the book on their windowsill and then go back home and from your window read it with binoculars. What's more it can be a good chance to chat a little with some new people.
Today one has to work scientifically, to study the microcosm and the macrocosm.
The three Americans had to leave Italy and Dennis especially was worried or maybe I'd better say beside himself. A centrifugal force had been

created in the group.
Sorry, I wound the film up backwards. This was the end.

. . .

I had another dream but this time a daydream. It's a village that really exists. The village has a very old tradition. The men are all painted white. They eat, drink, sleep, work, make love, reproduce and play. But all this is of secondary importance. They paint themselves white. They are obsessed by colors, spend their lives defending themselves from colors. For them color is unbearable, it must be eliminated. It is the enemy. They are painted white so they can recognize each other. Whoever is painted white is a real man in this village. Fear lies in color, it's the symbol of danger. They've created deadly instruments and with these they defend themselves from colors. If somebody gets the idea of painting himself some color, he's had it. They get scared to death and react automatically. Of all colors, I'd say the opposite of white, black, is the most terrible for them. Black represents the void, chaos, terror, death.
The white man is determined, if he's not able to paint the inhabitants of other villages white he kills them and he sacrifices his own life to defend white which is against death. Saint Silvester's Eve. The high command has declared the final and total war for the destruction of all colors.
Long live absolute white. Hurrah.
I'm a living example of survival. Yesterday I said to Mike: The State should replace the draft with an obligation of community life, that is, instead of going into the army one should go and stay for the same period of time in an experimental community. He replied: yes, I did both things, my horoscope tells me that those born under my sign always end up falling into some organization of that sort, the army, hospitals, or prisons.
Maybe we didn't understand each other.

. . .

I didn't choose the rags and cloths because they're poor, I chose them because they're beautiful, like sounds, but maybe there's someone who believes rags are good only for dressing the poor. They believe that if a person is dressed in rags he's poor. Then we must consider that poverty is . . . but excuse me I was speaking of rags, because there is dialectic and then if a person doesn't give meaning to rags he's had it because he doesn't know what meaning to give to gold. It's all a game, one sells rags to buy gold and one sells gold to buy rags, but both are good subjects for a novel.

. . .

The exercises in *The Minus Man* lasted four months. When everybody had worked out their own piece and their own part, at the first rehearsals, each entered into the character of the minus man.
I wrote a nice piece, I mean a long piece on those four months in Corniglia and on the work *The Minus Man* but not here, I wrote it in the white notebook, I'm very embarrassed to discuss it here, it's too delicate, I can't talk about the life of other people even if it was life in common, I can't decide for the others that way, I can't carry out *The Minus Man* here alone in spite of everything and everyone. The phenomena should be isolated from every possibility of judgment on people but this is difficult when speaking of the people themselves and it could be very bad for others to feel themselves placed at the mercy of just any reader. Maybe I'll succeed in discussing the phenomenon without describing the people and the facts. Right now I'm meeting the two extremes of unbearableness.
On one hand the necessity to tell the whole story in detail, which would become a speculation on what happened, a story of tactless reproduction that I couldn't bear and on the other the necessity to express the sense of unbearableness that arose from *The Minus Man* facing pure contingency and immediacy.
People struggle between the too old and the too new and even this state let's say in the middle, neither too old nor too new, has something.
We can make speculation unscrupulous like in politics when the right wing starts to look progressive. Or make impulsiveness into a system like when the extreme left in politics becomes fascism. Or else consider as secure the space that lies between the two extremes and struggle like the parties in the center, between left and right. On the other hand in politics the center is unbearable for the opposite sides. I really think it's a closed circle, like the one the minus man traced on the ground with chalk, every point of which is unbearable. Maybe this circle is the sense of the prison that Dennis had perceived in Fondi. The circle of unbearableness, of politics, in which every point is in contradiction with itself and with other points. This book is my circle, my contradiction. My liberation and my prison. People compelled to trace their own circle inside the larger one compelled to build their own prison, to make themselves a little community to escape from the prison of the large community to find themselves only seeing a condensed version of phenomena that perhaps escaped them before.
But does it still end up the same way?
Maybe the centrifugal force that flung us out of Lo Zoo creates a more convenient I'd say more comic design.

. . .

Art, what is art.
Nothing bad has ever been done in the name of art.

Art is the science closest to man. Man makes mistakes, he can't help making mistakes, his very energetic charge leads him to err, but art allows him to free himself from his errors, to understand them and to want a better state.
Bill is American he never leaves his saxophone case, not even when he stops at the autogrill along the freeway for a cup of coffee. One evening when I was very melancholy, Bill hugged the case that contained his saxophone, we were sitting in a trattoria, and then he told me: if I didn't have this saxophone I wouldn't be here. Right now I'd be in Vietnam carrying a machine-gun. It is thanks to the discovery of art. He's twenty-one and knows all the modern artists, he saw my works before seeing me. "It is thanks to the discovery of art," he told me, "that I saved myself from violence and war."

. . .

But the circle comes alive and burns for those people who realize the unbearableness of every point. For these people the circle becomes a centrifugal force. They take action to escape from it. Over the four months in Corniglia the game of minus man became a circular situation. The freedom of each person was closed in the circle of a freedom organized for everyone, by turns. What does someone do when it isn't his turn to be free? He isn't free.
And there were twelve of us. Each person got a moment of freedom in every twelve. Think of how many of us there are on the earth and what percentage of freedom remains.
Then there was the freedom of one's own turn that entered into a circle of repetition of actions, that became the performance of one's own freedom in a possible play.
The opening scene of the minus man marking out the circle and all the others inside the circle become participants in a competition, planned in advance, that ends with a revolt and the lynching of the winner and then everyone goes to sleep powerless because in the circle of the game there'll be another minus man, immediately afterward while one sleeps, even if the person will always be new and different it'll be the idea that lives again in dream, in the unconscious of the company.
I was saying all this was symbolic, but so close to reality as to bring out in four months of work all the unbearableness of the circular system. I think we all understood that.
Because when Dennis became the minus man for a week he didn't mark out a circle on the floor, but a spiral.
The Spiral expands its points from the center outward and suggests a centrifugal motion.

. . .

And if we are illiterate, we don't have a common language, we've only had fear in common never another voice. Just one word is a bit too late. These words I'm writing are many but they have just one meaning. Fear. If you open yourself you get a punch in the stomach. If you give a hungry person something to eat you give him the strength to bust your nose. We have to keep ourselves from being together. If we come together it's only to exterminate another race. We proved it with the crusades, with Naziism, and we're continually proving it.
Maybe I should start painting I have to think of becoming a real painter I have to lock the door and take this canvas hundreds of years thick and put it back on the wall. Opaque deaf like an impenetrable barrier, without wondering anymore what's behind it, not to think about it. That there's a closed door behind it. I have to take these paints thickened and dried by thousands of years, scrape off a bit of crust to make a powder, dilute it in a little water, add some glue and spread these paints over the canvas.

. . .

How much money do you have? Do you have a lot? Lots and lots of money? Who knows how much money you have, I think you have a whole lot of money. I'm sure you have so much money, you possess money and money and more money and cash and money and lots of money, cash, lots of cash, you have lots of cash, you have cash, cash, you have wealth, a lot of money. Honey I love and adore you.
How many things do you possess? How many things do you have to lose? What are the things you have to reproach others for? What are the things the others have to reproach you for? Do you think there's somebody that wants to hurt you? I don't think so, nobody wants to hurt you, everyone is good and kind to you, aren't they? Then you don't have anything to lose do you? Oh I knew it. Cause for those who hurt others there are prisons, society is well organized, there's justice, you're not in prison so you don't do anything wrong, you've never done anything wrong, otherwise you'd be in jail. You have a clean conscience, security, tranquility, you live in peace. Then you're a little smarter than the others and you always manage fairly well. I like that. If that's really the way it is I think you must really like it.
I know the semantics of the future. Here we live the unbearable. We have to find a peaceful relationship with forms this is the medicine.
We have to find a peaceful relationship with forms
we have to find a peaceful relationship with forms
we have to find a peaceful relationship with forms
we have to find a peaceful relationship with forms

. . .

There were eight of us. At the bar Maria heard that somebody had to move boxes and couldn't find a porter to do it. How much are you paying? says Maria. Three thousand liras, there's a full day of work, eight hours for a laborer, says the bartender.
Where are the boxes? says Maria. They're over there, says the other pointing to a mountain of crates. We'll do it replies Maria. An hour later the boxes had reached their destination. Moral: a single man moves boxes all day (8 hours) earns three thousand liras that he spends the next day for his essential needs: eating sleeping and dressing. Eight people in an hour do the same job. For eight people that eat together three thousand liras are enough to live a day on. What can these eight people do for the remaining seven hours? Whatever they want.
So don't tell me the experience of a small community is worthless.
It's true it reproduces the defects of the large community but there's also the possibility of finding some solutions to them. But the solutions at this point can't be seen by one person only everybody has to see them everybody has to feel they're necessary otherwise you don't get anywhere. Everybody works too much because they don't know what the essential is and what the sacred superfluous is.
The economy in our civilization is the most disorganized thing that exists. Ditto the mental economy of one's own individual time.
Everyone is a victim of it, industrialists and laborers, statesmen policemen and artists. Now let me tell you one of my almost daydreams. A company of young people gets together to do some theater. But not traditional theater, to do living, directly creative dramas.
This company has on hand, by virtue of past circumstances, a sum of money that allows them to be self-sufficient for a fairly long time.
The group moves to a small village where there's a house available where they can rehearse and work creatively. The group appears in the village in a way that's definitely a little strange for the eyes of the inhabitants used to a closed and provincial tradition.
The new arrivals are suspicious characters, dressed a little crazily, the beards, the hair, strange costumes, trunks, canvas duffle bags, musical instruments.
Day after day the group goes around playing music amid the olive trees eating pizza in the square buying cigarettes swimming in the sea. There are only a few tourists but they're different from the tourists.
The tourists bring some money but they also bring another atmosphere, they bring the fascination of the big city, of industry, the sense of comfort of accommodations cleaned with who knows what miraculous appliances. The money, the smooth made-up skin the beautiful clothing of the department stores full of light of the shops with kind clerks, the movie-houses the luxurious theaters music, the choice of the good and the beautiful, security.

But at night only the young people of the village stay for hours seated at the tables left in the center of the square by the bar that closed a while ago. One sees the group of young people who speak in small groups around the chairs and tables, softly in order not to wake people. It's summer, even the young people that have just arrived wander still between the woods and the square. Someone in the group of artists says hello to the kids sitting around in passing, while another comes over and asks to sit down with them.
Every night's the same. When it's not too late the young people of the village and the others form a circle around the artists who play some music on their guitars and sing some songs, then give a somewhat strange concert. The people pay attention don't make comments then still another evening the artists find themselves sitting around with the young people and talking together well into the night.
The local kids, curious, ask questions, are polite. Then they talk about themselves about their problems like all the other evenings about politics and work. One talks about the wine the good wine of the place, the effort of making it. The young people say: twenty years ago the hill was one big vineyard, well kept. But it was a dog's life keeping it up then the vegetable gardens and then going up into the mountains, there were cows and sheep, they made milk and cheese there are chestnut groves and olive trees, thousands of olive trees, the harvest. The oil made here is scented. But now only the old people cultivate the earth and they're tired, they keep doing it for tradition's sake but there are no more cows, little oil is made and the vineyards are largely abandoned. Even the old people are tired. They don't want to work like that anymore. In ten years they say nobody will work the land here. None of us young people wants to go farm, everything's going to ruin. Then the political discussions, on the parties, on the factories, on the possibilities of finding work.
"There's no room for us, already in town here at the arsenal the old people live in the fear that that little will be taken away from them from one moment to the next because there's less and less work. We young people study and we really want to work but it's hard too hard to fit in, we want to fit into society but the possibility doesn't exist for us, it's terribly hard to enter into and work society."
Every day the group of artists rehearses in the square behind the church, the women the children the old people, every day invariably are seated on the steps to watch the daily drama, toward evening the spectators are joined by the young people who come back from town or from fishing and the men who have finished work.
Then a little more chatting in the street or at the café or in the grocery store. Some local kid becomes particularly close to someone in the group and shows special attention and interest for this strange society that seems to have problems so different from those to which they are tied. Little by little these young people begin to see in the group almost an

alternative to that society which while attracting them doesn't allow them any possibility to fit in. This one they have before their eyes is also a kind of society, but it appears more carefree, with fewer problems and fewer demands.

At the evening meetings less and less talk centers on politics, a different atmosphere, a different understanding is slowly established. A young villager by this time passes much of his time, when he doesn't have to study or help his father, with the group, brings a few flasks of wine, helps out with some job.

The group decides to give up the idea of touring with their plays and to remain in the village to realize a kind of life different from that of fitting into the windmill of the alienating machine of consumption. Corresponding with the theaters becomes an absurd task for those of the group. Paper that goes, paper that comes, bureaucratic relations, dates fixed in advance, negotiating prices, calculating expenses, always greater than the expected earnings. Relations with the world, cold, mediated, difficult. The village boy is a witness, he hears sees participates. The group decides not to go away, to stay, after all the works can be performed in the square, the spectators are certainly no less noble than those of any theater in any city and the encounter is in any case more direct more true, more immediate.

The problem of surviving in that place arises. One of the group one morning gets out of bed and makes some proposals to the others, the proposals are taken into consideration and steps are taken to carry them out. The group speaks to the boy from the village: you own a lot of land, we don't possess any land. Or better yet, your father has some land, for him it's hard to work it as it is for you, so a lot of the land goes unfarmed. We'll work your land with you one day a week and you can go on doing what you want, study or whatever and we'll live together on the harvest. As a beginning we'll go and do a few days all together to live until the first harvest. But it wasn't necessary to do this, to work by the day, because a little later, when the village folk saw that somebody really wanted to work that land everybody began to bring something to the kids in the group and other young people joined them to work the land and shifts were set up. Those who worked Monday let the others work Tuesday, ten each day and every day the same amount of work was accomplished that a farmer would have taken ten days to do. In a short time the life of the village had changed a new force animated the young people and the women. The older men were happy to see their land flourish once more and let their children and the others work in accordance with their expert advice. A pioneer atmosphere, a consciousness in this sense vibrated in the air every day it seemed that these people had come to a virgin land like the pioneers of the United States of America. In the village there was theater, music, some studied some read some wrote and parties began for everybody at night and on sunny days, some made instruments, some painted, some laid

bricks, some built objects, furniture, each according to his own aptitude, and the idea came up to use what money there was to buy cows and sheep for the following years, everyone without realizing it became proprietors of all the land because the labor and the food were shared.
But often dreams repeat themselves and have different endings.
In the last few days I dreamed the same dream again, exactly the same up to the point in which the group came to consider the absurd job of the correspondence, written paper that goes, written paper that comes, bureaucratic relations, dates made weeks ahead of time, negotiations for prices, calculations of expenses always greater than the expected earnings, relations with the world cold mediated difficult. At this point the group decided to leave immediately and to try to work wherever they could, without advance organization, taking advantage of whatever possibilities presented themselves. The majority felt the need to leave to have new experiences, see new people different places meet women. When the group left the village appeared deserted.
The grindstone of society swallowed up the group which disappeared in the crowd.

. . .

You always expect everything of me, you want me to teach you, to stimulate you, to help you and then if I don't do what you want you kick me in the teeth. But get out, get away from me. I'm not going to talk to you about love because it bores me, all we do is talk about it. Words, words only and always words: uniforms with braids on the cap or braids in uniform. Wash my feet slave and I'll even give you a tip. Yes, I'll give you a tip that's more than everything you own. What do you want. I don't have anything for you, this is literature.
Why couldn't I do my work in Venice, you stupid jerk, because you didn't understand a thing. I'm an artist, goddammit, haven't you understood that yet? I wanted to make poetry in Venice with my friends, not show my handsome face not challenge the old sclerotics or protest against the protesters. I don't have anything to protest about, protesting disgusts me, the only thing that didn't disgust me was the freedom to create, to fly in poetry, but no, I couldn't do that. With me was a gang of artists, poor penniless, where were we all going to stay in Venice when in addition to everything else all the hotels were booked? So then we wanted to go sleep during the day in the room that by George they'd placed at my disposal. The visitors would have seen living sculptures, wouldn't they? Us as we slept, and then in the evening, when they closed the gates we'd go around the town and all night we'd do small poetic things, small sculptures or paintings, to leave on the doors or on the windows of the houses, so the Venetians in the morning would have a little poetic gift and would have felt the pleasure a child feels when he wakes up on Christmas morning and

finds a present on the edge of his bed or under the tree. But what do you want? If we'd gone up to the gates with our sleeping bags they would have thought we wanted to take advantage of my room to occupy the Biennale. Because there were all those people who wanted to occupy it. So we gave up.
The police called me yesterday to charge me with giving hospitality to three Americans without reporting their presence in my house to headquarters within twenty-four hours of their arrival.

. . .

Metaphorically Lo Zoo signified the state or prison in which man the animal finds himself today when he realized his vital needs for creative expansion. The need to start out from an exhibition hall to go out into the open and set down his own creations is still a metaphor and an exercise at the same time in liberating primary human needs. The superstructures exist, and how, but an artist doesn't try to attack them, he simply tries to free himself from them. The task is a very delicate one can't go at it heavy handedly and run the risk of losing the essential, losing the space for poetry. Be more artistic in your politics and more political in your art.
But don't get me wrong again, I'm not talking about party politics, guerrilla warfare, power or protest, I'm talking about politics in the deep sense, that is, one of the economy of relations between human needs and the things that condition them.

. . .

I mean there's always time to start everything all over again.
To bear well in mind that the Minusman must never be the protagonist of a possible staging of this volume.
He's to be represented as a little puppet that lives in the pocket of one character after another, maybe once by mistake he can fall out of the pocket while a character takes out his handkerchief to blow his nose with a roar.
That's all. On the playbill he mustn't be mixed up with the other actors, uh-uh. His name has to appear far away from the others.
There must be the name of the work at the top then the name of the theater then the date the street the city and the telephone. Below, the list of actors flanked by the characters they play, then further below the prices of the seats: front stalls, rear stalls, first tier boxes, second tier boxes, gallery and entrances. Then below everything in fine print but not too fine: with the participation of the Minusman.
In short the Minusman is something to be kept in a pocket. Don't be led into hanging him on the rearview mirror of your car or using him as a keychain, at most you can touch him when you're afraid, like people touch

iron, also because it's becoming more and more difficult to touch iron, it can be steel or aluminum and even plated, or it can actually be plastic disguised as metal. And then if it's iron there's the risk that it's painted with some cunning substance that takes away all its effect. By contrast with the little black man you have in your pocket you can touch safely and not have to worry.

. . .

The minus man has gone away, by himself, he didn't have anything left to do or say. But if you listen to me I'll speak. Now there are serious people around doing serious things, people doing jobs they know how to do. Done right, well finished useful for all. In the stupendous madness that arises. The moons of the future. A gang of artists. The meetings didn't fail. The meetings are being born tomorrow we'll be calm. Do you think languages are changing? Look at the light. A gesture a movement, a sound, a grimace. The increasingly live irony waits a moment. I'm an optimist at this point, it can't go wrong anymore. If you think it's going wrong it's an illusion you'll get over. I know people want to be well. They're still a little silly shy a little timid. But the world at this point has changed, all we can do is go ahead. This is what I believe, I'm not sad anymore I understand that everything's going to be alright. Believe me I'm sincere. I'm convinced that everything will be okay I have faith I have faith in you in your madness. White man I'm talking to you, black man I'm listening, blue man I'm watching you, in your double-breasted jacket, in gray. Hippies. Gagà. Soubrettes, sidewalk cigarette vendors who dream of a job with Fiat, all will love our madness and theirs. We'll bring the peasants our madness in movies, in dances, we'll put on serious dramas at the fair. The gendarmes will be men. Buses will still be buses. The police will still be police. But on the trolleycars and buses will travel men with more imagination and the bus-drivers will come to see our movies, they'll visit our exhibitions, buy our collages, multiples, posters. The bus-drivers will build hot-air balloons and will give light shows for their children. It won't be Carnival all year round, but something magic. Choose to open the car-door for the well-dressed gentleman. The ragamuffin bows. The gentleman in the double-breasted suit, a dignified gesture, the wind sweeps away his hat, lets the hat go by itself.

. . .

Sterility is the most serious illness of our time. What does a rich person who buys an artwork today think he's doing? Unfortunately every work of art that one brings home is a trinket. It's not the thought of today's man. The time has come to put our money to work in the right way.
Money can be useful for giving birth together. You eat and I eat but the money will have worked wonders, brought good humor, greater more

complete feelings. You will have participated in the creation of art. I want to make a movie two movies and you should say to me here's the money, as long as it's done don't ask anything else of yourself. The rest will take care of itself. The rest will grow up on its own like a child. What kind of relationship still exists today between artists and industrialists, artists and the wealthy? They're little employees too, like the office workers who endure the alienation wrought by the bosses. What can one person alone do? Just be a clown, what can many artists do together, claim the money to make art together.

It's not true that industrialists are a privileged group, they have no hope in their life, they're sterile no matter how hard they try not to be, the workers have more hopes, more freshness less to lose, more to gain.

It's better to play the clown in the street for sincere people who understand you and give you what little they can without expecting to take anything home, except a new thought.

The Deposito d'Arte Presente (Warehouse of Present Art) was created in Turin and some people worked hard to put it together, even to furnish it, but the right approach wasn't made to the capitalists who had put up their little share. It was the time and place in which they had to realize that to have a part in culture they had to give money to the artists for every creative project without expecting anything preordained in exchange. And they would have had much much more, they would have participated directly in the creation.

I saw them, limited, closed in an alienating pace of work, without outlets without hopes without light, sad in their family routine or at most their escapade with a mistress. Obtuse faces. Conditioned by giving and taking. But we weren't capable of asking them to dig up their love.

. . .

Art is alright if it changes the forms but it's not alright if it changes the structure. But if you're patient enough to wait a couple of years your attempt to change a structure will become a change of forms and everything will work out fine for everyone.

I said some things once and I entitled them "Famous Last Words," they were supposed to be the last words I said, but here I am writing words upon words, here are my famous last words.

But I was bankrupt then as I am now. I'm always bankrupt. This is my ad: big banners in the windows: bankruptcy—money off today—clearance sale, all goods must go. This too is a way to sell. My merchandise is third choice, it's not good merchandise, but in bankruptcies there's always the hope of getting a good deal and one rushes in and buys in order not to have problems. Do something, anything and then have patience enough to wait at least two years, everyone will be talking about you. New art is always truly new and, new art is always the art of always. What we did is the best

that could be done. But we got bored, so let's do something else that's right. I noticed that everyone likes to change, change clothes, furniture, change the old model of something for the new model. People love to change, they feel the need.
It's not true that changes are contrary to people's needs. One changes the form of the vase in the living room, one changes the painting on the wall, one changes one's car for a car with newer styling.
One changes haircuts. But nobody wants to change something deeper more internal. Nobody wants to change structures.
So did you go ahead John? And "do you understand now John that it's serious?" To manage to finish this book in three days is crazy and yet I can't escape, there are still many very many pages and I have a thousand things to do, paint, look for money, talk to Tom, Dick, and Harry, prepare the objects to send off for the show, think of the material the photos the vita the essays. Last night Maria, with a cold, told me as she went to bed: strange we even find time to sleep. Yes it's true, strange, I agreed. But just look how bad people are, malicious all the time, they said I had opened my studio to others because I didn't have any more ideas and I wanted to exploit the ideas of others. Malicious, huh? Do you think I'm the kind of person who lacks ideas? That's maliciousness for you.
Sure enough people are just a little too malicious.

. . .

This book is not a diet, it is not for those who have to eat unseasoned food. I'm writing for those who have holes in their pockets, who always spend twice as much as they have. I'm writing for those who sit like a pope and walk like a king. Bet everything at the roulette table and tomorrow to tell it to your friends. I'm writing for those who sleep heavily, who snore at night with their mouths open. I'm writing for those who defend themselves by themselves who beat you up if you make a mistake. I rub grease on my boots and cream on my hair, I go to the john in the backyard, I bought an expensive dog in an expensive shop. I want to buy a bell tower to paint long tall paintings in sitting up between the mullioned windows.
Simple but succulent dishes, varied and well seasoned. The tourists love good Italian cuisine, I'm writing for them, I court and spark them. A drop of grappa? A sambuca sir? It's on the house and come back soon. I'm not writing for those with a delicate stomach or for those who never know where to put their hands. I'm writing for those who eat salt onions and radishes at six in the morning at the flower market and for those who put their hands on the asses of buxom women. I'm writing spicy tales for the fourteen-year-old daughters. I'm not writing for those who suffer in silence. I'm writing for those who walk at a quick pace. I'm not writing for the corns. I'm writing for the strong, sturdy feet, I'm writing for shoes above size ten. I'm writing for the brains of the peasants who use only

fresh manure and put sulphur on the grapevines. I'm not writing for chemical fertilizers, for supermarket chickens. I'm not writing.
People always talked about liberty and liberalism was born. People always talked about community and communism was born. People always talked about life and vitalism was born.
I'm not writing for tired, lazy people, without a future, without desires, without ambitions, I'm not writing for them. Writing is not doing a good deed. It's not music for the deaf. I'm writing for people in good health, strong, sanguine people. I'm writing for Parma hams, I'm writing for sausage and sauerkraut. I'm writing Russian salad and spaghetti and tomato sauce in the same dish. I'm writing for the Italian well-to-do, laborers or peasants who love hot sauce with their boiled meat.
These lines smell of garlic a mile away, they smell of grappa.
These lines are a hundred and fifty proof. I'm writing for the palate of the average Italian who rises to power, who goes to parliament with red cheeks.

. . .

The direct connection between thought and sign of a being and between sign and thought of another is semantics. The essentiality of the signs and the will that these be clear requires the will to pursue a slow but exact intention of substituting the crystallized and at this point confused signs of semantics
a thousand reasons never to reveal ourselves. I try to recognize myself, I try to make myself be recognized. The only system I've managed to find till now seems actually to contradict the claim I've just made. I've faced life as though it were theater. I've worn countless masks. Sometimes people don't recognize me, because I changed my mask, my costume, my pose. But it's instinctive, I know only masks, I see only masks, poses, costumes. I never see a face, a person. Maybe if I saw one I'd be too frightened, anyone would be frightened, because we're not accustomed to it.
But at least by changing masks I come close to feeling what the pretense is. My work more or

. . .

Solerosso: huh!
Albarosa: what do you mean, huh?
Solerosso: I'm thinking of those people who manage to keep their interest alive as long as they live themselves, there are ninety-year-olds who speak with the same enthusiasm as kids of twenty and speak to the kids as though they were one of them. People like Bertrand Russell who believe in peace like a child and knew well where and who failed in the
going the wrong way makes my head spin a little like when I used to

dance the waltz and I go really fast, I saw everything spin around until all the forms dissolved, then all of a sudden I started spinning fast in the opposite direction. This was fun for me. Maybe if I'd continued I would have been able to make it to the moon, that's a little like the exercises they do at Cape Kennedy to train the astronauts. How great it would be if the waltz came back into style I'm still one of those who know how to dance it. Indeed I remember very well the first time I danced it. A young friend of my mother's made me do it one day when we went to visit her at her house. She had a gramophone you had to wind up by hand and the record was a tango. She taught me that you take two steps to the left and one to the right and that I had to put my arm around her waist and with the other hand hold her hand.

How many pages left to write there still were at the time. What sweet fear and how much certainty of wonderful women for my future life and how much respect.

Know what I did? I started writing on the last page and so I'll go on writing on the page before and so on. Except that the size of these pages doesn't correspond to the printed pages so I'm curious to see how it comes out. Anyway at this point I could say that the book is finished because I'm writing the last page, but instead almost a third of the book remains to be written before I find the point from which I skipped here. The point is where I was talking about rhythm as the essential element in life and art. Something you have to take into consideration if you want to become a great artist. Yes but there's no need for me to say it because at that point, that is where the book will be finished I'll sign my name.

This translation follows previously published translations, with slight variations to accord with the style followed elsewhere in this volume.

CHRONOLOGY OF MICHELANGELO PISTOLETTO, 1956–74

Marco Farano

Background

Michelangelo Pistoletto was born in Biella on June 25, 1933, the only child of Ettore Olivero Pistoletto (1898–1984) and Livia Fila (1896–1971). His father was a painter from Gravere di Susa who had moved to Turin in the 1920s to improve his technique at the Accademia del Nudo. He stayed in Biella for a lengthy period to realize various works, including a series of graffito pieces in the Ermenegildo Zegna plant on the history of wool-making. During this time he met Livia Fila, to whom he gave painting lessons; they married in Biella in March 1932.

One year after Michelangelo's birth, the family moved to Turin, where Ettore continued to paint and opened a restoration studio. As a child, Michelangelo learned the fundamentals of drawing and painting from his father. On Sunday mornings he accompanied Ettore on his usual visits to the Galleria Sabauda, where the works on display began with a collection of gilded altarpieces from the thirteenth and fourteenth centuries. These visits would have a significant influence on his future work as an artist.

During the World War II aerial bombings of 1943, after an explosive device struck the restoration studio, the family moved to Susa, which was safer but nonetheless subject to continuous strafings and where the Nazis held partisan hangings in the main piazza. The family returned to Turin in late 1946. At the age of fourteen, Michelangelo began working in his father's restoration studio and drew his first self-portrait; he started collecting antique wood sculptures with his initial earnings. The study and practice of restoration provided him with a firm knowledge of the Western pictorial tradition, in particular medieval and Renaissance art. During a visit to the Palazzo Ducale in Urbino when he was about eighteen, he saw Piero della Francesca's *Flagellation of Christ* (see fig. 56), a work that would exert a lasting influence on him.

At age twenty, on his mother's advice, he enrolled in a school of advertising design recently opened in Turin under the direction of Armando Testa. After about a year, he opened his own advertising studio, which he ran until 1958. His contact with the world of advertising, which at that time was closely attuned and extremely receptive to contemporary art, led him to frequent galleries in Turin that were offering an international, up-to-date view of contemporary art. In 1953, he saw a work from Lucio Fontana's Holes series in the yearly exhibition *Arte in vetrina* (*Art in the Window*), organized in Turin's downtown shops. This work, which aroused heated debate, inspired Pistoletto to seek a personal response in his art to the existential questions he saw expressed in various contemporary art currents. While he experienced the oppositional pull of abstract and figurative art that was then polarizing artistic debate in Turin as well as elsewhere, he saw in figurative painting a path more consistent with his own background and culture.

In 1954, he met Marzia Calleri in Turin and with her made his first trip abroad, to Greece and Turkey. They married the following year. In December 1955, he began his career as an artist by participating in an exhibition at the Circolo degli Artisti in Turin, where his father had often shown his own paintings. The piece included in the exhibition was a self-portrait created that year.

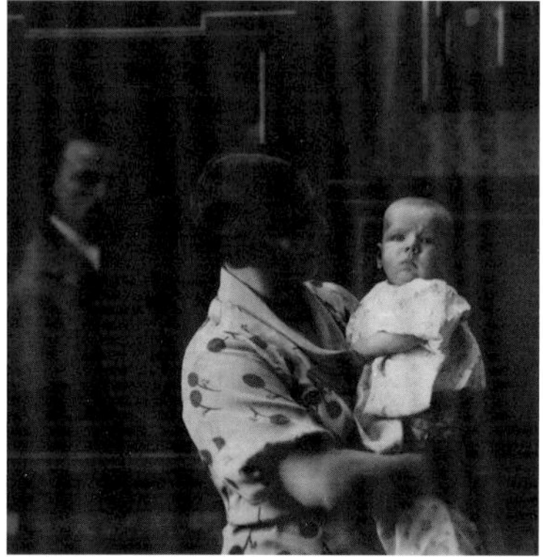

FIG. 212. Pistoletto at age three months in the arms of his mother, Livia Fila, Biella, 1933. Behind them is a self-portrait by his father, Ettore Olivero Pistoletto. Courtesy of Cittadellarte-Fondazione Pistoletto, Biella

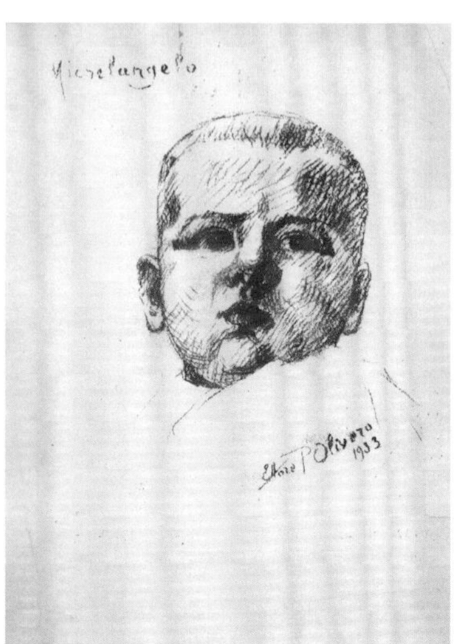

FIG. 213. A portrait of Pistoletto at the age of three months, realized by his father, Ettore Olivero Pistoletto, and adapted by Pistoletto in 1973 as *Autoritratto attraverso mio padre* (*Self-Portrait through My Father*). Courtesy of Cittadellarte-Fondazione Pistoletto, Biella

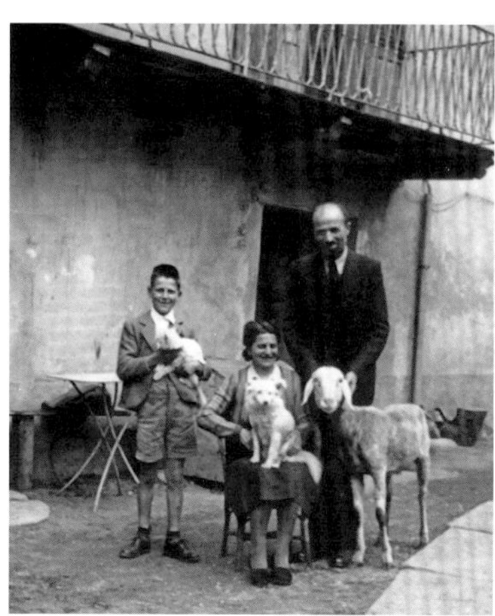

FIG. 214. Pistoletto with his parents during their stay in Susa during World War II, August 1944. Courtesy of Cittadellarte-Fondazione Pistoletto, Biella

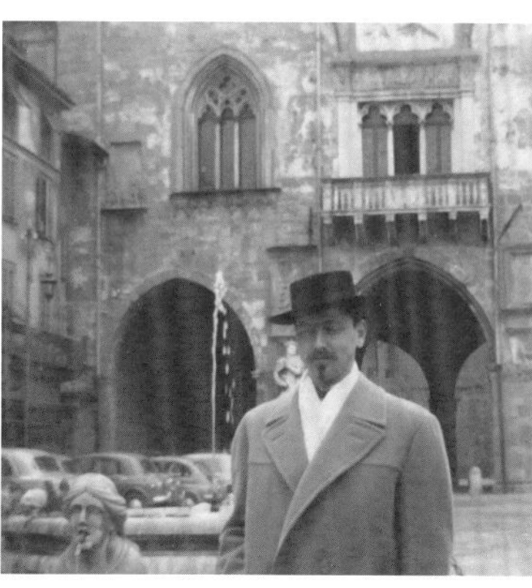

FIG. 215. Pistoletto in Verona, 1955. Courtesy of Cittadellarte-Fondazione Pistoletto, Biella

CHRONOLOGY OF ITALY, 1956–74

Luigia Lonardelli

Background

After years of civil war and the German occupation during World War II, Italy attained political and economic stability only with great effort. Following its liberation by Italian partisan movements and Allied forces, the country embarked on the complicated path of rebuilding its government and industry, with essential support from the Marshall Plan. Disputes arose over the handling of contributions from the U.S.-administered plan (also called the European Recovery Program, or ERP), specifically over pressure from the United States to prevent the installation of a government supported by the left—a condition tied to the assignment of funds. These disputes would have a profound effect on the political debate of the 1950s.

In April 1948, the first democratic elections were held in Italy, with the Christian Democrats, a party of the center, defeating the Popular Democratic Front, a coalition of the Communist and Socialist parties. The victory of the Christian Democrats reflected the views of the Catholic Church, which in 1949 announced the excommunication of all Catholics who voted for the Communists. The Vatican's influential role during these years was accomplished through organization of its widespread network of parishes.

The first parliamentary tasks proceeded amid reform efforts and episodes of violent repression, attempts at collaboration, and a tense dialogue strongly focused on such themes as the apportioning of uncultivated lands, the signing of the Atlantic Pact (against Communism), and the political legacy of the Italian Resistance.

The artistic environment of these years was fully enmeshed with the political climate. In 1948, after a long period of isolation and censorship, the Venice Biennale resumed, offering Italy an opportunity to experience an international ambience once again. This year's Biennale, the 24th, included Picasso's first solo exhibition in Italy; a showing of Peggy Guggenheim's collection, which presented a synthesis of early-twentieth-century art movements; and the introduction of the group Fronte Nuovo delle Arti (New Art Front), which brought together a heterogeneous mix of artists who were united by their dislike of the aesthetics of the previous Fascist regime, and who, through a post-Cubist sensibility, sought a path toward a new realism.

Two tendencies immediately formed within the Fronte, mirroring the already heated debate over realism versus abstraction and, later, over a lyrical type of abstraction versus a more concrete approach that absorbed the example of Piet Mondrian. The particular vehemence of this period arose from the movement's proximity to the Communist party, which supported an aesthetic orthodoxy close to a Soviet-style figurative realism. In 1948, the attack by the leader of the Italian Communist party, Palmiro Togliatti, on abstract art, which he accused of formalism and distance from the masses, precipitated profound second thoughts within the group.

The 1951 exhibition *Arte astratta e concreta in Italia* (*Concrete and Abstract Art in Italy*) at the Galleria Nazionale d'Arte Moderna in Rome took stock of current developments, particularly in Concrete art. The abstract fringe of the Fronte, under the aegis of Lionello Venturi, coalesced in 1952 in the Gruppo degli Otto, a group of eight Italian painters who followed an abstract-concrete style.

Occurring in concert with these collective artistic endeavors was a series of more individual investigations, such as those carried out by Giuseppe Capogrossi, Alberto Burri, and Lucio Fontana. The latter created his first *Ambiente spaziale a luce nera* (*Spatial Environment in Black Light*) in 1949 at Milan's Galleria del Naviglio, an installation that conquered another dimension—that of space—for the field of artistic activity.

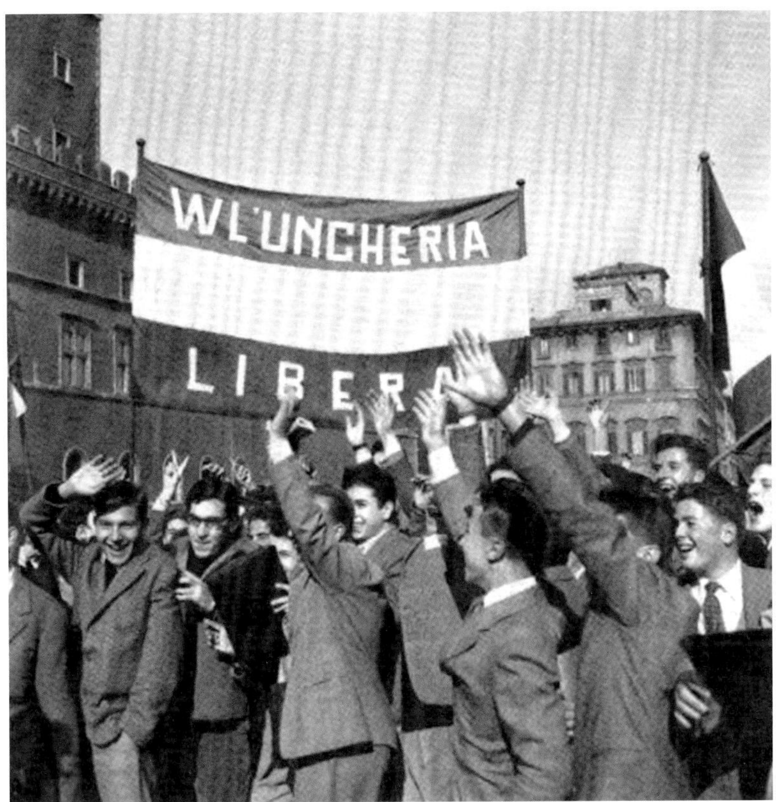

FIG. 216. Student demonstration in solidarity with Hungary's revolt against the oppressive policies of Soviet rule, Rome, October 29, 1956. Courtesy of the Archivio Cicconi, Rome

1956

Pistoletto rents his first studio, an attic space in a residential building on via Bava in Turin. His artistic investigations increasingly center on the self-portrait, and he produces paintings at the limits of Art informel—large canvases that emphasize material and in which the face occupies almost the entire surface of the painting (see fig. 32; plate 1).

1957

Among the works he produces this year, two self-portraits, *Sacerdote* (*Priest*; see fig. 36) and *Il santo* (*The Saint*; see fig. 37), are particularly significant. In these works, the face no longer occupies the entire surface of the canvas, and there are obvious references to sacred iconography. Both paintings are reproduced in the second issue of the magazine *Presenze*, published in Turin by Pistoletto, his wife Marzia, and a group of friends that includes the photographer Renato Rinaldi, whom Pistoletto had met while attending Testa's design school. The same issue of the magazine includes a text by Pistoletto that focuses on the present impasse in abstract art—on the danger of reducing abstraction to sterile formalism and the importance of reviving art's essential social and spiritual functions.

During the year he sees the exhibitions *Yves Klein: proposte monochrome, epoca blu* (*Yves Klein: Proposition Monochrome, Blue Epoch*) at Galleria Apollinaire in Milan (January); *Dipinti e ceramiche di Lucio Fontana* (*Paintings and Ceramics by Lucio Fontana*) at Il Prisma in Turin (June); and *Opere di Alberto Burri* (*Works by Alberto Burri*) at La Bussola, also in Turin (November).

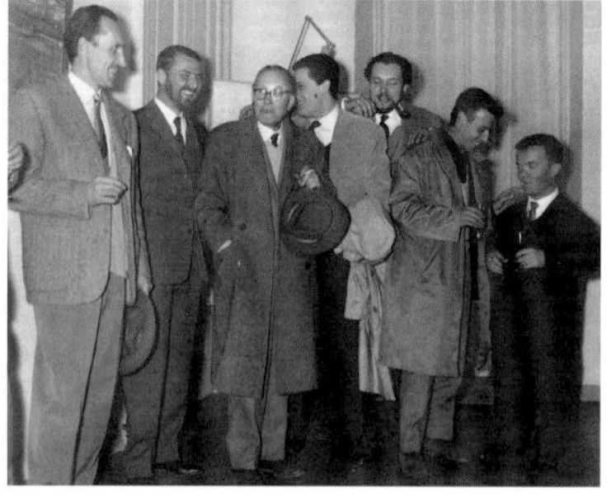

FIG. 217. Pistoletto and others in the house of the collector Aldo Buzzacchino, Turin, 1959. From left to right are Aldo Buzzacchino, Pistoletto, Francesco Menzio (a painter and founder in 1928 of the Turin group of artist called "Gruppo dei sei"), and the Turin painters Sergio Saroni, Francesco Casorati, Nino Aimone, and Francesco Tabusso. Courtesy of Cittadellarte-Fondazione Pistoletto, Biella

1958

In his paintings he begins to confront the relationship between the human figure (now depicted at full scale) and the background, ceaselessly experimenting with different solutions to the figure-ground problem. In both *Uomo coricato sotto la finestra* (*Man Lying beneath the Window*, 1957–58; see fig. 35) and *Uomo sul sofà* (*Man on the Sofa*, 1958; see fig. 117), the background includes a luminous stained-glass window that radiates light behind the represented figure.

January: He sees Francis Bacon's first exhibition in Italy, at Galleria Galatea in Turin. Stimulated by the dramatic nature of Bacon's representation, he continues his own investigations of the human figure, while eliminating any form of dramatic expression of the type found in Bacon's work.

November 8: His painting *Uomo seduto* (*Seated Man*, 1958) is included in an exhibition at Galleria San Fedele in Milan and wins the San Fedele Prize. Afterward, Luigi Carluccio, a member of the jury and an authoritative and influential critic and curator in Turin, visits his studio and introduces him to Mario Tazzoli, owner of Galleria Galatea, who purchases *Uomo seduto* and offers Pistoletto an exclusive contract.

Pistoletto closes his advertising agency, leaves the studio on via Bava, and acquires a new, larger workspace adjacent to his house on via Cibrario.

During this period he meets Tommaso Trini Castelli, the future critic and publisher of the magazine *Data*. Between 1958 and 1960, Castelli, Pistoletto, Rinaldi, and the poet Piera Opezzo experiment with cinematography.

1959

His artistic research focuses on the creation of the background. Significant works from this period include *La folla ingrata* (*The Thankless Crowd*, 1958–59; see fig. 34) and *La folla* (*The Crowd*, 1959; plate 2), in which the figure multiplies and interweaves with the background over the entire surface of the canvas; and *Esperimento* (*Experiment*, 1959; plate 3), in which the figure is reduced to a simple silhouette and the background to a silver monochrome.

The group exhibitions he participates in this year include *Premio Morgan's Paint* in Rimini (opening July 15), whose catalogue includes, for the first time, a brief text about his works; and *Premio Lorenzo Dellani* in Biella (opening September 19), where his painting *Piazza Duomo in Biella* (1959) wins the exhibition prize and is acquired by the Museo Civico in Biella.

1956

Turin is the site of the major Italian publishing houses dealing with nonfiction, such as Einaudi, Loescher, Utet, and Boringhieri.

June: Pressures within the Communist party, spurred by the publication of the Khrushchev report, which denounced the crimes of Stalinism that were revealed during the 20th Congress of the CPSU (Communist Party of the Soviet Union), force Palmiro Togliatti cautiously to criticize Stalinism and seek a national approach to Communism.

September 2: In Alba, in Piedmonte, the Movimento internazionale per una Bauhaus immaginista (International Movement for an Imaginist Bauhaus), founded in 1955 by Pinot Gallizio and Asger Jorn, convenes the first worldwide congress of free artists, which establishes the basis for collaboration with Guy Debord and Gil Wolman's Internationale Lettriste (Lettrist International), a Paris-based group of radical artists and thinkers. The following year the merger of the two movements results in the Situationist International.

November 4: The Soviet Red Army harshly represses a Hungarian revolt against the oppressive Communist regime. Much of the Italian left organizes demonstrations in support of the Hungarian people, and the failure of the party to condemn the situation alienates many intellectuals.

1957

January 2: The exhibition *Yves Klein: proposizioni monocrome, epoca blu* (*Yves Klein: Proposition Monochrome, Blue Epoch*) at Galleria Apollinaire in Milan marks the beginning of Klein's "blue era."

July 4: In Turin, the Italian automaker Fiat begins production of the Nuova 500, which during the 1960s becomes one of the symbols of Italy's *miracolo economico* (economic miracle). By the time production ceases in 1975, 4,250,000 models of this compact city car will have been produced.

September: The conceptual artist Piero Manzoni, along with the group Arte nucleare—the latter formed in opposition to the powers unleashed by the nuclear age and promoting a fantastical form of avant-garde art—signs the manifesto *Contro lo stile* (*Against Style*).

December 10: In Turin, Luciano Pistoi's Galleria Notizie opens with a Wols exhibition. It will subsequently provide a venue for Art informel, a European development highlighting a spontaneous or expressive abstraction over the formal rationalism of geometric abstraction.

1958

January 23: Francis Bacon's first solo exhibition in Italy opens at Mario Tazzoli's Galleria Galatea in Turin. The show subsequently travels to Beatrice Monti's Galleria Ariete in Milan and Irene Brin's and Gaspero Del Corso's Galleria L'Obelisco in Rome.

May 17: Cy Twombly's first solo exhibition in Europe opens at Plinio De Martiis's Galleria La Tartaruga in Rome.

May 25: The Christian Democratic party wins Italy's elections with 42 percent of the vote.

May 31: In Turin, Pinot Gallizio presents his first "Industrial Painting"—a roll of paint-spattered canvas sold by the meter—at Galleria Notizie.

November: The country begins a phase of growing modernization. At Latina in central Italy, construction begins on the country's first nuclear plant. A few weeks later, the first section of the "autostrada del Sole" (highway of the Sun) opens. Also this month, the American avant-garde composer John Cage, invited by the Italian composer Luciano Berio, works at the phonology studio of the Italian public broadcaster RAI (Radiotelevisione italiana) in Milan, composing the piece *Fontana Mix*.

November 24: Alberto Burri shows his latest pieces, created with iron, in the exhibition *Burri: ferri* at Galleria Blu in Milan.

1959

February: Lucio Fontana exhibits his first *tagli* (cuts)—canvases that have been slashed—in Milan at Carlo Cardazzo's Galleria del Naviglio.

March 14: Aldo Moro becomes secretary of the Christian Democratic party.

May 5: Michel Tapié and Luciano Pistoi organize the exhibition *Arte nuova* (*New Art*) at the Circolo degli artisti in Turin, where they exhibit *art autre*, American action painting, and Japanese experimental art.

May 23: Mario Schifano's first solo exhibition opens at Emilio Villa's Galleria Appia Antica in Rome, with canvases that recall Art informel painting but already presage work that will move beyond it. At the end of the month, Galleria La Tartaruga in Rome shows Robert Rauschenberg's combine paintings, which mix paint with found objects and other nontraditional materials.

May 25: The *Daily Mail* describes the well-being achieved by Italy as an "economic miracle."

October 31: In Turin, the new facility for the Galleria Civica d'Arte Moderna opens. Over the course of the 1960s it will become the most important experimental exhibition space in Italy.

December 4: Following the publication of the first issue of Agostino Bonalumi, Enrico Castellani, and Piero Manzoni's avant-garde art magazine *Azimuth*, the homonymous exhibition space opens in Milan. Piero Manzoni shows his *Linee* (Lines), created on strips of rolled paper, in the new gallery.

1960

March 30–April 15: Pistoletto has his first solo exhibition, at Galleria Galatea in Turin, exhibiting twenty works created between 1958 and 1960, including self-portraits, some figures of athletes (see fig. 1), landscapes, and a still life. The catalogue has an introductory text by Luigi Carluccio.

In subsequent paintings of this year, Pistoletto's figures take on an increasingly immobile and inexpressive character, as if they were prototypes of ordinary human beings, while the backgrounds evolve from a repetition of decorative markings to a monochrome format in such works as *Autoritratto linoleum, Autoritratto oro, Autoritratto argento,* and *Autoritratto bronzo* (*Linoleum Self-Portrait*, *Gold Self-Portrait*, *Silver Self-Portrait*, and *Bronze Self-Portrait;* see fig. 41; plates 4–6).

June 30: His daughter, Cristina, is born.

1961

After applying a thick layer of black varnish to a canvas he is working on, he realizes he can see himself reflected on the surface where he is painting his own face. Over the course of the year he will use the technique of the reflective surface to create a series of self-portraits in which the title includes the phrase *Il presente* (*The Present*) to indicate the instantaneous relationship these works create between the viewer, his or her reflection, and the painted figure (see fig. 46; plates 7–9).

He continues to investigate new solutions to the problem of the figure-ground relationship, now with a tendency to make the background more reflective, as in *Uomo grigio di schiena* (*Gray Man from the Back*, 1961; see fig. 48), in which the figure is painted on a sheet of aluminum applied to the canvas.

May: He goes to Paris with Antonio Carena, a Turinese painter with whom he is friendly at this time. While there, he visits some galleries, including Galerie J, where the important Nouveau Réalisme exhibition *À 40° au-dessus de Dada* (*At 40° above Dada*), organized by the critic Pierre Restany, is being held.

Through Luigi Carluccio, he meets the artist Mario Merz. The two visit each other's studios and will continue to see each other over the years.

The group exhibitions he participates in this year include *III Biennale internazionale d'arte contemporanea* in San Marino (July).

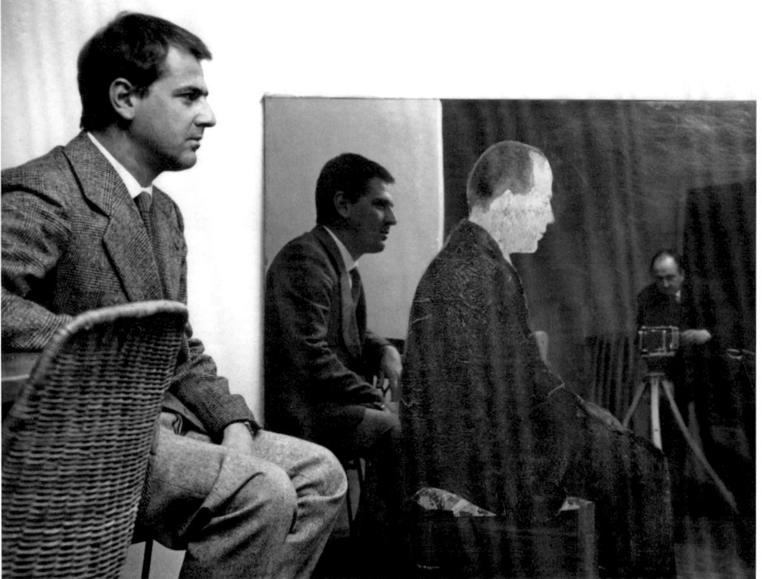

FIG. 218. Pistoletto in front of the mirror painting *Persona seduta* (*Seated Person*, 1962), whose subject is his friend Renato Rinaldi, in his house in Turin, 1962. The reflections in the work are of Pistoletto (seated at left) and the photographer, Paolo Bressano. Courtesy of Cittadellarte-Fondazione Pistoletto, Biella

1962

He fine-tunes the technique he uses to create his reflecting paintings, now employing a sheet of stainless steel polished to a mirror finish, to which he applies an image obtained by tracing and then painting details of a photograph, enlarged to life-size, onto tissue paper that he cuts out and affixes to the steel panel. Until the end of the 1960s, the photographs used for the mirror paintings are created under the direction of the artist in the studio of Paolo Bressano, whom Pistoletto had met in the 1950s, thanks to his father, who used the photographer to document works he was restoring.

He meets Gian Enzo Sperone, a young assistant at Galleria Galatea in Turin. During the following year he will support Sperone's appointment as director of Galleria Il Punto.

His exhibitions this year include the *XIII Mostra internazionale d'arte, Premio Fiorino* at the Palazzo Strozzi, Florence (April).

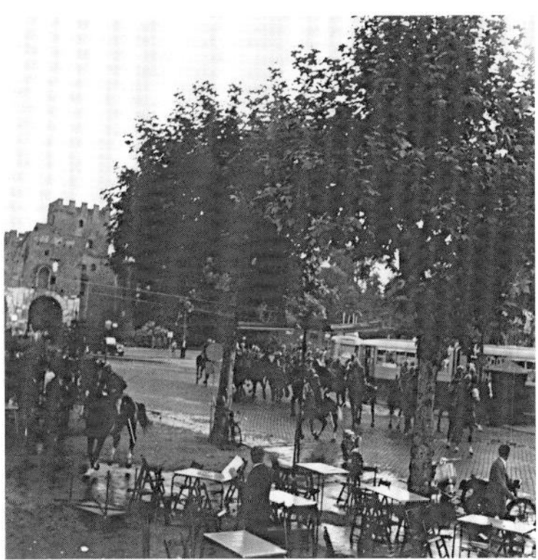

FIG. 219. Demonstrators clash with police at the Porta San Paolo, Rome, July 6, 1960. Courtesy of the Archivio Cicconi, Rome

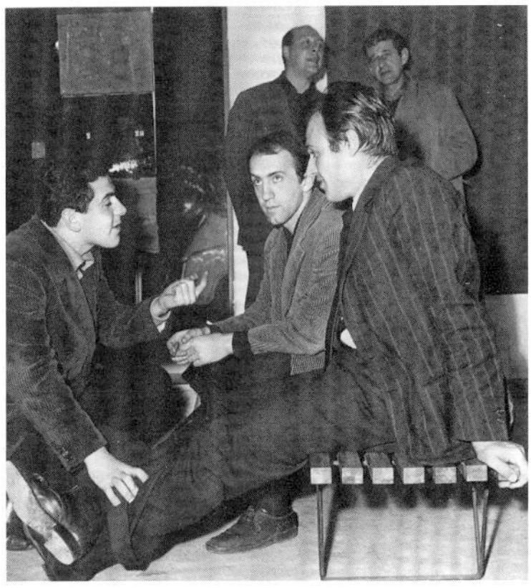

FIG. 220. Tano Festa, Francesco Lo Savio, and Mario Schifano at the opening of the exhibition *5 Pittori-Roma '60* at Galleria La Salita, Rome, 1960. In the background are Piero Dorazio and Giulio Turcato.

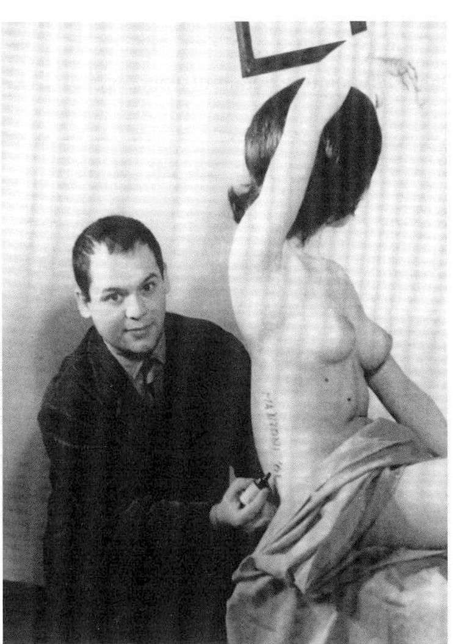

FIG. 221. Piero Manzoni, *Living Sculptures*, 1961. Courtesy of the Fondazione Piero Manzoni, Milan, in collaboration with the Gagosian Gallery, New York

1960

At the beginning of the decade, more than half the population of Turin lives directly off work from the Fiat industry.

April 16: In Milan, Guido Le Noci's Galleria Apollinaire holds the first exhibition of the work of the Nouveaux réalistes, a group formally established in Paris in October 1960 by the critic Pierre Restany.

June 4: Jannis Kounellis has his first solo exhibition, at Galleria La Tartaruga in Rome, showing his "alphabets," which are made using typographic stencils on canvas.

June 20: In Turin, Michel Tapié, together with the architects Luigi Moretti and Carlo Mollino, founds the Centro Internazionale per la ricerca estetica (International Center for Aesthetic Research, or ICAR), which promotes experimental music, dance, and *art autre*.

June 29: Michelangelo Antonioni releases his film *L'avventura* (*The Adventure*), which analyzes the alienation of modern man in the contemporary landscape and the new industrial reality in Italy. It is the first film in a trilogy that will include *La notte* (*The Night*), released in 1961, and *L'eclisse* (*The Eclipse*), of 1962.

July 6: During an antifascist demonstration in Porta San Paolo in Rome, the police attack demonstrators with a cavalry charge, an episode that confirms the Fernando Tambroni government's hard line against public protests.

November 18: The exhibition *5 pittori—Roma '60* (*5 Painters—Rome '60*) opens at Gian Tommaso Liverani's Galleria La Salita, featuring works by Giuseppe Uncini, Franco Angeli, Tano Festa, Francesco Lo Savio, and Mario Schifano. The latter four will become part of the Scuola di Piazza del Popolo group (School of the Piazza del Popolo) in Rome, young artists who exceed Art informel through the adoption of icons arising from consumer society.

1961

February 10: The abolition of emigration limits leads to a new wave of migration from southern Italy to cities in the Milan-Turin-Genoa industrial triangle.

February 24: The censorship campaign that had opposed the screening of many films during the previous year—including *Rocco e i suoi fratelli* (*Rocco and His Brothers*) by Luchino Visconti, *La dolce vita* by Federico Fellini, and *L'avventura* by Michelangelo Antonioni—culminates in suspension of production of the theater piece *L'Arialda* by Giovanni Testori at the Teatro nuovo in Milan for its alleged obscenity.

April 22: Piero Manzoni presents his *Sculture viventi* (*Living Sculptures*) at Galleria La Tartaruga in Rome, signing the bodies of the models and some of the people who are present, including the writer Umberto Eco, the artist Mario Schifano, and the critic Emilio Villa.

June 13: In Italy for the first time, the Living Theatre, founded in 1947 by the American Abstract Expressionist painter Julian Beck and the actress Judith Malina, presents *The Connection* and *Many Loves* at Club Teatro Parioli in Rome.

1962

March: The publication of Umberto Eco's essay *Opera aperta* (*The Open Work*) opens up aesthetic studies to new information theories, according to which artistic creations can be interpreted as linguistic systems in their own right.

April 11: Mario Merz's first paintings are shown at Galleria Notizie in Turin, presented by the critic Carla Lonzi.

May: The exhibition *Arte programmata* (*Programmed Art*), organized by Bruno Munari at the showroom of the typewriter and computer manufacturer Olivetti in Milan, focuses on developments in kinetic art in Italy. It will also be shown at Olivetti in New York.

July 7: In Turin, a large workers' strike is held in the Piazza Statuto in collaboration with various unions; this is a time when new forms of social conflict are making their appearance.

September 11: A Francis Bacon retrospective opens at Galleria Civica d'Arte Moderna in Turin.

December: The Marlborough Gallery in Rome shows Alberto Burri's first plastic "Combustions," made by burning their material with an oxyhydrogen torch.

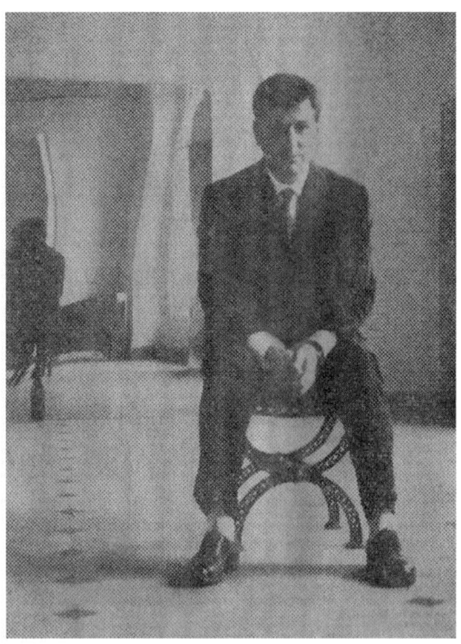

FIG. 222. Pistoletto at Galerie Ileana Sonnabend, Paris, 1964. Courtesy of Cittadellarte-Fondazione Pistoletto, Biella

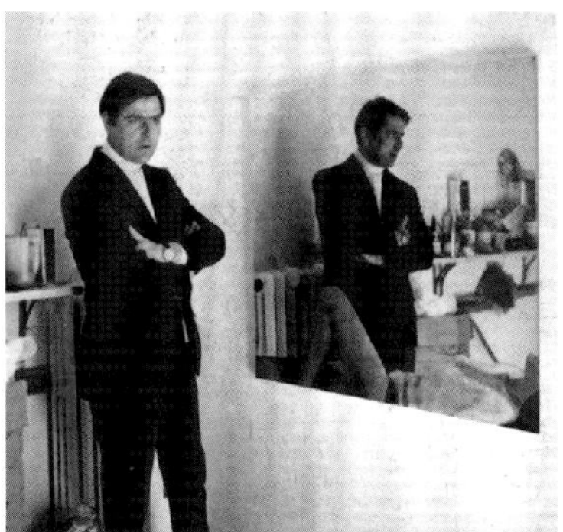

FIG. 223. Pistoletto in front of his mirror painting *Donna sdraiata* (*Reclining Woman*), 1964, in his studio on via Cibrario in Turin, 1964. Photograph by Paolo Bressano. Courtesy of Cittadellarte-Fondazione Pistoletto, Biella

1963

April 27: Pistoletto shows his mirror paintings for the first time, in a solo exhibition at Galleria Galatea in Turin. The catalogue includes an introductory text by Luigi Carluccio and four different photographic reproductions of one of the exhibited works, *Persona seduta* (*Seated Person*, 1962), in which the reflections in the mirroring surface of the steel are of Pistoletto, Paolo Bressano, and Aldo Mondino, a Turinese painter with whom he is socializing at this time.

After the opening of his Galatea show he goes to Paris, where he visits Galerie Sonnabend during the installation of the exhibition *Pop Art Américain*. He meets Ileana and Michael Sonnabend, who a few days later travel to Turin, where they visit his Galatea show, buy all the works there, and take over the contract between Pistoletto and the gallery.

June: He accompanies Sperone to Galerie Sonnabend, which is holding an exhibition of Roy Lichtenstein's work, and encourages Sperone to show the American artist at Il Punto. This is the beginning of Sperone's collaboration with the Sonnabend gallery, leading to a Turin–Paris–New York relationship (New York is where the gallery of Leo Castelli, Sonnabend's U.S. partner, is located) that will end up being decisive for the dissemination of new Italian art in Europe and the United States and for American art in Italy.

November: He is the sole European artist to participate in the exhibition *Dessins Pop* at Galerie Sonnabend, a show that includes the American artists Lee Bontecou, Jim Dine, Jasper Johns, Roy Lichtenstein, Claes Oldenburg, Robert Rauschenberg, George Segal, and Andy Warhol.

1964

March 4: He has a solo exhibition at Galerie Sonnabend, in which he exhibits a group of ten mirror paintings. The catalogue contains critical texts by Michael Sonnabend and Tommaso Trini, as well as the writer-artist Alain Jouffroy. Several of the exhibited works are acquired by important collectors, such as the architect Phillip Johnson (*La signora Lichtenstein* [*Mrs. Lichtenstein*], 1963) and the Houston philanthropist and collector John de Menil (*Due Persone* [*Two People*], 1963–64; plate 20). A number of major collectors and museums in the United States and Europe soon acquire his mirror paintings. Visitors to the exhibition include the composer John Cage, whom Pistoletto first meets on this occasion and with whom he will remain friends.

May 9: Galleria Gian Enzo Sperone opens in Turin with the exhibition *Lichtenstein, Mondino,*

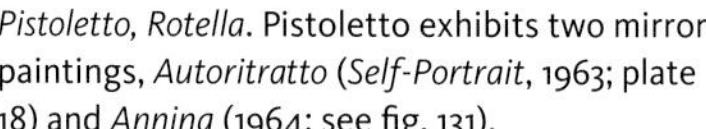

Pistoletto, Rotella. Pistoletto exhibits two mirror paintings, *Autoritratto* (*Self-Portrait*, 1963; plate 18) and *Annina* (1964; see fig. 131).

Between summer 1964 and spring 1965, he participates in a series of large European exhibitions devoted to New Figuration, Pop art, and Nouveau Réalisme, including *Neuwe Realisten* at the Gemeentemuseum in The Hague (opening June 24); *Figuration et défiguration: la figure humaine dépuis Picasso* (*Figuration and Defiguration: The Human Figure since Picasso*) at the Musée des Beaux-Arts in Ghent (opening July 10); *Mythologies quotidiennes* (*Daily Mythologies*) at the Musée d'art moderne de la ville de Paris (in July); and *Neuer Realismus und Pop Art* (*New Realism and Pop Art*) at the Museum des 20. Jahrhunderts in Vienna (opening September 19).

September 4: He has a solo exhibition at Galleria del Leone in Venice, which is owned by Attilio Codognato and Giorgio Camuffo.

September: He makes his first trip to New York, along with Ileana Sonnabend and the artists Christo and Jean Claude, whom he had met in Paris and who are moving to New York.

October 2: At his solo exhibition at Galleria Sperone in Turin, he exhibits a group of seven new works titled *I plexiglass* (see plates 68–74), along with some mirror paintings. The new works, made of photographs affixed to transparent Plexiglas panels, represent a first step in his exploration within real space of the new phenomenological dimension he had identified in the mirror paintings. His text in the catalogue contains a position statement regarding the current practice of using everyday objects in an artistic setting, leading to considerations about the conceptual nature of art.

October 30: He exhibits his work in the United States for the first time, showing the mirror painting *Gruppo di persone* (*Group of People*, 1963) in *International Exhibition of Contemporary Painting* at the Carnegie Institute Museum of Art in Pittsburgh.

Late in the year, Leo Castelli, who is involved with disseminating Pistoletto's work in the United States through the Sonnabend Gallery in New York, urges the artist to produce new mirror paintings so that he can organize an exhibition at the New York gallery.

A number of critical texts on the artist appear in journals this year, including Annina Nosei, "Pistoletto," *Collage* (Palermo) 2 (March); Annette Michelson, "Paris Letter: Pistoletto," *Art International* 8, no. 3 (April), p. 70; and Ettore Sottsass, Jr., "Pop e non pop, a proposito di Michelangelo Pistoletto," *Domus*, May.

1963

February 15: Federico Fellini's film *8½*—a reflection on the condition of the intellectual in mass society and his difficulty in reconciling himself to an industrial culture—is released.

July 7: The 4th San Marino Biennale, organized by the critic Giulio Carlo Argan, is dedicated to the theme *Oltre l'informale* (*Beyond Art informel*), signaling that critics are ready to move away from the latter tendency and opening the field to more object-related investigations. The December issue of the Milan literary magazine *Il verri* will be devoted to the same theme.

September 21: Giulio Carlo Argan opens the proceedings of the 12th Convegno di Verucchio, which examines the social function of art.

October 6: Gruppo 63, an avant-garde literary movement that follows structuralist theory, is established in Palermo. Members include Luciano Anceschi, Alberto Arbasino, Nanni Balestrini, Renato Barilli, Furio Colombo, Gillo Dorfles, Umberto Eco, Gastone Novelli, Lamberto Pignotti, and Eduardo Sanguineti. The group will publish the review *Quindici* from June 1967 to July 1969.

November: In Genoa, on the initiative of the art critic Eugenio Battisti, publication of *Marcatrè*, a bulletin of contemporary culture, begins. The bulletin covers various areas of creativity, divided into thematic sections.

December 4: The first center-left government is formed, with Aldo Moro as Presidente del Consiglio (prime minister). In Turin, the Museo sperimentale d'arte contemporanea (Experimental Museum of Contemporary Art) opens, under the leadership of Eugenio Battisti, while in Palermo, the journal *Collage* is born. The magazine covers new music and contemporary art and is under the direction of Antonino Titone and Paolo Emilio Carapezza.

1964

January: The German philosopher Herbert Marcuse's 1955 essay *Eros and Civilization* is published in Italian. The liberated society it describes makes it a classic of the student movement of 1968.

June 20: At the 32nd Venice Biennale, the United States pavilion, organized by Alan Solomon, shows the work of Pop artists. Robert Rauschenberg wins the Grand Prix for painting. This biennial has a strong impact on Italian artists, who have an opportunity to gain in-depth knowledge of the latest American work and establish contacts with U.S. galleries.

August: In response to the United States broadening its involvement in the war in Vietnam, Italian pacifist groups organize a series of protest demonstrations.

August 21: Palmiro Togliatti dies and his *Memoriale di Yalta*, in which he criticizes Soviet foreign policy, is published in the magazine *Pravda*, the official organ of the CPSU, the Communist party of the Soviet Union.

September: Umberto Eco publishes his essay *Apocalittici e integrati* (titled *Apocalypse Postponed* in English), an analysis of mass culture and the processes by which it includes or excludes the individual.

October 2: The writer and director Pier Paolo Pasolini's film *Il vangelo secondo Matteo* (*The Gospel According to Matthew*) is interpreted as a metaphor for the contrast between the Church as a power structure and evangelical Christianity.

November: In Turin, the association Amici torinesi dell'arte contemporanea (Turinese Friends of Contemporary Art) is founded. It will support the organization of exhibitions at the Galleria Civica d'Arte Moderna, inaugurating a new public-private form of collaboration.

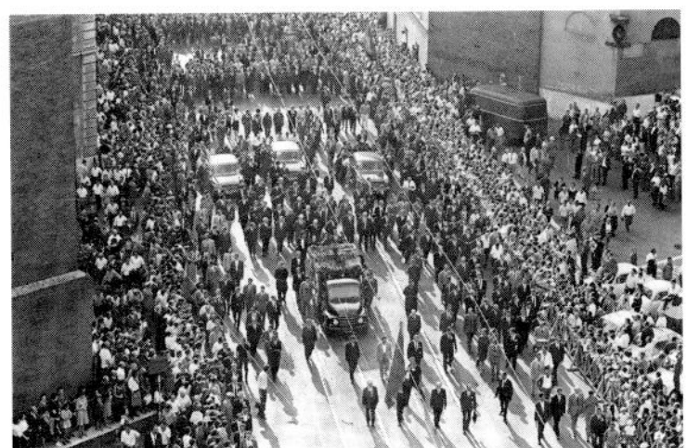

FIG. 224. The funeral of Palmiro Togliatti, leader of the Italian Communist party, Rome, August 25, 1964. Courtesy of the Archivio Cicconi, Rome

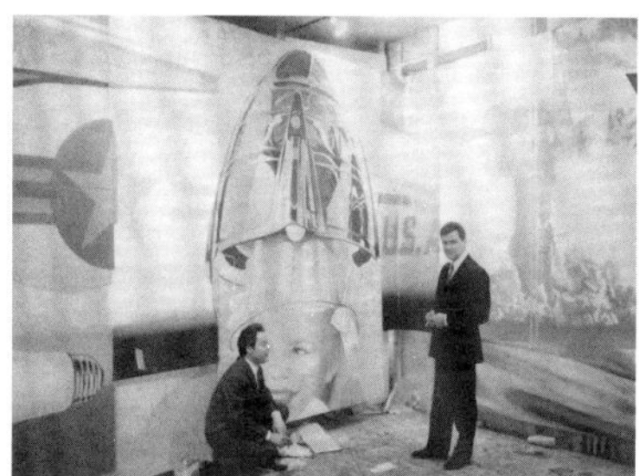

FIG. 225. The French critic Otto Hahn and Pistoletto in James Rosenquist's studio, New York, 1965. Polaroid taken by James Rosenquist. Courtesy of Cittadellarte-Fondazione Pistoletto, Biella

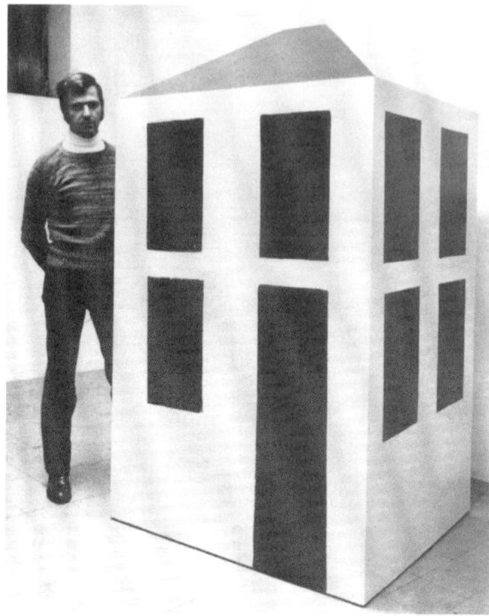

FIG. 226. Pistoletto beside the Minus Object *Casa a misura d'uomo* (*House on a Human Scale*, 1965–66; plate 93), in his studio on via Reymond in Turin, 1966. Courtesy of Cittadellarte-Fondazione Pistoletto, Biella

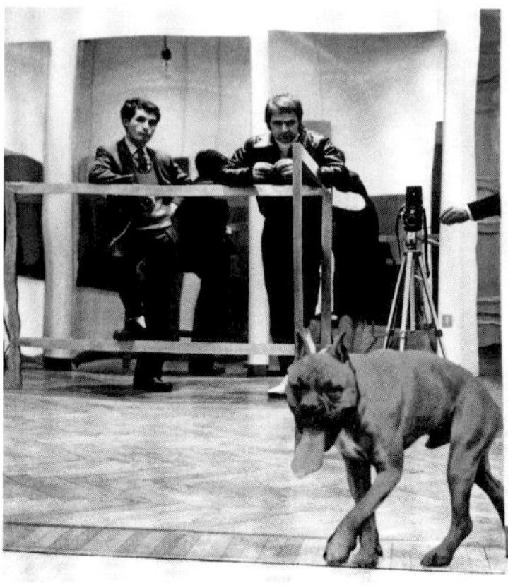

FIG. 227. Gian Enzo Sperone and Pistoletto leaning on *Struttura per parlare in piedi* (*Structure for Talking while Standing*, 1965–66; plate 87), reflected in the mirror painting *Cane* (*Dog*, 1965), during Pistoletto's solo exhibition at Galleria Sperone, Milan, November 1966. Courtesy of Cittadellarte-Fondazione Pistoletto, Biella

1965

Pistoletto travels to New York a few times this year and meets and befriends, among other artists, Roy Lichtenstein, Claes Oldenburg, Robert Rauschenberg (who purchases one of his mirror paintings), and James Rosenquist—all artists whose works are shown with his in various group exhibitions during this time. On one of his New York sojourns, Leo Castelli tells him that in order to secure an American exhibition and not compromise his work's success in the United States, he must move to New York permanently. Pistoletto rejects his suggestion and subsequently distances himself from the art scene in the United States, where he nonetheless continues to exhibit continuously for the remainder of the decade.

February–March: He has a solo exhibition in the Sala Espressioni-Ideal Standard, an exhibition space in the center of Milan conceived by the architect and designer Gio Ponti. Pistoletto shows four mirror paintings from 1964, all of people looking out over balconies: *Uomo appoggiato alla balconata* (*Man Leaning on a Balcony*), *Due persone alla balconata* (*Two People on a Balcony*), *Tre ragazze alla balconata* (*Three Girls on a Balcony*; plate 27), and *Quattro persone alla balconata* (*Four People on a Balcony*; plate 26). The introductory text is by the architect Ettore Sottsass, Jr.

Spring: He rents a former printing establishment at via Reymond 13 consisting of three spaces, which he uses as his studio and residence.

May–July: He participates in various group exhibitions in the spring and early summer, including *Beyond Realism* at the Pace Gallery, New York (opening May 4); *Carena, Castellani, Fontana, Gilardi, Pistoletto, Sottsass Jr.* at Galleria Sperone, Turin (opening May 13); and *Accardi, Castellani, Paolini, Pistoletto, Twombly* at Galleria Notizie, Turin (opening May 28). The catalogue of the latter includes some photographs of the critic Carla Lonzi and the artist Carla Accardi shot in Pistoletto's studio during a visit by Luciano Pistoi (owner of Galleria Notizie).

August: The Swedish magazine *Konstrevy* devotes its cover and considerable space inside to Pistoletto. The essay is by Michael Sonnabend.

Winter: He meets the artist Pino Pascali and convinces Sperone to exhibit in his Turin gallery a group of Pascali's works titled *Armi* (Weapons), which Galleria La Tartaruga in Rome had hesitated to show. The friendship between Pistoletto and Pascali will contribute to the creation of the first ties between artists in Turin and Rome, leading to the Arte Povera movement.

December 1965–January 1966: He produces and exhibits his *Oggetti in meno* (Minus Objects) in his studio-residence. Created through a working process connected to the temporal dimension and contingency, and each different from the others, the Minus Objects break with the dogma that dictates that an artist's work must be stylistically recognizable, like a standardized commercial brand. The Minus Objects initially receive a cool reception from critics and are greeted with incomprehension on the part of gallery owners. The critic Germano Celant, who visits the exhibition in Pistoletto's studio and stays in close touch with the artist during this period, considers the Minus Objects a fundamental stage for the birth of Arte Povera, whose principles he first expresses in his theoretical manifesto "Arte Povera: Appunti per una Guerriglia" (Arte Povera: Notes for a Guerrilla War), published in the magazine *Flash Art* in November 1967.

1966

January: With the exhibition of his Minus Objects, Pistoletto's studio increasingly becomes a meeting place for various artists, some of whom he knows, such as Mario and Marisa Merz, Piero Gilardi, Gianni Piacentino, and Gilberto Zorio, and others, such as Alighiero Boetti, whom he meets for the first time.

April 4: A major exhibition of his work, *Michelangelo Pistoletto: A Reflected World*, opens at the Walker Art Center in Minneapolis with thirty-two mirror paintings created between 1963 and 1965; the director Martin Friedman writes the text for the catalogue. The previous day, the *Minneapolis Sunday Tribune* had featured his work on its front page.

April 4: His mirror painting *Uomo con pantaloni gialli* (*Man with Yellow Pants*, 1964; see fig. 134), acquired by the Museum of Modern Art (MoMA) in New York the previous year, is included in its exhibition *Recent Acquisitions*.

June: He participates in a second exhibition at MoMA, *The Object Transformed*, and also takes part in the exhibition *Arte abitabile* (*Inhabitable Art*) at Galleria Sperone in Turin, where some of his Minus Objects are exhibited for the first time outside his studio, along with works by Gianni Piacentino and Piero Gilardi (see fig. 68).

June 10: He exhibits mirror paintings and some Plexiglas pieces in a solo exhibition at Galleria del Leone in Venice.

June 18: His new mirror painting *Biennale 66* (1966; plate 39) is exhibited at the Venice Biennale in a room dedicated to his work.

November 8: In a solo exhibition at the new Milan venue of Galleria Sperone (opened from spring of this year until June 1967), he exhibits mirror paintings, some Plexiglas works, and the Minus Object *Struttura per parlare in piedi* (*Structure for Talking while Standing*, 1965–66; plate 87).

December: He exhibits a group of *versioni* (versions) of the Minus Objects and some mirror paintings in a solo exhibition at Galleria La Bertesca in Genoa, run by Francesco Masnata and Nicola Trantalance. The catalogue, edited by Germano Celant, has a text by Pistoletto on the Minus Objects and the first anthology of critical texts on his work. On this occasion he meets the artist Pier Paolo Calzolari, who is working as an assistant on the installation of the show.

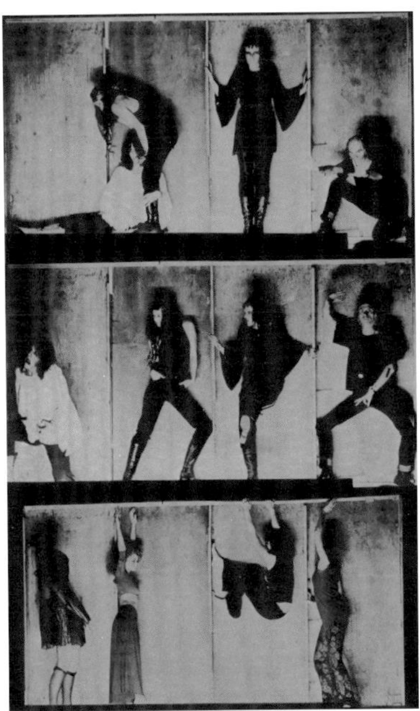

FIG. 228. The Living Theatre at Teatro Eliseo, Rome, March 1965. Courtesy of the Living Theatre

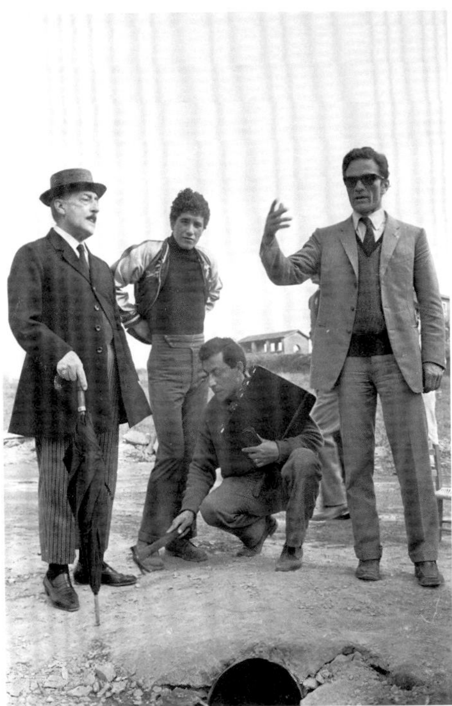

FIG. 229. Totò, Ninetto Davoli, an unidentified man, and Pier Paolo Pasolini during the filming of *Uccellacci e uccellini* (*The Hawks and the Sparrows*), 1966. Courtesy of the Archivio Cicconi, Rome

1965

Donald Judd publishes his essay "Specific Objects" in *Arts Yearbook*, theorizing the birth of an art that is neither sculpture nor painting but an object in itself and which therefore creates new relationships with the exhibition space.

January 11: Pino Pascali's first solo exhibition at Galleria La Tartaruga in Rome presents his "sculptural paintings," as well as *Teatrino* (*Puppet Theater*; see fig. 22), *Colosseo* (*Colosseum*), and *Ruderi sul prato* (*Ruins on the Meadow*)—works of art that reference stage sets and investigate new territory for art.

February 20: An Andy Warhol exhibition opens at Galleria Sperone in Turin.

March 13: At the Teatro Eliseo in Rome, the Living Theatre stages *Mysteries . . . and Smaller Pieces*, a collective creation that relies on nonverbal sounds and improvised actions.

April 20: Luciano Fabro exhibits his works made of glass in his first solo show, at Galleria Vismara in Milan.

October 31: In his film *I pugni in tasca* (*Fist in His Pocket*), the director Marco Bellocchio portrays a middle-class family in which familial tensions are experienced with extreme violence, anticipating the protest-laden atmosphere of 1968.

December 7: The Second Vatican Council ends. Its resolutions will open up the Church to social themes and greater religious freedom.

1966

January: Walter Benjamin's 1936 essay "Das Kunstwerk im Zeitalter seiner technischen Reproduzierbarkeit" (The Work of Art in the Age of Mechanical Reproduction) is translated into Italian. His insights are interpreted in relation to the dissemination of mass culture during this period.

January 26: At Galleria Sperone in Turin, Pino Pascali exhibits his *Cannoni* (Cannons), weapons made from assembling scrap metal and toys.

February: Robert Morris publishes his first "Notes on Sculpture" in *Artforum*, proposing the use of industrial materials and products in sculpture.

April: Students begin occupying universities. On the 27th, the Socialist student Paolo Rossi is killed during clashes with neo-Fascists at the University of Rome. He will become a symbol of protest.

May 3: In his first solo exhibition, at the Galleria Sperone in Turin, Piero Gilardi shows his "tappeti-natura" (nature-carpets)—expanded polyurethane carpets that simulate nature.

May 4: Fiat signs an agreement with the Soviet Union to build a factory in Togliattigrad, the Russian city named after the secretary of the Italian Communist party. On the same day, Pier Paolo Pasolini's film *Uccellacci e uccellini* (*The Hawks and the Sparrows*)—which reflects on the incomprehension and impossibility of dialogue between the committed intellectual and the common man and features the actor Totò—is released.

June: The exhibition *Arte abitabile* (*Inhabitable Art*) opens at Galleria Sperone in Turin.

September 20: The exhibition *Eccentric Abstraction*, organized by Lucy Lippard, opens at the Fischbach Gallery in New York, showing work by Alice Adams, Louise Bourgeois, Eva Hesse, Gary Kuehn, Bruce Nauman, Don Potts, Keith Sonnier, and Frank Lincoln Viner and laying the foundations for art that will be called "anti-form."

November 4: In Florence, the Arno River floods, damaging thousands of books and works of art and taking many lives. Following the flood, hundreds of young volunteers arrive in the city to help save works of art. It is the first sign of the youth gatherings that will characterize protests at the end of the decade.

December 1: The Beat '72 theater in Rome shows Carmelo Bene's film *Nostra signora dei turchi* (*Our Lady of the Turks*), in which the action on stage is experienced as a flaunting of behavior.

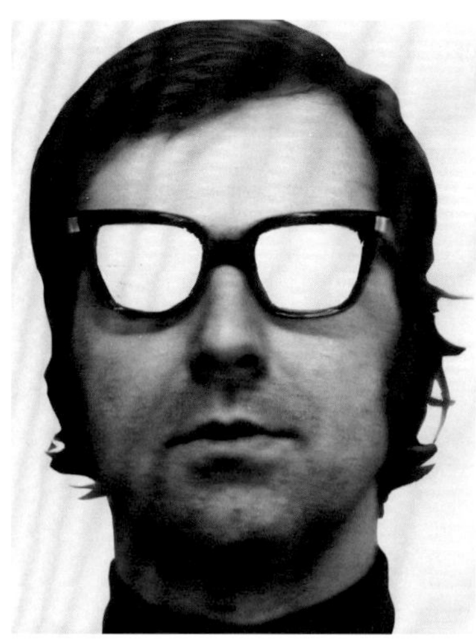

FIG. 230. The mask of Pistoletto's face used by participants in the action *La fine di Pistoletto* (*The End of Pistoletto*), Piper Pluriclub, Turin, March 6, 1967. Courtesy of Cittadellarte-Fondazione Pistoletto, Biella

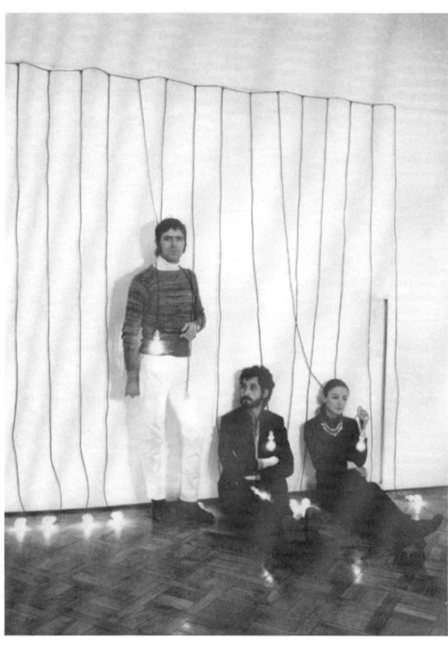

FIG. 231. Pistoletto, Gian Enzo Sperone, and Maria Pioppi with *Quadro di fili elettrici* (*Painting of Electric Wires*, 1967; plate 105), at Galleria Sperone, Turin, 1967. Courtesy of Cittadellarte-Fondazione Pistoletto, Biella

The principal critical texts on the artist that appear this year are Maurizio Fagiolo, "Il dramma fisico di Pistoletto," *Avanti!* (Rome), May 7; John Ashbery, "Talking of Michelangelo," *ARTnews* 65, no. 4 (Summer 1966), pp. 42–43, 64–65; Sidney Simon, "Michelangleo Pistoletto," *Art International* 10, no. 6 (Summer 1966), pp. 69–71; and Tommaso Trini, "Pistoletto," *Quadrum* (Brussels) 20 (1966), pp. 152–53.

1967

February 22: His solo exhibition at Galleria del Naviglio in Milan (owned by Carlo Cardazzo) includes some Minus Objects along with mirror paintings.

March 6: He presents his first action piece, *La fine di Pistoletto* (*The End of Pistoletto*), at the Piper Pluriclub in Turin. Thirty people wearing masks that reproduce Pistoletto's face are arranged along the edges of the dance floor holding up sheets of reflective steel that are used to produce sounds. During the event, the people begin dancing and gradually rest the sheets of steel on the dance floor, and both they and the public dance on them. Some mirror paintings are aligned along a portion of the room.

March 15: At the Piper Pluriclub, he sees a performance by the Living Theatre for the first time, *Mysteries . . . and Smaller Pieces*. He subsequently gets to know the members of the group and has them stay at his studio on numerous occasions in the following months, when the troupe is in Turin for other performances.

April 14: He exhibits thirty-four mirror paintings, some Minus Objects, and his Plexiglas works in a solo exhibition at the Palais des Beaux-Arts, Brussels, and receives the Belgian Critics Prize. The exhibition catalogue includes texts by Jean Dypréau, Henry Martin, and himself.

April 22: His solo exhibition at the Kornblee Gallery in New York includes a group of mirror paintings, among them the diptych *Uomo che legge* (*Man Reading*, 1967) and the triptych *Lampadina che oscilla* (*Swinging Lightbulb*, 1967), each work composed of a sheet of reflective steel on which a figure is depicted and adjacent or flanking "empty" sheets of steel.

April 26: The exhibition *Flavin, Rosenquist, Chamberlain, Warhol, Fontana, Pistoletto, Gilardi, Piacentino, Fabro, Pascali, Anselmo, Zorio* opens at Galleria Sperone in Turin. Pistoletto shows the Minus Object *Pozzo* (*Well*, 1966).

May 26: His solo exhibition at Galerie Zwirner in Cologne, Germany, opens. Among the mirror paintings exhibited is *Ragazza seduta per terra* (*Girl Sitting on the Floor*, 1967; plate 46), which is reproduced in the exhibition announcement.

June 8: The group exhibition *Fuoco immagine acqua terra* (*Fire Image Water Earth*), which includes Pistoletto's *Due persone alla balconata* (*Two People at the Balcony*, 1964), opens at Fabio Sargentini's Galleria L'Attico in Rome.

July 2: He exhibits *Cinque pozzi* (*Five Wells*, 1966) in *Lo spazio dell'immagine* (*The Space of the Image*) at the Palazzo Trinci in Foligno.

July 15: His mirror painting *Autoritratto con Souzka* (*Self-Portrait with Souzka*, 1967; see fig. 14) is included in the exhibition *Nuove tecniche d'immagine* (*New Techniques of Representation*) at the Palazzo del Kursaal of the San Marino Biennale.

September 2: In Tokyo, he participates in *Exhibition of Contemporary Italian Art* at the National Museum of Modern Art, showing his mirror painting *Meeting IX* (1965); it is his first exhibition in Japan.

September 23: He shows the mirror paintings *Ragazza che cammina* (*Girl Walking*, 1966; plate 40), *Lui e lei che parlano* (*He and She Talking*, 1967; plate 43), and *Uomo che aggiusta un camion* (*Man Fixing a Van*, 1967; see fig. 149) in the *IX Biennale—Artistas italianos de hoje* (*IX Biennial: Italian Artists of Today*) at the Museu de Arte Moderna in São Paolo and receives the Biennial prize.

Fall: He exhibits a group of mirror paintings in a solo exhibition at the J. L. Hudson Gallery in Detroit.

November: In Rome, he meets Maria Pioppi, who the following month moves to Turin and becomes his companion in life and work. Born in Rome on October 4, 1938, daughter of an antiquarian, she had studied at the Accademia di Belle Arti in Rome from 1956 to 1959. After spending the years 1961–65 in Iran, she returned to Rome, where she worked first at Plinio De Martiis's Galleria La Tartaruga and then at Mara Coccia's Galleria Arco D'Alibert.

December 4: During the exhibition *Con-temp-l'azione*, which takes place simultaneously in three galleries in Turin—Galleria Sperone, Galleria Stein, and Il Punto—his *Sfera di giornali* (*Newspaper Sphere*, 1966) is renamed *Scultura da passeggio* (*Walking Sculpture*) and is rolled by Pistoletto and other artists along the route that connects the galleries (see fig. 65).

December 12: He shows six mirror paintings as well as *Pozzi* (*Wells*, 1966) and *Sarcofago* (*Sarcophagus*, 1966; plate 94) in a solo exhibition at Galerie Sonnabend in Paris.

December 13: In the auditorium of the Università-Istituto di Storia dell'Arte in Genoa, a public gathering of Arte Povera artists takes place, titled *Collage I* and organized by Germano Celant. When it is time for him to participate, Pistoletto cuts Marzia Calleri's hair while she is seated in the audience as his daughter, Cristina, moves around the room on roller skates cutting her doll's hair.

December 22: His solo exhibition opens at Galleria Sperone in Turin. As an announcement for the exhibition, he publishes a manifesto in which he states: "Con questa mostra io ho liberato il mio studio, che si apre per accogliervi i giovani che vogliono presentare il loro lavoro, fare delle cose, trovarsi" (With this exhibition I have liberated my studio, which is open to young people who want to present their work, do things, be together). Initially, a single work is exhibited at the center of the gallery, *Pietra miliare* (*Milestone*, 1967; plate 98), a curbstone

1967

During the year, 60,000 immigrants from the south arrive in Turin in search of work.

January 19: At Galleria Stein in Turin, Alighiero Boetti's first solo exhibition presents sculptures created through the juxtaposition and superimposition of industrial components.

February 7: Students occupy the University of Pisa. On this occasion the political movement "Potere operaio" (Workers' Power) is born. Its extreme fringe will split into various terrorist groups in 1973.

March 13: In Turin, the Living Theatre presents its version of *Antigone* at the Unione culturale (Cultural Union).

April: The artists Ben Vautier and Ugo Nespolo organize *le parole le cose fluxus—arte totale* (*words things fluxus—total art*), performance evenings at Galleria Il Punto and the Teatro Stabile in Turin.

June: The translation of the Canadian philosopher Marshall McLuhan's *Understanding Media* (1964) is published in Italian as *Gli strumenti del comunicare*. McLuhan's innovative approach to media theory will have a profound influence on Italian critics.

Summer: In the American journal *Artforum*, Sol LeWitt publishes "Paragraphs on Conceptual Art," which theorizes the predominance of the idea over the object.

June: In Milan, the first issue of the international magazine *Flash Art* is published. In the coming years it will become a fundamental resource for knowledge about international developments in the arts.

June 8: The exhibition *Fuoco immagine acqua terra* (*Fire Image Water Earth*; see fig. 24), curated by Alberto Boatto and Maurizio Calvesi, opens at Fabio Sargentini's Galleria L'Attico in Rome. Included are works by Umberto Bignardi, Mario Ceroli, Piero Gilardi, Jannis Kounellis, Pino Pascali, Pistoletto, and Mario Schifano—artists who share a search for a new approach to the use of the exhibition space.

June 30: Marisa Merz's first solo exhibition, at Galleria Sperone in Turin, includes a piece created with large sheets of aluminum foil that invade the gallery space.

July 2: The exhibition *Lo spazio dell'immagine* (*The Space of the Image*) opens in Foligno at the Palazzo Trinci.

September 27: In Genoa, the exhibition *Arte Povera e Im-spazio* at Galleria La Bertesca, organized by Germano Celant, brings together a group of artists—Umberto Bignardi, Alighiero Boetti, Mario Ceroli, Luciano Fabro, Jannis Kounellis, Renato Mambor, Eliseo Mattiacci, Giulio Paolini, Pino Pascali, and Emilio Prini—who examine the intrinsic quality of materials, reflecting on a pared-down understanding of the archetype.

November: In Turin, in the spaces of the Museo sperimentale d'arte contemporanea, acquired by the Galleria Civica d'Arte Moderna this year, Mario Merz exhibits his first neon works. Germano Celant's manifesto "Arte Povera: Appunti per una guerriglia" (Arte Povera: Notes for a Guerilla War) is published in *Flash Art*.

December 4: The exhibition *Con-temp-l'azione*, curated by Daniela Palazzoli, opens simultaneously in three galleries in Turin—Sperone, Stein, and Il Punto.

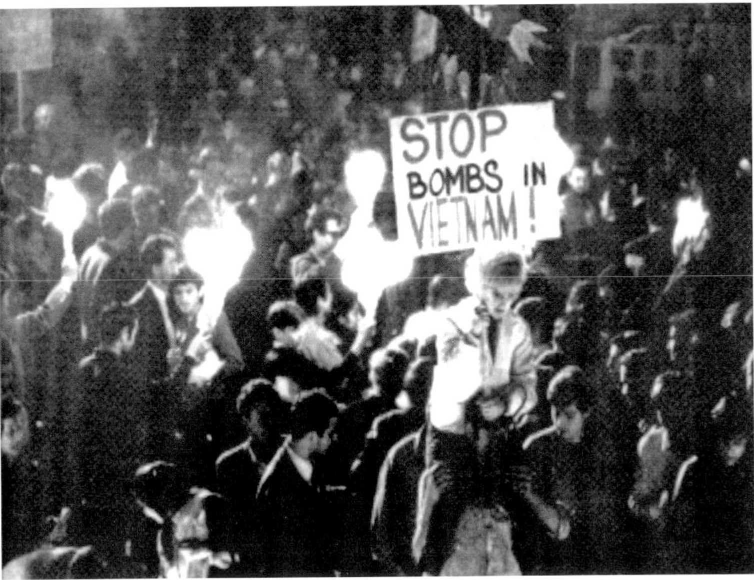

FIG. 232. Demonstration against the war in Vietnam, Rome, 1967

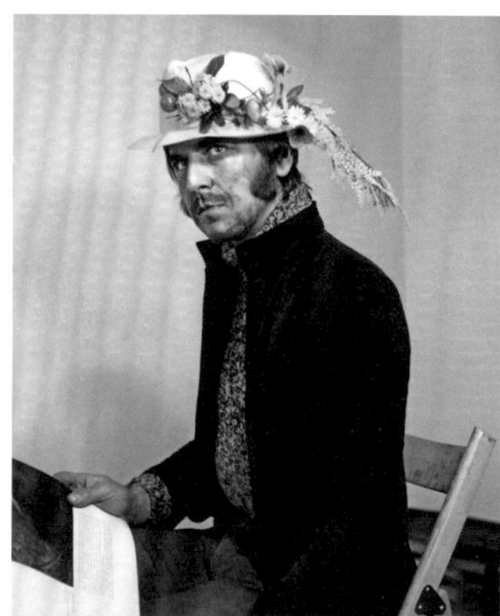

FIG. 233. Pistoletto in his studio in Turin, February 1968, during shooting of the film *Pistoletto & Sotheby*, by Pia Epremiam. Photograph published on the cover of the catalogue for Pistoletto's solo exhibition at Galleria L'Attico, Rome, February 1968. Courtesy of Cittadellarte-Fondazione Pistoletto, Biella

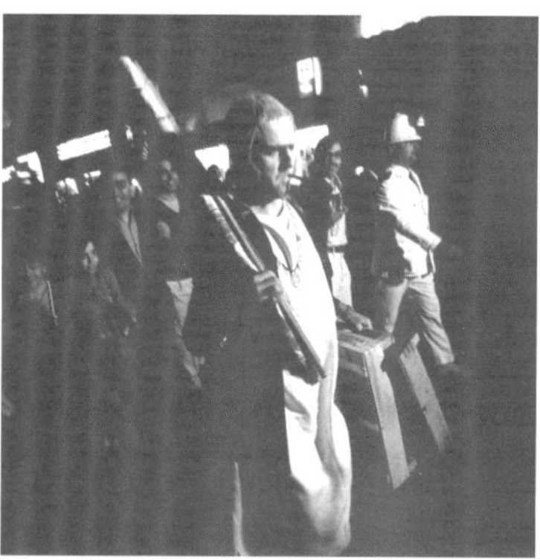

FIG. 234. Lo Zoo, *L'Uomo ammaestrato* (*The Trained Man*) performed on a street in Amalfi, with Pistoletto at center, October 5, 1968. Photograph by Claudio Abate. Courtesy of Cittadellarte-Fondazione Pistoletto, Biella

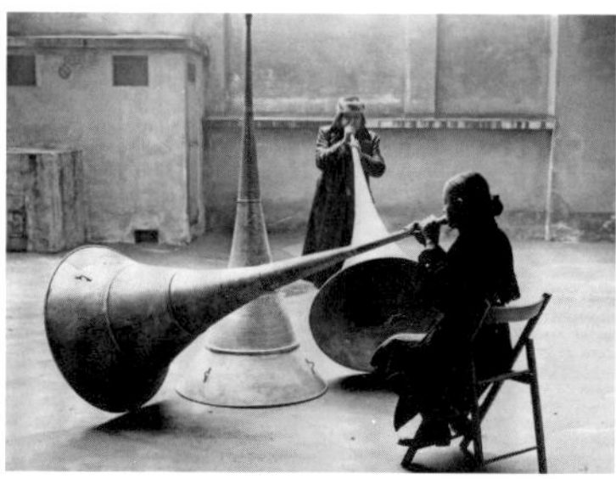

FIG. 235. Pistoletto and Maria Pioppi in the performance *Le trombe del giudizio* (*The Trumpets of Judgment*), in the courtyard of the artist's studio on via Reymond, Turin, 1968. Courtesy of Cittadellarte-Fondazione Pistoletto, Biella

with the date 1967 carved on top. During the course of the exhibition, he creates a group of works based on light and its reflections directly in the gallery.

December: He publishes his text "Le ultime parole famose" ("Famous Last Words"), printing it himself in English and Italian.

The principal critical texts on the artist this year are Henry Martin, "Mirror, Mirror," *Art and Artists* (London), April 1967; Tommaso Trini, "No Man's Mirror," *Domus* 449 (April), with a cover dedicated to the artist; and "Visitors to a Pistoletto Show Get Right into His Paintings," *Horizon* (New York) 9, no. 2 (Spring).

1968

January–April: Pistoletto's studio in Turin is the site of intense activity, with meetings and art actions in which actors, musicians, poets, filmmakers, and Pistoletto himself participate. Among those taking part are future members of Lo Zoo, including Carlo Colnaghi, Lionello Gennero, and Gianni Milano.

January: He has a solo exhibition at Galleria Christian Stein in Turin in which he exhibits mirror paintings and Minus Objects.

January 23: The show *Young Italians*—which includes Pistoletto's mirror paintings *Scopa* (*Broom*, 1967; plate 42), *Alighiero Boetti che guarda un negativo* (*Alighiero Boetti Looking at a Negative*, 1967; plate 44), *Donna sdraiata* (*Reclining Woman*, 1967), and *Autoritratto con Souzka* (*Self-Portrait with Souzka*, 1967; see fig. 14)—opens at the Institute of Contemporary Art in Boston. It will travel to the Jewish Museum, New York, in May.

February 12: A solo exhibition of his work opens at Galleria L'Attico in Rome. The catalogue text is written by the art historian Guilio Carlo Argan. For the opening, Pistoletto installs in the first room of the gallery a coatrack hung with costumes from Cinecittà that visitors are invited to put on; they thus become actors in the second room, where there are twenty chairs, some set pieces from Cinecittà, and three of Pistoletto's mirror paintings. During the month of the exhibition, working with ten young Turinese filmmakers, Pistoletto creates ten short films, shot for the most part in his Turin studio; these are shown at L'Attico during the show's final days.

February 24: He participates in the second Arte Povera exhibition, at Galleria de' Foscherari in Bologna, showing *Bagno-barca* (*Bath-Ship*, 1966–68), a Minus Object made of fiberglass, polished steel, lightbulbs, water, and bath salts. On March 23, the show opens at Centro Arte Viva Feltrinelli in Trieste.

March 23: Some of the Arte Povera artists from Turin, including Pistoletto, are among the exhibitors participating in *Percorso* (*Journey*) at Mara Coccia's Galleria Arco D'Alibert in Rome.

April 2: He is invited to exhibit at the Venice Biennale, where a space is to be devoted to his work, and publishes his "Manifesto of Collaboration," a poster distributed by mail and by hand to those who visit his studio. In the end, he will refuse to create the Biennale project because of the political protests that are taking place, which he feels would have led to his work being misunderstood.

May 8: He performs *Cocapicco e vestitorito* at the Piper Pluriclub in Turin with, among others, Carlo Colnaghi, Gianni Milano, and Maria Pioppi. This constitutes the initial core group of what will become Lo Zoo, the collective with which Pistoletto will create actions and performances from 1968 to 1970 at various venues—in the streets, in theaters, and in galleries. The presentations will be conceived as creative collaborations among artists working in different disciplines.

June 22: The group show *Options* opens at the Milwaukee Art Center, with Pistoletto exhibiting *Uomo che legge* (*Man Reading*, 1967) and *Lampadina che oscilla* (*Swinging Lightbulb*, 1967). It will travel to the Museum of Contemporary Art in Chicago in September.

June 27: He exhibits some of the Minus Objects—*Sarcofago* (*Sarcophagus*, 1966; plate 94), *Portico* (1966), and *Pozzi* (*Wells*, 1966)—along with the mirror painting *Ragazza seduta per terra* (*Girl Sitting on the Floor*, 1967; plate 46) and the rag work *Muretto di stracci* (*Small Wall of Rags*, 1968; plate 102)—at *Documenta 4* in Kassel, Germany. The latter work, not reproduced in the catalogue, was created on-site and is exhibited here for the first time outside his studio.

August 17: Lo Zoo—with Carlo Colnaghi, Gianni Milano, Maria Pioppi, and Pistoletto— performs *L'Uomo ammaestrato* (*The Trained Man*) in the piazza of Vernazza, a small town in Cinque Terre in Liguria.

Over the course of the year he acquires a house in the nearby village of Corniglia, which will be the base for Lo Zoo's activities and, beginning in the 1970s, the site of numerous collaborations between the artist and local inhabitants.

September 27: He shows the mirror painting *Padre e madre* (*Father and Mother*, 1968) in the traveling exhibition *European Painters Today*, which opens at the Musée des Arts Décoratifs in Paris and will travel in 1969 to the Jewish Museum, New York; the Smithsonian Institution, Washington, D.C.; the Museum of Contemporary Art, Chicago; the High Museum of Art, Atlanta; and the Dayton Art Institute, Dayton, Ohio.

October 4: At the exhibition *Arte Povera + Azioni Povere* in the Arsenali dell' Antica Repubblica in Amalfi he creates works on site, integrating them with some Roman ruins that are present in the exhibition space (see figs. 63, 79–81). The town's main piazza is the setting for a production of *L'Uomo ammaestrato* (*The Trained Man*), whose main character is on this occasion played by the critic Henry Martin (see fig. 82).

October 25–26: Invited to create an action with Lo Zoo at Galleria L'Attico, Pistoletto extends the invitation to Musica Elettronica Viva (MEV), a group formed in Rome by some American

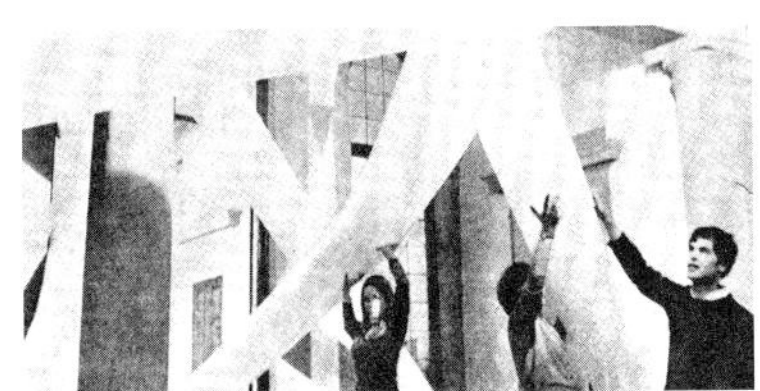

FIG. 236. A group event by the collective UFO in Florence, February 1968

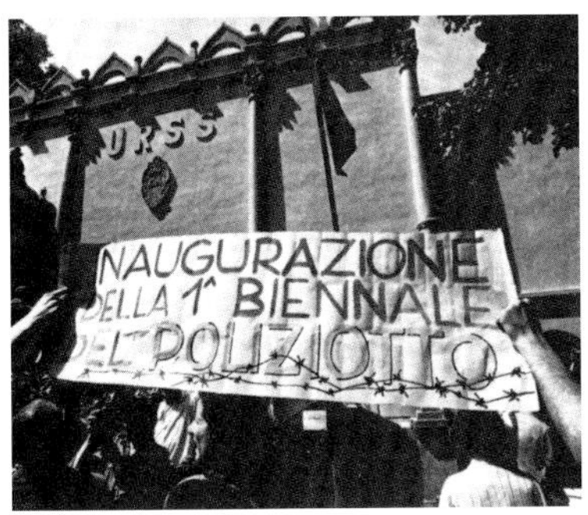

FIG. 237. Protests in front of the Soviet Pavilion at the Venice Biennale, June 1968

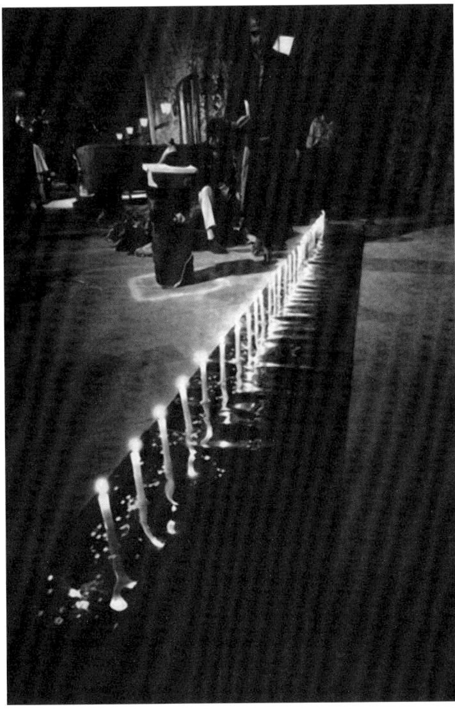

FIG. 238. Pistoletto lighting *Candele* (*Candles*), a site-specific sculpture created for *Arte Povera + Azioni Povere*, Arsenali dell'Antica Repubblica, Amalfi, October 4, 1968. Photograph by Claudio Abate. Courtesy of Cittadellarte-Fondazione Pistoletto, Biella

1968

February 12: UFO, a collective of architects who advocate radical architecture, carries out an action at the School of Architecture in Florence, redesigning the space with a series of elements that disrupt the habits and rituals of its use.

February 12: The actor and director Luca Ronconi presents his *Richard III* at the Teatro Alfieri in Turin. The sets are by the artist Mario Ceroli, who creates a series of wood structures that reverse the perspectival system of the Elizabethan theater.

March 1: One of the most violent incidents of student protest takes place at the Valle Giulia school of architecture in Rome, when the students, having been expelled from the building they had occupied for most of February, attempt in turn to expel the police. Many students and police are injured. Pier Paolo Pasolini expresses his perplexity regarding the authenticity of the movement in a poem published in the newsmagazine *L'Espresso* in June. Also in March, the art journal *Cartabianca* begins publication. Through its five issues, until January 1969, it will be a fundamental vehicle for militant debate on contemporary art.

April 6: In Turin, a series of large-scale strikes begins at Fiat. Students unite with workers protesting in front of the gates of the Mirafiori plant.

May: Throughout the month, Galleria La Tartaruga in Rome presents a survey show titled *Il teatro delle mostre* (*The Theater of the Exhibition*), with the participation of a different artist every day.

May 30: The 14th Milan Triennale opens. Dedicated to the theme of *Grande Numero*, and curated by Giancarlo De Carlo with Marco Zanuso, the exhibition analyzes how artists and architects confront the problem of the industrialization of the art object and its consequent quantitative growth; students occupy the Palazzo dell'Arte, destroying the exhibition.

June 18: In the days prior to the opening of the 34th Venice Biennale (June 21), there is an escalation of tension with student protestors, the main criticism focusing on the Biennale as a bourgeois institution. Many artists decide to withdraw from the show or to cover up their works as a sign of protest against student intimidation. The protests continue at Documenta 4 in Kassel, Germany, which opens on June 27.

August 20: The Soviet Union invades Czechoslovakia with the intention of putting an end to a period of reform there known as the Prague Spring, which had begun in January.

October 4: On the occasion of the exhibition *Arte Povera + Azioni Povere*, the spaces of the Arsenali in Amalfi are interpreted as a theatrical arena in which artistic participation becomes an event. The exhibition includes works by Giovanni Anselmo, Alighiero Boetti, Jan Dibbets, Luciano Fabro, Piero Gilardi, Paolo Icaro, Pietro Lista, Richard Long, Gino Marotta, Plinio Martelli, Mario Merz, Giulio Paolini, Gianni Piacentino, Pistoletto with Lo Zoo, Ger van Elk, and Gilberto Zorio.

November 25–26: In Turin, the Deposito d'arte presente (Warehouse of Present Art), one of the most important alternative spaces in Italy, backed by Marcello Levi in collaboration with gallery owner Gian Enzo Sperone and other figures in experimental art circles in the city, holds the premiere for Pier Paolo Pasolini's *Orgia* (*Orgy*).

December 4: The works of Giovanni Anselmo and Gilberto Zorio are shown together with those of major figures of American post-minimalism—Bill Bollinger, Eva Hesse, Stephen Kaltenbach, Bruce Nauman, Alan Saret, Richard Serra, and Keith Sonnier—in the exhibition *9 at Leo Castelli* at the Leo Castelli Gallery in New York.

December 19: Italy's law against female adultery is nullified (there was no comparable law for men).

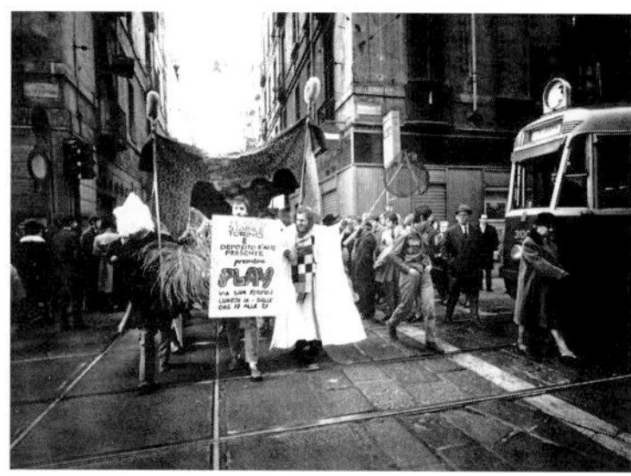

FIG. 239. *Teatro baldacchino* (*Canopy Theater*), a performance by Lo Zoo and Musica Elettronica Viva (MEV), Turin, December 15, 1968. Photograph by Claudio Abate. Courtesy of Cittadellarte-Fondazione Pistoletto, Biella

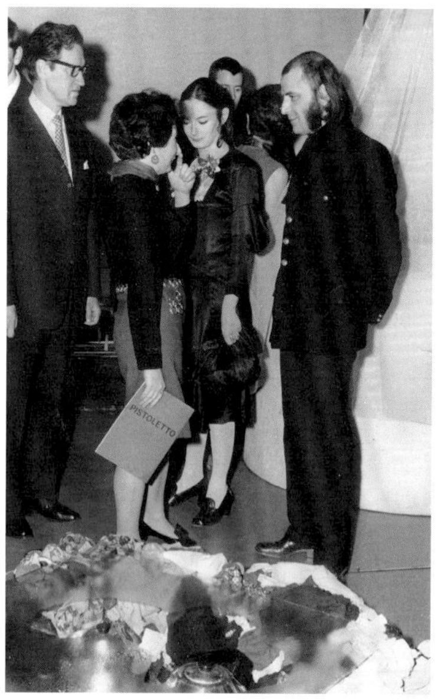

FIG. 240. The opening of Pistoletto's solo exhibition at the Museum Boijmans Van Beuningen, Rotterdam, March 1969. Pistoletto is on the right, and Maria Pioppi is at center. In the foreground is *Orchestra di stracci* (*Orchestra of Rags*, 1968; plate 100), and behind the figures, at the right, is *Pozzo culla* (*Well Cradle*, 1966–68; see fig. 62). This photograph was used in making *Visitatrice con catalogo* (*Visitor with Catalogue*, 1969; plate 49). Courtesy of Cittadellarte-Fondazione Pistoletto, Biella

composers and musicians—including Alvin Curran, Steve Lacy, Jon Phetteplace, Frederic Rzewski, and Richard Teitelbaum—whom Pistoletto had met a few months earlier at the club in Rome where MEV practiced and performed. The resulting piece, *Zuppa* (*Soup*), is a succession of musical and gestural improvisations among the participants, during which Pistoletto revives and develops certain earlier motifs, such as the ladder on which Maria Pioppi is positioned and the electrical wires and lightbulbs he uses to create a structure that traverses the gallery space.

December 15–16: On two successive days in Turin, Lo Zoo and MEV create two performances, *Teatro baldacchino* (*Canopy Theater*; see figs. 77, 78, 239) and *Play*. The former takes place in the streets of downtown Turin, from the city market of Porta Palazzo to the central station of Porta Nuova. The latter takes place at the Deposito d'arte presente (Warehouse of Present Art), a large, 4,800-square-foot space in a former garage in Turin that was opened earlier this year by the collector Marcello Levi, inspired by Pistoletto and Gian Enzo Sperone and financed by an association of collectors and entrepreneurs led by Levi. (In June, the work of the Turinese Arte Povera artists—and the Bolognese artist Pier Paolo Calzolari—had been shown there, attracting the attention of various curators and gallery owners, many of whom visited during the summer while en route from the Venice Biennale to Documenta in Kassel, Germany; these visitors included the gallery owners Ileana Sonnabend, Leo Castelli, and Fabio Sargentini. In October, the artists' work was taken down to accommodate the premiere of the performance of Pasolini's *Orgia* [*Orgy*].) To create *Play*, some of the Minus Objects (1965–66), the *Venere degli stracci* (*Venus of the Rags*, 1967; plate 99), *Orchestra di stracci* (*Orchestra of Rags*, 1968; plate 100), and other objects, either taken from Pistoletto's studio or found for the occasion, are brought to the Deposito d'Arte Presente. Some of these are used during the action as musical instruments for collective sound improvisations. Alvin Curran, for example, "plays" some of the steel sheets or frames used for making the mirror paintings, while Pistoletto—reclining in an old bathtub—plays the bass clarinet. The performance lasts approximately five hours and is illuminated solely by the headlights of Lo Zoo's minibus and by candles and flashlights used during the event.

Winter: Lo Zoo is joined by the dancer and choreographer Simone Forti, whom Pistoletto had met on the occasion of Lo Zoo's October performance at L'Attico, and Beppe Bergamasco and Lionello Gennero, actors and directors from Turin. For several months the group conducts an intensive program of rehearsals and experimental work, which will result in the following year's new performances.

The principal texts on Pistoletto this year include Michael Sonnabend, "Michelangelo Pistoletto: A Strange Shock," *Metro* (Venice) 12; Alberto Boatto, "Pistoletto: dissipazione come procedimento," *Cartabianca* (Rome), March, pp. 9–12; Lia Vergine, "Torino' 68—Nevrosi e sublimazione," *Metro* 14 (June); and Michelangelo Pistoletto, "Risposta a 'E' il momento della negazione?'" *Sipario* (Milan) 268–69 (August–September).

1969

January 25: Pistoletto has a second solo exhibition at the Kornblee Gallery in New York, again showing a group of mirror paintings.

February 28–March 1: Lo Zoo presents *Il principe pazzo* (*The Crazy Prince*, see figs. 85–88) and *Il tè di Alice* (*Alice's Tea*, see figs. 74, 75) at Galleria Il Centro, Naples; the critic Achille Bonito Oliva writes a text for the playbill. *Il tè di Alice* will be presented again in May at the Stedelijk Museum, Amsterdam; the Kolpinghaus, Offenbach; and Galerie Senatore, Stuttgart. On this occasion, Lo Zoo is joined by the actress Claudia Fiorelli and the musicians William Hagans, Guido Scategni, Nino Peluffo, Dennis Kaufman, and Mike Wotell.

March 22: His solo exhibition at the Museum Boijmans Van Beuningen in Rotterdam opens. Included in the show are twenty mirror paintings created between 1962 and 1968; some of the Minus Objects, along with two giant posters of the objects photographed in his studio; *Pietra miliare* and *Tenda di lampadine* (*Milestone*, 1967 [plate 98], and *Lightbulb Curtain*, 1967 [see fig. 80]); *Orchestra di stracci* and *Colonne di stracci* (*Orchestra of Rags* and *Column of Rags*, 1968); and *Labirinto e megafoni* (*Labyrinth and Megaphones*, 1968–69), within which he places the three megaphones used the year before for an action in the courtyard of his studio, *Le trombe del giudizio* (*The Trumpets of Judgment*; see fig. 235). He revives the latter, together with Lionello Gennero and Maria Pioppi, on the day of the opening. The exhibition catalogue includes texts by Henry Martin and the artist.

April 18: Lo Zoo's action *Bella gente* (*Beautiful People*) is presented at the Salone delle Mostre of the Istituto Bancario San Paolo in Turin on the occasion of the opening of the exhibition *Linee della giovane arte torinese* (*Lines of the Young Turinese Artists*). For this action, the members of Lo Zoo show up wearing bourgeois clothing, put on their Zoo garments and together paint a group work, change clothes again, copy the just-created painting onto sheets of drawing paper, put their Zoo clothing back on, and leave.

May 9: In Amsterdam, at Paradiso, one of the best-known European clubs for alternative youth culture at this time, Lo Zoo presents *Concerto da gabbia* (*Cage Concert*).

May 13–June 15: The Albright-Knox Art Gallery in Buffalo exhibits a group of Pistoletto's mirror paintings. The catalogue essay is by the curator Robert M. Murdock.

May 13: Lo Zoo's performance *I ratti baratti* (*The Bartering Rats*; see fig. 91) is presented at De Lantaren in Rotterdam. It is performed again in Heidelberg on May 18 as part of Festival Intermedia 69. This occasion marks the first appearance of a large sheet—subsequently used

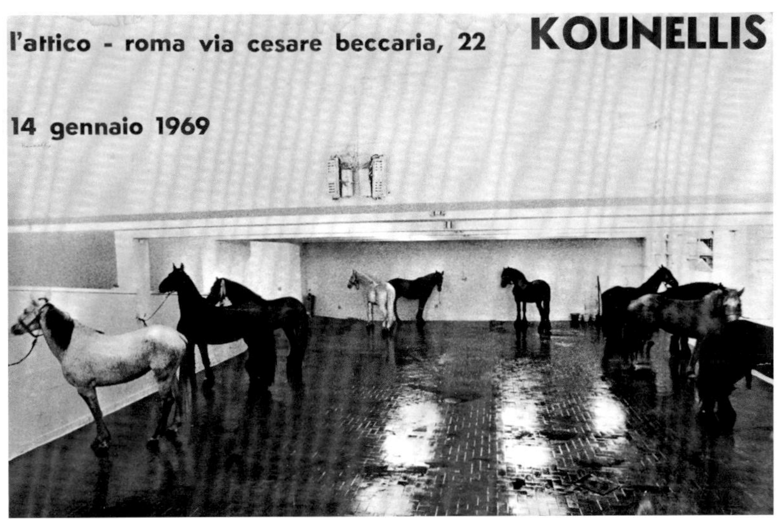

FIG. 241. Poster for Jannis Kounellis's solo exhibition at Galleria L'Attico's new space, Rome, January 14, 1969. Courtesy of L'Attico Archive-Fabio Sargentini, Rome

1969

At the end of the 1960s, Turin becomes a critical site for social conflict in Italy.

January 14: On the occasion of the inauguration of Galleria L'Attico's new space in Rome—a garage—Jannis Kounellis brings in twelve horses. Visitors are invited to interact with the animals, offering them food and petting them.

February 27: Richard Nixon's visit to Rome provokes a series of demonstrations during which one student dies.

March 22: At the Kunsthalle Bern, the exhibition *Live in Your Head: When Attitudes Become Form* —organized by Harald Szeemann, the director of the Kunsthalle—focuses on conceptual tendencies, presenting research at the boundaries between concept, process, and information. At the same time, the exhibition *Op Losse Schroeven Situaties en Cryptostructuren* (*On Loose Screw Situations and Cryptostructures*), under the direction of Wim Beeren, is on view at the Stedelijkmuseum, Amsterdam.

April 2: The exhibition *New-dada e pop art newyorkesi*, organized by Luigi Mallé, opens at the Galleria Civica d'Arte Moderna in Turin.

May 2: In Rome, Galleria L'Attico presents the wall drawings of Sol LeWitt.

May 31: The Galleria Nazionale d'Arte Moderna in Rome holds an important retrospective, curated by Palma Bucarelli, of the work of Pino Pascali, who had died in a motorcycle accident in September 1968.

July: The publication of Carla Lonzi's *Autoritratto* (*Self-Portrait*)—an unedited transcript of her dialogues with various artists—marks the beginning of an important critical practice that rejects interpretation in favor of the direct recording of events.

September 11: A large strike by workers in the engineering industry marks the beginning of the first "autunno caldo" (hot autumn), which will lead in December to the signing of a national labor contract. During these demonstrations, the leftwing group Lotta continua (Continuous Struggle) is founded and in November begins publication of a homonymous magazine.

September 21: The event *Campo urbano: interventi estetici nella dimensione collettiva urbana* (*Urban Field: Aesthetic Interventions in a Collective Urban Dimension*), curated by Luciano Caramel, Ugo Mulas, and Bruno Munari, provides for a series of actions in the historic center of Como in northern Italy, as well as interactions between artists and the people.

October 1: The playwright and composer Dario Fo's *Il Mistero buffo* (*The Comic Mystery*)—a miscellany of proletarian theater texts—is presented in Sestri Levante in Liguria, opening up a new line of experimentation in the theater.

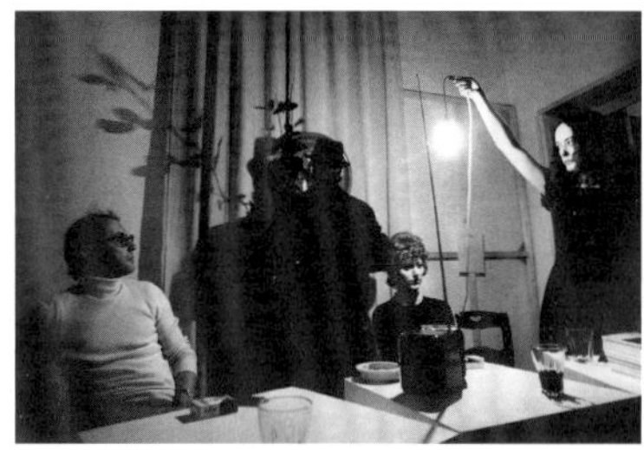

FIG. 242. Presentation of Pistoletto's book *L'Uomo nero, il lato insopportabile* (*The Minus Man, the Unbearable Side*) at Galleria dell'Ariete, Milan, March 24, 1970. From left to right are Tommaso Trini, Pistoletto (from the back), Franca Sacchi, and Maria Pioppi. Photograph by Ugo Mulas © Ugo Mulas Heirs. All rights reserved

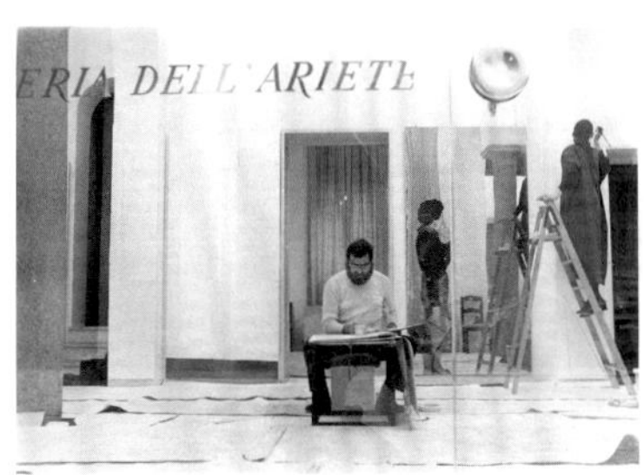

FIG. 243. Pistoletto and Maria Pioppi during the exhibition *Tutte le donne* (*All the Women*) at Galleria dell'Ariete, Milan, March 1970. Photograph by Ugo Mulas © Ugo Mulas Heirs. All rights reserved

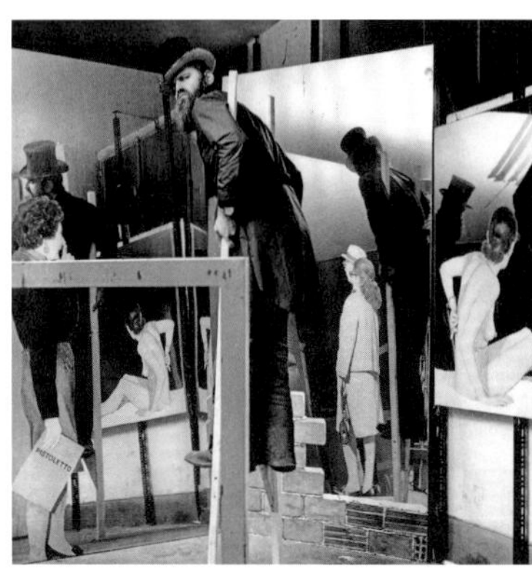

FIG. 244. Pistoletto in his studio in Turin, fall 1970, with the costume and short stilts used in Lo Zoo's performance *Bello e basta* (*Beautiful and Enough*; see figs. 93–95). Around him are some of his mirror paintings, including *Visitatrice con catalogo* (*Visitor with Catalogue*, 1969; plate 49), *Uomo e donna con occhiali neri* (*Man and Woman with Dark Glasses*, 1970; see fig. 151), *Maria* (1969), and *Muretto di mattoni* (*Small Wall of Bricks*, 1970; plate 53). Photograph by Ugo Mulas © Ugo Mulas Heirs. All rights reserved

in other Zoo performances—made from raw, unprimed canvases sewn together.

May–October: After its European tour, Lo Zoo spends several months in Corniglia, where, working in a piazza in the town, the group experiments with a theater method they call *Il gioco dell'Uomo nero* (*The Game of the Minus Man*), conceived to allow each person the greatest possible creative participation.

October 25: *Lo Zoo scopre l'Uomo nero* (*The Zoo Discovers the Minus Man*) is presented at Galleria Sperone in Turin. This is an attempt to bring the game *l'Uomo nero* from Corniglia, where it was created and practiced, into the gallery.

November 14: At a staging of *L'Uomo nero* at Pio Monti's Artestudio in Macerata, the police interrupt the performance and order the American members of Lo Zoo to leave Italy. The police had been called in when the public, crowding around the entrance to the gallery, were blocking traffic. The American members of the group are ordered to leave the country on the pretext of an old law related to the residency permits of foreigners, although the real reason is their long hair and unconventional appearance.

December 1969–January 1970: In precisely one month, in final draft form on 365 pages of a diary, Pistoletto writes the book *L'Uomo nero, il lato insopportabile* (*The Minus Man, the Unbearable Side*). It will be published in 1970 by Rumma Editore, the art dealer Marcello Rumma's publishing house.

Between 1969 and 1970, Pistoletto creates his first "multiple" and begins to experiment with silkscreen, creating a mirror-painting self-portrait issued in two different editions by Gabriele Mazzotta in Milan: an edition of thirty on gold-plated silver, and an edition of one hundred on nickel-plated copper (see fig. 6).

The principal texts on the artist this year, written by critics and the artist himself, include Grace Glueck, "Highways, Mirrors and . . . Gee," *New York Times*, February 2; Henry Martin, "Pistoletto," *Art International* 13, no. 2 (February 20, 1969), pp. 29–32; Guido Boursier, "Far scattare nella gente meccanismi di liberazione," *Sipario* (Milan), no. 276 (April); and Michelangelo Pistoletto, "Lo Zoo," *Teatro* (Milan) 1.

The first monograph on Pistoletto's work, *Pistoletto: dentro/fuori lo specchio* (*Pistoletto: Inside/Outside The Mirror*), is published. Written by Alberto Boatto, with the text in Italian, French, and English, it is released by Fantini Editrice in Rome.

1970

January 31: The first installation of *Ufficio dell'Uomo nero* (*Office of the Minus Man*; see fig. 67) takes place at the Museo Civico in Bologna on the occasion of the *III Biennale: January '70*.

February: During the opening of his solo exhibition *Operazione subacquea* (*Underwater Operation*), organized by Lucio Amelio at the Naples gallery Modern Art Agency, Pistoletto installs the show in the presence of the public while dressed as a scuba diver.

March 6: He has a solo exhibition at Galleria Sperone in Turin titled *Padre Figlio Spirito Santo e Le Tre Grazie* (*Father Son Holy Spirit and the Three Graces*), in which he exhibits six canvases covered with mica, created between 1966 and 1970.

March 24: His solo exhibition at Beatrice Monti's Galleria dell'Ariete in Milan opens. During the month of the exhibition, titled *Tutte le donne* (*All the Women*), Maria Pioppi, assisted by Pistoletto, paints large canvases that cover the walls of the gallery. The opening features a launch/performance of the book *L'Uomo nero, il lato insopportabile*, in collaboration with the critic Tommaso Trini and the musician Franca Sacchi.

May 31: On the occasion of the group exhibition *Processi di pensiero visualizzati* (*Thought Processes Visualized*) at the Kunstmuseum, Lucerne, he exhibits a banner that reads "Si può partecipare a tutte le mostre" (One can participate in all exhibitions) inside the museum, and one that reads "Non si può partecipare a tutte le mostre" (One cannot participate in all exhibitions) outside the museum.

June 12: The exhibition *Conceptual Art, Arte Povera, Land Art* opens at Galleria Civica d'Arte Moderna in Turin. Organized by Germano Celant, it includes works by the artists Joseph Beuys, Bruce Nauman, Pino Pascali, Pistoletto, and Robert Smithson, among many others.

July 2: For the exhibition *Information* at the Museum of Modern Art in New York, giant posters of the pages of Pistoletto's text "Le ultime parole famose" (Famous Last Words) are glued to the floor.

September 12 and 15: Lo Zoo presents *Chi sei tu?* (*Who Are You?*) at Bitef (the Belgrade International Theatre Festival) and at a theater in Novi Sad, north of Belgrade. The Naples gallery owner Lucio Amelio participates in the Belgrade performance.

October 21–28: Lo Zoo's final performance, *Bello e basta* (*Beautiful and Enough*; see figs. 93–95), takes place at Teatro Uomo in Milan.

November: On the occasion of the exhibition *Vitalità del negativo* (*Vitality of the Negative*) at the Palazzo delle Esposizioni in Rome, Ugo Mulas creates his famous photograph in which he is reflected in Pistoletto's mirror painting *Donna nuda di schiena* (*Nude Woman from the Back*, 1966).

Summer: Pistoletto rents an apartment in Turin, on via Provana, where he lives and exhibits his collection of works by Arte Povera artists from Turin.

A book on his father's work, written by Giovanni Petrillo, is published by Toso Editore in Turin.

Principal critical texts on the artist that appear in journals this year are Germano Celant, "Lo Zoo di M. Pistoletto," *Sipario* 291 (October), whose cover features side-by-side photographs of Lo Zoo and El Teatro Campesino; Franco Quadri, "Le sperimentazioni di Pistoletto," *NAC* (Notiziario Arte Contemporanea) 3 (December); and Achille Bonito Oliva, "Gesti di liberazione," *Sipario* 296 (December), pp. 56–59.

November 28: Italy's Camera dei Deputati (Chamber of Deputies) approves the law legalizing divorce.

December 11: The student movement obtains open access for high-school graduates to all university divisions.

December 12: In Milan, in the headquarters of the Banca Nazionale dell'Agricoltura in Piazza Fontana, a bomb kills seventeen people.

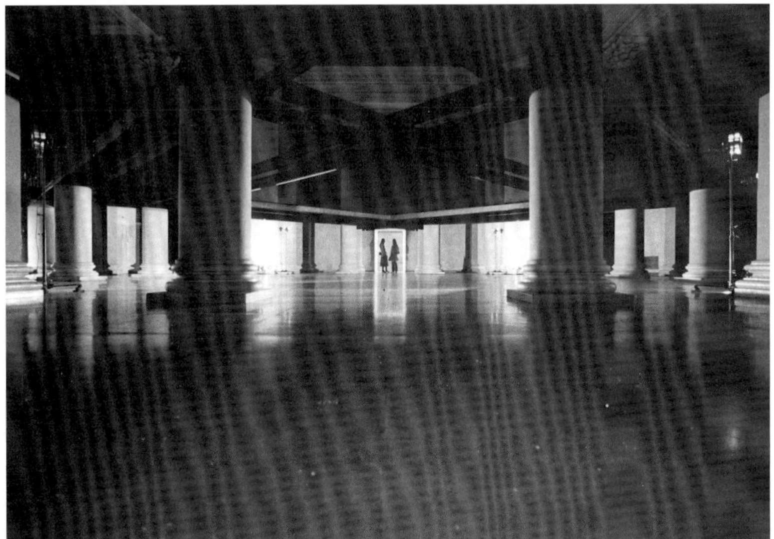

FIG. 245. The courtyard of the Palazzo delle Esposizioni during the exhibition *Vitalità del negativo* (*Vitality of the Negative*), installed by the architect Piero Sartogo, Rome, 1970. Photograph by Ugo Mulas © Ugo Mulas Heirs. All rights reserved

1970

February 25: In Turin, Galleria Sperone organizes American artist Bruce Nauman's first solo exhibition in Italy, featuring the work *Touch and Sound Walls*.

April 4: At Galleria L'Attico in Rome, the artist Gino De Dominicis presents *Lo Zodiaco*, in which the zodiac signs are personified tautologically by things and people.

June 12: The exhibition *Conceptual Art, Arte Povera, Land Art*, organized by Germano Celant at the Galleria Civica d'Arte Moderna in Turin, marks a moment of conjunction between the Arte Povera tendency and international developments in the arts.

November: *Re nudo*, an Italian magazine dedicated to the counterculture, begins publication. Two years later, it will organize the Festival del proletariato giovanile (Festival of the Young Proletariat).

November 30: The exhibition *Vitalità del negativo nell'arte italiana, 1960–1970* (*The Vitality of the Negative in Italian Art, 1960–1970*) opens at the Palazzo delle Esposizioni in Rome. It is promoted by the association Incontri Internazionali d'Arte, founded by Graziella Lonardi Buontempo, and is curated by Achille Bonito Oliva. The exhibition brings together Italian works from the 1960s that share an anthropological approach to reality.

December 8: An attempted military coup, known as Golpe Borghese, is thwarted by a neo-Fascist group but is not publicized until the following March.

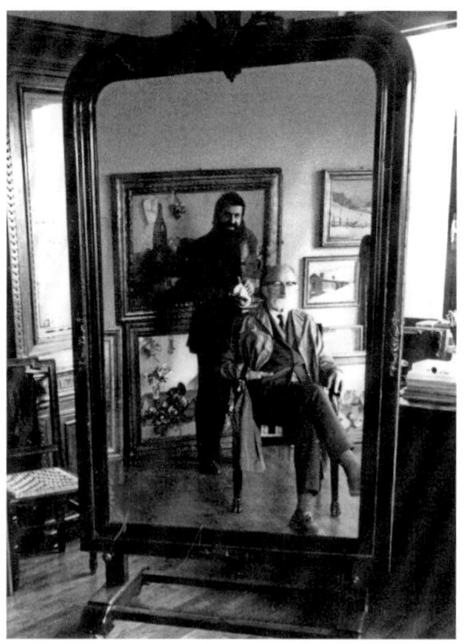

FIG. 246. Michelangelo and his father, Ettore Olivero Pistoletto, in the latter's study, Susa, 1971. A photograph from the same session is later published in the exhibition catalogue for *Padre e figlio* (*Father and Son*), Galleria Sperone, Turin, June 1973. Photograph by Paolo Mussat Sartor. Courtesy of Cittadellarte-Fondazione Pistoletto, Biella

1971

February 28–April 18: Pistoletto's Minus Object *Metrocubo d'infinito* (*Cubic Meter of Infinity*, 1966; plate 96) and the mirror painting *Cordone* (*Cord*, 1970) are included in the exhibition *Elf Italiener Heute* (*Eleven Italians Today*) at the Museum am Ostwall in Dortmund, Germany. The other artists represented are Getulio Alviani, Agostino Bonalumi, Enrico Castellani, Mario Ceroli, Lucio Del Pezzo, Ugo La Pietra, Gino Marotta, Giulio Paolini, Gianni Piacentino, and Pino Spagnulo.

March 5–April 4: He participates in the exhibition *Multiples: The First Decade* at the Philadelphia Museum of Art, showing a work titled *Gold Nails* that consists of a Plexiglas cylinder containing eleven gold nails. The work is issued in an edition of ninety.

March 25: He exhibits the mirror painting *Uomo e donna con occhiali neri* (*Man and Woman with Dark Glasses*, 1970; see fig. 151) in *20 artistas italianos* (*20 Italian Artists*) at the Museo de Arte Moderno in Mexico City.

April 22: His mirror painting *Tenda rosa* (*Red Curtain*, 1966) is included in the exhibition *Métamorphose de l'object* (*Metamorphosis of the Object*) at the Palais des Beaux-Arts in Brussels.

May 26: *Arte Povera: 13 Italienische Kunstler* (*Arte Povera: 13 Italian Artists*) opens at the Kunstverein, Munich. Pistoletto exhibits *Metrocubo d'infinito* (*Cubic Meter of Infinity*, 1966; plate 96) and creates additional works on site that focus on the relationship between communication, imagination, visibility, and the art object.

September 8: His mother dies at age seventy-five.

September 21: His twin daughters, Armona and Pietra, are born.

October 4: An exhibition of his mirror paintings opens at Galerie M. E. Thelen in Cologne.

December: The Milan magazine *L'uomo e l'arte* (no. 7) publishes a lengthy piece on his work that includes critical texts by Germano Beringheli, Franco Quadri, Gualtiero Schönenberg, and Tommaso Trini.

1972

January 6: He participates in the exhibition *Sharp-Focus Realism* at the Sidney Janis Gallery in New York, showing the mirror painting *Uomo con pantaloni gialli* (*Man with Yellow Pants*, 1964; see fig. 134).

February: In Barberino Valdelsa (Siena) in Tuscany, he renovates an abandoned farm, where he lives for a few months with his family and his artist friends Stefano Giolitti and Franco Volontè and their families. The farm is owned by the Corsini princes, to whom he pays a symbolic rent of 1,000 lire a year.

November: He moves with his family to his house in the mountains in San Sicario, in Val di Susa, where he lives and works until 1978, while continuing to use his studio on via Reymond in Turin during trips to the city. Pistoletto had acquired the house in San Sicario in 1968 in order to pursue his passion for skiing. San Sicario is at the center of one of the largest skiing regions in Europe, via Lattea. In 1974, Pistoletto will create the mirror painting *Autoritratto con gli sci* (*Self-Portrait with Skis*).

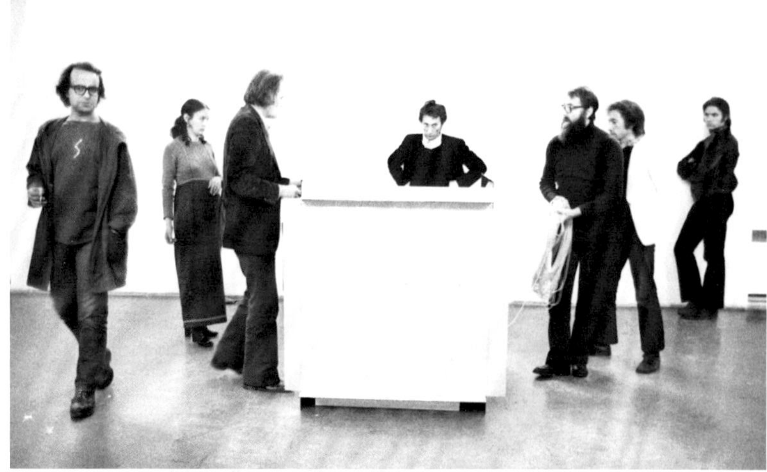

FIG. 247. The preparation of *Metrocubo d'infinito* (*Cubic Meter of Infinity*, 1966; plate 96) in the exhibition *Arte Povera*, Kunstverein München, May 1971. From left to right are Emilio Prini, Maria Pioppi, Mario Merz, Giovanni Anselmo, Pistoletto, an unidentified man, and Fabio Sargentini. Photograph by Claudio Abate. Courtesy of Cittadellarte-Fondazione Pistoletto, Biella

1971

February: The first National Women's Liberation Conference is held in Rome.

April 2: Fabio Mauri presents the performance *Che cos'è il fascismo* (*What Is Fascism?*)—a representation of the organization of power and its mechanisms of coercion and propaganda—at the Safa Palatino film studios in Rome.

April 27: On the occasion of his debut at the Teatro Eliseo in Rome, the avant-garde director Robert Wilson stages *Deafman Glance*, a theater work without words.

June 13: In Italian local elections, a large segment of the electorate votes for the party of the extreme right, Movimento Sociale Italiano (MSI).

September: The magazine *Data* begins publication. It is under the direction of the critic Tommaso Trini, who will dedicate the cover of each issue to a photograph of the work of a particular artist, thus promoting photography's documentary role.

September 17: Elio Petri's film *La classe operaia va in paradiso* (*The Working Class Goes to Heaven*) condemns the commitment of the student movement and the unions, who are characterized as guilty of a failure to recognize the true reality in which workers live.

1972

March 3: The left-wing terrorist group Brigate Rosse (Red Brigades) organizes its first kidnapping, subjecting Idalgo Macchiarini, a director of Sit-Siemens in Milan, to a political trial for several hours before releasing him.

March 17: Enrico Berlinguer becomes national secretary of the Italian Communist party. In subsequent years he will be a proponent, along with Aldo Moro, of a meeting of the various parties in the center of the political spectrum as part of the strategy known as *compromesso storico* (historic compromise).

March 18: At Lucio Amelio's gallery Modern Art Agency in Naples, the experimental films of the Belgian poet and artist Marcel Broodthaers are screened for the first time in Italy.

April 3: In Rimini, during a meeting of the far-left group Lotta Continua (Continuous Struggle), the participants are invited to prepare for combat. This moment is considered the beginning of a second phase of a more openly violent and militaristic struggle.

June 11: At the 36th Venice Biennale, the exhibition *Opera e comportamento* (*Artwork and Behavior*), curated by Francesco Arcangeli, Renato Barilli, and Marco Valsecchi, marks the official inclusion of photography and video at the Biennale.

June 30: Harald Szeemann, the secretary general of Documenta 5 in Kassel, Germany, proposes a new way of thinking about the quinquennial exhibition, opening it up to a reflection on the entire territory of visual production and the power of the media to invade the imagination.

December 15: The law establishing the right of conscientious objection is passed in Italy, giving young people eligible for the draft the option of declining military service.

1973

March–April: He exhibits the mirror painting *I voyeurs* (*The Voyeurs*, 1971) in the group show *Combattimento per un'immagine: fotografi e pittori* (*Fighting for an Image: Photographers and Painters*) at Galleria Civica d'Arte Moderna in Turin.

May: An exhibition of works resulting from a collaboration between Pistoletto and the artist Vettor Pisani is on view at the Marlborough Gallery in Rome. Titled *Plagio* (*Plagiarism*), the exhibition includes a catalogue with text by Maurizio Calvesi. The two artists had begun collaborating in 1970 and will continue to work together until 1976.

June 7: In a solo exhibition at Galleria dell'Ariete in Milan, he exhibits a group of new mirror paintings, the first created using the silkscreen process that are not issued as multiples but rather as unique works. These are prepared in the print shop of Renato Volpini, where Alberto Serighelli works as an art printer. (In September of this year, Serighelli will open his own studio in Milan, which Pistoletto continues to use to this day to produce his mirror paintings.) The catalogue contains a text by Pistoletto and photographs by Antonia Mulas that document certain phases of the works' production.

June: He has an exhibition with his father, titled *Padre e figlio* (*Father and Son*), at Galleria Sperone in Turin. Michelangelo shows mirror paintings, and his father shows oil paintings—still lifes depicting metal objects that reflect the surrounding space and the artist in the act of painting.

October: Pistoletto's *La venere con la pipa* (*The Venus with the Pipe*, 1973) is illustrated on the cover of the Milan magazine *Data*.

November 23: His solo exhibition opens at the Kestner Gesellschaft in Hanover, Germany. It is the most extensive exhibition of the mirror paintings to date, consisting of forty-two works created between 1962 and 1974. The catalogue includes an essay by Wieland Schmied, an interview with the artist by Mirella Bandini, and an anthology of critical essays.

November 30: He includes a group of mirror paintings in the exhibition *Contemporanea*, which takes place in the parking lot of the Villa Borghese in Rome.

1974

January 25: His solo exhibition at Galerie Gunter Sachs in Hamburg, Germany, includes a group of mirror paintings.

March 2: He has a solo exhibition at Galerie Löwenadler in Stockholm, his first in Sweden.

April 27: He shows forty-one mirror paintings in a solo exhibition at the Mathildenhöhe in Darmstadt, Germany. The catalogue includes an essay by Bernd Krimmel and extensive photographic documentation of the installation of the exhibition.

November 6: The exhibition *New Paintings by Pistoletto* opens at the Sidney Janis Gallery in New York. It includes the mirror paintings *Marcel Duchamp seduto su un Brancusi* (*Duchamp Seated on a Brancusi*, 1974), which was created using a photograph by Ugo Mulas, and *Gabbia* (*Cage*, 1969; plate 50), a work made up of twenty-nine steel panels, eight of which are exhibited here lined up along the gallery walls. The text of the accompanying catalogue is by Tommaso Trini.

Translated from the Italian by Marguerite Shore.

For a complete listing of Pistoletto's exhibitions, see the artist's Web site at www.pistoletto.it

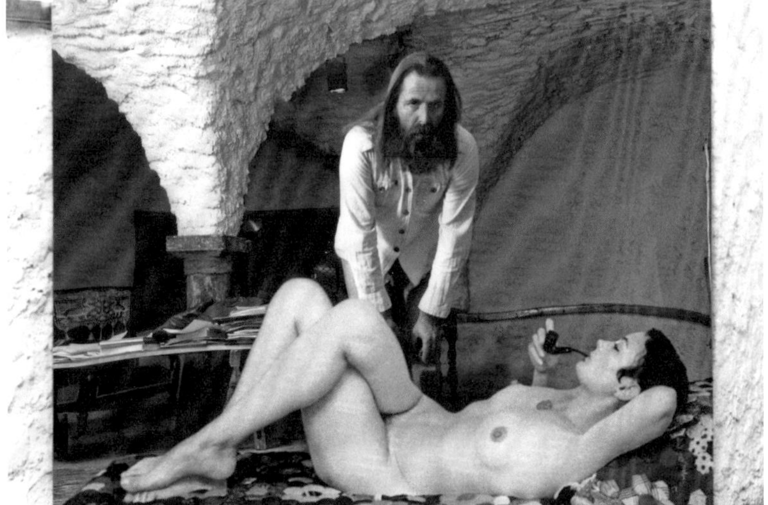

FIG. 248. Pistoletto reflected in the mirror painting *La venere con la pipa* (*The Venus with the Pipe*, 1973) in his studio in San Sicario, 1974. Photograph by Paolo Mussat Sartor. Courtesy of Cittadellarte-Fondazione Pistoletto, Biella

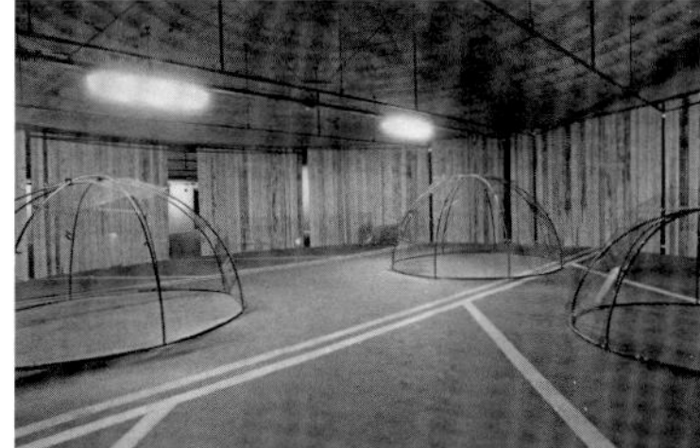

FIG. 249. Works by Mario Merz in the exhibition *Contemporanea* in the parking lot of the Villa Borghese, Rome, 1973. Photograph by Massimo Piersanti. Courtesy of Incontri Internazionali d'Arte

1973

The first cooperative gynecological centers in Italy open in several towns.

March: The exhibition *Combattimento per un'immagine: fotografi e pittori* (*Fighting for an Image: Photographers and Painters*), curated by Luigi Carluccio and Daniela Palazzoli, opens at the Galleria Civica d'Arte Moderna in Turin, sparking debate in Italy on the role of photography—on its relation to the other arts and its formal autonomy.

April 16: Two sons of a right-wing militant die in a fire set in their house in Rome. The homicide is attributed to the radical left-wing group Potere Operaio (Workers' Power)

September: In Florence, Maria Gloria Bicocchi opens art/tapes/22, a center for video production that will make a fundamental contribution to video art in Italy.

November 22: Following the Yom Kippur War, which disrupts oil production and shipping and thus causes an increase in oil prices, a state of austerity is proclaimed in Italy and energy-saving measures are imposed.

November 30: *Contemporanea*, an event promoted by the association Incontri Internazionali d'Arte and organized by a curatorial group coordinated by Achille Bonito Oliva—whose other members include Bruno Corà, Mario Diacono, Yvon Lambert, Alessandro Mendini, Daniela Palazzoli, and Fabio Sargentini—opens in the parking lot of the Villa Borghese in Rome. It is part festival and part exhibition and presents the most innovative work of the moment in various creative fields: visual arts, theater, poetry, music, and dance. For the occasion, the artist Christo "wraps" a stretch of the Aurelian wall.

December 10: The Brigate Rosse kidnap Ettore Amerio, the personnel manager of Fiat.

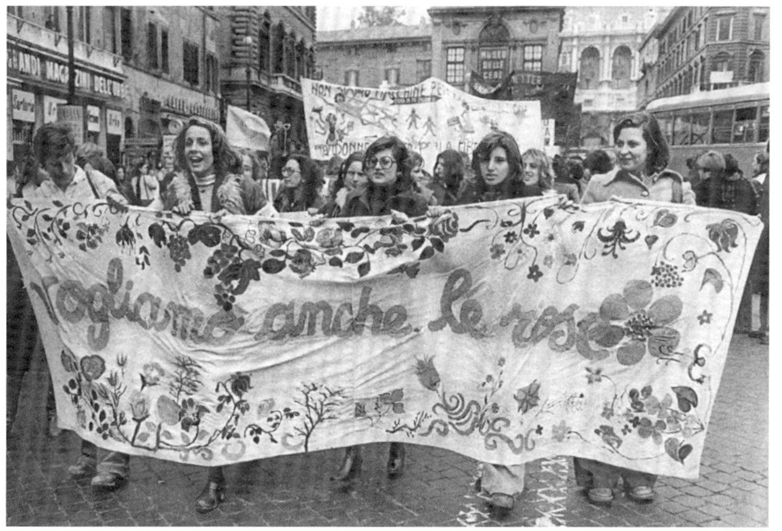

FIG. 250. Demonstration by feminists, Rome, 1973. Photograph by Tano D'Amico. Courtesy of Tano D'Amico

1974

The first forms of civil disobedience in Italy, such as the deliberate underpayment of bills, take place, especially in Turin.

May 12: A referendum on the abolition of the divorce law results in a victory for pro-divorce proponents in Italy.

September 8: In Pinerolo, in the province of Turin, the Brigate Rosse members Renato Curcio and Alberto Franceschini are arrested. Subsequent investigations reveal Turin to be the organizational center of left-wing terrorism.

October: Following various demands for modernization, the Venice Biennale of this year, dedicated to Chile, opens without a precise installation program. As a sign of solidarity with those resisting the dictatorship in Chile, artists are asked to create a series of murals in Venice dedicated to Chilean culture. Among this Biennale's distinctive features are the lack of both an identifying number in its title and a catalogue.

December 10: Luchino Visconti's film *Gruppo di famiglia in un interno* (translated in English as *Conversation Piece*), paints a picture of the disintegration of the family and the impossibility for an intellectual who has survived the war to coexist with the youth culture and modern lifestyles produced by the movement of 1968.

Translated from the Italian by Marguerite Shore.

BIBLIOGRAPHY

Celant, Germano, ed. *Identité italienne: l'art en Italie depuis 1959*. Exh. cat. Florence: Centro Di, 1981.

—— ed. *The Italian Metamorphosis, 1943–1968*. Exh. cat. New York: Solomon R. Guggenheim Museum, 1994.

Flood, Richard, and Francis Morris, eds. *Zero to Infinity: Arte Povera, 1962–1972*. Exh. cat. Minneapolis: Walker Art Center, 2001.

Gianelli, Ida, ed. *Un'avventura internazionale: Torino e le arti, 1950–1970*. Exh. cat. Milan: Charta, 1993.

Linee della ricerca artistica in Italia, 1960–1980, vol. 2, *Documentazione*. Exh. cat. Rome: De Luca, 1981.

Sabbatucci, Giovanni, and Vidotto, Vittorio, eds. *Storia d'Italia*, vol. 5, *La Repubblica, 1943–1963*. Rome-Bari: Laterza, 1997.

—— eds. *Storia d'Italia*, vol. 6, *L'Italia contemporanea, dal 1963 a oggi*. Rome-Bari: Laterza, 1999

Tranfaglia, Nicola, ed. *Storia di Torino*, vol. 9, *Gli anni della Repubblica*. Turin: Einaudi, 1999.

CHECKLIST OF THE EXHIBITION

Jennifer Wilkinson

Note to the Reader

The information in the checklist represents ongoing research.

The alternate titles listed have appeared in previous publications inaccurately; they are listed here for research purposes.

Absence of a provenance field indicates that the work has never left the artist's collection. Galleries that showed Pistoletto's works in the early years (1960s) may have held ownership of them and are therefore included in the provenance.

In the 1960s Galleria Sperone changed names a number of times. In 1964 it was called Gian Enzo Sperone—Arte moderna; in April 1965 the name was shortened to Gian Enzo Sperone; and in June 1967 it became Galleria Sperone. For the purposes of simplicity, it is referred to as Galleria Sperone throughout the checklist.

Exhibition catalogues are listed under References if a work was illustrated in the catalogue but was not included in the exhibition. Citations included under References correspond to illustrations of the work.

EARLY WORKS

1
Autoritratto (*Self-Portrait*), 1956
Oil and acrylic on canvas
55⅛ x 35 7/16 inches (140 x 90 cm)
Collection of the artist

Solo exhibitions: Palazzo Grassi, Venice, 1976; p. 5, cat. 1 (repr.).
References: Forte di Belvedere, Florence, 1984; p. 16, cat. 2 (repr.).

2
La folla (*The Crowd*), 1959
Oil and acrylic on canvas
78¾ x 47¼ inches (200 x 120 cm)
Private collection

Provenance: Acquired by the present owner, directly from the artist, n.d.
Solo exhibitions: Palazzina della Società delle Belle Arti and Castello di Rivoli Museo d'Arte Contemporanea, Rivoli-Turin, 2000–2001; p. 43 (color repr.).

3
Esperimento (*Experiment*), 1959
Silver, acrylic, rope, wood, and canvas
29⅛ x 23⅝ inches (74 x 60 cm)
Collection of the artist

4
Autoritratto argento (*Silver Self-Portrait*), 1960
Oil, acrylic, and silver on wood
78¾ x 78¾ inches (200 x 200 cm)
Collection of the artist

Solo exhibitions: Forte di Belvedere, Florence, 1984; p. 25, cat. 13 (color repr.). The Institute for Contemporary Art, P.S. 1 Museum, New York, 1988; p. 36 (color repr.). Museu d'Art Contemporani de Barcelona, 2000; p. 17 (color repr.). Palazzina della Società delle Belle Arti and Castello di Rivoli Museo d'Arte Contemporanea, Rivoli-Turin, 2000–2001; p. 44 (color repr.).
References: Centre d'Art Santa Monica, Barcelona, 1991; p. 25 (repr.).

5
Autoritratto oro (*Gold Self-Portrait*), 1960
Oil, acrylic, and gold on canvas
78¾ x 59 1/16 inches (200 x 150 cm)
Collection of the artist

Solo exhibitions: Forte di Belvedere, Florence, 1984; p. 28, cat. 16 (color repr.). The Institute for Contemporary Art, P.S. 1 Museum, New York, 1988; p. 37 (color repr.). Galleria Nazionale d'Arte Moderna, Rome, 1990; p. 73, cat. 1 (color repr.). Museu d'Art Contemporani de Barcelona, 2000; p. 16 (color repr.). Palazzina della Società delle Belle Arti and Castello di Rivoli Museo d'Arte Contemporanea, Rivoli-Turin, 2000–2001; p. 45 (color repr.). Musée d'Art Moderne et d'Art Contemporain, Nice, 2007; p. 49 (color repr.).
References: Corà 1986; p. 65, no. 28 (repr.). Staatliche Kunsthalle, Baden-Baden, 1988; p. 26 (color repr.). Museu d'Art Contemporani de Barcelona, 2000; p. 16 (repr.). Palazzo Grassi, Venice, 2006; p. 124 (color repr.).

6
Autoritratto bronzo (*Bronze Self-Portrait*), 1961
Oil, bronze, and acrylic on canvas
78¾ x 47¼ inches (200 x 120 cm)
Private collection

Provenance: Marcello and Lia Rumma, Naples, n.d. To the present owner, October 1988.
Solo exhibitions: The Institute for Contemporary Art, P.S. 1 Museum, New York, 1988; p. 34 (repr.).

7
Verso il presente (*Toward the Present*), 1961
Acrylic and plastic varnish on canvas
59 1/16 x 59 1/16 inches (150 x 150 cm)
Collezione La Gaia, Busca, Italy

Provenance: Galleria Giorgio Persano, Turin, n.d. Sold to Collezione La Gaia, Busca, n.d.

8
Il presente—Autoritratto in camicia (*The Present—Self-Portrait in Shirt*), 1961
Acrylic and plastic varnish on canvas
78¾ x 59 1/16 inches (200 x 150 cm)
Collection of the artist

Alternate titles: Autoritratto in camicia; Autoritratto in camicia—Il presente; Uomo in camicia (Il presente); Uomo in camicia [Il presente].

Solo exhibitions: Forte di Belvedere, Florence, 1984; p. 22, cat. 9 (repr.), as *Autoritratto in camicia*. Galleria Nazionale d'Arte Moderna, Rome, 1990; p. 75, cat. 3 (color repr.), as *Uomo in camicia (Il presente)*. The National Museum of Contemporary Art, Seoul, 1994; p. 29 (repr.), as *Uomo in camicia (Il presente)*. Museum Moderner Kunst Stiftung Ludwig, Vienna, 1995; p. 21, cat. 1 (color repr.), as *Autoritratto in camicia—Il presente*. Palazzina della Società delle Belle Arti and Castello di Rivoli Museo d'Arte Contemporanea, Rivoli-Turin, 2000–2001; p. 46 (color repr.), as *Autoritratto in camicia—Il presente*.
References: Forte di Belvedere, Florence, 1984; p. 22, cat. 9 (repr.), as *Autoritratto in camicia*. Kunstnernes Hus, Oslo, 1986; cat. 19 (repr.), as *Selvportrett med skjorte*. Staatliche Kunsthalle, Baden-Baden, 1988; p. 28 (repr.), as *Selbstbildnis mit Hemd*. Castello di Rivoli Museo d'Arte Contemporanea, Rivoli-Turin, 1993; p. 143 (repr.), as *Un olio esposto nel 1960*. Città di Castello (Perugia), 2001; p. 15 (repr.). Musée d'Art Moderne et d'Art Contemporain, Nice, 2007; p. 14 (repr.), as *Le Présent. Autoportrait à la chemise*.
Note: Reproductions of the image have often been reversed.

9
Il presente—Uomo di schiena (*The Present—Man from the Back*), 1961
Acrylic and plastic varnish on canvas
78¾ x 59 1/16 inches (200 x 150 cm)
Collection of the artist

Alternate titles: Il presente. Uomo di schiena; Uomo di schiena—Il presente; Uomo di schiena—Il presente—.

Solo exhibitions: Palazzina della Società delle Belle Arti and Castello di Rivoli Museo d'Arte Contemporanea, Rivoli-Turin, 2000–2001; p. 47 (color repr.), as *Uomo di schiena—Il presente*. Museu d'Art Contemporani de Barcelona, 2000; p. 18 (color repr.), as *Uomo di schiena—Il presente—*, 1960–61. Musée d'Art Moderne et d'Art Contemporain, Nice, 2007; p. 50 (color repr.), as *Il presente. Uomo di schiena*.
References: Fundação de Serralves, Porto, Portugal, 1993; p. 23 (color repr.).

10
Disegno 5 (*Drawing 5*), 1962
Pencil on paper
25 13/16 x 18 11/16 inches (65.5 x 47.5 cm)
Private collection

Alternate title: Disegno.

Provenance: Galleria Il Punto, Turin, by 1962. To the present owner, 1962.
References: Carluccio, Gribaudo, and Sanguineti 1963; (repr.). Forte di Belvedere, Florence, 1984; p. 23, cat. 12 (repr.), as *Disegno*. Corà 1986; p. 29, no. 8 (repr.).

11
Disegno (Drawing), 1962
Pencil on paper
23⅝ x 17¾ inches (60 x 45 cm)
Private collection

Provenance: Galleria Galatea, Turin, by April 1963. To Studio Simonis, Paris, n.d. To the present owner by 2001.
References: Arte Club, Catania, 1993; (repr.).

12
Disegno I (Drawing I), 1962
Pencil on paper
26⅜ x 18⅞ inches (67 x 48 cm)
Collection of Giorgio and Giorgiana Persano

Alternate title: Disegno.

Provenance: Galleria Galatea, Turin, by April 1963. Sold by 1974. To Giorgio Persano, Milan, n.d.
References: Carluccio, Gribaudo, and Sanguineti 1963; (repr.). Corà 1986; p. 29, no. 6 (repr.). Galleria Nazionale d'Arte Moderna, Rome, 1990; p. 20 (repr.), as *Disegno*. Arte Club, Catania, 1993; (repr.).

QUADRI SPECCHIANTI / MIRROR PAINTINGS

13
Figura di profilo (Figure in Profile), 1962
Painted tissue paper on polished stainless steel
24 7/16 x 20½ inches (62 x 52 cm)
François Pinault Foundation

Alternate titles: Persona di profilo; Specchio con figura.

Provenance: Galleria Galatea, Turin, by April 1963. To Galleria Christian Stein, Turin, by January 1968. To Jean Dypréau, Linkebeek, Belgium, by March 1969. To the François Pinault Foundation by November 1998.
Solo exhibitions: Galleria Galatea, Turin, 1963; cat. 13, as *Persona di profilo*, 1963. Galleria Christian Stein, Turin, 1968. Museum Boijmans Van Beuningen, Rotterdam, 1969; cat. IV, as *Figuur en profil*, 1963.
Group exhibitions: Palazzo delle Esposizioni, Rome, 1972–73; p. 126 (repr.), as *Specchio con figura*. Nouveau Musée, Villeurbanne, 1992; p. 221 (color repr.). Fine Arts Museum, Taipei, 1998; pl. 24, p. 64 (color repr.). Palazzo Grassi, Venice, 2006; p. 122 (repr.).

14
Particolari di persone (Details of People), 1962
Painted tissue paper on polished stainless steel
49 3/16 x 48 13/16 inches (125 x 124 cm)
San Francisco Museum of Modern Art. Gift of Edwin Janss, 1978

Alternate title: Due uomini.

Provenance: Galleria Galatea, Turin, by April 1963. To Edwin Janss, Thousand Oaks, Calif., by 1964, through Galerie Ileana Sonnabend, Paris. To the San Francisco Museum of Modern Art, as a gift, in 1978.
Solo exhibitions: Galleria Galatea, Turin, 1963; cat. 6, dated 1963.
Group exhibitions: Museum des 20. Jahrhunderts, Vienna, 1964–65; dated 1963.
References: Boatto 1969; cat. 11 (repr.), as *Due uomini*. Levoy 1991; (repr.).

15
Ritratto di Clino (Portrait of Clino), 1963
Painted tissue paper on polished stainless steel
31½ x 21 11/16 inches (80 x 55 cm)
Private collection

Alternate title: Portrait

Provenance: Acquired by the present owner directly from the artist, 1963.

16
Sacra conversazione, 1963
Painted tissue paper on polished stainless steel
67 x 39⅜ inches (170 x 100 cm)
Albright-Knox Art Gallery, Buffalo. Gift of Seymour H. Knox, Jr., 1964

Alternate title: Gruppo di persone.

Provenance: Robert Elkon Gallery, New York, n.d. To Seymour H. Knox, Jr., Buffalo, n.d. To the Albright-Knox Art Gallery, Buffalo, as a gift, in 1964.
Solo exhibitions: Galleria Galatea, Turin, 1963; cat. 3, as *Gruppo di persone*, 1962. Walker Art Center, Minneapolis, 1966; cat. 2, as *Sacred Conversation*. Albright-Knox Art Gallery, Buffalo, 1969; cat. 2 (repr.).
Group exhibitions: Museum of Art, Carnegie Institute, Pittsburgh, 1964; cat. 159, as *Gruppa di Persone*. J. L. Hudson Gallery, Detroit, 1967; cat. 25, as *Group of People*. National Gallery of Art, Washington, D.C., 1968; p. 94 (repr.). Museo Nacional de Bellas Artes, Buenos Aires, 1969; p. 72, cat. 61 (repr.). Albright-Knox Art Gallery, Buffalo, 1972.

17
Donna seduta di spalle (Seated Woman from Behind), 1963
Painted tissue paper on polished stainless steel
78¾ x 47¼ inches (200 x 120 cm)
The Sonnabend Collection

Alternate title: Donna seduta.

Provenance: Galerie Ileana Sonnabend, Paris, by March 1964. To Galleria Sperone, Turin, by April 1966. To Galleria del Leone, Venice, by September 1966. To the Kornblee Gallery, New York, by April 1967. To the J. L. Hudson Gallery, Detroit, by fall 1967. To the Sonnabend Collection, New York, by October 1988.
Solo exhibitions: Galerie Ileana Sonnabend, Paris, 1964; as *Donna seduta*. Galleria del Leone, Venice, 1964; (repr.). Walker Art Center, Minneapolis, 1966; cat. 7 (repr.), as *Seated Woman*. Kornblee Gallery, New York, 1967. J. L. Hudson Gallery, Detroit, 1967; cat. 3 (repr.), as *Seated Woman*. The Institute for Contemporary Art, P.S. 1 Museum, New York, 1988; p. 40 (repr.), as *Seated Woman*.
Group exhibitions: Centro de Arte Reina Sofía, Madrid, 1990; p. 458 (color repr.). The Solomon R. Guggenheim Museum, New York, 1994–95; cat. 192 (repr.). Montreal Museum of Fine Arts, 2006; p. 257 (repr.).
References: Boatto 1969; cat. 15 (repr.). Forte di Belvedere, Florence, 1984; p. 43, cat. 32 (repr.).
Note: A second, slightly smaller mirror painting from 1963 titled *Donna seduta*, in the collection of the Walker Art Center, Minneapolis, shows the same figure seated facing toward the viewer.

18
Autoritratto (Self-Portrait), 1963
Painted tissue paper on polished stainless steel
47¼ x 47¼ inches (120 x 120 cm)
Private collection. On long-term loan to MART—Museo di Arte Moderna e Contemporanea de Trento e Rovereto, Rovereto, Italy

Alternate titles: Autoportrait; Autoritratto (uomo accovacciato).

Provenance: Giancarlo Ferraresi, n.d. Sold to Galleria Christian Stiein, Milan, and Studio Casoli, Rome, in the 1980s. Sold at "Arte Moderna e Contemporanea," Sotheby's, Milan, November 27, 1990, lot 186 (color repr.). To a private collection, by March 1999. On long-term loan to MART—Museo d'Arte Moderna e Contemporanea di Trento e Rovereto, Rovereto, Italy.
Solo exhibitions: Galleria Sperone, Turin, 1964, (repr.), as *Autoritratto (uomo accovacciato)*. Galleria del Leone Arte Contemporanea, Venice, 1966. Palais des Beaux-Arts, Brussels, 1967, as *Autoportrait*, 1965. Studio Casoli, Rome, 1998, p. 7 (color repr.). Palazzina della Società delle Belle Arti and Castello di Rivoli Museo d'Arte Contemporaea, Rivoli-Turin, 2001, p. 52 (color repr.), dated 1964.
Group exhibitions: Naviglio 2, Milan, 1966; (repr.), dated 1964. Chiostro del Bramante, Rome, 1999; p. 177 (color repr.). Museo d'Arte Moderna e Contemporanea di Trento e Rovereto, Rovereto, 2005. Museo d'Arte Moderna e Contemporanea di Trento e Rovereto, Rovereto, 2007; p. 125, cat. 47 (repr.). Villa e Collezione Panza, Varese, 2010; p. 69 (repr.). Museo d'Arte Moderna e Contemporanea di Trento e Rovereto, Rovereto, 2008. Villa e Collezione Panza, Varese, 2009, fig. 15, pp. 68–69, 90 (repr.).
References: Naviglio 2, Milan, 1966. Boatto 1969; cat. 19 (repr.), dated 1964. Minola et al. 2000; p. 82 (repr.), dated 1964. Le Musée d'Art Moderne et d'Art Contemporain, Nice, 2007; p. 30 (repr.), dated 1964.

19
Bottiglia per terra (*Bottle on the Floor*), 1963
Photographic paper on polished stainless steel
90 9/16 x 47¼ inches (230 x 120 cm)
The Sonnabend Collection

Provenance: Galerie Ileana Sonnabend, Paris, by March 1964. To the Leo Castelli Gallery, New York, by April 1966. To the Kornblee Gallery, New York, by April 1967. To The New Gallery, Cleveland, by May 1969. To the Sonnabend Collection, New York, by March 1984.
Solo exhibitions: Galerie Ileana Sonnabend, Paris, 1964; (repr.). Walker Art Center, Minneapolis, 1966; cat. 8, as *Bottle on the Floor*. Kornblee Gallery, New York, 1967. Albright-Knox Art Gallery, Buffalo, 1969; cat. 3, as *Wine Bottle (Bottle on the Floor)*. The Institute for Contemporary Art, P.S. 1 Museum, New York, 1988; p. 54 (repr.). Galleria Nazionale d'Arte Moderna, Rome, 1990; p. 80, cat. 8 (repr.). The National Museum of Contemporary Art, Seoul, 1994; pp. 32–33 (repr.).
Group exhibitions: Royal Academy of Arts, London, 1989; p. 353, cat. 200 (color repr.). Centro de Arte Reina Sofía, Madrid, 1990; p. 459 (color repr.)
References: Forte di Belvedere, Florence, 1984; p. 32, cat. 20 (repr.). Corà 1986; p. 52, no. 13 (repr.). Staatliche Kunsthalle, Baden-Baden, 1988; p. 29 (repr.), as *Flasche auf dem Boden*. Centre d'Art Santa Monica, Barcelona, 1991; p. 33 (color repr.). Museum Moderner Kunst Stiftung Ludwig, Vienna, 1995; p. 22 (color repr.).
Note: Two other mirror paintings exist with the same title. One is a photograph on polished stainless steel (1963) in the collection of the artist; the other is a silkscreen on polished stainless steel (1975) in the collection of Cittadellarte-Fondazione Pistoletto, Biella.

20
Due persone (*Two People*), 1963–64
Painted tissue paper on polished stainless steel
78¾ x 47¼ inches (200 x 120 cm)
The Menil Collection, Houston

Alternate titles: Due persone n. 1; Due persone di schiena; uomo e donna.

Provenance: Kornblee Gallery, New York, by 1967. Sold to John and Dominique de Menil, 1968. To the Menil Foundation, Inc.
Solo exhibitions: Galerie Ileana Sonnabend, Paris, 1964; (repr.). Walker Art Center, Minneapolis, 1966; cat. 10, dated 1963–64. Rice Museum, Houston, 1979; cat. 3, dated 1963–64. The Institute for Contemporary Art, P.S. 1 Museum, New York, 1988; p. 49 (repr.), as *Two People*.
Group exhibitions: Contemporary Arts Museum, Houston, 2001; cat. 19 (color repr.). The Menil Collection, Houston, 2010; p. 59 (repr.).
References: Lippard 1966; p. 190, no. 179 (repr.). Corà 1986; p. 52, no. 13 (repr.), as *Due persone di schiena*. Palazzo Fabroni, Pistoia, 1996; p. 27 (repr.).

21
Chassis (*Frame*), 1964
Photography on polished stainless steel
78¾ x 39⅜ inches (200 x 100 cm)
Private collection

Provenance: Galleria del Leone, Venice, by September 1964. To Galleria Toninelli, Milan, by 1973. To the present owner after 1969.
Solo exhibitions: Galleria del Leone, Venice, 1964. Modern Art Agency (Galleria Lucio Amelio), Naples, 1970. Galleria Toninelli, Rome, 1972. Kestner Gesellschaft, Hanover, Germany, 1973–74; cat. 3, as *Keilrahmen / Telai di quadro (Châssis)*. Studio Casoli, Rome, 1998; p. 8 (color repr.). Studio Casoli, Milan, 2000.
Group exhibitions: Ateneumin Taidemuseo, Helsinki, 1969; cat. 124, as *Kilakehys/Kilram/ Chassis*. Museo Cantonale d'Arte, Lugano, 2006; p. 247, cat. 83 (color repr.).

22
Lampadina (*Lightbulb*), 1964
Painted tissue paper and photograph on polished stainless steel
78¾ x 39⅜ inches (200 x 100 cm)
Estate of Robert Rauschenberg

Provenance: Galleria Sperone, Turin, by October 1964. To Robert Rauschenberg, New York, by April 1966. To the Estate of Robert Rauschenberg, Mount Vernon, Virginia, as a bequest, in May 2008.
Solo exhibitions: Galleria Sperone, Turin, 1964; (repr.). Walker Art Center, Minneapolis, 1966; cat. 13, as *Hanging Light Bulb*. Albright-Knox Art Gallery, Buffalo, 1969; cat. 4, as *Hanging Light Bulb*. The Institute for Contemporary Art, P.S. 1 Museum, New York, 1988; p. 55 (repr.), as *Hanging Lightbulb*.
Note: A number of mirror paintings feature lamps or lightbulbs.

23
Due donne nude che ballano (*Two Nude Women Dancing*), 1964
Painted tissue paper on polished stainless steel
86⅝ x 47¼ inches (220 x 120 cm)
Collection of Beatrice Monti della Corte von Rezzori

Alternate titles: 2 donne nude che ballano; Due donne nude che ballano (da una foto di Muybridge); Donne nude che ballano.

Provenance: Galleria Sperone, Milan, by November 1966. To Galleria Ariete, Milan, by 1973. Sold by the artist to Beatrice Monti della Corte von Rezzori, Florence, by June 1976.
Solo exhibitions: Galleria Sperone, Milan, 1966; as *Donne nude che ballano*. Kestner Gesellschaft, Hanover, Germany, 1973–74; cat. 4, as *Zwei nackte Tänzerinnen / Donne nude che ballano*, 1966. Mathildenhöhe, Darmstadt, 1974; cat. 2 (repr.), as *Donne nude che ballano*, 1966. Palazzo Grassi, Venice, 1976; p. 13, cat. 21 (repr.). Galleria Nazionale d'Arte Moderna, Rome, 1990; p. 82, cat. 10 (repr.), as *Donne nude che ballano*.
Group exhibitions: Badischer Kunstverein, Karlsruhe, 1969; cat. 35 (repr.). Galleria Civica d'Arte Moderna, Turin, 1970; (repr.), as *2 donne nude che ballano*, 1966. Museum am Ostwall, Dortmund, Germany, 1971; cat. 35, as *Due donne nude, che ballano*, 1966. Mura Aureliane, Rome, 1982; p. 97, cat. 158 (repr.).
References: Centre Georges Pompidou, Paris, 1981; p. 195 (repr.), as *Deux femmes nues dançant*, 1966, p. 518 (repr.), as *La balle*. Corà 1986; p. 196, no. 174 (repr.). Fundação de Serralves, Porto, Portugal, 1993; p. 74 (repr.), as *Due donne nude che ballano (da una foto di Muybridge)*.

24
Marzia con la bambina (*Marzia with the Baby*), 1964
Painted tissue paper on polished stainless steel
78¾ x 47¼ inches (200 x 120 cm)
The Sonnabend Collection

Alternate titles: Donna con bambina; Marzia con bambina.

Provenance: Galerie Ileana Sonnabend, Paris, by March 1964. To Galleria Sperone, Turin, by October 1964. To Galerie Ileana Sonnabend, Paris, by October 1966. Transferred to the Sonnabend Collection, New York, by 1988.
Solo exhibitions: Galerie Ileana Sonnabend, Paris, 1964. Galleria Sperone, Turin, 1964; (repr.), as *Donna con bambina*. Walker Art Center, Minneapolis, 1966; cat. 12 (repr.), as *Woman with Child*. J. L. Hudson Gallery, Detroit, 1967; cat. 1 (repr.), as *Woman with Baby*. Museum Boijmans Van Beuningen, Rotterdam, 1969; cat. VI, as *Wandeling met kind*. The Institute for Contemporary Art, P.S. 1 Museum, New York, 1988; p. 53 (repr.).
Group exhibitions: Royal Academy of Arts, London, 1989; p. 352, cat. 199 (repr.). Centro de Arte Reina Sofía, Madrid, 1990; p. 460 (color repr.), as *Marzia con bambina*. Castello di Rivoli Museo d'Arte Contemporanea, Rivoli-Turin, 2000; p. 189 (repr.).
References: Minola et al. 2000; p. 83 (repr.). Miriam and Ira D. Wallach Art Gallery, New York, 2001; p. 43, cat. 7 (color repr.), as *Marzia con bambina*. Lumley 2004; p. 62, cat. 43 (repr.). Musée d'Art Moderne et d'Art Contemporain, Nice, 2007; p. 30 (repr.), as *Marzia à l'enfant*.

25
Persona appoggiata (*Person Leaning*), 1964
Painted tissue paper on polished stainless steel
78¾ x 39⅜ inches (200 x 100 cm)
Collection of Keith L. and Katherine Sachs

Alternate title: Uomo appoggiato.

Provenance: Galerie Ileana Sonnabend, Paris, by March 1964. To the Leo Castelli Gallery, New York, by April 1966. To Dr. and Mrs. Malcolm A. McCannel, Minneapolis, by May 1966. Consigned to Flanders Contemporary Art, Minneapolis, summer 2008. To Keith L. and Katherine Sachs, Philadelphia, fall 2008.
Solo exhibitions: Galerie Ileana Sonnabend, Paris, 1964. Galleria del Leone, Venice, 1964; (repr.),

as *Uomo appoggiato*. Walker Art Center, Minneapolis, 1966; cat. 11, as *Man with Cigarette*.
References: Minola et al. 2000; p. 24 (repr.), as *Uomo appoggiato*, 1962–66.

26
Quattro persone alla balconata (*Four People on a Balcony*), 1964
Painted tissue paper on polished stainless steel
78¾ x 78¾ inches (200 x 200 cm)
Collection of Martin Z. Margulies, Miami

Provenance: Galleria Sperone, Turin, by April 1966. To the Kornblee Gallery, New York, by June 1967. To the J. L. Hudson Gallery, Detroit, by fall 1967. Sold at Sotheby Parke Bernet, New York, November 2, 1978, lot 216. To Martin Z. Margulies, Miami, n.d.
Solo exhibitions: Sala Espressioni—Ideal Standard, Milan, 1965. Walker Art Center, Minneapolis, 1966; cat. 15, as *Four People on a Balcony*. J. L. Hudson Gallery, Detroit, 1967; cat. 12, as *Four People on a Balcony*.
Group exhibitions: The Larry Aldrich Museum of Contemporary Art, Ridgefield, 1967; cat. 61 (repr.), as *Four People on a Balcony*.
References: Forte di Belvedere, Florence, 1984; p. 44, cat. 34 (repr.).
Note: The Sala Espressioni—Ideal Standard, Milan, 1965, debuted four works: *Uomo appogiato alla balconata*, *Due persone alla balconata*, *Quattro persone alla balconata*, and *Tre ragazze alla balconata*.

27
Tre ragazze alla balconata (*Three Girls on a Balcony*), 1964
Painted tissue paper on polished stainless steel
78¾ x 78¾ inches (200 x 200 cm)
Walker Art Center, Minneapolis. Gift of Mrs. Julius E. Davis, 1999

Alternate title: Ragazze alla balconata

Provenance: Galleria Sperone, Turin, by April 1966. To Mrs. Julius E. Davis, around summer 1966. To the Walker Art Center, Minneapolis, as a gift, in 1999.
Solo exhibitions: Sala Espressioni—Ideal Standard, Milan, 1965; as *Ragazze alla balconata*. Walker Art Center, Minneapolis, 1966; cat. 14 (repr.), as *Three Girls on a Balcony*. Palazzo Grassi, Venice, 1976; p. 15, cat. 23 (repr.), as *Ragazze alla balconata*. Walker Art Center, Minneapolis, 2002; pp. 307, 357, cat. 123 (repr.).
Group exhibitions: Walker Art Center, Minneapolis, 1999–2001. Walker Art Center, Minneapolis, 2002; p. 307, cat. 123 (color repr.). Walker Art Center, Minneapolis, 2010.
References: Forte di Belvedere, Florence, 1984; p. 44, cat. 33 (repr.), as *Ragazze alla balconata*. Galleria Nazionale d'Arte Moderna, Rome, 1990; p. 21 (repr.), as *Ragazze alla balconata*. Centre Georges Pompidou, Paris, 1992; p. 54 (repr.). Città di Castello (Perugia), 2001; p. 20 (repr.), as *Ragazze alla balconata*.
Note: An artist's inscription on the verso reads "3 ragazze alla balconata."

28
Due persone in coda (*Two People in Line*), 1964
Painted tissue paper on polished stainless steel
$86\frac{13}{16}$ x 47¼ inches (220.5 x 120 cm)
Museum Boijmans Van Beuningen, Rotterdam

Provenance: Galleria Sperone, Turin, by April 1966. To the Kornblee Gallery, New York, by April 1967. To the J. L. Hudson Gallery, Detroit, by fall 1967. To Galerie Ileana Sonnabend, Paris, by March 1969. To Erasmusstichting, Rotterdam, in May 1969. To the Museum Boijmans Van Beuningen, Rotterdam, as a gift, in 1969.
Solo exhibitions: Walker Art Center, Minneapolis, 1966; cat. 16 (repr.), as *Two People in a Queue*. Kornblee Gallery, New York, 1967. J. L. Hudson Gallery, Detroit, 1967; cat. 15, as *Two People in a Queue*. Museum Boijmans Van Beuningen, Rotterdam, 1969; cat. V, as *Twee mensen achterelkaar*. Fundação de Serralves, Porto, Portugal, 1993.
Group exhibitions: The Larry Aldrich Museum of Contemporary Art, Ridgefield, 1967; cat. 60, as *Two People in a Queue*. Museum Boijmans Van Beuningen, Rotterdam, 1972; p. 127, fig. 174, cat. 233 (repr.), as *Twee mensen achterelkaar*. Museum Boijmans Van Beuningen, Rotterdam; *Een prikkelcollectie. De doorbraak van de moderne kunst in Museum Boijmans*; June 10–September 2, 2000; no cat. Hata International Co. Ltd., Kyoto; *Boijmans Exhibition 2002*, 2002; no cat.

29
Scala (*Ladder*), 1964
Painted tissue paper on polished stainless steel
$90\frac{9}{16}$ x 47¼ inches (230 x 120 cm)
Courtesy of Fondazione Marconi, Milan

Provenance: Galleria del Leone, Venice, by September 1964. To Galerie Ileana Sonnabend, Paris, after May 1969. To a private collection, n.d. To Giorgio Marconi, Milan, n.d.
Solo exhibitions: Galleria del Leone, Venice, 1964. Galleria del Leone, Venice, 1966. Palais des Beaux-Arts, Brussels, 1967; as *Escalier*, 1966.
References: Boatto 1969; cat. 21 (repr.).
Note: Pistoletto made two similar works, both titled *Scala* and dated 1964, but with different dimensions. The other *Scala* is in the collection of Cittadellarte-Fondazione Pistoletto, Biella.

30
Filodendro (*Philodendron*), 1965
Painted tissue paper on polished stainless steel
47¼ x 47¼ inches (120 x 120 cm)
Albright-Knox Art Gallery, Buffalo. Gift of The Seymour H. Knox Fondation, Inc., 1971

Provenance: Leo Castelli Gallery, New York, by April 1966. To Mr. and Mrs. Seymour H. Knox, Buffalo, by May 1969. To the Seymour H. Knox Foundation, Inc., as a gift, in 1971.
Solo exhibitions: Walker Art Center, Minneapolis, 1966; cat. 30. Albright-Knox Art Gallery, Buffalo, 1969; cat. 8 (repr.).
Group exhibitions: Palazzo del Kursaal, San Marino, 1965; cat. 286. Albright-Knox Art Gallery, Buffalo, 1972.

31
Autoritratto con pianta (*Self-Portrait with Plant*), 1965
Painted tissue paper on polished stainless steel
$77\frac{15}{16}$ x 47¼ inches (198 x 120 cm)
Private collection

Provenance: Galerie Ileana Sonnabend, Paris, by April 1966. To the Kornblee Gallery, New York, by April 1967. To the J. L. Hudson Gallery, Detroit, by fall 1967. To a private collection, probably by 1970. Sold at "Contemporary Art, Part Two," Sotheby's, New York, May 15, 2002, lot 199, p. 121 (color repr.). To the present owner by fall 2008.
Solo exhibitions: Walker Art Center, Minneapolis, 1966; cat. 28 (repr.), as *Self Portrait with Plant*. Kornblee Gallery, New York, 1967. L. Hudson Gallery, Detroit, 1967; cat. 5 (repr.). Nordjyllands Kunstmuseum, Aalborg, 1978; cat. 11, as *Selvportræt med portætter*.
References: Boatto 1969; cat. 23 (repr.).

32
Vietnam, 1965
Painted tissue paper on polished stainless steel
$86\frac{5}{8}$ x 47¼ inches (220 x 120 cm)
The Menil Collection, Houston

Provenance: Leo Castelli, Inc., New York, n.d. Sold to John and Dominique de Menil, 1964. To Menil Foundation, Inc., 1998
Solo exhibitions: Walker Art Center, Minneapolis, 1966; cat. 22. J. L. Hudson Gallery, Detroit, 1967; cat. 2. Albright-Knox Art Gallery, Buffalo, 1969; cat. 10, as "University of St. Thomas Collection, Houston." Palazzo Grassi, Venice, 1976; p. 16, cat. 6 (repr.). High Museum of Art, Atlanta, 1979; p. 10, cat. 5 (repr.). Palacio de Cristal et Istituto Italiano di Cultura, Parque del Retiro, Madrid, 1983; p. 43 (repr.), p. 154, cat. 6 (color repr. detail). The Institute for Contemporary Art, P.S. 1 Museum, New York, 1988; p. 45 (color repr.).
Group exhibitions: The Larry Aldrich Museum of Contemporary Art, Ridgefield, Conn., 1967; cat. 62. The Museum of Fine Arts, Houston, 1968; cat. 110, p. 123 (repr.). Galeries Nationales du Grand Palais, Paris, 1984; cat. 594, p. 413 (repr.). Royal Academy of Arts, London, 1989; p. 351, cat. 198 (color repr.). Los Angeles Museum of Art, 1996. The Menil Collection, Houston, 2004. The Menil Collection, Houston, 2005. Kunsthaus Zürich, 2008; p. 119 (color repr.).
References: Forte di Belvedere, Florence, 1984; p. 46, cat. 36 (repr.). Corà 1986; p. 198, no. 179 (repr.). Staatliche Kunsthalle, Baden-Baden, Germany, 1988; p. 21 (repr.). Centro de Arte Reina Sofía, Madrid, 1990; p. 174 (color repr.). Centre Georges Pompidou, Paris, 1994–95; p. 236 (repr.). Lenbachhaus, Munich, 1996; p. 21 (color repr.). Musée d'Art Moderne et d'Art Contemporain, Nice, 2007; p. 16 (repr.).

33
Ragazzo (Boy), 1965
Painted tissue paper on polished stainless steel
86⅝ x 47¼ inches (220 x 120 cm)
The Robert B. Mayer Family Collection, Chicago

Alternate title: Comizio.

Provenance: Leo Castelli Gallery, New York, by April 1966. To the Kornblee Gallery, New York, by April 1967. To the J. L. Hudson Gallery, Detroit, by fall 1967. To Mr. and Mrs. Robert B. Mayer, Winnetka, Ill., October 1967. To The Robert B. Mayer Family Collection, Chicago, by descent, in 1974.
Solo exhibitions: Walker Art Center, Minneapolis, 1966; cat. 17, as *Procession*. Kornblee Gallery, New York, 1967. J. L. Hudson Gallery, Detroit, 1967; cat. 14 (repr.), as *Boy*. Albright-Knox Art Gallery, Buffalo, 1969; cat. 6, as *Boy Walking*. Palazzo Grassi, Venice, 1976; p. 16, cat. 27 (repr.), as *Comizio*.
References: Forte di Belvedere, Florence, 1984; p. 47, cat. 38 (repr.), as *Comizio*.

34
No all'aumento del tram (No to the Raise of the Tram Fare), 1965
Painted tissue paper on polished stainless steel
47¼ x 86⅝ inches (120 x 220 cm)
The Detroit Institute of Arts. Gift of Mr. and Mrs. Richard A. Manoogian

Provenance: Galerie Ileana Sonnabend, Paris, by April 1966. To the J. L. Hudson Gallery, Detroit, by fall 1967. Purchased by Mr. and Mrs. Richard A. Manoogian, Detroit, Ill., from the Kornblee Gallery, 1967. Given to The Detroit Institute of Arts, as a gift, in 1967.
Solo exhibitions: Walker Art Center, Minneapolis, 1966; cat. 21. J. L. Hudson Gallery, Detroit, 1967; cat. 8. Albright-Knox Art Gallery, Buffalo, 1969; cat. 7 (repr.). Palazzo Grassi, Venice, 1976; p. 16, cat. 25 (repr.).

35
Persone che guardano (People Looking), 1965
Painted tissue paper on polished stainless steel
47¼ x 86⅝ inches (120 x 220 cm)
Private collection

Alternate titles: Comizio; Persone che ascoltano.

Provenance: Acquired by the present owner by 1979.
Solo exhibitions: Palazzo Grassi, Venice, 1976; p. 17, cat. 28 (repr.), as *Comizio*. High Museum of Art, Atlanta, 1979; as *Men Looking at a Demonstration*. Palacio de Cristal et Istituto Italiano di Cultura, Parque del Retiro, Madrid, 1983; p. 153, cat. 5 (repr.), as *Persone che ascoltano*. Galleria Nazionale d'Arte Moderna, Rome, 1990; p. 89, cat. 17 (repr.).
References: Boatto 1969; cat. 26 (repr., and frontispiece). Celant 1985; p. 148, no. 147 (repr.), as *Comizio*.

36
Person—Back View, 1965
Painted tissue paper on polished stainless steel
22½ x 16¼ inches (57.2 x 41.3 cm)
Collection of Suzanne Weil, New York

Provenance: Leo Castelli, New York, before April 1966. Sold to Suzanne Weil, New York, by May 1966.
Solo exhibitions: Walker Art Center, Minneapolis, 1966; (no cat.).
Note: Another, larger work with the same title was shown in the 1966 Walker Art Center exhibition and is included in the catalogue checklist; it is currently in a private collection.

37
Bandiera rossa (Comizio I) (Red Flag [Demonstration I]), 1966
Painted tissue paper on polished stainless steel
47¼ x 39⅜ inches (120 x 100 cm)
François Pinault Foundation

Alternate title: Bandiera rossa.

Provenance: Galleria Sperone, Turin, by April 1966. To Galleria La Bertesca, Genoa, by June 1966. To a private collection, Switzerland, by May 2004. To the François Pinault Foundation, by October 2006.
Solo exhibitions: Walker Art Center, Minneapolis, 1966; as *Procession III*, 1965. Galleria del Leone, Venice, 1966, as *Bandiera rossa*.
Group exhibitions: Montreal Museum of Fine Arts, 2003–4; p. 121, cat. 150 (color repr.), as *Bandiera rossa*. Palazzo Grassi, Venice, 2006; p. 127 (repr.).

38
Due persone che passano (Two People Passing By), 1966
Painted tissue paper on polished stainless steel
47¼ x 90$\frac{9}{16}$ inches (120 x 230 cm)
Private collection

Alternate title: Due uomini che passano.

Provenance: Galleria Sperone, Milan, by November 1966. Galleria La Bertesca, Genoa, by December 1966. To Galleria L'Attico, Rome, by 1985. To the present owner, 1985.
Solo exhibitions: Galleria Sperone, Milan, 1966; as *Due uomini che passano*. Galleria La Bertesca, Genoa, 1967; (repr.), as *Due uomini che passano*. Palais des Beaux-Arts, Brussels, 1967; as *Deux passants*.
References: Sonnabend 1966; pp. 91–93, no. 12 (repr.).

39
Biennale 66 (Biennial 66), 1966
Painted tissue paper on polished stainless steel, four panels
Overall: 90$\frac{9}{16}$ x 189 inches (230 x 480 cm)
The Sonnabend Collection

Alternate titles: Biennale '66.

Provenance: Galerie Ileana Sonnabend, Paris, by 1966. To the Sonnabend Collection, New York, by transfer, by 1988.
Solo exhibitions: Palais des Beaux-Arts, Brussels, 1967. Palacio de Cristal et Istituto Italiano di Cultura, Parque del Retiro, Madrid, 1983; pp. 155, 225, cat. 7 (repr.).
Group exhibitions: La Biennale di Venezia, 1966, cat. 6, fig. 106 (detail repr.). Musée d'Art Moderne de la Ville de Paris, 1967. The Frances Young Tang Teaching Museum and Art Gallery, Saratoga Springs, N.Y., 2002; p. 115 (color repr.).
References: Boatto 1969; cat. 30 (repr.), as *biennale '66*. Spazio Risonanze, Rome, 2009; p. 68 (color repr.), as *Biennale '66*.

40
Ragazza che cammina (Girl Walking), 1966
Painted tissue paper on polished stainless steel
90$\frac{9}{16}$ x 47¼ inches (230 x 120 cm)
Fondazione per l'Arte Moderna e Contemporanea—CRT, on loan to Castello di Rivoli Museo d'Arte Contemporanea, Rivoli-Turin; GAM—Galleria Civica d'Arte Moderna e Contemporanea, Turin

Provenance: Private collection, n.d. To a private collection, around 1970. Bought by Fondazione CRT—Project for Contemporary Art, at Sotheby's, Milan, November 23, 2004, lot 137, cat. 133. On long-term loan to Castello di Rivoli Museo d'Arte Contemporanea, Rivoli-Turin, since 2004.
Group exhibitions: Museu de Arte Moderna, São Paulo, 1967; cat. 64, as *Moça caminhando*. Hayward Gallery, London, 2007; pp. 78–79 (color reprs.), dated c. 1960.
References: Boatto 1972; p. 41, no. 33 (repr.). Casagrande 2008; p. 432 (color repr.).
Note: A second mirror painting bears the same title, date, materials, and dimensions and reproduces the same figure, positioned at the right edge of the work.

41
Uomo che si tocca il piede (Man Touching His Foot), 1966
Painted tissue paper on polished stainless steel
90$\frac{9}{16}$ x 47¼ inches (230 x 120 cm)
Private collection

Alternate title: Uomo che si tocca una scarpa.

Provenance: Private collection, Milan, acquired directly from the artist, n.d. To a private collection, United Kingdom, n.d. To the present owner around 2000.
Solo exhibitions: Galleria Sperone, Turin, 1964. Palais des Beaux-Arts, Brussels, 1967; as *Homme qui se touche un soulier*. Palazzo Grassi, Venice, 1976; p. 15, cat. 24 (repr.), as *Uomo che si tocca una scarpa*.

42
Scopa (Broom), 1967
Painted tissue paper on polished stainless steel
90$\frac{9}{16}$ x 47¼ inches (230 x 120 cm)
Private collection

Provenance: Galerie Ileana Sonnabend, Paris, 1968. Kornblee Gallery, New York, 1969. Sold to a private collection, 1969. Sold at "Contemporary Art, Afternoon Sale," Sotheby's, New York, May 16, 2007, lot. 572, p. 257 (color repr.), to the present owner.
Solo exhibitions: Galleria del Naviglio, Milan, 1967. Palais des Beaux-Arts, Brussels, 1967; cat. 24 as *Le balai / Bezem*. Likely Kornblee Gallery, New York, 1969. Albright-Knox

Gallery, Buffalo, 1969; cat. 13, as Broom.
Group exhibitions: Institute of Contemporary Art, Boston, 1968; no. 31, as *Broom (Scopa)*.
Note: Two other mirror paintings with the same dimensions present nearly identical brooms: *(La) Scopa* of 1966 and *Mani di uomo che scopa* of 1967.

43
Lui e lei che parlano (*He and She Talking*), 1967
Painted tissue paper on polished stainless steel
90⁹⁄₁₆ x 47¼ inches (230 x 120 cm)
Private collection

Alternate title: Due persone.

Provenance: Private collection, by April 1967. To the present owner at "Sale of 20th Century Contemporary Art," Sotheby's, London, October 20, 2008, lot 31, frontispiece (color repr.), p. 113 (color repr.).
Solo exhibitions: Palais des Beaux-Arts, Brussels, 1967; cat. 27, as *Elle et lui qui se parlent*. Palazzo Grassi, Venice, 1976; p. 17, cat. 28 (repr.), as *Due persone*.
Group exhibitions: Museu de Arte Moderna, São Paulo, 1967; cat. 67 (repr.), as *Ela e ele falando*.
References: Farano, Mundici, and Roberto 2005; p. 64 (repr.).

44
Alighiero Boetti che guarda un negativo (*Alighiero Boetti Looking at a Negative*), 1967
Painted tissue paper on polished stainless steel
90⁹⁄₁₆ x 47¼ inches (230 x 120 cm)
Abrams Family Collection

Alternate titles: Alighiero Boetti che guarda un negativo in trasparenza; Uomo che guarda un negativo; Uomo con negativo.

Provenance: Galerie Ileana Sonnabend, Paris, by May 1968. To the Kornblee Gallery, New York, n.d. Sold to Harry N. Abrams, New York, 1969. To the Abrams Family Collection, by transfer, by March 1979.
Solo exhibitions: Kornblee Gallery, New York, 1969. Palazzo Grassi, Venice, 1976; p. 57, cat. 111 (repr.), as *Alighiero Boetti che guarda un negativo in trasparenza*, 1970. High Museum of Art, Atlanta, 1979.
Group exhibtions: Institute of Contemporary Art, Boston, 1968; cat. 32 (repr.), as *Uomo che Guarda un Negativo*.
References: Boatto 1969; cat. 43 (repr.), as *Uomo con negativo*. Forte di Belvedere, Florence, 1984; p. 87, cat. 81 (repr.).
Note: Serigrafo bianco (1977), a silkscreened mirror painting with the same dimensions, reworks this theme, portraying three figures with their backs toward the viewer, holding up two negatives.

45
Maria nuda (*Maria Nude*), 1967
Painted tissue paper on polished stainless steel
47¼ x 59¹⁄₁₆ inches (120 x 150 cm)
Private collection

Alternate titles: Donna nuda sul letto; Maria; Nudo di donna.

Provenance: Private collection, 1967. Collection Camerana, Turin, 1973. To a private collection, by descent, n.d. To the present owner at the sale "Post-War and Contemporary Art: Evening Sale," Christie's, London, June 23, 2005, lot 14, p. 39 (color repr.).
Solo exhibitions: Kestner Gesellschaft, Hanover, Germany, 1973–74; cat. 14, as *Maria*, 1969.
Group exhibitions: Palazzo delle Espozisioni, Rome, 1970; cat. d. (repr.), as *Nudo di donna*.
References: Boatto 1969; cat 3 (repr.), as *Donna nuda sul letto*.

46
Ragazza seduta per terra (*Girl Sitting on the Floor*), 1967
Painted tissue paper on polished stainless steel
90⁹⁄₁₆ x 47¼ inches (230 x 120 cm)
Private collection

Alternate title: Donna seduta in mini gonna.

Provenance: Galerie Ileana Sonnabend, Paris, at Documenta 4, 1967. To the Helga and Walther Lauffs Collection, Bad Honnef, Germany, in 1968. On loan to the Kaiser Wilhelm Museum, Krefeld, 1968–2008. To David Zwirner, New York, 2008. To the present owner, 2010.
Solo exhibitions: Galerie Rudolf Zwirner, Cologne, 1967; (repr.). Palais des Beaux-Arts, Brussels, 1967; cat. 40 (repr.), as *Jeune fille assise par terre*. Galerie Ileana Sonnabend, Paris, 1967. *La fine di Pistoletto*, Piper Pluriclub, Turin, March 6, 1967; no cat.
Group exhibitions: Documenta 4, Kassel, Germany, 1968; p. 235, cat. 3 (repr.), as *Donna seduta in mini gonna*. Institute of Contemporary Arts, London, 1968; p. 65, no. 75, as *Jeune fille en mini-jupe*. Museum Haus Esters, Krefeld, Germany, 2001; p. 5 (repr.). David Zwirner, New York, May 2008; no cat. Zwirner & Wirth, New York, November–December 2008; no cat.
References: Wember 1973; p. 171, pl. 105 (repr.). Storck et al. 1983; no. 271 (repr.). Whitney 2009; vol. 1, p. 107 (color repr.), vol. 2, p. 168 (color repr.), p. 169 (repr.), as *Ragazza in minigonna / Ragazza seduta per terra*.

47
Lui e lei abbracciati (*He and She Embracing*), 1968
Painted tissue paper on polished stainless steel
47¼ x 39⅜ inches (120 x 100 cm)
Collezione Maramotti, Reggio Emilia, Italy

Provenance: Galleria del Naviglio, Milan, by February 1967. To Collezione Maramotti, Reggio Emila, Italy, n.d.
Group Exhibitions: Badischer Kunstverein, Karlsruhe, 1969; cat. 41.
Note: A similar work, *Lui e lei abbracciati di schiena*, was shown in the artist's 1968 exhibition at Galleria l'Attico, Rome. Since that work is smaller, it slightly crops the bottom of the image.

48
I visitatori (*The Visitors*), 1968
Painted tissue paper on polished stainless steel
90⁹⁄₁₆ x 94½ inches (230 x 240 cm)
GNAM—Galleria Nazionale d'Arte Moderna e Contemporanea, Rome. Courtesy of the Italian Ministry of Cultural Heritage and Activities

Provenance: Galleria Nazionale d'Arte Moderna, Rome, acquired directly from the artist, by March 1984.
Solo exhibitions: Galleria Nazionale d'Arte Moderna, Rome, 1990; p. 110, cat. 58 (repr.). Museum of Contemporary Art, Tokyo, 2001; p. 117 (repr.).
Group exhibitions: Palazzo delle Esposizioni, Rome, 1991; p. 228 (repr.).
References: Boatto 1969; cat. 51 (repr.). Forte di Belvedere, Florence, 1984; p. 58, cat. 49 (repr.).

49
Visitatrice con catalogo (*Visitor with Catalogue*), 1969
Painted tissue paper on polished stainless steel
90⁹⁄₁₆ x 47¼ inches (230 x 120 cm)
Collection of Pietro Valsecchi

Alternate title: Donna con catalogo.

Provenance: Galleria dellAriete, Milan, n.d. To Galleria Toninelli Arte Moderna, Milan, n.d. To a private collection, Switzerland, n.d. To a private collection at the sale "20th Century Italian Art," Sothebys, London, October 25, 2000, sale L00711, lot 41, p. 105 (repr.). To Pietro Valsecchi, Rome, at "Contemporary Evening Sale," Sothebys, London, Feburary 5, 2009, lot 4, p. 21 (color repr.).
Solo exhibitions: Galleria dellAriete, Milan, 1970. Galleria Toninelli, Rome, 1972. Kestner Gesellschaft, Hanover, Germany, 197374; cat. 12, as *Frau mit rotterdamer Katalog / Donna con catalogo*. Studio Casoli, Milan, 2000; (color repr., detail).
References: Corà 1986; p. 150, no. 103 (repr.).

50
Gabbia (*Cage*), 1969
Painted tissue paper on polished stainless steel
90⁹⁄₁₆ x 47¼ inches (230 x 120 cm)
Collection of the artist

Provenance: Beatrice Monti della Corte von Rezzori, Florence, n.d. To the artist after 1988.
Solo exhibitions: Palazzo Grassi, Venice, 1976; p. 47, cat. 100 (repr.). The Institute for Contemporary Art, P.S. 1 Museum, New York, 1988; p. 64 (repr.), as *The Cage*, 1963.
Group exhibitions: Walker Art Gallery, Liverpool, 1971; p. 105, cat. 67 (repr.), dated 1970.
Note: Other works on this theme have been made, among them later serigraphic mirror paintings, including the twenty-nine-panel *Gabbia* from 1974 and the four-panel *Gabbia* from 1975.

51
Il cane con la coda giù (*The Dog with Its Tail between Its Legs*), 1969
Painted tissue paper on polished stainless steel
90⁹⁄₁₆ x 47¼ inches (230 x 120 cm)
Courtesy of Fondazione Marconi, Milan

Alternate title: Cane.

Provenance: Gilberto Zorio, Turin, before November 1973. To Giorgio Marconi, Milan., n.d.
Solo exhibitions: Kestner Gesellschaft, Hanover, Germany, 1973–74; cat. 13, as *Ein Hund / Cane*. Mathildenhöhe, Darmstadt, Germany, 1974; cat. 9 (repr.), as *Cane*.
Group exhibitions: Moderna Museet, Stockholm, 2008; p. 133 (color repr.). Kunsthaus Zürich, 2009.
Note: The photograph of this dog was cropped and used in a smaller, earlier work, shown at Galerie Ileana Sonnnabend, Paris, 1967.

52
Saracinesca (*Iron Gate*), 1970
Painted tissue paper on polished stainless steel
90⁹⁄₁₆ x 47¼ inches (230 x 120 cm)
Private collection

Provenance: Galleria Toninelli, Milan, by 1973. Sold at the sale "Modern Oil Paintings, Watercolours and Scuplture," Sotheby's, Milan, November 27, 1990, lot 243. To the present owner, n.d.
Solo exhibitions: Galleria Toninelli, Rome, 1972. Kestner Gesellschaft, Hanover, Germany, 1973–74; cat. 16, as *Rolladen / Saracinesca*. Mathildenhöhe, Darmstadt, Germany, 1974; cat. 12. Palazzo Grassi, Venice, 1976; p. 62, cat. 115 (repr.), dated 1971.

53
Muretto di mattoni (*Small Wall of Bricks*), 1970
Painted tissue paper on polished stainless steel
90⁹⁄₁₆ x 47¼ inches (230 x 120 cm)
Private collection

Alternate titles: Muretto; Muro.

Provenance: Galleria Toninelli, Rome, n.d. To Banque Lambert, Brussels, n.d. To the Giorgio Persano gallery, Turin, n.d. To Galleria Christian Stein, Milan, n.d. To the present owner, n.d.
Solo exhibitions: Galleria Toninelli, Rome, 1972; as *Muretto*. Kestner Gesellschaft, Hanover, 1973–74; cat. 17, as *Mauer / Muro*. Mathildenhöhe, Darmstadt, 1974; cat. 13, as *Muro*. Nordjyllands Kunstmuseum, Aalborg, 1978; cat. 13, as *Mur*. Studio Casoli, Rome, 1998; p. 13 (color repr.). Museum of Modern Art, Oxford, 1999.
Group exhibitions: Rotonda della Besana, Milan, 2000; p. 227, cat. 13 (color repr.). Centre Cultural Contemporani Pelaires, Palma de Mallorca, 2005; p. 80 (color repr.), as *Muro de ladrillos*.
References: Museu d'Art Contemporani de Barcelona, 2000; p. 47 (color repr.).
Note: Another work with the same subject is titled *Muro di mattoni* and dates to 1967.

54
Donna che fugge (*Woman Escaping*), 1971
Painted tissue paper on polished stainless steel
90⁹⁄₁₆ x 47¼ inches (230 x 120 cm)
Private collection. Courtesy of Lia Rumma

Alternate titles: Ragazza che fugge; Ragazza che scappa.

Provenance: Acquired by the present owner by October 1988.
Solo exhibitions: The Institute for Contemporary Art, P.S. 1 Museum, New York, 1988; p. 65 (repr.), as *Woman on the Run*. Galleria Nazionale d'Arte Moderna, Rome, 1990; p. 114, cat. 62 (color repr.).
Group exhibitions: Palazzo delle Espozisioni, Rome, 1970; (repr.), as *Ragazza che cappa*, 1970.
References: Kestner Gesellschaft, Hanover, Germany, 1973–74; (repr.). Corà 1986; p. 54, no. 16 (repr.), as *Ragazza che fugge*, 1967.
Note: Differently painted, the figure in this work appears in another, untitled mirror painting of the same materials, dimensions, and date, currently in the collection of the Museo del Novecento, Milan.

55
Donna nuda che beve il tè (*Nude Woman Drinking Tea*), 1971
Painted tissue paper on polished stainless steel
90⁹⁄₁₆ x 47¼ inches (230 x 120 cm)
Private collection

Alternate title: Donna che prende il tè; Maria con la tazza di tè; Donna che beve il tè.

Provenance: collection of the artist until 1973; Galleria Sperone, Turin, by 1974. To the present owner by 1984.
Solo exhibitions: Kestner Gesellschaft, Hanover, Germany, 1973–74; cat. 22, as *Tee trinkende Frau / Donna che prende il tè*. Mathildenhöhe, Darmstadt, Germany, 1974; cat. 24, (repr.), as *Maria con tazza di tè*.
Group exhibitions: Walker Art Gallery, Liverpool, 1971; p. 106, cat. 68 (repr.), as *Nude Girl Drinking Tea*.
References: Forte di Belvedere, Florence, 1984; p. 87, cat. 80 (repr.), as *Donna che prende il tè*. Staatliche Kunsthalle, Baden-Baden, Germany, 1988; p. 23 (repr.), as *Tee trinkende Frau*.
Note: There is another work from 1971 with similar dimensions that shows the same subject seated drinking tea.

56
Catena (*Chain*), 1971
Painted tissue paper on polished stainless steel
90⁹⁄₁₆ x 47¼ inches (230 x 120 cm)
Private collection

Alternate title: La catena.

Provenance: Acquired by the present owner, directly from the artist, around 1971.
Solo exhibitions: Palazzo Grassi, Venice, 1976; p. 62, cat. 114 (repr.), as *La catena*.
Group exhibitions: Walker Art Gallery, Liverpool, 1971, p. 106, cat. 69 (repr.), as *La catena*. Parcheggio di Villa Borghese, Rome, 1973–74; p. 195 (repr.).

57
Graziella, 1971
Painted tissue paper on polished stainless steel
59¹⁄₁₆ x 47¼ inches (150 x 120 cm)
Private collection

Provenance: Acquired by the present owner, directly from the artist, around 1971.
Solo exhibitions: Forte di Belvedere, Florence, 1984; p. 72, cat. 64 (color repr.).
References: Corà 1986; p. 58, no. 23 (repr.).

58
Senza titolo (*Untitled*), 1972
Painted tissue paper on polished stainless steel
90⁹⁄₁₆ x 47¼ inches (230 x 120 cm)
Collection of Marco and Franca Brignone

Alternate title: *Lenzuolo*.

Provenance: Galleria Sperone, Turin, 1972. To the present owner, 1972.

59
Cappio (*Noose*), 1973
Silkscreen on polished stainless steel
90⁹⁄₁₆ x 47¼ inches (230 x 120 cm)
Collection of the artist

Alternate title: Il cappio.

Solo exhibitions: Galleria dell'Ariete, Milan, 1973. Galleria Sperone, Turin, 1973. Kestner Gesellschaft, Hanover, Germany, 1973–74. Mathildenhöhe, Darmstadt, Germany, 1974; cat. 26 (repr.), as collection of Galleria Sperone, Turin. Galleria Sperone, Rome, 1975. Tokyo Art Agency, Tokyo, 1975. Palazzo Grassi, Venice, 1976; p. 63, cat. 118 (repr.), as *Il cappio*. Nordjyllands Kunstmuseum, Aalborg, Denmark 1978; cat. 21, as *Løkken*. Nationalgalerie, Berlin, 1978; cat. 12, as *Schlinge*.
References: Mussat Sartor 1979; p. 230 (repr.). Palacio de Cristal et Istituto Italiano di Cultura, Parque del Retiro, Madrid, 1983; p. 87 (repr.), as *El Lazo*. Forte di Belvedere, Florence, 1984; p. 115, cat. 115 (repr.). Corà 1986; p. 56, no. 19 (repr.). Staatliche Kunsthalle, Baden-Baden, Germany, 1988; p. 8, fig. 1 (repr.), dated 1976. Centre d'Art Santa Monica, Barcelona, 1991; pp. 38–39 (reprs.). Neues Museum Weserburg, Bremen, 1997; p. 241 (repr.).
Note: This is the first non-editioned mirror painting Pistoletto produced using the silkscreen technique; before this work he had only used the technique for the production of multiples. A year after this work was created, Pistoletto created a multiple with the same theme.

60
Sacra conversazione (Anselmo, Zorio, Penone), 1973
Silkscreen on polished stainless steel
90⁹⁄₁₆ x 47¼ inches (230 x 120 cm)
Collection of the artist

Alternate titles: Sacra Conversazione; La Sacra Conversazione AZP; Sacra conversazione, Anselmo, Zorio e Penone.

Provenance: Galleria Toninelli, Milan, in 1974. Collection of the artist, n.d.
Solo exhibitions: Mathildenhöhe, Darmstadt, Germany, 1974; cat. 31, as *La Sacra Conversazione AZP*. Nordjyllands

Kunstmuseum, Aalborg, Denmark, 1978; cat. 14, as *Sacra Conversazione*. Palacio de Cristal et Istituto Italiano di Cultura, Parque del Retiro, Madrid, 1983; p. 159, cat. 11 (repr.). Galleria Nazionale d'Arte Moderna, Rome, 1990; p. 116, cat. 64 (color repr.). Palazzina della Società delle Belle Arti and Castello di Rivoli Museo d'Arte Contemporanea, Rivoli-Turin, 2000–2001; p. 54 (color repr.). Musée d'Art Contemporain, Lyon, 2001; pp. 28–30, 155, cat. 47 (reprs., color repr.). Musée d'Art Moderne et d'Art Contemporain, Nice, 2007; p. 72 (color repr.).

References: Forte di Belvedere, Florence, 1984; p. 89, cat. 83 (repr.), as *Sacra conversazione*. Corà 1986; p. 57, no. 21 (repr.). Fundação de Serralves, Porto, Portugal, 1993; p. 65 (color repr.). Miriam and Ira D. Wallach Art Gallery, New York, 2001; p. 18 (repr.). Città di Castello (Perugia), 2001; p. 33 (repr.).

Note: This work includes portraits of the Arte Povera artists Giovanni Anselmo (b. 1934), Gilberto Zorio (b. 1944), and Giuseppe Penone (b. 1947).

61
Deposizione (*Deposition*), 1973
Silkscreen on polished stainless steel
$90\frac{9}{16}$ x $47\frac{1}{4}$ inches (230 x 120 cm)
Collection of the artist

Solo exhibitions: Mathildenhöhe, Darmstadt, Germany, 1974; as collection of Galleria Toninelli, Milan. Galleria Nazionale d'Arte Moderna, Rome, 1990; p. 117, cat. 65 (repr.).

References: Corà 1986; p. 54, no. 15 (repr.). Centre d'Art Santa Monica, Barcelona, 1991; p. 28 (repr.), dated 1979. Musée d'Art Contemporain, Lyon, 2001; p. 157 (repr.).

Note: This image has been used in two other mirror paintings: the smaller *Particolari della deposizione* (1974) and *Deposizione in bianco e nero* (1979).

62
Donna che fa la cacca (*Woman Defecating*), 1973
Silkscreen on polished stainless steel
$90\frac{9}{16}$ x $47\frac{1}{4}$ inches (230 x 120 cm)
Collection of Constance R. Caplan

Alternate titles: Donna accovacciata—che defeca; Donna accovacciata (che defeca); Donna in maglia rossa; Gli escrementi.

Provenance: Galleria Sperone, Rome, directly from the artist, by June 1976. To Galleria dell'Ariete, Milan, n.d. To a private collection, n.d. To Constance R. Caplan, Baltimore, at "Post-War and Contemporary Art Day Sale," Christie's, London, July 1, 2009, lot 177, pp. 70, 71 (repr.).

Solo exhibitions: Galleria dell'Ariete, Milan, 1973; as *Donna in maglia rossa*. Galleria Sperone, Rome, 1975; as *Donna accovacciata (che defeca)*, 1974. Tokyo Art Agency, Tokyo, 1975; as *Donna accovacciata (che defeca)*, 1974. Palazzo Grassi, Venice, 1976; p. 65, cat. 120 (repr.), as *Donna accovacciata (che defeca)*, 1974. Nordjyllands Kunstmuseum, Aalborg, Denmark, 1978; cat. 15, as *Kvinde der sidder på hug*. Nationalgalerie, Berlin, 1978; cat. 4, as *Frau, ihre Notdruft verrichtend*, 1978. Galleria Il Ponte, Florence, 2003, p. 19 (color repr.).

References: Lenbachhaus, Munich, 1996; p. 22 (color repr.), as *Donna accovacciata—che defeca*. Minola et al. 2000; p. 251 (color repr.), as *Gli escrementi*, 1974.

Note: Another version of this work, of the same dimensions but slightly darker in tone, and a third, smaller version of the work are in the collection of the artist. The present version is signed, titled twice, dated, and inscribed: "già altrimenti catalogato sotto: / ›donna in maglia rossa‹ / Sono molto soddisfatto del risultato, / —ho portato in primo piano un particolare di / un quadro di Olivero artista piemontese del 1700 / naturalmente con l'intervento dell'occhio fotografico— / N. 6 / 1973 / cm 120 x 230 / Michelangelo Pistoletto / › donna che fa la cacca‹ / La fotografia di questo quadro è stata fatta da / Mussat nel suo studio di Torino, / da quando uso la serigrafia non lavoro più / in un mio studio ma uso vari studi o laboratori già / attrezzati. E mi avvalgo della collaborazione / di tecnici esperti, ognuno nel suo ambito. / Direi che la mia è un'operazione di regia." (Already otherwise catalogued under: "woman in red skirt." I am very satisfied with the result. I put in the foreground a detail of a painting by Olivero, a Piedmontese artist from the eighteenth century, obviously with the use of the camera lens. . . . The photograph for this painting was shot by Mussat in his studio in Turin. Since I use serigraphy, I no longer work in my studio but use various studios or laboratories that are already equipped. And I benefit from the collaboration of technical experts, each one with his own expertise. I would say that mine is the role of director).

63
Uomo che spara (*Man Shooting*), 1973
Silkscreen on polished stainless steel
$90\frac{9}{16}$ x $47\frac{1}{4}$ inches (230 x 120 cm)
Private collection. Courtesy of Rory Howard

Alternate title: L'agguato.

Provenance Galleria Sperone, Turin, n.d. To the present owner at "Post-War and Contemporary (Afternoon Sale)," Christie's, New York, 2002, lot 357, p. 62 (color repr.).

Solo exhibitions: Galleria dell'Ariete, Milan, 1973. Tokyo Art Agency, Tokyo, 1975. Galleria Sperone, Rome, 1975; as *L'agguato*. Galleria Il Centro, Naples, 1975.

References: Minola et al. 2000; p. 250 (color repr.), as *L'agguato*, 1974.

Note: There is an exhibition copy in the collection of the artist.

64
Cage, 1973
Silkscreen on polished stainless steel
$90\frac{9}{16}$ x $228\frac{3}{8}$ inches (230 x 580 cm)
Collection of the artist

Alternate titles: Cage; La Gabbia; La gabbia con mulatto che scopa.

Solo exhibitions: Galleria Sperone, Rome, 1975; as *Gabbia con mulatto che scopa*. Tokyo Art Agency, Tokyo, 1975; as *Gabbia con mulatto che scopa*. Palazzo Grassi, Venice, 1976; p. 66, cat. 121 (repr.), as *La gabbia con mulatto che scopa*, 1974. Nordjyllands Kunstmuseum, Aalborg, Denmark, 1978; cat. 20, as *Mulatdreng der fejer*. The National Museum of Contemporary Art, Seoul, 1994; p. 34 (repr.), as *Cage*, 1973. Palazzina della Società delle Belle Arti and Castello di Rivoli Museo d'Arte Contemporanea, Rivoli-Turin, 2000–2001; p. 50 (color repr.), as *La Gabbia*. Musée d'Art Moderne et d'Art Contemporain, Nice, 2007; p. 61 (repr.), as *Cage*, 1975.

Note: A single-panel mirror painting of 1967 titled *Uomo che scopa* might be considered a precursor to this work.

65
Sedia (*Chair*), 1974
Silkscreen on polished stainless steel
$90\frac{9}{16}$ x $49\frac{3}{16}$ inches (230 x 125 cm)
Collection of the artist

Note: The subject of this mirror painting is one of the chairs Pistoletto used in his studio and in works of art (such as *Piramide verde*, plate 80), as well as in important actions and exhibitions, such as the L'Attico exhibition in 1968. A 1967 mirror painting of the same subject shows the chair in a neutral color.

66
Pericolo di morte (*Danger of Death*), 1974
Silkscreen on polished stainless steel
$49\frac{3}{16}$ x $90\frac{9}{16}$ inches (125 x 230 cm)
Private collection

Provenance: Galleria Giorgio Persano, Turin, by 1983. To the present owner, n.d.

Solo exhibitions: Sidney Janis Gallery, New York, 1974; cat. 8 (repr.). Tokyo Art Agency, Tokyo, 1974.

Note: Two other serigraphic works with this motif also date to 1974, although they differ from this one in size. In addition, another mirror painting with the same dimensions and motif exists in the artist's collection. Pistoletto also used this theme in an editioned work.

67
Ragazzo che si gratta la schiena (*Boy Scratching His Back*), 1974
Silkscreen on polished stainless steel
$90\frac{9}{16}$ x $49\frac{3}{16}$ inches (230 x 125 cm)
Collection of the artist

Solo exhibitions: Sidney Janis Gallery, New York, 1974; cat. 13 (repr.). Nationalgalerie, Berlin, 1978; cat. 7, as *Mann, der sich den Rücken kratzt*. Hansen Fuller Golden Gallery, San Francisco, 1980.

PLEXIGLAS

68
Il muro (*The Wall*), 1964
Transparent Plexiglas
70⅞ x 47¼ inches (180 x 120 cm)
Cittadellarte-Fondazione Pistoletto, Biella.

Alternate titles: Il muro (I Plexiglas); Il muro (I plexiglass); Il Muro—Plexiglas.

Solo exhibitions: Galleria del Leone, Venice, 1964. Galleria Sperone, Turin, 1964; (repr.). L.A.I.C.A., Los Angeles, 1979. The Institute for Contemporary Art, P.S. 1 Museum, New York, 1988; p. 57 (repr.), as *The Wall (Plexiglass)*. Galleria Nazionale d'Arte Moderna, Rome, 1990; p. 83, cat. 11 (repr.), as *Il muro (I plexiglass)*. Fundação de Serralves, Porto, Portugal, 1993. Museum Moderner Kunst Stiftung Ludwig, Vienna, 1995; pp. 28, 31, cat. 4 (repr., color repr.), as *Il muro (I Plexiglas)*. Museu d'Art Contemporani de Barcelona, 2000; p. 60 (repr.), as *Il muro (I Plexiglas)*. Palazzina della Società delle Belle Arti and Castello di Rivoli Museo d'Arte Contemporanea, Rivoli-Turin, 2000–2001; p. 62 (color repr.), as *Il muro (I plexiglass)*.
References: Forte di Belvedere, Florence, 1984; p. 39, cat. 28 (repr.). Corà 1986; p. 88, no. 34 (repr.), as *Il muro (I plexiglass)*. Museo di Capodimonte, Naples, 1989; p. 20 (repr.), as *Il Muro—Plexiglas*.

69
Filo elettrico appeso al muro (*Electric Cord Hanging on the Wall*), 1964
Photograph on transparent Plexiglas
70⅞ x 47¼ inches (180 x 120 cm)
Cittadellarte-Fondazione Pistoletto, Biella.

Alternate titles: Filo elettrico appeso al muro (I plexiglass); Filo elettrico appeso al muro (I Plexiglas).

Solo exhibitions: Galleria Sperone, Turin, 1964; (repr.). Galleria Sperone, Milan, 1966. Palais des Beaux-Arts, Brussels, 1967; cat. 20. Kestner Gesellschaft, Hanover, Germany, 1973–74; (repr.). Palazzo Grassi, Venice, 1976; p. 8, cat. 11 (repr.). L.A.I.C.A., Los Angeles, 1979. The Institute for Contemporary Art, P.S. 1 Museum, New York, 1988; p. 60 (repr.), as *Electric Wire Hanging on the Wall (Plexiglass)*. Galleria Nazionale d'Arte Moderna, Rome, 1990; p. 84, cat. 12 (repr.), as *Filo elettrico appeso al muro (I plexiglass)*. Fundação de Serralves, Porto, Portugal, 1993; p. 69 (repr.). Museu d'Art Contemporani de Barcelona, 2000; p. 61 (repr.), as *Filo elettrico appeso al muro (I Plexiglas)*. Palazzina della Società delle Belle Arti and Castello di Rivoli Museo d'Arte Contemporanea, Rivoli-Turin, 2000–2001; p. 63 (color repr.), as *Filo elettrico appeso al muro (I plexiglass)*.
Group exhibitions: Palazzo delle Esposizioni, Rome, 1972–73; p. 128 (repr.).

70
Filo elettrico caduto (*Fallen Electric Cord*), 1964
Photograph on transparent Plexiglas
70⅞ x 47¼ x 15¾ inches (180 x 120 x 40 cm)
Cittadellarte-Fondazione Pistoletto, Biella.

Alternate titles: Filo elettrico per terra; Filo elettrico caduto (I plexiglass); Filo elettrico per terra (I Plexiglas).

Solo exhibitions: Galleria Sperone, Turin, 1964; (repr.). Galleria del Leone, Venice, 1964. L.A.I.C.A., Los Angeles, 1979. The Institute for Contemporary Art, P.S. 1 Museum, New York, 1988; p. 58 (repr.), as *Electric Wire on the Floor (Plexiglass)*. Galleria Nazionale d'Arte Moderna, Rome, 1990; p. 85, cat. 13 (repr.), as *Filo elettrico per terra (I Plexiglas)*. Fundação de Serralves, Porto, Portugal, 1993; as *Filo elettrico per terra*. Palazzina della Società delle Belle Arti and Castello di Rivoli Museo d'Arte Contemporanea, Rivoli-Turin, 2000–2001; p. 65 (color repr.), as *Filo elettrico caduto (I plexiglass)*. Museu d'Art Contemporani de Barcelona, 2000; (repr.), as *Filo elettrico per terra (I Plexiglas)*.
References: Forte di Belvedere, Florence, 1984; p. 39, cat. 27 (repr.), as *Filo elettrico per terra*. Corà 1986; p. 88, no. 33 (repr.), as *Filo elettrico per terra (I plexiglass)*.

71
Scala doppia appoggiata al muro (*Double Ladder Leaning against the Wall*), 1964
Photograph on two sheets of transparent Plexiglas
70⅞ x 47¼ inches (180 x 120 cm); 59¹⁄₁₆ x 47¼ inches (150 x 120 cm)
Cittadellarte-Fondazione Pistoletto, Biella.

Alternate titles: La scala; Scala appoggiata al muro; Scala doppia appoggiata; Scala doppia appoggiata al muro (I Plexiglas); Scala doppia appoggiata (I plexiglass).

Solo exhibitions: Galleria Sperone, Turin, 1964; (repr.), as *Scala doppia appoggiata*. Galleria Sperone, Milan, 1966, as *Scala doppia appoggiata*. Galleria del Leone, Venice, 1966; as *Scala appoggiata al muro*. Palais des Beaux-Arts, Brussels, 1967; cat. 21, as *Escalier in plexiglas*. Palazzo Grassi, Venice, 1976; p. 8, cat. 12 (repr.). L.A.I.C.A., Los Angeles, 1979. The Institute for Contemporary Art, P.S. 1 Museum, New York, 1988; p. 59 (repr.), as *Double Ladder Leaning Against the Wall (Plexiglass)*. Galleria Nazionale d'Arte Moderna, Rome, 1990; p. 86, cat. 14 (color repr.), as *Scala doppia appoggiata (I plexiglass)*. Fundação de Serralves, Porto, Portugal, 1993; p. 68 (repr.). Museu d'Art Contemporani de Barcelona, 2000; p. 58 (repr.), as *Scala doppia appoggiata al muro (I Plexiglas)*. Palazzina della Società delle Belle Arti and Castello di Rivoli Museo d'Arte Contemporanea, Rivoli-Turin, 2000–2001; p. 64 (color repr.), as *Scala doppia appoggiata (I plexiglass)*.
Group exhibitions: Palazzo delle Esposizioni, Rome, 1972–73; p. 188 (repr.). Centro de Arte Reina Sofía, Madrid, 1990; p. 190 (repr.), as *Los plexiglás*.
References: Centre Georges Pompidou, Paris, 1981; p. 128 (repr.), as *La scala*. Palacio de Cristal et Istituto Italiano di Cultura, Parque del Retiro, Madrid, 1983; p. 38 (repr.), as *Escalera doble apoyada sobre la pared*. Palazzo Fabroni, Pistoia, 1996; p. 48 (repr.). Castello di Rivoli Museo d'Arte Contemporanea, Rivoli-Turin, 2000; p. 298 (repr.).

72
Segnale rosso su plexiglass (*Red Signal on Plexiglas*), 1964
Red Plexiglas disc on transparent Plexiglas
70⅞ x 47¼ inches (180 x 120 cm)
Cittadellarte-Fondazione Pistoletto, Biella

Alternate titles: Plexiglas; Plexiglas—con punto rosso; Segnale sul plexiglass sul muro; Segnale rosso su plexiglass, sul muro (I plexiglass); Segnale rosso su plexiglass, sul muro (I Plexiglas).

Solo exhibitions: Galleria Sperone, Turin, 1964; (repr.). Palazzo Grassi, Venice, 1976; p. 10, cat. 16 (repr.), as *Segnale sul plexiglass sul muro*. L.A.I.C.A., Los Angeles, 1979. Museum Moderner Kunst Stiftung Ludwig, Vienna, 1995; p. 31, cat. 5 (color repr.), as *Plexiglas—con punto rosso*. Museu d'Art Contemporani de Barcelona, 2000; as *Segnale rosso su plexiglass, sul muro (I Plexiglas)*. Palazzina della Società delle Belle Arti and Castello di Rivoli Museo d'Arte Contemporanea, Rivoli-Turin, 2000–2001; p. 66 (color repr.), as *Segnale rosso su plexiglass, sul muro (I plexiglass)*.
References: Centre Georges Pompidou, Paris, 1981; p. 128 (repr.), as *Il punto*. Staatliche Kunsthalle, Baden-Baden, Germany, 1988; p. 31 (repr.), as *Plexiglas*. The Institute for Contemporary Art, P.S. 1 Museum, New York, 1988; p. 61 (repr.).

73
Tavolino con disco e giornale (*Small Table with Record and Newspaper*), 1964
Photographs and paint on transparent Plexiglas
13¾ x 23⅝ x 23⅝ inches (35 x 60 x 60 cm)
Cittadellarte-Fondazione Pistoletto, Biella

Alternate titles: Tavolino con disco e giornale (I plexiglass); Tavolino con disco e giornale (I Plexiglas).

Solo exhibitions: Galleria Sperone, Turin, 1964; (repr.). Galleria del Leone, Venice, 1966. Palazzo Grassi, Venice, 1976; p. 9, cat. 15 (repr.). The Institute for Contemporary Art, P.S. 1 Museum, New York, 1988; p. 76 (repr.). Galleria Nazionale d'Arte Moderna, Rome, 1990; p. 87, cat. 15 (repr.), as *Tavolino con disco e giornale (I plexiglass)*. Fundação de Serralves, Porto, Portugal, 1993. Museu d'Art Contemporani de Barcelona, 2000; as *Tavolino con disco e giornale (I Plexiglas)*. Palazzina della Società delle Belle Arti and Castello di Rivoli Museo d'Arte Contemporanea, Rivoli-Turin, 2000–2001; p. 67 (color repr.), as *Tavolino con disco e giornale (I plexiglass)*.
References: Centre Georges Pompidou, Paris, 1981; p. 128 (repr.), as *Table*. Palazzina della Società delle Belle Arti and Castello di Rivoli Museo d'Arte Contemporanea, Rivoli-Turin, 2000–2001; p. 67 (color repr.).

74
Pila di dischi (*Pile of Records*), 1964
Photograph on transparent Plexiglas, eleven elements
Each 15¾ x 15¾ inches (40 x 40 cm)
Cittadellarte-Fondazione Pistoletto, Biella.

Alternate titles: Dischi; *Pila di dischi (I plexiglass)*; *Pila di dischi (I Plexiglas).*

Solo exhibitions: Galleria del Leone, Venice, 1964. Galleria Sperone, Turin, 1964; (repr.). Galleria del Leone, Venice, 1966; as *Dischi*. Palazzo Grassi, Venice, 1976; p. 11, cat. 17 (repr.). L.A.I.C.A., Los Angeles, 1979. The Institute for Contemporary Art, P.S. 1 Museum, New York, 1988; p. 62 (repr.), as *Stack of Records (Plexiglass)*. Galleria Nazionale d'Arte Moderna, Rome, 1990; p. 88, cat. 16 (repr.), as *Pila di dischi (I plexiglass)*. Fundação de Serralves, Porto, Portugal, 1993. Museu d'Art Contemporani de Barcelona, 2000; p. 59 (repr.), as *Pila di dischi (I Plexiglas)*. Palazzina della Società delle Belle Arti and Castello di Rivoli Museo d'Arte Contemporanea, Rivoli-Turin, 2000–2001; p. 60 (repr.), as *Pila di dischi (I plexiglass)*.
References: Forte di Belvedere, Florence, 1984; p. 38, cat. 26 (repr.). Corà 1986; p. 89, no. 35 (repr.), as *Pila di dischi (I plexiglass)*. Minola et al. 2000; p. 82 (repr.). Città di Castello (Perugia), 2001; p. 17 (repr.).

OGGETTI IN MENO / MINUS OBJECTS

75
Quadro da pranzo (*Lunch Painting*), 1965
Wood
78¾ x 81¾ x 17⅜ inches (200 x 207.6 x 44.1 cm)
Walker Art Center, Minneapolis. T. B. Walker Acquisition Fund, 2002

Alternate titles: Quadro da pranzo (Ogetti [sic] in meno); *Quadro da pranzo (Oggetti in meno).*

Provenance: Sold by Pistoletto Onlus Foundation to the Walker Art Center, 2002
Solo exhibitions: Pistoletto's studio, Turin, 1966. Modern Art Agency (Galleria Lucio Amelio), Naples, 1970. Palazzo Grassi, Venice, 1976; p. 21, cat. 32 (repr.). L.A.I.C.A., Los Angeles, 1979. Forte di Belvedere, Florence, 1984. The Institute for Contemporary Art, P.S. 1 Museum, New York, 1988; p. 82 (repr.), as *Painting for Eating (Minus Objects)*. Kunsthalle, Bern, 1989; p. 30 (color repr.). Galleria Nazionale d'Arte Moderna, Rome, 1990; cat. 18. Deichtorhallen, Hamburg, 1992; p. 36 (color repr.). Museum Moderner Kunst Stiftung Ludwig, Vienna, 1995; p. 131, cat. 6 (repr.), as *Quadro da pranzo (Oggetti in meno)*. Museu d'Art Contemporani de Barcelona, 2000; p. 74 (color repr.), as *Quadro da pranzo (Ogetti [sic] in meno)*. Palazzina della Società delle Belle Arti and Castello di Rivoli Museo d'Arte Contemporanea, Rivoli-Turin, 2000–2001; pp. 76–77 (color repr.), as *Quadro da pranzo (Oggetti in meno)*. Musée d'Art Contemporain, Lyon, 2001; pp. 83, 213, cat. 11 (repr., color repr.). Musée d'Art Moderne et d'Art Contemporain, Nice, 2007; p. 89 (color repr.).
Group exhibitions: Museum Fridericianum, Kassel, Germany, 1997; p. 197 (repr.). Walker Art Center, Minneapolis, 2002; p. 310, cat. 124 (repr.). Walker Art Center, Minneapolis, 2005. Museo d'Art Contemporani, Barcelona, 2007; p. 238 (color repr.).
References: Corà 1986; p. 92, no. 42 (repr.). Corà 1989; p. 71 (repr.). Palazzo Fabroni, Pistoia, 1996; p. 38 (repr.). Città di Castello (Perugia), 2001; p. 18 (repr.). Palazzo Grassi, Venice, 2008; p. 64 (repr.).
Note: Two other versions of this work exist with the same title and date. One is in the collection of the artist; the other was last shown at the Musée d'Art Contemporain, Lyon, in 2001. The three versions of the work are included in the exhibition history above.

76
Rosa bruciata (*Burnt Rose*), 1965
Corrugated cardboard and spray paint
55⅛ x 55⅛ x 39⅜ inches (140 x 140 x 100 cm)
Cittadellarte-Fondazione Pistoletto, Biella.

Alternate titles: Rosa; *Rosa Bruciata*; *Rosa bruciata (Oggetti in meno).*

Solo exhibitions: Pistoletto's studio, Turin, 1966. Galleria La Bertesca, Genoa, 1967; (reprs.), as *Rosa* and *Rosa Bruciata*, 1966. Galleria del Naviglio, Milan, 1967. Palais des Beaux-Arts, Brussels, 1967; cat. 36, as *La rose*. Galleria Christian Stein, Turin, 1968. Museum Boijmans Van Beuningen, Rotterdam, 1969; cat. 2 (repr.). Palazzo Grassi, Venice, 1976; pp. 21–22, cats. 32, 34 (repr.). Mario Diacono, Bologna, 1979. L.A.I.C.A., Los Angeles, 1979. Palacio de Cristal et Istituto Italiano di Cultura, Parque del Retiro, Madrid, 1983; p. 168, cat. 20 (repr.), as *Rosa quemanda*. Forte di Belvedere, Florence, 1984; p. 54, cat. 44 (repr.). Galleria Giorgio Persano, Turin, 1985; cat. 8 (repr.). The Institute for Contemporary Art, P.S. 1 Museum, New York, 1988; p. 91 (color repr.). Kunsthalle, Bern, 1989; p. 31 (color repr.). Galleria Nazionale d'Arte Moderna, Rome, 1990; p. 91, cat. 20 (repr.), as *Rosa bruciata (Oggetti in meno)*. Deichtorhallen, Hamburg, 1992; p. 33 (color repr.). The Solomon R. Guggenheim Museum, New York, 1994–95; cat. 194 (repr.). Museu d'Art Contemporani de Barcelona, 2000; p. 84 (color repr.), as *Rosa bruciata (Oggetti in meno)*. Palazzina della Società delle Belle Arti and Castello di Rivoli Museo d'Arte Contemporanea, Rivoli-Turin, 2000–2001; pp. 74–75 (color repr.), as *Rosa bruciata (Oggetti in meno)*. Musée d'Art Contemporain, Lyon, 2001; p. 215, cat. 22 (color repr.). Musée d'Art Moderne et d'Art Contemporain, Nice, 2007; p. 91 (color repr.).
Group exhibitions: Galleria Stein, Galleria Sperone, Galleria Il Punto, Turin, 1967. Kunstverein, Munich, 1971; (repr.). Centre Georges Pompidou, Paris, 1981; p. 174 (repr.), as *La rose brûlée*. Palazzo delle Esposizioni, Rome, 1980; p. 154, cat. 183 (repr.). Kölnischer Kunstverein, Cologne, 1983; p. 98 (repr.), as *Verbrannte Rose/Rosabruciata*. Museum Fridericianum, Kassel, Germany, 1997; p. 172 (color repr.).
References: Kultermann 1968; p. 76, no. 110, as *Pistoletto's New Work*. Boatto 1969; cat. 34. (repr.). Corà 1986; p. 92, no. 46 (repr.). Kunstnernes Hus, Oslo, 1986; cat. 2 (repr.), as *Brent rose*. Nouveau Musée, Villeurbanne, 1992; p. 56 (repr.). Città di Castello (Perugia), 2001; p. 24 (repr.).

77
Paesaggio (*Landscape*), 1965
Cardboard, tissue paper, rags, and clay figures
27⁹⁄₁₆ x 15¾ x 7⅞ inches (70 x 40 x 20 cm)
Cittadellarte-Fondazione Pistoletto, Biella

Alternate titles: "l'ultimo presepio"; *Paesaggio-Presepe*; *Paesaggio (Oggetti in meno).*

Solo exhibitions: Pistoletto's studio, Turin, 1966. Kestner Gesellschaft, Hanover, Germany, 1973–74; (repr.). Palazzo Grassi, Venice, 1976; pp. 21–22, cats. 32, 37 (reprs.). Mario Diacono, Bologna, 1979. L.A.I.C.A., Los Angeles, 1979. Palacio de Cristal et Istituto Italiano di Cultura, Parque del Retiro, Madrid, 1983; p. 170, cat. 22 (repr.), as *Paesaggio-Presepe*. Forte di Belvedere, Florence, 1984; p. 55, cat. 45 (repr.), dated 1965–66. The Institute for Contemporary Art, P.S. 1 Museum, New York, 1988; p. 97 (color repr.), as *Landscape (Minus Object)*. Kunsthalle, Bern, 1989; p. 32 (color repr.). Galleria Nazionale d'Arte Moderna, Rome, 1990; p. 93, cat. 22 (repr.), as *Paesaggio (Oggetti in meno)*. Museu d'Art Contemporani de Barcelona, 2000; as *Paesaggio (Oggetti in meno)*. Palazzina della Società delle Belle Arti and Castello di Rivoli Museo d'Arte Contemporanea, Rivoli-Turin, 2000–2001; p. 77 (color repr.), as *Paesaggio (Oggetti in meno)*. Musée d'Art Contemporain, Lyon, 2001; p. 83, cat. 9 (repr.), p. 212 (color repr.). Musée d'Art Moderne et d'Art Contemporain, Nice, 2007; p. 92 (color repr.).
Group exhibitions: Galleria Stein, Galleria Sperone, Galleria Il Punto, Turin, 1967. Centre Georges Pompidou, Paris, 1981; p. 173 (repr.), as *La crèche*, 1966. Corà 1986; p. 92, no. 43 (repr.). The Solomon R. Guggenheim Museum, New York, 1994–95; cat. 194 (repr.).

78
Pozzo (*Well*), 1965
Corrugated cardboard, canvases, and broken frames
H. 39⅜ inches (100 cm); diam. 55⅛ inches (140 cm)
Cittadellarte-Fondazione Pistoletto, Biella

Alternate titles: Il pozzo; "il pozzo di cartone"; *Pozzo con cartone*; *Pozzo di cartone; Pozzo (Oggetti in meno)*; "un pozzo di cartone con tele spaccate al centro."

Solo exhibitions: Pistoletto's studio, Turin, 1966. Galleria La Bertesca, Genoa, 1967; dated 1966. Museum Boijmans Van Beuningen, Rotterdam, 1969; cat. 1, as *Pozzo con cartone*, 1966. Palazzo Grassi, Venice, 1976; p. 22, cat. 36 (repr.), as *Pozzo di cartone*. Museo Diego Aragona Pignatelli Cortez, Naples, 1977; as *Pozzo di cartone*, 1966. Nordjyllands

Kunstmuseum, Aalborg, Denmark, 1978; cat. 33, as *Kilde af pap*, 1966. Hayward Gallery, London, 1982–83; p. 179 (repr.), as *Il pozzo*, 1966. Forte di Belvedere, Florence, 1984; p. 50, cat. 41 (repr.). The Institute for Contemporary Art, P.S. 1 Museum, New York, 1988; p. 89 (repr.), as *Well (Minus Objects).* Kunsthalle, Bern, 1989; p. 36 (color repr.). Galleria Nazionale d'Arte Moderna, Rome, 1990; cat. 19, as *Pozzo (Oggetti in meno).* Camden Arts Centre, London, 1991; (repr.). Deichtorhallen, Hamburg, 1992; p. 38 (repr.). Museu d'Art Contemporani de Barcelona, 2000; p. 86 (repr.), as *Pozzo (Oggetti in meno).* Palazzina della Società delle Belle Arti and Castello di Rivoli Museo d'Arte Contemporanea, Rivoli-Turin, 2000–2001; pp. 88–89 (color repr.), as *Pozzo (Oggetti in meno).* Musée d'Art Contemporain, Lyon, 2001; pp. 68, 216, cat. 4 (repr., color repr.). Musée d'Art Moderne et d'Art Contemporain, Nice, 2007; p. 98 (color repr.).

References: Boatto 1969; cat. 35 (repr.), as *pozzo di cartone*, 1966. Centre Georges Pompidou, Paris, 1981; p. 171 (repr.), as *Puits*, 1966. Corà 1986; p. 92, no. 47 (repr.). Staatliche Kunsthalle, Baden-Baden, Germany, 1988; p. 35 (repr.), as *Teil der Minus-Objekte*.

79

Lampada a mercurio (*Mercury Lamp*), 1965
Aluminum, iron, and lightbulbs
H. 31½ inches (80 cm); diam. 17$\frac{11}{16}$ inches (45 cm)
Cittadellarte-Fondazione Pistoletto, Biella

Alternate titles: Lampa; *Lampada a mercurio a luce gialla*; *La lampada gialla*; *Lampada gialla*; *Lampada a mercurio (Oggetti in meno)*; "una lampada a luce di mercurio".

Solo exhibitions: Pistoletto's studio, Turin, 1966. Museum Boijmans Van Beuningen, Rotterdam, 1969; cat. 4, as *Lampa*, 1966. Modern Art Agency (Galleria Lucio Amelio), Naples, 1970. Palazzo Grassi, Venice, 1976; p. 21, cat. 32 (repr.), as *Lampada a mercurio a luce gialla*. L.A.I.C.A., Los Angeles, 1979. Forte di Belvedere, Florence, 1984. Kunsthalle, Bern, 1989; p. 33 (color repr.). Galleria Nazionale d'Arte Moderna, Rome, 1990; pp. 91–93, cat. 23 (repr.), as *Lampada a mercurio (Oggetti in meno)*, 1965–66. Deichtorhallen, Hamburg, 1992; p. 45 (color repr.). Museu d'Art Contemporani de Barcelona, 2000; p. 80 (color repr.), as *Lampada a mercurio (Oggetti in meno).* Palazzina della Società delle Belle Arti and Castello di Rivoli Museo d'Arte Contemporanea, Rivoli-Turin, 2000–2001; p. 92 (color repr.), as *Lampada a mercurio (Oggetti in meno).* Musée d'Art Contemporain, Lyon, 2001; cat. 18. Musée d'Art Moderne et d'Art Contemporain, Nice, 2007; p. 95 (color repr.).

Group exhibitions: Galleria Sperone, Turin, 1966. Deposito d'Arte Presente, Turin, 1968. Palacio de Cristal and Palacio de Velázquez, Madrid, 1985; p. 142, cat. 127 (repr.). Museum Fridericianum, Kassel, Germany, 1997; p. 175 (repr.).

References: Corà 1986; p. 91, no. 38 (repr.). Museo d'Art Contemporani, Barcelona, 2007; p. 238 (color repr.).

80

Piramide verde (*Green Pyramid*), 1965
Wood table and four wood chairs
51$\frac{3}{16}$ x 59$\frac{1}{16}$ x 59$\frac{1}{16}$ inches (130 x 150 x 150 cm)
Cittadellarte-Fondazione Pistoletto, Biella

Alternate titles: La piramide verde; *Piramide verde con tavolo e sedie (Oggetti in meno)*; *Piramide verde (Oggetti in meno).*

Solo exhibitions: Pistoletto's studio, Turin, 1966. Palazzo Grassi, Venice, 1976; p. 21, cats. 32, 33 (repr.), as *Piramide verde con tavolo e sedie.* Mario Diacono, Bologna, 1979. L.A.I.C.A., Los Angeles, 1979; as *La piramide verde*. Forte di Belvedere, Florence, 1984. Kunsthalle, Bern, 1989; p. 34 (color repr.). Galleria Nazionale d'Arte Moderna, Rome, 1990; pp. 90, 92, 93, cat. 24 (reprs.), as *Piramide verde con tavolo e sedie (Oggetti in meno).* Deichtorhallen, Hamburg, 1992; p. 34 (repr.). Museu d'Art Contemporani de Barcelona, 2000; as *Piramide verde (Oggetti in meno).* Palazzina della Società delle Belle Arti and Castello di Rivoli Museo d'Arte Contemporanea, Rivoli-Turin, 2000–2001; pp. 79–80 (color repr.), as *Piramide verde con tavolo e sedie (Oggetti in meno).* Musée d'Art Contemporain, Lyon, 2001; p. 215, cat. 24 (color repr.). Musée d'Art Moderne et d'Art Contemporain, Nice, 2007; p. 97 (color repr.).

References: Centre Georges Pompidou, Paris, 1981; p. 213 (repr.), as *structure vert + table*, 1965–66. Corà 1986; p. 93, no. 57 (repr.). Moderna Galerija, Ljubljana, Slovenia, 1996; (repr.), as *Keramika–Piramida/Ceramic–Pyramid*.

81

Colonne di cemento (*Concrete Columns*), 1965
Concrete, four elements
Each 94½ x 17$\frac{11}{16}$ x 17$\frac{11}{16}$ inches (240 x 45 x 45 cm)
Cittadellarte-Fondazione Pistoletto, Biella

Alternate titles: Colonna di cemento; *Colonne di cemento (Oggetti in meno)*; *Columns; Le colonne di cemento*; "pylons."

Solo exhibitions: Pistoletto's studio, Turin, 1966. Palais des Beaux-Arts, Brussels, 1967, cat. 39, as *Colonnes en ciment.* Museum Boijmans Van Beuningen, Rotterdam, 1969. Palazzo Grassi, Venice, 1976; p. 21, cat. 33 (repr.), as *Le colonne di cemento.* L.A.I.C.A., Los Angeles, 1979, (reconstructed in wood). Forte di Belvedere, Florence, 1984. The Institute for Contemporary Art, P.S. 1 Museum, New York, 1988; p. 96 (repr.), as *Concrete Columns (Minus Objects).* Kunsthalle, Bern, 1989; p. 37 (color repr.). Galleria Nazionale d'Arte Moderna, Rome, 1990; pp. 91, 92, cat. 21 (reprs.). Deichtorhallen, Hamburg, 1992; p. 41 (color repr.). Museu d'Art Contemporani, Barcelona, 2000, as *Colonne di cemento (Oggetti in meno).* Palazzina della Società delle Belle Arti and Castello di Rivoli Museo d'Arte Contemporaea, Rivoli-Turin, 2001; p. 91 (color repr.), as *Colonne di cemento (Oggetti in meno).* Musée d'Art Contemporain, Lyon, 2001; cat. 17. Le Musée d'Art Moderne et d'Art Contemporain, Nice, 2007; p. 93 (color repr.).

References: Corà 1986; p. 93, cat. 56 (repr.).

82

Semisfere decorative (*Decorative Semispheres*), 1965–66
Colored plastic semispheres, nine elements
Overall 84¼ x 92⅛ inches (214 x 234 cm)
Cittadellarte-Fondazione Pistoletto, Biella

Alternate title: Semisfere decorative (Oggetti in meno).

Solo exhibitions: Pistoletto's studio, Turin, 1966. Palazzo Grassi, Venice, 1976; pp. 20, 21, 97, cat. 33 (repr.), as *Pannelli decorativi*. Forte di Belvedere, Florence, 1984. The Institute for Contemporary Art, P.S. 1 Museum, New York, 1988; p. 83 (repr.), as *Decorative Semispheres (Minus Objects)*, 200 x 300 cm. Kunsthalle, Bern, 1989; p. 48 (color repr.). Palazzo Fabroni, Pistoia, 1996. Palazzina della Società delle Belle Arti and Castello di Rivoli Museo d'Arte Contemporanea, Rivoli-Turin, 2000–2001; pp. 81–82 (color repr.), as *Semisfere decorative (Oggetti in meno).* Musée d'Art Moderne et d'Art Contemporain, Nice, 2007; p. 100 (color repr.).

Group exhibitions: Galleria Sperone, Turin, 1966.

References: Corà 1986; p. 93, no. 52 (repr.). Museo di Capodimonte, Naples, 1989; p. 22 (repr.). Museu d'Art Contemporani de Barcelona, 2000; p. 76 (color repr.).

Note: A variation on this work, *Semisfere decorative sospese*, was created in 1966.

83

Teletorte (*Twisted Canvases*), 1965–66
Tempera on canvas, three elements
Each 90$\frac{9}{16}$ x 47¼ inches (230 x 120 cm)
Cittadellarte-Fondazione Pistoletto, Biella

Alternate titles: Le teletorte; *Panelli torti*; *Teletorte (Oggetti in meno).*

Solo exhibitions: Pistoletto's studio, Turin, 1966. Museum Boijmans Van Beuningen, Rotterdam, 1969; cat. 15 (repr.), as *Panelli torti*, 1966–67. Palazzo Grassi, Venice, 1976; p. 23, cat. 41 (repr.), as *Le teletorte.* Nordjyllands Kunstmuseum, Aalborg, Denmark, 1978; cat. 36, as *Forvredne lærreder*, "Le Teletorte," 1966. Akadamie der Künste, Berlin, 1978; cat. 15 (repr.), as *Die verderehten Leinwände.* L.A.I.C.A., Los Angeles, 1979; as *Le teletorte.* Forte di Belvedere, Florence, 1984. The Institute for Contemporary Art, P.S. 1 Museum, New York, 1988; p. 85 (repr.), as *Twisted Canvases (Minus Objects).* Kunsthalle, Bern, 1989; p. 50 (color repr.). Galleria Nazionale d'Arte Moderna, Rome, 1990; pp. 93, 95, cat. 34 (repr., color repr.), as *Teletorte (Oggetti in meno).* Deichtorhallen, Hamburg, 1992; p. 50 (repr.). Palazzina della Società delle Belle Arti and Castello di Rivoli Museo d'Arte Contemporanea, Rivoli-Turin, 2000–2001; pp. 72–73 (color repr.), as *Teletorte (Oggetti in meno)*. Museu d'Art Contemporani de Barcelona, 2000; p. 77 (color repr.), as *Teletorte (Oggetti in meno)*, 1966. Musée d'Art Contemporain, Lyon, 2001; pp. 83, 216, cat. 7 (repr., color repr.). Musée d'Art Moderne et d'Art Contemporain, Nice, 2007; p. 101 (color repr.).

References: Corà 1986; p. 93, no. 54 (repr.). Museo di Capodimonte, Naples, 1989; p. 20 (repr.). Lenbachhaus, Munich, 1996; p. 92 (repr.).

84
Mobile (Furniture), 1965–66
Wood, canvas, and velvet
33⅞ x 33⅞ x 33⅞ inches (86 x 86 x 86 cm)
Cittadellarte-Fondazione Pistoletto, Biella

Alternate titles: Il mobile; Mobile (Oggetti in meno).

Solo exhibitions: Pistoletto's studio, Turin, 1966. Palazzo Grassi, Venice, 1976; p. 21, cat. 32 (repr.), as *Il mobile*. L.A.I.C.A., Los Angeles, 1979. Forte di Belvedere, Florence, 1984. The Institute for Contemporary Art, P.S. 1 Museum, New York, 1988; p. 90 (color repr.), as *Furniture (Minus Objects)*. Kunsthalle, Bern, 1989; p. 49 (color repr.). Galleria Nazionale d'Arte Moderna, Rome, 1990; pp. 92, 93, cat. 36 (reprs.), as *Mobile (Oggetti in meno)*. Deichtorhallen, Hamburg, 1992; p. 49 (color repr.). Museu d'Art Contemporani de Barcelona, 2000; p. 65 (repr.), as *Mobile (Oggetti in meno)*. Palazzina della Società delle Belle Arti and Castello di Rivoli Museo d'Arte Contemporanea, Rivoli-Turin, 2000–2001; pp. 80–81 (color repr.), as *Mobile (Oggetti in meno)*. Walker Art Center, Minneapolis, 2002; p. 311, cat. 128 (color repr.), as *Mobile (Oggetti in meno)*. Musée d'Art Moderne et d'Art Contemporain, Nice, 2007; p. 103 (color repr.).

References: Corà 1986; p. 92, no. 44 (repr.).

85
Bagno (Bath), 1965–66
Fiberglass
23⅝ x 78¾ x 39⅜ inches (60 x 200 x 100 cm)
Cittadellarte-Fondazione Pistoletto, Biella

Alternate titles: Bagno (Oggetti in meno); Il Bagno; Il bagno; "Il Bagno"; "un bagno"; *Vasca da bagno.*

Solo exhibitions: Pistoletto's studio, Turin, 1966. Galleria Sperone, Milan, 1966. Nordjyllands Kunstmuseum, Aalborg, Denmark, 1978; cat. 35, as *Badekar*, 1966. Deutsche Oper, Berlin, 1978; cat. 18 (repr.), as *Il Bagno*, 1967, 1967. L.A.I.C.A., Los Angeles, 1979. Hayward Gallery, London, 1982–83; p. 179 (repr.), as *Il bagno / Das Bad*, 1966. Forte di Belvedere, Florence, 1984. The Institute for Contemporary Art, P.S. 1 Museum, New York, 1988; p. 87 (repr.), as *Bath (Minus Objects)*. Kunsthalle, Bern, 1989; pp. 40–41 (color repr.). Galleria Nazionale d'Arte Moderna, Rome, 1990; pp. 91, 92, cat. 35 (reprs.), as *Bagno (Oggetti in meno)*. Deichtorhallen, Hamburg, 1992; p. 51 (repr.). Museum Moderner Kunst Stiftung Ludwig, Vienna, 1995; pp. 34, 35, cat. 8 (color reprs.), as *Bagno (Oggetti in meno)*. Museu d'Art Contemporani de Barcelona, 2000; as *Bagno (Oggetti in meno)*. Palazzina della Società delle Belle Arti and Castello di Rivoli Museo d'Arte Contemporanea, Rivoli-Turin, 2000–2001; pp. 71–72 (color repr.), as *Bagno (Oggetti in meno)*. Walker Art Center, Minneapolis, 2002; p. 312, cat. 125 (color repr.), as *Bagno (Oggetti in meno)*. Musée d'Art Moderne et d'Art Contemporain, Nice, 2007; p. 102 (color repr.).

Group shows: Galleria Stein, Galleria Sperone, Galleria Il Punto, Turin, 1967. Galleria de'Foscherari, Bologna, 1968; (repr.). Centro Arte Viva Feltrinelli, Trieste, 1968. Centre Georges Pompidou, Paris, 1981.

References: Celant 1976; p. 69, fig. 75 (repr.), as "un bagno," dated 1967. Corà 1986; p. 92, no. 49 (repr.).

86
Mica, 1965–66
Mica on canvas
47¼ x 47¼ inches (120 x 120 cm)
Cittadellarte-Fondazione Pistoletto, Biella

Alternate titles: Mica (Oggetti in meno); "un corpo ricoperto di mica."

Solo exhibitions: Pistoletto's studio, Turin, 1966. Galleria Christian Stein, Turin, 1968. MATRIX University Art Museum, Berkeley, 1980. Forte di Belvedere, Florence, 1984; pp. 112, 199–200 (dated 1965–66), 209 (dated 1966). Galleria Giorgio Persano, Turin, 1985; cat. 1 (repr.). Kunstnernes Hus, Oslo, 1986; cat. 4 (repr.), as *Kråkesolv* (Sea Silver), 1966. Kunsthalle, Bern, 1989; p. 51 (color repr.). Galleria Nazionale d'Arte Moderna, Rome, 1990; p. 96, cat. 38 (color repr.), as *Mica (Oggetti in meno)*. Museu d'Art Contemporani de Barcelona, 2000; as *Mica (Oggetti in meno)*, 1965. Palazzina della Società delle Belle Arti and Castello di Rivoli Museo d'Arte Contemporanea, Rivoli-Turin, 2000–2001; pp. 75–76 (color repr.), as *Mica (Oggetti in meno)*. Musée d'Art Contemporain, Lyon, 2001; cat. 16. Musée d'Art Moderne et d'Art Contemporain, Nice, 2007; p. 107 (color repr.).

References: Museo di Capodimonte, Naples, 1989; p. 22 (repr.).

Note: Many other works by Pistoletto use mica, including *Tre Grazie (The Three Graces*, 1966), *Mica-Dyptich* (1966), other works titled *Mica* from 1966, and another *Mica*, from 1971–72.

87
Struttura per parlare in piedi (Structure for Talking while Standing), 1965–66
Welded and painted iron pipe
47¼ x 78¾ x 78¾ inches (120 x 200 x 200 cm)
Cittadellarte-Fondazione Pistoletto, Biella

Alternate titles: Struttura per chiacchierare in piedi; Struttura per Conversare in Piedi; Struttura per parlare in piedi, Oggetti in meno; Struttura per parlare in piedi (Oggetti in meno); "un struttura per parlare in piedi."

Solo exhibitions: Pistoletto's studio, Turin, 1966. Galleria Sperone, Milan, 1966. Galleria La Bertesca, Genoa, 1967. Palazzo Grassi, Venice, 1976; p. 21, cat. 32 (repr.). Nordjyllands Kunstmuseum, Aalborg, Denmark, 1978; cat. 34, as *Structure for talking while standing-up*, 1966. IDZ Internationales Design Zentrum, Berlin, 1978; cat. 20 (repr.), as *Struttura per Conversare in Piedi / Struktur um stehend mileinander zu reden / Struktur um stehend mileinander zu sprechen*, 1966. L.A.I.C.A., Los Angeles, 1979 (an approximate reconstruction of the work). Forte di Belvedere, Florence, 1984. The Institute for Contemporary Art, P.S. 1 Museum, New York, 1988; p. 93 (repr.), as *Structure for Talking while Standing (Minus Objects)*. Kunsthalle, Bern, 1989; p. 43 (color repr.). Museum Moderner Kunst Stiftung Ludwig, Vienna, 1995; p. 33, cat. 10 (repr.), as *Struttura per parlare in piedi (Oggetti in meno)*. Palazzo Fabroni, Pistoia, 1996; p. 36 (repr.). Museu d'Art Contemporani de Barcelona, 2000; p. 77 (color repr.), as *Struttura per parlare in piedi (Oggetti in meno)*, 1965. Palazzina della Società delle Belle Arti and Castello di Rivoli Museo d'Arte Contemporanea, Rivoli-Turin, 2000–2001; pp. 87–88 (color repr.), as *Struttura per parlare in piedi (Oggetti in meno)*. Musée d'Art Contemporain, Lyon, 2001; cat. 12; Musée d'Art Moderne et d'Art Contemporain, Nice, 2007; p. 105 (color repr.).

Group exhibitions: Galleria Sperone, Milan, 1966. Deposito d'Arte Presente, Turin, 1968. Palazzo delle Esposizioni, Rome, 1972–73; p. 193 (repr.). Neues Museum Weserburg, Bremen, Germany, 1998–99; p. 195 (color repr.). Museo Nacional Centro de Arte Reina Sofía, Madrid, 2001; p. 57 (color repr.), as *Struttura per parlare in piedi, Oggetti in meno*. Walker Art Center, Minneapolis, 2002; p. 309, cat. 131 (repr.), as *Struttura per parlare in piedi (Oggetti in meno)*. Astrup Fearnley Museet for Moderne Kunst, Oslo, 2002; p. 41 (color repr.). Museo d'Art Contemporani, Barcelona, 2007.

References: Centre Georges Pompidou, Paris, 1981; p. 172 (repr.), as *Structure pour parler assis*. Corà 1986; p. 91, no. 39 (repr.), dated 1966.

88
Vetrina (Display Case), 1965–66
Wood, iron, mirror, and clothes
92½ x 39⅜ x 31½ inches (235 x 100 x 80 cm)
Cittadellarte-Fondazione Pistoletto, Biella

Alternate titles: La vetrina; "vestiti in vetrina"; *Vetrina (Oggetti in meno).*

Solo exhibitions: Pistoletto's studio, Turin, 1966. Galleria del Naviglio, Milan, 1967. Palais des Beaux-Arts, Brussels, 1967; cat. 37, as *La vitrine*. Palazzo Grassi, Venice, 1976; pp. 21, 23, cat. 33, as *La vetrina*, cat. 40 (reprs.). Forte di Belvedere, Florence, 1984. The Institute for Contemporary Art, P.S. 1 Museum, New York, 1988. Kunsthalle, Bern, 1989; p. 55 (color repr.). Galleria Nazionale d'Arte Moderna, Rome, 1990; p. 92, cat. 29 (repr.), as *Vetrina*

(Oggetti in meno). Deichtorhallen, Hamburg, 1992; p. 52 (repr.). Museum Moderner Kunst Stiftung Ludwig, Vienna, 1995; pp. 33, 36, cat. 11 (repr., color repr.), as *Vetrina (Oggetti in meno)*. Palazzina della Società delle Belle Arti and Castello di Rivoli Museo d'Arte Contemporanea, Rivoli-Turin, 2000–2001; p. 70 (color repr.), as *Vetrina (Oggetti in meno)*. Museu d'Art Contemporani de Barcelona, 2000; as *Vetrina (Oggetti in meno)*. Musée d'Art Contemporain, Lyon, 2001; p. 214, cat. 25 (repr.). Musée d'Art Moderne et d'Art Contemporain, Nice, 2007; pp. 111 (repr.), 147.
References: Centre Georges Pompidou, Paris, 1981; p. 172 (repr.), as *La vitrine*, 1966. Corà 1986; p. 93, no. 55 (repr.).

89
Fontana luminosa (*Luminous Fountain*), 1965–66
Oil on canvas
31½ x 39⅜ inches (80 x 100 cm)
Cittadellarte-Fondazione Pistoletto, Biella

Alternate titles: La fontana luminosa; La Fontana Luminosa; Fontana luminosa (Oggetti in meno).

Solo exhibitions: Pistoletto's studio, Turin, 1966. Palazzo Grassi, Venice, 1976; p. 21, cat. 33 (repr.), as *La fontana luminosa*. Mario Diacono, Bologna, 1979. Palacio de Cristal et Istituto Italiano di Cultura, Parque del Retiro, Madrid, 1983; p. 171, cat. 23 (repr.). Forte di Belvedere, Florence, 1984; p. 56, cat. 46 (color repr.), as *La fontana luminosa*. The Institute for Contemporary Art, P.S. 1 Museum, New York, 1988; p. 95 (color repr.), as *Light Fountain (Minus Objects)*. Kunsthalle, Bern, 1989; p. 45 (color repr.). Galleria Nazionale d'Arte Moderna, Rome, 1990; pp. 92, 93, cat. 39 (reprs.), as *Fontana luminosa (Oggetti in meno)*. Museu d'Art Contemporani de Barcelona, 2000; as *Fontana luminosa (Oggetti in meno)*. Palazzina della Società delle Belle Arti and Castello di Rivoli Museo d'Arte Contemporanea, Rivoli-Turin, 2000–2001; p. 85 (color repr.), as *Fontana luminosa (Oggetti in meno)*. Musée d'Art Contemporain, Lyon, 2001; cat. 19. Musée d'Art Moderne et d'Art Contemporain, Nice, 2007; p. 108 (color repr.).
References: Corà 1986; p. 92, no. 50 (repr.).

90
Ti amo (*I Love You*), 1965–66
Acrylic on canvas
23⅝ x 27$^{9}/_{16}$ inches (60 x 70 cm)
Cittadellarte-Fondazione Pistoletto, Biella

Alternate title: Ti amo (Oggetti in meno).

Solo exhibitions: Pistoletto's studio, Turin, 1966. Palazzo Grassi, Venice, 1976; p. 22, cat. 38 (repr.). Amerika-Gedenk-Bibliothek, Berlin, 1978; cat. 16 (repr.), as *Ti Amo / Ich liebe dich, 1966*. Mario Diacono, Bologna, 1979. L.A.I.C.A., Los Angeles, 1979. Forte di Belvedere, Florence, 1984. The Institute for Contemporary Art, P.S. 1 Museum, New York, 1988; p. 101 (repr.), as *I Love You (Minus Objects)*. Kunsthalle, Bern, 1989; p. 38 (repr.). Galleria Nazionale d'Arte Moderna, Rome, 1990; p. 94, cat. 28 (color repr.), as *Ti amo (Oggetti in meno)*. Camden Arts Centre, London, 1991, (repr.). Deichtorhallen, Hamburg, 1992; p. 53 (repr.). Museum Moderner Kunst Stiftung Ludwig, Vienna, 1995; p. 135, cat. 9 (repr.), as *Ti amo (Oggetti in meno)*. Lenbachhaus, Munich, 1996; p. 19 (color repr.). Museu d'Art Contemporani de Barcelona, 2000; p. 75 (color repr.), as *Ti amo (Oggetti in meno)*, 1965; Palazzina della Società delle Belle Arti and Castello di Rivoli Museo d'Arte Contemporanea, Rivoli-Turin, 2000–2001; pp. 83–84 (color repr.), as *Ti amo (Oggetti in meno)*. Musée d'Art Contemporain, Lyon, 2001; pp. 83, 214, cat. 8 (repr., color repr.). Musée d'Art Moderne et d'Art Contemporain, Nice, 2007; p. 109 (color repr.).
Group exhibitions: Museum Fridericianum, Kassel, Germany, 1997; p. 175 (color repr.).
References: Centre Georges Pompidou, Paris, 1981; p. 174 (repr.), as *Je t'aime*, 1966. Corà 1986; p. 92, no. 45 (repr.), dated 1966.
Note: A smaller version of this work, painted in red and dated 1966, currently belongs to a private collection.

91
Scultura lignea (*Wood Sculpture*), 1965–66
Antique wood sculpture encircled by orange Plexiglas on a wood stand
39⅜ x 11$^{13}/_{16}$ x 9$^{13}/_{16}$ inches (100 x 30 x 25 cm)
Cittadellarte-Fondazione Pistoletto, Biella

Alternate title: Scultura lignea (Oggetti in meno); Statua lignea.

Solo exhibitions: Pistoletto's studio, Turin, 1966. Palazzo Grassi, Venice, 1976; p. 21, cat. 32 (repr.), as *Statua lignea*. Samangallery, Genoa, 1977. L.A.I.C.A., Los Angeles, 1979. Forte di Belvedere, Florence, 1984; p. 53, cat. 43 (color repr.). The Institute for Contemporary Art, P.S. 1 Museum, New York, 1988; p. 186 (color repr.), as *Wooden Sculpture (Minus Objects)*. Kunsthalle, Bern, 1989; p. 44 (color repr.). Galleria Nazionale d'Arte Moderna, Rome, 1990; p. 90, cat. 26 (repr.), as *Scultura lignea (Oggetti in meno)*. Museu d'Art Contemporani de Barcelona, 2000; as *Scultura lignea (Oggetti in meno)*. Palazzina della Società delle Belle Arti and Castello di Rivoli Museo d'Arte Contemporanea, Rivoli-Turin, 2000–2001; p. 84 (color repr.), as *Scultura lignea (Oggetti in meno)*, 1965. Musée d'Art Moderne et d'Art Contemporain, Nice, 2007; p. 115 (color repr.).
Group exhibitions: Gian Enzo Sperone—Arte Moderna, Turin, 1966. Solomon R. Guggenheim Museum, New York, 1994–95; cat. 193 (repr.). Walker Art Center, Minneapolis, 2002; p. 313, cat. 129 (color repr.), as *Scultura lignea (Oggetti in meno)*.
References: Corà 1986; p. 94, no. 60 (repr.). Musée d'Art Contemporain, Lyon, 2001; p. 85 (repr.). Farano, Mundici, and Roberto 2005; p. 43 (repr.).

92
Sfera sotto il letto (*Sphere under the Bed*), 1965–66
Wood, canvas, polyurethane, lightbulb, and pressed newspaper
Overall 17 x 78¾ x 40⅛ inches (43 x 200 x 102 cm); sphere 13⅜ inches (34 cm)
Private collection

Alternate titles: Sfera sotto il letto (Oggetti in meno); Sphere under the Bed (minus objects).

Provenance: The Institute for Contemporary Art, P.S. 1 Museum, New York, 1988. To the present owner, n.d.
Solo exhibitions: Galleria Nazionale d'Arte Moderna, Rome, 1990; pp. 92, 98, cat. 46 (repr., color repr.), as *Sfera sotto il letto (Oggett in meno)*. Deichtorhallen, Hamburg, 1992; p. 46 (repr.). Museu d'Art Contemporani de Barcelona, 2000; p. 81 (repr.), as *Sfera sotto il letto (Oggetti in meno)*.
Group exhibitions: Università-Instituto di storia dell'arte, Genoa, 1967.
References: Koninklijk Museum voor Schone Kunsten, Antwerp, 1993; p. 69 (color repr.), as *Sphere under the Bed (minus objects)*.
Note: This work exists in two versions; the other is in the collection of Cittadellarte-Fondazione Pistoletto, Biella.

93
Casa a misura d'uomo (*House on a Human Scale*), 1965–66
Wood and enamel
78¾ x 39⅜ x 47¼ inches (200 x 100 x 120 cm)
Cittadellarte-Fondazione Pistoletto, Biella

Alternate titles: Casa a misura d'uomo (Oggetti in meno).

Solo exhibitions: Pistoletto's studio, Turin, 1966. L.A.I.C.A., Los Angeles, 1979. Forte di Belvedere, Florence, 1984; p. 51, cat. 42 (repr.). The Institute for Contemporary Art, P.S. 1 Museum, New York, 1988; p. 104 (repr.), as *Man-sized House (Minus Objects)*. Kunsthalle, Bern, 1989; p. 42 (color repr.). Galleria Nazionale d'Arte Moderna, Rome, 1990; p. 93, cat. 31 (repr.), as *Casa a misura d'uomo (Oggetti in meno)*. Camden Arts Centre, London. Deichtorhallen, Hamburg, 1992; p. 37 (color repr.). Palazzo Fabroni, Pistoia, Italy, 1996; p. 132 (repr.). Museu d'Art Contemporani de Barcelona, 2000; p. 76 (color repr.), as *Casa a misura d'uomo (Oggetti in meno)*. Palazzina della Società delle Belle Arti and Castello di Rivoli Museo d'Arte Contemporanea, Rivoli-Turin, 2000–2001; p. 71 (color repr.), as *Casa a misura d'uomo (Oggetti in meno)*. Musée d'Art Contemporain, Lyon, 2001; p. 81, cat. 6 (repr.). Walker Art Center, Minneapolis, 2002; p. 310, cat. 126 (color repr.), as *Casa a misura d'uomo (Oggetti in meno)*. Musée d'Art Moderne et d'Art Contemporain, Nice, 2007; pp. 31 (repr.), 113 (color repr.), as *Maison à mesure humaine*.
Group exhibitions: Deposito d'Arte Presente, Turin, 1968. Centre Georges Pompidou, Paris, 1981. Kunstmuseum Kloster Unser Lieben Frauen, Magdeburg, Germany, 2003; p. 121, cat. 87 (repr.), as *Casa a misura d'uomo (Oggetto in meno)*.

References: Palacio de Cristal et Istituto Italiano di Cultura, Parque del Retiro, Madrid, 1983; p. 50 (repr.), as *Casa a medida del hombre*, 1966. Corà 1986; p. 93, no. 51 (repr.).

94
Sarcofago (*Sarcophagus*), 1966
Wood, cement, and mica
60⅝ x 78¾ x 29¹⁵⁄₁₆ inches (154 x 200 x 76 cm)
Cittadellarte-Fondazione Pistoletto, Biella

Alternate titles: Sarcofago (Oggetti in meno); "un sarcofago."

Solo exhibitions: Pistoletto's studio, Turin, 1966. Galerie Ileana Sonnabend, Paris, 1967. Forte di Belvedere, Florence, 1984; p. 200. The Institute for Contemporary Art, P.S. 1 Museum, New York, 1988; p. 94 (repr.). Kunsthalle, Bern, 1989; p. 58 (color repr.). Galleria Nazionale d'Arte Moderna, Rome, 1990; p. 93, cat. 40 (repr.), as *Sarcofago (Oggetti in meno)*. Deichtorhallen, Hamburg, 1992; p. 47 (repr.). Museu d'Art Contemporani de Barcelona, 2000; as *Sarcofago (Oggetti in meno)*. Palazzina della Società delle Belle Arti and Castello di Rivoli Museo d'Arte Contemporanea, Rivoli-Turin, 2000–2001; p. 93 (color repr.), as *Sarcofago (Oggetti in meno)*.
Group exhibitions: Museum Fridericianum, Kassel, Germany, 1968; pp. 234, 235, cat. 1 (repr.).
References: Koninklijk Museum voor Schone Kunsten, Antwerp, 1993; p. 68 (color repr.), as *Sarcophagus (minus objects)*.

95
Foto di Jasper Johns (*Photograph of Jasper Johns*), 1966
Photograph on paper
98 ⁷⁄₁₆ x 39⅜ inches (250 x 100 cm)
Cittadellarte-Fondazione Pistoletto, Biella

Alternate titles: "la foto gigante di Jasper Johns"; *Fotografia di Jasper Johns*; *Foto di Jasper Johns (Oggetti in meno)*.

Solo exhibitions: Pistoletto's studio, Turin, 1966. Palazzo Grassi, Venice, 1976; pp. 21, 23, cats. 32, 33, as *Fotografia di Jasper Johns*, 43 (reprs.). Mario Diacono, Bologna, 1979. Forte di Belvedere, Florence, 1984. Kunsthalle, Bern, 1989; p. 56 (color repr.). Galleria Nazionale d'Arte Moderna, Rome, 1990; pp. 90, 92, 93, cat. 33 (reprs.), as *Foto di Jasper Johns (Oggetti in meno)*. Deichtorhallen, Hamburg, 1992; p. 55 (repr.). Musée d'Art Contemporain, Lyon, 2001; p. 217, cat. 15 (color repr.). Musée d'Art Moderne et d'Art Contemporain, Nice, 2007; p. 116 (repr.).
Group exhibitions: Centro La Capella, Trieste, Italy, 1970; (repr.). Museum Fridericianum, Kassel, Germany, 1997; p. 174 (repr.).
References: Corà 1986; p. 91, no. 40 (repr.).

96
Metrocubo d'infinito (*Cubic Meter of Infinity*), 1966
Six mirrors turned inward and tied with string
47¼ x 47¼ x 47¼ inches (120 x 120 x 120 cm)
Cittadellarte-Fondazione Pistoletto, Biella

Alternate titles: Metro cubo di infinito; Metro Cubo d'Infinito; Metrocubo d'infinito (Oggetti in meno).

Solo exhibitions: Museum am Ostwall, Dortmund, Germany, 1971; p. 58 (repr.). Palazzo Grassi, Venice, 1976; pp. 23, 58–59, cat. 44 (repr.), cat. 112a–c (repr.), as *Metro cubo di infinito*. Museo Diego Aragona Pignatelli Cortez, Naples, 1977; as *Metro cubo d'infinito*, 1966–67. Zeiss-Planetarium Wilhelm-Forerster-Sternwarte, Berlin, 1978; cat. 27 (repr.), as *Metro Cubo d'Infinito / Ein Kublikmeter Unendlichkeit*. Nordjyllands Kunstmuseum, Aalborg, Denmark, 1978; cat. 37, as *Uendelighendens kubikmeter*. High Museum of Art, Atlanta, 1979; p. 16, cat. 12 (repr.) (reconstruction). Kunstnernes Hus, Oslo, 1986; as *Uendelighetens kube*, 1965. Grazer Kunstverein, Graz, 1988. Staatliche Kunsthalle, Baden-Baden, Germany, 1988; p. 129, cat. 8 (color repr.), as *Ein Kubikmeter Unendilchkeit*. The Institute for Contemporary Art, P.S. 1 Museum, New York, 1988; p. 86 (repr.), as *A Cubic Meter of Infinity (Minus Objects)*. Kunsthalle, Bern, 1989; p. 57 (color repr.). Galleria Nazionale d'Arte Moderna, Rome, 1990; p. 92, cat. 44 (repr.), as *Metrocubo d' infinito (Oggetti in meno)*. Deichtorhallen, Hamburg, 1992; p. 44 (color repr.). Fundação de Serralves, Porto, Portugal, 1993; p. 55 (repr.). The National Museum of Contemporary Art, Seoul, 1994; p. 43 (color repr.). Museum Moderner Kunst Stiftung Ludwig, Vienna, 1995; p. 23, cat. 12 (color repr.), as *Metrocubo d' infinito (Oggetti in meno)*. Lenbachhaus, Munich, 1996; p. 69 (color repr.). Museu d'Art Contemporani de Barcelona, 2000; p. 76 (color repr.), as *Metrocubo d'infinito (Minus Objects)*, 1965–66. Palazzina della Società delle Belle Arti and Castello di Rivoli Museo d'Arte Contemporanea, Rivoli-Turin, 2000–2001; p. 86 (color repr.), as *Metrocubo d'infinito (Minus Objects)*. Museum of Modern Art, Oxford, 2000; as *Metro Cubo di Infinito*. Musée d'Art Contemporain, Lyon, 2001; p. 82, cat. 13 (repr., color repr.). Various spaces, Città di Castello (Perugia), 2001; pp. 97–101, 124 (color reprs.). Musée d'Art Moderne et d'Art Contemporain, Nice, 2007; p. 118 (repr.), as *Mètre cube d'infini*, p. 119 (color repr.), as *Metrocubo di infinito*. Moderna Museet, Stockholm, 2008; p. 134 (color repr.).
Group exhibitions: Galleria de' Foscherari, Bologna, 1968. Deposito d'Arte Presente, Turin, 1968. Palazzo delle Espozizioni, Rome, 1970. Palacio de Cristal and Palacio de Velázquez, Madrid, 1985; p. 143, cat. 128 (repr.). Palazzo della Permanente, Milan, 1981; p. 121, cat. 3 (repr.), as *Metro cubo d'infinito*, dated 1966–76. Kunstverein München, Munich, 1991; pp. 18–19, pls. 1, 2 (reprs.). Museum Fridericianum, Kassel, Germany, 1997; p. 175 (color repr.). Museum of Contemporary Art, Sydney, 2002; p. 110 (color repr.), as *Metro Cubo d'Infinito*. Kunstmuseum Kloster Unser Lieben Frauen, Magdeburg, Germany, 2003; p. 120, cat. 88 (repr.), as *Metrocubo d'infinto (Oggetto in meno)*. Museu d'Art Contemporani, Barcelona, 2007.
References: Centre Georges Pompidou, Paris, 1981; p. 339 (repr.), as *Cube infini*, Rome, 1970. Forte di Belvedere, Florence, 1984; p. 59, cat. 50 (repr.), as *Metro cubo di infinito*. Celant 1985; p. 148, no. 146 (repr.). The Institute for Contemporary Art, P.S. 1 Museum, New York, 1985; p. 224 (repr.). Corà 1986; p. 92, no. 48 (repr.), as *Metro cubo d'infinito*. Centre d'Art Santa Monica, Barcelona, 1991; pp. 16, 17 (repr., color repr.). Centre Georges Pompidou, Paris, 1992; p. 56 (color repr.), as *Metro cubo di infinito*, 1964–65. Lenbachhaus, Munich, 1996; p. 69 (repr.). Museum Fridericianum, Kassel, Germany, 1997; p. 175 (color repr.). Neues Museum Weserburg, Bremen, Germany, 1998–99; p. 197 (color repr.), as "Metrocubo d'Infinitio," 1965–66. Musée d'Art Contemporain, Lyon, 2001; p. 214 (repr.). Walker Art Center, Minneapolis, 2002; p. 13 (repr.), p. 311 (color repr.), cat. 127, as *Metro cubo d'infinito (Oggetti in Meno)*. Farano, Mundici, and Roberto 2005; p. 174 (repr.), as *One Cubic Meter of Infinity/ One Cubic Yard of Finity*. Museo Cantonale d'Arte, Lugano, Switzerland, 2006; p. 69, fig. 8 (repr.). Musée d'Art Moderne et d'Art Contemporain, Nice, 2007; p. 20 (repr.), as *Mètre cube d'infini*. Palazzo Grassi, Venice, 2008; pp. 194–95 (color repr.), p. 305 (repr.).
Note: This work exists in five versions of varying colors. One is in the collection of the Musée National d'Art Moderne Centre Georges Pompidou, Paris; another is on long-term loan to MART—Museo per l'Arte Contemporanea di Trento e Rovereto, Rovereto, Italy, from a private collection; a third is in the collection of the artist; and the remaining two are in the collection of Cittadellarte-Fondazione Pistoletto, Biella.

97
Mappamondo (*Globe*), 1966–68
Newspaper and wire
Wire ball: diam. 70⅞ inches (180 cm); newspaper ball: diam. 39⅜ inches (100 cm)
Collection of Lia Rumma

Alternate titles: Il mappamondo; Mappamondo (Oggetti in meno); Sfera di giornali (Mappamondo); Palla di giornali (Mappamondo).

Provenance: Acquired by the present owner around 1968.
Solo exhibitions: Pistoletto's studio, Turin, 1966. Modern Art Agency (Galleria Lucio Amelio), Naples, 1970. Palazzo Grassi, Venice, 1976; p. 16, cat. 27 (repr.). Mario Diacono, Bologna, 1979. Palacio de Cristal et Istituto Italiano di Cultura, Parque del Retiro, Madrid, 1983; pp. 62, 173, cat. 25 (reprs.), as *Mapamundi*. The Institute for Contemporary Art, P.S. 1 Museum, New York, 1988; pp. 118 (color repr.), 127 (repr.), as *Globe*. Grazer Kunstverein, Graz, Austria, 1988. Kunsthalle, Bern, 1989; p. 71 (color repr.). Galleria Nazionale d'Arte Moderna, Rome, 1990;

pp. 91–93, 99, cat. 47 (reprs., color repr.), as *Sfera di giornali (Mappamondo) (Oggetti in meno)*. Deichtorhallen, Hamburg, 1992; p. 54 (color repr.). Museu d'Art Contemporani de Barcelona, 2000; p. 82 (color repr.), as *Mappamondo (Oggetti in meno)*. Palazzina della Società delle Belle Arti and Castello di Rivoli Museo d'Arte Contemporanea, Rivoli-Turin, 2000–2001; pp. 78–79 (color repr.), as *Mappamondo (Oggetti in meno)*. Musée d'Art Contemporain, Lyon, 2001; p. 74, cat. 5 (repr.). Walker Art Center, Minneapolis, 2002; p. 314, cat. 133 (color repr.), as *Palla di giornali (Mappamondo)*. Musée d'Art Moderne et d'Art Contemporain, Nice, 2007; p. 121 (color repr.).

Group exhibitions: Arsenali, Amalfi, Italy, 1968. Palazzo delle Espozisioni, Rome, 1970; cat. a. (repr.), dated 1967. Grande Halle de la Villette, Paris, 1985. Kunst- und Austellungshalle der Bundesrepublik Deutschland, Bonn, 1992; p. 136, cat. 136 (color repr.). The Solomon R. Guggenheim Museum, New York, 1994–95; cat. 195 (repr.), as *Sfera di giornali (Mappamondo)*. Museum Fridericianum, Kassel, Germany, 1997; p. 175 (color repr.).

References: Boatto 1969; cat. 56 (repr.). Forte di Belvedere, Florence, 1984; p. 69, cat. 60 (color repr.). Celant 1985; p. 93, no. 74 (repr.). Corà 1986; p. 100, no. 70 (repr.), as *Il mappamondo*. Kunstnernes Hus, Oslo, 1986; cats. 1, 3 (reprs.), as *Klode*. Koninklijk Museum voor Schone Kunsten, Antwerp, 1993; p. 69 (color repr.), as *Globe*. Museum Moderner Kunst Stiftung Ludwig, Vienna, 1995; p. 92 (color repr.). Centre National d'Art et Culture Georges Pompidou, Paris, 1996–97; p. 405 (repr.). Umjetnicka Galerija, Sarajevo, 2001; p. 12 (repr.). Città di Castello (Perugia), 2001; p. 27 (repr.).

PIETRA MILIARE

98
Pietra miliare (*Milestone*), 1967
Roadside post and mica
H. 31½ inches (80 cm); diam. 15¾ inches (40 cm)
Cittadellarte-Fondazione Pistoletto, Biella

Alternate titles: La pietra miliare; Pietra Miliare.

Solo exhibitions: Galleria Stein, Galleria Sperone, Galleria Il Punto, Turin, 1967. Museum Boijmans Van Beuningen, Rotterdam, 1969; cat. 11. Palazzo Grassi, Venice, 1976; p. 30, cats. 57–58 (repr.), as *La pietra miliare*; p. 32, cat. 61 (repr.), as *Conclusione della mostra della pietra miliare*. Nordjyllands Kunstmuseum, Aalborg, Denmark, 1978; cat. 40, as *Milesten, "la pietra miliare."* Hochschule der Künste Berlin, cat. 19 (repr.), as *Pietra Miliare / Meilenstein*. Forte di Belvedere, Florence, 1984; p. 65, cat. 56 (repr.). The Institute for Contemporary Art, P.S. 1 Museum, New York, 1988; pp. 107, 109 (reprs.), as *Milestone*. Galleria Nazionale d'Arte Moderna, Rome, 1990; p. 104, cat. 52 (repr.). Museu d'Art Contemporani de Barcelona, 2000; p. 91 (repr.). Palazzina della Società delle Belle Arti and Castello di Rivoli Museo d'Arte Contemporanea, Rivoli-Turin, 2000–2001; p. 103 (repr.). Musée d'Art Contemporain, Lyon, 2001; pp. 26–27, cat. 40 (color repr.). Musée d'Art Moderne et d'Art Contemporain, Nice, 2007; p. 79 (repr.).

Group exhibitions: Galleria Civica d'Arte Moderna, Turin, 1970. Palazzo delle Espozisioni, Rome, 1970; cat. b. (repr.), as *La pietra miliare*. Montreal Museum of Fine Arts, 2003–4; p. 131, cat. 151 (color repr.).

References: Boatto 1969; cat. 46 (repr.). Centre Georges Pompidou, Paris, 1981; p. 224 (repr.), as *Pierre miliaire*, 1967. Staatliche Kunsthalle, Baden-Baden, Germany, 1988; p. 37 (repr.), as *Meilenstein*. Museum Moderner Kunst Stiftung Ludwig, Vienna, 1995; pp. 43–44 (reprs.). Walker Art Center, Minneapolis, 2002; p. 44, fig. 6 (repr.).

STRACCI / RAGS

99
Venere degli stracci (*Venus of the Rags*), 1967
Marble and rags
Statue: 65¾ x 23⅝ x 19¹¹⁄₁₆ inches (167 x 6 x 50 cm); overall: 74¾ x 98⅜ x 55⅛ inches (190 x 250 x 140 cm)
Cittadellarte-Fondazione Pistoletto, Biella

Alternate titles: La Venere degli stracci; Venere degli specchi.

Solo exhibitions: Palazzo Grassi, Venice, 1976; p. 42, cat. 89 (repr.). Museo Diego Aragona Pignatelli Cortez, Naples, 1977. Nordjyllands Kunstmuseum, Aalborg, 1978; cat. 41, as *Venus med gamle klude*. Café EinStein, Berlin, 1978; cat. 17 (repr.), as *Venere degli Stracci, 1968*. MATRIX University Art Museum, Berkeley, 1980. Hayward Gallery, London, 1982–83; p. 181 (color repr.), as *Venus of rags*. Galerie Tanit, Munich, 1982. Palacio de Cristal et Istituto Italiano di Cultura, Parque del Retiro, Madrid, 1983; p. 74, cats. 30–31 (reprs.), as *Venus de los trapos*. Forte di Belvedere, Florence, 1984; pp. 64, 130, cat. 85a–b (repr., color reprs.). Kunstnernes Hus, Oslo, 1986; cat. 7 (repr.), as *Venus med filler*. The Institute for Contemporary Art, P.S. 1 Museum, New York, 1988; pp. 121 (repr.), 125 (repr.), 138–39 (reprs.), as *Venus of Rags*. Staatliche Kunsthalle, Baden-Baden, 1988; pp. 87, 127, cat. 6 (repr., color repr.), as *Lumpenvenus*; p. 19, fig. 21 (repr.), as *Venus der Lumpen*. Galleria Nazionale d'Arte Moderna, Rome, 1990; p. 108, cat. 56 (color repr.), p. 16 (repr.). Kunstverein München, Munich, 1991; p. 93, pl. 17 (color repr.). Musée Départemental d'Art Contemporain, Rochechouart, 1993; p. 29 (color repr.), as *Vénus aux chiffons*. Lenbachhaus, Munich, 1996; p. 41 (color repr.). Museu d'Art Contemporani de Barcelona, 2000; p. 28 (repr.). Palazzina della Società delle Belle Arti and Castello di Rivoli Museo d'Arte Contemporanea, Rivoli-Turin, 2000–2001; p. 111 (color repr.). Città di Castello (Perugia), 2001; pp. 113–15 (color reprs.). Musée d'Art Moderne et d'Art Contemporain, Nice, 2007; pp. 21 (repr), 76–77 (color repr.), as *Vénus aux chiffons*.

Group exhibitions: Palazzo delle Espozisioni, Rome, 1970; cat. c (repr.), dated 1969. Palazzo delle Esposizioni, Rome, 1972–73; p. 265 (repr.). Mura aureliane, Rome, 1982; p. 97, cat. 161 (repr.), as *La Venere degli stracci*. Hayward Gallery, London, 1982–83; p. 181 (repr.). Venice Biennale, 1984; p. 104, cat. 1 (color repr.). Lenbachhaus, Munich, 1984; cat. 23 (repr.). The Institute for Contemporary Art, P.S. 1 Museum, New York, 1985; p. 231 (repr.), as *Venere degli specchi*. Palacio de Cristal and Palacio de Velázquez, Madrid, 1985; p. 148, cat. 133 (color repr.). Hagia Irene, Istanbul, 1987; p. 32 (color repr.). Haus der Kunst, Munich, 1988; p. 225, fig. 166 (color repr.), as *Venus in Lumpen*. American Academy, Rome, 1992; (color reprs.). Kodama Gallery, Osaka, 1992; p. 99 (repr.). Museu Nacional de Belas Artes, Rio de Janeiro, 1992; p. 89 (color repr.), dated 1967–71. Schüttkasten–Galerie Thaddaeus Ropac, Salzburg, 1993; p. 109, cat. 74 (color repr.). Museum van Hedendaagse Kunst, Gent, 1995; p. 65 (color repr.). Fine Arts Museum, Taipei, 1998; p. 77, pl. 37 (color repr.). Hirshhorn Museum and Sculpture Garden, Washington, D.C., 1999; p. 43, cat. 45 (color repr.). Scuderie Papali al Quirinale Mercati di Traiano, Rome, 2000–2001; p. 26 (color repr.). Palazzo Ducale, Sassuolo, 2001; p. 71 (color repr.). Museum of Contemporary Art, Sydney, 2002; p. 105 (color repr.). Castello di Rivoli Museo d'Arte Contemporanea, Rivoli-Turin, 2000; p. 259 (color repr.). K21 Kunstsammlung Nordrhein-Westfalen, Düsseldorf, 2002; p. 72 (color repr.). CAPC—Musée d'Art Contemporain Entrepôt, Bordeaux, 2003; pp. 65, 403 (color repr.). Palazzo della Ragione, Padua, 2003; (color repr.). Kunstmuseum Kloster Unser Lieben Frauen, Magdeburg, 2003; pp. 117, 144–45, cat. 92 (color reprs.). Montreal Museum of Fine Arts, 2003–4; p. 135, cat. 152 (color repr.). Scuderie del Quirinale, Rome, 2005; p. 148 (color repr.).

References: Mussat Sartor 1979; p. 230 (repr.). MATRIX University Art Museum, Berkeley, 1980 (repr.). Centre Georges Pompidou, Paris, 1981; p. 286 (repr.), as *Vénus aux chiffons*, 1968. Bonita Oliva 1984; p. 44 (repr.). Celant 1985; p. 148, no. 147 (repr.). Corà 1986; p. 101, no. 72 (repr.). The Institute for Contemporary Art, P.S. 1 Museum, New York, 1988; pp. 125 (repr.), 139 (repr.). Corà 1989; p. 73 (repr.). Koninklijk Museum voor Schone Kunsten, Antwerp, 1993; p. 66 (color repr.), as *Venus of the Rags*. Museum Moderner Kunst Stiftung Ludwig, Vienna, 1995; pp. 13 (color repr.), 48 (color repr.). Henry Moore Institute, Leeds, 1999; p. 5, fig. 6 (repr.). Dorfles 1999; p. 44 (repr.). Umjetnicka Galerija, Sarajevo, 2001; p. 12 (repr.). Museum für Angewandte Kunst, Cologne, 2001; pp. 64–65 (color repr.). Farano, Mundici, and Roberto 2005; pp. 194–95 (repr.), as *Venus and the Big Digger (La Venere e il Gran Carro)*. Poli and Bernardelli 2005; p. 149 (color repr.), dated 1967–70. Lista 2006; p. 45, cat. 15 (color repr.), dated 1967–69. Casagrande 2008; p. 433 (color repr.). Spazio Risonanze, Rome, 2009; p. 77 (color repr.).

Note: There are six other works with the same title and date but with different materials and dimensions. Four are made with cement and rags and are in the following collections: Fondazione per l'Arte Moderna e Contemporanea—CRT, Turin, on permanent loan to Castello di Rivoli Museo d'Arte Contemporanea, Rivoli-Turin, and GAM—Galleria Civica d'Arte Moderna e Contemporanea, Turin; a private collection; collection of the artist, Biella; and the Ackermann Collection, K21 Kunstsammlung Nordrhein-Westfalen, Düsseldorf. Two are made with plaster and rags and are in the collections of the Hirshhorn Museum and Sculpture Garden, Smithsonian Institution, Washington, D.C., and the Toyota Museum of Municipal Art, Toyota City, Japan.

100

Orchestra di stracci—quartetto (*Orchestra of Rags—Quartet*), 1968
Rags, glass, teakettles, steam, and electric circuit
Four elements, dimensions variable
MART—Museo per l'Arte Contemporanea di Trento e Rovereto, Rovereto, Italy

Provenance: Private collection, on long-term loan to MART—Museo per l'Arte Contemporanea di Trento e Rovereto, Rovereto, Italy.

Solo exhibitions: Museum Boijmans Van Beuningen, Rotterdam, 1969; cat. 9, as *Orchestre di stracci*, 1968/69. Modern Art Agency (Galleria Lucio Amelio), Naples, 1970. Palazzo Grassi, Venice, 1976; p. 40, cat. 83 (repr.). Museo Diego Aragona Pignatelli Cortez, Naples, 1977. MATRIX University Art Museum, Berkeley, 1980. Palacio de Cristal et Istituto Italiano di Cultura, Parque del Retiro, Madrid, 1983; pp. 177–78, 226, cats. 29–30, (reprs.). Kunstnernes Hus, Oslo, 1986; cat. 10 (repr.), as *Karlsvognen*. The Institute for Contemporary Art, P.S. 1 Museum, New York, 1988; p. 123 (color repr.), as *Orchestra of Rags*. Grazer Kunstverein, Graz, 1988. Staatliche Kunsthalle, Baden-Baden, 1988; p. 44 (repr.), p. 130, cat. 11 (color repr.), as *Lumpenorchester*. Galleria Nazionale d'Arte Moderna, Rome, 1990; pp. 15, 16, 109, cat. 57 (reprs., color repr.). Kunstverein München, Munich, 1991; p. 49, pl. 36 (color repr.). Hayward Gallery, London, 1993; p. 101 (color repr.), as *Orchestra of rags—Trio*. Museum Moderner Kunst Stiftung Ludwig, Vienna, 1995; pp. 31 (repr.), 48 (repr.), 130. Lenbachhaus, Munich, 1996; p. 51 (color repr.), as *Orchester der Lumpen*. Museu d'Art Contemporani de Barcelona, 2000; p. 113 (color repr.), as *Orchestra degli stracci–Il grande carro*, 1969. Palazzina della Società delle Belle Arti and Castello di Rivoli Museo d'Arte Contemporanea, Rivoli-Turin, 2000–2001; pp. 112–13 (color repr.). Umjetnicka Galerija, Sarajevo, 2001; pp. 52–53 (color repr.). Musée d'Art Moderne et d'Art Contemporain, Nice, 2007; p. 82 (color repr.).

Group exhibitions: Galleria Civica d'Arte Moderna, Turin, 1970; (repr.), as *Concerto di stracci*. The Institute for Contemporary Art, P.S. 1 Museum, New York, 1985; cat. 3/4, p. 194–95 (color repr.), as *The Big Dipper (Seven Orchestras of Rags)*. Neues Museum Weserburg, Bremen, 1997; p. 179, cat. 179 (color repr.). Kunstmuseum Kloster Unser Lieben Frauen, Magdeburg, 2003; p. 44 (repr.), p. 142, cat. 93 (color repr.), as *Orchestra di Stracchi*.

References: Boatto 1969; cats. 9, 54 (reprs.). Celant 1969; p. 7 (repr.), p. 22. Centre Georges Pompidou, Paris, 1981; p. 241 (repr.), as *Concert de chiffons*. Forte di Belvedere, Florence, 1984; p. 61, cat. 52 (repr.). Lenbachhaus, Munich, 1984; (repr.). Corà 1986; p. 101, no. 71 (repr.). Royal Scottish Academy, Edinburgh, 1987; p. 122 (repr.). Centre d'Art Santa Monica, Barcelona, 1991; p. 45 (color repr.).

Note: The artist created different versions of the work, which are included in the exhibition history above. Their titles are *Orchestre di stracci*, *Orchestra degli stracci–Il grande carro*, and *Concerto di stracci*.

101

Monumentino (*Little Monument*), 1968
Rags, bricks, and shoe
37 x 17¾ x 8⅝ inches (94 x 45 x 22 cm)
Private collection

Alternate titles: Il Monumentino; *Piccolo monumento*.

Provenance: Acquired by the present owner, n.d.

Solo exhibitions: Museu d'Art Contemporani de Barcelona, 2000; p. 111 (color repr.). Palazzina della Società delle Belle Arti and Castello di Rivoli Museo d'Arte Contemporanea, Rivoli-Turin, 2000–2001; p. 112 (color repr.). Musée d'Art Moderne et d'Art Contemporain, Nice, 2007; p. 81 (color repr.).

Group exhibitions: Arsenali, Amalfi, 1968. Esoterick Collection, London, 2005; p. 55 (repr.).

References: Palacio de Cristal et Istituto Italiano di Cultura, Parque del Retiro, Madrid, 1983; p. 62 (repr.), as *Pequeño monumentino*. Forte di Belvedere, Florence, 1984; p. 71 (repr.). Kunstnernes Hus, Oslo, 1986, cat. 1 (repr.), as *Lite monument*. The Institute for Contemporary Art, P.S. 1 Museum, New York, 1988; p. 127 (repr.). Grazer Kunstverein, Graz; p. 43 (repr.), as *Kleines Monument*. Museum Moderner Kunst Stiftung Ludwig, Vienna, 1995; p. 46 (repr.). Lenbachhaus, Munich, 1996; p. 49 (repr.). Lumley 2004: p. 66, cat. 47 (repr.).

Note: Two other, different versions of this work exist, both in the collection of Cittadellarte-Fondazione Pistoletto, Biella.

102

Muretto di stracci (*Small Wall of Rags*), 1968
Bricks and rags
47¼ x 71⅞ x 9¼ inches (120 x 182.5 x 23.5 cm)
Fundação de Serralves—Museu de Arte Contemporânea, Porto, Portugal

Alternate titles: *Muro di stracci*; *Muro degli stracci*; *Muretto di Mattoni e stracci*; *Muretto di mattoni e stracci*.

Provenance: Sperone Westwater, New York, by September 1997. To the Fundação de Serralves–Museu de Arte Contemporânea, Porto, around 1997.

Solo exhibitions: Palazzo Grassi, Venice, 1976; pp. 42, 43, cat. 89 (repr.). The Institute for Contemporary Art, P.S. 1 Museum, New York, 1988; p. 122 (color repr.), as *Wall of Rags*.

Group exhibitions: Museum Fridericianum, Kassel, 1968. Palazzo delle Espozisioni, Rome, 1970; cat. c. (repr.), as *Muretto di mattoni e stracci*. Palazzo delle Esposizioni, Rome, 1972–73; p. 265 (repr.), dated 1972. Galleria in Arco, Turin, 1990; cat. 40. Musée Matisse, Le-Cateau-Cambrésis, and Musée des Beaux-Arts, Cambray, 1992; p. 200, cat. 464, pl. 66 (color repr.), as *Muro di stracci (Mur de chiffons)*. Sperone Westwater, New York, 1997. Musée des Beaux-Arts, Tourcoing, 2001; as *Muro di stracci*. Palais des Papes, Avignon, 2003; as *Muro di stracci*. FRAC Nord–Pas de Calais, Dunkirk, 2004; as *Muro di stracci*. Ecole d'Architecture et de Paysage de Lille, Villeneuve-d'Ascq, 2005; as *Muro di stracci*. Musée Départemental d'Art Contemporain, Rochechouart, 2007; as *Muro di stracci*. Hangar à Bananes, Nantes, 2008; no cat.; as *Muro di stracci*.

References: Forte di Belvedere, Florence, 1984; p. 61, cat. 51 (repr.). Staatliche Kunsthalle, Baden-Baden, 1988; p. 43 (repr.), as *Kleinses Monument*. Bouyer et al. 1990; (repr.). Museu d'Art Contemporani de Barcelona, 2000; p. 110 (color repr.), as *Muro degli stracci*. Minola et al. 2000; p. 470 (color repr.). Città di Castello (Perugia), 2001; p. 26 (repr.). Museo d'Arte Contemporanea di Villa Croce, Genoa, 2004; (repr.).

Note: Three versions of this work exist. One of the others is in the collection of the artist; the other in the collection of FRAC Nord–Pas de Calais, titled *Muro di stracci*.

LIGHTS AND REFLECTIONS

103

Candele (*Candles*), 1967
Candles on mirroring Mylar foil
Dimensions variable
Cittadellarte-Fondazione Pistoletto, Biella

Alternate titles: Le candele.

Solo exhibitions: Galleria Stein, Galleria Sperone, Galleria Il Punto, Turin, 1967. Museum Boijmans Van Beuningen, Rotterdam, 1969; cat. 14 (repr.). Palazzo Grassi, Venice, 1976; p. 33, cat. 64 (repr.), as *Le candele*. The Institute for Contemporary Art, P.S. 1 Museum, New York, 1988; pp. 108, 109, 127 (reprs.), as *Candles*. Galleria Nazionale d'Arte Moderna, Rome, 1990; p. 107, cat. 55 (repr.). Museu d'Art Contemporani de Barcelona, 2000; p. 106 (repr.). Palazzina della Società delle Belle Arti and Castello di Rivoli Museo d'Arte Contemporanea, Rivoli-Turin, 2000–2001;

p. 107 (repr.). Musée d'Art Contemporain, Lyon, 2001; pp. 26–27, 204, cat. 39 (color reprs.).
Group exhibitions: Arsenali, Amalfi, 1968. Galleria Civica d'Arte Moderna, Turin, 1970; (repr.), dated 1966.
References: Boatto 1969; cats. 42, 46, 56 (repr.). Celant 1969; p. 21 (repr.). Risso 1978; p. 11 (repr.). Palacio de Cristal et Istituto Italiano di Cultura, Parque del Retiro, Madrid, 1983; pp. 57, 62 (reprs.), as *Velas*. Forte di Belvedere, Florence, 1984; p. 67, cat. 58 (repr.). Corà 1986; p. 96, no. 62 (repr.), as *Le candele*. Kunstnernes Hus, Oslo, 1986; cat. 1 (repr.), as *Lys*. Staatliche Kunsthalle, Baden-Baden, 1988; p. 37 (repr.), as *Kerzen*. Museum Moderner Kunst Stiftung Ludwig, Vienna, 1995; pp. 44, 47 (reprs.). Minola et al. 2000; p. 117 (repr.).

104
Riflessi sul muro (*Reflections on the Wall*), 1967
Mirroring Mylar foil
Dimensions variable
Cittadellarte-Fondazione Pistoletto, Biella

Alternate title: Riflessi.

Solo exhibitions: Galleria Stein, Galleria Sperone, Galleria Il Punto, Turin, 1967. Palazzo Grassi, Venice, 1976; p. 32, cat. 62 (repr.). Hansen Fuller Golden Gallery, San Francisco, 1980. Galleria Nazionale d'Arte Moderna, Rome, 1990; p. 106, cat. 54 (repr.). Museu d'Art Contemporani de Barcelona, 2000; p. 107 (repr.). Palazzina della Società delle Belle Arti and Castello di Rivoli Museo d'Arte Contemporanea, Rivoli-Turin, 2000–2001; pp. 104–5 (repr.). Umjetnicka Galerija, Sarajevo, 2001; pp. 56–57 (color reprs.). Musée d'Art Contemporain, Lyon, 2001; pp. 26–27, cat. 41 (color reprs.), as *Riflessi*. Musée d'Art Moderne et d'Art Contemporain, Nice, 2007; p. 75 (repr.).
Group exhibitions: Galleria Civica d'Arte Moderna, Turin, 1970; (repr.).
References: Boatto 1969; cats. 40, 46 (reprs.), as *riflessi sul muro*. Forte di Belvedere, Florence, 1984; p. 67, cat. 59 (repr.). Corà 1986; p. 98, no. 66 (repr.). Museum Moderner Kunst Stiftung Ludwig, Vienna, 1995; p. 44 (repr.). Minola et al. 2000; p. 117 (repr.).

A note about the following two works: In the first decades after their conception, the name and size of the works changed depending on the way they were exhibited: *Quadro di fili elettrici* (*Painting of Electric Wires*) was shown against a wall, while *Tenda di lampadine* (*Curtain of Lightbulbs*) or *Tenda di fili elettrici* (*Curtain of Electric Wires*) was hung in a doorway. This was not always the case, however. There are four versions of this work: the two below and those in the collection of the artist and of FRAC Nord–Pas de Calais, Dunkirk (*Tenda di lampadine a muro*). The following exhibition histories are organized according to whether the work was called a *Quadro* or a *Tenda*.

105
Quadro di fili elettrici (*Painting of Electric Wires*), 1967
Twenty-one electric wires and lightbulbs
105½ x 173¼ x 3 15/16 inches (268 x 440 x 10 cm)
MAXXI—Museo Nazionale delle Arti del XXI Secolo, Rome. Courtesy of the Italian Ministry of Cultural Heritage and Activities

Alternate title: Fili elettrici e lampadine; *Quadro di Fili Elettrici.*

Provenance: Purchased directly directly from the artist.
Solo exhibitions: Galleria Stein, Galleria Sperone, Galleria Il Punto, Turin, 1967. Palazzo Grassi, Venice, 1976; p. 33, cat. 63 (repr.). 13 public sites, Berlin (this work at Kunstspedition Schlien), 1978; cat. 26 (repr.), as *Kunstspedition Schlien*. San Francisco Museum of Modern Art, 1980. The Institute for Contemporary Art, P.S. 1 Museum, New York, 1988; p. 109 (repr.), as *Painting of Electric Wires*. Galleria Nazionale d'Arte Moderna, Rome, 1990; p. 105, cat. 53 (repr.), as *Quadro di fili elettrici*. Kunstverein München, Munich, 1991; p. 51, pl. 38 (repr.). Musée Départemental d'Art Contemporain, Rochechouart, 1993; p. 34 (color repr.). Museu d'Art Contemporani de Barcelona, 2000; p. 105 (repr.). Palazzina della Società delle Belle Arti and Castello di Rivoli Museo d'Arte Contemporanea, Rivoli-Turin, 2000–2001; p. 106 (color repr.). Umjetnicka Galerija, Sarajevo, 2001; pp. 55–56 (color reprs.). Musée d'Art Contemporain, Lyon, 2001; pp. 26–27, cat. 42 (color repr.).
Group exhibitions: Galleria Civica d'Arte Moderna, Turin, 1977; p. 46 (repr.). Walker Art Center, Minneapolis, 2002; p. 315, cat. 134 (repr.). CAPC—Musée d'Art Contemporain de Bordeaux, 2003; p. 76 (repr.).
References: Boatto 1969; cats. 41, 46 (reprs.), as *Fili elettrici e lampadine*. Forte di Belvedere, Florence, 1984; p. 67, cat. 57 (repr.). Corà 1986; p. 98, no. 65 (repr.). The Institute for Contemporary Art, P.S. 1 Museum, New York, 1988; p. 109 (repr.). Staatliche Kunsthalle, Baden-Baden, 1988; p. 37 (repr.), as *Bild aus Elektrokabeln*. Museum Moderner Kunst Stiftung Ludwig, Vienna, 1995; p. 44 (repr.). Minola et al. 2000; p. 116 (repr.). Farano, Mundici, and Roberto 2005; p. 68 (repr.). Lista 2006; p. 44, cat. 8 (color repr.). Musée d'Art Moderne et d'Art Contemporain, Nice, 2007; p. 32 (repr.), as *Tableau de fils électriques*. Frezzotti, Italiano, and Rorro 2010, vol. 2, p. 553, as *Quadro di fili elettrici—Tenda di lampadine.*

106
Tenda di fili elettrici (*Curtain of Electric Wires*), 1967
Electric wire and lightbulbs
Dimensions variable, approx. 149½ x 157½ inches (379.7 x 400.1 cm)
Private collection

Alternate titles: Quadro di fili elettrici; *Tenda di lampadine*; *Tenda di lampadine a muro*; "una serie di lampadine."

Solo exhibitions: Museum Boijmans Van Beuningen, Rotterdam, 1969; cat. 16. Museo Diego Aragona Pignatelli Cortez, Naples, 1977; dated 1966. Museum of Modern Art, San Francisco, 1980. Musée d'Art Moderne et d'Art Contemporain, Nice, 2007; p. 74 (color repr.).
Group exhibitions: Galleria Civica d'Arte Moderna, Turin, 1970; (repr.). Musée Matisse Le-Cateau-Cambrésis, and the Musée des Beaux-Arts, Cambray, 1992; p. 260, cat. 463 (repr.), as *Tenda di lampadine a muro (Rideau de petites lampes murales)*. Hayward Gallery, London, 1993; (color repr.), as *Curtain of electric bulbs on the wall (Tenda di lampadine a muro)*. Palazzo Grassi, Venice, 2006; pp. 123 (color repr.), 125 (repr.), as *Tenda di fili elettrici*. Hangar à Bananes, Nantes, 2008; as *Tenda di lampadine a muro*.
References: Forte di Belvedere, Florence, 1984; p. 66 (repr.), p. 122, cat. 127 (repr.). The Institute for Contemporary Art, P.S. 1 Museum, New York, 1988; p. 126 (repr.), as *Lightbulb Curtain*. Bouyer et al. 1990; (repr.). Musée d'Art Moderne et Contemporain, Nice, 1992; as *Tenda di lampadine a muro*. Hayward Gallery, London, 1993; p. 97 (repr.), as *Curtain of electric bulbs on the wall (Tenda di lampadine a muro)*. Anciens Etablissements, Brussels, 1995; as *Tenda di lampadine a muro*. Lenbachhaus, Munich, 1996; p. 30 (repr.). Palazzo Fabroni, Pistoia, 1996; p. 170 (repr.). Musée d'Art Moderne et Contemporain, Strasbourg, 1998; as *Tenda di lampadine a muro*. Musée des Beaux-Arts, Arras, 2000; as *Tenda di lampadine a muro*. Palais des Papes, Avignon, 2003; as *Tenda di lampadine a muro*. Museo d'Arte Contemporanea di Villa Croce, Genoa, 2004; p. 44 (repr.), as *Tenda di lampadine a muro*. Hangar à Bananes, Nantes, 2008; as *Tenda di lampadine a muro*.

107
Slitta di acqua e sapone (*Sled of Water and Soap*), 1968
Frosted glass, soap, water, and aluminum
11 13/16 x 78¾ x 39 3/8 inches (30 x 200 x 100 cm)
Cittadellarte-Fondazione Pistoletto, Biella

Alternate title: Slitta d'acqua e sapone.

Solo exhibitions: Museum Boijmans Van Beuningen, Rotterdam, 1969; cat. 10 (repr.). Modern Art Agency (Galleria Lucio Amelio), Naples, 1970. Palacio de Cristal et Istituto Italiano di Cultura, Parque del Retiro, Madrid, 1983; p. 175, cat. 27 (repr.). The Institute for Contemporary Art, P.S. 1 Museum, New York, 1988; p. 109 (repr.), as *Soap and Water Sled*. Museu d'Art Contemporani de Barcelona, 2000; p. 108 (repr.).
Group exhibitions: Galleria Civica d'Arte Moderna, Turin, 1970; (repr.).
References: Boatto 1969; cat. 50 (repr.), as *slitta d'acqua e sapone*. Forte di Belvedere, Florence, 1984; p. 82, cat. 76 (repr.). Corà 1986; p. 99, no. 67 (repr.). Museum Moderner Kunst Stiftung Ludwig, Vienna, 1995; p. 44 (repr.). Lenbachhaus, Munich, 1996; p. 28 (repr.).

AUTORITRATTO DI STELLE

108

Autoritratto di stelle (*Self-Portrait of Stars*), 1973
Photograph on transparent plastic
78¾ x 41⁵⁄₁₆ inches (200 x 105 cm)
Cittadellarte-Fondazione Pistoletto, Biella

Solo exhibitions: Palazzo Grassi, Venice, 1976; p. 73, cat. 132 (repr.). Crown Point Gallery, Oakland, Calif., 1981. The Institute for Contemporary Art, P.S. 1 Museum, New York, 1988; p. 184 (repr.), as *Self-Portrait of Stars*. Fundação de Serralves, Porto, Portugal, 1993; p. 62 (repr.). Palazzo Fabroni, Pistoia, 1996; p. 152 (repr.), dated 1973–75. Città di Castello (Perugia), 2001; p. 111 (color repr.).
Group exhibitions: Association du Méjan, Arles, 2004; p. 167 (color repr.).
References: Palacio de Cristal et Istituto Italiano di Cultura, Parque del Retiro, Madrid, 1983; p. 91 (repr.), as *Autoretrato de estrellas*, 1973–75. Forte di Belvedere, Florence, 1984; p. 113, cat. 113 (repr.), dated 1973–75. Corà 1986; p. 151, no. 104 (repr.), dated 1973–75. Galleria Nazionale d'Arte Moderna, Rome, 1990; p. 24 (repr.). The National Museum of Contemporary Art, Seoul, 1994; p. 10 (repr.). Museum Moderner Kunst Stiftung Ludwig, Vienna, 1995; p. 64 (repr.), dated 1973–75. Museo L. Pecci, Prato, 1996; p. 71 (repr.). Pinacoteca Comunale, Volterra, 1996; p. 100, cat. 49 (color repr.).

ACTIONS AND PERFORMANCES

Pistoletto's performances and actions were represented in the exhibition with ephemera (flyers, posters, and photographs) and by the following works, props, and films.

Le trombe del giudizio (*The Trumpets of Judgment*), 1968
Aluminum, three elements
Each 39⅜ x 78¾ inches (100 x 200 cm)
Cittadellarte-Fondazione Pistoletto, Biella
Fig. 229

Valigia dell'Uomo nero (*Suitcase of the Minus Man*), 1969
Suitcase with writing in chalk
7½ x 26¾ x 16⁹⁄₁₆ inches (19 x 68 x 42 cm)

shown together with

Il direttore d'orchestra (*The Conductor*), 1976
Silkscreen on paper
91⅜ x 47¼ inches (232 x 120 cm)
Private collection
Fig. 29

Manuscript of "L'Uomo nero, il lato insopportabile" (*The Minus Man, the Unbearable Side*), 1970
Book
Cittadellarte-Fondazione Pistoletto, Biella
Fig. 30

Maria Fotografia (*Maria Photography*), by Plinio Martelli, 1968
16mm film, black-and-white with sound, transferred to DVD
18 minutes
Restoration of film by Museo Nazionale del Cinema, Turin
Courtesy of Cittadellarte-Fondazione Pistoletto, Biella

La vestizione (The Rite of Dressing), by Antonio De Bernardi, 1968
8mm film, color with sound, transferred to DVD
25 minutes
Restoration of film by Museo Nazionale del Cinema, Turin
Courtesy of Cittadellarte-Fondazione Pistoletto, Biella

Pistoletto & Sotheby, by Pia Epremiam De Silvestris, 1968
8mm film, color with sound, transferred to DVD
25 minutes
Restoration of film by Museo Nazionale del Cinema, Turin
Courtesy of Cittadellarte-Fondazione Pistoletto, Biella

Buongiorno, Michelangelo (Good Morning, Michelangelo), by Ugo Nespolo, 1968
16mm film, black and white and color with sound, transferred to DVD
18 minutes
Courtesy of Ugo Nespolo
Fig. 65

Comunicato speciale (*Special Message*), by Renato Ferraro, 1968
16mm film, color with sound, transferred to DVD
8 minutes
Courtesy of Cittadellarte-Fondazione Pistoletto, Biella

Vernissage, by Franco Giachino Nichot and Cesare Tacchi, 1968
8mm, color, transferred to DVD
15 minutes
Restoration of film by Museo Nazionale del Cinema, Turin
Courtesy of Cittadellarte-Fondazione Pistoletto, Biella

REFERENCES CITED IN THE CHECKLIST

Boatto, Alberto. *Pistoletto: dentro / fuori lo specchio*. Rome: Fantini, 1969.

Bonito Oliva, Achille. *Dialoghi d'artista: incontri con l'arte contemporanea, 1970–1984*. Milan: Electa, 1984.

——. *Territorio Magico: comportamenti alternativi dell'arte*. Florence: Stampa Stiav, 1971.

Bouyer et al. *Catalogue FRAC Nord—Pas de Calais: Acquisitions 1988/89/90*. Lille, France: FRAC Nord—Pas de Calais, 1990.

Carluccio, Luigi, Ezro Gribaudo, and Edoardo Sanguineti. *Disegni e parole*. Turin: Edizioni d'Arte Fratelli Pozzo, 1963.

Casagrande, Gaia, ed. *The Castle—The Collection: Castello di Rivoli Museo d'Arte Contemporanea*. Milan: Skira, 2008.

Celant, Germano. *Arte dall'Italia*. Milan: Feltrinelli, 1988.

——. *Arte Povera*. Milan: Gabriele Mazzotta, 1969.

——. *Precronistoria, 1966–69: minimal art, pittura sistemica, arte povera, land art, conceptual art, body art, arte ambientale e nuovi media*. Florence: Centro Di, 1976.

——. *Arte Povera / Art Povera*. Milan: Electa, 1985.

Corà, Bruno. *Michelangelo Pistoletto: lo spazio della reflessione nell'arte*. Ravenna: Essegi, 1986.

——. *Pistoletto: sette rilievi*. Milan: Electa, 1989.

——. *Michelangelo Pistoletto—anno bianco*. Rome: I Libri di AEIUO, 1990.

Dorfles, Gillo. *Ultime tendenze nell'arte d'oggi: dall'informale al neo-oggettuale*. Rev. ed. Milan: Feltrinelli, 1999.

Farano, Marco, Maria Cristina Mundici, and Maria Teresa Roberto. *Michelangelo Pistoletto: il varco dello specchio; azioni e collaborazioni, 1967–2004*. Turin: Fondazione Torino Musei, 2005.

Frezzotti, Stefania, Carolina Italiano, and Angelandreina Rorro, eds. *Galleria nazionale d'arte moderna e MAXXI, Roma: le collezioni, 1958–2008*. 2 vols. Milan: Electa, 2010.

Kultermann, Udo. *The New Sculpture: Environments and Assemblages*. New York: Praeger, 1968.

Lippard, Lucy. *Pop Art*. New York: Praeger, 1966.

Lista, Giovanni. *Arte Povera*. Milan: 5 Continents, 2006.

Lumley, Robert. *Arte Povera*. London: Tate Publishing, 2004.

Minola, Anna, et al. *Gian Enzo Sperone: Torino–Roma–New York*. Turin: hopefulmonster, 2000.

Museum Ludwig. *Kunst des 20. Jahrhunderts: Museum Ludwig Köln*. Cologne: Taschen, 1996.

Mussat Sartor, Paolo. *Paolo Mussat Sartor fotografo, 1968–1978: arte e artisti in Italia*. Turin: Stampatori, 1979.

Oellers, Adam C., Alfred M. Fischer, et al. *Handbuch Museum Ludwig: Kunst des 20. Jahrhunderts; Gemälde, Skulpturen, Collagen, Objekte, Environments*. 2 vols. Cologne: Museen der Stadt, 1979–83.

Osten, Gert von der, and Horst Keller. *Kunst der sechziger Jahre: Sammlung Ludwig im Wallraf-Richartz Museum Köln / Art of the Sixties*. 4th ed. Cologne: Wallraf-Richartz-Museum, 1970.

Poli, Francesco, and Francesco Bernardelli. *Arte contemporanea: le ricerche internazionali dalla fine degli anni '50 a oggi*. Milan: Electa, 2005.

Risso, Giuseppe. *L'arte assume la religione*. Turin: Giorgio Persano, 1978.

Ruhrberg, Karl, et al. *Art of the 20th Century*. Edited by Ingo F. Walther. Translated by John William Gabriel. New York: Taschen, 1998.

Schwabsky, Barry. *The Widening Circle: Consequences of Modernism in Contemporary Art*. New York: Cambridge University Press, 1997.

Storck, Gerhard, et al. *Sammlung Helga und Walther Lauffs im Kaiser Wilhelm Museum Krefeld: Amerikanische und europäische Kunst der sechziger und siebziger Jahre*. Krefeld: Kaiser Wilhelm Museum, 1983.

Weiss, Evelyn. *Katalog der Gemälde des 20. Jahrhunderts: Die jüngeren Generationen ab 1915 im Museum Ludwig*. Cologne: Wallraf-Richartz-Museum, 1976.

Wember, Paul. *Kunst in Krefeld: Öffentliche und private Kunstsammlungen*. Cologne: DuMont-Schauberg, 1973.

Whitney, Alexandra, ed. *The Helga and Walther Lauffs Collection*. 2 vols. Göttingen: Steidl, 2009.

EXHIBITIONS CITED IN THE CHECKLIST

For a complete listing of Pistoletto's exhibitions, see the artist's Web site at www.pistoletto.it.

Solo Exhibitions

1963
Turin, Italy, Galatea–Galleria d'Arte Contemporanea. *Pistoletto*. April 27–May 14, 1963. Catalogue, with texts by Alain Jouffroy, Michael Sonnabend, and Tommaso Trini.

1964
Paris, Galerie Ileana Sonnabend. *Pistoletto*. March 1964. Catalogue, with essays by Tommaso Trini Castelli and Alain Jouffroy.

Venice, Galleria del Leone. *Pistoletto*. Opened September 4, 1964. Catalogue.

Turin, Galleria Sperone. *Pistoletto*. Opened October 2, 1964. Brochure, with text by Michelangelo Pistoletto.

1965
Milan, Sala Espressioni–Ideal Standard. *Michelangelo Pistoletto*. February–March 1965. Catalogue, with essay by Ettore Sottsass Jr.

1966
Turin, Italy, Pistoletto's studio. *Oggetti in meno*. January 1966.

Minneapolis, Walker Art Center. *Michelangelo Pistoletto: A Reflected World*. April 4–May 8, 1966. Catalogue, with essay by Martin Friedman.

Venice, Galleria del Leone Arte Contemporanea. *Michelangelo Pistoletto*. June 10–17, 1966. Catalogue.

Milan, Galleria Sperone. Opened November 8, 1966. Brochure.

Genoa, Italy, Galleria La Bertesca. *Michelangelo Pistoletto*. December 1966–January 1967. Catalogue, with essays by L. Ashbery, et al.

1967
Milan, Galleria del Naviglio. *Pistoletto*. February 22–March 7, 1967. Catalogue, with essay by Tommaso Trini.

Brussels, Palais des Beaux-Arts. *Michelangelo Pistoletto*. April 14–March 7, 1967. Catalogue, with essays by Jean Dypreau, Henry Martin, and Michelangelo Pistoletto.

New York, Kornblee Gallery. *Standing Man: 7 Perception*. April 22–May 18, 1967. Catalogue.

Cologne, Galerie Rudolf Zwirner. *Michelangelo Pistoletto*. May 26, 1967. Brochure.

Detroit, J. L. Hudson Gallery. *Recent Works:, Michelangelo Pistoletto*. Fall 1967. Catalogue, with essay by Martin Friedman.

Paris, Galerie Ileana Sonnabend. 1967.

1968
Turin, Italy, Galleria Christian Stein. *Quadri specchianti, rosa bruciata, palla di giornali*. January 1968.

1969
New York, Kornblee Gallery. *Michelangelo Pistoletto*. January 25–February 13, 1969. Catalogue.

Rotterdam, The Netherlands, Museum Boijmans Van Beuningen. *Michelangelo Pistoletto*. March 22–May 4, 1969. Catalogue, with essays by Renilde Hammacher van den Brande, Henry Martin, and Michelangelo Pistoletto.

Buffalo, Albright-Knox Art Gallery. *Michelangelo Pistoletto*. May 13–June 15, 1969. Catalogue, edited by Ethel Moore, with essay by Robert M. Murdock.

1970
Trieste, Italy, Centro La Capella. *Fotografia creativa*. February 21–March 14, 1970. Catalogue, with essays by Gillo Dorfles and Daniella Palazzoli.

Naples, Modern Art Agency: Galleria Lucio Amelio. *Michelangelo Pistoletto*. February 1970. Brochure.

Turin, Italy, Galleria Sperone. *Padre Figlio Spirito Santo e Le Tre Grazie*. Opened March 6, 1970.

Milan, Galleria dell'Ariete. *Tutte le donne. . . .* March 24–April 21, 1970. Catalogue, with essay by Tommaso Trini.

1972
Rome, Galleria Toninelli. 1972. Brochure.

1973
Milan, Galleria dell'Ariete. *Pistoletto*. Opened June 7, 1973. Catalogue, with text by Michelangelo Pistoletto.

Turin, Galleria Sperone. *Padre e figlio*. June 1973.

Hanover, Germany, Kestner Gesellschaft. *Michelangelo Pistoletto*. November 23, 1973–January 13, 1974. Catalogue, edited by Wieland Schmied.

1974
Darmstadt, Germany, Mathildenhöhe. *Michelangelo Pistoletto*. April 27–May 26, 1974. Catalogue, with essay by Bernd Krimmel.

New York, Sidney Janis Gallery. *New Paintings by Pistoletto*. November 6–30, 1974. Catalogue, with essay by Tommaso Trini.

1975
Rome, Galleria Sperone. *La prigione, il suicidio, il pericolo della morte, l'agguato, il decadimento, gli escrementi, il cimitero, la cattura*. Opened January 14, 1975.

Tokyo, Tokyo Art Agency. May 13–June 7, 1975.

Naples, Galleria Il Centro. 1975.

1976
Venice, Palazzo Grassi. *Michelangelo Pistoletto*. June 16–July 31, 1976. Catalogue, with essays by Germano Celant and Michelangelo Pistoletto.

1977
Naples, Museo Diego Aragona Pignatelli Cortes. *Michelangelo Pistoletto*, February–March 1977. Brochure.

Genoa, Samangallery. *L'alto in basso, il basso in alto, il dentro fuori*. Opened October 12, 1977. Brochure.

1978
Aalborg, Denmark, Nordjyllands Kunstmuseum. *Pistoletto*. February–March 1978. Catalogue, with essays by Mirella Bandini et al.

Turin, Italy, Galleria Giorgio Persano. *L'arte assume la religione*. March 1978. Catalogue, with essays by Michelangelo Pistoletto and Giuseppe Risso.

Berlin, Nationalgalerie. *Reflexionen*. August 4–November 12, 1978. Additionally, 13 public sites in the city. *Pistoletto in Berlin: Arbeiten aus den Jahren 1962–1978*. October 12–November 12, 1978. Catalogue (*Pistoletto in Berlin*), edited by Helga Retzer.

Bologna, Italy, Galleria Mario Diacono. *Michelangelo Pistoletto: mostra antilogica*. December 9, 1978–January 6, 1979. Catalogue, with essays by Mario Diacono and Michelangelo Pistoletto.

1979
Houston, Institute for the Arts, Rice University. *Michelangelo Pistoletto: Mirrors-Works*. February 16–April 15, 1979. Traveled to Atlanta, High Museum of Art and other locations, as *Creative Collaborations*, March 1–April 7, 1979; Athens, Georgia Museum of Art, University of Georgia, as *Furniture Environment*, April 15–May 10, 1979. Catalogue (*Michelangelo Pistoletto: Mirror-Works, Creative Collaborations, Furniture Environments*; published 1983), with essays by Dave Hickey et al.

Los Angeles, Los Angeles Institute of Contemporary Art (L.A.I.C.A.). *Minus Objects*. December 15, 1979–January 18, 1980. Brochure.

1980
Berkeley, Calif., University Art Museum. *Michelangelo Pistoletto*. January 16–March 2, 1980. Catalogue, with essay by Germano Celant.

San Francisco, Hansen Fuller Golden Gallery. *Reflections*. February 7–March 1980.

San Francisco Museum of Modern Art. February 29–March 30, 1980. Brochure.

1981
Oakland, Calif., Crown Point Gallery. 1981.

1982
Rome, Galleria Pieroni. *Michelangelo Pistoletto: la mano, la testa, la spalla*. February, 1982. Catalogue.

Munich, Galerie Tanit. *Michelangelo Pistoletto*. December 2, 1982–January 29, 1983. Catalogue, with text by Enrico R. Comi.

1983
Madrid, Palacio de Cristal, Parque del Retiro. *Michelangelo Pistoletto*. October 28–December 1, 1983. Catalogue, edited by Aurora García.

1984
Geneva, Centre d'Art Contemporain. *Michelangelo Pistoletto: Sculptures 1981-1982-1983*. January 28–February 29, 1984. Catalogue, with essay by Fulvio Salvadori.

Florence, Forte di Belvedere. *Pistoletto*. March 24–May 27, 1984. Catalogue, edited by Germano Celant.

1985
Paris, Galerie de France. *Michelangelo Pisoletto: les quatre saisons*. March 14–April 28, 1985. Catalogue, with essay by Giuseppe Conte.

Turin, Italy, Galleria Giorgio Persano. *Michelangelo Pistoletto: quarta generazione*. May–June 1985. Catalogue, with texts by Rudi Fuchs and Michelangelo Pistoletto.

1986
Oslo, Kunstnernes Hus. *Pistoletto: Skulptur/Malerei*. January 25–February 23, 1986. Catalogue, with essay by Demetrio Paparoni.

Toronto, Art Gallery of Ontario and Istituto Italiano di Cultura. *Michelangelo Pistoletto: The Big Dipper*. February 28–April 20, 1986. Catalogue, with essays by Roald Nasgaard, F. Valente, and R. F. Welsh.

1987
Antwerp, Belgium, Galerie Montevideo. *Dentro*. September 12–October 24, 1987. Catalogue (*Michelangelo Pistoletto*), with essays by Wim Van Mulders and Michelangelo Pistoletto.

1988
Graz, Austria, Grazer Kunstverein. *Michelangelo Pistoletto*. January 20–February 14, 1988. Catalogue, with essays by Bruno Corà, Peter Pakesch, and Michelangelo Pistoletto.

Long Island City, N.Y., The Institute for Contemporary Art: P.S. 1 Museum. *Michelangelo Pistoletto: Division and Multiplication of the Mirror*. October 2–November 27, 1988. Catalogue, with essays by Germano Celant, Alana Heiss, and Michelangelo Pistoletto.

Baden-Baden, Germany, Staatliche Kunsthalle. *Michelangelo Pistoletto*. October 8–November 27, 1988. Catalogue, edited by Jochen Poetter.

1989
Naples, Museo di Capodimonte. *Pistoletto: sette rilievi*. March 12, 1989. Catalogue, with essay by Bruno Corà.

Bern, Switzerland, Kunsthalle. *Michelangelo Pistoletto: Oggetti in meno, 1965–1966*. October 21–December 3, 1989. Traveled to Vienna, Wiener Secession, January 25–February 25, 1990. Catalogue, with essays by Ulrich Loock, Michelangelo Pistoletto, and Denys Zacharopoulos.

1990
Rome, Galleria Nazionale d'Arte Moderna. *Michelangelo Pistoletto*. June 8–October 30, 1990. Catalogue, with essays by F. Fiorani, Anna Imponente, and Augusto Monferini.

Barcelona, Centre d'Art Santa Monica. *L'arquitectura del mirall: Pistoletto*. November 22, 1990–January 10, 1991. Catalogue, with essays by Antonio D'Avossa and J. M. Garcia.

1991
London, Camden Arts Centre. *Michelangelo Pistoletto: Oggetti in meno (Minus Objects), 1965–1966*. September 13–November 3, 1991. Traveled to Oslo, Museet for Samtidskunst, November 23, 1991–January 26, 1992. Brochure.

1992
Hamburg, Deichtorhallen. *Michelangelo Pistoletto: gli oggetti in meno, lo specchio, la gabbia / Die Minus-Objekte, Spiegel, Gitter*. March 11–May 10, 1992. Catalogue, with essays by Zdenek Felix and Michelangelo Pistoletto.

1993
Porto, Portugal, Fundação de Serralves. *Pistoletto e la fotografia*. January 21–March 14, 1993. Traveled to Rotterdam, The Netherlands, Witte de With, Centrum voor Hedendaagse Kunst, April 3–May 16, 1993. Catalogue, with essays by Jean-François Chevrier et al.

Catania, Italy, Arte Club. *Pistoletto*. February 18–March 10, 1993. Catalogue, with essay by Francesco Gallo.

Rochechouart, France, Musée Départemental d'Art Contemporain. *Il segno arte*. July 7–September 30, 1993. Catalogue, with essays by Laurence Gateau, Dominique Marchès, and Jean-Marc Prévost.

1994
Seoul, The National Museum of Contemporary Art. *Pistoletto through the Mirror*. July 20–August 21, 1994. Catalogue, edited by Anna Imponente.

1995
Vienna, Museum Moderner Kunst Stiftung Ludwig Wien. *Michelangelo Pistoletto: Zeit-Räume*. June 1–September 10, 1995. Catalogue, with essays by Monika Faber et al.

Pistoia, Italy, Palazzo Fabroni. *Michelangelo Pistoletto: le porte di Palazzo Fabroni*. November 18, 1995–February 11, 1996. Catalogue, edited by Bruno Corà.

1996
Munich, Lenbachhaus. *Michelangelo Pistoletto: Memoria, intelligentia, praevidentia*. March 27–June 23, 1996. Catalogue, with essays by Helmut Friedel and Michelangelo Pistoletto.

Prato, Italy, Centro per l'Arte Contemporanea Luigi Pecci. *Habitus, abito, abitare: Progetto arte*. September 20, 1996–February 10, 1997. Catalogue, with essays by Bruno Corà and Michelangelo Pistoletto.

Ljubljana, Slovenia, Moderna Galerija. *Michelangelo Pistoletto: "44 fotokeramik—po Minus objektih, 1965/66" / "44 Photoceramics—from Minus Objects, 1965/1966."* November 15–December 8, 1996. Catalogue, with essay by Zdenka Badovinac.

1998
Rome, Studio Casoli. *Michelangelo Pistoletto: quadri specchianti*. October 1998. Catalogue, with essay by Tommaso Trini.

1999
Innsbruck, Austria, Galerie im Taxispalais. *Michelangelo Pistoletto: azioni materiali*. August 11–October 10, 1999. Catalogue, edited by Sylvia Eiblmayr, with essays by Gillo Dorfles et al.

Oxford, Museum of Modern Art. *Michelangelo Pistoletto: Shifting Perspective ("I am the Other")*. October 17–December 30, 1999. An expanded form of this exhibition was shown in Barcelona in 2000 under the title *Michelangelo Pistoletto*. Catalogue, with essays by Robert Hopper and Michael Tarantino.

2000
Milan, Studio Casoli. *Michelangelo Pistoletto*. Opened January 18, 2000. Brochure.

Barcelona, Museu d'Art Contemporani de Barcelona. *Michelangelo Pistoletto*. January 27–March 29, 2000. Catalogue, edited by Anna Jiménez Jorquera and Anna Tetas, with essays by Véronique Goudinoux et al.

Turin, Italy, Palazzina della Società delle Belle Arti and Castello di Rivoli Museo d'Arte Contemporanea. *Io sono l'altro: Michelangelo Pistoletto*. November 18, 2000–February 4, 2001. Catalogue, with essays by Michelangelo Pistoletto and Angela Vettese.

2001
Sarajevo, Bosnia and Herzegovina, Umjetnicka Galerija. *Michelangelo Pistoletto—la porta dello specchio*. January 29–February 15, 2001. Traveled to Budapest, Ludwig Museum of Contemporary Art, May 4–July 1, 2001. Catalogue, with essays by E. R. Comi et al.

Lyon, France, Musée d'Art Contemporain. *Continenti di tempo / Continents de temps / Continents of Time: Michelangelo Pistoletto*. March 8–May 6, 2001. Catalogue, with essays by Isabelle Bertolotti et al.

Perugia, Città di Castello, Italy, various exhibition spaces. *Pistoletto—Codice Inverso*. April 8–June 9, 2001. Catalogue, with essays by Michelangelo Pistoletto and Giuliano Serafini.

2003
Florence, Galleria Il Ponte. *Michelangelo Pistoletto: superfici specchianti, 1962–2000*. October 4–November 8, 2003. Exh. cat., with essay by Chiara Bertola.

2005
Rome, Galleria Oredaria. *Michelangelo Pistoletto: Azione-comunic-azione*. March 11–May 31, 2005. Catalogue, with essay by Achille Bonito Oliva.

2007
Nice, France, Le Musée d'Art Moderne et d'Art Contemporain. *Michelangelo Pistoletto*. June 30–November 4, 2007. Catalogue, interview with Michelangelo Pistoletto by Gilbert Perlein, Pierre Padovani, and Michèle Brun and essay by Marco Farano.

Group Exhibitions

1964

Turin, Italy, Galleria Sperone. *Lichtenstein, Mondino, Pistoletto, Rotella*. Opened May 9, 1964.

Vienna, Museum des 20 Jahrhunderts. *POP etc.* September 19–October 31, 1964. Catalogue, with essays by O. A. Graf and W. Hofmann.

Pittsburgh Museum of Art, Carnegie Institute. *The 1964 Pittsburgh International Exhibition of Contemporary Painting and Sculpture*. October 30, 1964–January 10, 1965. Catalogue, with essay by Gustave von Groschwitz.

Vienna, Museum des 20 Jahrhunderts. *New Realism and Pop Art / Neuer Realismus und Pop Art*. November 20, 1964–January 3, 1965. Catalogue, with essays by Friedrich Ahlers-Hestermann and W. Hofmann.

1965
Detroit, J. L. Hudson Gallery. *International '65, Part I*. February 10–March 6, 1965. Brochure.

San Marino, Italy, Palazzo del Kursaal. *V Biennale internazionale d'arte contemporanea*. July 31–September 30, 1965. Catalogue.

1966
Milan, Naviglio 2. *Nuove tendenze in Italia*. June 6–30, 1966. Catalogue, with essay by Gillo Dorfles.

Turin, Italy, Galleria Sperone. *Arte abitabile*. June–July 1966.

Milan, Galleria Sperone. *Pistoletto, Gilardi, Piacentino, Fabro*. 1966.

1967
Ridgefield, Conn., The Larry Aldrich Museum of Contemporary Art. *Highlights of the 1966–67 Art Season*. June 18–September 4, 1967. Catalogue, with essay by Larry Aldrich.

San Marino, Italy, Palazzo dei Congressi. *Nuove tecniche d'immagine*. July 15–September 30, 1967. Catalogue, edited by Sandra Pinto, with essays by Lawrence Alloway et al.

Paris, Musée d'Art Moderne de la Ville de Paris. *V Biennale d'art contemporain*. September 30–November 5, 1967. Catalogue, with essay by Palma Bucarelli.

Sao Paulo, Museu de Arte Moderna. *9a Bienal: artistas italianos de hoje*. September 1967–January 1968. Catalogue, edited by Umbro Apollonio, with essay by Gillo Dorfles.

Turin, Italy, Galleria Stein, Galleria Sperone, Galleria Il Punto. *Con-temp-l'azione*. December 1967. Pamphlet.

Genoa, Italy, Universita-Instituto di Storia dell'Arte. *Arte Povera, im-spazio*. 1967. Catalogue, with an essay by Germano Celant.

1968
Boston, Institute of Contemporary Art. *Young Italians*. January 23–March 23, 1968. Traveled to New York, The Jewish Museum, May 20–September 2, 1968. Catalogue, with essay by Alan R. Solomon.

Bologna, Italy, Galleria de' Foscherari. *Arte Povera*. February 24–March 15, 1968. Catalogue, with essay by Germano Celant.

Trieste, Italy, Centro Arte Viva Feltrinelli. *Arte Povera*. March 23–April 11, 1968. Catalogue.

London, Institute of Contemporary Arts. *The Obsessive Image, 1960–1968*. April 10–May 29, 1968. Catalogue, with essay by Mario Amaya.

Washington, D.C., National Gallery of Art. *Paintings from the Albright-Knox Art Gallery, Buffalo, New York*. May 19–July 21, 1968. Catalogue, with an essay by Gordon M. Smith.

Kassel, Germany, Galerie an der Schönen Aussicht, Museum Fridericianum, and Orangerie im Auepark. *4. Documenta*. June 27–October 6, 1968. Catalogue (2 vols.), with essays by Arnold Bode et al.

Amalfi, Italy, Arsenali. *Arte Povera più azioni povere*. Opened October 4, 1968. Catalogue, with essay by Germano Celant.

Houston, Museum of Fine Arts. *A Young Teaching Collection*. November 7, 1968–January 12, 1969. Exh. cat.

Turin, Italy, Deposito d'Arte Presente. *Play*. Opened December 16, 1968. Pamphlet.

Rome, Galleria Nazionale d'Arte Moderna. *Cento opere d'arte italiana dal Futurismo ad oggi*. December 20, 1968–January 20, 1969. Catalogue, edited by Sandra Pinto.

1969
Karlsruhe, Germany, Badischer Kunstverein. *5 Italiener*. February 21–March 23, 1969. Catalogue, with essay by Georg Bussmann.

Helsinki, Ateneumin Taidemuseo. *Ars 69 Helsinki: International Exhibition of Contemporary Art*. March 8–April 13, 1969. Traveled to Tampere, Finland, Nykytaiteen Museo, April 20–May 11, 1969. Catalogue, with essay by Salme Sarajas-Korte.

Buenos Aires, Museo Nacional de Bellas Artes. *109 obras de Albright-Knox Art Gallery*. October 23–November 30, 1969. Catalogue, with essays by S. H. Knox, S. F. Oliver, and G. M. Smith.

1970
Turin, Italy, Galleria Civica d'Arte Moderna. *Conceptual Art, Arte Povera, Land Art*. June 12–July 12, 1970. Catalogue, edited by Germano Celant.

Rome, Palazzo delle Esposizioni. *Vitalità del negativo nell'arte italiana, 1960/1970*. November 1970–January 1971. Catalogue, edited by Achille Bonito Oliva, with essays by Giulio Carlo Argan et al.

1971
Dortmund, Germany, Museum am Ostwall. *Elf Italiener heute*. February 28–April 18, 1971. Catalogue, with essay by Gillo Dorfles.

Munich Kunstverein. *Arte povera: 13 Italienische Künstler*. May 26–June 27, 1971. Catalogue, edited by Armin M. Börne, Eva Madelung, and Peter Nemetschek, with essay by Alberto Boatto.

Liverpool, England, Walker Art Gallery. *New Italian Art, 1953–71*. July 22–September 11, 1971. Catalogue, with essay by Giovanni Carandente.

1972
Rome, Palazzo delle Esposizioni. *X quadriennale nazionale d'arte: la ricerca estetica dal 1960 al 1970*. April 11–May 27, 1973. Catalogue, with essay by Ernesto Valentino.

Buffalo, Albright-Knox Art Gallery. *Continental Painting and Sculpture, 1942–1972*. July 21–August 27, 1972. Catalogue, with essays by Lawrence Alloway and R. W. D. Ozenaar.

Rotterdam, The Netherlands, Museum Boijmans Van Beuningen. *Kunst van de 20e eeuw*. Summer 1972. Catalogue, with essay by Renild Hammacher van den Brande.

1973
Recklinghausen, Germany, Städtische Kunsthalle. *Mit Kamera, Pinsel und Spritzpistole: Realistische Kunst in unserer Zeit*. May 4–June 17, 1973. Catalogue, edited by Thomas Grochowiak and Anneliese Schröder.

Rome, Parcheggio di Villa Borghese. *Contemporanea*. November 30, 1973–February 1974. Catalogue, with essays by Achille Bonito Oliva and Piero Sartogo.

1977
Turin, Italy, Galleria Civica d'Arte Moderna. *Dall'opera al coinvolgimento: l'opera; simboli e immagini; la linea analitica*. May–September 1977. Catalogue, with essays by Renato Barilli et al.

1978
Venice, La Biennale di Venezia. *Artenatura*. June–October 1978. Catalogue, edited by Achille Bonito Oliva, with essays by Jean-Christophe Ammann et al.

1979
Tel Aviv, The Tel Aviv Museum. *Art of the Sixties: Europe and the USA; from the Collection of the Museum Ludwig, Cologne*. May–July 1979. Catalogue.

1980
Rome, Palazzo delle Esposizioni. *Linee della ricerca artistica in Italia, 1960–1980*. February 14–April 15, 1981. Catalogue, edited by Nello Ponente, with essays by Maurizio Calvesi et al.

1981
Paris, Centre Georges Pompidou. *Identité italienne: l'art en Italie depuis 1959*. June 25–September 7, 1981. Catalogue, edited by Germano Celant, with essays by Graziella Lonardi Buontempo et al.

Milan, Palazzo della Permanente. *In labirinto*. June–August 1981. Catalogue (*Luoghi del silenzio imparziale*), edited by Achille Bonito Oliva, with essays by Umberto Eco et al.

Tokyo, National Museum of Modern Art. *Cento anni d'arte italiana moderna, 1880–1980*. 1981. Catalogue, with essay by Giorgio de Marchis.

1982
Rome, Mura Aureliane. *Avanguardia, transavanguardia*. April–July 1982. Catalogue, edited by Achille Bonito Oliva, with essays by Alberto Arbasino et al.

London, Hayward Gallery. *Arte Italiana, 1960–1982*. October 20, 1982–January 9, 1983. Traveled to London, Institute of Contemporary Arts, October 12–24, 1982. Catalogue, with essays by Guido Ballo et al.

Rome, Istituto di Storia dell'Arte. *Generazione a confronto*. 1982.

1983
Cologne, Kölnischer Kunstverein. *Eine Kunst-Geschichte in Turin, 1965–1983*. October 8–November 13, 1983. Catalogue, edited by Wulf Herzogenrath, with essays by Germano Celant and Marlis Grüterich.

1984
Paris, Galeries Nationales du Grand Palais. *La rime et la raison: les Collections Ménil (Houston-New York)*. April 17–July 30, 1984. Catalogue.

Munich, Städtische Galerie im Lenbachhaus. *Der Traum des Orpheus: Mythologie in der italienischen Gegenwartskunst.* May 16–July 1, 1984. Catalogue, edited by Helmut Friedel, with essays by Helmut Friedel et al.

Turin, Italy, Mole Antonelliana. *Coerenza in coerenza: dall'Arte Povera al 1984.* June 12–October 14, 1984. Catalogue, with essay by Germano Celant.

Venice, XLI Biennale di Venezia. *Arte allo specchio.* June–October 1984. Catalogue, with essays by Maurizio Calvesi and Marisa Vescovo.

1985
Madrid, Palacio de Cristal and Palacio de Velázquez. *Del Arte Povera a 1985.* January 24–April 7, 1985. Catalogue, with essay by Germano Celant.

Paris, Grande Halle de la Villette. *Nouvelle Biennale de Paris.* March 22–May 21, 1985. Catalogue, edited by Georges Boudaille.

Long Island City, N.Y., P.S. 1. *The Knot: Arte Povera at P.S. 1.* October 6–December 15, 1985. Catalogue, with essay by Germano Celant.

Turin, Italy, Castello di Rivoli Museo d'Arte Contemporanea. *Il museo sperimentale di Torino: arte italiana degli anni Sessanta nelle collezioni della Galleria Civica d'Arte Moderna.* December 1985–January 1986. Catalogue, edited by Mirella Bandini, with essays by Mirella Bandini, Eugenio Battisti, and Rosanna Maggio Serra.

1987
Istanbul, Istanbul Foundation for Culture and Arts. *1 International Istanbul Contemporary Art Exhibitions.* September 25–November 15, 1987. Catalogue, with essays by Nejat F. Eczaciba i, A. Gün, and Sezer Tansu.

Edinburgh, Scotland, Royal Scottish Academy. *Edinburgh International: Reason and Emotion in Contemporary Art.* December 19, 1987–February 14, 1988. Catalogue, edited by Douglas Hall, with essays by Michael Compton and Martin Kunz.

1988
Munich, Haus der Kunst. *Mythos Italien: Wintermärchen Deutschland.* March 24–May 29, 1988. Catalogue, edited by Carla Schulz-Hoffmann, with essays by Germano Celant et al.

1989
London, Royal Academy of Arts. *Italian Art in the 20th Century.* January 14–April 9, 1989. Catalogue, edited by Emily Braum and Alberto Asor Rosa, with essays by Paolo Baldacci et al.

1990
Turin, Italy, Galleria in Arco. *Arte Povera.* May 14–September 15, 1990. Catalogue, edited by Sergio Bertaccini, with essay by Floriana Piqué.

Rome, Palazzo delle Esposizioni. *Roma anni '60: al di là della pittura.* December 20, 1990–February 15, 1991. Catalogue, edited by Rosella Siligato.

Madrid, Centro de Arte Reina Sofía. *Memoria del futuro: arte italiano desde las primeras vanguardias a la posguerra.* 1990. Catalogue, edited by Germano Celant and Ida Gianelli with essays by Maurizio Fagiolo dell'Arco et al.

1991
Munich, Kunstverein München. *Arte Povera 1971 und 20 Jahre danach.* April 26–June 23, 1991. Catalogue, with essays by Hannes Böhringer et al.

Pori, Finland, Porin Taidemuseo. *Borealis V: Material and Its Radiance.* August 23–October 13, 1991. Catalogue, with essays by Germano Celant et al.

1992
Rome, American Academy in Rome. *Joseph Kosuth, Michelangelo Pistoletto.* January 28–March 13, 1992. Catalogue, discussion with Joseph Kosuth, Michelangelo Pistoletto, and Pier Luigi Tazzi.

Le Cateau-Cambrésis, Musée Matisse et Cambrai and Musée des Beaux-Arts. *De Matisse à aujourd'hui: la sculpture du XXème siècle dans les collections des Musées et du Fonds Régional d'Art Contemporain du Nord-Pas-de-Calais.* February 15–April 26, 1992. Traveled to Tourcoing, Musée des Beaux-Arts, May 8–June 28, 1992; Calais, Musée des Beaux-Arts et Dunkerque and Musée d'Art Contemporain et Musée des Beaux-Arts, July 10–September 14, 1992; Arras, Musée des Beaux-Arts, September–October 1992. Catalogue, edited by Jean Etienne Grislain, with essays by Roger Benjamin et al.

Rio de Janeiro, Museu Nacional de Belas Artes. *—Reperti—Environment through the Eyes of 18 of the World's Major Artists.* June 5–July 5, 1992. Catalogue, edited by Barbara Lösel, with essays by Daniel Machado do Freitas, Maria Lucia Verdi, and Maria Christina Sampaio Lopes.

Paris, Centre Georges Pompidou. *Manifeste 4: l'Arte Povera, antiform.* June 18–September 28, 1992. Catalogue (*L'Arte Povera*), with essay by Didier Semin.

Bonn, Germany, Kunst- und Ausstellungshalle der Bundesrepublik Deutschland. *Territorium Artis.* June 19–September 20, 1992. Catalogue, edited by Pontus Hultén, with essays by B. des Innern, W. Jacob, and R. Seiters.

Villeurbanne, France, Nouveau Musée. *La collection Christian Stein: un regard sur l'art italien.* June 24–October 31, 1992. Catalogue, with essay by Catherine Francblin.

Graz, Austria, Künstlerhaus Neue Galerie Stadtmuseum. *Identität, Differenz: Tribüne Trigon, 1940–1990; Eine Topografie der Moderne.* October 3–November 8, 1992. Catalogue, with essays by Peter Weibel and Christa Steinle.

Osaka, Japan, Kodama Gallery. *Arte Povera.* October 19–December 12, 1992. Catalogue, with essay by Luigi Meneghelli.

1993
London, Hayward Gallery. *Gravity and Grace: The Changing Condition of Sculpture, 1965–1975.* January 21–March 14, 1993. Catalogue, edited by Susan Ferleger Brades, with essays by Yehuda Safran, Jon Thompson, and William Tucker.

Turin, Italy, Castello di Rivoli Museo d'Arte Contemporanea. *Un'avventura internazionale: Torino e le arti, 1950–1970.* February 5–April 25, 1993. Catalogue, with essays by M. Agnelli et al.

Salzburg, Austria, Schüttkasten–Galerie Thaddaeus Ropac. *Utopia: arte italiana, 1950–1993.* July 24–August 31, 1993. Traveled to Paris, Galerie Thaddaeus Ropac, September 18–October 31, 1993. Catalogue, edited by Hella Preimesberger.

Antwerp, Belgium, Koninklijk Museum voor Schone Kunsten. *The Sublime Void: On the Memory of the Imagination.* July 25–October 10, 1993. Catalogue, edited by Bart Cassiman, Greet Ramael, and Frank Vande Veire.

1994
New York, The Solomon R. Guggenheim Museum. *The Italian Metamorphosis, 1943–1968.* October 7, 1994–January 22, 1995. Traveled to Milan, Triennale di Milano, February–May 1995; Wolfsburg, Germany, Kunstmuseum, May–September 1995. Catalogue, edited by Germano Celant, with essays by Pandora Tabatabai Asbaghi et al.

Paris, Centre Georges Pompidou. *Hors limites: l'art et la vie, 1952–1994.* November 9, 1994–January 23, 1995. Catalogue, edited by Jean de Loisy, with essays by François Barré, Jean de Loisy, and Pierre Restany.

1995
Brussels, Anciens Etablissements. *Les fragments du désir: Old England.* June 2–September 17, 1995.

Ghent, Museum van Hedendaagse Kunst. *Corpus delicti: twee privé-verzamelingen; een dialoog noord/zuid / Due collezioni private; un dialogo nord/sud.* July 1–September 3, 1995. Catalogue edited by Norbert de Dauw et al., with essays by Jan Hoet, Steven Jacobs, and Giorgio Verzotti.

1996
Hamburg, Deichtorhallen. *Sammlung Sonnabend: Von der Pop-art bis Heute, amerikanische und europäische Kunst seit 1954.* February 23–May 5, 1996. Catalogue, edited by Zdenek Felix, with essay by Michel Bourel.

Munich, Kunsthalle der Hypo-Kulturstiftung and Staatsgalerie Moderner Kunst. *Amerika Europa: Sammlung Sonnabend.* July 5–September 8, 1996. Catalogue, with essays by Carla Schulz-Hoffmann and Corinna Thierolf.

Siena, Italy, Palazzo Patrizi; San Gimignano, Palazzo Comunale; Volterra, Fortezza di Montalcino and Pinacoteca Comunale. *Arte all'arte.* September 22–October 22, 1996. Catalogue, with essay by Laura Cherubini.

Los Angeles Museum of Art. *Hidden in Plain Sight: Illusion in Art from Jasper Johns to Virtual Reality.* November 27, 1996–January 12, 1997. Catalogue, with essays by Virginia Rutledge and Maurice Tuchman.

Paris, Centre Georges Pompidou. *Face à l'histoire, 1933–1996: l'artiste moderne devant l'événement historique.* December 19, 1996–April 7, 1997. Catalogue, edited by Jean-Paul Ameline, with essays by Jean-Jacques Aillagon et al.

1997
Kassel, Germany, Museum Friedericianum. *Politics-Poetics: Documenta X.* June 21–September 28, 1997. Catalogue, with essays by Jean-François Chevrier and Catherine David.

Bremen, Germany, Neues Museum Weserburg. *Arte Povera: Arbeiten und Dokumente aus der Sammlung Goetz, 1958 bis Heute.* June

22–September 7, 1997. Traveled to Nuremberg, Germany, Kunsthalle, October 2–December 7, 1997; Cologne, Kölnischer Kunstverein, February 2–April 26, 1998; Vienna, Museum Moderner Kunst Stiftung Ludwig Wein, July 19–August 30, 1998; Gothenburg, Sweden, Konsthallen, September 19–October 10, 1998. Catalogue, edited by Ingvild Goetz and Christiane Meyer-Stoll, with essays by Nike Bätzner et al.

New York, Sperone Westwater. *Anselmo, Boetti, Laib, Merz, Nauman, Paolini, Pistoletto, Vital, Zorio.* September 13–October 18, 1997.

1998
São Paulo, Paço das Artes. *Memória—presente.* August 26, 1998–October 3, 1999. Traveled to Rio de Janeiro, Museu de Arte Moderna, November 25, 1999–January 5, 2000. Catalogue, with essay by Jean-Marc Prévost.

Taipei Fine Arts Museum. *Invisible: Post-War Italian Art.* September 19–November 15, 1998. Catalogue, with essays by S. Chern et al.

Bremen, Germany, Neues Museum Weserburg. *Minimal Maximal: Die Minimal Art und ihr Einfluss auf die internationale Kunst der 90er Jahre / Minimal Art and Its Influence on International Art of the 1990s.* October 11, 1998–January 3, 1999. Traveled to Baden-Baden, Germany, Kunsthalle, January 22–March 21, 1999; Santiago de Compostela, Spain, Centro Galego de Arte Contemporanéa, April 16–July 4, 1999. Catalogue, edited by Peter Friese, with essays by Manuel Bamming et al.

Strasbourg, France, Musée d'Art Moderne et Contemporain. *Sentimentale journée.* November 6, 1998–February 15, 1999.

1999
Leeds, England, Henry Moore Institute. *Sampled: The Use of Fabric in Sculpture.* February 6–March 28, 1999. Catalogue, with essays by Gill Nicol, Fiona Russell, and Gerard Williams.

Rome, Centro Culturale Internazionale Chiostro del Bramante. *I Love Pop: Europa–USA anni '60; mitologie del quotidiano.* March 24–June 27, 1999. Catalogue, edited by Wolfgang Becher et al.

Washington, D.C., Hirshhorn Museum and Sculpture Garden, Smithsonian Institution. *Regarding Beauty: A View of the Late Twentieth Century.* October 7, 1999–January 17, 2000. Traveled to Munich, Haus der Kunst, February 11–April 30, 2000. Catalogue, with essays by Neal David Benezra, Arthur Coleman Danto, and Olga M. Viso.

Minneapolis, Walker Art Center. *Art in Our Time: 1950 to the Present.* September 5, 1999–September 2, 2001.

2000
Turin, Italy, Castello di Rivoli Museo d'Arte Contemporanea. *Quotidiana: immagini della vita di ogni giorno nell'arte del XX secolo / The Continuity of the Everyday in 20th Century Art.* February 5–May 21, 2000. Catalogue, edited by David Ross, with essays by Marcella Beccaria et al.

Milan, Rotonda della Besana. *Stanze e segreti.* April 11–May 7, 2000. Catalogue, edited by Achille Bonito Oliva, with essays by Marina Abramovic et al.

Lucerne, Switzerland, Neues Kunstmuseum Luzern. *Mixing Memory and Desire / Wunsch und Erinnerung.* June 20–September 24, 2000. Catalogue, edited by Ulrich Loock et al., with essays by Cornelia Dietschi et al.

Arras, France, Musée des Beaux-Arts. *La poétique de l'Italie.* September 1–December 31, 2000.

Turin, Italy, Castello di Rivoli Museo d'Arte Contemporanea. *Arte Povera in collezione / Arte Povera in Collection.* December 6, 2000–March 25, 2001. Catalogue, edited by Ida Gianelli, with essays by Jean-Christophe Ammann et al.

Rome, Scuderie Papali al Quirinale and Mercati di Traiano. *Novecento: arte e storia in Italia.* December 30, 2000–April 1, 2001. Catalogue, edited by Federica Pirani, with essays by Maurizio Calvesi and Paul Ginsborg.

2001
Krefeld, Germany, Museum Haus Esters. *Die Sammlung Lauffs I.* March 4–April 29, 2001. Brochure.

Houston, Contemporary Arts Museum. *Subject Plural: Crowds in Contemporary Art.* March 10–April 29, 2001. Catalogue, with essay by Paola Morsiani.

Cologne, Museum für Angewandte Kunst Köln. *Untragbar: Mode als Skulptur.* July 14–September 6, 2001. Catalogue, edited by Susanne Anna and Markus Heinzelmann, with essays by Susanne Anna et al.

Madrid, Museo Nacional Centro de Arte Reina Sofía. *Minimalismos: un signo de los tiempos.* July 11–October 8, 2001. Catalogue, edited by Marta González, with essays by Tom Johnson, Javier Rodríguez Marcos, and Anatxu Zabalbeascoa.

Sassuolo, Italy, Palazzo Ducale. *Presenze italiane / Italian Presences.* September 16–November 18, 2001. Catalogue, edited by Filippo Trevisani.

Tokyo Museum of Contemporary Art. *A History of Italian Art in the 20th Century.* September 22–December 2, 2001. Catalogue.

New York, Miriam and Ira D. Wallach Art Gallery, Columbia University. *Arte Povera: Selections from the Sonnabend Collection.* October 2–December 8, 2001. Catalogue, with essay by Claire Gilman.

Rome, Foro di Cesare, Foro di Augusto, Templum Pacis, Foro di Nerva, Foro di Traiano. *Giganti: arte contemporanea nel Fori Imperiali.* October 9–November 25, 2001. Catalogue, with essays by Ludovico Pratesi, Alessandra Maria Sette, and Angela Vettese.

Minneapolis, Walker Art Center. *Zero to Infinity: Arte Povera, 1962–1972.* October 13, 2001–January 13, 2002. Traveled to London, Tate Modern, May 31, 2000–August 19, 2001; Los Angeles, The Museum of Contemporary Art, March 10–August 11, 2002; Washington, D.C., Hirshhorn Museum and Sculpture Garden, October 17, 2002–January 12, 2003. Catalogue, edited by Richard Flood and Frances Morris, essays by Carolyn Christov-Bakargiev et al.

Tourcoing, France, Musée des Beaux-Arts. *Sous le drap, le temps des plis.* October 20, 2001–January 7, 2002.

2002
Oslo, Astrup Fearnley Museet for Moderne Kunst. *Passasjer: Beterakteren som deltaker / Passenger: The Viewer as Participant.* January 19–April 21, 2002. Catalogue, with essay by Øystein Ustvedt.

Saratoga Springs, N.Y., Frances Young Tang Teaching Museum and Art Gallery. *From Pop to Now: Selections from the Sonnabend Collection.* June 22–September 29, 2002. Traveled to Columbus, Wexner Center for the Arts at Ohio State University, November 3, 2002–February 2, 2003. Catalogue, edited by Margaret Sundell, with essay by Charles Ashley Stainback and texts by Rachel Haidu.

Sydney, Museum of Contemporary Art. *Arte Povera: Art from Italy, 1967–2002.* August 23–November 11, 2002. Catalogue, with essays by Germano Celant and Carolyn Christov-Bakargiev.

Bordeaux, France, CAPC Musée d'Art Contemporain, L'Entrepôt. *Les années 70: l'art en cause.* October 18, 2002–January 19, 2003. Catalogue, with essay by Maurice Fréchuret.

Providence, Rhode Island, David Winton Bell Gallery, Brown University. *Toward Uncertainty.* November 9–December 29, 2002. Catalogue, with essays by Chiara Bertola et al.

Düsseldorf, K21 Kunstsammlung Nordrhein-Westfalen, Germany. *Sammlung Ackermans.* 2002. Catalogue, edited by Julian Heynen, with essays by Iwona Blazwick et al.

Naples, Museo Nazionale di Capodimonte. *Museo Nazionale di Capodimonte: arte contemporanea.* 2002. Catalogue, with essay by Angela Tecce.

2003
Padua, Italy, Palazzo della Ragione. *La grande svolta—anni '60: viaggio negli anni Sessanta in Italia.* June 7–October 19, 2003. Catalogue, with essays by Virginia Baradel et al.

Turku, Finland, Wäinö Aaltosen Museo. *Pop International.* June 18–October 19, 2003. Catalogue, edited by Allan D'Arcangelo, with essays by Alfred M. Fischer et al.

Avignon, France, Palais des Papes. *Les 20 ans des Frac: esprits des lieux.* June 27–October 12, 2003.

Magdeburg, Germany, Kunstmuseum Kloster Unser Lieben Frauen. *La poetica dell'Arte Povera.* September 14–December 7, 2003. Catalogue, edited by Annegret Laabs, with essays by Nike Bätzner et al.

Montreal Museum of Fine Arts, Jean-Noël Desmarais Pavilion. *Global Village: The 1960s.* October 2, 2003–January 18, 2004. Traveled to the Dallas Museum of Art, February 19–May 23, 2004. Catalogue, with essays by Stéphane Aquin and Anna Detheridge.

2004
Dunkerque, France, FRAC Nord—Pas de Calais. *Interlude 1: Arte Povera, variations sur la collection du FRAC Nord—Pas de Calais.* April 3–July 31, 2004.

Genoa, Italy, Museo d'Arte Contemporanea di Villa Croce. *Arredare la casa, abitare il museo: selezione di opere dalle collezioni di arte e design del FRAC Nord—Pas de Calais.* April 22–June 6, 2004. Catalogue, edited by Sandra Solimano.

Grenoble, France, Musée de Grenoble. *L'art au futur antérieur—Liliane et Michel Durand-Dessert, l'engagement d'une galerie, 1975–2004*. July 10–October 4, 2004. Catalogue, interview with Guy Tosatto, Michel Durand-Dessert, and Liliane Durand-Dessert.

Arles, France, Association du Méjan. *Arles rencontres de la photographie 2004*. July 18–September 19, 2004. Catalogue, with essays by François Barré, François Hébel, and Martin Parr.

Houston, The Menil Collection. *Contortion and Distortion: Postwar European Art from The Menil Collection*. September 22, 2004–January 9, 2005.

London, Whitechapel Gallery. *Faces in the Crowd: Picturing Modern Life from Manet to Today / Volti nella folla: immagini della vita moderna da Manet a oggi*. December 3, 2004–March 6, 2005. Traveled to Turin, Italy, Castello di Rivoli Museo d'Arte Contemporanea, April 6–July 10, 2005. Catalogue, edited by Michele Abate and Melissa Larner, with essays by Iwona Blazwick et al.

2005

Naples, PAN–Palazzo delle Arti Napoli. *The Giving Person / Il dono dell'artista*. March 26–August 28, 2005. Catalogue, edited by Lóránd Hegyi.

Minneapolis, Walker Art Center. *The Shape of Time*. April 15, 2005–October 27, 2009.

Modena, Italy, Galleria Civica. *Pop Art Italia, 1958–1968*. April 17–July 3, 2005. Catalogue, with essays by Luca Massimo Barbero and Walter Guadagnini.

Villeneuve d'Ascq, France, École Nationale Supérieure d'Architecture et de Paysage de Lille. *Le goût des choses*. April 25–June 8, 2005.

Milan, Catello Sforzesco. *Alice nel Castello delle meraviglie: il mondo fuori forma e fuori tempo nell'arte italiana del Novecento*. May 25–September 18, 2005. Catalogue, with essays by Carlo Birrozzi, Marina Pugliese, and Marta Ragozzino.

Carrara, Italy, Palazzo Benelli. *Il disegno della scultura contemporanea da Fontana a Paladino*. June 26–July 31, 2005. Catalogue, with an essay by Walter Guadagnini.

Benevento, Italy, Piazza Vari. *Lingue taglienti, lingue avvelenate*. August 25–September 11, 2005. Catalogue, edited by Demetrio Paparoni and Gianni Mercurio.

Palma de Mallorca, Spain, Centre Cultural Contemporani Pelaires. *La forma restituita: arte italiano de fin de milenio*. August–November 2005. Catalogue, with an essay by Marco Meneguzzo.

London, Estorick Collection. *Marcello Levi: ritratto di un collezionista; dal Futurismo all'Arte Povera / Portrait of a Collection; From Futurism to Arte Povera*. September 14–December 18, 2005. Catalogue, edited by Robert Lumley and Francesco Manacorda.

Rovereto, Italy, Museo d'Arte Moderna e Contemporanea di Trento e Rovereto. *Dalla Pop alla Minimal: opere dalla collezione permanente del Mart*. September 28, 2005–January 29, 2006.

Houston, The Menil Collection. *Robert Gober: The Meat Wagon*. October 28, 2005–January 12, 2006. Catalogue, with essays by Matthew Drutt and Robert Gober.

Rome, Scuderie del Quirinale. *Burri: gli artisti e la materia, 1945–2004*. November 17, 2005–February 16, 2006. Catalogue, edited by Maurizio Calvesi and Italo Tomassoni.

2006

Biella, Italy, Museo del Territorio Biellese. *Premio Biella per l'incisione 2006: arte nell'età dell'ansia / Art in the Age of Anxiety*. March 19–June 4, 2006. Catalogue, edited by Jeremy Lewison.

Venice, Palazzo Grassi. *"Where Are We Going?" Selections from the François Pinault Collection*. April 29–October 1, 2006. Catalogue, edited by Jack Bankowsky and Alison M. Gingeras.

Montreal Museum of Fine Arts, Jean-Noël Desmarais Pavilion. *Il Modo Italiano: Italian Design and Avant-garde in the 20th Century*. May 4–August 27, 2006. Traveled to Toronto, Royal Ontario Museum, October 28, 2006–January 7, 2007; Rovereto, Italy, Mart–Museo di Arte Moderna e Contemporanea di Trento e Rovereto, March 3–June 3, 2007. Catalogue, edited by Giampiero Bosoni, with essays by Paola Antonelli et al. and conversations with Mario Bellini et al.

Rovereto, Italy, Museo d'Arte Moderna e Contemporanea di Trento e Rovereto. *Scultura e pittura*. May 16–October 29, 2006.

Lugano, Switzerland, Museo Cantonale d'Arte. *L'immagine del vuoto: una linea di ricerca nell'arte in Italia, 1958–2006 / The Image of the Void: An Investigation on Italian Art, 1958–2006*. October 7, 2006–January 7, 2007. Catalogue, edited by Bettina Della Casa, with essays by Bruno Corà et al.

2007

Rochechouart, France, Musée Départemental d'Art Contemporain. *Après la pluie*. March 1–June 10, 2007.

Milan, Palazzo Reale. *Camera con vista: arte e interni in Italia, 1900–2000*. April 18–July 1, 2007. Catalogue, edited by Rachele Ferrario and Luigi Settembrini.

Schaulager, Basel. May 12–October 14, 2007. *Robert Gober: Work, 1976–2007*. Catalogue (*Robert Gober: Sculptures and Installations, 1979–2007*), edited by Theodora Vischer, with essay by Elizabeth Sussman.

Barcelona, Museu d'Art Contemporani. *A Theater without Theater*. May 25–September 11, 2007. Traveled to Lisbon, Museu Colecção Berardo–Arte Moderna e Contemporânea, November 16, 2007–February 17, 2008. Catalogue, with essays by Bernard Blistène et al.

Rovereto, Italy, MART–Museo di Arte Moderna e Contemporanea di Trento e Rovereto. *Percorsi privati: lo sguardo di un collezionista da Balla a Chen Zhen*. June 23–October 7, 2007. Catalogue, with essays by Gabriella Belli and Alberto Fiz.

London, Gagosian Gallery. *Pop Art Is. . . .* September 27–November 21, 2007. Catalogue, edited by Mark Francis and Stefan Ratibor.

London, Hayward Gallery. *The Painting of Modern Life: 1960s to Now*. October 4–December 30, 2007. Traveled to Turin, Italy, Castello di Rivoli Museo d'Arte Contemporanea, February 6–May 4, 2008. Catalogue, with essays by Carolyn Christov-Bakargievet al.

2008

Zurich, Kunsthaus Zürich. *Europop*. February 15–May 12, 2008. Catalogue, with essays by Tobia Bezzola et al.

Rovereto, Italy, Museo d'Arte Moderna e Contemporanea di Trento e Rovereto. *100 anni: opere dalla collezione permanente del Mart*. April 26 – October 12, 2008.

New York, David Zwirner and Zwirner & Wirth. *Selections from the Collection of Helga and Walther Lauffs*. May 1–22, 2008.

Stockholm, Moderna Museet. *Time and Place: Milano–Torino, 1958–1968*. May 1–September 7, 2008. Catalogue, edited by Luca Massimo Barbero.

Nantes, France, Le Hangar à Bananes. *Living Box*. July 12–October 12, 2008.

Venice, Palazzo Grassi. *Italics: Italian Art between Tradition and Revolution, 1968–2008*. September 27, 2008–March 22, 2009. Traveled to Chicago, Museum of Contemporary Art, November 14, 2009–February 14, 2010. Catalogue, with essays by Francesco Bonami et al.

New York, David Zwirner and Zwirner & Wirth. *Minimal and Conceptual Art in Europe: The Helga and Walther Lauffs Collection*. November 5–December 23, 2008.

2009

Rome, Spazio Risonanze. *Risonanze 3: Michelangelo Pistoletto and Giovanni Sollima*. May 29– June 15, 2009. Catalogue, edited by Marcello Smarrelli.

Rome, Galleria Nazionale d'Arte Moderna. *Palma Bucarelli: il museo come avanguardia*. June 26–November 1, 2009. Catalogue, edited by Mariastella Margozzi.

Varese, Italy, Villa e Collezione Panza. *Arte Povera: energia e metamorfosi dei materiali; opere dalle collezioni del MART*. December 17, 2009–March 28, 2010. Catalogue, with essays by Beatrice Avanzi et al.

2010

Houston, The Menil Collection. *Maurizio Cattelan: Is There Life Before Death?* February 12–August 15, 2010. Catalogue, with essay by Franklin Sirmans.

Minneapolis, Walker Art Center. *1964*. March 25–October 24, 2010.

ACKNOWLEDGMENTS

Michelangelo Pistoletto: From One to Many, 1956–1974 was organized with the collaboration, enthusiasm, and support of a large number of extraordinarily generous individuals who were gracious with their time, efforts, and resources. Together with the Philadelphia Museum of Art, I would like to thank those listed below for their invaluable assistance with the scholarship, planning, and implementation of the exhibition and catalogue.

First and foremost, I thank the artist, Michelangelo Pistoletto, who worked closely, patiently, and enthusiastically with me over the past four years to develop this project. We were also greatly aided by the staff of Cittadellarte-Fondazione Pistoletto. I would like to acknowledge especially Maria Pioppi, the artist's wife, as well as Marco Farano, Alessandro Lacirasella, and Cristina Mirandola.

Since the very inception of this project, Anna Mattirolo, the Director of MAXXI Arte, was a source of both critical advice and encouragement with this endeavor. It is thanks largely to her support that this exhibition has been realized as an intercontinental collaboration between our two institutions in the United States and Italy.

The following lenders to the exhibition demonstrated great generosity in parting with treasured works for the duration of the show: Abrams Family Collection, New York; Albright-Knox Art Gallery, Buffalo; Marco and Franca Brignone; Constance R. Caplan; Cittadellarte-Fondazione Pistoletto, Biella; Collezione La Gaia, Busca; Collezione Maramotti, Reggio Emilia; The Detroit Institute of Arts; Fondazione Marconi, Milan; Fondazione per l'arte moderna e contemporanea CRT and Castello di Rivoli Museo d'arte contemporanea, Turin; Fundação de Serralves—Museu de Arte Contemporânea, Porto, Portugal; GAM—Galleria civica d'arte moderna e contemporanea, Turin; GNAM—Galleria nazionale d'arte moderna, Rome, courtesy of the Italian Ministry of Cultural Heritage and Actitivies; Martin Z. Margulies; MART—Museo per l'arte contemporanea di Trento e Rovereto, Rovereto, Italy; MAXXI—Museo nazionale delle arti del XXI secolo, Rome, courtesy of the Italian Ministry of Cultural Heritage and Actitivies; The Robert B. Mayer Family Collection, Chicago; The Menil Collection, Houston; Beatrice Monti della Corte von Rezzori; Museum Boijmans Van Beuningen, Rotterdam; Giorgio and Giorgiana Persano; François Pinault Foundation, Paris; Michelangelo Pistoletto, Biella; Estate of Robert Rauschenberg, Mount Vernon, New York; Lia Rumma; Keith L. and Katherine Sachs; San Francisco Museum of Modern Art; The Sonnabend Collection; Pietro Valsecchi; Walker Art Center, Minneapolis; Suzanne Weil; and private individuals.

I would also like to thank the following persons for their invaluable assistance in facilitating loans, conducting research, providing photographs, and supplying source materials, all of which contributed greatly to the original scholarship reflected in both the exhibition and this catalogue: Barbara Abbondanza; Roland Augustine, Luhring Augustine, New York; Paolo and Gabriella Basilico; Mariolina Bassetti, Christie's, Milan; Gianfranco Benedetti, Christian Stein Gallery, Milan; Francesco Bonami; Caroline Bourgeois and Odile de Labouchère, François Pinault Foundation, Paris; Kerry Brougher and Valerie Fletcher, Hirshhorn Museum and Sculpture Garden, Smithsonian Institution, Washington, D.C.; Ben Brown, Ben Brown Fine Arts, London; Brunella Buscicchio Scherer; Irene Calderoni, Fondazione Sandretto Re Rebaudengo, Turin; Sergio Casoli; Chiara Castagna; Germano Celant;

Eleonora Charans; Mario Codognato; Irene Damiani; Maria De Vivo; Jeffrey Deitch, Deitch Projects, New York; Roberta Dell'Acqua, Sotheby's, Milan; Piero Derossi and Anna Licata, Studio Derossi Associati, Turin; Liliane Durand-Dessert; Marcella Ferrari; Danilo Eccher, Director, GAM—Galleria civica d'arte moderna e contemporanea, Turin; Nicoletta Fiorucci; Richard Flood, New Museum, New York; Martin Friedman; Sandra Frimmel, Kunstmuseum Liechstenstein; Martin Halusa; Marla Hand, Curator of the Robert B. Mayer Family Collection, Chicago; Katherine Hinds, Curator of the Martin Z. Marguiles Collection, Miami; Jane Holzer; Antonio Homem, Sonnabend Gallery, New York; Rory Howard; Agnes Husslein-Arco, Director, Gallerie Belvedere, Vienna; Harold Joffe; Valentina Lacorte, Sotheby's Milan; Marcello Levi; Stefania Levi; Graziella Lonardi Buontempo; Robert Lumley; Pepi Marchetti Franchi, Gagosian Gallery, Rome; Paolo di Marzio, GNAM, Rome; Museo Nazionale del Cinema, Turin; Paolo Mussat Sartor; Ugo Nespolo; Chiara Oliveri Bertola, Castello di Rivoli Museo d'Arte Contemporanea, Turin; Sara Paulucci; Riccardo Passoni and Franco Stella, Fondazione Torino musei, Turin; Paolo Pellion di Persano; Pier Luigi Pero; Valentina Pero; Giorgio Persano; Suzanne Quigley, Curator of the Abrams Family Collection, Chicago; Lia Rumma, Galleria Lia Rumma, Naples and Milan; Fabio Sargentini; Marina Saviano; Silvia Simoncelli, Sotheby's, Milan; Gian Enzo Sperone; Simona Tarantino; Giulio Tega; Clino Trini Castelli; Paolo Vedovi, Galerie Vedovi, Brussels; Cordula Von Keller; Jill Vuchetich, Walker Art Center, Minneapolis; Thomas Walker, The Living Theatre; Angela Westwater, Sperone Westwater Gallery, New York; David White and Thomas Buehler, Estate of Robert Rauschenberg; Elena Zonca, Zonca & Zonca, Milan; and David Zwirner and Veronique Ansorge, David Zwirner Gallery, New York.

I am extremely grateful for the generosity of those who supported the Philadelphia Museum of Art's presentation of the work of Michelangelo Pistoletto: The Pew Center for Arts & Heritage through the Philadelphia Exhibitions Initiative, The Andy Warhol Foundation for the Visual Arts, The Kathleen C. and John J. F. Sherrerd Fund for Exhibitions, and Lynne and Harold Honickman, as well as Galleria Lia Rumma, Christie's, Luhring Augustine, Galleria Christian Stein, Simon Lee Gallery, Jane and Leonard Korman, Harriet and Larry Weiss, Sankey and Connie Williams, the Philip and Muriel Berman Foundation, Jill and Sheldon Bonovitz, and Jaimie and David Field. For their support of the catalogue, I thank illycaffè and The Andrew W. Mellon Fund for Scholarly Publications.

At the Philadelphia Museum of Art, many individuals played key roles in helping the exhibition come to fruition. In the Department of Modern and Contemporary Art, Erica F. Battle and Roberta Nuzzaci worked with me closely on the exhibition, initially aided by Jennifer Wilkinson. I am also thankful for the enthusiasm and support of Michael Taylor, Adelina Vlas, Ashley Carey, Claire Howard, Jennifer Ginsberg, John Vick, and intern Samantha Gainsburg.

The staff of many other departments within the Museum also lent their efforts and expertise to this endeavor: in Audio-Visual, Stephen A. Keever and Jennifer Schlegel; in Communications, Norman Keyes, Marcia L. Birbilis, Mia Gannon, Shen Shellenberger, Lindsay Warner, and Kari Molvar; in Conservation, Suzanne Penn, Sally Malenka, Melissa S. Meighan, Nancy Ash, Scott Homolka, and Sara Reiter; in Development, Kelly M. O'Brien, Peter Dunn, V. Susan Fisher, Molly C. Dixon, and

Christina Morrison; in Editorial and Graphic Design, Ruth Abrahams, Barb Metzger, Maia Wind, and Cynthia Rodríguez; in Education, Marla K. Shoemaker, Mary Teeling, Esperanza Altamar, Barbara A. Bassett, and Emily Schreiner; in Installation Design, Jack Schlechter, Aimee Keefer, Jeffrey Sitton, and Andrew Slavinskas; in Installation and Packing: David Gallagher, Martha Masiello, and many dedicated art handlers; in the Library, Richard B. Seiber, Ryan McNally, Evan B. Towle, and Mary Wassermann; in the Office of the Registrar, Irene Taurins and Wynne Kettell Grant; and in Special Exhibitions Planning, Suzanne F. Wells, Zoë Kahr, and Eliza D. Johnson.

Last but not least, the content and design of this striking catalogue owe much to the knowledge, persistence, and resilience of the following people: catalogue authors Jean-Francois Chevrier, Claire Gilman, Gabriele Guercio, Suzanne Penn, and Angela Vettese; catalogue contributors Marco Farano, Luigia Lonardelli, and Jennifer Wilkinson; in the Museum's Department of Publishing, Sherry Babbitt, Richard Bonk, and Kathleen Krattenmaker with assistance from David Frankel and Corinne Filipek; translators Marguerite Shore and Michael Gilson; designers Abbott Miller and Christine Moog of Pentagram, New York; and, in the Museum's Rights and Reproductions Department and Photography Studio, Graydon Wood, Conna Clark, Constance Mensh, Jason Wierzbicki, Holly Frisbee, Amanda Jaffe, and Giema Tsakuginow.

Carlos Basualdo
The Keith L. and Katherine Sachs Curator of Contemporary Art

INDEX OF ILLUSTRATED WORKS BY MICHELANGELO PISTOLETTO

PHOTOGRAPHY CREDITS

Photographs have been supplied by the owners and/or the following:

Claudio Abate: figs. 58, 63, 77, 79–82, 84, 92, 112, 234, 238, 239, 247

Roland Aellig: figs. 99, 100

Albright-Knox Art Gallery (Biff Henrich): plates 16, 30

Giorgio Benni: fig. 3

Paul Bijtebier: fig. 4

Paolo Bressano: figs. 5, 11, 15, 26, 27, 32, 52, 59, 60, 64, 103, 109, 111, 123, 124, 128–30, 131, 133, 135, 137, 139, 140, 142, 155, 157, 158, 160, 164, 166, 171, 174, 175, 182, 183, 186, 189, 194, 198, 199, 218, 223, 226, 227, 231, 235; plates 10–12, 76, 77, 79, 95, 101, 103, 104, 107

Santi Caleca: plate 106

Riccardo Capitelli: fig. 104

Clino Trini Castelli: fig. 10; plate 15

Christie's Images Limited: figs. 138, 153; plates 45, 62, 63

Archivio Cicconi, Rome: figs. 216, 219, 224, 229

Mario Cresci: fig. 72

Tano d'Amico: figs. 114, 250

Detroit Institute of Arts (R. H. Hensleigh): plate 34

Fabio Donato: figs. 86–88

Fondazione Piero Manzoni, Milan, in collaboration with the Gagosian Gallery, New York: fig. 221

Galleria L'Attico Archive—Fabio Sargentini: figs. 24, 241

Piero Gilardi: figs. 68, 97, 98

Paul Hester, Houston: fig. 190; plate 20

George Hixson, Houston: plate 32

Mimmo Jodice: figs. 30, 62; plate 97

Jacques Lathion: fig. 43

Living Theatre: fig. 228

Maurizio Malagoli: fig. 115

Attilio Maranzano: fig. 101; plate 23

Ari Marcopoulos: fig. 45; plate 96

Herbert Michel; fig. 149

Raul Morichetti: fig. 28

Ugo Mulas: figs. 93, 95, 163, 191, 242–45

Paolo Mussat Sartor: figs. 29, 31, 49, 66, 67, 89, 90, 94, 151, 152, 184, 197, 201–4, 210, 246, 248; plate 98

Ugo Nespolo: figs. 19, 65, 83, 93, 95, 163

Monica Nikolic: fig. 70

Paolo Pellion di Persano: figs. 27, 207; plates 1–5, 8, 9, 50, 52, 59–61, 64, 66–74, 78, 80–94, 99

Suzanne Penn: figs. 116, 118–21, 126, 127, 154

Philadelphia Museum of Art: figs. 53, 125; plate 44 (Constance Mensh); plates 22, 36, 39 (Graydon Wood)

Massimo Piersanti: fig. 249

Angelika Platen: figs. 162, 200

Heinz Preute: plate 55

Renato Rinaldi: figs. 16, 17, 18, 141, 143, 176, 187, 188, 193

James Rosenquist: fig. 225

Silvio Scafoletti: fig. 23

B. Scagliola: figs. 71, 73

Giuseppe Schiavinotto: fig. 57; plate 48

Sotheby's, Milan, reproduced by permission: plates 43, 49

Margherita Spiluttini: figs. 61, 102

Eric Sutherland: figs. 2, 106, 110, 156, 169, 170, 172, 178–80

Patrizia Tocci: plates 6, 31, 56–58

ARTISTS' COPYRIGHTS